NEOLIBERALISM, GLOBALIZATION, AND INEQUALITIES
Consequences for Health and Quality of Life

Edited by
Vicente Navarro

POLICY, POLITICS, HEALTH AND MEDICINE SERIES
Vicente Navarro, Series Editor

Baywood Publishing Company, Inc.
Amityville, New York

Baywood Publishing Company, Inc.
26 Austin Avenue
P.O. Box 337
Amityville, NY 11701
(800) 638-7819
E-mail: baywood@baywood.com
Web site: baywood.com

Library of Congress Catalog Number: 2007005970

ISBN 978-0-89503-338-3 (cloth)
ISBN 978-0-89503-344-4 (paper)

Library of Congress Cataloging-in-Publication Data

Neoliberalization, globalization, and inequalities : consequences for health and quality of life / edited by Vicente Navarro.
    p. ; cm. -- (Policy, politics, health, and medicine series)
Includes bibliographical references and index.
  ISBN 978-0-89503-338-3 (cloth : alk. paper -- ISBN 978-0-89503-344-4 (pbk. : alk. paper) 1. Neoliberalism--Health aspects. 2. Globalization--Health aspects. 3. Equality--Health aspects. 4. Health services accessibility. 5. Public health--Economic aspects. 6. Public health--Public aspects. 7. Quality of life. 8. Welfare state. 9. World health. I. Navarro, Vicente. II. Series: Policy, politics, health, and medicine series (Unnumbered)
  [DNLM: 1. Health Services Accessibility. 2. Health Policy. 3. Politics. 4. Socioeconomic Factors. W 76 N438 2007]

  RA418.N385 2007
  362.1--dc22

                                                        2007005970

About the Book

Since U.S. President Reagan and U.K. Prime Minister Thatcher, a major ideology (under the name of economic science) has been expanded worldwide that claims that the best policies to stimulate human development are those that reduce the role of the state in economic and social lives: privatizing public services and public enterprises, deregulating the mobility of capital and labor, eliminating protectionism, and reducing public social protection. This ideology, called "neoliberalism," has guided the globalization of economic activity and become the conventional wisdom in international agencies and institutions (such as the IMF, World Bank, World Trade Organization, and the technical agencies of the United Nations, including the WHO). Reproduced in the "Washington consensus" in the United States and the "Brussels consensus" in the European Union, this ideology has guided policies widely accepted as the only ones possible and advisable.

This book assembles a series of articles that challenge that ideology. Written by well-known scholars, these articles question each of the tenets of neoliberal doctrine, showing how the policies guided by this ideology have adversely affected human development in the countries where they have been implemented.

About the Editor

Vicente Navarro is Professor of Health and Public Policy, Sociology, and Policy Studies at The Johns Hopkins University, USA, and Professor of Political and Social Sciences at the Pompeu Fabra University, Spain. He has also been Professor of Economics at Barcelona University, Spain. Dr. Navarro has served as consultant to the United Nations and to many of its agencies, such as the WHO and UNICEF, and been a member of many international commissions dealing with human development areas. He has written extensively on political economy, public policy, and human development, and his books have been translated into many different languages. His most recent volumes include *The Political Economy of Social Inequalities: Consequences for Health and Quality of Life* and *The Politics of Health Policy.*

Contents

Introduction

Vicente Navarro

At the end of the 1970s and beginning of the 1980s, an ideology originating in the United States (first with a Democratic president, Jimmy Carter, then with a Republican president, Ronald Reagan) and the United Kingdom (with Prime Minister Margaret Thatcher) spread worldwide. According to this ideology, the role of the state in all dimensions of economic and social life should be reduced in order to free up the enormous potential of market forces (usually referred to as "free" market forces), by deregulating world trade, increasing the mobility of capital and labor, and eliminating social arrangements (such as social pacts and protectionism) that stood in the way of the full development and expansion of capitalism. Capitalism without borders became the name of the game in world affairs, reproducing a narrative that became known as *neoliberalism*—adding the *neo* prefix to indicate that this was indeed a new, broader, more advanced form of the old liberalism.

Such ideology became the guiding force behind international economic relations, a process facilitated by the collapse of the Soviet Union, which until then had been the other pole in a bipolar world. From that point there was only one pole, and only one alternative. The application of neoliberal policies to the international economic order became known as *globalization.* Neoliberal globalization has now been around for more than 30 years. Indeed, its hegemony is evident not only in the international institutions that manage the globalization process (such as the International Monetary Fund, World Bank, World Trade Organization, and United Nations—including its technical agencies such as the World Health Organization, UNICEF, UNESCO, and others), but also in the majority of governments of both the developed and the developing countries. Such hegemonic ideology has been promoted as the *Washington consensus,* supported by all U.S. administrations (Carter, Reagan, Bush senior, Clinton, and Bush junior), and on the other side of the Atlantic (in the European Union) as the *Brussels consensus*—and, indeed, it has guided the establishment of the European Union.

1

The defenders of neoliberal policies (i.e., most academic and mainstream media, both in North America and in Europe) have presented these policies as a great success: they have given rise, it is said, to an unprecedented increase in economic development and social well-being. These perceptions are uncritically presented as obvious facts and realities in the major economic and political forums and in the establishment media.

An exception to this choir of complacency is the *International Journal of Health Services (IJHS)*, established in 1970 and remaining loyal to its critical vocation. Despite its name (kept for historical reasons), the *IJHS* covers a much broader range of topics than health services. As indicated by its subtitle, the *IJHS* covers health and social policy, political economy and sociology, history and philosophy, and ethics and law. In summary, it covers any subject related to population's health and quality of life. And neoliberalism and globalization do indeed affect the health and quality of life of our populations, as is the theme of this volume. This book (with the exception of one chapter) is a collection of articles published in the *IJHS*.

The book opens, in Part I, with a chapter by Vicente Navarro (Professor of Health and Public Policy at the Johns Hopkins University and Professor of Political and Social Sciences at the Pompeu Fabra University, Spain), which explains the origins and nature of neoliberalism and globalization—two sides of the same coin. Chapter 1 challenges the widely held assumption among liberal authors (reproduced on occasion by sectors of the anti-globalization movement, such as Susan George and Ignacio Ramonet of *Le Monde Diplomatique*) that in the new globalized order, nation-states have lost their importance and have been replaced by multinational corporations, which are now the main motors of economic activity. Navarro questions the disappearance of the state and shows how states (heavily influenced by the classes and economic groups dominant in each nation-state) play a critical role in the international order— or, better, disorder. Moreover, he postulates that neoliberalism is the ideology of the dominant classes of both developed countries (the North) and developing countries (the South). These dominant classes have established an alliance that governs today's world, and neoliberalism is the ideology of this class alliance.

Part II shows how states (and thus politics) play a critical role in defining what happens in each country. Chapter 2, by Vicente Navarro, John Schmitt (Visiting Professor in the Public and Social Policy Program of the Pompeu Fabra University and economist at the Center for Economic and Policy Research in Washington, D.C.) and Javier Astudillo (Professor of Political Science at the Pompeu Fabra University), shows there is no convergence toward a uniform, reduced set of welfare state interventions (such as social security, labor market interventions, health and medical care, education, social services, housing, prevention of social exclusion and immigration), as neoliberal authors claim. Rather, there continue to be different types of welfare states (with different levels of public social expenditures), depending on the political traditions that have governed in each country and the class interests those traditions represent.

Chapter 3, by Francis G. Castles (Professor in the Department of Social Policy of the University of Edinburgh, Scotland), further expands on the continuing centrality of political factors in the configuration of social policies. There is no economic determinism (globalization) that forces all governments to do the same thing (i.e., to carry out neoliberal policies). The relations of power, including class power, continue to have a critical role. Many of the heralded crises of the welfare state are overblown by governments that have used "globalization" as a way of justifying and carrying out unpopular, class-oriented policies.

Part III consists of three chapters by Robert Hunter Wade (Professor at the London School of Economics) that analyze the adverse effects of neoliberalism and globalization on economic efficiency, social cohesion, and inequality. Chapter 4 challenges the basic economic assumptions of neoliberalism and globalization, presenting empirical information that invalidates the intellectual arguments used to sustain the theoretical framework on which neoliberalism is based. Chapter 5 challenges the argument that free trade in goods and services (including financial services) makes for better overall economic performance at the level of the world economy or national economies. It shows that neoliberal policies have increased inequalities and poverty, a position further documented in Chapter 6, in which Wade also challenges the neoliberal position that inequalities are desirable because of their beneficial effects on incentives and innovation. This chapter presents empirical evidence that falsifies the liberal position and emphasizes that redistribution within each nation-state is a critical condition for economic efficiency.

Part IV presents the consequences of neoliberalism and globalization for the quality of life of the world's populations. Chapter 7, by Mark Weisbrot, Dean Baker, and David Rosnick (economists at the Center for Economic and Policy Research, Washington, D.C.), documents the enormous human costs of neoliberalism and globalization for health, education, and other indicators of social well-being and quality of life. The authors demonstrate these costs by comparing the evolution of social indicators in the period 1980–2005 with the period 1960–1980, stressing that improvement in economic and social indicators for countries at equal levels of development at the beginning of each period was much lower (and even, on occasions, negative) in the later than in the earlier period.

Chapter 8, by Vicente Navarro, critically analyzes the consequences of neoliberalism for health around the world. This also includes a critique of the "humanism" of many initiatives coming from neoliberal establishments (such as the AIDS campaigns), which reproduce a "technological bullet" approach to solving enormous health problems—problems that are rooted in the unequal power relations (class power as well as gender power) supported by the liberal establishments. The chapter also includes a critique of the WHO for its reproduction of neoliberal policies (a point elaborated on in Part IX).

In Part V, the authors analyze the situation of monetary and economic integration in the European Union. Chapter 9, by Vicente Navarro and John Schmitt, challenges the widely held view in neoliberal discourse that there is a necessary trade-off between higher efficiency and lower reduction of inequalities. The chapter empirically shows that the liberal U.S. model has been less efficient economically (slower economic growth, higher unemployment) than the social model existing in the European Union and in most of its member states. Based on the data presented, Navarro and Schmitt criticize the adoption of features of the neoliberal model (such as deregulation of labor markets and reduction of public social expenditures) by some European governments. They go on to analyze the causes for the slowdown of economic growth and increased unemployment in the European Union—the application of monetarist and neoliberal policies in the institutional frame of the European Union, including the Stability Pact, the objectives and modus operandi of the European Central Bank, and the very limited resources available to the European Commission for stimulatory and distributive functions. Finally, the authors detail the reasons for these developments, including (besides historical considerations) the strong influence of financial capital in the E.U. institutions and the very limited democracy. Proposals for change are included.

Chapter 10, by John Schmitt and Ben Zipperer (economist at the Center for Economic and Policy Research, Washington, D.C.) gives a detailed analysis of the neoliberal model, presented by its advocates as the model the European Union should follow, and highlights the huge deficiencies of that model.

In Part VI, the discussion focuses on the social and economic situation of the United States, the point of reference in the neoliberal narrative. Chapter 11, by John Schmitt, analyzes the most unequal of the world's advanced capitalist economies, the United States, showing how inequality has increased substantially over the past 30 years. Schmitt also documents trends in the inequality of three key economic distributions—hourly earnings, annual incomes, and net wealth—and relates these developments to changes in economic and social policy over the past three decades. The primary cause of high and rising inequality is the systematic erosion of the bargaining power of lower- and middle-income workers relative to their employers, reflected in the erosion of the real value of the minimum wage, the decline in unions, wide-scale deregulation of industries such as airlines and trucking, privatization and outsourcing of many state and local government activities, increasing international competition, and periods of restrictive macroeconomic policy.

Chapter 12, by Vicente Navarro, discusses the political context in which health inequalities research has historically operated in the United States. The discussion focuses on the limitations of research that uses income, consumption, and status as the primary categories of research practice. Navarro concludes that it is essential to use categories of analysis that focus on class relations, as well as race and gender relations, and their reproduction through international and national institutions, in order to study their impact on the health and well-being of populations. In fact, a major weakness of most health inequalities research in the United States is its profound apoliticism. The actual causes of inequalities (in class, gender, and race power relations) are systematically ignored or downplayed. Even the term *inequalities* has disappeared from the narrative, replaced by the term *disparities*.

Part VII describes one of the most interesting alternatives to neoliberalism that has appeared in the developing world. Venezuela's health policies are based on an active public intervention with active mobilization of the population. Several scholars from the United States, Europe, and Venezuela present and analyze these experiences: in Chapter 13, Oscar Feo (Professor at the University of Carabobo, Venezuela) and Carlos Eduardo Siqueira (Professor at the University of Massachusetts, Lowell); and in Chapter 14, Carles Muntaner (Professor at the University of Toronto), René M. Guerra Salazar (Professor at the University of Toronto), Joan Benach (Professor at the Pompeu Fabra University, Spain), and Francisco Armada (Minister of Health of Venezuela).

The focus of Part VIII is the experience of neoliberalism and its negative effects on the African continent. In Chapter 15, Patrick Bond (Professor at the University of KwaZulu-Natal, South Africa) describes the dispossession of Africa's resources at the cost of its populations' health. The international establishments, including the International Monetary Fund and the World Bank are hypocritical—as Demba Moussa Dembele (from the African Forum on Alternatives) clearly shows in Chapter 17—in having pushed and imposed neoliberal policies on African countries and now lamenting the widespread crises and calling for more aid to these countries. It is neoliberalism itself that has worsened the health of African populations, as is further documented by Patrick Bond and George Dor (activist with Jubilee South Africa and the African Social Forum) in Chapter 16.

Part IX, Section A, critically analyzes proposals put forward by the WHO to resolve health crises at the world level. Indeed, three major commissions established by the WHO have had an major influence on the configuration of health policies. And, as the chapters here show, two of these commissions, heavily influenced by neoliberalism, are wrong, and the third is clearly insufficient.

In Chapter 18, Alison Katz (former consultant to the WHO) critically analyzes the Sachs report *Investing in Health for Economic Development*. This report, the product of the WHO Commission on Macroeconomics and Health, reproduces a set of highly dubious assumptions, one of which is that the primary cause of poverty in countries is a lack of resources. Thus, the report calls for aid to developing countries. Completely absent is any analysis of the class power relations existing within each country, as well as globally, as causes of underdevelopment. This lack of attention to the political factor accompanies a lack of questioning of the basic assumptions of the neoliberal project (perhaps because of Jeffrey Sachs's leadership in imposing neoliberal policies on the Soviet Union, policies that resulted in half a million deaths in just two years). It is an indication of the enormous hegemony of the neoliberal discourse that Sachs was asked to chair the WHO commission. Debabar Banerji (Emeritus Professor, Jawaharlal Nehru University, India) also criticizes the WHO Commission on Macroeconomics and Health (Chapter 19), as well as the WHO Commission on Social Determinants of Health (Chapter 21), from the viewpoint of a long-time public health professional working in a developing country. Chapter 20 presents a critique by Vicente Navarro (first published in the *Lancet*) of the WHO report *Health Systems: Improving Performance,* a document that, again, reproduced the neoliberal ideology of the WHO.

The critique of neoliberal policies ends with Section B of Part IX, a critical analysis of Jeffrey Sachs's manifesto *The End of Poverty,* by Doug Henwood (of the *Left Business Observer*).

These, then, are the contents of the volume. As indicated at the beginning of the introduction, the objective of this collection is to critically analyze the conventional wisdom in the political, economic, and academic establishments of the Western world. The chapters in this volume differ from and frequently are in conflict with mainstream explanations that present neoliberalism and globalization as good for people's health and quality of life. The data presented here challenge such assumptions. We hope that this contribution stimulates a much needed debate on the impact of economic, social, and political determinants on health and quality of life, focusing on how two major developments—neoliberalism and globalization—are adversely affecting the human development of our population.

Finally, we wish to thank the many persons who have labored in the preparation of this volume, starting with Linda Strange and Jean McMahon, copy editor and managing editor, respectively, of the *International Journal of Health Services.* Their work has been essential. Special thanks are also owed to Bobbi Olszewski and the staff of Baywood Publishing, who have been crucial to the editing, production, indexing, and promotion of the book. And, of course, out thanks to the President of Baywood, Stuart Cohen, who has always been a strong supporter of the *International Journal of Health Services,* the major forum for the topics discussed in this volume. We are grateful to Sule Calikoglu, a doctoral candidate at Johns Hopkins University, for her assistance in the collection and preparation of the articles. We thank the *Lancet* for allowing us to publish one of their articles as a chapter in this book.

PART I

What Is Neoliberalism?

CHAPTER 1

Neoliberalism as a Class Ideology; Or, The Political Causes of the Growth of Inequalities

Vicente Navarro

A trademark of our times is the dominance of *neoliberalism* in the major economic, political, and social forums of the developed capitalist countries and in the international agencies they influence—including the International Monetary Fund (IMF), the World Bank, the World Trade Organization (WTO), and the technical agencies of the United Nations, such as the World Health Organization (WHO), Food and Agriculture Organization, and UNICEF. Starting in the United States during the Carter administration, neoliberalism expanded its influence through the Reagan administration and, in the United Kingdom, the Thatcher administration, to become an international ideology. Neoliberalism holds to a theory (though not necessarily a practice) that posits the following:

1. The state (or what is wrongly referred to in popular parlance as "the government") needs to reduce its interventionism in economic and social activities.
2. Labor and financial markets need to be deregulated in order to liberate the enormous creative energy of the markets.
3. Commerce and investments need to be stimulated by eliminating borders and barriers to allow for the full mobility of labor, capital, goods, and services.

Following these three tenets, according to neoliberal authors, we have seen that the worldwide implementation of such practices has led to the development of a "new" process: a globalization of economic activity that has generated a period of enormous economic growth worldwide, associated with a new era of social progress. For the first time in history, we are told, we are witnessing a worldwide economy, in which states are losing power and are being replaced by a worldwide market centered in multinational corporations, which are the main units of economic activity in the world today.

This celebration of the process of globalization is also evident among some sectors of the left. Michael Hardt and Antonio Negri, in their widely cited

9

Empire (1), celebrate the great creativity of what they consider to be a new era of capitalism. This new era, they claim, breaks with obsolete state structures and establishes a new international order, which they define as an imperialist order. They further postulate that this new imperialist order is maintained without any state dominating or being hegemonic in that order. Thus, they write (1, p. 39):

> We want to emphasize that the establishment of empire is a positive step towards the elimination of nostalgic activities based on previous power structures; we reject all political strategies that want to take us back to past situations such as the resurrection of the nation-state in order to protect the population from global capital. We believe that the new imperialist order is better than the previous system in the same way that Marx believed that capitalism was a mode of production and a type of society superior to the mode that it replaced. This point of view held by Marx was based on a healthy despisement of the parochial localism and rigid hierarchies that preceded the capitalist society, as well as on the recognition of the enormous potential for liberation that capitalism had.

Globalization (i.e., the internationalization of economic activity according to neoliberal tenets) becomes, in Hardt and Negri's position, an international system that is stimulating a worldwide activity that operates without any state or states leading or organizing it. Such an admiring and flattering view of globalization and neoliberalism explains the positive reviews that *Empire* has received from Emily Eakin, a book reviewer for the *New York Times,* and other mainstream critics, not known for sympathetic reviews of books that claim to derive their theoretical position from Marxism. Actually, Eakin describes *Empire* as the theoretical framework that the world needs to understand its reality.

Hardt and Negri celebrate and applaud, along with neoliberal authors, the expansion of globalization. Other left-wing authors, however, mourn rather than celebrate this expansion, regarding globalization as the cause of the world's growing inequalities and poverty. It is important to stress that even though the authors in this latter group—which includes, for example, Susan George and Eric Hobsbawm—lament globalization and criticize neoliberal thinking, they still share with neoliberal authors the basic assumptions of neoliberalism: that states are losing power in an international order in which the power of multinational corporations has replaced the power of states, operating within a global market that is responsible for the international order (which neoliberals applaud) or disorder (which some left-wing critics lament).

THE CONTRADICTION BETWEEN THEORY AND PRACTICE IN NEOLIBERALISM

Let's be clear right away that neoliberal *theory* is one thing and neoliberal *practice* another thing entirely. Most members of the Organization for Economic Cooperation and Development (OECD)—including the U.S. federal government—have seen state interventionism and state public expenditures *increase* during the past 30 years. My area of scholarship is public policy, and, as such, I study the nature of state interventions in many parts of the world. I can testify to the expansion of state intervention in most countries in the developed capitalist world. Even in the United States, Reagan's neoliberalism did not translate into a decline of the federal public sector. As a matter of fact, federal public expenditures increased under his mandate, from 21.6 to 23 percent of gross national product (GNP), as a consequence of a spectacular growth in military expenditures from 4.9 to 6.1 percent of GNP during the Reagan years (2). This growth in public expenditures was financed by an increase in the federal deficit (creating a burgeoning of the federal debt) and increase in taxes. As the supposedly anti-tax president, Reagan in fact increased taxes for a greater number of people (in peace time) than any other president in U.S. history. And he increased taxes not once, but twice (in 1982 and in 1983). In a demonstration of class power, he reduced the taxes of the top 20 percent (by income) of the population enormously, at the cost of increasing taxes for the majority of the population.

It is not accurate, therefore, to say that President Reagan reduced the role of the state in the United States by reducing the size of the public sector and lowering taxes. What Reagan (and Carter before him) did was dramatically change the nature of state intervention, such that it benefited even more the upper classes and the economic groups (such as military-related corporations) that financed his electoral campaigns. Reagan's policies where indeed class policies that hurt the majority of the nation's working class. Reagan was profoundly anti-labor, making cuts in social expenditures at an unprecedented level. It bears repeating that Reagan's policies were not liberal: they were Keynesian, based on large public expenditures and large federal deficits. Also, the federal government intervened very actively in the nation's industrial development (mainly, but not exclusively, through the Defense Department). As Caspar Weinberger (3), secretary of defense in the Reagan administration, once indicated (in response to criticisms by the Democratic Party that the U.S. government had abandoned the manufacturing sector), "Our Administration is the Administration that has a more advanced and extended industrial policy in the western world." He was right. No other Western government had such an extensive industrial policy. And today, the huge growth of the U.S. biomedical industry is to a large degree stimulated by an active state intervention. Indeed, the U.S. federal state is one of the most interventionist states in the Western world.

There exists very robust scientific evidence that the United States is not a liberal state (as it is constantly defined) and that the U.S. state is not reducing its key role in developing the national economy, including in the production and distribution of goods and services by large U.S. corporations—which, incidentally, are wrongly referred to as "multinationals" but are actually "transnationals." *This empirical evidence shows that the U.S. federal government's interventionism (in the economic, political, cultural, and security spheres) has increased over the past 30 years.* In the economic sphere, for example, protectionism has not declined. It has increased, with higher subsidies to the agricultural, military, aerospace, and biomedical sectors. In the social arena, public interventions to weaken social rights (and most particularly labor rights) have increased enormously (not only under Reagan, but also under Bush Senior, Clinton, and Bush Junior), and surveillance of the citizenry has increased exponentially. Again, there has been no diminution of federal interventionism in the United States, but rather an even more skewed class character to this intervention during the past 30 years.

Neoliberal narrative about the declining role of the state in people's lives is easily falsified by the facts. Indeed, as John Williamson, one of the intellectual architects of neoliberalism, once indicated, "We have to recognize that what the U.S. government promotes abroad, the U.S. government does not follow at home," adding that "the U.S. government promotes policies that are not followed in the U.S." (4, p. 213). It could not have been said better. In other words, if you want to understand U.S. public policies, look at what the U.S. government does, not what it says. This same situation occurs in the majority of developed capitalist countries. Their states have become more, not less, interventionist. The size of the state (measured by public expenditures per capita) has increased in most of these countries. Again, the empirical information on this point is strong. What has been happening is not a reduction of the state but rather a change in the nature of state intervention—further strengthening its class character.

DETERIORATION OF THE WORLD ECONOMIC AND SOCIAL SITUATION

Another correction that needs to be made as a rebuttal to neoliberal dogma is that neoliberal public policies have been remarkably unsuccessful at achieving what they claim to be their aims: economic efficiency and social well-being. If we compare the period 1980–2000 (when neoliberalism reached its maximum expression)[1] with the immediately preceding period, 1960–1980, we can easily see that 1980–2000 was much less successful than 1960–1980 in most developed and

---

[1] The starting point of neoliberalism and of the growth in inequalities was July 1979, with Paul Volker's dramatic increase in interest rates that slowed down economic growth—plus the two oil shocks that particularly affected countries highly dependent on imported oil (see 5). Volker increased interest rates (thus creating a worldwide recession) as an anti-working class move to weaken labor in the United States and abroad. The rate increase also initiated, as Arrighi (6) noted, a flow of capital to the United States, making it very difficult for other countries, especially poor countries, to compete for the limited capital. The fact that petrol Euro dollars (which increased enormously with the oil shocks) were deposited in the United States made the scarcity of capital particularly hard for poor countries to adapt to. This is the time when the stagnation of the poor countries started. The countries most affected by these neoliberal public policies were the Latin American countries, which followed these policies extensively, and the African countries (the poorest of the poor), which saw extremely negative economic growth. In 2000, 24 African countries had a smaller GNP per capita than 25 years earlier.

Table 1

Economic growth, 1960–2000

	1960–1980	1980–2000
Rate of economic growth in developing countries (except China):		
Annual economic growth	5.5%	2.6%
Annual economic growth per capita	3.2%	0.7%
Rate of economic growth in China:		
Annual economic growth	4.5%	9.8%
Annual economic growth per capita	2.5%	8.4%

Sources: World Bank, *World Development Indicators,* 2001; R. Pollin, *Contours of Descent,* Verso, 2003, p. 131.

developing capitalist countries. As Table 1 shows, the rate of growth and the rate of growth per capita in all developing (non-OECD) countries (excluding China) were much higher in 1960–1980 (5.5 percent and 3.2 percent) than in 1980–2000 (2.6 percent and 0.7 percent). Mark Weisbrot, Dean Baker, and David Rosnick (7) have documented that the improvement in quality-of-life and well-being indicators (infant mortality, rate of school enrollment, life expectancy, and others) increased faster in 1960–1980 than in 1980–2000 (when comparing countries at the same level of development at the starting year of each period). And as Table 2 shows, the annual rate of economic growth per capita in the developed capitalist countries was lower in 1980–2000 than in 1960–1980. But, what is also important to stress is that due to the larger annual economic growth per capita in the OECD countries than in the developing countries (except China), the difference in their rates of growth per capita has been increasing dramatically. This means, in practical terms, that income inequalities between these two types of countries have grown spectacularly, and particularly between the extremes (see Table 2). But, most important, inequalities have increased dramatically not only among but *within* countries, developed and developing alike. Adding both types of inequalities (among and within countries), we find that, as Branco Milanovic (8) has documented, the top 1 percent of the world population receives 57 percent of the world income, and the income difference between those at the top and those at the bottom has increased from 78 to 114 times.

It bears emphasizing that even though poverty has increased worldwide and within countries that are following neoliberal public policies, this does not mean the rich within each country (including developing countries) have been adversely affected. As a matter of fact, the rich saw their incomes and their distance from the non-rich increase substantially. Class inequalities have increased greatly in most capitalist countries.

Table 2.

I. Average annual rate of per capita economic growth in the OECD and developing countries

	1961–1980	1981–2000
(A) OECD countries	3.5%	2.0%
(B) Developing countries (except China)	3.2%	0.7%
Growth differential (A – B)	0.3%	1.3%

II. Growth in world income inequalities, 1980–1998 (excluding China)

Income of richest 50% as share of poorest 50%	4% more unequal
Income of richest 20% as share of poorest 20%	8% more unequal
Income of richest 10% as share of poorest 10%	19% more unequal
Income of richest 1% as share of poorest 1%	77% more unequal

Sources: World Bank, *World Development Indicators,* 2001; R. Sutcliffe, *A More or Less Unequal World?* Political Economy Research Institute, 2003; R. Pollin, *Contours of Descent,* Verso, 2003, p. 133.

NEOLIBERALISM AS THE ROOT OF INEQUALITIES

In each of these countries, then, the income of those at the top has grown spectacularly as a result of state interventions. Consequently, we need to turn to some of the categories and concepts discarded by large sectors of the left: class structure, class power, class struggle, and their impact on the state. These scientific categories continue to be of key importance to understanding what is going on in each country. Let me clarify that a scientific concept can be very old but not antiquated. "Ancient" and "antiquated" are two different concepts. The law of gravity is very old but is not antiquated. Anyone who doubts this can test it by jumping from the tenth floor. There is a risk that some sectors of the left may pay an equally suicidal cost by ignoring scientific concepts such as class and class struggle simply because these are old concepts. We cannot understand the world (from the Iraq War to the rejection of the European Constitution) without acknowledging the existence of classes and class alliances, established worldwide between the dominant classes of the developed capitalist world and those of the developing capitalist world. *Neoliberalism is the ideology and practice of the dominant classes of the developed and developing worlds alike.*

But before we jump ahead, let's start with the situation in each country. Neoliberal ideology was the dominant classes' response to the considerable gains achieved by the working and peasant classes between the end of World War II and the mid-1970s. The huge increase in inequalities that has occurred since then is the direct result of the growth in income and well-being of the dominant classes, which is a consequence of class-determined public policies such as: (a) *deregulation of labor markets,* an anti–working class move; (b) *deregulation of financial markets,* which has greatly benefited financial capital, the hegemonic branch of capital in the period 1980–2005; (c) *deregulation of commerce in goods and services,* which has benefited the high-consumption population at the expense of laborers; (d) *reduction of social public expenditures,* which has hurt the working class; (e) *privatization of services,* which has benefited the top 20 percent of the population (by income) at the expense of the well-being of the working classes that use public services; (f) *promotion of individualism and consumerism,* hurting the culture of solidarity; (g) *development of a theoretical narrative and discourse that pays rhetorical homage to the markets,* but masks a clear alliance between transnationals and the state in which they are based; and (h) *promotion of an anti-interventionist discourse,* that is in clear conflict with the actual increased state interventionism, to promote the interests of the dominant classes and the economic units—the transnationals—that foster their interests. Each of these class-determined public policies requires a state action or intervention that conflicts with the interests of the working and other popular classes.

THE PRIMARY CONFLICT IN TODAY'S WORLD: NOT BETWEEN NORTH AND SOUTH BUT BETWEEN AN ALLIANCE OF DOMINANT CLASSES OF NORTH AND SOUTH AGAINST DOMINATED CLASSES OF NORTH AND SOUTH

It has become part of the conventional wisdom that the primary conflict in the world is between the rich North and the poor South. The North and the South, however, have classes with opposing interests that have established alliances at the international level. This situation became clear to me when I was advising President Allende in Chile. The fascist coup led by General Pinochet was not, as was widely reported, a coup imposed by the rich North (the United States) on the poor South (Chile). Those who brutally imposed the Pinochet regime were the dominant classes of Chile (bourgeoisie, petit bourgeoisie, and upper-middle professional classes), with the support not of the United States (U.S. society is not an aggregate of 240 million imperialists!) but of the Nixon administration (Nixon as spokesperson for the dominant classes of the United States)—which at that time was very unpopular in the United States, having sent the Army to put down the coalminers' strike in Appalachia.

A lack of awareness of the existence of classes often leads to condemnation of an entire country, frequently the United States. But, in fact, the U.S. working class is one of the first victims of U.S. imperialism. Some will say that the U.S. working class benefits from imperialism. Gasoline, for example, is very cheap (although increasingly less so) in the United States. It costs me $35 to fill my car in the United States and 52 euros to fill the same-model car in Europe. But, by contrast, public transportation in the United States is practically nonexistent in many regions. The working class of Baltimore (where the Johns Hopkins University is located), for example, would benefit much more from first-class public transportation (which it does not have) than dependency on a car, whatever the price of gasoline. And let's not forget that the energy and automobile industry interests have been major agents in opposing and destroying public transport systems in the United States. The U.S. working class is a victim of its nation's capitalist and imperialist system. It is not by chance that no other country in the developed capitalist world has such an underdeveloped welfare state as the United States. More than 100,000 people die in the United States every year due to a lack of public health care.

The tendency to look at the distribution of world power while ignoring class power within each country is also evident in the frequent criticism that the international organizations are controlled by the rich countries. It is frequently pointed out, for example, that the 10 percent of the world population living in the richest countries has 43 percent of the votes in the IMF, but it is not the 10 percent of the population living in the so-called rich countries that controls the IMF. It is the dominant classes of those rich countries that dominate the IMF, putting forward public policies that hurt the dominated classes of their own countries as well as those of other countries. The director of the IMF, for example, is Rodrigo Rato, who while Spain's minister of economy in the ultra-right government of José María Aznar (who partnered with Bush and Blair to support the Iraq War) carried out the brutal austerity policies that severely reduced the standard of living of the Spanish popular classes (9).

Let me also clarify another point. Much has been written about the conflict within the WTO between rich and poor countries. The governments of the rich countries, it is said, heavily subsidize their agriculture while raising protective barriers for industries such as textiles and foods that are vulnerable to products coming from the poor countries. While these obstacles to world trade do indeed adversely affect poor countries, it is wrong to assume that the solution is freer worldwide trade. Even without the barriers, the higher productivity of the rich countries would guarantee their success in world trade. What poor countries need to do is to change from export-oriented economies (the root of their problems) to domestic-oriented growth—a strategy that would require a major income redistribution and is thus resisted by the dominant classes of those (and of the rich) countries. It is extremely important to realize that most countries already have the resources (including capital) to break with their underdevelopment. Let me quote from an unlikely source. The *New York Times,* in the middle of the Malthusian highs (when population explosion was held to be the cause of world poverty), published a surprisingly candid assessment of the situation in Bangladesh, the poorest country in the world. In this extensive article, Ann Crittenden (10) touched directly on the root of the problem: the patterns of ownership of the production asset—the land:

> The root of the persistent malnutrition in the midst of relative plenty is the unequal distribution of land in Bangladesh. Few people are rich here by Western standards, but severe inequalities do exist and they are reflected in highly skewed land ownership. The wealthiest 16% of the rural population controls two thirds of the land and almost 60% of the population holds less than one acre of property.

Crittenden is not hopeful that the solution is technological. Quite to the contrary, technology can make things even worse:

> The new agricultural technologies being introduced have tended to favor large farmers, putting them in a better position to buy out their less fortunate neighbors.

Why does this situation persist? The answer is clear.

> Nevertheless, with the government dominated by landowners—about 75% of the members of the Parliament hold land—no one foresees any official support for fundamental changes in the system.

Let me add that in the U.S. State Department's classification of political regimes, Bangladesh is placed in the democratic column. Meanwhile, hunger and underweight are the primary causes of child mortality in Bangladesh. The hungry face of a child in Bangladesh has become the most common poster used by many charitable organizations to shame people in developed countries into sending money and food aid to Bangladesh. With what results?

> Food aid officials in Bangladesh privately concede that only a fraction of the millions of tons of food aid sent to Bangladesh has reached the poor and hungry in the villages. The food is given to the Government, which in turn sells it at subsidized prices to the military, the police, and the middle class inhabitants of the cities.

The class structure of Bangladesh and the property relations that determine it are the causes of the enormous poverty. As Ann Crittenden concludes:

> Bangladesh has enough land to provide an adequate diet for every man, woman and child in the country. The agricultural potential of this lush green land is such that even the inevitable population growth of the next 20 years could be fed easily by the resources of Bangladesh alone.

Most recently, Bangladesh has been much in the news as having undergone high economic growth due primarily to its exports in the world market. But that growth has been limited to a small, export-oriented sector of the economy and has left untouched the majority of the population. Malnutrition and hunger, meanwhile, have increased.

THE STATES AND CLASS ALLIANCES

In the establishment of class alliances, states play a key role. U.S. foreign policy, for example, is oriented toward supporting the dominant classes of the South (where, incidentally, 20 percent of the world's richest persons live). These alliances include, on many occasions, personal ties among members of the dominant classes. Examples are many—among them, the traditional support of the Bush family for the Middle East feudal regimes; Clinton's support for the United Arab Emirates (UAE), one of the major supporters of the Clinton Library in Arkansas and major donor to Clinton in speaking fees (up to a million dollars) and to causes favoring Clinton (11). The UAE is one of the world's most oppressively brutal regimes. The dominant classes deny citizenship to 85 percent of the working population (called "guest workers"). Needless to say, international agencies (heavily influenced by the U.S. and European governments) promote such alliances based on the neoliberal rhetoric of free markets. Cutting public social expenditures (including health expenditures), as advocated by the IMF and the World Bank, is part of the neoliberal public policies pushed by the dominant classes of the North and South at the expense of the well-being and quality of life of the dominated classes of both North and South. In all these examples, the states of the North and the South play a critical role.

Another example of alliances among dominant classes is the current promotion of for-profit health insurance by the Bush administration, both to the U.S. population and, increasingly, to the developing world. This is done with the advice and collaboration of conservative governments in Latin America on behalf of their dominant classes, which benefit from private insurance schemes that select clientele and exclude the popular classes. Those popular classes, in the United States and Latin America, profoundly dislike this push toward for-profit health care. (The movie *John Q* relates the hostility toward health insurance companies among the U.S. working class.) The fact that the dominant classes in the developed and developing countries share class interests does not mean they see eye-to-eye on everything. Of course not. They have major disagreements and conflicts (just as there are disagreements and conflicts among the different components of the dominant classes in each country). But these disagreements cannot conceal the commonality of their interests, as clearly exposed in the neoliberal focus (such as at Davos) and neoliberal instruments that have a hegemonic position (such as the *Economist* and the *Financial Times*).

IS THERE A DOMINANT STATE IN THE WORLD TODAY?

More than globalization, what we are witnessing in the world today is the *regionalization* of economic activities around a dominant state: North America around the United States, Europe around Germany, and Asia around Japan—and soon China. Thus there is a hierarchy of states within each region. In Europe, for example, the Spanish government is becoming dependent on public policies of the European Union, in which the German state predominates. This dependency creates an ambivalent situation. On the one hand, the states of the European Union chose to delegate major policies (such as monetary policies) to a higher institution (the European Central Bank, which is dominated by the German Central Bank). But this does not necessarily mean that the Spanish state loses power. "Losing power" means you had more power before, which is not necessarily the case. Spain, for example, is more powerful with the euro as currency than it was with the peseta. Indeed, Spain's President Zapatero would have paid a very high cost in his confrontation with Bush (in withdrawing Spanish troops from Iraq) if Spain still had the peseta as its national currency. Sharing sovereignty can increase power. On the other hand, the European government is frequently used by Europe's dominant classes as excuse and justification for unpopular policies that they want to implement (such as reducing public expenditures as a consequence of the European Stability Pact, which forces countries to maintain a central government deficit below 3 percent of GNP); these policies are presented as coming from European legislation rather than from any of the member states, thus diluting the responsibility of each government. Class alliances at the European level are manifested through the operation of E.U. institutions heavily committed to neoliberal ideology and public policies. The "no" vote on the proposed European Constitution was the response of the working classes of some member states to the European institutions that operate as alliances for Europe's dominant classes.

Within the hierarchy of states, some are dominant. The U.S. state has a dominant place that is maintained through a set of alliances with the dominant classes of other states. Neoliberal ideology provides the linkage among these classes. Needless to say, there are conflicts and tensions among them. But these tensions cannot outweigh the commonality of their class interests. Among the practices that unite them are aggressive policies against the working class and left-wing instruments. The 1980–2005 period was characterized by an aggressive campaign against left-wing parties that had been successful in the earlier, 1960–1980, period. During the "neoliberal" period, the alliance of the dominant classes has promoted multi-class religious movements that have used religion as a motivating force to stop socialism or communism. It was the administration of President Carter that began to support the religious fundamentalists in Afghanistan against the communist-led government. From Afghanistan to Iraq, Iran, the Palestinian Territories, and many other Arab countries, the dominant classes of the United States and Europe, through their governments, funded and supported the religious fundamentalists—often not only out of their own class interests, but out of their own religiosity. The "moral majority" in the United States was supposed to become the moral majority worldwide. These profoundly anti-left fundamentalist movements developed their own dynamics, channeling the enormous frustrations of the Arab masses with their oppressive, feudal regimes, to replace those regimes with equally oppressive religious theocracies, as has happened in many Arab countries.

But it is wrong to see the support by the dominant classes for the feudal regimes as simply a product of the Cold War. It was much more than that. It was a class response. The best evidence for this is that the support continued even after the collapse of the Soviet Union. The Cold War was an excuse and justification for carrying on the class struggle at the world level—as its continuation proves. Class war has indeed become an extremely active component of U.S. interventionism. It was the "shock therapy" pushed by Lawrence Summers and Jeffrey Sachs in Russia during the Clinton administration that led to the shortening of life expectancy in Russia, a consequence of the dramatic decline in the standard of living of the Russian popular classes. (That Sachs was asked to chair the WHO Commission on Macroeconomics and Health illustrates the enormous influence of neoliberalism. Another example of such influence is the WHO report on health systems performance, co-authored by Christopher Murray and Julio Frenk (12) and critiqued by Navarro (13).) The increased privatization of major public assets was part of that class war in Russia, as it has been in Iraq. The chief of the U.S. occupation in Iraq, Paul Bremer, fired half a million government workers, slashed business taxes, gave investors extraordinary new rights, and eliminated all import restrictions for all business except the oil industry. As Jeff Faux relates in *The Global Class Struggle* (14), the only laws from the brutal Iraqi dictatorship that the occupation did not supplant were those that were anti–labor union, including a restrictive collective-bargaining agreement that took away all workers' bonuses and food and housing subsidies. As the *Economist* (15) editorialized, "The occupation of Iraq is a capitalist's dream."

Recently, another version of the North-South divide appears in the writings of one of the most influential thinkers in the United States, the philosopher John Rawls, who divides the countries of the world into *decent* and *non-decent* countries. The decent countries (mostly located in the developed capitalist world) are those that have democratic rights and institutions, while the non-decent countries (mostly located in the developing capitalist world) are those that do not. After dividing the world into these two categories, Rawls concludes that the non-decent countries had better be ignored, although he admits "a moral responsibility to help poor countries that are prevented by poverty from organizing themselves as liberal or decent society." I find such positions and statements remarkable for their overwhelming ignorance of past and present international relations, as well as of the class relations in each of those countries. Rawls further confuses governments with countries (a confusion that occurs frequently in the assumption that the primary conflict is between North and South). What he calls non-decent countries (characterized by brutal and corrupt dictatorships) have classes; their dominant classes have not been ignored in activities cultivated and supported by the dominant classes of the decent countries, which have also hurt the quality of life and well-being of their own dominated classes. Also, in Rawls's so-called non-decent countries, there are class-based movements that endure enormous sacrifices, carrying out a heroic struggle for change, struggling constantly while handicapped and opposed by the dominant classes of the so-called decent countries. I find it remarkable (but predictable) that such an intellectual figure defines the moral compass of these indecent classes. The latest example of this indecency is the reported support of the U.S. and U.K. governments for the King of Nepal, in their concern to stop a mass revolt led by left-wing parties.

INEQUALITIES AMONG COUNTRIES AND THEIR SOCIAL CONSEQUENCES

That inequalities contribute to a lack of social solidarity and increase social pathology is well documented. Many people, including myself, have documented this reality (16). The scientific evidence supporting this position is overwhelming. In any given society, the greatest number of deaths would be prevented by reducing social inequalities. Michael Marmot studied the gradient of heart disease mortality among professionals at different authority levels, and he found that the higher the level of authority, the lower the heart disease mortality (17). He further showed that this mortality gradient could not be explained by diet, physical exercise, or cholesterol alone; these risk factors explained only a small part of the gradient. The most important factor was the position that people held within the social structure (in which class, gender, and race play key roles), the social distance between groups, and the differential control that people had over their own lives.

This enormously important scientific finding, which builds upon previous scholarly work, has many implications; one of them is that the major problem we face is not simply eliminating poverty but rather reducing inequality. The first is impossible to resolve without resolving the second. Another implication is that poverty is not just a matter of resources, as is wrongly assumed in World Bank reports that measure worldwide poverty by quantifying the number of people who live on a standardized U.S. dollar a day. The real problem, again, is not absolute resources but social distance and the different degrees of control over one's own resources. And this holds true in every society.

Let me elaborate. An unskilled, unemployed, young black person living in the ghetto area of Baltimore has more resources (he or she is likely to have a car, a mobile phone, a TV, and more square feet per household and more kitchen equipment) than a middle-class professional in Ghana, Africa. If the whole world were just a single society, the Baltimore youth would be middle class and the Ghana professional would be poor. And yet, the first has a much shorter life expectancy (45 years) than the second (62 years). How can that be, when the first has more resources than the second? The answer is clear. It is far more difficult to be poor in the United States (the sense of distance, frustration, powerlessness, and failure is much greater) than to be middle class in Ghana. The first is far below the median; the second is above the median.

Does the same mechanism operate in inequalities among countries? The answer is increasingly, yes. And the reason for adding "increasingly" is communication—with ever more globalized information systems and networks, more information is reaching the most remote areas of the world. And the social distance created by inequalities is becoming increasingly apparent, not only within but also among countries. Because this distance is more and more perceived as an outcome of exploitation, we are facing an enormous tension, comparable with that of the 19th and early 20th centuries, when class exploitation became the driving force for social mobilization. The key element for defining the future is through what channels that mobilization takes place. What we have seen is a huge mobilization, instigated and guided by an alliance of the dominant classes of the North and South, aimed at—as mentioned earlier—stimulating multi-class religious or nationalistic mobilizations that leave key class relations unchanged. We saw this phenomenon at the end of the 19th and beginning of the 20th centuries. Christian Democracy in Europe, for example, appears as the dominant classes' response to the threat of socialism and communism. The birth of Islamic fundamentalism was also stimulated for the same purposes.

The progressive alternative must be centered in alliances among the dominated classes and other dominated groups, with a political movement that must be built upon the process of struggle that takes place in each country. The struggle for better health in any country has to be part of that broader struggle to build a better world, emphasizing that another world—based on solidarity—is possible. But, to intervene in and change current reality, we have to understand it, with a critical evaluation of the conventional wisdom that reproduces neoliberalism worldwide—an evaluation that should be uncompromising in the sense that it should fear neither its own results nor conflict with the powers that be. In that respect, this evaluation should include the political analysis rarely seen in scholarly work. And here, I am concerned that the newly established WHO Commission on Social Determinants of Health (18) is not looking at the basis of the problems that determine poor health, problems that are rooted in class as well as in race and gender power relations and in the political instruments through which such power is exercised and reproduced. The political determinants of health need to be understood and acted upon, however uncomfortable or risky this may be. Such is the intention of this chapter.

Note — A modified version of this chapter has been published in *Monthly Review*.

REFERENCES

1. Hardt, M., and Negri, A. *Empire.* Harvard University Press, Cambridge, 2000.
2. Congressional Budget Office National Accounts 2003.
3. Weinberger, C. *Washington Post,* July 13, 1983.
4. Williamson, J. What Washington means by the policy reform. In *Latin America Adjustment: How Much Has Happened?* ed. J. Williamson. Institute for International Economics, Washington, DC, 1990.
5. Harvey, D. *A Brief History of Neoliberalism.* Oxford University Press, New York, 2005.
6. Arrighi, G. The African crisis: World systemic and regional aspects. *New Left Review,* May–June, 2002.
7. Weisbrot, M., Baker, D., and Rosnick, D. The scorecard on development: 25 years of diminished progress. *Int. J. Health Serv.* 36:211–234, 2006.
8. Milanovic, B. *Worlds Apart: Measuring International and Global Inequality.* Princeton University Press, Princeton, NJ, 2005.
9. Navarro, V. Who is Mr Rato? *CounterPunch,* June 2004.
10. Crittenden, A. *New York Times,* September 12, 1992.
11. *Financial Times,* March 4, 2006.
12. Murray, C., and Frenk, J. *World Health Report 2000: Health Systems—Improving Performance.* World Health Organization, Geneva, 2000.
13. Navarro, V. Assessment of the World Health Report 2000. *Lancet* 356:1598–1601, 2000.
14. Faux, J. *The Global Class Struggle.* Wiley, New York, 2006.
15. *Economist,* September 25, 2003.
16. Navarro, V. (ed.). *The Political Economy of Social Inequalities: Consequences for Health and Quality of Life.* Baywood, Amityville, NY, 2002.
17. Marmot, M. *The Status Syndrome: How Social Standing Affects Our Health and Longevity.* Owl Books, New York, 2005.
18. WHO Commission on Social Determinants of Health. *Towards a Conceptual Framework for Analysis and Action on Social Determinants of Health.* World Health Organization, Geneva, 2005.

PART II

Neoliberalism, Globalization, and the Welfare State

Is Globalization Undermining the Welfare State? The Evolution of the Welfare State in Developed Capitalist Countries during the 1990s

Vicente Navarro, John Schmitt,
and Javier Astudillo

INTRODUCTION

*Is Globalization Forcing a Retrenchment of
the Welfare State? An Ongoing Debate*

A major debate appeared in important academic, political, and economic circles during the 1980s and 1990s concerning the impact of the globalization of economic activities (whether commercial, productive, or financial) on the ability of the world's developed economies to sustain their welfare states. Many authors have argued that deregulation of international capital flows and trade has considerably narrowed the scope of governments to pursue expansionist and redistributive policies, forcing all governments to cut public social expenditures and deregulate labor markets in order to make their countries more competitive.[1] According to this interpretation of the impact of globalization on public social policies, the political coloration of governing parties loses its importance, since left- and right-wing parties, once in government, are compelled to follow the same or similar policies. As stated by a major proponent of the process of globalization, Prime Minister Tony Blair of Britain's New Labour government: "There is no right or left politics in the globalized economy of today. There is only good or bad politics" (4; see 5 for a critical discussion of Blair's speech).

This position, however, has been challenged by many authors, such as Hirst and Thompson (6; see 7 for a critique), who have questioned the concept and

---

[1] There is an extensive list of publications to support this position. For representative views, see 1–3.

extent of globalization; Pierson (8) and Castles (9), who have questioned the existence of a retrenchment of the welfare states; Huber and Stephens (10), who have raised questions about the dwindling importance of political parties in government as an explanation of the evolution of welfare states; and Scharpf and Schmidt (11) and others, who have questioned the convergence of welfare state policies in developed capitalist countries.

In this chapter we contribute to this debate by analyzing the evolution of macro-indicators of social and economic well-being during the 1990s in the majority of developed capitalist countries. Our primary goal is to use the most recent data available to test two competing explanations for recent developments in the welfare state. The first view is that globalization in the 1990s acted as the great equalizer, forcing cutbacks in the welfare state in the face of the new economic realities of that decade. The second view is that "politics still matters," that the principal determinant of recent developments in the welfare state has been the state of internal political forces, particularly the strength or weakness of national labor movements. To assess these two explanations, we first sketch some of the main economic and social predictions of each framework, then review the relevant data. Since the main interest here is in analyzing the importance of politics as a primary determinant of the welfare state, the analysis of the national data groups countries according to their political traditions.

Globalization versus Politics

The competing explanations for the recent evolution of the welfare state make sharply different predictions about a host of national economic and social indicators. Those holding the view that globalization is the main determinant of the limits of the welfare state generally believe that globalization will force states to reduce their total levels of taxation and, especially, to shift taxation away from mobile factors such as capital and toward less mobile factors such as labor. This fiscal reality, the argument goes, will make it harder and harder for governments to finance their welfare states, independent of their political leanings, and will lead, ultimately, to convergence toward considerably smaller welfare states financed to a much greater degree by a country's workforce.

The competing view is that "politics still matters"; that the ability to tax, the composition of taxes, and the level and growth of state expenditure and government employment all respond primarily to internal political circumstances, rather than to global economic and technological forces. According to this view, we should continue to see significant diversity in the welfare states of the advanced capitalist countries. More specifically, the share of total taxation, the source of those tax revenues, the size of public expenditures on health, education, and welfare, and the size of public-sector employment should all vary systematically, depending primarily on political forces.

The Political Traditions

In grouping the welfare states of the developed capitalist countries, we follow the path-breaking typology developed by Gosta Esping-Andersen (12), later modified by Castles and Mitchell (to include the antipodean type of "wage-earner welfare state") (13) and by Huber and Stephens (who renamed Esping-Andersen's "conservative/corporatist" group the "Christian democratic" group) (14). In our typology, we are particularly indebted to Huber and Stephens, who emphasize the importance of political variables in configuring the different types of welfare states; we present these political variables (such as the political partisanship of governments) as primarily (although not exclusively) an expression of class forces and root our analysis in the theoretical school of class power resources first developed by Walter Korpi (15, 16; see also 17, 18). We modify Huber and Stephens's typology, however, to include a new group of countries: ex-dictatorial right-wing southern European conservative regimes. This group includes Spain, Portugal, and Greece, all governed by right-wing dictatorships or authoritarian conservative regimes for most of the years during the formative period of the welfare states (1945–80) and all having welfare states with specific characteristics different from those of the other groups, as we will show. Also, in this chapter we do not include the antipodean countries, but instead focus primarily on North America (Canada and the United States), Japan, and the Western European countries. The reason for this focus is that these are the countries we know best; we admit our ignorance or incomplete knowledge about the countries we have excluded.

Consequently, and following Huber and Stephens, we divide our selected countries into four groups:

1. *Countries in the social democratic tradition* (SDCs), including Sweden, Denmark, Norway, Finland, and Austria, which have been governed by social democratic parties (either alone or in partnership with other parties) for the majority of years during 1945–80. By including Austria, we depart from Huber and Stephens, who include Austria among the Christian democratic countries. We differ with them in this respect because, during 1945–80, Austria was governed for 20 years by social democratic parties and for only 15 years by Christian democrats. We are sensitive, however, to the arguments put forward by Huber and Stephens for including Austria among the Christian democratic countries. Indeed, the social democratic and Christian democratic parties have governed that country in coalition for many years, which explains why its social policies are a mix of social democratic and Christian democratic. Moreover, the hegemonic culture in Austria is a Christian culture, which gives a strong imprimatur to its social policies and explains, for example, the relatively low percentage of women in the labor force. Still, we keep Austria in the SDC column to stress the dominance of the social democratic party in that coalition for most of the welfare states' formative period, 1945–80.

2. *Countries in the Christian democratic tradition* or *conservative tradition rooted in Christian values* (CDCs); this has two subgroups. One group of countries—Belgium, Netherlands, and Germany—has been governed by Christian democratic parties during most of the 1945–80 period, but has also had powerful social democratic parties with which the Christian democratic parties have governed in alliance for variable periods of time. The other group of countries—France, Italy, and Switzerland—has been governed by Christian democratic parties or by conservative parties (rooted in the Christian tradition) for most of the 1945–80 period. In France and Italy, the left was characterized by the dominance of the communist parties for the majority of years in the 1945–80 period. In all three countries (although particularly in France), the left was very powerful and, immediately after World War II, had considerable influence in shaping the economic and social policies of that period. In France, for example, the combined socialist and communist vote in the first elections after the war made up 55 percent of the poll. Moreover, De Gaulle's first government adopted the Resistance Program, which included the nationalization of banks, insurance companies, and the major utilities, establishing indicative planning and economic modernization as the main elements of its program (19). In all these countries, where the communist party was the major force on the left, the Cold War—which divided the socialist from the communist parties— greatly weakened the labor movement.

3. *Countries in the liberal tradition* (LCs), including Canada, Ireland, the United Kingdom, the United States, and Japan, in which neither social democratic nor Christian democratic parties played a major role in the development of their welfare states. (The exceptions were the Labour Party in the United Kingdom, which in 1948 established the National Health Service, and Canada's Social Democratic Party, which established a provincial—later national—health insurance system.) These countries were governed by conservative parties of liberal persuasion for the majority of years during 1945–80.

Two clarifications are needed regarding the composition of this group of LCs. One is the inclusion of the United Kingdom, in spite of its being governed by a social democratic party for 16 years. Our rationale for including Britain in this group—as did Huber and Stephens—is that the country was governed by a liberal-oriented Conservative Party for most of the 1945–80 period, which explains the low level of public and social expenditures as well as the residual nature of the welfare state, with the exception of the National Health Service. Despite public pronouncements that the British welfare state was "the envy of the world," even during the Labour government of 1945–50 the United Kingdom was spending less on social security (by the late 1950s) than were any of the major continental European democracies (20). The liberal economist John Maynard Keynes wrote that the Beveridge proposals (the basis for the British welfare state) were "the cheapest alternative open to us . . . and there is no doubt that Beveridge's definition of subsistence conformed to a very basic Spartan minimum" (quoted in 21).

The other clarification concerns the inclusion of Japan in this group of liberal countries. We do this for internal consistency, since Japan was governed by conservative parties of liberal persuasion for the majority of years in the 1945–80 period, while accepting that Japan has many characteristics that differentiate it from the other, Anglo-Saxon liberal countries.

4. *The ex-dictatorial conservative southern European countries* (EDCs), Spain, Portugal, and Greece. These countries were governed by right-wing dictatorships that imposed scarcely developed welfare states.

THE SOCIAL DEMOCRATIC TRADITION

Is There Still a Social Democratic Type of Welfare State in the 1990s?

The social democratic countries have long had a unique combination of strong labor movements and open, export-oriented economies.[2] Strong trade union movements have guaranteed a comprehensive, universalistic welfare state, despite a high and rising level of "globalization" in these economies since the 1960s. The social democratic tradition has been based on a strong labor-union movement, whose strength, continuing through the 1990s, is characterized by:

1. *A high percentage of unionization of the workforce.* Table 1 shows that in all the SDCs except Austria, more that 50 percent of the workforce continued to be unionized during the 1990s, reaching in 1994 (the latest year for which the OECD has published complete data on unionization rates) extremely high levels in Sweden (91 percent), Finland (81 percent), and Denmark (76 percent). The rise in unionization between 1980 and 1994 was particularly accentuated in Sweden and Finland (increasing from 80 to 91 percent in Sweden, and from 70 to 81 percent in Finland).

2. *An even higher share of the workforce still covered by collective bargaining agreements,* ranging from 69 percent in Denmark to 98 percent in Austria, with 89 percent in Sweden, 74 percent in Norway, and 95 percent in Finland (Table 1).

3. *Inheritance of a strong social democratic tradition, reflected in a very large percentage of the electoral share won by social democratic parties in general elections,* with an average for the 1980–90 period of 44.6 percent in Austria, 44.5 percent in Sweden, 32.2 percent in Denmark, 37.4 percent in Norway, and 25.4 percent in Finland. The percentages were, on average, practically the same for the entire 1945–90 period, except in Norway, where the percentage declined from 44.2 percent in 1945–73 to 37.4 percent in 1980–90. In Sweden and Denmark, shares of the electoral vote going to social democratic parties were only slightly lower in the 1980–90 period

---

[2] "Openness" refers here primarily to trade in goods. Below we discuss problems associated with the opening up of capital flows.

Table 1

Union information, as percentage of wage-and-salary workforce

	Union density			Coverage by collective bargaining		
	1980	1994	Change	1980	1994	Change
Social democratic						
Austria	56	42	−14	98	98	0
Denmark	76	76	0	69	69	0
Finland	70	81	11	95	95	0
Norway	57	58	1	75	74	−1
Sweden	80	91	11	86	89	3
Average	68	70	2	85	85	0
Christian democratic						
Belgium	56	53	−3	90	90	0
France	18	9	−9	85	95	10
Germany	36	29	−7	91	92	1
Italy	49	39	−10	85	82	−3
Netherlands	35	26	−9	76	81	5
Switzerland	31	27	−4	53	50	−3
Average	38	31	−7	80	82	2
Liberal						
Canada	36	38	2	37	36	−1
United Kingdom	50	34	−16	70	47	−23
Ireland	—	—	—	—	—	—
Japan	31	24	−7	28	21	−7
United States	22	16	−6	26	18	−8
Average	35	28	−7	40	31	−10
Ex-dictatorship						
Greece	—	—	—	—	—	—
Portugal	61	32	−29	70	71	1
Spain	9	19	10	76	78	2
Average	35	26	−10	73	75	2

Source: OECD, *OECD Employment Outlook,* Paris, July 1997, Table 3.3.

(44.5 and 32.2 percent, respectively) than in the 1945–73 period (46.3 and 37.7 percent, respectively) (19, Table 9.1, p. 215).

4. *As a result of this strong electoral tradition, long periods of government by social democratic parties:* 23.5 years as an average during the formative years 1945–80, when the social democratic parties governed either alone or in alliance with agrarian or communist parties. This includes 30 years in Sweden, 28 years in Norway, 25 years in Denmark, 14 years in Finland, and 20 years in Austria. None of these countries (except Austria) were ever governed by Christian democratic parties (in Austria, Christian democrats governed for 15 years) (14, Table 4.1, p. 110).

Consequent to this strength of the labor movement, the SDCs have large welfare states grounded for the most part on the principle of *universality, with benefits provided as a matter of citizenship.*[3] This universality of benefits was a response to the demand of the less-favored sectors in society (such as blue-collar workers) for the same benefits as the most-favored sectors (white-collar workers), using the law (rather than the labor market) as the instrument for attaining such equalization. The principle of universality was therefore rooted in the principles of solidarity and equality among classes (and later, from the 1950s, between the sexes) (10, p. 119). As a result of this universalism, in the 1990s the SDCs continued to have the largest *social public expenditures* (Table 2) among the developed capitalist countries, an average of 29.3 percent of GDP in 1997, up from 24.2 percent in 1980. The most dramatic growth in public expenditure took place in Finland and Norway, where social expenditures were the lowest of the group during this period.

Some authors, such as Clayton and Pontusson (23), have questioned the value of regarding social expenditures as an indicator of commitment to the welfare state, since universal social transfers such as pensions may be more a result of the aging of the population, for example, than of the generosity of pensions. Castles (9), however, has shown that the growth of social expenditures in these countries is, in general, above that required to cover the increased numbers of older persons. Moreover, we have also looked at the growth of public employment (which is less related to aging) and have found, as Table 2 shows, that in the 1990s the SDCs also continued to have the *largest percentage of employment in the public sector,* at 20 percent of overall employment in 1997. While social expenditures in 1997 were somewhat larger in the SDCs than in the CDCs (on average, 29.3

---

[3] Dani Rodrik (22) argues that it was precisely the strong welfare states of these countries, a result of the universalization of benefits, that made high levels of globalization politically feasible. In Rodrik's view, more-open economies are prone to higher economic and social adjustment costs and larger economic swings. Since strong welfare-state institutions can protect workers against these potential problems, the welfare state helps to ensure political support for opening countries to the world economy.

Table 2

Social expenditure and employment

	Public social exps., % GDP			Government employment, % total employment		
	1980	1997	Change	1974	1997	Change
Social democratic						
Austria	23.9	26.2	2.3	9.6	15.4	5.8
Denmark	29.4	30.8	1.4	16.4	23.4	7.0
Finland	18.9	29.5	10.6	9.9	16.1	6.2
Norway	18.8	26.5	7.7	12.8	23.6	10.8
Sweden	29.8	33.7	3.9	18.7	21.3	2.6
Average	24.2	29.3	5.2	13.5	20.0	6.5
Christian democratic						
Belgium	25.6	25.1	−0.5	9.5	10.6	1.1
France	23.5	29.6	6.1	11.5	14.8	3.3
Germany	25.4	27.7	2.3	8.8	9.9	1.1
Italy	18.4	26.9	8.5	7.5	8.3	0.8
Netherlands	28.9	25.9	−3.0	7.0	8.3	1.3
Switzerland	16.7	27.2	10.5	6.9	11.1	4.2
Average	23.1	27.1	4.0	8.5	10.5	2.0
Liberal						
Canada	13.3	16.9	3.6	12.4	12.9	0.5
United Kingdom	18.4	21.9	3.5	14.0	10.1	−3.9
Ireland	17.6	17.9	0.3	7.5	7.0	−0.5
Japan	10.5	14.8	4.3	4.4	4.4	0.0
United States	13.9	16.5	2.6	10.5	9.8	−0.7
Average	14.7	17.6	2.9	9.8	8.8	−0.9
Ex-dictatorship						
Greece	11.5	22.2	10.7	—	—	—
Portugal	11.6	19.1	7.5	6.2	11.4	5.2
Spain	16.3	20.9	4.6	5.6	7.3	1.7
Average	13.1	20.7	7.6	5.9	9.4	3.5

Sources: Public and mandatory private social expenditures as a share of GDP from OECD, *OECD Social Expenditure Database 1980–1997,* Paris, 2000. Government employment as a percentage of total employment from OECD, *OECD Historical Statistics 1960–1997,* Paris, 1999, Table 2.13, multiplied by employment-to-population rate from OECD, *OECD Historical Statistics 1970–1999,* Paris, 2000, Table 2.13.

Note: Data for Austria, Norway, the Netherlands, Great Britain, Spain, and Portugal in column for 1997 refer to 1995.

percent of GDP in the SDCs vs. 27.1 percent of GDP in the CDCs), public employment as percentage of overall employment was much larger in the SDCs (20.0 percent) than in the other groups of countries—almost double the level in the CDCs (10.5 percent) and more than double that of the LCs (8.8 percent) and the EDCs (9.4 percent). This difference arises because, although both the SDCs and CDCs are rich in social transfers and social expenditures, the SDCs rely heavily on the public sector for the provision of welfare-state services—that is, most public services are provided by public employees—while the CDCs and other countries supply these services primarily through private providers. Moreover, the extent and coverage of welfare-state services is much larger in the SDCs than in the other groups of countries. "Family-friendly and women-friendly services," such as childcare and home care services, for example, are far more extensive in the SDCs than in the other groups of countries. As Kohl (20), Esping-Andersen (12), Castles (24), Huber and Stephens (10), and Scharpf (25) have shown, the SDCs *are not only transfer rich but also services rich.* This latter characteristic explains why the SDCs are also public-employment rich. *The data presented in Table 2 show that the SDCs, for most of the 1990s, remained the countries with the largest social public transfer and social services (provided primarily in the public sector).*

The large size of the public social services in the SDCs also helps explain why *the overall employment in services also remains very high in the SDCs*—in 1999 an average of 68.7 percent of all workers were in the services sector—about the same as in the CDCs (69.0 percent) and the LCs (69.3 percent), and well above that in the EDCs (55.4 percent) (Table 3). These differences in services employment, particularly public-sector employment, are strongly related to differences in women's participation in the labor force, which continues to be much higher in the SDCs (72.4 percent) than in the CDCs (60.7 percent), LCs (64.5 percent), and EDCs (54.2 percent). In general, a simple regression analysis of the data in Table 3 indicates that a 1 percentage-point increase in a country's service-sector employment is associated with a 0.6 percentage-point increase in the corresponding female labor-force participation rate. This positive correlation exists for several reasons: first, because services are the major suppliers of jobs for women (especially the personal and social services); second, because family- and women-friendly services such as childcare and home care enable women to combine their family and professional responsibilities; and third, because, as Esping-Andersen (26) has noted, participation of women in the labor market stimulates the demand for jobs in the personal-services sector (cleaning, restaurants, and so forth). Moreover, the public nature of much services employment in the SDCs appears to be associated with even higher rates of female labor-force participation than in the CDCs or the LCs, which have comparable levels of total service-sector employment but lower female participation rates than the SDCs.

The percentage of women in the labor force continued to be very high in the SDCs during the 1990s, even though it declined somewhat in Finland and in

Table 3

Service-sector employment and women's participation in the labor force

	Employment in services sector, % of total employment, 1999	Female participation rate, %, 1999
Social democratic		
Austria	61.9	62.7
Denmark	70.0	76.1
Finland	65.9	71.2
Norway	73.2	76.1
Sweden	72.3	76.0
Average	68.7	72.4
Christian democratic		
Belgium	72.6	56.0
France	71.0	61.3
Germany	62.6	62.3
Italy	62.2	45.6
Netherlands	75.9	64.4
Switzerland	69.5	74.5
Average	69.0	60.7
Liberal		
Canada	73.6	69.8
United Kingdom	72.4	68.4
Ireland	62.9	54.3
Japan	63.2	59.5
United States	74.4	70.7
Average	69.3	64.5
Ex-dictatorship		
Greece	59.2	49.7
Portugal	45.2	63.0
Spain	61.9	49.9
Average	55.4	54.2

Sources: See Table 2 for participation rates. Service-sector employment from OECD, *Labor Force Statistics 1979–1999,* Paris, 2000, pp. 32–34.

Note: Regression analysis indicates that a 1 percentage-point increase in service-sector employment is associated with a 0.6 percentage-point increase in women's labor-force participation; the relationship is statistically significant at the 5% level. Service-sector employment for Greece refers to 1998. Population figures for the United States refer to ages 16 to 64.

Sweden. Still, in 1999, women's employment rates in the SDCs (67.3 percent) remained higher, on average, than in the LDCs (61.8 percent), the CDCs (54.1 percent), and the EDCs (46.1 percent) (Table 4). Actually, women's employment rate is particularly low in Spain (37.7 percent), among the EDCs, and in Italy (38.8 percent), among the CDCs, which are also the two countries with the lowest fertility rates. This situation, in which Spain and Italy have very low fertility and low female participation in the labor force, challenges the widely held assumption in conservative religious circles, including the Spanish and Italian churches, that women's participation in the labor force is the cause of the "deterioration" of the family and decline of fertility rates. Table 5 shows that the SDCs have higher female participation and higher fertility rates than Italy and Spain. Moreover, the table also shows that the SDCs have much lower overall female and young female (15 to 24 years of age) unemployment than do Italy and Spain. These data would seem to confirm for the 1990s the thesis advanced by Bettio and Villa (27) that low fertility in Italy and Spain is primarily related to the stability (or lack of stability) of employment among young women (15 to 24 years of age) rather than to their participation rate in the labor force.

From the data presented thus far, we can conclude that *in the decade of the 1990s, the welfare states in SDCs remained strong and expansive.* A look at Table 6 reveals that the standard of living in the SDCs—as measured by compensation and growth of compensation—was not adversely affected in the 1990s by the strength of their welfare states. As the table shows, the annual growth in real compensation for the 1989–98 period was much higher in the SDCs (1.7 percent) than in the CDCs (0.8 percent) or the LCs (1.0 percent). Only the low-wage EDCs managed faster real-compensation growth in 1989–98 (2.4 percent). It is worth noting that the SDCs were also the top performers in the 1980s, when annual growth in real compensation averaged 1.4 percent in the SDCs, 1.0 percent in the CDCs, 1.1 percent in the LCs (–0.3 percent in the United States), and just 0.1 percent in the EDCs. In 1999, the SDCs were the group with the highest hourly compensation in manufacturing: 116 (cf. 100 in the United States), compared with 112 in the CDCs, 89 in the LCs, and 47 in the EDCs. The SDCs continued with the lowest wage differentials and lowest household-income inequalities in the 1990s, with the second lowest (after the CDCs) number of hours worked per worker (an indication of quality of life at the workplace). The SDCs also had the lowest poverty rates among all age groups, elderly and children.

Economic Performance of the SDCs and Their Welfare States: Are They Still Competitive under Globalization?

The rate of growth of real GDP per capita in the SDCs during the 1990s fell between the higher rates in the LCs and EDCs, on the one hand, and the lower rates in the CDCs, on the other (Table 7). Per capita GDP growth over the period was particularly low in Sweden, averaging 1.1 percent per year. Some critics of

Table 4

Employment rates: percentage employed as share of working-age population

	Men			Women		
	1979	1989	1999	1979	1989	1999
Social democratic						
Austria	80.4	77.7	76.1	47.6	52.3	59.1
Denmark	82.5	81.1	79.7	64.1	70.1	70.5
Finland	74.3	77.1	68.4	65.2	71.9	63.7
Norway	84.9	79.1	80.7	60.2	67.9	73.9
Sweden	86.3	83.9	73.3	71.1	79.5	69.5
Average	81.7	79.8	75.6	61.6	68.3	67.3
Christian democratic						
Belgium	73.1	65.4	64.4	40.2	44.4	49.1
France	76.1	67.2	64.6	49.8	50.2	52.8
Germany	80.1	74.9	72.6	49.9	51.9	57.0
Italy	75.7	69.4	66.9	33.6	36.1	38.8
Netherlands	72.9	72.8	79.7	31.2	45.1	59.5
Switzerland	94.1	99.6	93.4	52.8	62.8	67.7
Average	78.7	74.9	73.8	42.9	48.4	54.1
Liberal						
Canada	79.5	77.8	75.3	50.9	61.7	64.5
United Kingdom	83.9	80.0	76.5	56.0	61.4	63.4
Ireland	82.6	66.8	75.0	33.2	35.4	51.9
Japan	87.1	85.1	88.0	53.5	57.8	60.9
United States	78.8	79.2	80.2	54.7	64.4	68.4
Average	82.4	77.8	79.0	49.7	56.1	61.8
Ex-dictatorship						
Greece	78.0	71.7	69.8	31.7	38.1	39.6
Portugal	81.3	79.6	78.1	47.0	54.8	61.0
Spain	73.0	65.6	64.9	29.5	30.1	37.7
Average	77.4	72.3	71.0	36.1	41.0	46.1

Source: OECD, *Labor Force Statistics 1979–1999,* Paris, 2000, Part 2.

Note: Data for Greece in column for 1999 refer to 1996. Data for Netherlands in column for 1999 refer to 1997. Data for Portugal in column for 1979 refer to 1980; data for 1999 refer to 1998. Data for Great Britain in column for 1999 refer to 1998.

Table 5

Women's labor-force participation, fertility, and unemployment

	Female participation, %, ages 15–64		Fertility rate		Female unemployment, %, average 1996–99	
	1974	1999	1970–75	1995–2000	All	Ages 15–24
Social democratic						
Austria	53	62	2.02	1.41	5.3	7.0
Denmark	63	76	1.97	1.72	6.8	10.1
Finland	66	71	1.62	1.73	12.8	24.4
Norway	50	76	2.25	1.85	3.8	10.7
Sweden	65	75	1.89	1.57	8.6	18.4
Average	59	72	1.95	1.66	7.5	14.1
Christian democratic						
Belgium	42	58	1.93	1.56	11.5	23.9
France	51	61	2.31	1.75	14.0	31.1
Germany	51	63	1.64	1.33	9.9	8.7
Italy	34	46	2.28	1.22	16.6	39.0
Netherlands	30	65	1.97	1.47	6.5	9.9
Switzerland	54	70	1.82	1.47	4.0	5.2
Average	44	60	1.99	1.47	10.4	19.6
Liberal						
Canada	48	70	1.97	1.57	8.4	13.8
United Kingdom	55	68	2.04	1.72	5.6	10.7
Ireland	34	55	3.82	1.90	8.8	12.9
Japan	52	64	2.07	1.46	4.0	7.1
United States	52	72	2.02	1.93	4.9	10.3
Average	48	66	2.38	1.72	6.3	11.0
Ex-dictatorship						
Greece	33	49	2.32	1.24	15.9	40.4
Portugal	51	67	2.75	1.32	7.2	15.4
Spain	33	49	2.89	1.13	27.0	43.9
Average	39	55	2.65	1.23	16.7	33.2

Sources: Updated information for the article by Bettio and Villa (27, p. 139). Participation rates from OECD, *OECD Historical Statistics 1970–1999,* Paris, 2001, Table 2.7. Unemployment rates updated using *OECD Employment Outlook,* Paris, July 2000, Table B; unemployment rates for 15- to 24-year-olds from Table C. Estimated and projected fertility rates from the United Nations, *World Population Prospects, the 1998 Revision, Volume 1: Comprehensive Tables,* as reported in the WISTAT4 database, Table 4.4

Note: Labor-force participation and unemployment rates for the United States refer to the population of age 16 to 64. Labor-force participation rates for Greece in column for 1999 refer to 1998.

Table 6

Characteristics of the labor market: earnings, income, hours worked, and poverty

	Annualized growth in real compensation, %		Relative hourly compensation in manufacturing, at market exchange rates, U.S. = 100			Change in earnings ineq., % change		Household income ineq. (90:10 ratio)	Average annual hours of work		Relative poverty rate, % of population, 1990s		
	1979–89	1989–98	1980	1990	1999	Early 80s to late 80s	Late 80s to mid 90s	Early to mid 1990s	1979	1999	Total	Elderly	Children
Social democratic													
Austria	1.9	1.4	90	119	114	1.7	4.3	2.89	—	—	2.8	6.8	2.6
Denmark	0.2	1.6	110	121	120	1.9	—	2.84	—	1,730	3.6	3.7	2.1
Finland	3.0	2.3	83	141	110	4.5	-8.9	2.68	1,837	1,395	—	—	—
Norway	0.4	1.7	117	144	125	-3.9	—	2.82	1,514	1,635	3.0	0.7	2.2
Sweden	1.3	1.3	127	140	112	3.9	4.2	2.59	1,516	1,587	4.6	0.7	1.3
Average	1.4	1.7	105	133	116	1.6	-0.1	2.76	1,622	1,587	3.5	3.0	2.1
Christian democratic													
Belgium	0.9	1.5	133	129	119	—	4.0	2.76	—	1,562	1.9	4.2	1.6
France	1.0	1.0	91	104	94	1.2	-6.7	3.32	1,806	1,399	3.2	3.6	2.6
Germany	1.2	1.2	124	147	140	-8.6	-5.7	3.18	1,633	1,634	4.2	4.0	6.0
Italy	1.4	0.5	83	117	86	-26.5	29.6	4.68	1,722	1,343	8.9	4.7	14.1
Netherlands	0.0	0.4	122	121	109	—	-0.8	3.08	1,591	—	4.7	3.1	4.6
Switzerland	1.5	0.0	112	140	123	—	1.9	3.39	—	1,588	4.0	3.1	4.4
Average	1.0	0.8	111	126	112	-11.3	3.7	3.40	1,688	1,505	4.5	3.8	5.6

Liberal													
Canada	0.5	0.8	88	107	81	9.7	-4.5	3.90	1,832	1,785	6.6	1.2	8.5
United Kingdom	2.1	1.3	77	85	86	17.6	2.7	4.52	1,815	1,719	5.7	4.0	8.3
Ireland	1.6	1.7	60	78	71	—	—	4.20	—	—	—	—	—
Japan	1.4	0.4	56	86	109	5.0	-4.4	4.17	2,126	1,840	6.9	—	—
United States	-0.3	0.6	100	100	100	13.4	7.0	5.64	1,845	1,877	10.7	12.0	14.7
Average	1.1	1.0	76	91	89	11.4	0.2	4.49	1,905	1,805	7.5	5.7	10.5
Ex-dictatorship													
Greece	0.1	—	38	45	48	—	—	—	—	—	—	—	—
Portugal	0.1	3.2	21	25	29	—	16.0	—	—	—	—	—	—
Spain	0.1	1.5	60	76	63	—	—	3.96	2,022	1,812	5.1	3.9	7.0
Average	0.1	2.4	40	49	47	—	16.0	3.96	2,022	1,812	5.1	3.9	7.0

Sources: Real compensation from analysis of OECD data in Mishel, Bernstein, and Schmitt, *The State of Working America*, Economic Policy Institute, 2001, Table 7.5. Relative hourly compensation from U.S. BLS, ftp://ftp.bls.gov/pub/special.requests/ForeignLabor/ind2000.txt, p. 6. Change in earnings inequality adapted from analysis of OECD data in Mishel, Bernstein, and Schmitt, Table 7.9. Household earnings inequality from Smeeding, T. M., *Changing Income Inequality in OECD Countries*, Luxembourg Income Study Working Paper No. 252, March 2000, Figure 1. Poverty rates from Smeeding, T., Rainwater, L., and Burtless, G., United States Poverty in a Cross-National Context, paper prepared for the IRP conference volume *Understanding Poverty in America: Progress and Problems*, September 28, 2000, Table 2.

Note: Relative hourly compensation data for Germany refer to western Germany only; data for Greece and Portugal in column for 1999 refer to 1998. Earnings inequality is defined as the ratio of the 90th percentile to the 10th percentile of the earnings distribution. Average annual hours worked data are for all workers, except in the Netherlands and Germany, where they refer to dependent employment; German data refer to western Germany. Poverty measured as adjusted disposable personal income below 40 percent of the median.

Table 7

Economic growth: annualized percentage growth in real GDP per capita

	1960–73	1973–79	1979–89	1989–99
Social democratic				
Austria	4.3	3.0	2.0	1.8
Denmark	3.6	1.2	1.4	1.7
Finland	4.5	1.9	3.2	1.2
Norway	3.5	4.3	2.3	2.7
Sweden	3.4	1.5	1.8	1.1
Average	3.9	2.4	2.1	1.7
Christian democratic				
Belgium	4.4	2.2	2.1	1.7
France	4.3	2.3	1.8	1.3
Germany	3.7	2.5	1.9	1.3
Italy	4.6	3.0	2.3	1.2
Netherlands	3.6	1.9	1.3	2.2
Switzerland	3.0	−0.1	1.7	0.2
Average	3.9	2.0	1.9	1.3
Liberal				
Canada	3.6	2.6	1.7	1.1
United Kingdom	2.6	1.5	2.2	1.6
Ireland	3.7	3.3	2.7	6.1
Japan	8.3	2.4	3.1	1.4
United States	2.6	2.0	2.0	2.0
Average	4.2	2.4	2.3	2.4
Ex-dictatorship				
Greece	7.1	2.6	1.2	1.4
Portugal	6.9	1.0	2.9	2.7
Spain	6.2	1.2	2.3	2.3
Average	6.7	1.6	2.1	2.1

Sources: Data for 1960–73 from OECD, *OECD Historical Statistics 1960–1997,* Paris, 1996, Table 3.2. Other data from OECD, *OECD Historical Statistics 1970–1999,* Paris, 2000, Table 3.2.

the SDC model have attributed the relatively poor performance of the SDCs, especially Sweden, to "excessive" welfare states, with too much government intervention and regulation of the SDC economies. Lindbeck and Henrekson, in particular, have argued that the deceleration in growth in Sweden in the 1990s is a sign of the "exhaustion" of the Swedish welfare state and, indirectly, of the failure of the social democratic model (28; see 29–32 for a full discussion of Lindbeck's thesis and critiques; see also 33, 34).

The unweighted average growth rate in the SDCs during the 1990s was lower than the corresponding unweighted average for the LCs; however, this result depends entirely on the rapid growth in Ireland, where real per capita GDP rose at an average annual rate of 6.1 percent in the 1990s (Table 7). Excluding Ireland, the LCs actually grew more slowly, at 1.5 percent per year, than did the SDCs (1.7 percent). In fact, during the 1990s, Austria, Denmark, and Norway all grew faster than Canada, Japan, and the United Kingdom. The fastest growing SDC economy, Norway (2.7 percent), grew faster than the United States (2.0 percent); and Austria (1.8 percent) and Denmark (1.7 percent) were not far behind. Both groups of countries also had laggards: just as Finland (1.2 percent) and Sweden (1.1 percent) put in disappointing performances in the 1990s, so too did Canada (1.1 percent) and Japan (1.4 percent). As such, the national evidence on growth rates suggests that the SDCs fared no worse than did the LCs in the 1990s. The idea that the evident deceleration in growth rates in the 1990s responded to "exhaustion" under the weight of the welfare state is not supported by the available data. Real GDP growth rates decelerated in the 1990s in almost every OECD economy, regardless of the type and extent of their welfare states. Even in the United States (a laggard in its welfare state), real per capita GDP growth was no greater in the 1990s than in the 1973–79 and 1979–89 periods, and was well below what it had been in 1960–73. The case for exhaustion in Sweden is particularly problematic, because the low real-GDP growth rate in the 1990s was the product of a sharp and sudden recession in the early 1990s (–1.1 percent change in real GDP in 1991, –1.7 percent in 1992, and –1.8 percent in 1993) and a sustained and energetic boom at the end of the 1990s (2.1 percent real growth in 1997, 3.6 percent in 1998, 4.1 percent in 1999, and 3.6 percent in 2000). If the Swedish model was exhausted by the end of the 1980s, it somehow managed to catch its breath at some point in the mid-1990s and did so without a significant restructuring of its labor markets or its welfare states (see 35, chapt. 3, for evidence that Sweden has fallen far short of OECD hopes for internal reform).[4]

Actually, the thesis that the welfare state has hindered economic performance conflicts also with the analysis of the employment performance of the SDCs. As a group, the SDCs, for most of the period since 1960, including the 1990s,

---

[4] Moreover, the largest employment growth took place primarily in the export-oriented sectors, maintaining a percentage of the adult population working in such sectors above the OECD-18 average (see 25, pp. 89, 345).

have provided high employment levels (Table 4), low unemployment rates (except Finland; see Table 8), and rapid compensation growth that has been widely shared (Table 6). The institutional structures that have helped to generate these egalitarian outcomes may also have contributed to—and certainly have not hindered—the SDCs' strong participation in nearly all aspects of the "New Economy."[5]

If Not the Welfare State, What Caused the Slowdown
of the SDCs (and Other Countries) in the 1990s?

The expansion of social expenditures that occurred in all the SDCs (and in most other countries, except the United States, Ireland, and Great Britain) was not the reason for the general slowdown of economic growth and increase of unemployment in the European Union in the 1990s. The actual reasons included high continent-wide interest rates following German Unification; the creation of a European Central Bank with a mandate to focus exclusively on inflation; the fiscal austerity required by the Maastricht Treaty; the collapse of the Soviet Union (which particularly affected countries, such as Finland, that had substantial trade with the Soviet bloc); the late transition out of agriculture (especially in the EDCs); and the deregulation of the financial markets, a point especially emphasized by Huber and Stephens and by Scharpf (10, 25). According to these authors, the deregulation of capital markets has led to higher interest rates in deregulated markets (making it more difficult for investors to borrow) as well as higher levels of instability in capital markets, which has reinforced the negative effects of higher interest rates. Table 9 shows that gross fixed capital formation (as percentage of GDP) declined in the 1990s in the overwhelming majority of developed capitalist countries considered in this study. Only Belgium, Germany, and Spain saw an increase of investment during this decade, consistent with the thesis that recent financial-market developments have been detrimental to real investment. The countries with the most important decline in investment were the SDCs, where gross fixed capital formation fell from an average of 23.4 percent of GDP in 1980–89 to 20.1 percent of GDP in 1990–99; between the same two periods, gross fixed capital formation fell from 21.9 to 20.9 percent in the CDCs, from 21.9 to 20.3 percent in the LCs, and from 24.4 to 22.4 percent in the EDCs. The liberalization of capital markets had a larger negative impact in the SDCs than it did elsewhere, because the SDCs had historically relied on public credit policies—a major component of what is usually referred to as "supply-side socialism"—which were particularly adversely affected by the deregulation of financial markets. Moreover, liberalization of capital markets weakened the

---

[5] According to a recent OECD review of the "New Economy," for example, in the 1990s Sweden (*a*) trailed only Japan (first) and the United States (second) in the number of patents granted relative to GDP; (*b*) led the OECD in business spending on research and development (R&D) as a share of GDP; and (*c*) was second, after the United States, in government-financed R&D as a share of GDP (see 36, chapt. 3).

Table 8

Unemployment rate: average annual standardized unemployment rate,
as percentage of labor force

	1964–73	1974–79	1980–89	1990–99	1998–00
Social democratic					
Austria	—	—	—	—	4.1
Denmark	—	—	—	7.4	5.0
Finland	2.3	5.1	5.4	11.9	10.5
Norway	1.7	1.8	2.8	4.9	3.3
Sweden	2.0	1.9	2.6	7.3	7.1
Average	2.0	2.9	3.6	7.9	6.0
Christian democratic					
Belgium	2.3	7.1	9.8	8.7	8.4
France	2.2	4.5	8.9	11.2	10.8
Germany	0.8	3.2	5.8	7.5	8.6
Italy	5.5	6.6	8.0	10.6	11.2
Netherlands	1.3	5.4	7.9	5.7	3.4
Switzerland	—	—	—	—	3.3
Average	2.4	5.4	8.1	8.7	7.6
Liberal					
Canada	4.8	7.2	9.4	9.5	7.6
United Kingdom	3.0	4.7	9.8	8.2	6.0
Ireland	—	—	—	12.1	5.8
Japan	1.2	1.9	2.5	3.0	4.5
United States	4.5	6.8	7.3	5.8	4.2
Average	3.4	5.2	7.3	7.7	5.6
Ex-dictatorship					
Greece	—	—	—	—	—
Portugal	—	—	—	5.7	4.6
Spain	—	—	17.7	19.8	16.3
Average	—	—	17.7	12.8	10.5

Sources: Data for 1964–73 and for 1974–79 for France, Germany, and Italy, from OECD, *OECD Historical Statistics 1960–1994,* Paris, 1996, Table 2.20. Other data from OECD, *OECD Historical Statistics 1970–1999,* Paris, 2000, Table 2.19.

Table 9

Gross fixed capital formation, as percentage of GDP

	1960–73	1973–79	1980–89	1990–99
Social democratic				
Austria	26.7	25.3	22.9	23.6
Denmark	23.8	23.2	19.7	18.8
Finland	26.4	28.6	26.5	19.4
Norway	27.5	32.7	27.0	21.5
Sweden	23.3	22.1	20.9	17.2
Average	25.5	26.4	23.4	20.1
Christian democratic				
Belgium	21.6	24.6	19.4	21.0
France	23.8	24.2	21.7	19.6
Germany	24.6	21.2	20.8	22.5
Italy	24.6	25.5	22.6	19.2
Netherlands	25.6	23.0	21.5	21.3
Switzerland	27.9	23.5	25.1	22.0
Average	24.7	23.7	21.9	20.9
Liberal				
Canada	21.8	23.5	21.7	18.9
United Kingdom	22.4	20.1	18.5	17.1
Ireland	20.0	24.9	21.0	18.6
Japan	32.6	31.8	29.1	29.1
United States	18.4	19.4	19.2	17.7
Average	23.0	23.9	21.9	20.3
Ex-dictatorship				
Greece	27.8	28.3	24.2	20.8
Portugal	26.5	26.7	26.7	23.4
Spain	24.1	26.0	22.3	22.9
Average	26.1	27.0	24.4	22.4

Sources: Data for 1960–73 from OECD, *OECD Historical Statistics 1960–1994,* Paris, 1996, Table 6.8. Other periods from OECD, *OECD Historical Statistics 1970–1999,* Paris, 2000, Table 6.8.

relationship between banking and industry that had been a characteristic of the SDCs, as well as the CDCs (10, 25).

Even though the SDCs have lagged behind the CDCs, LCs, and EDCs with respect to investment, unemployment in the SDCs continues to be among the lowest in the developed capitalist countries. One important reason for the strong employment performance of the SDCs in the face of low investment is the large services sector, especially public-services sector, in the SDCs. Even though financial-market deregulation has forced the SDCs to abandon key components of their "supply-side socialism," such as credit policies, financial deregulation has not had an adverse effect on social policies. The SDCs still have the highest levels and growth rates of social expenditures, which have been sustained primarily by the SDCs' tax policies, as demonstrated below. Indeed, public consumption—a good indirect indicator of the size of a welfare state, since it includes expenditure on public transfers plus public employment (Table 10)—was, in the 1990s, higher in the SDCs than in the other developed capitalist countries. Moreover, public consumption continued to grow in the SDCs in the 1990s, even as it declined in the CDCs and LCs over the same period.

Although the deregulation of financial markets, usually referred to as global-ization of finance, has adversely affected the continuation of major elements of "supply-side socialism" in the SDCs, without affecting their welfare states, other dimensions of globalization, such as globalization of trade in goods and services, have not had any obvious adverse effects on the development of social democratic policies. As is evident in Table 11, which shows exports as share of GDP for each group of countries, in the 1990s SDCs, after the CDCs, continued to be the most globalized of the developed capitalist countries with respect to trade. At the same time, the SDCs also maintained the most extensive welfare states.

How Could the SDCs Continue Their Welfare State
Expansion in an Era of Financial Globalization?

One of the most striking changes in the 1990s in the developed capitalist countries, including the SDCs, was with respect to fiscal policies. As Table 12 shows, tax revenues increased in the SDCs and in all the groups of countries except the LCs, where they actually declined during the 1990s, and the Netherlands (among the CDCs), where taxes also diminished. Taxes represented the highest share of GDP in the SDCs (47.0 percent, on average), followed by the CDCs (41.3 percent), with the LCs (32.0 percent) and EDCs (34.0 percent) at much lower rates. These data, incidentally, challenge the widely held assumption that countries seem to have exhausted their capacity to raise public revenues.[6]

---

[6] An example of that perception appears in Scharpf's statement that "the share of taxes and social security contributions in GDP has risen steeply until the mid-1980s, but stagnated thereafter" (25, p. 73). Our Table 12 does not show that stagnation. Actually, Scharpf's own data—in his Table A.23: total taxation as percent of GDP (25, p. 360)—do not support his thesis of stagnation.

Table 10

Growth in public consumption: government final consumption
expenditure as percentage of GDP, annual average

	1960–73	1974–79	1980–89	1990–99
Social democratic				
Austria	14.0	17.8	19.4	19.9
Denmark	17.6	24.9	26.7	25.9
Finland	14.0	18.2	20.0	23.1
Norway	15.3	19.0	19.4	21.1
Sweden	19.5	26.6	28.2	27.3
Average	16.1	21.3	22.7	23.5
Christian democratic				
Belgium	13.2	21.5	22.9	21.2
France	14.6	19.9	22.9	23.6
Germany	16.0	20.0	20.2	19.5
Italy	13.5	15.9	18.5	19.0
Netherlands	14.2	26.4	25.9	23.7
Switzerland	10.4	12.4	13.1	14.3
Average	13.7	19.4	20.6	20.2
Liberal				
Canada	16.1	21.7	22.0	21.9
United Kingdom	17.5	21.0	21.1	19.7
Ireland	13.1	18.8	19.6	16.2
Japan	7.9	9.7	9.6	9.6
United States	17.8	17.1	17.3	15.6
Average	14.5	17.7	17.9	16.6
Ex-dictatorship				
Greece	8.7	10.7	13.4	14.6
Portugal	11.8	13.7	14.9	18.6
Spain	8.9	12.2	15.5	17.9
Average	9.8	12.2	14.6	17.0

Sources: Data for 1960–73 from OECD, *OECD Historical Statistics 1960–1994,* Paris, 1996, Table 6.2. Other data from OECD, *OECD Historical Statistics 1970–1999,* Paris, 2000, Table 6.2.

Table 11

Export information: exports as percentage of GDP, average over period

	1960–73	1974–79	1980–89	1990–99
Social democratic				
Austria	27	33	37	40
Denmark	29	29	34	36
Finland	22	27	29	33
Norway	40	37	40	39
Sweden	23	29	33	36
Average	28	31	35	37
Christian democratic				
Belgium	38	51	70	71
France	14	20	21	23
Germany	—	25	30	27
Italy	14	20	21	23
Netherlands	46	49	56	54
Switzerland	30	34	36	37
Average	29	33	39	39
Liberal				
Canada	20	24	27	34
United Kingdom	20	28	26	26
Ireland	35	47	55	72
Japan	10	13	13	10
United States	5	8	8	11
Average	18	24	26	30
Ex-dictatorship				
Greece	10	17	21	18
Portugal	22	20	27	26
Spain	10	14	19	23
Average	14	17	22	22

Source: International Monetary Fund, *International Financial Statistics* (CD), July 2001.

Table 12

Tax revenue as percentage of GDP, three-year moving average

	1969	1979	1989	1998
Social democratic				
Austria	34.8	39.9	40.5	44.3
Denmark	37.4	44.0	49.0	50.1
Finland	32.2	37.0	43.2	46.3
Norway	34.4	41.7	42.1	42.6
Sweden	39.5	48.8	53.4	51.8
Average	35.7	42.3	45.6	47.0
Christian democratic				
Belgium	35.1	44.3	43.4	45.7
France	35.3	39.8	43.0	45.5
Germany	33.0	36.3	32.9	37.2
Italy	26.5	28.2	37.8	43.3
Netherlands	36.4	44.0	43.9	41.1
Switzerland	22.1	29.3	31.3	34.7
Average	31.4	37.0	38.7	41.3
Liberal				
Canada	30.4	31.4	35.1	37.2
United Kingdom	35.8	33.5	36.5	36.4
Ireland	28.8	30.5	35.0	32.3
Japan	19.0	24.6	30.6	28.3
United States	27.0	26.8	26.9	25.7
Average	28.2	29.4	32.8	32.0
Ex-dictatorship				
Greece	21.1	24.2	27.9	33.5
Portugal	18.2	23.2	29.3	34.0
Spain	16.5	23.0	32.5	34.4
Average	18.6	23.5	29.9	34.0

Source: OECD, *Revenue Statistics 1965–1999* (CD), Paris, 2000.

The source of tax revenues also changed significantly over the period (Tables 13–17) and, generally, not along the lines predicted by the globalization theorists such as Gray, Greider, or Mann (1–3). Contrary to the conventional wisdom, which says that taxation of mobile factors such as capital should fall relative to taxation of less mobile factors such as labor, the share of revenue from taxes on capital actually *increased* during the 1990s in most of the advanced capitalist countries, including the SDCs (which are among the most "globalized" as a group).The only exception was the LCs (Table 14). Meanwhile, revenue from social security and payroll taxes, which are less mobile than capital and therefore supposedly better targets for taxation in the globalized economy, increased during the 1990s in most of the SDCs, while decreasing in most of the CDCs (except Germany). This suggests that international competitiveness forced a decline of payroll taxes in countries that supported their welfare states through those taxes (as do the CDCs; see Table 15). Also, and against expectations, the contribution of income taxes to total tax revenue declined in most countries (though not in Austria, France, the United Kingdom, the United States, Greece, and Portugal) (Table 13). It is worth stressing that the changes in taxation of property—even less mobile than labor—also give little support to the globalization view. The tax share from property taxes did increase in 11 countries, but it fell in eight, including in four of the five SDCs (Table 16). Consumption taxes, incidentally, also declined in the SDCs as well as, on average, in the other groups of countries (Table 17).

These data challenge many of the positions that assume globalization requires reductions in taxes and shifts in the tax base toward less mobile factors. The data show that taxes increased during the 1990s in the majority of SDCs, CDCs, and EDCs, while remaining practically the same in the LCs. Only in Sweden, the Netherlands, the United Kingdom, Ireland, Japan, and the United States did taxes decrease—a decrease, incidentally, that was unrelated to any obvious component of globalization. Also, taxes on capital (as percentage of all taxes) increased in all the countries except Italy, Switzerland, the United Kingdom, Japan, and Spain. Again, none of these increases can be explained by the needs of the process of globalization.

As an obvious derivation from the data on taxes and expenditures, one can conclude that larger welfare states, with higher public social expenditures and higher public employment, as in the SDCs, require higher levels of taxation. In this respect we should stress that it has not been a common practice of the SDCs to support their welfare states by sustaining large public deficits, as Giddens (37) has wrongly accused what he calls the "traditional" social democracies of doing (see 38 for a critique of Giddens's economic assumptions, and 39 for Giddens's response). Table 18 shows that for most of the 1960–89 period, the majority of the SDCs ran budget surpluses; and even in the 1990s, when most of the developed capitalist countries were running deficits, the SDCs had lower deficits than the CDCs, LCs, and EDCs.

Table 13

Taxes on individual incomes and capital gains as percentage of total tax revenue

	1969	1979	1989	1998
Social democratic				
Austria	19.9	23.0	19.8	22.5
Denmark	42.7	50.6	51.8	51.5
Finland	38.5	38.8	38.4	32.3
Norway	38.8	31.1	27.8	27.3
Sweden	47.5	42.4	39.3	35.0
Average	37.5	37.2	35.4	33.7
Christian democratic				
Belgium	23.9	35.4	31.4	30.7
France	11.7	11.2	10.5	17.4
Germany	26.5	28.9	29.5	25.0
Italy	11.8	22.7	26.7	25.0
Netherlands	27.2	26.5	21.3	15.2
Switzerland	32.6	35.7	33.8	31.8
Average	22.3	26.7	25.5	24.2
Liberal				
Canada	29.2	33.6	38.3	37.8
United Kingdom	31.4	32.8	26.0	27.5
Ireland	17.3	29.9	31.7	30.9
Japan	21.4	23.7	24.7	18.8
United States	36.8	38.4	37.5	40.5
Average	27.2	31.7	31.6	31.1
Ex-dictatorship				
Greece	9.1	12.9	13.1	13.2
Portugal	—	—	13.9	17.1
Spain	10.6	18.5	22.8	20.8
Average	9.9	15.7	16.6	17.0

Source: OECD, *Revenue Statistics 1965–1999* (CD), Paris, 2000.
Note: Data for Greece in column for 1998 refer to 1997.

Table 14

Taxes on corporate profits and capital gains as percentage of total tax revenue

	1969	1979	1989	1998
Social democratic				
Austria	4.4	3.5	3.9	4.8
Denmark	2.9	3.1	4.2	5.6
Finland	4.8	3.7	3.6	9.0
Norway	3.3	6.7	5.4	9.7
Sweden	4.9	3.1	3.8	5.7
Average	4.1	4.0	4.2	7.0
Christian democratic				
Belgium	6.5	6.2	6.5	8.4
France	4.9	4.8	5.5	6.0
Germany	7.9	6.0	5.5	4.4
Italy	7.2	8.3	10.0	7.0
Netherlands	8.1	5.8	7.2	10.6
Switzerland	7.2	5.9	6.4	6.0
Average	7.0	6.2	6.9	7.1
Liberal				
Canada	14.0	11.5	8.4	9.9
United Kingdom	8.0	7.7	12.6	10.9
Ireland	7.9	5.7	3.4	10.7
Japan	25.1	20.8	24.3	13.3
United States	15.2	11.9	8.9	9.0
Average	14.0	11.5	11.5	10.8
Ex-dictatorship				
Greece	1.6	3.5	4.6	6.3
Portugal	—	—	4.5	11.6
Spain	8.5	4.9	8.6	7.3
Average	5.1	4.2	5.9	8.4

Source: OECD, *Revenue Statistics 1965–1999* (CD), Paris, 2000.
Note: Data for Greece in column for 1998 refer to 1997.

Table 15

Social security and payroll taxes as percentage of total tax revenue

	1969	1979	1989	1998
Social democratic				
Austria	33.5	37.4	39.3	40.3
Denmark	4.4	1.5	3.3	3.9
Finland	12.9	19.2	19.8	25.2
Norway	16.1	23.6	27.4	23.3
Sweden	16.4	29.7	29.2	33.5
Average	16.7	22.3	23.8	25.2
Christian democratic				
Belgium	29.1	29.5	32.3	31.6
France	37.3	44.5	45.7	38.5
Germany	28.4	34.5	36.3	40.4
Italy	35.4	37.0	33.6	29.5
Netherlands	34.8	38.1	41.2	39.9
Switzerland	23.7	30.5	32.1	35.7
Average	31.5	35.7	36.9	35.9
Liberal				
Canada	9.3	10.8	13.4	15.9
United Kingdom	17.7	22.3	17.4	17.6
Ireland	8.0	14.2	15.8	13.8
Japan	21.9	29.2	28.1	38.4
United States	15.1	21.3	25.6	23.7
Average	14.4	19.6	20.1	21.9
Ex-dictatorship				
Greece	30.6	32.6	33.8	32.3
Portugal	24.0	31.6	26.3	25.5
Spain	38.1	50.2	34.6	35.2
Average	30.9	38.1	31.6	31.0

Source: OECD, *Revenue Statistics 1965–1999* (CD), Paris, 2000.
Note: Data for Greece in column for 1998 refer to 1997.

Table 16

Property taxes as percentage of total tax revenue

	1969	1979	1989	1998
Social democratic				
Austria	4.0	3.0	2.7	1.3
Denmark	6.0	5.9	4.4	3.6
Finland	2.3	2.0	3.4	2.4
Norway	2.7	1.9	2.9	2.4
Sweden	1.5	0.9	3.4	3.7
Average	3.3	2.7	3.4	2.7
Christian democratic				
Belgium	3.5	2.7	2.8	3.2
France	4.1	4.8	6.4	7.3
Germany	5.3	3.4	3.0	2.4
Italy	6.2	3.8	2.3	4.8
Netherlands	3.5	3.8	3.8	4.9
Switzerland	8.7	7.4	8.8	8.3
Average	5.2	4.3	4.5	5.2
Liberal				
Canada	12.5	9.4	9.7	10.4
United Kingdom	13.4	12.4	12.7	10.7
Ireland	13.1	6.1	4.8	5.2
Japan	7.6	8.6	10.2	10.5
United States	13.7	11.1	10.9	10.6
Average	12.1	9.5	9.7	9.5
Ex-dictatorship				
Greece	8.6	5.5	3.4	3.8
Portugal	4.5	1.5	1.5	2.9
Spain	6.2	5.0	5.1	6.0
Average	6.4	4.0	3.3	4.2

Source: OECD, *Revenue Statistics 1965–1999* (CD), Paris, 2000.
Note: Data for Greece in column for 1998 refer to 1997.

Table 17

Taxes on goods and services, including value-added tax (VAT),
as percentage of total tax revenue

	1969	1979	1989	1998
Social democratic				
Austria	37.6	32.1	32.5	27.9
Denmark	43.9	38.7	33.0	33.2
Finland	41.4	35.9	34.5	30.7
Norway	38.6	36.7	36.5	37.2
Sweden	29.7	23.7	24.2	21.6
Average	38.2	33.4	32.1	30.1
Christian democratic				
Belgium	36.7	25.9	27.0	24.9
France	39.0	31.6	28.7	26.6
Germany	31.9	27.2	25.6	27.4
Italy	39.3	28.3	27.0	27.4
Netherlands	26.1	25.4	26.2	27.7
Switzerland	27.8	20.4	18.9	18.2
Average	33.5	26.5	25.6	25.4
Liberal				
Canada	32.9	32.6	28.3	24.7
United Kingdom	30.3	25.9	31.0	32.6
Ireland	53.7	44.1	44.3	38.7
Japan	24.0	17.5	12.5	18.8
United States	19.3	17.4	17.1	16.2
Average	32.0	27.5	26.6	26.2
Ex-dictatorship				
Greece	49.8	45.0	44.6	41.0
Portugal	44.5	42.0	45.2	41.4
Spain	36.1	21.0	28.8	29.4
Average	43.5	36.0	39.5	37.3

Source: OECD, *Revenue Statistics 1965–1999* (CD), Paris, 2000.
Note: Data for Greece in column for 1998 refer to 1997.

Table 18
Updating government budget surplus information: net lending of
government as a percentage of GDP, average over period

	1960–73	1974–79	1980–89	1990–99
Social democratic				
Austria	0.7	–2.0	–3.1	–3.2
Denmark	2.1	0.5	–2.1	–1.0
Finland	3.0	5.0	3.6	–2.0
Norway	4.1	2.5	5.2	2.7
Sweden	3.8	1.3	–1.6	–3.7
Average	2.7	1.5	0.4	–1.4
Christian democratic				
Belgium	–2.8	–6.0	–10.7	–4.6
France	0.5	–0.9	–2.3	–3.7
Germany	0.5	–3.0	–2.1	–3.3
Italy	–3.1	–9.2	–10.8	–7.2
Netherlands	–0.6	–2.0	–5.1	–3.1
Switzerland	—	—	—	—
Average	–1.1	–4.2	–6.2	–4.4
Liberal				
Canada	–0.1	–2.0	–4.8	–4.2
United Kingdom	–0.8	–3.9	–2.3	–3.6
Ireland	–3.5	–8.4	–9.4	–1.1
Japan	1.0	–3.4	–1.5	–2.0
United States	–0.6	–1.5	–3.4	–3.4
Average	–0.8	–3.8	–4.3	–2.9
Ex-dictatorship				
Greece	—	—	—	–9.0
Portugal	0.6	–5.3	–5.5	–4.2
Spain	—	–0.7	–4.4	–5.1
Average	0.6	–3.0	–5.0	–6.1

Sources: Data for 1960–73 from OECD, *OECD Historical Statistics 1960–1994*, Paris, 1996, Table 6.7. Other data from OECD, *OECD Historical Statistics 1970–1999*, Paris, 2000, Table 6.7.
Note: Data are net lending of government as a percentage of GDP. In 1990–99 column, data for Canada and Japan refer to 1990–98; data for the United States, to 1990–97; data for Spain, to 1990–96.

THE CHRISTIAN DEMOCRATIC TRADITION AND ITS WELFARE STATE IN THE 1990s

The Christian democratic tradition, based on parties representing a multi-class coalition, was established at the beginning of the 20th century as an alternative to the labor- or class-based—social democratic, socialist, or communist—parties (which claimed to represent primarily the working class, whose interests were perceived, at least until the 1960s, as antagonistic to those of the employer class). Denying the existence of class conflict, the Christian democratic parties called on the support of different classes mobilized by the social doctrine of the Christian churches. These political parties have enjoyed considerable support among the middle and working classes, through unions led by Christian democrats, wherever these churches are influential—as in central and southern Europe. The influence of these parties among the working classes seemed to decline in the 1980s and 1990s. Also, the percentage of the labor force that was unionized in the CDCs declined during this period (from 38 percent in 1980 to 31 percent in 1994; see Table 1). Still, the degree of unionization in the 1990s, while lower than in the SDCs, remained higher in the CDCs (with the exception of France) than in the LCs and EDCs. In most of the CDCs in the 1990s, the unions remained divided along confessional (Christian democratic, social democratic, communist), territorial, or ethnic lines, a divide that weakened their power and influence. Moreover, in countries where the communist party played the major role on the left, such as Italy and France, the Cold War culture also divided the union movement and weakened labor, a situation that changed after the 1980s with the growing separation between the communist parties and the Soviet Union and the later collapse of the U.S.S.R.

Social transfers and some social services in the CDCs (excluding education) were once based (and still are in many CDCs) on the position of the individual in the labor market. In this sense, the welfare state reproduces the hierarchies and status existing in the labor market, and this situation is further reproduced by the system of funding of much of the welfare state in the CDCs. The laborer and employer contribute, via payroll taxes, to social security trust funds (controlled by labor, employees, and the government), each sector and hierarchy of employment having its own trust fund. The state has intervened only when civil society, structured around the family and the labor market, has failed to intervene. In this scheme, the male breadwinner or wage earner, through contributions to his social security trust fund, paid for pensions and health care for himself and his family, while his wife stayed at home to care for infants, adolescents, adults, and elderly family members. In the CDCs, the state generally does not provide family-oriented services that would assist the integration of women into the labor force. Thus the *CDCs continue to be strong on social transfers and expenditures and weak on public services,* as indicated in the previous section. Table 2 shows that in 1997 the CDCs had almost the same level of social expenditures as the SDCs, but much less public employment than the SDCs (about half), because the public-services sectors are less developed in the CDCs. Consequently, the degree of women's participation in the labor force is also much lower in the CDCs than in the SDCs. Only the EDCs have a lower percentage of women in the labor force.

These characteristics of the CDCs have been modified during the last 30 years, of course, primarily through the influence of social democratic parties that have pressed for expansion of benefits coverage toward a universalization of social services. Also, the increasing incorporation of women into the labor market in the CDCs has forced an expansion of family- and women-friendly services, such as home care and childcare services, which in the CDCs are usually funded and provided by private sources. One example is France, which established an extensive network of childcare services in the 1950s and 1960s as part of the natalist policies of the de Gaulle regime.

The heavy dependency of state revenues on payroll taxes (35.9 percent of all taxes) in the CDCs (Table 15), the highest percentage among all developed capitalist countries for financing welfare states, explains why the social policies of the CDCs were the most directly affected by changes in the labor market in the 1990s. Indeed, for a long period after World War II, a young man traditionally started work at 16 years of age and retired at the age of 65. During these 49 years of working life, he paid (assuming that his employer's contribution to the social security fund was derived primarily from his wages) for his own and his family's medical care, plus his pension and his wife's pension. Changes in the life cycle, however, seem to threaten that model. As Esping-Andersen (26) has indicated in his discussion of the laborer's life cycle, the average young person now enters the labor market at the age of 20 or 22 years, following an extended public education, and retires earlier, as early as 60 years of age (in Germany), 58 (in France), or 62 (in Spain). This shortening of the period of contribution to the social security trust fund, from 49 to 38 years, along with a seven-year increase in average life expectancy in these countries, has put some pressure on the funding of the welfare state in general and of the pension system in particular. During the 1990s, the major intervention in the CDCs for addressing these new financing needs was the increased number of women in the labor force and the increased productivity, which resulted in rising wages that fed through the tax system in the form of greater tax revenues. These policies were already in existence in the SDCs, whose welfare states are less vulnerable to the reduced length of lifetime employment per worker, because of the high percentage of the adult population that is working and the heavy dependency of the welfare state on general revenues.

Some authors, such as Esping-Andersen (40), consider these measures to address the new funding needs of the welfare state insufficient, and they recommend discontinuing mandatory retirement at 65 years of age, delaying obligatory retirement. Aware of the unpopularity of such measures, Esping-Andersen (40, p. 130) has recommended that the policy be adopted at the E.U. level. This shifting of the decision point to the European level, however, would further contribute to the decline in popularity of the European project that is already evident in most European countries.[7] By contrast, it is remarkable that during the 1990s the major welfare-state programs have continued to enjoy substantial popular support. Polling data consistently demonstrate a high level of support for the welfare state from the 1980s through the 1990s (41, 42). Public support has been even greater for pensions and health care, which are practically universal, than it has been for programs that benefit only some sectors of the population, such as unemployment benefits. This support for welfare-state institutions is evident among both men and women and across all social classes and age groups, although it is more pronounced among the working class and women than among other groups (43).

As indicated in the discussion of taxes in the SDCs, it is far from clear that most countries, including the CDCs, have exhausted their ability to raise the revenues that would allow the continued smooth functioning of their welfare states. Actually, taxes on individual income are rather low (24.2 percent of all tax revenues) in the CDCs compared with the SDCs (33.7 percent) and even the LCs (31.1 percent) (Table 13). The same situation is evident for consumption taxes: lower in the CDCs (25.4 percent) than in the SDCs (30.1 percent), LCs (26.2 percent), and EDCs (37.3 percent) (Table 17). In the light of these data, *it is questionable to assume that the CDCs have exhausted their capacity to raise revenues to finance their very popular welfare states.* Given the great popularity of such social programs and the still-untapped potential for public revenues, the case for regressive increases in the retirement age has not been established. Opposition to raising the official retirement age does not imply an opposition to some flexibility in the mandatory age of retirement, making later retirement voluntary—that is, permissible for those who so wish. But we are concerned that *mandating later retirement* would be a class-biased policy that would hurt primarily those whose work is physically challenging, as is the case for large sectors of the unskilled working class, and even for many of those in the services sector.[8]

THE LIBERAL TRADITION AND ITS WELFARE STATE

The LCs have been governed by less "labor-friendly" parties than the groups discussed thus far. The degree of unionization in these countries (28 percent of the

---

[7] According to a recent poll on the popularity of the European Union among the populations of its member countries (EUROSTAT, "Popular Opinion in the EU Institutions"), in the 1990s the European project was losing popularity very rapidly in most countries, including Italy and Spain, where the E.U. had been a very popular project. The percentage of people who thought E.U. institutions had improved their lives was less than 18 percent on average.

[8] Johnson and Hall (44), for example, have shown that 52 percent of the labor force is "burned out" after working for 35 to 40 years; the percentage is even larger among blue-collar workers.

workforce in 1994) continued to be lower during the 1990s than in any other group except the EDCs (26 percent, compared with 70 percent in the SDCs and 31 percent in the CDCs; see Table 1). In all the LCs (with the exception of Canada), the rate of unionization declined in the 1990s, particularly in the United Kingdom. The low proportions of unionization in the LCs translate into a greatly weakened labor movement. This weakness is evident in the low percentage of the working population covered by collective-bargaining agreements, a percentage that has declined in all the LCs, particularly the United Kingdom. Coverage in the United Kingdom fell from 70 percent in 1980 to 47 percent in 1994, a process that has continued under the New Labour government (45).

The weakness of the labor movement in the LCs is the main reason for these countries' low levels of social expenditures (17.6 percent of GDP, on average, in 1997; see Table 2) and slow rate of increase in social expenditures between 1980 and 1997 (up an average of 2.9 percentage points between 1980 and 1997). The LCs also have the lowest share of public employment (8.8 percent in 1997) as a percentage of total employment and are the only group of countries that, on average, underwent a decline in the share of public employment between 1974 and 1997. At the same time, many labor-market indicators in the LCs performed poorly in the 1980s and 1990s. During these decades, for example, the LCs had the lowest annual growth of labor compensation (along with the CDCs), the lowest hourly compensation in manufacturing (after the EDCs), the highest wage dispersion, the greatest degree of household income inequality, the longest work year per worker, and the highest rates of poverty (Table 6).

In general, the LCs are not labor-friendly countries—a result of weak labor movements, weak unions, weak social democratic parties, and weak welfare states. The level of public consumption is the lowest among all the developed capitalist countries (Table 10).

The LCs also have, on average, the lowest share of taxes as percentage of GDP—(32 percent) (Table 12). Of the LCs, the United States has the lowest share, with tax revenues representing just 25.7 percent of GDP in 1998. Some authors, such as Giddens (46), have praised the U.S. tax system's progressivity compared with that of other advanced capitalist economies. This progressivity, however, is a dubious distinction, a result mainly of a tax system that raises far less revenue than do those of comparable economies. The low level of income taxation in the United States is even more remarkable given the very high percentage of the adult population that works, a result of the very high level of women's participation in the labor force (70.7 percent in 1999, comparable to the 76.0 percent in Sweden for the same year; see Table 3). Most of this female labor-force participation takes place in the services sector (where women represent 74 percent of all employment), with a high concentration in low-wage jobs such as personal and social services. This results in a highly polarized labor market and a polarized income distribution—characteristic of the LCs in general and the United States in particular (Table 6).

FORMER ULTRA-RIGHT SOUTHERN EUROPEAN
DICTATORSHIPS

The EDCs were governed for most of the 1945–80 period by very repressive conservative and authoritarian, labor-hostile regimes. Labor-friendly parties were brutally repressed; free unions were not allowed in Spain and were heavily controlled in Greece and Portugal. Consequently, in all these countries, social expenditures and public employment were extremely scarce at the time democracy was instituted, a scarcity that appeared most dramatically in social public employment. All these countries converted to democracies in the late 1970s, and for most of the 1980s were governed by social democratic parties intent on correcting the enormous underdevelopment of their welfare states. During the 1980s, the average electoral support for social democratic parties in these southern European countries (Spain, Greece, and Portugal) was 32.9 percent—lower than in the SDCs (Norway, Sweden, Denmark, Finland, and Austria), at 39.7 percent, but much higher than in the CDCs, at 23.6 percent (47). A primary objective of the social democratic parties in the EDCs was to correct the substantial deficits in their welfare states. But the point of departure in the mid-1970s and early 1980s was so low that, even with a quite impressive growth of social expenditures (the highest in the developed capitalist countries) and of public employment (the second highest after the SDCs), in the 1990s these countries continued to have *very low social transfers and low public employment, putting them in a separate category from the SDCs, CDCs, and LCs.* The social expenditures in the EDCs in 1997 (20.7 percent of GDP) were the lowest, after the LCs, among the developed capitalist countries, and their public employment (9.4 percent) was also among the lowest in the developed capitalist countries (though higher than in the LCs) (Table 2).

The proportion of the labor force that was unionized was low in the EDCs, although it increased considerably in Spain (from 9 percent in 1980 to 19 percent in 1994), where a social democratic party governed for most of the 1980s and 1990s. A major difference from the LCs, however, is that collective-bargaining agreements cover the great majority of the labor force in the EDCs (in 1994, 75 percent vs. 31 percent in the LCs) (Table 1). The growing strength of the labor movements in the EDCs contributed to a large annualized growth (2.4 percent) of real labor compensation in the 1990s, with reductions in household-income inequalities, in number of working hours per worker, and in poverty—although child poverty remains high due to the poor labor conditions facing single mothers (a situation also much in evidence in Italy) (Table 6). We should stress that while much improvement took place in the EDCs during the 1990s, still, because of the underdeveloped welfare states and deteriorated labor markets existing under the ultra-right-wing dictatorships, household-income inequalities and working hours per worker remain high, the second highest (after the LCs).

The EDCs, poor in social transfers and in social services, are undergoing a transition along either Christian democratic or social democratic paths, depending on the coalition of forces in the coming decades. Nor can we discount the possibility that they may evolve toward LCs. Indeed, the conservative party that has governed Spain since 1996 (in coalition with Catalan and Basque Christian democratic parties until 2000 and on its own since that year) has reduced social expenditures and public employment considerably.

All the EDCs increased their tax revenues during the 1990s, surpassing the LCs in their level of taxation (in 1998, 34.0 percent of GDP in the EDCs vs. 32.0 percent in the LCs) but remaining much lower than the SDCs (47.0 percent) and CDCs (41.3 percent) (Table 12). Income taxes in the EDCs, however, remain very low, at 17.0 percent of all taxes in 1998, compared with 31.1 percent in the LCs, 24.2 percent in the CDCs, and 33.7 percent in the SDCs (Table 13). This is a result of the enormous income tax evasion in the EDCs (particularly among high-income households), the highest among the developed capitalist countries. The EDCs (with the exception of Portugal) also have lower capital taxes than most of the SDCs, CDCs, and LCs (Table 14). To compensate for the low percentage of income and capital taxes, the consumption taxes as percentage of all taxes are very high in the EDCs (the highest among the developed capitalist countries)—except in Spain, whose consumption taxes are high but comparable to those in the LCs and CDCs, although lower than those in most SDCs (except Sweden) (Table 17). It is clear from these figures that *the EDCs have far from exhausted their capacity to generate revenues for expanding their still under-developed welfare states. This will require major efforts to correct tax evasion by high-income households and to tax capital more highly.*

A prominent characteristic of the EDCs, shared with Italy, is what Esping-Andersen (26) has called "familialization"—that is, the large role played by families in taking care of infants, adolescents, adults, and the elderly. These responsibilities place a very heavy burden on women, who are overstressed in these societies. Familialization contributes significantly to the low percentage of women in the labor force, which in turn helps to explain the underdevelop-ment of services employment (Table 3)—the lowest in the developed capitalist countries—and of personal and social services. The underdevelopment of these services further inhibits the entrance of women into the labor force, lowering the supply of women for employment and retarding their entrance into a deteriorated and unstable labor market. All of this together encourages women to postpone having children, leaving the EDCs with the lowest fertility rates among the developed capitalist countries (Table 5).

SUMMARY AND CONCLUSIONS

The data presented in this chapter confirm that during the 1990s, despite a con-vergence in some of their components, the welfare states of the four groups of developed capitalist countries retained important differences—differences based on their structural characteristics, which are shaped primarily by the dominant political forces in each group. As our analysis shows, countries retain, for the most part (with the partial exception of the EDCs), the same major characteristics first used to classify them in the typology constructed by Esping-Andersen and modified by Huber and Stephens (and to which we have added further modifications). We found that, in the 1990s, the SDCs continued to be rich in social public transfers and public services; the CDCs continued to be rich in social public transfers but poorer than the SDCs in public employment, including public-services employment (although less poor than in the 1980s); and the LCs continued to be poor both in social public transfers and in public employment and public-services employment (with a further decline of public employment in some countries, including the United States and United Kingdom). The countries that are most changed are the EDCs. They have undergone a transition from very low social transfers and low public employment (in the 1970s, lower than in all other developed capitalist countries), including very low public services, to a much improved situation in the 1990s—although still with a considerable deficit compared with the SDCs and CDCs. Across the country types, developments reflected the correlation of national political forces, particularly the relative strength of national labor movements—and not economic pressures brought on by globalization. Stronger labor power has meant larger and more redistributive welfare states; weaker labor power has led to poorer, less extensive, and less redistributive welfare states. If globalization has played any role, the national experiences reviewed here suggest that the combined forces of globalization are a weaker determinant of the future of the welfare state than are organized labor and pro-labor political parties.

In describing these differences, we do not deny the similarities and even convergences that occurred in the 1990s in response to factors other than labor power. One such factor was the globalization of finance, which has been associated with a decline in the rate of capital formation in most countries, especially the SDCs, which historically have relied more than the other countries on financial controls and financial stimuli for the development of their economic policies. Political variables, however, continue to be central in explaining how countries responded to the globalization of finance in the 1990s to protect, strengthen, or weaken their welfare states. Even given the globalization of finance, the SDCs still have the strongest welfare states.

Another change in the 1990s that affected all the welfare states was the continuing integration of women into the labor force, in which both class and cultural (religion-related) factors play key roles. In countries where labor is strong and traditional Christian values are weak (as in the SDCs), family-friendly policies are well developed and facilitate the largest participation of women in the labor force. In countries where families are overburdened and much of the funding is based on payroll taxes (as in the CDCs), we find lower participation of women in the labor force. The CDCs have been the countries most directly affected by the increasing participation of women in the labor market. These changes have forced major accommodations in their welfare states to better respond to the needs of working women and of multi-wage-earner families so as to guarantee the viability of labor-market-based social security. The CDCs have also been most affected by international competitiveness, forcing them to rely less on social security taxes for the funding of their welfare states.

By contrast, the LCs, the least labor-friendly countries (especially the United States and United Kingdom, but with the exception of Canada), continue on the road to further polarization of their labor markets and their societies, becoming the least developed welfare states. In this, they have lost ground to the EDCs, which have been improving many components of their welfare states in the 20 years since they became democratic countries. The EDCs have caught up rapidly, but their welfare states still exhibit many gaps, reflecting the correlation of class forces in each country.

This chapter has also questioned the thesis that countries have "exhausted" their ability to raise public revenues and to redistribute public resources. As we have indicated, the universalistic programs of the welfare state remain highly popular. And we must challenge the conclusion that people are not supportive of redistributive policies, when that conclusion is derived from polls in which people are asked whether they favor policies that take from the rich to give to the poor (so as "to reduce income differences between rich and poor"), as in Taylor-Gooby's recent study (43, p. 139). Given that most people are neither rich nor poor, such a question is not a good way to measure popular support for redistribution. However, if people are asked whether they believe that those in the top two income deciles should pay higher taxes for programs that benefit the remaining 80 percent of the population, in most countries the majority of responses are in the affirmative.[9] The conclusion that public support for expansion and redistribution declined in the 1990s is highly questionable. The popularity or unpopularity of taxes depends on the purpose of raising those revenues. Most polls show that large majorities support the universalistic programs of the welfare state and favor larger expenditures for them. In that respect, people's feelings about taxes clearly depend on the perceived benefits they obtain from public revenues. Supporters of the supposed anti-tax mood of western populations usually refer to the British Labour Party victory of 1997, wrongly attributing this to Labour's pledge not to increase taxes, while ignoring the big win by the Swedish Social Democrats in 1994 with an explicit commitment to increase taxes. The progressive, universalistic Swedish welfare state (which benefits the middle classes as well as the working classes) triggers more popular support for taxes

---

[9] Since the 1980s, Gallup Polls have asked about people's opinions on different tax policies. The most popular, or least unpopular, policies are those that tax high-income groups for the benefit of middle- and low-income groups.

than do the limited welfare states, regressively financed, such as the Anglo-Saxon model existing in the United Kingdom. Actually, even in the United Kingdom and the United States, wide support exists for increasing taxes for universal types of programs such as public pensions, education, and health care, which provide benefits to the majority of the population.

Finally, we have also demonstrated the importance of political variables for explaining the changes in the extent and composition of public revenues, challenging the notion that the globalization of financial capital has led to a reduction of taxes on the mobile factors of production. Here again, the political factors are the most important ones for explaining the taxation of mobile versus nonmobile factors of production and consumption. In summary, then, politics remains extremely important in explaining countries' responses to globalization and their maintaining and expanding their welfare states.

Note — This chapter is a modified and expanded version of a paper published in *Cambridge Journal of Economics* 28, 2004.

REFERENCES

1. Gray, J. *False Dawn: The Delusions of Global Capitalism.* Granta Books, London, 1998.
2. Greider, W. *One World Ready or Not: The Manic Logic of Global Capitalism.* Simon and Schuster, New York, 1997.
3. Mann, M. Globalization after September 11. *New Left Rev.* 12:51–73, November–December 2001.
4. Blair, T. Speech to the French National Assembly, March 24, 1998.
5. Editorial. *Le Monde Diplomatique,* April 2, 1998.
6. Hirst, P., and Thompson, G. *Globalization in Question.* Polity Press, Cambridge, 1996.
7. Perraton, T. The global economy—myths and realities. *Camb. J. Econ.* 25:669–684, 2001.
8. Pierson, P. The new politics of the welfare state. *World Polit.* 98(2):143–179, 1996.
9. Castles, F. G. On the political economy of recent public sector development. *J. Eur. Soc. Policy* 11(3):195–211, 2001.
10. Huber, E., and Stephens, J. D. *Development and Crisis of the Welfare State: Parties and Policies in Global Markets.* University of Chicago Press, Chicago, 2001.
11. Scharpf, F. W., and Schmidt, V. A. (eds). *Welfare and Work in the Open Economy: Vol 1. From Vulnerability to Competitiveness.* Oxford University Press, Oxford, 2000.
12. Esping-Andersen, G. *The Three Worlds of Welfare Capitalism.* Princeton University Press, Princeton, 1990.
13. Castles, F. G., and Mitchell, D. Three worlds of welfare capitalism or four? In *Families of Nations: Public Policy in Western Democracies,* ed. F. G. Castles. Brookfield, VC, Dartmouth, 1993.

14. Huber, E., and Stephens, J. Welfare state and production regimes in the era of retrenchment. In *The New Politics of the Welfare State,* ed. P. Pierson. Oxford University Press, Oxford, 2001.
15. Korpi, W. *The Working Class in Welfare Capitalism: Work, Unions and Politics in Sweden.* Routledge and Kegan Paul, London, 1978.
16. Korpi, W. *The Democratic Class Struggle.* Routledge and Kegan Paul, London, 1983.
17. Hicks, A. *Social Democracy and Welfare Capitalism.* Cornell University Press, Ithaca, 1999.
18. Bartolini, S. *The Political Mobilization of the European Left, 1960–1980.* Cambridge University Press, Cambridge, 2000.
19. Callaghan, J. *The Retreat of Social Democracy.* Manchester University Press, Manchester, 2000.
20. Kohl, J. Trends and problems in postwar public expenditures development in western Europe and North America. In *The Development of Welfare States in Europe and North America,* ed. P. Flora and A. J. Heideriheimer, pp. 307–344. Transaction Publishers, Somerset, NJ, 1981.
21. Harris, J. Social planning in war time. In *War and Economic Development,* ed. J. M. Winter. Cambridge University Press, Cambridge, 1975.
22. Rodrik, D. *Has Globalization Gone Too Far?* Institute for International Economics, 1997.
23. Clayton, R., and Pontusson, J. Welfare state retrenchment revisited. *World Polit.* 51(1):67–98, 1998.
24. Castles, F. G. *Comparative Public Policy: Patterns of Postwar Transformation.* Edward Elgar, Cheltenham, UK, 1998.
25. Scharpf, F. W. Economic changes, vulnerabilities and institutional capabilities. In *Welfare and Work in the Open Economy: Vol I. From Vulnerability to Competitiveness,* ed. F. W. Scharpf and V. A. Schmidt. Oxford University Press, Oxford, 2000.
26. Esping-Andersen, G. *Social Foundations of Post Industrial Economics.* Oxford University Press, Oxford, 1999.
27. Bettio, F., and Villa, P. A. A Mediterranean perspective on the breakdown of the relationship between participation and fertility. *Camb. J. Econ.* 22:137–171, 1998.
28. Lindbeck, A. The Swedish experiment. *J. Econ. Lit.* 35(3):1273–1319, 1997.
29. Korpi, W. Eurosclerosis and the sclerosis of objectivity: On the role of values among economic experts. In *Controversies in Microeconomics: Growth, Trade and Policy,* ed. D. H. Dixon. Oxford University Press, Oxford, 2000.
30. Henrekson, M. Sweden's relative economic performance: Lagging behind or staying on top. In *Controversies in Microeconomics: Growth, Trade and Policy,* ed. D. H. Dixon. Oxford University Press, Oxford, 2000.
31. Agell, T. Why Sweden's welfare state needed reform. In *Controversies in Microeconomics: Growth, Trade and Policy,* ed. D. H. Dixon. Oxford University Press, Oxford, 2000.
32. Domrick, S. Swedish economic performance and Swedish economic debate. In *Controversies in Microeconomics: Growth, Trade and Policy,* ed. D. H. Dixon. Oxford University Press, Oxford, 2000.
33. Henrekson, M. Swedish economic growth. *Challenge,* July-August 2001, pp. 38–58.

34. Korpi, W. The economic consequences of Sweden's welfare states. *Challenge,* November-December 2001, pp. 104–112.
35. OECD. Structural reform: A review of the progress. In *OECD Economic Surveys: Sweden.* Paris, 1999.
36. OECD. *The New Economy: Beyond the Hype.* Paris, 2001.
37. Giddens, A. *The Third Way.* Polity Press, Cambridge, 1998.
38. Navarro, V. Is there a Third Way? A response to Giddens's *The Third Way.* In *The Political Economy of Social Inequalities,* ed. V. Navarro, pp. 419–429. Baywood, Amityville, NY, 2002.
39. Giddens, A. *A Third Way and Its Critics.* Polity Press, Cambridge, 2000.
40. Esping-Andersen, G. Comments. In Bertola, T., Jimeno, G., Marinon, R., and Pissarides, C. EU welfare systems and labor markets: Diverse in the past, integrated in the future? In *Welfare and Employment in a United Europe,* ed. G. Bertola, T. Boeri, and G. Nicoletti. MIT Press, Boston, 2001.
41. Pierson, P. The politics of the new welfare state. *World Polit.* 48(2):143–179, 1996.
42. Ross, F. Interest and choice in the not quite so new politics of welfare. *W. Eur. Polit.* 23(2):11–34, 2000.
43. Taylor-Gooby, P. Sustaining state welfare in hard times: Who will foot the bill? *J. Eur. Soc. Policy* 11(2), May 2001.
44. Johnson, J., and Hall, E. *The Sociophysiological Dimensions of Work.* HPM Papers No. 32. Johns Hopkins University, Baltimore, 1994.
45. Toynbee, P., and Walker, D. Did things get better? In *An Audit of Labour's Successes and Failures.* Penguin Books, London, 2001.
46. Giddens, A. Just carry on being new. *New Statesman,* June 11, 2001, p. 29.
47. Merkel, W. Evolution electoral de los partidos social democratas. In *Final de la Social Democracia,* Table 3, p. 62. Ediciones Alfonso el Magnamim, 1995.

CHAPTER 3

The Future of the Welfare State:
Crisis Myths and Crisis Realities

Francis G. Castles

The welfare state has been perceived as being in crisis for more than two decades now. In the late 1970s and 1980s, the crisis was variously conceived as resulting from democratic overload (1, 2), economic slowdown (3, 4), and a fiscal crisis of the state (5, 6). In the 1990s, the major foci of crisis warnings have been economic internationalization, supposedly making it impossible for large welfare states to remain competitively viable (7, 8; cf. 9) and population aging, seen as leading to insatiable and unsustainable demands on the public purse (10, 11).

The first wave of crisis predictions petered out in the face of evidence that the more advanced welfare states were among the most successful in weathering the economic storms of the 1970s and 1980s and that the majority of nations of the Organization for Economic Cooperation and Development (OECD) were able to contain public expenditure growth in this period. Evidence is now beginning to emerge that neither the "race to the bottom" predicted by the globophobes nor the expenditure blowout predicted by the gerontophobes is occurring on anything like the scale assumed by the crisis scenarios. Continued national diversity resting on substantial national autonomy and, in many countries, a real capacity to effect needed reforms are the keynote findings of two surveys of the state of the welfare state in Europe and beyond (12, 13).

These findings have been based largely on individual case studies of national social policy developments in recent years. Past and future trends in public expenditure have also been the subject of more systematic cross-national comparison. Recently reported pooled time-series analyses of welfare state development over three or more decades have highlighted political differences among nations and economic factors other than internationalization as the main factors shaping postwar expenditure trajectories (14–16). Scenarios of predicted demographic development over the next few decades are the main substance of World Bank (10) and OECD (11) anxieties concerning the impact on expenditure of population aging.

There have not been many studies focusing exclusively on public expenditure trends in recent decades. This is, in many ways, quite strange, since it is in the 1980s and 1990s—and not in what has come to be seen as the "Golden Age" (17) of welfare state development—that one would expect to encounter the clearest manifestations of the supposed stresses produced by emergent trends toward economic globalization and population aging. The objective of the first two sections of this chapter is to take some initial, modest steps to remedying this deficiency. The assumption underlying the argument is that, if the internationalization of the economy and population aging have had only modest effects on public expenditure trends in recent decades, they are unlikely to portend an unmanageable crisis in the immediate future.

The final section of the chapter looks beyond the immediate future to the prospects of the welfare state in the coming century as a whole. Here, I argue that, at the opposite end of the demographic spectrum from population aging, a real crisis of societal development is beginning to emerge: a crisis of low and declining fertility. In what is necessarily a brief survey of the issues, I discuss some of the potentially serious consequences of prolonged periods of below-reproduction-level fertility. On the basis of some preliminary modeling of fertility data for the 1980s and 1990s, I seek to demonstrate that the best hope of averting or, at least, minimizing the adverse consequences of such a development is to take immediate action to modify the institutional priorities of the welfare state.

GLOBALIZATION AND RECENT PUBLIC
EXPENDITURE TRENDS

The belief that global integration of the world economy is producing a general tendency toward downsizing of the state and, in particular, a roll-back in its welfare commitments does not survive even the most cursory examination of the relevant data. Table 1 provides information on levels and growth of total government spending and total public social expenditure, measured as percentages of gross domestic product (GDP), for 17 OECD countries over the period 1984–97. This period of 13 years is chosen with a view to examining the most recent spending data available as of 2002, while avoiding the bias that would result from the selection of a period in which unemployment was trending either markedly upward or downward. Between 1984 and 1997, the average change in levels of unemployment in these 17 OECD nations was an increase of just 0.6 of a percent of the labor force (data calculated from 18).

Focusing initially on total outlays, we see persisting resemblances among expenditure levels in groups of nations bound by common historical, cultural, and geographical ties, with the countries of continental western Europe and Scandinavia generally characterized by substantially larger public sectors than the countries of southern Europe and, especially, the English-speaking world.

Table 1

Total outlays of general government and total public social expenditure
as percentages of GDP in 17 OECD countries, 1984–1997

	Total outlays			Social expenditure		
Country[a]	1984	1997	Change, 1984–97	1984	1997	Change, 1984–97
Australia	36.4	33.2	-3.2	13.7	18.1	4.4
Canada	45.3	42.4	-2.9	16.2	16.9	0.7
Ireland	47.7	33.2	-14.5	22.9	17.9	-5.0
United States	33.1	31.4	-1.7	14.1	16.0	1.9
Finland	40.2	51.8	11.6	22.3	29.3	7.0
Norway	42.1	44.1	2.0	19.7[b]	25.4	5.7
Sweden	59.2	59.0	-0.2	30.0	33.3	3.3
Austria	49.3	49.8	0.5	24.3[b]	25.4	1.1
Belgium	60.7	51.4	-9.3	26.7	23.6	-3.1
France	51.5	52.6	1.1	26.4	29.6	3.2
Germany	47.4	48.1	0.7	23.6	26.6	3.0
Italy	49.4	50.0	0.6	21.0	26.8	5.8
Netherlands	53.8	44.6	-9.2	30.2	25.1	-5.1
Greece	43.1	50.4	7.3	16.9	22.2	5.3
Portugal	41.1	43.5	2.4	11.4	18.7	7.3
Spain	35.2	39.9	4.7	17.8	20.9	3.1
Japan	32.3	35.0	2.7	11.4	14.4	3.0
Mean	**45.2**	**44.7**	**-0.5**	**20.5**	**22.9**	**2.4**

Sources: Total outlays of general government from OECD (18); total public social expenditure from OECD Secretariat, Social Expenditure Database (SOCX).
[a]Missing outlays data for Denmark, New Zealand, Switzerland, and the United Kingdom made it necessary to omit these countries from the study.
[b]1985 data.

These family-of-nations patterns (see 19) are strongly indicative of the fact that universalizing forces such as globalization have yet to dissolve national differences based on cultural and political preferences. Looking at changes in total outlays, we note the quite considerable diversity of public expenditure trajectories over the period, with no clearly observable patterns in either Scandinavia or continental western Europe. By contrast, there is a clear downward trend in the

English-speaking world and an expansive trend in southern Europe. The former was possibly associated with the greater success of parties committed to neoliberal ideologies in these nations during these years. The latter was probably a consequence of attempts by these late democratizers to catch up to the rest of the OECD in social infrastructure development. Contrary to the notion of a wholesale retreat of the state in the 1980s and 1990s, the average decrease in public sector expenditure over the period was just 0.5 of a percent of GDP.

The story that is told by the social expenditure data in Table 1 is, in many respects, quite similar. Once again, levels of expenditure manifest distinct family-of-nations patterns. While the countries of southern Europe spent less than those of continental western Europe, by the end of the period they were both spending distinctly more than the nations of the English-speaking world and Japan. The Scandinavian countries, as befits their reputation as welfare state leaders, were spending most. With respect to change over time, there appear to be two broad groupings: the Scandinavian and southern European nations, in which welfare state expansion was quite pronounced over the period, and the English-speaking world and continental western Europe, in which, with a few exceptions, the expansion was more modest. Confounding the notion of a general social expenditure rollback, only three countries—Belgium, Ireland, and the Netherlands—experienced any decline in total social spending thereafter. Between the mid-1980s and the latter part of the 1990s, these 17 OECD countries experienced an average increase in levels of social spending of 2.4 percentage points of GDP.

This hardly suggests a decline in welfare state commitment on the part of national governments. Indeed, as shown by the calculations in Table 2, by the late 1990s, the combination of modestly declining levels of total outlays and more markedly increasing levels of total public social expenditures meant that, in all of these OECD nations, welfare state expenditure represented a larger proportion of the total than had previously been the case. In 12 of these 17 OECD nations, social programs now cost more than all other government functions combined, and this total does not include educational spending, an area widely regarded as an integral part of the welfare state. Thus, contrary to the view that the welfare state has been forced onto the defensive by globalization, it is everywhere becoming more central to the tasks of modern government. Together with the strong upward trend in social expenditure as a percentage of GDP, this is a finding consonant with the continuingly high level of support for the welfare state shown in many recent surveys of mass opinion (20, 21) and accords well with Paul Pierson's conclusions (22–24) that client support for particular social programs makes welfare an area in which governments find it extremely difficult to effect major cutbacks.

The absence of any clear indication of a general rollback of public expenditure as a whole or of the welfare state in particular does not necessarily imply that trends toward globalization were without effect. The change columns in Table 1 demonstrate considerable cross-national variation in recent public expenditure trends, and it could well be that vulnerability to world market forces was among

Table 2

Total social expenditure as percentage of
total outlays of government in 17 OECD
countries, 1984 and 1997

Country	1984	1997
Australia	37.6	54.5
Canada	35.8	39.9
Ireland[a]	48.0	53.9
United States	42.6	51.0
Finland	55.5	56.6
Norway[a]	46.8	57.6
Sweden	50.7	56.4
Austria[a]	49.3	51.0
Belgium	44.0	45.9
France	51.3	56.3
Germany	49.8	55.3
Italy	42.5	53.6
Netherlands	56.1	56.3
Greece	39.2	44.0
Portugal	27.7	43.0
Spain	50.6	52.4
Japan	35.3	41.1
Mean	**44.8**	**51.1**

Sources: Calculated from the data in Table 1.
[a]1985 data.

the factors responsible for this variation. The measure of vulnerability that has featured most prominently in the literature on the size of the state and its welfare effort has been the extent of national exposure to international trade. Over time, however, there has been a major turnaround in the way in which the impact of this variable has been theorized. Originally, the linkage was viewed as a positive one, with political actors on the left seen as mobilizing against the effects of trade openness by establishing public programs designed to protect against externally induced economic fluctuation (see 25, 26). More recently, the linkage has been identified in more negative terms, with an emphasis on the need for exporting nations to reduce the size of their public programs to maintain a competitive edge in world markets (see 27, 28). This has been seen as leading to a "race to the bottom," with even minimum standards of social protection under pressure as enterprise economies seek ever greater efficiency. Examining correlations between trade openness in 1984 and subsequent change in total outlays of government and total social expenditure, we find that the latter interpretation appears closest to contemporary realities. In both instances (see figures in parentheses under the "1984 Trade Openness" variable in Figure 1), the reported relationships are negative and statistically significant at the .01 level, despite the relatively small number of cases examined.

A single-variable model is, of course, far too simplistic to provide any real insight into the mechanisms by which trade openness affects expenditure change. The critical path models reported in Figure 1 take account of three additional variables: prior expenditure level, economic growth, and change in unemployment level. Prior expenditure is important because of the strong convergence tendency noted in most cross-national studies of expenditure change. A plausible interpretation of such findings is that convergence is a function of timing differentials in program adoption combined with a plateauing effect as programs in early-adopting nations reach maturity (see 19, pp. 315–316). Economic growth is likely to be significant simply because of the way in which expenditure change is measured. Because outlays and social expenditures are reported as proportions of GDP, it follows that, all other things being equal, the more rapid the growth of national product in a given period, the slower will be the reported growth of spending as a percentage of GDP. Extraordinary rates of economic growth explain why Japan, the OECD nation with much the highest rate of postwar real social expenditure growth, has, for more than half a century, remained among the smallest of the OECD's welfare states measured in terms of percentage of GDP. Finally, unemployment was, almost certainly, the major policy problem confronted by OECD economic and social policymakers in this period. It had immediate public expenditure implications for expenditure growth, as displaced workers claimed social insurance entitlements and as governments put in place active labor market training programs designed to reduce open unemployment.

Focusing initially on the direct effects in Figure 1, the first point to note is that, in both models, the significant impact of trade openness disappears in the presence of these other variables. In the case of total outlays (Figure 1a), expenditure is a positive function of unemployment and a negative function of economic growth and the prior size of the state. This last effect is the strongest. In the case of total social expenditures (Figure 1b), the positive impact of unemployment on expenditure growth is marginally the strongest effect, but the negative relationship with initial spending levels is almost as great. The relationship between economic growth and social expenditure is, however, quite negligible. The strong relationship between unemployment and social expenditure is not surprising, given that social expenditure is clearly where unemployment most directly affects the budget. The absence of an economic growth effect in the case of social

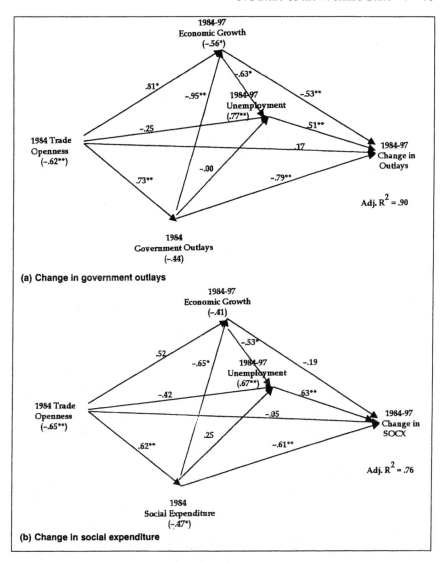

(a) Change in government outlays

(b) Change in social expenditure

Figure 1. Critical path analysis of (a) change in general government outlays, 1984–97, and (b) change in total social expenditure (SOCX), 1984–97. Figures in parentheses are correlation coefficients for the relationships between independent and dependent variables. Otherwise figures are standardized regression coefficients (significance levels: *.05; **.01). *1984–97 Unemployment* is the change in unemployment as a percentage of the labor force between 1984 and 1997; *1984 Trade Openness* is imports plus exports as a percentage of GDP; *1984–97 Economic Growth* is average annual real GDP; 1984 and *1984–97 Government Outlays* and *1984 and 1984–97 Social Expenditure (SOCX)* from Table 1. *Other sources:* 1984 Trade Openness from OECD, *Historical Statistics 1960–1994,* Paris, 1996; 1984–97 Economic Growth from OECD (18).

expenditure again seems indicative of the priority that modern governments give to social spending programs. In this period, governments seem to have used the fruits of economic growth to engineer a relative decline in the salience of the public sector as a whole, but appear to have resisted the temptation to use this mechanism as a means of downsizing the welfare state.

In terms of our understanding of the impact of international trade, it is the indirect effects that are most interesting. Causal paths going immediately via economic growth and unemployment are negative and significant for change in outlays, although not for social expenditure. In this period, greater trade enhanced economic growth and minimized unemployment, in both cases moderating the overall growth of the state. In contrast, causal paths going via the prior extension of the state on through economic growth and unemployment are positive, with higher spending militating against economic growth and, via that route, promoting higher unemployment. In both models, negative indirect effects mediated through economic conditions slightly—but only slightly—outweigh positive impacts. This means that, in both models, the key to the significant bivariate negative association between trade openness and expenditure change lies in the mediating effect of prior expenditure levels. The finding is a paradoxical one, seemingly simultaneously confirming conflicting hypotheses on the effects of trade vulnerability. The story is one of open economies spawning large public sectors and substantial social expenditure growth up to 1984, but of these very developments leading to lower public sector growth and weaker welfare state expansion in the years thereafter.

This paradox is only resolvable once we realize that both hypotheses are incorrect, because both fail to capture a cross-national variation that is simultaneously one of place and time. What we are observing here is not the working out of invariant economic laws linking trade exposure to expenditure growth, but rather stages in a process of convergent program maturation. Trade exposure leads not so much to permanently higher levels of public and social expenditure as to the early adoption of programs for coping with the economic fluctuation that results from such exposure. Analysis focusing on a period in which only the early adopters have expanded their programs gives the impression that trade openness is a determinant of higher levels of expenditure. The research studies reported by both Cameron (25) and Katzenstein (26), as well as the linkages between 1984 trade openness and 1984 expenditure levels located in the critical path models above, seem to imply such a conclusion, because they draw their evidence only from such a period.

What that conclusion misses is what happens next. As programs in the early-adopting countries mature, rates of expenditure development decline, while rates in later-adopting countries accelerate. Catch-up processes of this kind are captured by the negative association between prior expenditure levels and subsequent expenditure change and help to explain why commentators who focus exclusively on recent patterns of expenditure development are so pessimistic about the effects of globalization. Such catch-up effects may well be exacerbated by the fact that early adopters are also likely to be the first to experience any adverse effects of program adoption and to respond to them. As I note in the next section, the institutional design of pensions systems varies considerably, with some having a far greater potential for expenditure growth than others. Successful reform efforts in countries in which pension costs have become politically and economically intolerable contribute to the process of catch-up by bringing the high spenders back to the pack.

What is important about this account of expenditure convergence is that it tells a story in which globalization and international trade are not the enemies of the state. Once the process of program maturation is completed, much of the negativity of the relationship between trade openness and expenditure change is likely to disappear. The part that does not—mediated via higher economic growth and lower unemployment—cannot easily be seen as a threat to welfare objectives of the kind implied by "a race to the bottom" in standards of social protection. Higher rates of economic growth spell a decline in spending as a percentage of GDP, but not in real expenditure terms. Lower unemployment brings with it not only lower public and social expenditure but also reduced poverty and inequality. A positive role model for the future of an increasingly globalized economy could well be the Netherlands, whose levels of public and social expenditure, measured as percentages of GDP, have fallen markedly in recent years, largely because of high rates of economic growth and a rate of unemployment decline greater than any other in the OECD, and which, despite—or, perhaps, partly because of—these changes, has achieved real welfare outcomes markedly superior to those of most other Western nations (29).

THE SPECTRE OF AN AGING POPULATION

Over the life cycle of the postwar baby boom generation, the OECD has experienced and will continue to experience a major process of population aging. In 1960, in the 17 OECD countries featured in the earlier analysis, those aged 65 years and over averaged 9.5 percent of the population, and in only seven of those countries was more than a tenth of the total population in this age bracket. By 1995, the average had increased to 14.6 percent and, in all 17 countries, between a fifth and a tenth of the population was now in the elderly category. The estimates on which OECD pension expenditure predictions rest suggest that, by 2030, the average will be 23.7 percent and only Ireland will have less than a fifth of its population in the 65-plus age group (1960 and 2030 figures calculated from 30; 1995 figure from 31). Although the scenario of demographic change in coming decades is often presented as creating a problem of wholly unprecedented magnitude, these figures, as they stand, do not suggest a startling acceleration in the rate of population aging.[1] In the 35 years between 1960 and 1995, there was a 54 percent increase in the proportion of the population aged 65 and over. Between 1995 and 2030, the projected increase will be of the order of 62 percent. Whether this justifies talk of an "old age crisis," as has been forcefully argued by the World Bank (10), or merits consideration as "a critical policy challenge" to the future of the welfare state, as has been suggested by the OECD Secretariat (11), clearly depends on the extent to which the size of public programs catering to the needs of the elderly is a direct function of population demography. The tacit assumptions that give such crisis warnings their urgency are that age structure translates directly into expenditure and that increased aging translates no less directly into increased spending. The findings presented here suggest that, even in the case of public pensions, the program most directly meeting the needs of the elderly, such assumptions are by no means as self-evident as the crisis discourse presumes.

Table 3 presents data for public spending on pensions for the elderly for the same period and the same countries featured in the previous analysis. Apart from sample means, the table also contains a summary measure—the adjusted R-squared—of the association between spending and age structure. Means of 6.3 percent of GDP in 1984 and 7.5 percent in 1997 demonstrate the extent of OECD cash expenditure on the aged. In fact, pensions are the biggest single program of the welfare state, contrasting with 6.0 percent of GDP for public health and 5.9 percent for public education (1993 figures from 19). However, closer examination of Table 3 shows that, in this instance, averages do not mean very much. What is really extraordinary about pensions, in contrast to other major contemporary welfare state programs, is the extent of their cross-national variation, which can, again, be conveniently described in terms of family-of-nations patterns. Throughout the period, the high spenders were the countries of continental western Europe and the low spenders were the English-speaking nations, with the former outspending the latter by a ratio of more than two to one. Initially, the countries of southern Europe and those of Scandinavia are difficult to distinguish, but by the end of the period spending in southern Europe is beginning to move ahead. Change is less easily described in family-of-nations terms. Nevertheless, there's a clear pattern, with the most pronounced increases in spending occurring in the Mediterranean region, including the "new" southern Europe plus France and Italy. Again, there is a huge range of cross-national

---

[1] It is, however, quite possible that the real average for 2030 will be somewhat higher than the estimate given here and that OECD estimates of pension spending beyond that date will be increasingly inaccurate and optimistic. Bos and colleagues (30), on whom the OECD (11) relies for its demographic projections, assume that fertility rates presently below replacement levels will return to replacement levels by 2030. I argue forcefully in the final section of this chapter that this is most unlikely to occur unless there are substantial changes in cultural values concerning employment and in welfare state arrangements themselves.

Table 3

Public spending on cash benefits to the aged as
percentage of GDP in 17 OECD countries, 1984–1997

Country	1984	1997	Change, 1984–97
Australia	3.3	4.4	1.1
Canada	3.3	4.4	1.1
Ireland	4.5	2.9	–1.6
United States	5.7	5.6	–.1
Finland	6.4	7.5	1.1
Norway	4.8	5.6	.8
Sweden	7.2	8.0	.8
Austria	9.6	10.1	.5
Belgium	6.8	7.4	.6
France	8.7	10.7	2.0
Germany	10.2	10.5	.3
Italy	8.9	13.2	4.3
Netherlands	6.8	6.6	–.2
Greece	7.7	9.4	1.7
Portugal	3.8	6.5	2.7
Spain	5.8	8.6	2.8
Japan	3.6	5.5	1.9
Mean	**6.3**	**7.5**	**1.2**
Adj. R^2	**.36**	**.41**	**.37**

Sources: Cash benefits to the aged from OECD Secretariat,
Social Expenditure Database (SOCX).

Note: Adjusted *R*-squared is a measure of the association
between spending on the aged and the proportion of the population
over age 65 at a given time-point or over time.

variation, with Italy increasing its pension commitment by nearly a half and
Ireland reducing its expenditure effort by somewhat more than a third.

The important question here is the extent to which this variation is a consequence of age structure. An approximate answer is given by the adjusted
R-squared figures in Table 3, which indicate the degree of association between
cross-national variation in pensions spending and pensions spending change,
on the one hand, and cross-national variation in age structure and age structure

change, on the other. These figures tell a consistent story. At both time-points and with respect to change over time, population aging accounts for about 40 percent of spending differences. What that means, of course, is that somewhat more than half the observed cross-national variation is due to factors other than aging. In principle, we know precisely what these factors are. Pensions expenditure is, effectively, an identity of the proportion of a given population covered by a benefit scheme, the generosity of the benefit provided, and the size of the population entitled to benefit. The size of the population entitled to benefit from pensions for the elderly is roughly captured by the proportion of the population over age 65. This means that unexplained differences among nations must be a function of differential coverage and generosity of national pensions systems. Such differentials have nothing to do with demography and everything to do with the institutional design of welfare state programs.

A simple measure of the joint extent of these differentials is provided in Table 4, which calculates the ratio of spending on pensions as a percentage of GDP to the size of the population age 65 years and over. The resulting age generosity expenditure (AGE) ratio can most easily be thought of as an indicator of relative national spending on pensions per aged person. Table 4 demonstrates the very considerable differences in the joint impact of coverage and program generosity in the OECD nations. Italy, France, and Austria, for example, spend a far greater share of their national product per pensioner than Ireland, Japan, and Norway. Using the 1997 AGE ratio as a benchmark, we can calculate that when Italy achieves the OECD mean level of population aging for 2030 (and, for Italy, that will occur almost a decade earlier than 2030), that country will be spending approximately 20 percent of its GDP on pensions. If Ireland's population were to age to the same extent (and current estimates suggest that it will not), that country's spending would still be only around 6 percent of GDP. The story, then, is of some countries facing potential crises and others not, and of a crisis potential that appears to stem more from cross-national differences in the structure of provision than from differences in the age structure of the population. The aged are not the problem; some pension systems are.

The danger of the misdiagnosis, of course, is that it leads to inappropriate treatment. Having determined the cause of the welfare state's malaise as population aging, a more or less universal—and, insofar as it results from increased life expectation, a highly desirable—feature of societal development, the World Bank (10) sees the only solution as a wholesale redesign of pension systems the world over. If, however, the real public expenditure problem is a question of weaknesses of institutional design in some countries, the proper answer is pension reform in these countries and not in others. There are signs that this may be what is actually happening. Table 4 shows that four of the six big-spending continental western European family of nations were successful in reducing their AGE ratios in the period under examination here, and some preliminary modeling

Table 4

AGE ratio (pension spending to aged population)
in 17 OECD countries, 1984–1997

Country	1984	1997	Change, 1984–97
Australia	.327	.364	.037
Canada	.330	.358	.028
Ireland	.417	.254	−.162
United States	.483	.467	−.016
Finland	.516	.517	.001
Norway	.310	.354	.045
Sweden	.424	.460	.036
Austria	.671	.656	−.015
Belgium	.496	.454	−.042
France	.674	.690	.016
Germany	.694	.648	−.046
Italy	.690	.841	.151
Netherlands	.571	.493	−.079
Greece	.579	.595	.016
Portugal	.325	.436	.111
Spain	.492	.541	.049
Japan	.364	.350	−.013
Mean	**.492**	**.499**	**.007**

Sources: Calculated from data on cash benefits to the aged in
Table 3 and information on the size of the over-65 population
from Bos et al. (30) and OECD (31).

further suggests the possibility of a systematic *negative* relationship between prior
levels of social spending and change in the AGE ratio thereafter.[2]

Perhaps the most cheering story for welfare state buffs comes from Italy, the
OECD country combining the most extreme trajectory of future aging with the
highest level of present generosity to its pensioners. The 1996 OECD baseline

[2] 1984–97 Change in the AGE ratio = .354 − .008 (.002) [1984 total social expenditure] − .071 (.016)
[1984–97 real economic growth]. Adjusted R-squared = .54. Figures in parentheses are standard errors.
Data are from sources cited in earlier tables and figures.

predictions for expenditure (11, Table 2.3) estimated that Italian pensions spending would peak in 2040 at 21.4 percent of GDP. However, a long series of pension reform packages during the course of the 1990s has made for a trajectory of future spending that will now peak at somewhat below 16 percent of GDP at some point in the early 2030s. A knowledgeable commentator, describing this extended process of piecemeal reform and its outcomes, argues that it has "planted important institutional seeds that may trigger off a sort of spontaneous and self-sustaining dynamic of internal re-equilibration" and suggests that "the virtual stabilisation" of expenditure removes the threat of national bankruptcy, even if it does not cure all the imbalances of the Italian welfare state (32, pp. 176–177).

The Italian case is important just because it is the most extreme case. If the nation with the worst prognosis on the grounds of both demography and institutional design can pull back from the brink, so can other nations. This challenge is undoubtedly a real one for a number of the countries of continental western Europe and southern Europe, especially since these are the countries where current trends toward low fertility are most extreme. However, in the English-speaking world and Scandinavia, where both demography and institutional design are less conducive to high spending, the notion of a demographically induced crisis occurring over the course of the next few decades makes far less sense (see 33). Indeed, the real institutional design problem for the majority of English-speaking countries is that levels of coverage and generosity are far too low. A cynic might wonder whether the recent prominence, in precisely these countries, of an official discourse highlighting the adverse expenditure effects of population aging was not, in some measure, designed to preempt popular demands that such shortcomings be rectified.

THE COMING CRISIS AND HOW TO AVOID IT

The argument of the previous section that, for most Western nations, the threat of public insolvency caused by population aging is much exaggerated applies in the short and medium term but not necessarily in the longer term. Current projections of numbers in older and labor-market-active age cohorts are likely to be reasonably accurate for the years up to 2030. Thereafter things become considerably more uncertain, with increasing question marks over the size of the active population, which arise from unknowns about future rates of labor force participation, migration, and fertility. It is the latter that chiefly concerns us here, because, although still "through a glass darkly," there is increasing evidence that fertility rates in the majority of economically advanced countries are on trajectories that, unless reversed or in some other way alleviated, will lead to crises of population aging and population decline several orders of magnitude more serious than any currently contemplated by the World Bank and the OECD.

Fertility decline is generally considered a direct consequence of economic and scientific modernity. A standard interpretation is that offered by "demographic transition theory," which suggests that, as mortality and disease decline as a result of improvements in public hygiene and medical practice, parents will opt for smaller families because of a reduced risk of children failing to survive to maturity (34, 35). Although the wide dissemination of clinical and supply methods of contraception now gives families—and, in particular, women—the means of controlling their own fertility, it has, until recently, been widely assumed that fertility rates would not decline much below the level of population reproduction. Under the conditions of mortality obtaining in present-day Western nations, that level is about 2.06 children per woman.

Table 5 shows that total fertility rates across the OECD have been declining continuously since 1960. The beginning of the period coincides with the height of the "baby boom" and, in 1960, the average fertility rate for the 17 countries examined here was 2.85, well above the rate required for population reproduction. By 1980, the average fertility rate had declined to 1.87, and by 1999, on the brink of the new millennium, it was down to 1.56 children per woman, well below reproduction level. While some part of the recent reduction in measured fertility is clearly a function of changes in the age at which women choose to have children—that is, to delayed rather than foregone fertility—fertility decline in the advanced nations during the past quarter of a century has, in general, been of too great a magnitude and too prolonged to be attributable to this cause alone.

The potential seriousness of these figures is hard to exaggerate. For the majority of these nations, the implication is of population decline on a major scale. Assuming that fertility rates stabilize at 1995 levels and are maintained over the next 100 years, McDonald calculates that, in the absence of migration, Italy's population will be a mere 14 percent of what it was in 1995, with corresponding figures for Spain of 15 percent, Germany 17 percent, and Japan 28 percent (36, p. 2). This would mean that Italy and Spain would be reduced from medium-sized powers to mini-powers, with Italy's population dropping from about 55 million to just 8 million and Spain's from 40 million to about 6 million. By the same token, Germany and Japan would cease to be economic super-powers, the former declining in population from 82 to 14 million and the latter from 135 to 35 million.

These are countries with really low fertility rates, but even a rate as relatively high as 1.70 implies a halving of population over 100 years. Judging by the figures in Table 5, and in the absence of a major reversal of existing trends, this appears to be a likely scenario for the majority of these countries and for the OECD region as a whole, excluding the United States. Moreover, any reversal of trends needs to occur sooner rather than later. Demographic projections suggest that fertility rates of the order of 1.40 will produce what may be described as "coffin-shaped" age structures (37, p. 272), with increasingly smaller younger-age cohorts finding it more and more difficult to replace larger older-age cohorts. This "momentum for population decline" (38) will markedly exacerbate existing trends in population aging while rapidly undermining future demographic sustainability.

Table 5

Total fertility rates in 17 OECD countries, 1960–1999

Country	1960	1980	1999	Change, 1960–80	Change, 1980–99
Australia	3.48	1.89	1.75	−1.59	−0.14
Canada	3.90	1.67	1.55	−2.23	−0.12
Ireland	3.73	3.30	1.89	−0.43	−1.41
United States	3.65	1.80	2.05	−1.85	0.25
Finland	2.71	1.60	1.74	−1.11	0.14
Norway	2.90	1.70	1.84	−1.20	0.14
Sweden	2.13	1.70	1.50	−0.43	−0.20
Austria	2.69	1.60	1.34	−1.09	−0.24
Belgium	2.58	1.70	1.54	−0.88	−0.16
France	2.73	2.00	1.77	−0.73	−0.23
Germany	2.36	1.60	1.37	−0.76	−0.23
Italy	2.41	1.60	1.21	−0.81	−0.39
Netherlands	3.12	1.60	1.64	−0.52	0.04
Greece	2.28	2.20	1.30	−0.08	−0.90
Portugal	3.01	2.20	1.48	−0.81	−0.72
Spain	2.86	2.20	1.19	−0.66	−1.01
Japan	2.00	1.80	1.40	−0.20	−0.40
Mean	**2.85**	**1.87**	**1.56**	**−0.98**	**−0.31**

Sources: 1960 data from World Health Organization, 1993; 1980 and 1999 data from Eurostat, *Statistics in Focus,* Theme 3, 10/2000, 5, supplemented by further information from Professor Peter McDonald of the Australian National University Demography Program.

How we view such likely population changes depends on many considerations. Environmentalists are likely to welcome the reduced pressure on resources that a declining population will bring. On the other hand, it is most unlikely that national populations will be allowed to implode without intervention. Initially, population decline will mean reduced rates of growth of the labor force and national product. Very soon, it will come to mean labor market contraction and negative rates of economic growth. Employers and governments will increasingly see such trends as reasons to promote migration in areas where skills are in short supply. Attempts to counter the public expenditure effects of population aging by maintaining ratios of the active to the elderly population will be feasible only through similar means.

By the middle of the century, the rates of migration required to redress economic decline and population aging in southern Europe, continental western Europe, and northeast Asia (Korea and Taiwan are in the same boat as Japan) are likely to be very high indeed.

Such developments, in turn, suggest the probability of rising political tensions around issues of migration and a strong basis for the emergence of anti-immigrant populist movements, especially since, as history teaches us, migrant populations are likely to be blamed for bringing about precisely the economic circumstances their recruitment is designed to redress. Population change is also likely to affect the balance of economic and military might over the course of the next 100 years. The United States is presently the only one of the major OECD countries that seems relatively immune from population decline. As earlier noted, in terms of population size alone, many of the other big players in the contemporary international arena are going to find themselves downgraded to what amount to bit parts well before the end of the coming century. Economic stagnation resulting from rapid population decline will also make it harder and harder for other countries to compete on even terms with what is likely to remain a continuingly dynamic American economy. Among the likely consequences may well be a "brain drain" westward and the depletion of much of Europe's and north Asia's human capital base. At the same time, Europe, on its eastern and southern borders, will be facing nations with rapidly growing populations and declining living standards, both resulting from high (or, at least, much higher than European) levels of fertility. The prospect for increasing jealousies, mounting tensions, and ultimately, perhaps, armed confrontation between have and have-not nations is very real indeed.

The more extreme consequences of a low-fertility scenario can properly be seen as a crisis waiting to happen and one that will be harder to reverse with each passing decade. While a few countries, such as the United States, may presently see themselves as exempt from such scenarios, that could well be a case of premature optimism. The overall trend of OECD fertility remains strongly downward, and downward movements can be large and quite sudden. In 1993, Sweden's fertility rate was 2.00, only just behind Ireland and the United States, and the country was lauded as a model for sound population policy. As Table 5 shows, only six years later, the Swedish fertility rate had fallen to 1.50 and well into the area for serious concern. Nor can we simply assume, as the OECD has done until recently (see footnote 1 on p. 78), that fertility decline below reproduction level is some sort of aberration that will automatically right itself with the passage of a few decades. Austria, Germany, Italy, and the Netherlands, for example, have been on a path that implies at least a halving of their present population levels for two decades now, with no obvious signs of revival.

As should also be clear, solutions cannot simply involve reversals of the known causes of fertility decline over the past four decades. There may be those who would like to halt the tide of modernity, and many who believe that "small is beautiful," but there are unlikely to be many votes for a return to pre-1960s' standards of medical practice and the higher levels of infant mortality that might motivate parents to opt for more children. Nor, in this secular age, does it seem likely that policymakers will find it easy to reimpose restrictions on the distribution of clinical and supply methods of contraception, although abortion might possibly be a different matter. Some conservative politicians, remembering back to the "good old days" of the "baby boom," clearly do hanker for a world in which women's attachment to the labor force is less and attachment to the home and family is greater. When in office, they have sometimes tinkered with tax schedules and family allowance systems to make the "home duties" option somewhat more financially attractive—although only, of course, for married women. But nowhere have such schemes had any real impact on reversing the trend toward greater female employment or, indeed, had any notable impact on fertility.

Conservative proposals are unsuccessful because they do not recognize the new realities of the labor market, which link female labor force attachment to fertility in an entirely novel way. Until recently, it was a verity of those labor market texts that bothered to consider issues of women's employment that female labor force participation was strongly negatively correlated with fertility. This was because the standard cultural imperatives of the time made employment and child-bearing and, to a greater or lesser extent, employment and child-rearing mutually exclusive choices. This no longer seems to be the case. Cross-national research does, indeed, identify negative and significant correlations between female labor force participation and fertility rates for both the early 1960s and the mid-1970s. However, by the early 1990s, the relationship appears to have been wholly transformed, with an association that continues strongly statistically significant but which has now become positive (see 19, p. 272). Still more recent evidence, showing a correlation of .57 between levels of female labor force participation in 1999 (39) and fertility levels for the same year (data from Table 5), demonstrates that the latter finding was no aberration. This recent evidence of a changed relationship between female labor force attachment and fertility strongly suggests the need for a convincing account of a world in which women appear to be more likely to have children and build families in those societies in which they have the greatest opportunities to engage in gainful employment.

Positive correlations between women's participation in the labor force and fertility are of particular interest because they suggest that changes in the culture and organization of the labor force may have a role to play in accounting for trends toward below reproduction-level fertility. Identifying such changes and the potential they offer for purposive policy intervention to modify fertility trends has now become a topic of active debate among comparative researchers in the fields of social and public policy and demographers interested in the population dynamics of economically advanced nations. An obvious difficulty is that the range of evidence available for this debate is restricted to the relatively small number of countries at or below reproduction levels of fertility. This means that the findings of comparative analysis are, at best, broadly indicative and, quite often, open to a range of legitimately divergent interpretations. Figure 2, which provides specifications for alternative models of change in total fertility between 1980 and 1999, illustrates both the direction of the sorts of findings that are emerging and some of their ambiguities.

Both models contain a term of similar magnitude expressing the strong catchup—or, rather, catch-down—trajectory of fertility over these years. Essentially, that term accounts for the marked decline in fertility in Ireland, Greece, Portugal, and Spain, where the decline took place later than for other OECD nations in this group. The distinctive features of model 1 are a positive term for Protestant adherence and a negative term for the growth of female unemployment in the 1980s and 1990s. Model 2, apart from its catch-up term, is all about employment, demonstrating a tendency for fertility to increase in countries in which female employment levels had already reached high levels by 1980 and in which female employment increased most rapidly in subsequent decades. Ostensibly, the models have very different implications, since Protestant adherence is a relatively unchanging parameter, whereas female employment and unemployment profiles have changed quite markedly during the postwar era. In reality, the models are quite compatible once the strong identity between female employment and Protestantism is recognized. A story compatible with the evidence provided by

---

Model 1

1980–99 Change in total fertility = .941 − .729 (.105) [1980 total fertility]
+ .005 (.001) [Protestantism] − .021 (.008) [1980–99 change in female unemployment]

Adj. R^2 = .87

Model 2

1980–99 Change in total fertility = .065 − .749 (.119) [1980 total fertility]
+ .017 (.005) [1980 female employment] + .021 (.008) [1980–99 change in female unemployment]

Adj. R^2 = .83

Figure 2. Alternative models of change in total fertility in 17 OECD countries, 1980–99. Female employment is measured as a percentage of the female population aged 15 to 64. Figures in parentheses are standard errors. *Sources:* 1980–99 change in total fertility from Table 5; Protestantism (Protestant adherence as a percentage of the population) from D. B. Barrett, *World Christian Encyclopedia,* Oxford University Press, 1982; other variables from, or calculated from, OECD (11, 39).

both models is that fertility has declined least in those Protestant countries in which public policy has favored high levels of employment for women.

The theoretical underpinnings of this story have been interpreted in a variety of ways. Esping-Andersen sees the main source of change as increasing levels of female educational attainment combined with a demand for economic independence, which in countries of traditional familialism may be satisfied only by forgoing maternity altogether (40, p. 69). McDonald (36) identifies the major change as a shift from a breadwinner to a partnership conception of marital relationships, with women rejecting fertility unless they see it as compatible with shared responsibilities for paid work and parenting. I have told the story as that of women's liberation triumphant, with a demand for careers on the same terms as men leading women to delay or, in some instances, forgo fertility altogether (19, p. 269). In all these accounts, the reason that greater fertility is associated with higher levels of women's participation in the labor force is that the changing culture of female labor force attachment makes it more and more likely that the bulk of fertility will occur among women who can find a way of combining maternity with employment. In all of these accounts, policy is crucial. In countries where policies permit women to combine labor force and family roles, there will be both higher levels of female employment and higher levels of fertility. In countries where traditional cultural restraints get in the way of instituting "family friendly" policies, women who seek employment will find it much more difficult to achieve a balanced redefinition of roles and may end up opting for labor force participation without fertility.

In a sense, then, the correlation between female labor force attachment and fertility is a spurious one. What seems to matter is whether the institutions governing access to the labor market permit women to redefine their roles in ways compatible with both work and family. The kinds of institutions that are important in this context are, for the most part, welfare state measures such as public child care, maternity and parental leave, and legal guarantees of reentry into the labor force after childbirth, which provide women with the time and resources required for maternity while minimizing concomitant risks of labor force detachment. One nonwelfare measure with possibly similar effects is great flexibility in forms, hours, and conditions of employment, which may well help account for the United States' simultaneously high levels of fertility and female employment. Cultures shaped by Protestant values have been more welcoming of welfare innovation in support of women's employment and more tolerant of employment flexibility than cultures imbued by Catholic values—which is why it is the Catholic countries of southern Europe, once seen as fixated on maternity, that now languish at the foot of the low-fertility league table. Measures to promote full employment may also contribute to fertility, since high levels of female unemployment give women in economically marginal occupations a compelling reason to put off having children in order to maintain their existing workforce attachment. Arguably, full employment has been as important as positive welfare measures in accounting for the recent success of the Scandinavian countries in maintaining fertility rates reasonably close to reproduction level. Certainly, the recent massive drop in Swedish fertility followed that country's first experience of mass unemployment for nearly 60 years.

An optimistic reading of my argument in this section is that potentially serious postwar fertility trends in advanced Western societies may be contained or even marginally reversed by public policy measures that encourage and enable women to combine work and families. Even if such measures are insufficient to return all these nations to reproduction-level fertility, their wider adoption in countries of exceptionally low fertility may help reduce the risk of "coffin-shaped" population structures leading to irreversible social decline. Were that to be the case, it would be a natural step in the historical development of the Western welfare state, whose dominant theme has been not the continuity of internal crisis but the evolution of successive and successful societal responses to the major transformations that have periodically afflicted capitalist development and are likely to do so in the future.

Note — This chapter is expanded from a paper presented at the conference Re-Inventing Society in a Changing Global Economy, University of Toronto, March 8–10, 2001, and delivered as a keynote address to the meeting of Research Committee 19 (on Poverty, Social Welfare, and Social Policy) of the International Sociological Association, University of Oviedo, September 6–9, 2001.

REFERENCES

1. Crozier, M., Huntington, S. P., and Watanuki, S. *The Crisis of Democracy: Report to the Trilateral Commission on the Governability of Liberal Democracies.* New York University Press, New York, 1975.
2. Brittan, S. *The Economic Consequences of Democracy.* Temple Smith, London, 1977.
3. Organization for Economic Cooperation and Development. *The Welfare State in Crisis.* Paris, 1981.
4. Organization for Economic Cooperation and Development. *Social Expenditure 1960–1990: Problems of Growth and Control.* Paris, 1985.
5. O'Connor, J. *The Fiscal Crisis of the State.* St. Martin's Press, New York, 1973.
6. Offe, C. *Contradictions of the Welfare State.* Hutchinson, London, 1984.
7. Boyer, R., and Drache, D. (eds.). *States against Markets: The Limits of Globalization.* Routledge, London, 1996.
8. Rhodes, M. Globalization and west European welfare states: A critical review of recent debates. *J. Eur. Soc. Policy* 6(4):305–327, 1996.
9. Pfaller, A., Gough, I., and Therborn, G. (eds.). *Can the Welfare State Compete?* Macmillan, London, 1991.
10. World Bank. *Averting the Old Age Crisis.* Oxford University Press, New York, 1994.
11. Organization for Economic Cooperation and Development. *Ageing in OECD Countries: A Critical Policy Challenge.* Social Policy Studies, No. 2. Paris, 1996.
12. Kuhnle, S. (ed.). *Survival of the European Welfare State.* Routledge, London, 2000.

13. Liebfried, S. (ed.). The future of the welfare state. *Eur. Rev.* 8(2), 2000.
14. Huber, E., Ragin, C., and Stephens, J. D. Social democracy, Christian democracy, constitutional structure and the welfare state. *Am. J. Sociol.* 99(3):711–749, 1993.
15. Schmidt, M. G. When parties matter: A review of the possibilities and limits of partisan influence on public policy. *Eur. J. Polit. Res.* 30: 155–183, 1996.
16. Garrett, G. *Partisan Politics in the Global Economy.* Cambridge University Press, Cambridge, 1998.
17. Esping-Andersen, G. (ed.). *The Welfare State in Transition.* Sage, London, 1996.
18. Organization for Economic Cooperation and Development. *Economic Outlook.* Paris, 1999.
19. Castles, F. G. *Comparative Public Policy: Patterns of Post-war Transformation.* Edward Elgar, Cheltenham, UK, 1998.
20. Kaase, M., and Newton, K. What people expect from the state: Plus, ça change. In *British—and European—Social Attitudes: How Britain Differs,* ed. R. Jowell et al. Ashgate, Aldershot, UK, 1998.
21. Svallfors, S., and Taylor-Gooby, P. (eds.). *The End of the Welfare State? Responses to State Retrenchment.* Routledge, London, 1999.
22. Pierson, P. *Dismantling the Welfare State?* Cambridge University Press, Cambridge, 1994.
23. Pierson, P. The new politics of welfare state. *World Polit.* 48:143–179, 1996.
24. Pierson, P. (ed.). *The New Politics of the Welfare State.* Oxford University Press, Oxford, 2001.
25. Cameron, D. The expansion of the public economy: A comparative analysis. *Am. Polit. Sci. Rev.* 72(4):1243–1261, 1978.
26. Katzenstein, P. *Small States in World Markets.* Cornell University Press, Ithaca, 1985.
27. Gourevitch, P. *Politics in Hard Times: Comparative Responses to International Economic Crises.* Cornell University Press, Ithaca, 1986.
28. Rodrik, D. *Has Globalisation Gone Too Far?* Institute for International Economics, Washington, DC, 1997.
29. Goodin, R. E., et al. *The Real Worlds of Welfare Capitalism.* Cambridge University Press, Cambridge, 1999.
30. Bos, E., et al. *World Population Projections, 1994–95.* World Bank, New York, 1994.
31. Organization for Economic Cooperation and Development. *Labour Force Statistics 1960–1995.* Paris, 1997.
32. Ferrera, M. Reconstructing the state in southern Europe. In *The Survival of the European Welfare State,* ed. S. Kuhnle, pp. 166–181. Routledge, London, 2000.
33. Castles, F. G. Public expenditure and population ageing: Why families of nations are different? In *What Future for Social Security? Cross-National Perspectives,* ed. J. Clasen. Kluwer, The Hague, 2001.
34. Chesnais, J.-C. *The Demographic Transition: Stages, Patterns, and Economic Implications.* Clarendon Press, Oxford, 1992.
35. Van de Kaa, D. J. Anchored narratives: The story and findings of half a century of research into the determinants of fertility. *Popul. Stud.* 50(3):389–432, 1996.
36. McDonald, P. Gender equity, social institutions and the future of fertility. *J. Popul. Res.* 17:1–16, 2000.

37. McDonald, P. The shape of an Australian population policy. *Aust. Econ. Rev.* 33(3):272–280, 2000.
38. McDonald, P., and Kippen, R. *Population Futures for Australia: The Policy Alternatives.* Parliamentary Library, Canberra, 1999.
39. Organization for Economic Cooperation and Development. *Employment Outlook.* Paris, 2000.
40. Esping-Andersen, G. *Social Foundations of Postindustrial Economies.* Oxford University Press, Oxford, 1999.

PART III

The Growth of Inequalities

CHAPTER 4

Should We Worry About Income Inequality?

Robert Hunter Wade

The liberal approach to economic policy, which has dominated policy thinking in developed and developing countries for the past 25 years, claims that income inequality is itself not something to worry about. "Don't mind the gap" is its motto. Until the 1970s microeconomists even claimed that distribution and efficiency should be considered quite separately; and avowed that the economist should "stick to his last" and recommend policies that increased efficiency regardless of the distributive effects, provided that the gainers could *potentially* compensate the losers. That separation has more recently been questioned by academic economists, but it retains its potency in wider liberal circles. And liberals still emphasize that inequality is, first, an inevitable consequence of private property rights, and second, a necessary condition for effort, risk-taking, and entrepreneurship, and thereby for efficiency and innovation—indeed, for the whole thrust of Western panache. Liberals (in the European sense) therefore tend to dismiss questions about the growing gap between rich and poor as "the politics of envy." They say that public policy should not worry about income inequality as long as it results from "fair" market processes, including fair access to opportunities to earn income; and as long as it does not reach the point where popular resentment of great gaps threatens the liberal order.

What matters in liberal eyes is not income inequality as such but inequality of *opportunities* for earning income. Public policy should try to "even up" opportunities, so that one's country of birth, or class, or gender counts for less and less in determining one's wealth, health, and privileges. Inequalities of income not due to "predetermined" characteristics are presumed to be the result of differences in effort and talent or just plain luck, and here the moral case for greater equality falls away.

The exception is at the bottom. Just about everyone agrees that reducing extreme poverty should be a high priority for international and national action.

95

Jeffrey Sachs's *The End of Poverty* (1) shows that only very small amounts of additional resources—amounting to only a few U.S. dollars or so per year per person in the West—could make a dramatic cut in the number of people in the world living on less than $1 or $2 per day. Relatedly, just about everyone can agree that reducing inequality in life expectancy should be a high priority, for there is something compellingly unjust about a world in which one-quarter of the world's population living in low-income countries (excluding China and India) has a life expectancy at birth of around 55 years and the one-sixth of the world's population living in high-income countries has more than 20 years longer. But reducing income inequality not due to predetermined characteristics is apparently another story.

As applied to developing countries, the liberal policy reform agenda is known as the "Washington Consensus"—a set of mainly macroeconomic policy reforms to do with making markets work better ("getting the prices right"), including strengthening property rights, liberalizing domestic markets, privatizing state-owned enterprises, and opening the economy to free trade and investment. The Consensus was augmented in the late 1990s by reforms of certain institutions ("getting the institutions right"), especially to make the judiciary more rule-bound and the government more responsive and accountable; plus more emphasis on state responsibility for the supply of certain public goods, including primary health and education ("social sectors").[1] In the context of middle-income countries, the Augmented Washington Consensus supports a strong push towards the "financialization" of the economy: stock markets are to be the institutional pivot of the economy, company performance is to be judged primarily by return on capital, corporate law should facilitate hostile takeovers, pension systems should move away from the principle of taxation-financed "defined benefit" towards individual "defined contribution" retirement accounts invested in stock-market portfolios, and collective bargaining and other labor market "rigidities" should be removed.[2] The sub-text is that the share of capital income should rise relative to labor income.

The Augmented Washington Consensus leaves the economic core of the Washington Consensus untouched, focused on macroeconomic market liberalization, free trade, and privatization. This agenda has come to be accepted as so universally valid that the word "reform" is used exclusively to refer to policy changes in this direction. Other changes (higher protection as part of an industrial strategy, for example) are described as deviant, not as "reforms."

---

[1] When I say that the liberal (or neoliberal) paradigm sets the dominant approach to development strategy, and refer to this approach as the Washington Consensus, I am not talking about academic growth theory. I am talking about the dominant ideas of organizations, media, and writers close to policy making, as academic growth theorists are not.

[2] There has been a less than full consensus on the issue of how quickly middle-income countries should move to free capital mobility and free trade in financial services.

To quote Martin Wolf of the *Financial Times,* "What the successful countries all share is a move towards the market economy, one in which private property rights, free enterprise and competition increasingly took the place of state ownership, planning and protection. They chose, however haltingly, the path of economic liberalization and international integration. This is the heart of the matter. All else is commentary" (2, pp. 143–144).

The Consensus is forged in the echo chamber of the Washington-based organizations, including the World Bank, the International Monetary Fund (IMF), the U.S. Treasury,[3] USAID, and assorted think tanks; amplified through transatlantic components including the *Financial Times,* the *Economist,* the U.K. Treasury; and bandwagoned into finance and development ministries in many developing countries.

In this "climate of opinion," arguments and evidence consistent with liberalism are accepted at face value, with little critical scrutiny. Protracted recession in Japan? Obviously due to labor market rigidities, excessive regulation of industry, and high nonperforming loans (NPLs) in the banking system. Chronic unemployment in Germany? Due to labor market rigidities. Is executive pay in the United States too high in relation to average pay? No, because optimal-contracting theory shows how high pay helps to align the interests of managers with those of the owners, overcoming the "principal-agent problem" that bedevils the relationship between shareholders and managers.

But what about alternative hypotheses? For example, to explain chronic unemployment in Germany, "labor market rigidities" should be weighed against "excessively contractionary monetary policy by the European Central Bank." In Japan, "excessive regulation of industry" as a cause of continuing recession should be weighed against the argument that regulation in old-economy industries is needed to prevent hidden underemployment becoming overt unemployment, and high-technology, telecommunications, and other growth industries are not obstructed by regulation. NPLs as a cause of insufficient bank lending should be weighed against macroeconomically induced unwillingness to borrow. In the United States, "present levels of executive pay are justified by optimal-contracting theory" should be weighed against "executives inflate their pay beyond any contribution to efficiency and dividends thanks to their power to influence the board members who set their pay."

Serious testing of liberal against other hypotheses is rare. Inside the World Bank, the researcher who finds empirical evidence that confirms standard liberal prescriptions can send his paper off to the editorial office of the *Economist* with

---

[3] For example, the statement of U.S. Treasury Secretary John Snow: "Free trade is an essential component of the drive for stronger global economic growth . . . Developed and developing countries alike need to be prepared to reduce their trade barriers and subsidies. Financial services liberalization offers particular promise, and I look for good offers in this area as a key ingredient for a successful conclusion of the Round" (3).

the approval only of his head of division, whereas the one who finds evidence not consistent with standard liberal prescriptions has to send the paper off through rounds of "internal reviews." Should it survive, approval for outside release has to come from much higher up the hierarchy and may be delayed by months or even years. The signal to researchers is clear: you get ahead by going along, and you go along by finding just enough evidence to justify liberal conclusions. The criterion is, "Can I believe this (a liberal conclusion)? not "Must I believe this?"

This is faith-based social science. It smacks of the spirit of the George W. Bush White House, as articulated by a person identified by *New York Times* journalist Ron Suskind as "a senior advisor to Bush." The advisor told Suskind that people like him (Suskind) were "in what we call the reality-based community," which he defined as people who "believe that solutions emerge from your judicious study of discernible reality." The advisor continued, "That's not the way the world really works anymore. We're an empire now, and when we act, we create our own reality. And while you're studying that reality— judiciously, as you will—we'll act again, creating other new realities, which you can study too, and that's how things will sort out" (4).

At the risk of seeming old-fashioned, I shall assess the liberal claims in three reality-based ways. First, I examine the argument that a liberal policy regime is good for economic growth and development, good for poverty reduction, and good for keeping a lid on income inequality. Here I treat inequality as a "dependent" variable. If the liberal argument holds up, there is not much of a case for public policy measures targeted at lowering inequality per se, for inequality will be contained by "the market" provided we stick to the liberal agenda. Second, I examine the evidence on the impacts of income inequality on other variables, treating inequality as an "independent" variable. If inequality has no significant bad effects on other variables, there is again not much of a case for public policy measures designed to reduce inequality. Third, I examine the liberal theory of capitalist politics and economics, and consider how adequately it deals with what we observe as central tendencies in the role of advanced capitalist states.

THE LIBERAL ARGUMENT ON GROWTH, POVERTY, AND INEQUALITY

Let us distinguish two periods: the first was the era of "managed capitalism," including "Rhenish capitalism," "Japanese capitalism," and "import-substituting industrialization" in developing countries, and ran from roughly 1960 to 1979; the second is the era of "globalization" and "liberal" policies worldwide, from 1980 to the present. If the liberal argument about the benefits of a liberal policy regime is true, we expect to see an improvement in world economic growth between the first and second periods. We also expect a fall in the number of poor people in the world, or at least a fall in the proportion of poor. Third, we expect a fall in income inequality between countries and between the world's individuals or households.[4]

These expectations are resoundingly confirmed by the evidence, say the liberal champions. For example, the World Bank said in 2002, "The number of people subsisting on less than $1 per day rose steadily for nearly two centuries, but in the past 20 years it has . . . fallen by as much as 200 million, even as the world's population has risen by about 1.6 billion" (8). Since the number of people in extreme poverty is moving in the right direction—and also the other big outcomes, including economic growth and income inequality—we can conclude that the world system in its current liberal configuration meets a "fairness" test. Martin Wolf makes the causality clear: "economic integration, where successful, has reduced poverty and global inequality, not increased it. The tragedy is that there has been too little successful economic integration, not too much" (9).

The liberal argument carries prophetic clout: provided we hold steady to the central thrust towards free markets and private property and lower taxes, extreme poverty will be eliminated, income gaps between countries will "level up," and income gaps within countries will also level up as the poor become better off. The proviso is important. National governments and GEMS (global economic multilaterals, including the World Bank, IMF, World Trade Organization) must press ahead with the liberal-globalization or Washington Consensus agenda, against the forces of special interests and anti-Enlightenment NGOs (nongovernmental organizations). As Wolf puts it, "The failure of our world is not that there is too much globalization, but that there is too little. *The potential for greater economic integration has barely been tapped.* We need more global markets, not fewer, if we want to raise the living standards of the poor of the world. Social democrats, classical liberals and democratic conservatives should unite to preserve and improve the liberal global economy against *the enemies mustering both outside and inside the gates*" (2, p. 4, emphasis added). Elsewhere Wolf goes even further, describing the arguments of "anti-globalists" as "the big lie," a viperous phrase usually reserved for a Nazi propaganda technique.

In liberal eyes, sub-Saharan Africa is a special case that has not shared in the general lifting of boats. Special efforts are needed to supplement the liberal-globalization agenda with more aid, debt forgiveness, and public health interventions.

TRENDS AND CAUSES

Growth

Has the worldwide shift towards free markets in the past 25 years been associated with an increase in the rate of world economic growth? No. We have seen a dramatic growth slowdown in both developed and developing countries.

---

[4] Some of the ground covered here is covered in more detail elsewhere (5, 6). Colin Crouch (7) warns against dichotomous distinctions of the kind I make here.

Between 1960–1978, the era of managed capitalism, and 1979–2000, the era of globalization, the world economic growth rate fell by almost half, from 2.7 to 1.5 percent (10). The median GDP (gross domestic product) per capita growth rate for OECD countries fell from 3.5 percent in 1965–1979 to 1.8 percent in 1980–1998; and the median for developing countries fell from 2.4 percent to zero (11)![5] Many more countries experienced negative growth in the second period than in the first, and longer, deeper, and more frequent recessions.

In the case of Latin America, real per capita income grew by 80 percent in the 19 years from 1960 to 1979, during the era of "bad" import-substituting industrialization; in the 24 years from 1980 to 2004, during the era of "good" liberal policies, real per capita income grew by just 12 percent. For the past 25 years Latin America has had trouble staying on the right side of zero growth; between 1980 and 2002, average per capita GDP growth in Latin America (in 1995 U.S. dollars) averaged just 0.2 percent. Indeed, all regions except (non-Japan) Asia had a slowdown in growth rates between the era of managed capitalism and the era of globalization. Liberal champions tend to ignore these awkward facts. Wolf, for instance, presents a table that shows the growth slowdown in all regions except Asia, but makes no comment on its implications for the liberal argument (2, Table 8.1).

Poverty

Has the number of people living in extreme poverty (less than PPP$1 (purchasing power parity dollars) per day) fallen substantially in the past 25 years, reversing the long-term trend? If we take World Bank numbers at face value, the answer is, "Yes, but the fall depends entirely on China." Take China out and the number rises between 1981 and 2001 (12). If we use the slightly more generous PPP$2 a day as the international poverty line, the number of people in poverty *increased* from 2.4 billion in 1981 to 2.7 billion in 2001, again taking World Bank figures at face value. However, this increase in numbers still amounted to a fall in the proportion of world population living on less than PPP$2 per day, from 67 to 53 percent, which is a remarkable achievement.

These are two big qualifications to the standard liberal claim about poverty trends, taking the World Bank's figures at face value. A third qualification is that the World Bank poverty numbers are of very uncertain reliability, but the Bank virtually never acknowledges the wide margins of error.[6] And it is quite likely—though this is a weaker conclusion than the one about margins of error—that they bias the poverty headcount downwards. The international extreme or

---

[5] The median for the second period is driven down by the former communist countries, many of which experienced negative growth in the 1990s as they underwent big-bang liberalization.

[6] Chen and Ravallion's report (12) begins, "A cloud of doubt hangs over our knowledge about the extent of the world's progress against poverty."

absolute poverty line of $1 per day is rather arbitrary, not closely related to the consumption or expenditure or income needed to avoid extreme poverty, not closely related to calorific or demographic characteristics. We have no way of knowing what proportion of food-clothing-shelter needs the Bank's international poverty line captures. But we can be fairly sure that if the Bank had used a "basic needs" poverty line rather than its present artificial one, the number of absolute poor would rise, because the national poverty lines equivalent to a global basic needs poverty line would rise (perhaps by 30 to 40 percent). A 30 to 40 percent increase in a basic-needs-based international poverty line would increase the world total of people in extreme poverty by at least 30 to 40 percent. A recent study for Latin America by the United Nations' Economic Commission for Latin America shows that national extreme poverty rates, using poverty lines based on calorific and demographic characteristics, are commonly more than *twice* as high as those based on the World Bank's $1 a day line (13; see also 14).

Inequality

What about income inequality between countries? "International income inequality" (using per capita income measured in PPP dollars, weighted by population, and the Gini coefficient) increased through the 1960s and 1970s and then started to fall in the 1980s and continued to fall thereafter. This seems to confirm the liberal argument.

Except that, as with the fall in the world extreme poverty headcount, the result depends entirely on China. If China is excluded, inequality between countries— even by this measure, the one most favorable for the liberal argument—increased after 1980. One cannot then say that world income distribution has become more equal thanks to a general process called globalization or economic integration or liberalization. Increasing equality between population-weighted country incomes is the result of one—massive—case, not a general trend.

Moreover, other plausible measures show a clear trend towards rising inequality. For example, the income of the top 90th percentile over that of the bottom 10th percentile, and regional per capita income over the OECD average, both show inequality increasing. The average income per head of the South (in PPP dollars) has fallen as a percentage of the North ever since 1950, with a leveling off in the 1990s. Latin America's percentage has fallen precipitously since 1980; also sub-Saharan Africa's, eastern Europe's, and central Asia's. East Asia is the exception: its percentage has risen since 1980, driven mainly by China (see Figure 1).

When data on income distribution between countries are combined with data on distribution within countries we get "global income distribution," or the distribution between all the world's individuals or households. Here the big story is that about 60 percent of world economic growth over the 1990s—more than half the increase in world income or consumption—accrued to individuals living

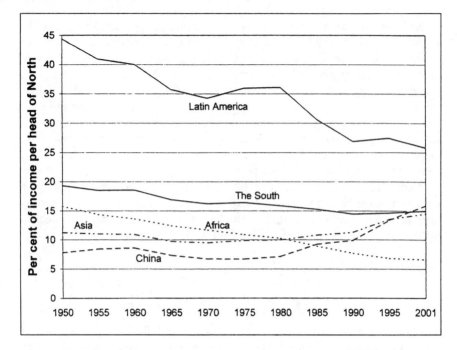

Figure 1. Income per head as percentage of North. Note: South includes the whole world except Western Europe, United States, Canada, Japan, Australia, and New Zealand. It includes Eastern Europe. (If Eastern Europe and the former Soviet Union are excluded, the line for the South remains much the same, except that it is a couple of percentage points less in 1950, falls less during the period, and rises to about the same as shown.) Asia includes everywhere east of Turkey, except Russia and Japan; specifically, it includes China. The separate line for China shows China's influence on the Asia line. The figures are weighted in the sense that they are calculated as total GDP per total population of the South (or other group) as a percentage of total GDP per total population of the North. The South goes down to begin with because all its elements go down. Asia starts rising in 1980, but the rest continue to go down, so the South as a whole levels off. Then in the 1990s Asia starts pulling the South average up slightly, though all its other components continue to go down, some of them (Eastern Europe, former USSR, and Africa faster than ever). With India now in the growth club and the Russia–Eastern Europe area growing again, the South line will probably rise noticeably in 2000–2005. I thank Bob Sutcliffe for discussions. *Source:* Bob Sutcliffe, World inequality and globalization, *Oxford Review of Economic Policy* 20(1), 2004; based on Angus Maddison, *The World Economy: Historical Statistics,* OECD, Paris, 2003.

on more than PPP$10,000 a year, most of them in the top half of the rich countries' income distribution; that is, to roughly 8 percent of the world's population. Most of the other half accrued to the burgeoning middle class of China, living on around PPP$3,000 to $5,000 per year. Again, the good news on a global scale depends largely on one case, China. The Indian middle class, by contrast, benefited very little in terms of its share of world economic growth. Hardly any of the additional world consumption accrued to people—wherever they lived—on less than about $1,000 a year.

The top few percentiles of the income distribution in the high-income states have benefited from a sharp swing in income distribution from labor income to capital income. For the OECD countries as a group, the share of labor remuneration in business revenue hovered around 70 percent for decades after the Second World War, increased to around 72 percent by 1980, and then—with Reagan and Thatcher forcing the rollback—fell steadily to about 64 percent today. On the other hand, the share of profits went up by 8 percentage points between 1980 and 2003, a very satisfactory result for shareholders (15). In the United States, the share of household income accruing to the top 0.01 percent of households fell from roughly 3 percent in 1929 to 0.5 percent by the early 1970s, flattened out, then—with globalization—shot back up to reach 3 percent by the early 2000s (16). A very satisfactory result for the top 0.01 percent.

In any case, our normal measures of inequality are misleading, because they measure only relative income, not absolute income gaps. To see this, take two countries, A with per capita income of $10,000, and B with per capita income of $1,000. Their relative income is 10:1, and the absolute gap is $9,000. If A's per capita income doubles to $20,000, the degree of income inequality remains constant provided B's increases to $2,000. In which case we conclude that income inequality has *not* become more unequal. But the absolute gap widens from $9,000 to $18,000. No one questions that absolute income gaps have been increasing fast—as between, for example, the average income of the top 20 percent of world income recipients and that of the bottom 20 percent, and also between the top 20 percent and the intermediate 60 percent. If, as is likely, people respond not only to relative income trends but also to trends in absolute gaps—those at the lower end feel more marginalized as absolute gaps increase even if relative incomes become more equal—our answer to the question, "What is happening to income inequality?" should not be blind to absolute gaps.

In short, plausible measures suggest that income inequality on a world scale has not fallen. Other measures that do indicate a fall get this result thanks to one case, China. In any case, single index numbers like the Gini coefficient are misleading, because they obscure where in the distribution the changes are taking place, or who is getting richer and who is not. Evidence on the distribution of the benefits of economic growth over the 1990s suggests that the growth has accrued largely to the richer half of the population of the high-income countries and to the emerging middle class of China.

All this is bad news for the argument that the worldwide shift towards liberal policies over the past quarter-century has generated higher economic growth, lower poverty, and lower world income inequality. Quite a lot of evidence suggests that the opposite is closer to the truth. Without China, the impact of globalization and liberalization on poverty and income distribution would look dismal. But China has got richer with a form of state-led capitalism very different from that enjoined by the liberal argument. Its big falls in poverty had little to do with China's integration into the world economy; they occurred in response to the decollectivization of agriculture in the 1980s and again in response to the increase in government procurement prices for food grains in the 1990s (though, of course, China's subsequent fast growth was enabled by rapid trade expansion). So if we are concerned to see better performance on poverty and inequality on a world scale, we should not place high confidence in the liberal policy agenda as a powerful engine of growth.

One other point. The liberal argument focuses on good and bad *policies*. But one can plausibly argue that geography and "institutions" count for relatively more—with the implication that large parts of the world not blessed with good geography and good institutions are unlikely to come close to, say, 50 percent of the average income of the North in the next century. One recent study finds that simply the age of states is a good predictor of recent growth performance. "In recent decades, 'old countries'—countries that gave rise to early states, kingdoms, and empires and those that maintained forms of political organization above the tribal level for large parts of the last two millennia— have been recording more rapid economic growth, on average, than have 'new countries.' This result is remarkably robust, standing up in multivariate regressions for both world samples and samples including developing countries only" (17).

THE IMPACTS OF INCOME INEQUALITY

We can present a moral case that the magnitude of inequalities in the world today is simply "unacceptable," especially in the light of the rather small cost to the rest of the world's population of substantially raising up the bottom tail of the distribution (eliminating extreme poverty). The size of the gaps is suggested in Table 1, which shows the income pyramid beneath the European Union in its "near abroad," with regional per capita income expressed both in market exchange rates and in PPP dollars.

What about the instrumental case, that inequality of income outcomes should be reduced—nationally and internationally—because of effects on other things?

The liberal argument stresses the desirable incentive effects of inequality. The counterargument is that this incentive effect applies only at moderate, Scandinavian-type levels of inequality. Above this, as in the United States over the past 20 years and still more at Brazil-type levels, the incentive effect is likely to be swamped by social costs. Inequality above a moderate level creates a kind

Table 1

The poverty pyramid below the European Union

| | Relative average income | |
Region/country	Market exchange rates	PPP$
E.U. 15	100	100
Eight new E.U. member states	22	46
Turkey	10	24
Russia	8	29
Ukraine, Belarus, Moldova	3	20
Caucasus	3	12
Central Asia	3	14
Magreb	6	17
Middle East	12	28
sub-Saharan Africa	2	7

Source: World Bank, World Bank Indicators, 2003.
Note: Middle East includes Iran, Saudi Arabia, and Yemen (others, no data).

of society that even crusty conservatives hate to live in, unpleasant and unsafe, coarsened by envy and distrust.

National Inequality

Does a higher initial level of income inequality cause slower subsequent growth? The cross-sectional evidence gives no robust answer. Too much "noise." Even if we found a strong relationship between higher inequality and slower subsequent growth, the causality is questionable: the effect on growth might be due to whatever caused the inequality to be high rather than the inequality itself. On the other hand, most economists do not now accept the once conventional belief that they should consider "efficiency" and "distribution" separately and base policy recommendations on efficiency impacts alone, provided the gainers from an efficiency-enhancing policy change could potentially compensate the losers and still be gainers. Economists today would more likely accept that today's inequality can drive tomorrow's allocation inefficiency through both market and political chains of causation.

The effects of income inequality on other variables are clearer. There is fairly good evidence that higher income inequality within countries goes with (*a*) higher poverty; and specifically, a lower contribution of economic growth to poverty reduction (lower "growth elasticity of poverty reduction"); (*b*) higher unemployment; (*c*) higher crime; (*d*) lower average health; (*e*) weaker property rights; (*f*) more skewed access to public services and state rule-setting fora, and lower standards of public services; and (*g*) slower transitions to democratic regimes, and more fragile democracies. (Some of this evidence is gathered together in 18, 19.)

Correlation is not causation, of course, and the causation in all these cases is probably two-way. But it is plausible that a strong causality does run from income inequality to the other variables.[7] In the case of crime, for example, we expect that higher inequality would raise the returns to crime (the rich have more to steal) and lower the opportunity cost of crime (the poor have fewer alternative livelihoods). And we do find that in the United States, cities with higher levels of income inequality also have higher rates of crime. In South Africa one study concluded that "policy-makers would do well to worry about the distribution of income—both within and between racial groups—when devising strategies for economic growth, as the welfare benefits from growth may be attenuated by decreased safety if such growth is accompanied by increased inequality" (22). Another study across many countries found that higher income inequality is associated with higher homicide rates and robbery rates, holding several other variables constant (23).

The link between inequality and crime comes partly through the inability of unskilled men in high-inequality societies to play traditional male economic and social roles, including a plausible contribution to family income. But higher crime and violence are only the tip of a distribution of social relationships skewed towards the aggressive end of the spectrum, with low average levels of trust and social capital. American states with more equal income distribution, like New Hampshire, also have more social trust.

There is good evidence that income inequality is bad for your health (see the new book by Richard Wilkinson; 24). The level of average health of a population rises with its average income and falls with higher income inequality; so higher income inequality is associated with lower average health, holding average income constant. Life expectancy in rich countries correlates closely with income inequality. Greece has an average income about half that of the United States, but its income distribution is more equal and its life expectancy is higher.

The evidence also suggests that other, non-income inequalities may be as or more important for health outcomes; notably, power inequalities and relative deprivation. People who perceive themselves to be lower in the social hierarchy

---

[7] But some recent research sounds a caution. David Lindauer and Lant Pritchett conclude from a wide-ranging study, "Estimates in the typical growth regressions are unstable over time and across countries" (20, p. 19). See also Mbabzi and coauthors: "The results are weak: we find no robust evidence that inequality, or indeed growth, are determinants of cross-country variations in poverty . . . any claims regarding growth and poverty or trade liberalization (even globalization) and poverty should be interpreted with extreme caution" (21, p. 113). "If we achieve no more than to convince readers to interpret cross-country evidence on inequality, growth and poverty with extreme caution and to eschew generalizations based on such evidence, we would be content" (21, p. 137).

tend to die younger than those just above them. Health is a function of stress, and stress is a function of insults, domination, low status, lack of control. High status and high control, on the other hand, seem to be good for health. A study in Sweden found that Ph.D.s live longer than those with master's degrees, who live longer than those with bachelor's degrees, who live longer than those with high school educations. Similar hierarchical effects have been found in other primates. Monkeys are happier and healthier when at the top of social hierarchies; their brains are found to produce more serotonin.

Societies with higher degrees of income inequality have societal institutions whose rules and resource allocations are more skewed in favor of the rich, because framed by the rich. For example, the poor pay more than the non-poor to get access to the courts and are less likely to receive a satisfactory outcome. At the same time, these societies have more difficulty in resolving collective-action problems, including getting contending groups to make credible commitments to coherent long-term development policies. The much higher coordinating capacity of Scandinavia and Japan compared with India, going back generations, may be linked to their much higher social homogeneity and economic equality.

Societies with high and rising levels of income inequality (including the United States and Britain) experience a vicious circle. People in the top fifth, say, of the income distribution become less tolerant of the idea of higher taxes to finance better public services, because they are increasingly able to exit—to go private. The government, whose policymakers come largely from this top quintile, responds to their preferences and promotes lower taxation, fudging the effects on public services. Over time the collective consciousness changes to regard levels of taxation that were once "acceptable" as "unacceptable." As the quality of public services falls, inequality rises and intolerance of "more progressive taxation for better public services" also rises.

Within Europe, Scandinavia has much lower after-tax income inequality than the rest. It has also shown better economic and social performance than both the rest of Europe and the United States by most of the important yardsticks—economic growth, labor productivity, research and development investment, product and service markets, performance in high-technology and telecommunications sectors, rates of employment, physical and social infrastructure, and quality of public services (from transport to education and health care). Scandinavia's better performance suggests that a relatively equal income distribution is compatible with relatively high economic growth, high labor productivity, and entrepreneurial incentives. Yet European governments and the European Commission remain fixated on the United States as the model of virile capitalism, and look hardly at all to Scandinavia.

In short, this evidence on the impacts of inequality at the national level supports the normative conclusion that income inequality above moderate levels should be reduced via public policy, even if just for the sake of the prosperous. The prosperous can indeed "do well by doing good."

Inequality between Countries

The liberal argument is even less concerned about widening inequality between countries than about inequality within countries, because we cannot do anything directly to lessen international inequality, as distinct from extreme poverty. But on the face of it, the more globalized the world becomes, the more the reasons why we should be concerned about within-country inequalities also apply between countries.

Increases in world inequality above moderate levels may constrain world demand and thereby world economic growth, producing a vicious circle of rising world inequality and lower world growth. Widening income inequality within developing countries results in a high marginal propensity to import sophisticated goods and services from rich countries. This sets a basic export imperative for developing countries to compete against each other, generating downward pressure on wage costs and exchange rates. Widening income inequality between countries—in particular the "missing middle" in world income distribution, only very slowly being filled by the upper percentiles of China's distribution—keeps down the demand for relatively unsophisticated goods of the kind that could be produced in developing countries. This dampener on world demand helps to hold demand for manufactured goods well below world supply capacity, resulting in intensifying competition, overproduction, falling prices, and falling profits. Crises of overproduction become more frequent—the only question is where they break out and whose production will be knocked out. As a Korean petro-chemical executive said when asked (in the 1980s) whether it was wise for Korea to be undertaking a massive expansion of petrochemical capacity at a time of excess world petrochemical capacity, "We are pretty sure that if there is blood to be spilled, it will not be ours."

Rising inequality between countries directly affects national political economy in the poorer states, as rich people who earlier compared themselves with others in their neighborhood now compare themselves with others in the United States or Western Europe, and feel deprived and perhaps angry. Inequality above moderate levels may, for example, predispose the elites to become more corrupt as they compare themselves with elites in rich countries and squeeze their own populations in order to sustain a comparable living standard, enfeebling whatever norms of citizenship have emerged. Likewise, rapidly widening between-country inequality in current exchange rate terms feeds back into stress in public services, as the increasing foreign exchange cost of imports, debt repayment, and the like has to be offset by cuts in budgets for health, education, and industrial policy.

Migration is a function of inequality, since the fastest way for a poor person to get richer is to jump across the border from a poor country to a rich country. Widening inequality may raise the incentive for the educated people of poor countries to migrate to the rich countries, and raise the incentive for unskilled people to seek illegal entry. Yet migration/refugees/asylum is the single most emotional, most atavistic issue in Western politics. Polls in Western countries commonly show that more than two-thirds of respondents agree that there should be fewer "foreigners" living in their countries (25). For all the resistance, migration into the rich countries will continue to rise, bringing not only a supply of cheap labor but also disease pools from countries with decrepit health systems.

The effects of inequality within and between countries also depend on prevailing norms. Where prevailing norms sanction equality, the sense of relative deprivation associated with any given level of inequality is stronger than where power hierarchy and income inequality are thought to be the natural human condition. The significance for the future is that norms of equity and democracy are being energetically promoted by the prosperous democracies in the rest of the world, at the same time as the lived experience in much of the rest of the world belongs to another planet.

For what it is worth, evidence on the international distribution of happiness (the proportion of people who indicate satisfaction with their lives) could be taken to support the case for more international income redistribution on utility maximization grounds. It turns out that higher per capita income is associated with higher average happiness only in countries below about $15,000 per head (well below the United Kingdom, around the level of Spain and Portugal).

The effects of international income inequality on between-country inequality in participation and influence in international organizations are clear, at least in broad terms. In the case of the World Bank, for example, the biggest five shareholders are the United States, Japan, Germany, France, and the United Kingdom, with almost 40 percent of the vote, and each has its own executive director (5 out of the 24). Forty-two sub-Saharan African countries have two executive directors between them and 5.2 percent of the vote. Yet the biggest five shareholders do not borrow from the Bank, whereas the sub-Saharan African countries are heavily dependent on it. Also, two-thirds of the senior management positions at the World Bank are held by nationals of the non-borrowing countries, which account for less than a fifth of world population. These voting shares are worked out using per capita incomes expressed in *market exchange rates* (together with other variables). For all that economists say that PPP dollars are more accurate to measure relative welfare, the rich countries are not lining up to reallocate shares to developing countries according to their PPP$ incomes, which are relatively much higher than their market exchange rate incomes (see Table 1).

More basically, the widening inequality between the United States and most developing regions apart from East Asia—especially when incomes are expressed in market exchange rate terms rather than in PPP dollars—helps the U.S. primacy (or empire) project. It facilitates U.S. intervention in other states to change their political economies, their weapons capabilities, or their security alignments, whether bilaterally or through multilateral organizations (26). American neoconservatives see this as a good outcome; others may beg to differ.

THE LIBERAL THEORY OF CAPITALIST POLITICS AND ECONOMICS

The liberal economic agenda derives from a coherent story about the appropriate role of the state in a market economy, but one that directs attention away from phenomena that question its validity. In the liberal story, juridically equal individuals engage in free-market exchanges to mutual benefit. The state, seen as external to the economy, acts as the agent of citizens in implementing their collective preferences, providing regulatory and policing functions, particularly with respect to property rights. The dilemma, however, is that the state's necessary coercive power—to enforce contracts and to protect the state and its citizens against external enemies—can be turned against citizens in a way that weakens the liberal order, whether by individual public officials seeking "rents" or by whole agencies of the state. This is the "state-market" dilemma: better markets need better states; but better states can undermine markets (27). Then the logic of the state interferes with the logic of the market, rather than supports it. Powerholders' grasp for resources impairs exchange and efficiency. This is the efficiency reason for sharply limiting the power and resource base of the state.

Underlying this notion of the appropriate role of the state is an assumption that markets—once private property rights and contracts are protected—are self-adjusting, tending towards equilibrium "by themselves"; and that competition is the driver of efficient use of resources (and not, for example, organizational loyalty). The perfectly competitive market is iconic in liberal thought, as the paradigm of a social order that works without power, where no actor is able to shape aggregate outcomes. In a world view founded on the distrust of power, the perfectly competitive market is a beguiling image of a social order with an underlying harmony of interests between its participants.

Looking back over the 19th and 20th centuries we can see that the liberal theory misses or trivializes some of the central drivers of industrial capitalism. For one, it trivializes the problem of order facing a state seeking to expand the economy. On the one hand, the state must provide sufficient predictability and security of property rights that the owners of capital are willing to "throw [their] property forward in time in the form of new investments which will produce profit only in the future rather than immediately" (28).[8] On the other hand, the state must contain the unrest of those without capital, who depend for their livelihood on selling their labor, massed in cities and susceptible to organization. These are much more demanding requirements than those faced by pre-capitalist states. The solution has been to go beyond legally legitimated violence, to identity politics: to convince the population that the state and its rulers are identical with them, and that they represent the wishes of the people—a very different conception to that in

---

[8] Gowan's paper (28) informs my discussion of the superficiality of the liberal theory of capitalist politics and economy.

pre-industrial states, where rulers emphasized their distinctiveness from their subjects and their affinity with God(s). Through identity politics, the capitalist state and its rulers try to obscure from view the conflict of interests between those who depend on capital income and those who depend on labor income.

Equally, the liberal story occludes the coordinating and entrepreneurial roles of the modern state in expanding and upgrading the national economy. It does so by assuming that producers face diminishing returns or constant returns, and hence that markets tend towards equilibrium "by themselves." In the real world, increasing returns to scale and scope, and hence "first mover advantages," are pervasive. ("First mover advantages" refer to the advantages reaped by the early entrants into a new sector or location, in being able to outcompete later entrants; 29). They drive the results of "free exchanges" in the direction of monopoly at the sector level, and of cumulative advantage for locations with early movers. But these increasing returns depend on mechanisms *outside* firms, in which the modern state and state resources have a big role—in providing cheap credit and tax incentives for lumpy or risky investments, supporting research and development, identifying key process or product frontiers important for the economy's future growth, supervising the supply of skilled labor and of transport and communications infrastructure, assisting the run-down of "sunset" industries, bankruptcy protection, industrial relations favorable to innovation, and more. This is a role of the state as coordinator and entrepreneur, well beyond the limits of the liberal role; but at the same time it cannot be dismissed with the standard gibes, "bureaucrats can't pick winners" or "protection protects inefficiencies," because it is not mainly about "picking winners" or about trade protection as such.

The U.S. state has been aggressive in its hypocrisy—using the cover of "national defense" to mount strategic industrial policy that deploys public resources and authority to enhance U.S. economic capacity in a whole array of frontier industries, while presenting itself as a champion of free markets and a regulatory state as the basis for the world economic order. And the World Trade Organization, steered by the G7 group of advanced states, has become an instrument for encouraging industrial upgrading in the industries relevant to the advanced countries, while discouraging industrial upgrading in the industries relevant to the developing countries. The Uruguay Round agreements—such as Trade-Related Investment Measures (TRIMs), Trade-Related Intellectual Property (TRIPs), Subsidies and Countervailing Measures (SCM)—provide plenty of scope for subsidies of the kind needed to promote high-tech frontier industries, but rule out most of the instruments appropriate for entry and upgrading in more basic industries (30, 31).

In these terms we can understand the unevenness of development noted earlier, in which a small portion of the world's population living in the advanced industrial states is able to enhance its preexisting international market dominance, with few new locations emerging in growth-intensive sectors with increasing returns. The most powerful states seek to expand legible property rights into the jurisdictions of other states with a view to expanding the room for *their* capitals to reap economies of scale and scope. Some of this entails cooperation with other states, legitimized with the liberal claim that free trade and investment are in the mutual interest of the participants. But particularly in relations between already developed states and "emerging markets," more arm-twisting may be involved. Developed states seek to shape the internal regimes of emerging markets in ways that favor the expansion of the property and profits of their own producers, through both bilateral relations and multilateral organizations (such as the World Bank and the IMF).

But some sections of the state and of the capitalist and labor classes may resist, seeking to counter the scale and scope advantages of producers based in the developed economies by giving their own producers various forms of assistance to compete and upgrade. The struggles to defend the legitimacy of free trade and investment, and of more powerful states shaping the internal political economies of weaker states, on the one hand, and concerted national development using an array of *non*-free trade and investment policies, on the other, become central to inter-state capitalist politics, and the source of a structural, not just contingent, conflict between states that "globalization" does not transcend.

CONCLUSIONS

I began by setting out a liberal argument about appropriate objectives and economic policy, in which reducing income inequality from current levels receives little weight. From the perspective of reality, rather than faith-based social science, I suggested that the argument could be appraised in at least three ways: first, the evidence for the claim that a liberal policy regime is good for economic growth, good for poverty reduction, and good for keeping a lid on income inequality; second, the evidence on the impacts of income inequality on other variables; third, the ability of the liberal theory of capitalist politics and economics to grasp central dynamics of 20th century industrial capitalism.

The liberal theory does not do well on any of these tests. There is plenty of evidence against the hypothesis that a very liberal policy regime—nationally, internationally—is good for economic growth, poverty, and inequality. There is plenty of evidence that, beyond quite moderate levels, further income inequality gives rise to a whole range of undesirable effects. And the liberal theory of capitalist politics and economics suffers from glaring inadequacies for grasping the central dynamics of industrial capitalism and late development.

In particular, I have argued that the dizzyingly steep income pyramid of countries is, by plausible measures, becoming even steeper. Globalization and market liberalization in 1980–2000 has not raised world economic growth rates compared with 1960–1978, and has yielded only a tiny increase in the share of world consumption accruing to those living on less than PPP$1,000 a year.

The Credibility of Economic Liberalism

Why, then, have economic policy norms shifted worldwide towards liberal policies, when supportive empirical evidence is rather weak? A good part of the answer must follow from, "cui bono?" Those who have the power and influence to shift the norms have seen their own income shares increase handsomely over the 1980s and 1990s. The evidence referred to earlier suggests that economic growth during the 1990s—and presumably the 1980s as well—has benefited mainly two categories of people: those in the upper half of the income distribution of the high-income states, and those who have made it into the swelling ranks of China's middle class. Obviously, the people whose authority and opinions have propelled the drive to liberalism worldwide are placed high up the income distribution of the high-income states. They and their reference group have benefited handsomely from liberal globalization.

The high and rising concentration of world income in the hands of the top few percentiles of the income distribution of the high-income states provides the impetus for a shift in national political economies towards the Anglo-American type. U.S. hedge funds and private equity funds—benefiting from the United States being both the world's largest economy and the most unequal of the high-income states—have become powerful actors in the world economy at large, including in Japan and Europe. They are using their shareholding power to demand changes in corporate governance law that would allow them more easily to buy up Japanese and European (especially German) companies. They want to buy them because they are cheap compared with U.S. companies. The companies are cheap because a much lower proportion of the shares of value added goes to the providers of capital: 8 percent to equity holders and creditors and 85 percent to employees (including managers) in Germany, compared with 21 percent and 68 percent, respectively, in Britain. Stock-market capitalizations adjust to give roughly equivalent returns, making Japanese and German firms look like real bargains for anyone determined to run them solely to maximize returns on capital.

The liberal ideology is deployed to say that companies *should* be run so as to maximize "capital efficiency"—and is persuasive to many in the business and political elites even in countries like Japan and Germany, awash with savings and in the grip of demand-deficiency deflation, stagnant wages, and falling consumer purchasing power and confidence! Even in Japan, the word "competition" now appears four times more frequently in business rhetoric than the word "cooperation," whereas before 1990 it was the reverse. The human resource departments of major companies now see themselves as handmaidens of the top managers, charged with devising incentive systems to get the most out of labor and managing the employment aspects of mergers and acquisitions and divestments, reversing the earlier concern to develop the firm's human resource base and make it a "learning community."

Still, the change at the level of norms has not gone as far as this might suggest. Japanese and American managers were asked, "Do you agree that corporations are the property of the shareholders, and employees merely one of the factors of production?" In the United States 67 percent of managers agreed; in Japan only 9 percent. That was in 1998. The Japanese percentage would be higher today, but a large gap would persist (32). And a national sample of Japanese people were asked (in September 2005), "Do you prefer a society based on equality or one based on competition?" Sixty-four percent opted for "equality," 18 percent opted for "competition." Presumably in the United States the proportions would be roughly reversed.

How Much Inequality Is Fair?

If inequality is an appropriate target of public policy, can we indicate, in the abstract, a level of inequality that is "fair" or "acceptable"? No one in this debate is advocating income equality, or a Gini coefficient of near zero. To give just one instrumental reason, as income distribution moves close to equality there are, one can presume, big disincentive effects on entrepreneurialism, innovation, and panache; so economic growth may well slow and perhaps go backwards. No one is presuming that a greater world income equality caused by the developed countries retrogressing towards African living standards would make the world a better place, or that China in the egalitarian communist period was somehow better off than today, however much liberal polemicists like to paint their opponents with this brush.

In the abstract, one can say little more than that the acceptable degree of inequality should be one that gives sufficient income incentive to take sufficient risk to generate sufficient economic growth to provide sufficient opportunities for the poorer to become less poor. But not so much difference in income outcomes that the rich can translate their income differential into a political oligarchy that sets rules that continuously fortify these differentials and keeps social mobility at low levels.

As the last point suggests, it would be widely agreed that higher levels of income inequality are more damaging for other desiderata the lower the rate of social mobility; conversely, the higher the rate of social mobility, the less the damage from relatively high levels of inequality. The empirical studies of the impact of inequality referred to earlier do not control for social mobility, however, not least because little cross-country evidence on social mobility is available.

Policy Conclusions

The liberal distinction between equality of income *opportunities* and equality of income *outcomes* is not viable. The bad effects of inequality follow from inequality of outcomes, not just of opportunities. Beyond rather modest degrees of inequality, more inequality of income outcomes makes the reduction of extreme poverty more difficult, causes higher levels of crime, and is associated with lower levels of average health. Further, in many countries, some redistribution of income through the tax system—to change *outcomes*—is going to be necessary to improve equality of opportunities. Greater equality of opportunities for education, for example, may well require a more progressive tax structure and less tax-avoidance by the rich.

It is easy enough to suggest policies that would improve equality of both opportunities and outcomes. In developed countries, more progressive taxation and earned income tax credits—cash assistance to working families—would help. In developing countries, land reform, and more emphasis on expanding domestic demand and relying less on export demand, would help the development of a mass consumer market capable of supporting self-sustaining growth.

The harder political economy question is to do with the politics of redistribution. Here a central component of a more egalitarian strategy is the strengthening of political parties, the strengthening of civil society organizations, and the strengthening of the links between civil society organizations and political parties, so as to bring redistributivist priorities onto the political agenda. Compulsory voting as a way of boosting turnout among disadvantaged groups is one option. In the United Kingdom, with no compulsory voting, the gap between turnout in the top social classes (AB) and bottom (DE) is large and growing; it increased from 13 percent in 1997 to 16 percent in 2005. In the Netherlands, voting was compulsory before 1970, and the turnout gap between top and bottom classes was about 4 percent; since compulsory voting was abolished in 1970 the gap has soared to 21 percent (33).

Perhaps the new coalition of prominent developing countries, the G20, can concert their actions to prompt a shift in the consensus on development strategy. The rules of the international development regime need to be changed so as to give developing-country governments scope to adopt policies designed to accelerate the economy's move into higher value-added activities, as most of today's developed-country governments did in earlier stages of their economies' evolution. Elites of the G7 states can be expected to resist any such attempt, in the spirit of Martin Wolf's characterization of "anti-globalists" as "the enemies mustering both outside and inside the gates." No wonder, when they preside over a global market economy that delivers to them—and the rest of the top half of the high-income states' income distribution, constituting less than 10 percent of the world's population—more than half of the world's increase in consumption during the 1990s.

On the other hand, a prolonged period of turbulence between the major currencies—which seems quite likely in view of the size of the current imbalances—may yet prompt the G7 to undertake an adjustment in their economic policies that puts them in touch with their responsibilities. Analysts can help by drawing attention to the body of evidence that is difficult to square with liberal expectations: not only trends in world economic growth, poverty, and income inequality, but also the performance of Scandinavia compared with the rest of Western Europe; the performance of New Zealand compared with Australia since the early 1980s (New Zealand underwent a much faster and thorough-going liberalization and has had worse economic performance, to the surprise of open-minded Australian economists); the performance of the "transitional" economies of Europe and Asia (within regions like Central Europe, Southeast Europe, and countries of the former Soviet Union, those economies that underwent faster liberalization have performed worse than those that underwent slower liberalization) (34); and much else besides. To be persuasive this counterevidence has to be combined into an alternative story about development, one that can plausibly be presented as furthering liberal ends as distinct from liberal means; and the alternative story has to be backed by organizations and social movements that matter. Failing that, much of the development policy debate will continue at the primitive level of Wolf's proposition: "The idea that everything would work well with development if developing countries did not have to liberalize or privatize is just wrong" (as if anyone was arguing for no liberalization or privatization). And it will continue to boost a misleading consensus on "the fundamentals," summarized by Wolf as, "if governments do the right things, development will normally happen, as China and now India are showing" (35).

Acknowledgment — I thank Martin Wolf for good debate. See "Are global poverty and inequality getting worse? Yes: Robert Wade, No: Martin Wolf," *Prospect,* March 2002, 16–21.

Note — This chapter is adapted from as essay in *Global Inequality: A Comprehensive Overview,* edited by David Held and Ayse Kaya, Polity Press, 2006.

REFERENCES

1. Sachs, J. *The End of Poverty.* Penguin, New York, 2005.
2. Wolf, M. *Why Globalization Works.* Yale University Press, New Haven, CT, 2004.
3. Snow, J. U.S. Treasury, April 16, 2005. www.ustreas.gov/press/releases/js2385.htm.
4. Suskind, R. Without a doubt. *New York Times Magazine,* October 17, 2004.
5. Wade, R. Is globalization reducing poverty and inequality? *World Dev.* 32(2): 567–589, 2004.
6. Wade, R. Globalization, poverty and inequality. In *Global Political Economy,* ed. J. Ravenhill. Oxford University Press, Oxford, 2005.
7. Crouch, C. Models of capitalism. *New Polit. Econ.* 10(4):439–456, 2005.
8. World Bank. *Globalization, Growth and Poverty,* p. 3. Oxford University Press, New York, 2002.
9. Wolf, M. A stepping stone from poverty. *Financial Times,* December 19, 2001.

10. Milanovic, B. *Worlds Apart: International and Global Inequality.* Princeton University Press, Princeton, NJ, 2005.
11. Easterly, W. The lost decades. *J. Econ. Growth* 6(2):135–157, 2001.
12. Chen, S., and Ravallion, M. How have the world's poorest fared since the early 1980s? *World Bank Res. Observer* 19(2):141–169, 2004.
13. Economic Commission for Latin America. *Panorama social de America Latina 2000–01*, p. 52. Santiago, 2001.
14. Reddy, S., and Pogge, T. How Not to Count the Poor. 2004. www.socialanalysis.org.
15. Bennhold, K. Richer companies, poorer workers. *International Herald Tribune,* April 10, 2005.
16. Dumenil, G., and Levy, D. Neoliberal income trends: Wealth, class and ownership in the USA. *New Left Rev.* 30(November/December):105–133, 2004.
17. Chanda, A., and Putterman, L. Effectiveness, economic growth, and the age of states. In *States and Development: Historical Antecedents of Stagnation and Advance*, ed. M. Lange and D. Rueschemeyer, pp. 69–91. Palgrave Macmillan, New York, 2005.
18. World Bank. *World Development Report 2006.* Washington, DC, September 2005.
19. UNCTAD. *Human Development Report 2005.* New York, 2005.
20. Lindauer D., and Pritchett, L. What's the big idea? The third generation of policies for economic growth. *Economia* 3(1):1–39, 2002.
21. Mbabzi, J., Morissey, O., and Milner, C. The fragility of empirical links between inequality, trade liberalization, growth and poverty. In *Perspectives on Growth and Poverty*, ed. R. van der Hoeven and A. Shorrocks. United Nations University Press, New York, 2003.
22. Demombynes, G., and Ozler, B. Crime and local inequality in South Africa. *J. Dev. Stud.* 76(2):265–292, 2005.
23. Fajnzylber, P., Lederman, D., and Loayza, N. Crime and victimization: An economic perspective. *Economia* 1(1):219–278, 1998.
24. Wilkinson, R. *The Impact of Inequality: How to Make Sick Societies Healthier.* New Press, New York, 2005.
25. Demeny, P. Population policy dilemmas in Europe at the dawn of the twenty-first century. *Popul. Dev. Rev.* 29(1):1–28, March 2003.
26. Wade, R. The invisible hand of the American empire. *Ethics Int. Affairs* 17(3):77–88, 2003.
27. Wade, R. Resolving the state-market dilemma in East Asia. In *The Role of the State in Economic Change*, ed. H.-J. Chang and R. Rowthorn. Clarendon Press, Oxford, 2005.
28. Gowan, P. The Pre-conditions for Transcending the Capitalist Inter-state System. Working paper, Department of International Relations, London Metropolitan University, August 2005.
29. Chandler, A. *Scale and Scope.* Harvard University Press, Cambridge, MA, 1990.
30. Wade, R. What strategies are viable for developing countries today? The WTO and the shrinking of "development space." *Rev. Int. Polit. Econ.* 10(4), 2003.
31. Weiss, L. Global governance, national strategies: How industrialised states make room to move under the WTO. *Rev. Int. Polit. Econ.* 12(5):1–27, 2005.
32. Jacoby, S. *People on Top.* Princeton University Press, Princeton, NJ, 2005.

33. Rogers, B. Turnout is really about class. *Guardian* (Manchester), May 14, 2005.
34. King, L. P. Explaining Postcommunist Economic Performance. William Davidson Working Paper No. 559. William Davidson Institute at the University of Michigan Business School, 2003.
35. Wolf, M. The case for optimism. In *Debating Globalization,* ed. D. Held, pp. 40, 42. Polity, Cambridge, 2005.

CHAPTER 5

The Causes of Increasing World Poverty and Inequality; Or, Why the Matthew Effect Prevails

Robert Hunter Wade

In the 1870s the U.S. economist Henry George remarked that "the association of poverty with progress is the great enigma of our time." Fortunately the enigma is today well on the way to being solved. World poverty and income inequality have both fallen during the past 20 years, thanks in large part to the third great wave of "globalization" (rising economic openness and integration of national economies).[1] This, at least, is the claim of the neoliberal argument, which supports the optimism about globalization that emanates from the pages of the World Bank, International Monetary Fund (IMF), World Trade Organization (WTO), *Financial Times, Economist,* and other organs of "thinking for the world."

For example, the World Bank says that the number of people in extreme poverty (living on an income of less than $1 a day in purchasing-power-parity [PPP] terms) has fallen in the past two decades for the first time in more than 150 years, from 1.4 billion in 1980 to 1.2 billion in 1998 (2). No ifs or buts. Or in another version, the Bank says that "the long trend of rising global inequality and rising numbers of people in absolute poverty has been halted and even reversed [since around 1980]" (1, p. 50). This reversal of the long trend is the "net effect," says the Bank, of surging globalization, as shown by the fact that the big falls in poverty and inequality—sufficient to reverse the long global trend—have occurred in the "new globalizers," that is, countries that had the biggest increases in the ratio of trade to gross domestic product (GDP) in 1977–1997 (the top one-third in a sample of developing countries ranked by trade/GDP increase). The "nonglobalizers" (the countries in the bottom two-thirds of the ranking) make little or no contribution to the reversal of the trend.

---

[1] The first wave was 1870–1914; the second, 1945–1980; the third, 1980 to the present (see 1).

The empirical evidence thus confirms the neoliberal predictions that openness is good and more openness is better, both at the level of the world economy and at the level of national economies. Those who oppose further liberalization (including trade unions, sections of business) must be acting—wittingly or unwittingly—out of "vested interests" or "rent seeking," and the few marginal academics who argue against only betray their incompetence. Those who care for the general interest of nations, the world, and especially the poor should properly ignore them. The mandates of the international financial institutions (including the IMF, World Bank, WTO) should continue to center on the drive to liberalize markets and keep markets deregulated (though perhaps subject to regulations for the protection of the environment and indigenous peoples). Insofar as they do this these institutions should receive public support, provided that they stick to this agenda (though some neoliberals still regard them as irredeemably "socialist" and in need of shrinking or even closing down).

The underlying theory rests on the notion of comparative advantage—that in an open economy resources will move to their most efficient uses. It further assumes that decreasing returns prevail, that beyond a certain point additional inputs yield decreasing marginal returns. So when a high-cost, high-wage, high-saving economy (A) interacts through free markets with a low-cost, low-wage, low-saving economy (B), capital tends to move from A to B in search of higher returns, and labor from B to A. This is good for world poverty and inequality.

In a previous essay I argued that world poverty—the number of people living in extreme poverty, known as the poverty headcount—may be increasing, and that world income inequality, measured in plausible ways, may also be increasing (3). This strikes at the heart of the neoliberal argument. It suggests that Henry George's enigma may be deepening; or in more analytic terms that, at the level of the world economy as a whole, increasing returns in income generation—the positive feedback of the Matthew effect, "To him that hath shall be given"—prevail over diminishing returns, despite the third wave of globalization. For economics this is bad news.

Leading theorist John Hicks considered introducing an assumption of increasing returns into economic theory in the late 1930s and drew back in alarm. "It must be remembered that the threatened wreckage is that of the greater part of general equilibrium theory," he warned, because "unless we can suppose . . . that marginal costs generally increase with output at the point of equilibrium . . . the basis on which economic laws can be constructed is shorn away" (4).[2] The need for determinate mathematical solutions bent economics, as the aspiring universal science of human behavior, away from the study of increasing returns, not for any

[2] Hicks continued, "We must be aware, however, that we are taking a dangerous step, and probably limiting to a serious extent the problems with which our subsequent analysis will be fitted to deal. Personally, however, I doubt if most of the problems we shall have to exclude for this reason are capable of much useful analysis by the methods of economic theory" (see also 5, 6).

reason to do with the real world but because increasing returns are difficult to treat mathematically. But the framework thus constructed also bolstered economists' normative faith in free markets and distrust of the state, based on the premise, convenient for the mathematics, that the market system is stable and therefore should be "interfered" with very little. This evidence on poverty and inequality—and quite a lot of other evidence as well—challenges the normative faith as well as the conceptual apparatus.

Having indicated what is at stake, I now summarize the earlier findings about levels and trends and then go on to talk about some of the bulldozer (not scalpel) causes.

WORLD POVERTY AND INEQUALITY

On poverty, the strong conclusion is that we must be agnostic about the poverty headcount—level and trend—because deficiencies in current statistics make for a large margin of error. The less strong conclusion is that the poverty numbers are higher than the World Bank says, and the numbers have risen over the past two decades. On the other hand, it is plausible that the *proportion* of the world's population in extreme poverty has fallen in the past two decades. The margin of error would have to be huge for this not to have happened.

On income distribution, the strong conclusion is that the only valid short answer to the question "What is the trend of world income distribution?" is, "It depends." It depends on the particular combination of measures, samples, and data sets. For example, on the choice between (*a*) incomes measured at market exchange rates or in terms of PPP; (*b*) inequality measured in terms of average country incomes ("between-country" distribution) or in terms of both between-country and within-country distributions (i.e., the distribution between all individuals or households in the world regardless of where they live); (*c*) countries weighted equally or by population; (*d*) inequality measured as an average across the distribution (such as the Gini coefficient) or as a ratio of top to bottom (such as top decile to bottom decile, or "core" zone to "peripheral" zone); (*e*) national income distribution calculated from household surveys or national income accounts. *There is no single "best" combination.* At least ten combinations are plausible, and they yield different conclusions about magnitudes and trends.

One combination does indeed yield the neoliberal answer. It uses (*a*) PPP incomes, (*b*) average GDP, (*c*) countries weighted by population, and (*d*) Gini or other average coefficient. World income inequality measured in this way very likely fell in 1980–2000, having risen for many decades previously.

There are just two problems. First, take out China from the sample and the Gini rises; take out India as well and the trend goes up like a July the Fourth rocket. Hence falling inequality is not a *generalized* feature of the world economy in the third (post-1980) wave of globalization, even using the most favorable combination. Second, this combination is not interesting because it ignores trends in distribution within countries. We would not be interested in a statement about U.S. income distribution based on average state income weighted by state population if we had data on individuals or households.

From here on the neoliberal argument fares even worse. World inequality is certainly increasing—fast—when incomes are measured in current exchange rates. But most economists say that this is irrelevant, because incomes should always be measured at purchasing power parity, not at market exchange rates. This is true in principle if we are interested in income as a proxy for well-being, though the margins of error in current measures of PPP incomes (especially for China, India, and the former Soviet Union before 1990) are probably not much less than those in market-exchange rate incomes. But we are often interested in income as a proxy for *international* purchasing power, because this is more relevant than PPP for measuring relative effects of one part of the world on others, including the ability of one set of people (e.g., in a developing country) to import, to borrow, to repay loans, and also to participate in international rule-making forums. The difficulty that developing country governments face in staffing offices in the rule-making centers and in hiring consultants and lawyers to advise them in international negotiations is directly related to the widening of inequality in market-exchange-rate terms, because they must pay in U.S. dollars bought at current market exchange rates, not PPP-adjusted U.S. dollars. And creditors have not been lining up to accept debt repayment in PPP-adjusted dollars.

Income inequality is also increasing when PPP-adjusted inequality is measured in terms of ratios of richer to poorer income deciles, which captures the idea of polarization better than the Gini or some other average.

The several other plausible combinations of measures yield more ambiguous results, more contingent on things such as the time period and the countries included in the sample. But several recent studies, using different methodologies, different samples, and different time periods, do find that world income inequality has risen in the period since the early 1980s (7–10).

It is therefore disingenuous to say, *tout court,* that world income distribution has become more equal in the third wave of globalization. More likely, a rising proportion of the world's population is living at the ends of the world income distribution and a rising share of the world's income is going to those at the top. Most of the population of China and India are still at PPP incomes that put them in the bottom third, not the middle, of the world distribution.

However, the whole discussion about inequality misleads by considering only relative incomes. Absolute income gaps between the West and the rest of the world are widening, even in the case of the fast-growing countries such as China and India, and are likely to go on widening for another half century. No one disputes this, but it is treated as a fact of no significance.

STRUCTURE AND AGENCY IN
GLOBAL INEQUALITY

The development economics and modernization theory of the 1950s to the 1970s would point to failure to industrialize as the likely cause of negative trends, on the assumption that (market-friendly) industrialization is the vehicle to carry developing countries close to the prosperity of the developed world.

No. Taking manufacturing's share of GDP or of employment, we find a remarkable convergence—developing countries as a group now have a *bigger* share than developed countries (11). But each additional increment of manufacturing in developing countries is yielding less income over time. This is not what one would expect if manufacturing in developing countries was embedded in a dynamic capitalism. The failure of this prediction may help to explain why industrialization has disappeared to the margins of the "international community's" development agenda. The World Bank scarcely mentions it. In the Bank's eyes, development is about liberalized markets, open economies, poverty alleviation, market access, good governance, and environmental protection, not about capitalist industrialization as such.

If failure to industrialize is not the culprit, what other factors might explain rising income inequality between countries? A large part of the answer must relate to the determinants of the world location of qualitatively different activities (different in terms of their contribution to growth)—in particular, the world location of activities subject to increasing returns and those subject to decreasing returns. We know that, in the general case, location patterns can be understood in terms of the relative strength of agglomeration and dispersion tendencies. We also know that there have indeed been powerful dispersion tendencies at work in "manufacturing" as a whole, but that the dispersion has not yielded income convergence. To understand why, we must disaggregate the manufacturing value chain and factor in the increasing dominance of finance in the advanced economies. And we also have to weave through these "structural" factors some others with more "agency"—the American "primacy" strategy and certain design features of the architecture of the world economic order that came out of the strategy.

I consider the following: (*a*) "sticky" locations for high value-added/increasing return activities; (*b*) decreasing returns in the middle levels of the manufacturing value chain; (*c*) continuing, perhaps even increasing concentration of big multinational corporations in the markets of advanced economies; (*d*) financialization of the advanced economies; (*e*) East Asia; (*f*) population growth; and (*g*) the American "primacy" project and international regimes. With such a stretch the discussion is necessarily schematic.

STICKY LOCATIONS IN INCREASING-RETURN/HIGH VALUE-ADDED ACTIVITIES

In the simple version of neoliberal theory, capital and technology move from high-income, high-cost zones to low-income, low-cost zones, and low-cost labor moves in the opposite direction. The result is convergence of factor incomes, eventually. If this were the dominant trend in today's world—as dominant as in economic models—we should see falling poverty and inequality.

To understand the "fact" of nonconvergence—or uneven development, or failure of catch-up—we have to understand a general property of modern economic growth. Some kinds of economic activities and production methods have more positive effects on growth and productivity than others. They are activities rich in increasing returns (to scale, to agglomeration), in contrast to activities with decreasing returns. To oversimplify, increasing-return activities are characterized by falling marginal costs as output rises; diminishing returns, by rising marginal costs with output. Increasing-return activities tend to have large unpriced "spillover" benefits that can be captured by other firms in the locality (which therefore enjoy lower costs than otherwise); and they tend to yield higher value added than diminishing-return activities.

Countries and regions with higher proportions of increasing-return activities enjoy higher levels of real incomes, in a virtuous circle; countries and regions with higher proportions of diminishing-return activities have lower incomes, in a vicious circle. The central national-level development problem is to shift the resources of a national economy, at the margin, away from diminishing-return activities and toward increasing-return activities; away from the activities that Malthus wrote about and toward those that Schumpeter wrote about. As a first approximation, this means to shift resources out of agriculture and primary commodities and into manufacturing, food processing, processing of primary commodities, and certain kinds of services related to these activities (as distinct from shoe-shine services).

To understand the paradox of substantial catch-up in manufacturing/GDP of developing countries as a group to developed country levels without a corresponding catch-up in income, one has to start with the manufacturing value chain. The value chain is the sequence of operations that go into making final products, including research and development (R&D), design, procurement, manufacturing, assembly, distribution, advertising, and sales. Thanks in part to the communications advances associated with globalization, manufacturing value chains have become spatially disarticulated, and value added has "migrated" to the two ends of the value chain—to R&D and design, distribution and advertising (12). Activities within the value chain that are more subject to diminishing returns have been shifting to low-wage zones, while those more subject to increasing returns tend to stay at home.

In other words, the increasing-returns/high value-added activities in manufacturing and in services continue to cluster in the high-cost, high-wage zone of the world economy, even when markets are working well (and not as a result of "market imperfections"). German skilled workers cost more than 15 times more to employ than Chinese skilled workers, yet Germany remains a powerful manufacturing center. Japanese skilled workers cost even more, yet Japan too remains a powerful center of manufacturing, despite being only 700 kilometers from Shanghai across the East China Sea.

Why then are locations sticky for the increasing-return/high value-added activities? First, costs per unit of output may not be lower in the lower wage zone, because lower wages may be more than offset by lower productivity. In any case, the cost of employing people has fallen to a small proportion of total costs in automated assembly operations, often 10 percent or less. As the technology content of many engineering products—such as vehicle parts and aircraft—becomes increasingly sophisticated, this raises the premium on the company keeping highly skilled workers to develop and manufacture these products; and one way to keep them is to pay them highly. The fact that wages are a small part of total costs means that higher wage payments do not have much effect on the net incentive to move to the low-wage zone of the world economy.

Second, the "capability" of a firm relative to its rivals (the maximum quality level it can achieve, and its cost of production) depends not only on the sum of the skills of its workforce, but also on the *collective* or firm-level knowledge and social organization of its employees. In the case of increasing-return/higher value-added activities, much of this knowledge and social organization is *tacit*, transferred mainly through face-to-face relationships—not transferred easily between people in different places in the form of machinery or (technical and organizational) blueprints. The value of tacit knowledge typically increases as a share of total value even as the ratio of tacit to codified knowledge falls with computerization. If a firm or plant were to move its increasing-return activities to a lower wage zone and some of its employees were not mobile, the costs to the firm's capacity, including the loss of tacit knowledge, might outweigh the advantages of relocation.

Third, tacit knowledge transfer is bigger the shorter the physical and cultural distance, and some other forms of transactions costs fall in the same way. This is a powerful driver of spatial clustering in increasing-return activities. Firms in a network of spatially concentrated input-output linkages can derive (unpriced) spillover benefits from the presence of the other firms and supporting infrastructure. They all get access to nests of producers' goods and services, ranges of skills, people practiced at adapting and innovating, and tacit knowledge—in short, to the external economies of human capital that are a major source of increasing returns to location in the high-wage zone (13). These spillover benefits compound the tendency for any one firm not to move to a low-wage zone, or to transplant only its *low* value-added assembly activities by outsourcing or establishing subsidiaries while holding at home the core activities that depend on varied inputs, tacit knowledge, social contacts, and closeness to consumers. Further, as skill shortages develop in the core and the supply of skilled people rises in the low-wage zone, firms nowadays can remain rooted in the core because skilled people are increasingly crossing borders to find them.

Firm immobility is reinforced by the fact that, for many products and services, quality and value added go up not continuously but in steps. (Ballbearings below a quality threshold are useless.) Getting to higher steps may require big investments, critical masses, targeted assistance from public entities, and long-term supply contracts with multinational corporations seeking local suppliers. "Normal" market processes—now fortified by WTO agreements that make many forms of industrial policy illegal (14)—can therefore prevent firms and countries in the low-wage zone from transforming themselves into attractive sites for higher quality work.

The empirical significance of these effects is suggested by the fact that about two-thirds of manufacturing output in the Organization for Economic Cooperation and Development (OECD) is sold by one firm to another firm within the OECD. In addition, parent companies based in the OECD, especially in some of the biggest manufacturing sectors (including electronics and vehicles), have formed increasingly concentrated vertical production networks in which they shift a rising proportion of routine manufacturing operations to lower tier suppliers in the low-wage zone, often locally owned companies, while keeping control of the high value-added activities of proprietary technology, branding, and marketing. They then use their market power and intense competition among the lower tier suppliers to extract more value added from them. The lower tier suppliers are first to suffer in a recession.

This is not the end of the sticky location story. At the next round, the greater wealth and variety of economic activities in the high-wage zone—not to mention institutions that manage conflict and encourage risk-taking, such as legally guaranteed civil rights, social insurance, a legal system that supports limited liability, and socially more homogeneous populations—mean that the high-wage zone can more readily absorb the Schumpeterian shocks from innovation and bankruptcies, as activity shifts from products and processes with more intense competition to those with less competition closer to the innovation end of the process. There is less resistance to the "creative destruction" of market processes, despite the fact that organizing people to resist tends to be easier than in the low-wage zone. Enron may go bankrupt, but there are plenty more companies to take on its business and its employees.

DIMINISHING RETURNS IN THE MIDDLE RUNGS OF
THE MANUFACTURING VALUE CHAIN

Over the 1980s and 1990s, many firms in the North moved the more labor-intensive parts of their value chains to low-wage locations, and many analysts expected that the plants and firms in developing countries that undertook this work would be able to move up the chain, undertaking progressively higher value-added work. (In apparel, this would mean moving from stitching of imported cut pieces, to cutting and stitching, to "full package" production including designs; e.g., 15.) They also expected that this upward mobility would be developmentally nutritious, and that the trade flows associated with the expansion of North-South production networks would be as good for development as the arms-length trade assumed in the standard economic models.

The evidence suggests that plants and firms in the low-wage zone have indeed moved up the chain—but the resulting increase in competition between low-wage producers in the higher stages of manufacturing has caused a fall in returns at these higher stages (16). One study of "a decade's worth of hard data" found "an almost uniform wage meltdown in the apparel industry in the Third World" (17). The trends in apparel also apply in other assembly-intensive industries, including consumer electronics.

China is often held up as the prime example of an economy that has benefited massively from the expansion of production tied to northern value chains. But, in fact, exports from foreign-funded enterprises have yielded much less value added for the national economy than the roughly equal value of exports from national firms, because the import content of the foreign-funded enterprises remains much higher (18).

Here is a microeconomic explanation of the macro trend to worldwide convergence of manufacturing but non-convergence of incomes. Each increment of manufacturing in developing countries is yielding less value added in the South and more in the North.

In short, the several mechanisms described here—particularly the combination of spatial clustering of high value-added activities in the prosperous zone and the fall in returns to the middle stages of manufacturing as more southern producers enter them—help to explain a stably divided world in which high wages remain high in one zone while low wages elsewhere remain low, even as the industrialization gap has closed. The important point is that well-functioning free markets in a highly economically globalized world produce, "spontaneously," an equilibrium division of activities between the high-wage zone and the low-wage zone that is hardly desirable for the low-wage zone, although economists would not call this "market failure."

To spell out the causality further, one might hypothesize that rising ratios of (especially manufacturing) trade to GDP raise the income share of the rich in low-income developing countries—those who have education and control over critical trade-related services—while shrinking the share of the bulk of the population with minimal or no education. The consumption preferences of the rich lock the low-income countries into dependence on sophisticated imports from the high-income countries, restricting the replacement of imports by national production that is a key to expanding prosperity rooted in diversifying production from the national economy rather than in narrow export specialization for foreign markets. Oligopolistic industrial organization in the high-income zone reinforces the inequalities by supporting mark-up pricing, which generates falling terms of trade for the low-wage zone.

The falling terms of trade facing developing countries is a major proximate cause of the persistence of the North-South divide. The prices of exports from developing countries, not only of primary commodities but also of manufacturing goods, have fallen sharply over the past two decades in relation to the prices of exports from developed countries, depressing the share of world income going to the low-income zone (19). The harnessing of China's vast reservoirs of labor has particularly depressed the terms of trade for developing-country manufactures. The sharp fall in the developing countries' manufacturing terms of trade soon after 1984 is largely due to China's dramatic entry into manufacturing exports. At a stretch one could say that China's biggest export is deflation.

REGIONAL, NOT GLOBAL, FOCUS OF MULTINATIONAL CORPORATIONS

Not only are multinational corporations based in the high-cost zone keeping their high value-added activities in the high-cost zone, they are also depending more, not less, on the high-cost, high-income zone for their sales. Contrary to the common idea of markets and firms becoming increasingly global, most of the Fortune 500's biggest multinational corporations depend for most of their sales on their home region, whether North America, the European Union, or East Asia (the "Triad") (20). Less than a dozen are "global" in their sales, even in the restricted sense of having 20 percent or more of total sales (from parents and subsidiaries) in each of these three regions. And virtually none depend to any significant degree on markets in developing countries outside East Asia (more evidence of the skewness of world income distribution).

Moreover, their focus on just one or two of the Triad regions intensified in the second half of the 1990s compared with the first half. The foreign operations of the multinationals became less profitable than their home-based operations in the second half of the 1990s, having been more profitable in the first half.

The other side of this concentration of sales in one or two Triad regions is he concentration of the small proportion of total foreign private direct investment going to developing countries in only half a dozen. Most of it is for producing exports back to developed countries, not for sales in developing countries.

In a word, multinational corporations are "regionalizing" more than "globalizing," and their regions do not include developing countries outside East Asia. They have correspondingly little interest in the economic development of developing countries.

FINANCIALIZATION OF THE ECONOMY

More distant causes of the likely poverty and income inequality trends lie in the transformation of capitalism from assembly lines to information manipulation, from manufacturing to finance. This places higher premiums on skills and education and penalizes those without.

But at the top end of the world income distribution, the sharp shift of world income toward the very richest families cannot be explained by returns to education. It relates more to the shift in corporate culture from a norm of "earned differentials" to a norm of "winner take. all," such that senior management pay deals that are worth hundreds of times the pay of workers no longer provoke outrage (analogous to the way that sexual permissiveness no longer provoked outrage after the 1960s, except in southern parts of the United States) (21).

This in turn relates to the ascendancy of finance in the most powerful economies, or the "financialization of the economy." Financialization has occurred to the point where the financial sector is the pivot of the U.S. and U.K. economies, interlocked with the other sectors in ways that tend to preserve its preeminence. For example, finance is institutionally interlocked with the richest third of households via stock market–based pension funds, and normatively interlocked with the corporate sector via "return on capital" as the chief measure of corporate performance.[3] The financial sector accrues very high value added to the economies where it is dominant, because (retail financing aside) it faces only weak price competition, it operates worldwide with clients who, understanding little of the more esoteric of its products, are on the wrong side of "asymmetrical information" and easily duped (24), and it is subject to the increasing returns of reputation. Much of its income comes from transaction fees, so it gains from a regional bubble as it arranges the inflows of finance and gains from the subsequent crash as it arranges the outflows.

The norms and institutional models that underpin the dominance of finance in the West are then "internationalized" to the rest of the world, partly via the WTO, IMF, World Bank, and some bilateral aid agencies. For example, under the banner of "capital market development" the World Bank and U.S. Agency for International Development are promoting mandatory public or private pension funds even in countries, like Kazakhstan, that lack accountants and adequate

---

[3] The financial sector is also among the biggest sources of political finance in the United States. On financialization, see 22, 23.

record keeping, let alone a stock market (25, 26). This open honeypot is a sure way to make finance the sector of choice for predatory national elites.

This in turn makes it less likely that developing-country governments, often dominated or constrained by resource-based elites with easy financial exit options (capital flight, dollarization), will focus on development strategy—including long-gestation projects that intensify the internal articulation of the national economy through import replacement, production diversification, technological upgrading, and the like. Resource-based elites wanting cheap unskilled, unorganized labor, often tied to finance-based elites with quick exit options, erode both economic citizenship and development strategy.

EAST ASIA

Even when considering East Asia's ability to continue to defy economic gravity we should not get too optimistic. Only a minuscule portion of world R&D work is done in (non-Japan) East Asia. Virtually all of it continues to be done in the Triad countries of North America, Euroland, and Japan. Even Singapore, which looks to be an Asian center of R&D, does not do much "real" R&D. Its R&D labs mostly concentrate on adapting products developed in North America and Europe for the regional market and listening in on what competitors are doing (27). The much heralded "globalization of R&D" is really about movement within the high-income Triad.

China still relies heavily on foreign investment and imported components for its higher-tech manufactured output; and incoming foreign investment is still mainly seeking low-cost labor, tax breaks, and implied promises of protection, as distinct from rapidly rising skills. Even its information technology engineering complex around Shanghai depends heavily on Taiwanese and other foreign know-how. Japanese alarm bells have been ringing as graphs show Japan's personal computer exports to the United States falling as China's rise; but the figures conceal the fact that the computers are assembled in China using high value-added technology from Japan and elsewhere. Some of the technology is spilling into the heads of the millions of Chinese employees, almost certainly more than is occurring in other developing countries (China has 200 "technicians" per million people, using the UNESCO definition, compared with 108 in India, 30 in Thailand, 318 in South Korea, and 301 in Singapore; 18, p. 167). Nevertheless, if China is prevented by WTO rules from deploying the sorts of industrial policies used earlier in the capitalist economies of East Asia—used to generate productive "rent-seeking" in activities important for the economy's future growth—it may remain for a prolonged period as an assembly platform for low value-added exports. More likely, China will become adept at mutating its industrial policies to be beyond WTO range.

These qualifications should caution us about a scenario of declining world income inequality based on China's continued fast growth and transformation. But whether or not China does substantially upgrade the value added of its exports, it will continue to cause a widening of income inequality between many *other* developing countries and the West. As it becomes the world center for low-cost manufacturing, it is knocking out competing producers in higher wage countries, such as Mexico and Brazil. At the same time it is boosting demand for agricultural and mining commodities from these countries. The result may be a spatial shift of "comparative advantage" as developing countries outside East Asia lose comparative advantage in manufacturing and resume their earlier specialization as commodity suppliers, now not only to the West but also to China and the rest of East Asia. One analyst observed that a "paradigm shift" may be underway as Latin America moves away from efforts at economic diversification back to its area of historical comparative advantage—agricultural and industrial commodities (28). In the simple economic model that still informs development thinking, specialization in line with comparative advantage will benefit (almost) everyone. The developmental consequences of Latin America moving back toward the role of commodity supplier dramatize the failures of the model to take account of real-world increasing returns.

In short, the benign effects of free markets in spreading benefits around the world, as celebrated in the liberal argument, are probably offset by other tendencies, yielding divergence between, on the one hand, an increasing-returns, high value-added, highly versatile and high-wage zone and, on the other, a diminishing-returns, low value-added, narrowly specialized and low-wage zone— even as ratios of manufacture/GDP, total trade/GDP, and manufacturing exports/ total exports rise in the latter, and even as national income inequality in the high-wage zone rises toward the level of inequality in the low-wage zone.

POPULATION GROWTH

At the low-income end, population is growing many times faster than in the rich zone, raising the share of world population living in the low-income zone. Natural population growth (excluding migration) in the high-income zone is close to zero; in the low-income zone it is around 2 percent excluding China, or around 1.5 percent including China. With dreadful irony, some regions where high population growth used to be seen as a problem are now experiencing the opposite: AIDS is wiping out so many adults, including farmers, civil servants, judges, teachers, and other professionals, that development is going backwards. But within sub-Saharan Africa, this is occurring mainly in the eastern and southern regions; the population of the region as a whole continues to grow faster than any other, at around 2.5 percent, and is likely to continue to do so because the young age distribution imparts high growth momentum. India, even as its population growth rate slows dramatically, will experience another 500 to 600 million people in the next 50 years and will overtake China in population size.

THE U.S. "PRIMACY" PROJECT AND
INTERNATIONAL REGIMES

The factors considered so far are related to "structures" or "parameters," not agents. But structures do not make choices. Agents have an important role in the story. They have created rules, organizations, and structures that help them to win.

The U.S. government was the primary architect of the international monetary system in place since the breakdown of the Bretton Woods system around 1970—what Peter Gowan calls the Dollar–Wall Street Regime (29). One of the key features of this regime is the use of a debt currency (rather than an asset currency)—the U.S. dollar, not linked to gold—as the primary asset of foreign exchange reserves and the primary currency of international transactions. This feature has exempted the United States from the normal "debtor' s curse," whereby a country running sizable current deficits must either devalue the currency or undertake aggregate demand contraction or both. On the contrary, the United States has the magical "debtor's blessing," whereby the surplus countries at the other end of the U.S. deficits continue to accumulate U.S. dollar assets. Their central banks use surplus dollars to buy U.S. Treasury Bills issued to finance the deficits, so that they in essence lend back to the United States the finance with which to cover the U.S. deficits—the deficits themselves generate the finance with which to finance them. And yet they do not press the United States to lower the value of the dollar, because this would lower the competitiveness of their exports and the value of their existing reserves. Hence the United States does not have to contract aggregate demand. U.S. interest rates are kept lower than otherwise by the inflow of foreign finance, and the U.S. dollar is kept higher than otherwise. U.S. firms are able (thanks to the high dollar) to buy up foreign assets cheaply, and low U.S. interest rates give them a stronger incentive to do so. The United States has more autonomy than any other state to set key parameters of aggregate demand in accordance with its own domestic conditions and not worry about the reactions of others. And—the bottom line—it continues to have more guns and butter than anyone else, because it faces softer trade-offs between more consumption, more investment, and more military expenditure. If necessary it can "cash in" its military dominance for support from other states for its preferred international economic policies, in a way that no other state can.

At the same time, the Dollar–Wall Street regime, with its private (rather than public, through central banks) capital markets, puts pressure on the more success-ful developing countries—or those that have liberalized their capital account—to curb their growth rates so as to limit the risk of crisis triggered by sudden capital flight.

The Uruguay Round/WTO trade regime, under the banner of "free trade and level playing field," has tipped the playing field decisively in favor of the developed countries, as seen in the agreements about textiles, agriculture, and intellectual property, and the prohibition of most of the "performance requirements" that East Asian governments placed on foreign-invested firms, including local content and export requirement (also in services; see 14, 30). The pre-Uruguay Round norm of "special and differential treatment" of developing countries, *because* they are developing, has more or less disappeared, replaced by the norm of "reciprocity." As a *Financial Times* editorial said, endorsing reciprocity as the obvious principle of fairness, "They [developing countries] cannot have it both ways. *Unless developing countries . . . are ready to open their markets, it is unrealistic to expect industrialised ones to do so.* More to the point, liberalisation would do them good. The economics of trade, like freedom, are indivisible: there is not one set of rules for the rich and another for the poor" (31, emphasis added).

Almost all the multilateral economic organizations with clout take it for granted that more market access is always better, that differences in market regulations between national markets are an undesirable obstacle to trade, that harmonization should occur around "international best practice," and that poor countries should give high priority in terms of the use of scarce skills to meeting WTO conditions for market access.

The World Bank and the IMF have withdrawn support for industrial policies aimed at creating industries that replace imports and challenge established ones in the West—policies that might help to offset the centrifugal, polarizing forces described earlier. Yet their "structural adjustment" programs have forced adjusting countries to increase their exports quickly, and therefore to export unprocessed commodities, an effect reinforced by the tariff escalation in developed countries, which imposes higher tariffs on more processed products. The result is oversupply of commodities and falling terms of trade for commodity exporters, making a good deal for commodity consumers in rich countries.

Mongolia is a grim example. In 1991, following the break-up of the Soviet Union, Mongolia's government adopted a full-scale liberalization package. Within five years its industrial sector, built up over 50 years, was almost wiped out. As people were driven back into (diminishing-return) agriculture and herding, yields plunged. Its social indicators, which had been well above the norm for its per capita income, also plunged. The radically liberalizing government did, however, wish to retain one industrial policy instrument: a tax on the export of raw wool (a measure adopted by the English king in the 15th century, which accelerated the growth of the English textile industry). The Asian Development Bank announced it would hold up a loan until Mongolia's government removed the export ban. The government obliged. More than 50 textile mills were closed. The Chinese now process virtually all of Mongolia's wool (5).

At one remove, the development and stabilization strategies of the multilateral economic organizations can be understood as instruments of the American "primacy" strategy, which reached fruition during the Clinton administrations of the 1990s. Primacy refers not just to superordination, as in military and economic dominance, for superordination could be consistent with a range of political economies in other states. Rather, it refers to the establishment of a world economic order in which the political economy arrangements of other states are homogenized around an essentially Anglo-American political economic model, presented as the "natural" kind of capitalism, analogous to Rousseau's Noble Savage. As the Noble Savage is corrupted by society, so natural capitalism is corrupted by politics and government "intervention."

This bedrock belief of American elites supports the post–Cold War U.S. "enlargement" strategy. National Security Affairs Presidential Assistant Anthony Lake explained the strategy in 1993. During the Cold War, he noted, opening the rest of the world's markets had to be balanced against containing communism—the "containment" strategy. With the end of the Cold War, "The successor to a doctrine of containment must be a *strategy of enlargement,* enlargement of the world's free community of market democracies. . . . During the Cold War, even children understood America's security mission: as they looked at those maps on their schoolroom walls, they knew we were trying to contain the creeping expansion of that big, red blob. Today . . . we might visualize our security mission as promoting the enlargement of the 'blue areas' of market democracies (32, emphasis added). The interesting question is how the United States has been able to harness the multilateral economic organizations—meant to be cooperatives of states—to advance its national economic and security strategy with rather little opposition, and how the pursuit of the strategy has affected trends in world poverty and distribution (see 33).

CONCLUSIONS

If the number of people in extreme poverty seems not to be falling and if global inequality seems to be widening (in terms of several plausible measures, and emphatically in terms of absolute income gaps), we cannot conclude that globalization—the spread of free-market relations within the current framework—is moving the world in the right direction, with Africa's poverty as a special case for international attention. The balance of probability is that—like global warming—the world is moving in the wrong direction.

Should We Worry about Rising Inequality?

The neoliberal argument says that inequality provides incentives for effort and risk-taking, and thereby raises efficiency. We should not worry provided that it does not somehow make the poor worse off than otherwise. The counterargument is that this productive incentive effect applies only at moderate levels of inequality. At higher levels, such as in the United States over the past 20 years, it is likely to be swamped by social costs. Aside from the moral case against it, inequality above a moderate level creates a kind of society that even crusty conservatives hate to live in, unsafe and unpleasant.

Higher income inequality within nations goes with (*a*) higher poverty (using World Bank data and the number of people below the Bank's international poverty line) (34); (*b*) higher unemployment; (*c*) slower economic growth; and (*d*) higher crime (35–38). Evidence from across U.S. cities confirms that greater inequality is associated with higher rates of crime. The link to higher crime comes through the inability of unskilled men in high-inequality societies to play traditional male economic and social roles, including a plausible contribution to family income. But higher crime and violence is only the tip of a distribution of social relationships skewed toward the aggressive end of the spectrum, with low average levels of trust and social capital. In short, inequality at the national level should certainly be a target of public policy, even if just for the sake of the prosperous.

The neoliberal argument is even less concerned about widening inequality between countries than it is about inequality within countries, because we cannot do anything directly to lessen international inequality. But on the face of it, the more globalized the world becomes, the more the reasons why we should be concerned about within-country inequalities also apply between countries. If globalization within the current framework actually increases inequality within and between countries, as is consistent with a lot of evidence, increases in world inequality above moderate levels may cut world aggregate demand and thereby world economic growth, producing a vicious circle of rising world inequality and lower world growth.

And rising inequality between countries directly affects national political economy in the poorer states, as rich people who earlier compared themselves with others in their neighborhood or nation now compare themselves with others in the United States or Western Europe, and feel deprived and perhaps angry. Inequality above moderate levels may, for example, predispose the elites to become more corrupt as they compare themselves with elites in rich countries and squeeze their own populations in order to sustain a comparable living standard, enfeebling whatever norms of citizenship have emerged.

Likewise, rapidly widening between-country inequality in current exchange rate terms feeds back into stress in public services, as the increasing foreign exchange cost of imports, debt repayment, and the like has to be offset by cuts in budgets for health, education, and industrial policy.

Migration is a function of inequality, since the fastest way for a poor person to get richer is to move from a poor country to a rich country. Widening inequality may raise the incentive for the educated people of poor countries to migrate to the rich countries, and raise the incentive for unskilled people to seek illegal entry. Yet migration/refugees/asylum is the single most emotional, most atavistic issue in Western politics. Polls show that more than two-thirds of respondents agree that there should be fewer "foreigners" living in their countries (39).

Again, widening between-country inequality may intensify conflict between states and, because the market-exchange-rate income gap is so big, make it cheap for rich states to intervene to support one side or the other in civil strife. Rising inequality in market-exchange-rate terms—helped by a high U.S. dollar, a low (long-run) oil price, and the new intellectual property agreement of the WTO—allows the United States to finance the military sinews of its emerging empire more cheaply.

The effects of inequality within and between countries also depend on prevailing norms. Where power hierarchy and income inequality are thought to be the natural human condition, the negative effects can be expected to be lighter than where prevailing norms sanction equality and where the sense of relative deprivation is stronger. The significance for the future is that norms of equality and democracy are being energetically promoted by the prosperous democracies in the rest of the world, at the same time as the lived experience in much of the rest of the world belongs to another planet.

Development Economics

If sizable fractions of the world's population are to reach today's median income over the next half century, we need to revisit the theory and prescriptions of development economics. It is one of the ironies of our time that, during the great drive to mathematize economics in the 1940s to the 1970s, increasing returns, cumulative causation, and the like disappeared from the realm of high theory but remained in play in the subdiscipline of development economics (e.g., in the ideas of the "big push," "unbalanced growth," "industry first"). While, since the 1980s, much work in the realm of high theory investigates the heterodox world of increasing returns, linkages, monopolistic competition, and the like, these ideas more or less dropped out of the more applied variants of development economics. The dominant "structural adjustment" prescriptions of the Bretton Woods organizations assume orthodox decreasing returns, stable equilibria, and no significant non-market linkage effects. Sometimes the same economists straddle both worlds, setting aside their knowledge of the heterodox world of increasing returns when they deal with development policy in order to hammer home the orthodox "fundamentals" about efficient, rent-free markets implicitly assumed to operate in a world of diminishing-return activities and hence to be self-adjusting toward an optimal equilibrium.

Contemporary applied development economics teaches that (a) economic growth is a by-product of well-functioning markets; (b) countries should specialize in line with their comparative advantage; and (c) countries should practice free trade, for free trade is Pareto optimal—the only issue of trade policy is how fast and in what sequence to move to free trade.

In the 1990s, development economics added to these "fundamentals" a new concern with "good governance" in the form of slimmed down, decentralized, corruption-free public sectors and participatory procedures for public investments. The neoliberal development agenda, often called the Washington Consensus, takes as its central tasks the creation of (a) efficient, rent-free markets, (*b*) efficient, corruption-free public sectors able to supervise the delivery of a narrow set of inherently public services, and (*c*) decentralized arrangements of participatory democracy and civil society. The more these conditions are in place, the more development and prosperity are expected to follow.

But the argument flies in the face of the history of both the now advanced countries of western Europe and North America and the post–Second World War success stories. The history of development suggests, on the contrary, that deliberate, government-sponsored effort to create "rents" (returns above the normal market level) through various forms of infant industry nurturing—aimed in the first instance at replacing some current imports with local production and at shifting resources at the margin toward increasing-return activities—is an almost-necessary condition (40). Far from specializing in line with comparative advantage, successful developers have diversified their production base, right up to the per capita income of the lower levels of the World Bank's "high-income" countries (41).[4] They have not relied upon well-functioning markets to produce economic growth as a by-product, for the reason that markets are good at signaling relative profitability at the margin but bad at signaling the structural changes, the lumpy investments of the kind entailed by economic development. They have not practiced free trade, by and large, and one can see on theoretical grounds why free trade may not be Pareto optimal—because free trade, by raising risk and volatility, can make everyone worse off by prompting resource owners to reallocate into lower risk, less productive activities; not to mention that, in the real world, IMF and World Bank programs often require a cut-back in government transfer payments, and hence reduce the ability of the government to ensure that the gainers from the move to free trade really do compensate the losers.

We need to reintroduce a distinction that has dropped out of the development lexicon, between "external" integration and "internal" integration. In current usage "integration" refers to integration of a national economy into world markets, and more external integration is assumed automatically to stimulate internal integration between wages, consumption, and production, and between sectors such as rural and urban, consumer goods and intermediate goods. Much evidence suggests, on the contrary, that deliberately engineered increases in internal integration can propel higher external integration, especially through the replacement of some current imports with national production, thereby generating demands for new kinds of imports (40; see also 42–45). Some import replacement occurs "naturally" in response to transport costs, growing skills, and shifting relative costs. But the development experience of Latin America and Africa over the whole of the 20th century suggests that regions that integrate into the world economy as

---

[4] There are interesting analytical questions about how to integrate the advantages of diversification (economic activity spreading more equally across sectors as per capita income rises, in one country) with the advantages of a rising ratio of increasing- to decreasing-return activities, and interesting policy questions about how and when to accelerate diversification with infant industry promotion policies.

commodity supply regions are only too likely to remain stuck, their level of prosperity a function of access to rich-country markets and (falling) prices for their narrow portfolio of commodities. Deliberate efforts to accelerate import replacement, or internal integration more broadly, can certainly go awry, as much experience in Latin America, Africa, and South Asia shows. The response should be to do import replacement better, not less.

In the end, the central development problematique must be less about how to alleviate poverty, sustain the environment, and establish rent-free markets and corruption-free public sectors, and more about how to create forms of capitalism able to generate rising mass living standards in the low-wage zone of the world economy on the basis, mainly, of expanding domestic demand for domestic production. In this context, the rule of thumb is that an inefficient manufacturing sector is better than no manufacturing sector. For many economies (Mongolia is one), this is the choice, because an efficient manufacturing sector is nowhere in sight. It is remarkable how completely the issue of creating dynamic capitalisms has disappeared from the international development agenda. We need to re-engage with the issues that Malthus and Schumpeter were talking about.

Multilateral Economic Agreements

The question is how to reconfigure multilateral economic organizations so as to legitimize expanded "special and differential treatment" for developing countries and dilute requirements for "reciprocity," "national treatment," and "international best practice." The rules of the international economic regime must allow developing countries to accelerate import replacement by measures such as tariffs, subsidies, preferential government procurement for national firms, and targeted efforts to develop supply links between subsidiaries of multinational corporations and local firms (preferably all made conditional on improved performance of the assisted industries), and to impose restrictions on capital flows at times of surges (14). This is what developing-country representatives in international economic organizations should be concerting their agendas around.

All this policy prescription assumes, of course, that the structure of the world economy is open enough to permit the upward mobility of large demographic masses. It assumes that nothing in the functioning of world capitalism in the Dollar–Wall Street framework precludes movement toward a unipolar distribution of world income and a shrinking of the gap between bottom and top, or pushes some demographic masses down the income scale as others rise. What is the evidence?

Note — This is an abbreviated version of an essay of the same title in *New Political Economy* 9(2):163–188, 2004.

REFERENCES

1. World Bank. *Globalization, Growth, and Poverty: Building an Inclusive World Economy.* Washington, DC, 2002.
2. Wolfensohn, J. Foreword. In *World Development Indicators 2002.* World Bank, Washington, DC, 2002.
3. Wade, R. Is globalization reducing poverty and inequality? *World Dev.* 32(4), 2004.
4. Hicks, J. R. *Value and Capital.* Oxford University Press, London, 1946.
5. Reinert, E. Globalisation in the periphery as a Morgenthau Plan: The underdevelopment of Mongolia in the 1990s. In *Globalization, Economic Development and Inequality: An Alternative Perspective,* ed. E. Reinert. Edward Elgar, Cheltenham, UK, 2004.
6. Toner, P. *Main Currents in Cumulative Causation: The Dynamics of Growth and Development.* Macmillan, Basingstoke, UK, 1999.
7. Dowrick, S., and Akmal, M. Explaining Contradictory Trends in Global Income Inequality: A Tale of Two Biases. Faculty of Economics and Commerce, Australia National University, March 29, 2001. http://ecocomm.anu.edu.au/people/info.asp?Surname=Dowrick&Firstname=Steve.
8. Milanovic, B. True world income distribution, 1988 and 1993: First calculations based on household surveys alone. *Econ. J.* 112(476):51–92, 2002.
9. Milanovic. B. *Can We Discern the Effect of Globalization on Income Distribution? Evidence from Household Budget Surveys.* World Bank Policy Research Working Papers no. 2876. World Bank, Washington, DC, 2002. http://econ.worldbank.org.
10. Dikhanov, Y., and Ward, M. Evolution of the Global Distribution of Income in 1970–99. Proceedings of the Global Poverty Workshop, Initiative for Policy Dialogue, Columbia University, 2003. www-1.gsb.Columbia.edu/ipd/povertywk.html.
11. Arrighi, G., Silver, B., and Brewer, B. Industrial convergence, globalization and the persistence of the North-South divide. *Stud.Comp. Int. Dev.* 38(1):3–31, 2003.
12. Gereffi, G., and Korzeniewicz, M. (eds.). *Commodity Chains and Global Capitalism.* Praeger, Westport, CT, 1994.
13. Lucas, R. On the mechanics of economic development. *J. Monetary Econ.* 22(July): 3–42, 1988.
14. Wade, R. What strategies are viable for developing countries today? The WTO and the shrinking of development space. *Rev. Int. Polit. Econ.* 10(4):621–644, 2003.
15. Gereffi, G. International trade and industrial upgrading in the apparel commodity chain. *J. Int. Econ.* 48:37–70, 1999.
16. Schrank, A. Ready-to-Wear Development? Foreign Investment, Technology Transfer, and Learning-by-Watching in the Apparel Trade. Typescript, Sociology Department, Yale University, November 2002.
17. Tonelson, A. There's only so much that foreign trade can do. *Washington Post,* June 2, 2002.
18. United Nations Conference on Trade and Development. China's accession to the WTO: Managing integration and industrialization. *Trade and Development Report 2002: Developing Countries in World Trade,* chap. 5. Geneva, 2002.
19. Economic Commission for Latin America and the Caribbean. *Globalization and Development,* box 2.1, p. 38. Santiago, 2002.

20. Gestrin, M., Knight, R., and Rugman, A. M. The Templeton Global Perform-ance Index. Templeton College, University of Oxford, 1999, 2000, and 2001. www.templeton.ox.ac.uk.
21. Krugman, P. For richer. *New York Times,* October 20, 2002.
22. Wade, R. The U.S. role in the long Asian crisis of 1990–2000. In *The Political Economy of the East Asian Crisis and Its Aftermath,* pp. 195–226. Edward Elgar, Cheltenham, UK, 2001.
23. Dore, R. *Stock Market Capitalism: Welfare Capitalism—Japan and Germany vs. the Anglo-Saxons,* ed. A. Lukauskas and F. Rivera-Batiz. Oxford University Press, Oxford, 2000.
24. Partnoy, F. *F.I.A.S.C.O: Blood in the Water on Wall Street.* Norton, New York, 1997.
25. World Bank. *Averting the Old-Age Crisis.* Policy Research Report. Washington, DC, 1994.
26. Holzmann, R., and Stiglitz, J. (eds.). *New Ideas about Old Age Security.* World Bank, Washington, DC, 2001.
27. Amsden, A. H., Tschang, T., and Goto, A. *A New Classification of R&D Charac-teristics for International Comparison (with a Singapore Case Study).* Asian Development Bank Institute, Tokyo, December 2001.
28. Lapper, R. China begins to exert its influence on Latin America. *Financial Times,* September 26, 2003.
29. Gowan, P. *The Global Gamble.* Verso, London, 1999.
30. World Development Movement. *Out of Service: The Development Dangers of the General Agreement on Trade in Services.* London, March 2002.
31. WTO's yard a mess: Developing countries need to embrace trade reforms, too. *Financial Times,* August 8, 2003.
32. Lake, A., National Security Affairs Presidential Assistant. Speech of September 21, 1993.
33. Wade, R. The invisible hand of the American empire. *Ethics Int. Aff.* 17(2):77–88, 2003.
34. Besley, T., and Burgess. R. Halving world poverty. *J. Econ. Perspect.* 17(3):3–22, 2003.
35. Lee, M. R., and Bankston, W. Political structure, economic inequality, and homicide: A cross-sectional analysis. *Deviant Behavior: An Interdisciplinary Journal* 19:27–55, 1999.
36. Hsieh, C. C., and Pugh, M. Poverty, income inequality, and violent crime: A meta-analysis of recent aggregate data studies. *Criminal Justice Rev.* 18:182–202, 1993.
37. Fajnzylber, P., Lederman, D., and Loayza, N. *What Causes Violent Crime?* World Bank, Office of the Chief Economist, Latin America and the Caribbean Region, 1998.
38. Freeman, R. Why do so many young American men commit crimes and what might we do about it? *J. Econ. Perspect.* 10(1):25–42, 1996.
39. Demeny, P. Population policy dilemmas in Europe at the dawn of the twenty-first century. *Popul. Dev. Rev.* 29(1):1–28, 2003.
40. Wade, R. Creating capitalisms (introduction). In *Governing the Market.* Princeton University Press, Princeton, 2003.
41. Imbs, J., and Wacziarg, R. Stages of diversification. *Am. Econ. Rev.* 93(1):63–86, 2003.

42. Jacobs, J. *Cities and the Wealth of Nations: Principles of Economic Life.* Random House, New York, 1984.
43. Lall, S. *Competitiveness, Technology and Skill.* Edward Elgar, Cheltenham, UK, 2001.
44. Ha-Joon Chang. *Kicking Away the Ladder: Development Strategy in Historical Perspective.* Anthem, London, 2002.
45. Weiss, L. *The Myth of the Powerless State.* Polity, Cambridge, UK, 1998.

CHAPTER 6

Is Globalization Reducing Poverty and Inequality?

Robert Hunter Wade

Over the past 20 years the number of people living on less than $1 a day has fallen by 200 million, after rising steadily for 200 years.
James Wolfensohn, President, World Bank, 2002 (1)

The best evidence available *shows . . . the current wave of globalization, which started around 1980, has actually promoted economic equality and reduced poverty.*
Dollar and Kraay, 2002 (2, emphasis added)

Evidence suggests the 1980s and 1990s were decades of declining global inequality and reductions in the proportion of the world's population in extreme poverty.
Martin Wolf, *Financial Times,* 2002 (3)

[G]lobalization has dramatically increased inequality between and within nations.
Jay Mazur, U.S. union leader, 2000 (4)

The neoliberal argument says that the distribution of income between all the world's people has become more equal over the past two decades and the number of people living in extreme poverty has fallen, for the first time in more than a century and a half. It says that these progressive trends are due in large part to the rising density of economic integration between countries, which has made for rising efficiency of resource use worldwide as countries and regions specialize in line with their comparative advantage. Hence the combination of the "dollar–Wall Street" economic regime (5) in place since the breakdown of the Bretton Woods regime in the early 1970s, and the globalizing direction of change in the world economy since then, serves the great majority of the world's people well. The core solution for lagging regions, Africa above all, is freer domestic and international trade and more open financial markets, leading to deeper integration into the world economy.

Evidence from the current long wave of globalization thus confirms neoliberal economic theory—more open economies are more prosperous, economies that liberalize more experience a faster rate of progress, and people who resist further economic liberalization must be acting out of vested or "rent-seeking" interests. The world economy is an open system in the sense that country mobility up the income/wealth hierarchy is unconstrained by the structure. The hierarchy is in the process of being flattened, the North-South, core-periphery, rich country–poor country divide is being eroded away as globalization proceeds. The same evidence also validates the rationale of the World Trade Organization (WTO), the World Bank, the International Monetary Fund (IMF), and other multilateral economic organizations as agents for creating a global "level playing field" undistorted by state-imposed restrictions on markets. This line of argument is championed by the more powerful of the centers of "thinking for the world" that influence international policymaking, including the intergovernmental organizations like the World Bank, the IMF, and the WTO, also the U.S. and U.K. Treasuries, and opinion-shaping media like the *Financial Times* and the *Economist.*

The standard left assumption, in contrast, is that the rich and powerful countries and classes have little interest in greater equity. Consistent with this view, the "anti-globalization" (more accurately, "anti-neoliberal") argument asserts that world poverty and inequality have been rising, not falling, due to forces unleashed by the same globalization (e.g., union leader Jay Mazur's quote above; 4). The line of solution is some degree of tightening of public policy limits on the operation of market forces; though the "anti-neoliberal" camp embraces a much wider range of solutions than the liberal camp.

The debate tends to be conducted by each side as if its case was over-whelming, and only an intellectually deficient or dishonest person could see merit in the other's case. For example, Martin Wolf of the *Financial Times* claims that the "anti-globalization" argument is "the big lie" (6). If translated into public policy it would cause more poverty and inequality while pretending to do the opposite.

This chapter questions the empirical basis of the neoliberal argument. And it goes beyond the questions to suggest different conclusions about levels and trends, stated in terms not of certainties but of stronger or weaker probabilities. At the end it explains why we should be concerned about probably rising world inequality, and how we might think about the neglected subject of the political economy of statistics.

THE REGIONAL COLLAGE

The growth rate of world gross domestic product (GDP), measured in U.S. dollars and at current exchange rates, fell sharply from around 5.5 percent in 1970–1980 to 2.3 percent in 1980–1990 to 1.1 percent in 1990–2000 (7).[1] This is bad news, environmental considerations aside. But it still grew a little faster than world population over the past two decades; and the (population-weighted) GDP of developing countries as a group grew a little faster than that of the high-income countries. On the other hand, regional variation within the global South is large. Table 1 shows the trends of regional per capita gross national product (GNP) as a fraction of per capita GNP of the "core" regions (with incomes converted to U.S.$ at current exchange rates as a measure of *international* purchasing power (8). Between 1960 and 1999 the per capita incomes of sub-Saharan Africa, Latin America, and West Asia and North Africa fell as a fraction of the core's; South Asia's remained more or less constant; East Asia's (minus China) rose sharply; China's also rose sharply but from a very low base. The most striking feature is not the trends but the size of the gaps, testimony to the failure of "catch-up." Even success-story East Asia has an average income only about 13 percent of the core's.[2] It is a safe bet that most development experts in 1960 would have predicted much higher percentages by 2000.

The variation can also be shown in terms of the distribution of world income by regions and income percentiles. Figure 1 shows the regional distribution of people at each income percentile for two years, 1990 and 1999. Here incomes are expressed in "purchasing power parity" dollars (PPP$),[3] in order to measure, notionally at least, *domestic* purchasing power. One sees the African collapse in the increased share of the African population in the bottom quintile; also the falling back of the eastern and central European populations from the second to the third quintile; and the rising share of the East Asian population in the second quintile.

Figure 2 shows, in the top half, the world's population plotted against the log of PPP$ income, taking account of both between-country and within-country income distribution; and the breakdown by region. The bottom half shows the world's income plotted against income level, hence the share of income accruing to people at different income levels and in different regions. Residents of South Asia and East Asia predominate at income levels below the median, and residents of the OECD (Organization for Economic Cooperation and Development) countries predominate at the top.

---

[1] The trend is, however, highly sensitive to the dollar's strong depreciation in the 1970s and appreciation in the 1990s. When this is allowed for, the world growth rate may be closer to trendless.

[2] In more concrete terms, the number of hours of work it took for an entry-level adult male employee of McDonald's to earn the equivalent of one Big Mac around 2000 ranged as follows: Holland/Australia/New Zealand/United Kingdom/United States, 0.26 to 0.53 hours; Hong Kong, 0.68 hours; Malaysia/South Korea, 1.43 to 1.46 hours; Philippines/Thailand, 2.32 to 2.66 hours; China, 3.96 hours; India, 4 hours.

[3] Purchasing power parity is a method of adjusting relative incomes in different countries to take account of the fact that market exchange rates do not accurately reflect purchasing power—as in the common observation that poor Americans feel rich in India and rich Indians feel poor in the United States.

Table 1

GNP per capita for region as percentage of core's GNP per capita,[a] 1960–1999

Region	1960	1980	1999
Sub-Saharan Africa	5	4	2
Latin America	20	18	12
West Asia and North Africa	9	9	7
South Asia	2	1	2
East Asia (without China and Japan)	6	8	13
China	1	1	3
South	**5**	**4**	**5**
North America	124	100	101
Western Europe	111	104	98
Southern Europe	52	60	60
Australia and New Zealand	95	75	73
Japan	79	134	145
North (= core)	**100**	**100**	**100**

Source: Arrighi, Silver, and Brewer (8), based on World Bank data.
[a]GNP at current exchange rates.

Finally, Figure 3 shows the movement in the bimodal shape of the overall PPP$ income-to-population distribution between 1970 and 1999. The 1999 distribution has shifted forward compared to the 1970 one, especially the lower of the two income humps, reflecting the arrival of large numbers of South and East Asians into the middle deciles of the world income distribution.

How does the collage—positive world per capita growth and wide divergence of economic performance between developing regions—net out in terms of global trends in poverty and inequality?

POVERTY

Figure 2 shows the two standard international poverty lines, $1 per day and $2 per day; and also the line corresponding to an income of 50 percent of the world's median income. Notice that even the higher $2 per day absolute poverty line is below the conventional "minimum" *relative* poverty line of half of the median. Notice too how small a share of world income goes to those on less than $1 per day, and how small a share of the income of the richest earners would be needed to double the income of the poorest.

Figures 1 to 3 are based on a data set on income inequality compiled by the United Nation's World Institute for Development Economics Research

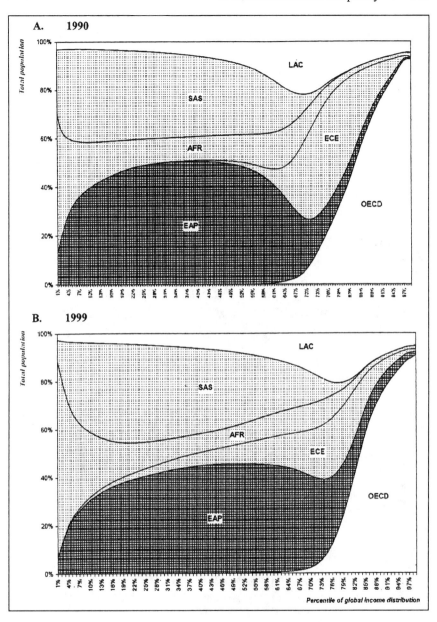

Figure 1. World income distribution, by region and by percentile of income distribution, 1990 and 1999. LAC, Latin America and Caribbean; SAS, South Asia; AFR, Africa; ECE, East and Central Europe; EAP, East Asia and Pacific; OECD, Organization for Economic Cooperation and Development. Based on World Institute for Development Economics Research (WIDER) data, PPP$. *Source:* Dikhanov and Ward (38).

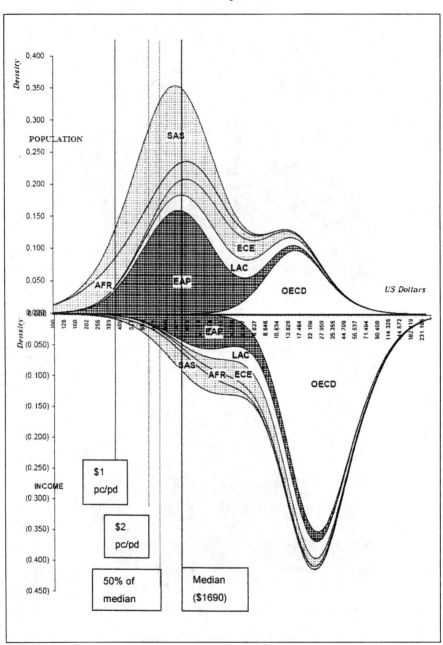

Figure 2. World income distribution, by region, 1999. Top half, distribution of world population against income; bottom half, distribution of world income against income. *Source:* Dikhanov and Ward (38).

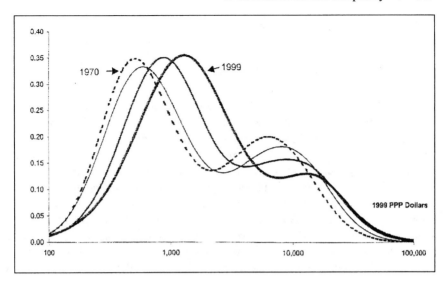

Figure 3. World income distribution, 1970, 1980, 1990, 1999. *Source:* Dikhanov and Ward (38).

(WIDER).[4] But the standard poverty numbers—the ones normally used in discussions about the state of the world—come from the World Bank's data set. This is the source of the claims that, in the words of Bank President James Wolfensohn, "Over the past 20 years the number of people living on less than $1 a day has fallen by 200 million, after rising steadily for 200 years" (1; also 9, p. 30). And "the proportion of people worldwide living in absolute poverty has dropped steadily in recent decades, from 29 percent in 1990 to a record low of 23 percent in 1998" (10). The opening sentence of the Bank's *World Development Indicators 2001* says, "Of the world's 6 billion people 1.2 billion live on less than $1 a day," the same number in 1987 and 1998 (11, p. 23; the $1 a day is measured in PPP; see also 12). No ifs or buts. I now show that the Bank's figures contain a large margin of error, and the errors *probably* flatter the result in one direction.[5]

To get the world extreme poverty headcount, the Bank first defines an international poverty line for a given base year by using purchasing power parity

---

[4] The WIDER data set marries consumption from household surveys with consumption from national income accounts, and makes an allowance for (non-public sector) unpriced goods and services.

[5] I am indebted to Sanjay Reddy for discussions about the Bank's poverty numbers (13; see also 14, 15). In this chapter I do not consider the additional problems that arise when estimating the impact of economic growth on poverty (see 16).

conversion factors (PPPs) to convert the purchasing power of an average of the official national poverty lines of a set of low-income countries into the U.S. dollar amount needed to have the same notional purchasing power in the United States in the same year. In its first global poverty estimation this procedure yielded a conveniently understandable U.S.$1 per day for the base year of 1985.[6] Then the Bank uses PPP conversion factors to estimate the amount of local currency, country by country, needed to have the same purchasing power in the same year as in the U.S. base case. This gives an international extreme poverty line equivalent to U.S.$1 per day, expressed in domestic currency. By way of illustration, Rs10 (rupees) may have the same purchasing power in India in 1985 as U.S.$1 in the United States in the same year, in which case India's international extreme poverty line is Rs10 per day. From household surveys the Bank then estimates the number of people in the country living on less than this figure. It sums the country totals to get the world total. It uses national consumer price indices to keep real purchasing power constant across time, and adjusts the international poverty line for each country upward with inflation.

Large Margin of Error

There are several reasons to expect a large margin of error, regardless of direction. First, the poverty headcount is very sensitive to the precise level of the international poverty lines. This is because the shape of income distribution near the poverty line is such that, in most developing countries, a given percentage change in the line brings a similar or larger percentage change in the number of people below it. Recent research on China suggests that a 10 percent increase in the line brings a roughly 20 percent increase in the poverty headcount.

Second, the poverty headcount is very sensitive to the reliability of household surveys of income and expenditure. The available surveys are of widely varying quality, and many do not follow a standard template. Some sources of error are well known, such as the exclusion of most of the benefits that people receive from publicly provided goods and services. Others are less well known, such as the sensitivity of the poverty headcount to the survey design. For example, the length of the recall period makes a big difference to the rate of reported expenditure— the shorter the recall period the higher the expenditure. A recent study in India suggests that a switch from the standard 30 day reporting period to a 7 day reporting period lifts 175 million people from poverty, a nearly 50 percent fall. This is using the Indian official poverty line. Using the higher $1 per day international line, the fall would be even greater (reported in 17). The point here is not that household surveys are less reliable than other possible sources (e.g., national income accounts); simply that they do contain large amounts of error.

---

[6] The Bank also calculates a poverty headcount with $2 per day, which suffers from the same limitations as the $1 per day line.

Third, China and India, the two most important countries for the overall trend, have PPP-adjusted income figures that contain an even bigger component of guess work than for most other significant countries. The main sources of PPP income figures (the Penn World Tables and the International Comparison Project) are based on two large-scale international price benchmarking exercises for calculating purchasing power parity exchange rates, one in 1985 in 60 countries, the other in 1993 in 110 countries. The government of China declined to participate in both. The purchasing power parity exchange rate for China is based on guesstimates from small, ad hoc price surveys in a few cities, adjusted by rules of thumb to take account of the huge price differences between urban and rural areas and between eastern and western regions. The government of India declined to participate in the 1993 exercise. The price comparisons for India are extrapolations from 1985 qualified by later ad hoc price surveys. The lack of reliable price comparisons for China and India—hence the lack of reliable evidence on the purchasing power of incomes across their distributions—compromises any statement about levels and trends in world poverty (13).

Fourth, the often-cited comparison between 1980 and 1998—1.4 billion in extreme poverty in 1980, 1.2 billion in 1998—is not valid. The Bank introduced a new methodology in the late 1990s which makes the figures noncomparable. The Bank has recalculated the poverty numbers with the new method only back to 1987.[7]

The change of method amounts to (a) a change in the way the international poverty line was calculated from the official poverty lines of a sample of low- and middle-income countries (and a change in the sample countries), which resulted in (b) a change in the international poverty line from PPP$1 per day to PPP$1.08 per day, and (c) a change in the procedure for aggregating, country by country, the relative price changes between 1985 and 1993 for a standard bundle of goods and services.

We do not know what the 1980 figure would be with the new method. However, we do know that the new method caused a huge change in the poverty count even for the same country in the same year using the same survey data (the new results were published in 18). Table 2 shows the method-induced changes by regions for 1993. Angus Deaton, an expert on these statistics, comments that "Changes of this size risk swamping real changes," "and it seems impossible to make statements about changes in world poverty when the ground underneath one's feet is changing in this way" (17, p. 128).

---

[7] Also "[Since 1980] the most rapid growth has occurred in poor locations. Consequently the number of poor has declined by 200 million since 1980" (2, p. 125).

Table 2

1993 poverty rate, calculated using old and new
World Bank methodology[a]

	Old poverty rate, %	New poverty rate, %
Sub-Saharan Africa	39.1	49.7
Latin America	23.5	15.3
Middle East/North Africa	4.1	1.9

Source: Deaton (17).
[a]Poverty rate is the proportion of the population living on less than $1 a day.

Downward Bias

Further sources of error bias the results downward, making the number of people in poverty seem lower than it really is; and the bias probably increases over time, making the trend look rosier than it is. There are at least three reasons.

First, the Bank's international poverty line underestimates the income or expenditure needed for an individual (or household) to avoid periods of food-clothing-shelter consumption too low to maintain health and well-being. (And it avoids altogether the problem that basic needs include unpriced public goods like clean water and access to basic health care.) The Bank's line refers to an "average consumption" bundle, not to a basket of goods and services that makes sense for measuring poverty (though "$1 per day" does have intuitive appeal to a western audience being asked to support aid). Suppose it costs Rs30 to buy an equivalent bundle of food in India (defined in terms of calories and micronutrients) as can be bought in the United States with $1; and that it costs Rs3 to buy an equivalent bundle of services (haircuts, massages) as $1 in the United States, such services being relatively very cheap in developing countries (I take this example from 19). Current methods of calculating purchasing power parity, based on an *average* consumption bundle of food, services, and other things, may yield a PPP exchange rate of PPP$1 = Rs10, meaning that Rs10 in India buys the equivalent average consumption bundle as $1 in the United States. But this is misleading, because the poor person, spending most income on food, can buy with Rs10 only a third of the food purchasable with $1 in the United States. To take the international poverty line for India as Rs10 therefore biases the number of poor downward.

We have no way of knowing what proportion of food-clothing-shelter needs the Bank's international poverty line captures. But we can be fairly sure that if the Bank used a basic needs poverty line rather than its present artificial one, the number of absolute poor would rise, because the national poverty lines equivalent to a global basic needs poverty line would probably rise (perhaps by 30 to 40 percent).[8] A 30 to 40 percent increase in a basic-needs-based international poverty line would increase the world total of people in extreme poverty by at least 30 to 40 percent. Indeed, a recent study for Latin America shows that national extreme poverty rates, calculated using poverty lines based on calorific and demographic characteristics, may be more than *twice* as high as those based on the World Bank's $1 per day line. For example, the World Bank estimates Brazil's extreme poverty rate (using its international poverty line) at 5 percent, while the Economic Commission for Latin America (ECLA), using a calories-and-demography poverty line, estimates the rate at 14 percent.[9]

In short, we can be reasonably confident that switching from the Bank's rather arbitrarily derived international extreme poverty line to one reflecting the purchasing power necessary to achieve elementary human capabilities would substantially raise the number of people in extreme poverty.

The second reason is that the Bank's new international poverty line of $1.08 per day probably increases the downward bias, leading the Bank to exaggerate the decline in the poverty headcount between the years covered by the old methodology and those covered by the new one. The new international poverty line of PPP$1.08 *lowers* the equivalent national poverty lines in most countries compared to the earlier PPP$1 line. It lowers them in 77 percent of the 94 countries for which data are available, containing 82 percent of their population. It lowers the old international poverty line for China by 14 percent, for India by 9 percent, and for the whole sample by an average of 13 percent (13). As noted, even a small downward shift in the poverty line removes a large number of people out of poverty.

Third, future "updating" of the international poverty line will continue artificially to lower the true numbers, because average consumption patterns (on which the international poverty line is based) are shifting toward services whose prices relative to food and shelter are lower in poor than in rich countries, giving the false impression that the cost of the basic consumption goods required by the poor is falling.[10]

All these problems have to be resolved in one way or another in any estimate of world poverty, whoever makes it. But the fact that the World Bank is the near-monopoly provider introduces a further complication. The number of poor

[8] The 30 to 40 percent figure is Reddy and Pogge's estimate, the range reflecting calculations based on PPP conversion factors for 1985 and 1993, and for "all-food" and "bread-and-cereals" indices.

[9] Also, Bolivia's extreme poverty rate according to the World Bank line was 11 percent, and according to the ECLA line, was 23 percent; Chile, 4 percent and 8 percent; Colombia, 11 percent and 24 percent; Mexico, 18 percent and 21 percent (20, p. 51).

[10] This effect is amplified by the widespread removal of price controls on "necessities" and the lowering of tariffs on luxuries.

people is politically sensitive. The Bank's many critics like to use the poverty numbers as one of many pointers to the conclusion that it has accomplished "precious little," in the words of U.S. Treasury Secretary O'Neill; which then provides a rationale for tighter U.S. control of the Bank, as in the statement by the head of the U.S. Agency for International Development, "Whether the U.S. way of doing things drives some multilateral institutions, I think it should, because, frankly, a lot of the multilateral institutions don't have a good track record" (21).

A comparison of two recent Bank publications suggests how the Bank's statements about poverty are affected by its tactics and the ideological predispositions of those in the ideas-controlling positions. *The World Development Report 2000/2001: Attacking Poverty* (18) says that the number of people living on less than $1 per day *increased* by 20 million from 1.18 billion in 1987 to 1.20 billion in 1998. When it was being written in the late 1990s, the key ideas-controlling positions in the Bank were held by Joe Stiglitz and Ravi Kanbur (respectively, chief economist and director of the *World Development Report 2000/2001*), not noted champions of neoliberal economics.[11] At that time the Bank was trying to mobilize support for making the Comprehensive Development Framework the new template for all its work, for which purpose *lack* of progress in development helped. Then came the majority report of the Meltzer Commission, for the U.S. Congress, which said the Bank was failing at its central task of poverty reduction and therefore should be sharply cut back—as shown by the fact that the number of people in absolute poverty remained constant at 1.2 billion between 1987 and 1998 (23).[12] Now the Bank needed to emphasize progress. The next major Bank publication, *Globalization, Growth, and Poverty: Building an Inclusive World Economy* (12), claimed that the number of people living in poverty *decreased* by 200 million in the 18 years from 1980 to 1998 (see 25). By this time Stiglitz and Kanbur were gone and David Dollar, a prominent Bank economist, was ascendant. He was chief author of *Globalization, Growth, and Poverty*.[13]

---

[11] Wade (22) uses Stiglitz's firing and Kanbur's resignation to illuminate the U.S. role in the Bank's generation of knowledge.

[12] Meltzer later described the fall in the proportion of the world's population in poverty from 28 percent in 1987 to 24 percent in 1998 as a "modest" decline, the better to hammer the Bank (24).

[13] Dollar was ascendant not in terms of bureaucratic position but in terms of epistemic influence, as seen in the Human Resource department's use of him as a "metric" for judging the stature of other economists. When reporters started contacting the Bank to ask why it was saying different things about the poverty numbers—specifically, why two papers on the Development Research Complex's website gave different pictures of the trends—the response was not, "We are a research complex, we let 100 flowers bloom," but rather an assertion of central control. Chief economist Nick Stern gave one manager "special responsibility" for making sure the Bank's poverty numbers were all "coherent" (e-mail from Stern to research managers, April 4, 2002).

Conclusions about Poverty

We can be fairly sure that the Bank's poverty headcount has a large margin of error in *all* years, in the sense that it may be significantly different from the headcount that would result from the use of PPP conversion factors based more closely on the real costs of living of the poor (defined in terms of income needed to buy enough calories, micronutrients, and other necessities in order not to be poor). By the same token we should question the Bank's confidence that the trend is downward.

We do not know for sure how the late 1990s revision of the method and the PPP numbers alter the poverty headcount in any one year and the trend. But it is likely that the Bank's numbers substantially underestimate the true numbers of the world's population living in extreme poverty, and make the trend look brighter.

On the other hand, it is quite plausible that the *proportion* of the world's population living in extreme poverty has fallen over the past 20 years or so. For all the problems with Chinese and Indian income figures, we know enough about trends in other variables—including life expectancy, heights, and other non-income measures—to be confident that their poverty headcounts have indeed dropped dramatically over the past 20 years. And if it is the case (as some experts claim) that household surveys are more likely to miss the rich than the poor, their results may *overstate* the proportion of the population in poverty. The magnitude of world population increase over the past 20 years is so large that the Bank's poverty numbers would have to be *huge* underestimates for the world poverty rate not to have fallen. Any more precise statement about the absolute number of the world's people living in extreme poverty and the change over time currently rests on quicksand.

INEQUALITY

The world poverty headcount could move in one direction while world income inequality moves in the other. The neoliberal argument says that they have both dropped.[14] But in the past several years, world income distribution has become a hot topic of debate in international economics and in sociology (much hotter than trends in world poverty). Disagreements about the overall inequality trend should not be surprising given the variation in regional economic performance—different ways of measuring emphasize different parts of the collage.

The only valid short answer to the question, "What is the trend of world income distribution?" is, "It depends on which combination out of many, plausible combinations of measures and countries we choose" (in addition to studies cited

[14] Non–World Bank champions of the idea that globalization improves global income distribution include Martin Wolf of the *Financial Times* (3, 6, 26, 27); also Anthony Giddens, described by some as a leading social theorist of his generation (28, p. 72); and Ian Castles, former Australian Statistician, who claims that "most studies suggest that the past 25 years have seen a reversal in the trend towards widening global inequalities which had been proceeding for two centuries" (29).

elsewhere, I here draw on 30–37). Whereas we *could* get better data on the poor to the extent that the poverty headcount would command general agreement, there is no single best measure of world income inequality.

The choices include (*a*) alternative measures of income (GDP per capita converted to U.S. dollars using market exchange rates, or GDP per capita adjusted for differences in purchasing power across countries); (*b*) alternative weightings of countries (each country weighted as one unit or by population); (*c*) alternative measures of distribution (including the Gini or some other average coefficient, or ratios of the income of richer deciles of world population to that of poorer deciles, or average income of a set of developing countries as a fraction of that of a set of developed countries); (*d*) alternative sources of data on incomes (national income accounts or household surveys); (*e*) alternative samples of countries and time periods.

We can be reasonably confident of the following six propositions.

Proposition 1: *World income distribution has become rapidly more unequal, when incomes are measured at market exchange rates and expressed in U.S. dollars.*

No one disputes this. The dispute is about what the figures mean. Most economists say that exchange-rate-based income measures are irrelevant, and hence would dismiss the data in Table 1. GDP incomes should always be adjusted by PPP exchange rates to take account of differences in purchasing power, they say.[15] This makes a big difference to the size of the gap between rich and poor. As noted, the PPP adjustment is made by computing the relative prices for an average bundle of goods and services in different countries. The PPP adjustment substantially raises the relative income of poor countries. India's PPP GDP, for example, is about four times its market-exchange-rate GDP. The PPP adjustment thus makes world income distribution look much more equal than the distribution of market-exchange-rate incomes.

---

[15] A reviewer comments, "The idea of using market exchange rates to calculate international inequality is unbelievably stupid, and it is amazing that it still makes an appearance here. The U.N. had a commission of enquiry on this, which concluded unambiguously that using market exchange rates was wrong." However, the World Bank continues to use market exchange rates, adjusted by the "Atlas" methodology, to calculate the per capita incomes that it then uses to rank countries by their degree of development; and hence as a criterion for its lending decisions. Member countries' voting shares in the Bank are based largely on their IMF quotas, which in turn are based largely on relative GDP at market exchange rates. So the Bank's practice does imply that it thinks that relative per capita incomes calculated through market exchange rates are meaningful proxies for well-being (and the practice has the benefit of holding down the voting share of developing countries). Moreover, as the text explains, incomes converted at market exchange rates do give meaningful measures of *international* purchasing power. Businesses making exporting and foreign direct investment (FDI) decisions (auto makers, for example) pay more attention to relative incomes at market exchange rates than to PPP incomes.

Market-exchange-rate-based income comparisons do suffer from all the ways in which official exchange rates do not reflect the "real" economy: from distortions in the official rates, exclusion of goods and services that are not traded, and sudden changes in the official exchange rate driven more by capital than by trade movements. Nevertheless, we should reject the argument that incomes converted via PPP exchange rates should always be used in preference to incomes converted at market exchange rates.

The practical reasons concern the weaknesses of the PPP numbers. Plausibly constructed PPP numbers for China differ by a factor of two. Estimates for countries of the former Soviet Union before the 1990s also differ by a wide margin; and India's too. So if incomes converted via market exchange rates do not give an accurate measure of relative purchasing power, neither do the PPP numbers for countries that carry heavy weight in world trends. Confidence in world PPP income distribution should be correspondingly limited.

Practical problems aside, PPP adjustment is in principle preferable when one is interested in domestic purchasing power or, more generally, material well-being. However, we may be interested in income not only as a measure of material well-being. We may *also* be interested in income as a proxy for the purchasing power of residents of different countries over goods and services produced in other countries—for example, the purchasing power of residents of developing countries over advanced-country products compared to the purchasing power of residents of advanced countries over developing-country products. If we are interested in any of the questions about the economic and geopolitical impact of one country (or region) on the rest of the world—including the cost to developing countries of repaying their debts, importing capital goods, and participating in international organizations—we should use market exchange rates.

The reason why many poor small countries are hardly represented in negotiations that concern them directly is that they cannot afford the cost of hotels, offices, and salaries in places like Washington, D.C., and Geneva, which must be paid not in PPP dollars but in hard currency bought with their own currency at market exchange rates. And the reason they cannot afford to pay the foreign exchange costs of living up to many of their international commitments—hiring foreign experts to help them exercise control over their banking sectors so that they can implement their part of the anti-money-laundering regime, for example—likewise reflects their low market-exchange-rate incomes. On the other hand, international lenders have not been lining up to accept repayment of developing-country debts in PPP dollars, which would reduce their debt repayments by 75 percent or more in many cases.

These same "foreign" impacts feed back to domestic state capacity. For example, we should use market exchange rates to pick up the key point that the long-run deterioration in the exchange rates of most developing countries is putting developing countries under increasing *internal* stress. When a rising amount of real domestic resources has to go into acquiring a given quantity of imports—say, of capital goods—other domestic uses of those resources are squeezed, including measures to reduce poverty, to finance civil services and schools and the like. This backwash effect is occluded in PPP calculations.

Hence we do need to pay attention to what is happening to market-exchange-rate world income distribution. It is widening fast.

The next four propositions refer to inequality of PPP-adjusted incomes, as an approximation to domestic purchasing power.

Proposition 2: *World PPP-income polarization has increased, with polarization measured as ratio of richest to poorest decile.*

The broad result is hardly surprising: the top 10 percent is comprised almost entirely of people living in the core countries of North America, western Europe, and Japan, where incomes have grown over the past 20 to 30 years, while a large chunk of the bottom 10 percent is comprised of African countries where incomes have stagnated or fallen. According to one study, the trend of ratio of richest to poorest decile goes like this: 1970, 92; 1980, 109; 1990, 104; 1999, 104 (38). Another study finds a jump in the ratio of 25 percent between 1988 and 1993 (39). The change is made up of the top decile pulling sharply up from the median and the bottom decile falling away from the median. The polarizing trend would be much sharper with the top 1 percent rather than the top decile.

Proposition 3: *Between-country world PPP-income inequality has increased since at least 1980, as calculated using per capita GDPs, equal country weights (China = Uganda), and a coefficient such as the Gini for the whole distribution.*

Of course, we would not weight countries equally if we were interested simply in relative well-being. But we would weight them equally—treat each country as a unit of observation, analogous to a laboratory test observation—if we were interested in growth theory and the growth impacts of public policies, resource endowments, and the like. We might, for example, arrange (unweighted) countries by the openness of their trade regime and see whether more open countries have better economic performance.

The same inequality-widening trend is obtained using a somewhat different measure of inequality—the dispersion of per capita GDPs across the world's (equally weighted) countries. Dispersion increased over the long period 1950–1998, and especially fast over the 1990s. Moreover, the dispersion of per capita GDP growth rates has also risen over time, suggesting wider variation in performance among countries at each income level. A study by the

Economic Commission for Latin America using these dispersion measures concludes that there is "no doubt as to the existence of a definite trend towards distributive inequality worldwide, both across and within countries" (40, p. 85).[16]

Proposition 4: *Between-country world PPP-income inequality has been constant or falling since around 1980, with countries weighted by population.*

This is the result that the neoliberal argument celebrates. There are just two problems. First, exclude China and even this measure shows a widening since 1980; also exclude India and the widening is pronounced. Therefore, *falling income inequality is not a general feature of the world economy, even using the most favorable combination of measures.*[17]

Second, this measure—the average income of each country weighted by population—is interesting only as an approximation to what we are really interested in, which is income distribution among all the world's people or households regardless of which country they reside in. We would not be interested in measuring income inequality within the United States by calculating the average income for each state weighted by population if we had data for all U.S. households.

Proposition 5: *Several serious studies find that world PPP-income inequality has increased over a period within the past two to three decades, taking account of both between- and within-country distributions.*

Studies that attempt to measure income distribution among all the world's people show widely varying results, depending on things like the precise measure of inequality, the sample of countries, the time period, and the sources of income data. But several studies, which use a variety of data sources and methods, point to widening inequality.

Steve Dowrick and Muhammad Akmal (42) make an approximation to the distribution of income among all the world's people by combining (population-weighted) between-country inequality in PPP-adjusted average incomes with within-country inequality. They find that world inequality widened between

---

[16] The dispersion of per capita GDP/PPP is measured as the average logarithmic deviation, the dispersion of growth rates as the standard deviation.

[17] In an earlier debate with Martin Wolf I wrongly said that the result depends on both China and India. Wolf commented, "Here you argue that if we exclude China and India, there is no obvious trend in inequality. But why would one want to exclude two countries that contained about 60 percent of the world's poorest people two decades ago and still contain almost 40 percent of the world's population today? To fail to give these giants their due weight in a discussion of global poverty alleviation or income distribution would be *Hamlet* without the prince" (41). This misconstrues my argument.

1980 and 1993 using *all of four* common measures of inequality over the whole distribution.[18]

Branko Milanovic (43) uses the most comprehensive set of data drawn only from household income and expenditure surveys (it does not mix data from these surveys with data from national income accounts). He finds a sharp rise in world inequality over as short a time as 1988 to 1993, using both the Gini coefficient and ratio (or polarization) measures.[19] Some of his findings are shown in Table 3. Preliminary analysis of 1998 data suggests a slight fall in inequality in 1993–1998, leaving a large rise over 1988–1998.

We have to be cautious about Milanovic's results, partly because household surveys have the kind of weaknesses described above (though these weaknesses do not make them worse than the alternative, national income accounts, which have their own problems), and partly because even a ten-year interval, let alone a five-year interval, is very short, suggesting that some of the increase may be noise.

Yuri Dikhanov and Michael Ward (38) combine micro-level household survey data with national income accounts, using the WIDER data set, a different statistical technique from the earlier authors, and a longer time period, 1970–1999. They find that the Gini coefficient increased over this period from 0.668 to 0.683.

Proposition 6: *Pay inequality within countries was stable or declining from the early 1960s to 1980–1982, then sharply and continuously increased to the present; 1980–1982 is a turning point toward greater inequality in manufacturing pay worldwide.*[20]

Pay data have the great advantage over income data that pay is a much less ambiguous variable, it has been collected systematically by the United Nations Industrial Development Organization (UNIDO) since the early 1960s, and gives many more observation points for each country than any data set on incomes. (The standard data set for world poverty and inequality, the World Bank's Deininger-Squire set, has few observation points for most of Africa, West Asia, and Latin America during the 1980s and 1990s, requiring the analyst to guess the intervening years.) The disadvantage of pay data, of course, is that they treat only a small part of the economy of many developing countries, and provide only a proxy for incomes and expenditure. Pay is of limited use if our interest is only

---

[18] Dowrick and Akmal find that world inequality increased between 1980 and 1993 based on Gini, Theil, coefficient of variation, and the variance of log income.

[19] Milanovic's preliminary analysis of 1998 data and an associated reworking of 1988 and 1993 data have produced the following Gini coefficients (and standard deviations): 1988: 61.9 (1.8); 1993: 65.2 (1.8); 1998: 64.2 (1.9). The trend for the Theil coefficient is similar (personal communication, June 9, 2003). Sala-i-Martin (44) finds a fall in both extreme poverty and inequality. His findings have been rejected by Milanovic (45) and Nye and Reddy (46).

[20] See the work of James Galbraith and collaborators in the University of Texas Inequality Project, http://utip.gov.utexas.edu (see also 47).

Table 3

World income distribution by households,
1988 and 1993

	1988	1993	% Change
Gini	0.63	0.67	+6
Richest decile/median	7.28	8.98	+23
Poorest decile/median	0.31	0.28	−10

Source: Milanovic (43).

in relative well-being (though of more use if our interest is in the effects of trade, manufacturing innovation, etc.) But not as limited as may seem at first sight, because what is happening to pay rates in formal-sector manufacturing reflects larger trends, including income differences between countries and income differences within countries (since the pay of unskilled, entry-port jobs in manufacturing is closely related to the opportunity cost of time in the "informal" or agricultural sectors).[21]

China and India

With 38 percent of world population, China and India shape world trends in poverty and inequality. They have grown very fast over the past decade (India) or two (China), if the figures are taken at face value. China's average purchasing power parity income rose from 0.3 of the world average in 1990 to 0.45 in 1998, or 15 percentage points in only eight years.

We can be sure that world poverty and inequality are less than they would be had China and India grown more slowly. About any stronger conclusion we have to be cautious. First, recall that China's and India's purchasing power parity numbers are even more questionable than those for the average developing country, because of their nonparticipation in the international price comparisons on which the PPP calculations rest. Second, China's growth in the 1990s is probably overstated. Many analysts have recently been revising China's growth statistics downward. Whereas government figures show annual real GDP growth of 7 to 8 percent in 1998 and 1999, one authority

---

[21] This is the answer to a reviewer's remark, "The work of Galbraith and his collaborators at Texas is essentially worthless for the purposes currently being discussed. We are interested in people's command over resources, not the earnings of people in work in the formal sector. The latter is transparently irrelevant in most of the poor countries of the world, including India and China."

on Chinese statistics estimates that the economy may not have grown at all (48, 49).[22]

Even the Chinese government says that the World Bank has been overstating China's average income, and the Bank has recently revised its numbers downward. Table 4 shows the Bank's estimates for China's average GNP in U.S.$ for 1997–1999 and the corresponding growth rates (11, 51, 52). The level of average (exchange-rate-converted) income *fell* sharply between 1997 and 1998, while the corresponding growth rate between 1997 and 1998 was plus 6.4 percent. The Bank reduced China's per capita income partly because it believed that China's fast growth campaign begun in 1998 had unleashed a torrent of statistical falsification. Also, the Chinese government arm-twisted the World Bank (especially after the allegedly accidental U.S. bombing of the Chinese embassy in Belgrade in May 1999) to lower average income below the threshold of eligibility for concessional International Development Association (IDA) lending from the Bank—not for cheap IDA loans but for the privilege extended to companies of IDA-eligible countries to add a 7.5 percent uplift on bids for World Bank projects.[23]

Over the 1990s, China's annual growth rate is more likely to have been around 6 to 8 percent than the 8 to 10 percent of the official statistics. This one change lowers the probability that world interpersonal distribution has become more equal.[24]

We have to be cautious about going from China's fast growth to falls in world income inequality, not only because China's growth rates and income level may be overstated but also because the rise in inequality within both China and India partly offsets the reduction in world income inequality that comes from their relatively fast growth of average income—though careful calculations of the relative strength of the two contrary effects have yet to be made.[25] China's surging inequality is now greater than before the Communists won the civil war in 1949, and inequality between regions is probably higher than in any other sizable country. The ratio of the average income of the richest to

[22] As another example from Rawski's analysis, Chinese government figures show total real GDP growth of 25 percent between 1997 and 2000, whereas energy consumption figures show a drop of 13 percent (not all of which is likely to be due to replacement of inefficient coal-fired furnaces). Rawski estimates the growth rate since 2000 has been about half the official rate. (See also 50.)

[23] This information is from Bank sources who request anonymity. During negotiations for China's joining the WTO, Chinese economists argued against the insistence of the United States and other rich countries that its average income be expressed in terms of purchasing power parity—and hence that China should be under the same obligations as "middle-income" countries, tougher than those on "low-income" countries. This is another example of the politics of statistics.

[24] In addition, taking account of even just the obviously big and roughly measurable environmental costs lowers China's official GDP by roughly 8 percent, India's by 5 percent (see 53).

[25] Evidence for rising inequality in India over the past two decades is set out by Jha (54). Deaton (25) agrees that inequality in India has been increasing "in recent years" and that consumption by the poor did not rise as fast as average consumption.

Table 4

China's GNP per capita and growth rate, 1997–1999[a]

	1997	1998	1999
GNP per capita PPP, U.S.$	3,070	3,050	3,550
GNP per capita, U.S.$	860	750	780
Annual growth rate of GNP per capita, %	7.4	6.4	6.1

Source: World Bank, World Development Indicators (11, 51, 52).
[a]Note that each report gives figures for only one year, so the discrepancy can be seen only by compiling one's own table.

poorest province (Guangdong to Guizhou) rose from around 3.2 in 1991 (current yuan) to 4.8 in 1993, and remained at 4.8 in 1998–2001.[26] The corresponding figure for India in the late 1990s was 4.2; for the United States, 1.9.

The United States and Other Anglo Political Economies

Canada excepted, all the countries of English settlement, led by the United States, have experienced big increases in income inequality over the past 20 to 30 years. In the United States, the top 1 percent of families enjoyed a growth of after-tax income of almost 160 percent between 1979 and 1997, while families in the middle of the distribution had a 10 percent increase (55). Within the top 1 percent, most of the gains have been concentrated in the top 0.1 percent. This is not a matter of reward to education. Inequality has expanded hugely among the college-educated. Whatever the causes, the fact is that the United States is now back to the same level of inequality of income as in the decades before 1929, the era of the "robber barons" and the Great Gatsby. Income distribution in the United Kingdom grew more unequal more quickly than even in the United States during the 1980s, and is now the most unequal of the big European countries.

Country Mobility

How much do countries move in the income hierarchy? One study uses real GNP per capita data (GNP deflated in local currency to a common base year, then

[26] Some sources give ratios of 7:1 in the early 1990s to 11:1 in the late 1990s. But these figures take Shanghai as the richest province. With Shanghai province-city as the numerator, the ratio reflects not only regional disparity but also rural-urban disparity, and more specifically, the growth of a new Hong Kong within China (one whose average income is exaggerated because nonpermanent residents are not included in its population). For these points I thank Andrew Fischer, Ph.D. candidate, Development Studies Institute, London School of Economics.

converted to dollars at the exchange rate for that base year) and finds a robustly trimodal distribution of world population against the log of GNP per capita during 1960–1999 (56). The three income zones might be taken as empirical correlates of the conceptual zones of core, semi-periphery, and periphery. Of the 100 countries in the sample, 72 remained in the same income zone over the whole period sampled at five-yearly intervals (e.g., Australia remained in zone 1, Brazil in zone 2, Bolivia in zone 3). The remaining 28 countries moved at least once from one zone to another (e.g., Argentina from 1 to 2). No country moved more than one zone. (South Korea, Hong Kong, and Singapore in 1960 were already in the middle, not the low zone.) There are about as many cases of upward movement as downward. Compared to the rate of potential mobility (each country moving one zone at each measurement date), the rate of actual mobility was 3 percent.

Of the 28 out of 100 countries that moved at least once between zones, about half had "stable" moves, in the sense that their position in 1990 and 1999 was one zone above or below their position in 1960 and 1965. Greece moved stably up from zone 2 to 1, Argentina moved stably down from 1 to 2, El Salvador moved stably down from 2 to 3. As many countries moved stably up as down.

The Absolute Income Gap

Our measures of inequality refer to relative incomes, not absolute incomes. Inequality between developing countries as a group and developed countries as a group remains constant if the ratio of developing-country income to developed-country income remains at 5 percent. But this of course implies a big rise in the absolute size of the gap. The absolute gap between a country with average income of $1,000 growing at 6 percent and a country with average income of $30,000 growing at 1 percent continues to widen until after the 40th year!

China and India are reducing the absolute gap with the faltering middle-income states such as Mexico, Brazil, Russia, and Argentina, but not with the countries of North America, western Europe, and Japan. Dikhanov and Ward's figures show that, overall, the absolute gap between the average income of the top decile of world population and the bottom decile increased from PPP$18,690 in 1970 to PPP$28,902 in 1999 (38). We can be sure that—a seventh proposition—absolute gaps between people and countries are widening fast and will continue to widen for at least two generations.

Conclusions about Inequality

The evidence does support the liberal argument when inequality is measured with population-weighted countries' per capita PPP-adjusted incomes, plus a measure of average inequality, taking China's income statistics at face value. On the other hand, polarization has clearly increased. And several studies that measure inequality over the whole distribution and use either cross-sectional household survey data or measures of combined inequality between countries and within countries show widening inequality since around 1980. The conclusion is that world inequality measured in plausible ways is probably rising, despite China's and India's fast growth. The conclusion is reinforced by evidence of a quite different kind. Dispersion in pay rates within manufacturing has become steadily wider since the early 1980s, having remained roughly constant from 1960 to the early 1980s. Meanwhile, absolute income gaps are widening fast.

GLOBALIZATION

I have raised doubts about the liberal argument's claim that (a) the number of people living in extreme poverty worldwide is currently about 1.2 billion, (b) that it has fallen substantially since 1980, by about 200 million, and (c) that world income inequality has fallen over the same period, having risen for many decades before then. Let us consider the other end of the argument—that the allegedly positive trends in poverty and inequality have been driven by rising integration of poorer countries into the world economy, as seen in rising trade/GDP, foreign direct investment/GDP, and the like.

Clearly the proposition is not well supported at the world level if we agree that globalization has been rising while poverty and income inequality have not been falling. Indeed, it is striking that the pronounced convergence of economic policy toward "openness" worldwide over the past 20 years has gone with divergence of economic performance. But it might still be possible to argue that globalization explains differences between countries: that more open economies or ones that open faster have a better record than less open ones or ones than open more slowly.

This is what World Bank studies claim. The best known, *Globalization, Growth, and Poverty* (12), distinguishes "newly globalizing" countries, also called "more globalized" countries, from "nonglobalizing" countries or "less globalized" countries. It measures globalizing by *changes* in the ratio of trade to GDP between 1977 and 1997. Ranking developing countries by the amount of change, it calls the top third the more globalized countries, the bottom two-thirds, the less globalized countries. It finds that the former have had faster economic growth, no increase in inequality, and faster reduction of poverty than the latter. "Thus globalization clearly can be a force for poverty reductions," it concludes.

The conclusion does not follow (for this discussion I draw on the arguments of Rodrik (57, 58)). First, using "change in the trade/GDP ratio" as the measure of globalization skews the results. The globalizers then include China and India, as well as countries such as Nepal, Côte d'Ivoire, Rwanda, Haiti, and Argentina. It is quite possible that "more globalized" countries are *less* open than many "less globalized" countries, both in terms of trade/GDP and in terms of the magnitude of tariffs and nontariff barriers. A country with high trade/GDP and very free trade policy would still be categorized as "less globalized" if its *increase* in trade/GDP over 1977–1997 put it in the bottom two-thirds of the sample. Many of the globalizing countries initially had very *low* trade/GDP in 1977 and still had relatively low trade/GDP at the *end* of the period in 1997 (reflecting more than just the fact that larger economies tend to have lower ratios of trade/GDP). To call relatively closed economies "more globalized" or "globalizers" and to call countries with much higher ratios of trade/GDP and much freer trade regimes "less globalized" or even "nonglobalizers" is an audacious use of language.

Excluding countries with high but not rising levels of trade/GDP from the category of more globalized eliminates many poor countries dependent on a few natural resource commodity exports, which have had poor economic performance. The structure of their economy and the low skill endowment of their population make them dependent on trade. If they were included as globalized, their poor economic performance would question the proposition that the more globalized countries do better. On the other hand, including China and India as globalizers— despite relatively low trade/GDP and relatively protective trade regimes— guarantees that the globalizers, weighted by population, show better performance than the nonglobalizers. Table 5 provides an illustration.

The second problem is that the argument fudges almost to vanishing point the distinction between trade quantities and trade policy, and implies, wrongly, that rising trade quantities—and the developmental benefits thereof—are the consequence of trade liberalization.

Third, the argument assumes that fast trade growth is the major cause of good economic performance. It does not examine the reverse causation, from fast economic growth to fast trade growth. Nor does it consider that other variables

Table 5

Trade-dependent nonglobalizers and less-trade-dependent globalizers

	Exports/GDP			GNP growth, 1988–99, %
	1990	1999	% Change	
Nonglobalizers				
Honduras	36	42	17	−1.2
Kenya	26	25	−0.04	0.5
Globalizers				
India	7	11	57	6.9
Bangladesh	6	14	133	3.3

Source: World Bank (18, Tables 1 and 13).

correlated with trade growth may be important causes of economic performance: quality of government, for example. One reexamination of the Bank's study finds that the globalizer countries do indeed have higher quality of government indicators than the nonglobalizer countries, on average (59).[27] Finally, trade does not capture important kinds of "openness," including people flows and ideas flows. Imagine an economy with no foreign trade but high levels of inward and outward migration and a well-developed diaspora network. In a real sense this would be an open or globalized economy, though not classified as such.

Certainly many countries—including China and India—have benefited from their more intensive engagement in international trade and investment over the past one or two decades. But this is not to say that their improved performance is largely due to their more intensive external integration. They began to open their own markets *after* building up industrial capacity and fast growth behind high barriers.[28] And throughout their period of so-called openness, they have maintained protection and other market restrictions that would earn them a bad report card from the World Bank and IMF were they not growing fast. China began its fast growth with a high degree of equality of assets and income, brought about in distinctly nonglobalized conditions and unlikely to have been achieved in an open economy and democratic polity (57).

Their experience—and that of Japan, South Korea, and Taiwan earlier—shows that countries do not have to adopt liberal trade policies in order to reap large benefits from trade (60). They all experienced relatively fast growth behind protective barriers; a significant part of their growth came from replacing imports of consumption goods with domestic production; and more and more of their rapidly growing imports consisted of capital goods and intermediate goods. As they became richer they tended to liberalize their trade—providing the basis for the misunderstanding that trade liberalization drove their growth. For all the Bank study's qualifications (such as, "We label the top third 'more globalized' without in any sense implying that they adopted pro-trade policies. The rise in trade may have been due to other policies or even to pure chance"), it concludes that trade liberalization has been the driving force of the increase in developing countries' trade. "The result of this trade liberalization in the developing world has been a large increase in both imports and exports," it says. On this shaky basis the Bank rests its case that developing countries must push hard toward near-free trade as a core ingredient of their development strategy, the better to enhance competition in efficient, rent-free markets.

---

[27] Besley (59) uses indicators such as press freedom, democratic accountability, corruption, civil rights.

[28] Cf. "As they reformed and integrated with the world market, the 'more globalized' developing countries *started to grow rapidly,* accelerating steadily from 2.9 percent in the 1970s to 5 percent through the 1990s" (12, p. 36, emphasis added).

Even when the Bank or other development agencies articulate the softer principle—trade liberalization is the necessary direction of change but countries may do it at different speeds—all the attention remains focused on the liberalization part, none on how to make protective regimes more effective (other than just by liberalizing them).

In short, the Bank's argument about the benign effects of globalization on growth, poverty, and income distribution does not survive scrutiny at either end. And a recent cross-country study of the relationship between openness and income distribution strikes another blow. It finds that among the subset of countries with low and middle levels of average income (below $5,000 per capita in PPP terms, that of Chile and the Czech Republic), higher levels of trade openness are associated with *more* inequality, while among higher-income countries more openness goes with less inequality (39).[29]

CONCLUSION

It is plausible, and important, that the proportion of the world's population living in extreme poverty has probably fallen over the past two decades or so, having been rising for decades before then. Beyond this we cannot be confident, because the World Bank's poverty numbers are subject to a large margin of error, are probably biased downward and probably make the trend look rosier than it really is. On income distribution, several studies suggest that world income inequality has been rising during the past two to three decades, and a study of manufacturing pay dispersions buttresses the same conclusion from another angle. The trend is sharpest when incomes are measured as market-exchange-rate incomes. This is less relevant to relative well-being than PPP-adjusted incomes, in principle; but it is highly relevant to state capacity, interstate power, and the dynamics of capitalism. One combination of inequality measures does yield the conclusion that income inequality has been falling—PPP-income per capita weighted by population, measured by an averaging coefficient such as the Gini. But take out China and even this measure shows widening inequality. Falling inequality is thus not a *generalized* feature of the world economy even by the most favorable measure. Finally, whatever we conclude about income inequality, absolute income gaps are widening and will continue to do so for decades.

If the number of people in extreme poverty may not be falling and if global inequality may be widening, we cannot conclude that globalization in the context of the dollar–Wall Street regime is moving the world in the right direction, with Africa's poverty as a special case in need of international attention. The

---

[29] Milanovic (39) finds that in countries below the average income of about PPP$5,000, higher levels of openness (imports plus exports/GDP) are associated with lower income shares of the bottom 80 percent of the population.

balance of probability is that—like global warming—the world is moving in the wrong direction.

The failure of the predicted effects aside, the studies that claim globalization as the driver are weakened by (*a*) the use of *increases* in the trade/GDP ratio or FDI/GDP ratio as the index of globalization or openness, irrespective of level (though using the level on its own is also problematic, the level of trade/GDP being determined mainly by country size); (*b*) the assumption that trade liberalization drives increases in trade/GDP; and (*c*) the assumption that increases in trade/GDP drive improved economic performance. The problems come together in the case of China and India, whose treatment dominates the overall results. They are classed as "globalizers," their relatively good economic performance is attributed mainly to their "openness," and the deviation between their economic policies— substantial trade protection and capital controls, for example—and the core economic policy package of the World Bank and the other multilateral economic organizations is glossed.

At the least, analysts have to separate out the effect of country size on trade/GDP levels from other factors determining trade/GDP, including trade policies, because the single best predictor of trade/GDP is country size (population and area). They must make a clear distinction between statements about (*a*) levels of trade, (*b*) changes in levels, (*c*) restrictiveness or openness of trade policy, (*d*) changes in restrictiveness of policy, and (*e*) the content of trade—whether a narrow range of commodity exports in return for a broad range of consumption imports, or a diverse range of exports (some of them replaced imports) in return for a diverse range of imports (some of them producer goods to assist further import replacement).

Should We Worry about Rising Inequality?

The neoliberal argument says that inequality provides incentives for effort and risk-taking, and thereby raises efficiency. As Margaret Thatcher put it, "It is our job to glory in inequality and see that talents and abilities are given vent and expression for the benefit of us all" (quoted in 61). We should worry about rising inequality only if it somehow makes the poor worse off than otherwise.

The counterargument is that this productive incentive effect applies only at moderate, Scandinavian, levels of inequality. At higher levels, such as in the United States over the past 20 years, it is likely to be swamped by social costs. Aside from the moral case against it, inequality above a moderate level creates a kind of society that even crusty conservatives hate to live in, unsafe and unpleasant.

Higher income inequality within nations goes with: (*a*) higher poverty (using World Bank data and the number of people below the Bank's international poverty line) (62); (*b*) slower economic growth, especially in large countries like China, because it constrains the growth of mass demand; (*c*) higher unemployment; and (*d*) higher crime (63–66). The link to higher crime comes through the inability of unskilled men in high-inequality societies to play traditional male economic and social roles, including a plausible contribution to family income. But higher crime and violence is only the tip of a distribution of social relationships skewed toward the aggressive end of the spectrum, with low average levels of trust and social capital. In short, inequality at the national level should certainly be a target of public policy, even if just for the sake of the prosperous.

The liberal argument is even less concerned about widening inequality between countries than it is about inequality within countries, because we cannot do much to lessen international inequality directly. But on the face of it, the more globalized the world becomes, the more do the reasons why we should be concerned about within-country inequalities also apply between countries. If globalization within the current framework actually increases inequality within and between countries, as some evidence suggests, increases in world inequality above moderate levels may cut world aggregate demand and thereby world economic growth, making a vicious circle of rising world inequality and slower world growth.

And rising inequality between countries impacts directly on national political economy in the poorer states, as rich people who earlier compared themselves to others in their neighborhood now compare themselves to others in the United States or western Europe, and feel deprived and perhaps angry. Inequality above moderate levels may, for example, predispose the elites to become more corrupt as they compare themselves to elites in rich countries and squeeze their own populations in order to sustain a comparable living standard, enfeebling whatever norms of citizenship have emerged and preventing the transition from an "oligarchic" elite, concerned to maximize redistribution upward and contain protests by repression, to an "establishment" elite, concerned to protect its position by being seen to operate fairly. Likewise, rapidly widening between-country inequality in current exchange rate terms feeds back into stress in public services, as the increasing foreign exchange cost of imports, debt repayment, and the like has to be offset by cuts in budgets for health, education, and industrial policy.

Migration is a function of inequality, since the fastest way for a poor person to get richer is to move from a poor country to a rich country. Widening inequality may raise the incentive for the educated people of poor countries to migrate to the rich countries, and raise the incentive for unskilled people to seek illegal entry. Yet migration/refugees/asylum is the single most emotional, most atavistic issue in western politics. Polls show that more than two-thirds of respondents agree that there should be fewer "foreigners" living in their countries (67).

Rising inequality may generate conflict between states, and—because the *market-exchange-rate* income gap is so big—make it cheap for rich states to intervene to support one side or the other in civil strife. Rising inequality in market-exchange-rate terms—helped by a high U.S. dollar, a low (long-run) oil price, and the WTO agreements on intellectual property rights, investment, and trade in services—allows the United States to finance the military sinews of its postimperial empire more cheaply (68, 69).

The effects of inequality within and between countries depend on prevailing norms. Where power hierarchy and income inequality are thought to be the natural human condition, the negative effects can be expected to be lighter than where prevailing norms affirm equality. Norms of equality and democracy are being energetically internationalized by the Atlantic states, at the same time as the lived experience in much of the rest of the world is from another planet.

In the end, the interests of the rich and powerful should, objectively, line up in favor of greater equity in the world at large, because some of the effects of widening inequality may contaminate their lives and those of their children. This fits the neoliberal argument. But the route to greater equity goes not only through the dismantling of market rules rigged in favor of the rich—also consistent with the neoliberal argument—but through more political (nonmarket) influence on resource allocation in order to counter the tendency of free markets to concentrate incomes and power. This requires international public policy well beyond the boundaries of neoliberalism.

The need for deliberate international redistribution is underlined by the evidence that world poverty may be higher in absolute numbers than is generally thought, and quite possibly rising rather than falling; and that world income inequality is probably rising too. This evidence suggests that the income and prosperity gap between a small proportion of the world's population living mainly in the North and a large proportion living entirely in the South is a structural divide, not just a matter of a lag in the South's catch-up. Sustained preferences for the South may be necessary if the world is to move to a single-humped and more narrowly dispersed distribution over the next century.

The Political Economy of Statistics

Concerns about global warming gave rise to a coordinated worldwide project to get better climatological data; the same is needed to get better data on poverty and inequality. The World Bank is one of the key actors. It has moved from major to minor source of foreign finance for most developing countries outside Africa. But it remains an important global organization because it wields a disproportionate influence in setting the development agenda, in offering an imprimatur of "sound finance" that crowds in other resources, and in providing finance at times when other finance is not available. Its statistics and development research are crucial to its legitimacy (70). Other regional development banks and aid agencies have largely given up on statistics and research, ceding the ground to the World Bank. Alternative views come only from a few "urban guerrillas" in pockets of academia and the U.N. system.[30] Keynes's dictum on

---

[30] For a good example of a heterodox book from a corner of the U.N. system, see UNDP (71); the WTO lobbied to prevent its publication.

practical men and long-dead economists suggests that such intellectual monopolization can have a hugely negative impact.

Think of two models of a statistical organization that is part of a larger organization working on politically sensitive themes. The "exogenous" model says that the statistics are produced by professionals exercising their best judgment in the face of difficulties that have no optimal solutions, who are managerially insulated from the overall tactical goals of the organization. The "endogenous" model says that the statistics are produced by staff who act as agents of the senior managers (the principals), the senior managers expect them to help advance the tactical goals of the organization just like other staff, and the statistics staff therefore have to massage the data beyond the limits of professional integrity, or quit.

Certainly the simple endogenous model does not fit the Bank; but nor does the other. The Bank is committed to an Official View of how countries should seek poverty reduction, rooted in the neoliberal agenda of trade opening, financial opening, privatization, deregulation, with some good governance, civil society, and environmental protection thrown in; it is exposed to arm-twisting by the G7 member states and international nongovernmental organizations; it must secure their support and defend itself against criticism (72). It seeks to advance its broad market opening agenda not through coercion but mainly by establishing a sense that the agenda is right and fitting. Without this it would lose the support of the G7 states, Wall Street, and fractions of developing country elites. The units of the Bank that produce the statistics are partly insulated from the resulting pressures, especially by their membership in "epistemic communities" of professionals inside and outside the Bank; but not wholly insulated. To say otherwise is to deny that the Bank is subject to the Chinese proverb, "Officials make the figures, and the figures make the officials"; or to Goodhart's law, which states that an indicator's measurement will be distorted if it is used as a target. (Charles Goodhart was thinking of monetary policy, but the point also applies to variables used to make overall evaluations of the performance of multilateral economic organizations.) To say otherwise is equally to deny that the Bank is affected by the same pressures as the IMF, about which a former Fund official said, "The managing director makes the big decisions, and the staff then puts together the numbers to justify them" (73). But little is known about the balance between autonomy and compliance in the two organizations, or the latitude of their statisticians to adjust the country numbers provided by colleagues elsewhere in the organization which they believe to be fiddled (as in the China case, above).[31]

Some of the Bank's statistics are also provided by independent sources, which provide a check. Others, including the poverty numbers, are produced only

---

[31] Key experts in the relevant statistical unit thought that colleagues had fiddled the China income numbers reported in Table 4, but their boss ignored their objections.

by the Bank, and these are more subject to Goodhart's law. The Bank should appoint an independent auditor to verify its main development statistics or cede the work to an independent agency, perhaps under U.N. auspices (but if done by, say, UNCTAD, the opposite bias might be introduced). And it would help if the Bank's figures on poverty and inequality made clearer than they do the possible biases and the likely margins of error.

All this, of course, only takes us to the starting point of an inquiry into the causes of the probable poverty and inequality trends (see 74, 75), their likely consequences, and public policy responses; but at least we are now ready to ask the right questions. Above all, we have to go back to a distinction that has all but dropped out of development studies, between increasing returns and decreasing returns or, more generally, between positive and negative feedback mechanisms. The central question is why, at the level of the whole, the increasing returns of the Matthew effect—"To him who hath shall be given"—continues to dominate decreasing returns in the third wave of globalization.

Acknowledgments — I thank without implicating Sanjay Reddy, Michael Ward, Branko Milanovic, Ron Dore, David Ellerman, Martin Wolf, Timothy Besley, and James Galbraith; and the Institute for Advanced Study, Berlin, and the Crisis States Program, DESTIN, London School of Economics, for financial support.

Note — This chapter is modified from a paper published in *World Development,* April 2004.

REFERENCES

1. World Bank. *World Development Indicators 2002.* Washington DC, 2002.
2. Dollar, D., and Kraay, A. Spreading the wealth. *Foreign Affairs,* January/February 2002, pp. 120–133.
3. Wolf, M. Doing more harm than good. *Financial Times,* May 8, 2002.
4. Mazur, J. Labor's new internationalism. *Foreign Affairs* 79(1):79–93, 2000.
5. Gowan, P. *The Global Gamble.* Verso, London, 1999.
6. Wolf, M. The big lie of global inequality. *Financial Times,* February 8, 2000.
7. International Monetary Fund. *World Economic Outlook.* Database. Washington, DC, April 2003.
8. Arrighi, G., Silver, B., and Brewer, B. Industrial convergence, globalization an the persistence of the North-South divide. *Stud. Comp. Int. Dev.* 38(1):3–31, 2003.
9. World Bank. *Global Economic Prospects and the Developing Countries 2002: Making Trade Work for the World's Poor.* Washington, DC, 2002.
10. Wolfensohn, J. Responding to the Challenges of Globalization: Remarks to the G-20 Finance Ministers and Central Governors. Ottawa, November 17, 2001.
11. World Bank. *World Development Indicators 2001.* Washington, DC, 2001.
12. World Bank. *Globalization, Growth, and Poverty: Building an Inclusive World Economy.* World Bank and Oxford University Press, New York, 2002.

13. Reddy, S. and Pogge, T. How Not to Count the Poor. 2003. www.socialanalysis.org.
14. Ravallion, M. Reply to Reddy and Pogge. 2003. www.socialanalysis.org.
15. Reddy, S., and Pogge, T. Reply to Ravallion. 2003. www.socialanalysis.org.
16. Deaton, A. Measuring Poverty in a Growing World (or Measuring Growth in a Poor World). NBER Working Paper 9822. 2003. http://d.repec.org/n?u=RePEc:nbr:nberwo:9822&r=dev
17. Deaton, A. Counting the world's poor: Problems and possible solutions. *World Bank Research Observer* 16(2):125–147, 2001.
18. World Bank. *World Development Report 2000/2001: Attacking Poverty.* Washington, DC, 2001.
19. Pogge, T., and Reddy, S. Unknown: The Extent, Distribution, and Trend of Global Income Poverty. 2003. www.socialanalysis.org.
20. Economic Commission for Latin America. *Panorama Social de America Latina 2000–01.* Santiago, 2001.
21. Gopinath, D. Poor choices. *Institutional Investor,* 2002, pp. 41–50.
22. Wade, R. H. US hegemony and the World Bank: The fight over people and ideas. *Rev. Int. Polit. Econ.* 9(2):201–229, 2002.
23. Meltzer Commission (U.S. Congressional Advisory Commission on International Financial Institutions. Report to the U.S. Congress on the International Financial Institutions. 2002. www.house/gov/jec/imf/ifiac
24. Meltzer, A. The World Bank one year after the Commission's report to Congress. Hearings before the Joint Economic Committee, U.S. Congress, March 8, 2001.
25. Deaton, A. Is world poverty falling? *Finance Dev.* 39(2), 2002. www.imf.org/external/pubs/ft/fandd/2002/06/deaton.htm.
26. Wolf, M. Growth makes the poor richer: Reversing the effects of globalization might increase equality as the critics claim, but it would be an equality of destitution. *Financial Times,* January 24, 2001.
27. Wolf, M. A stepping stone from poverty. *Financial Times,* December 19, 2001.
28. Giddens, A. *Where Now for New Labour?* Polity Press, Cambridge, 2002.
29. Castles, I. Letter. *Economist,* May 26, 2001.
30. Firebaugh, G. Empirics of world income inequality. *Am. J. Sociol.* 104(6):1597–1630, 1999.
31. Jones, C. On the evolution of world income distribution. *J. Econ. Perspect.* 11(3):19–36, 1997.
32. Pritchett, L. Divergence: Big time. *J. Econ. Perspect.* 11(3):3–17, 1997.
33. Quah, D. Empirics for growth and distribution: Stratification, polarization, and convergence clubs. *J. Econ. Growth* 2(1):27–57, 1997.
34. United Nations Development Program. *Human Development Report 1999.* United Nations, New York, 1999.
35. Kanbur, R. Conceptual Challenges in Poverty and Inequality: One Development Economist's Perspective. WP2002-09. Department of Applied Economics, Cornell University, 2002.
36. Korzeniewicz, R., and Moran, T. World-economic trends in the distribution of income, 1965–1992. *Am. J. Sociol.* 102(4):1000–1039, 1997.
37. Korzeniewicz, R., and Moran, T. Measuring world income inequalities. *Am. J. Sociol.* 106(1):209–214, 2000.

38. Dikhanov, Y., and Ward, M. Evolution of the global distribution of income in 1970–99. In *Proceedings of the Global Poverty Workshop*. Initiative for Policy Dialogue, Columbia University, 2003. www-l.gsb.Columbia.edu/ipd/povertywk.html.

39. Milanovic, B. Can We Discern the Effect of Globalization on Income Distribution? Evidence from Household Budget Surveys. World Bank Policy Research Working Papers 2876. 2002. http://econ.worldbank.org.

40. Economic Commission for Latin America. *Globalization and Development*. Santiago, 2002.

41. Wolf, M. Are global poverty and inequality getting worse? Yes: Robert Wade, No: Martin Wolf. *Prospect,* March 2002, pp. 16–21.

42. Dowrick, S., and Akmal, M. Explaining Contradictory Trends in Global Income Inequality: A Tale of Two Biasses. Faculty of Economics and Commerce, Australia National University, March 29, 2001. http://ecocomm.anu.edu.au/people/info.asp?Surname=Dowrick&Firstname=Steve

43. Milanovic, B. True world income distribution, 1988 and 1993: First calculations based on household surveys alone. *Econ. J.* 112(476):51–92, 2002.

44. Sala-i-Martin, X. The Disturbing "Rise" in Global Income Inequality. NBER Working Paper 8904. April 2002. http://papers.nber.org/papers/w8904.

45. Milanovic, B. The Ricardian Vice: Why Sala-i-Matin's Calculations Are Wrong. Typescript Development Research Group, World Bank, 2002. www.ssrn.com.

46. Nye, H., and Reddy, S. Weaknesses of Recent Global Poverty Estimates: Xavier Sala-i-Martin and Surjit Bhalla. 2003. www.socialanalysis.org.

47. Galbraith, J. K. A perfect crime: Inequality in the age of globalization. *Daedalus,* Winter 2002, pp. 11–25.

48. Kynge, J. Pyramid of power behind numbers game. *Financial Times,* February 27, 2002.

49. Rawski, T. Measuring China's Recent GDP Growth: Where Do We Stand? 2002. www.pitt.edu/~tgrawski.

50. Waldron, A. China's disguised failure: Statistics can no longer hide the need for Beijing to instigate painful structural reforms. *Financial Times,* July 4, 2002.

51. World Bank. *World Development Indicators 1999*. Washington, DC, 1999.

52. World Bank. *World Development Indicators 2000*. Washington, DC, 2000.

53. Hommann, K., and Brandon, C. The Cost of Inaction: Valuing the Economy-wide Cost of Environmental Degradation in India. Paper presented at Modelling Global Sustainability Conference, United Nations University, Tokyo, 1995.

54. Jha, R. Reducing Poverty and Inequality in India: Has Liberalization Helped? 2000. www.wider.unu.edu/research/1998-1999-3.1.publications.htm.

55. Krugman, P. For richer. *New York Times,* October 20, 2002.

56. Babones, S. The Structure of the World-Economy, 1960–1999. Paper presented at 97th Annual Meeting of the American Sociological Association, Chicago, 2002.

57. Rodrik, D. *The New Global Economy and Developing Countries: Making Openness Work*. Policy Essay 24, Overseas Development Council. Johns Hopkins University Press, Baltimore, 1999.

58. Rodrik, D. Trading in illusions. *Foreign Policy* 123(March/April):55–62, 2001.

59. Besley, T. Globalization and the Quality of Government. Manuscript. Economics Department, London School of Economics, March 2002.

60. Wade, R. H. *Governing the Market.* Princeton University Press, Princeton, 2003 [1990].
61. George, S. How to win the war of ideas: Lessons from the Gramscian right. *Dissent* 44(3):47–53, 1997.
62. Besley, T., and Burgess, R. Halving world poverty. *J. Econ. Perspect.* 17(3):3–22, 2003.
63. Lee, M. R., and Bankston, W. Political structure, economic inequality, and homicide: A cross-sectional analysis. *Deviant Behavior: An Interdisciplinary Journal* 19:27–55, 1999.
64. Hsieh, C. C., and Pugh, M. Poverty, income inequality, and violent crime: A meta-analysis of recent aggregate data studies. *Criminal Justice Rev.* 18:182–202, 1993.
65. Fajnzylber, P., Lederman, D., and Loayza, N. What Causes Violent Crime? Typescript. Office of the Chief Economist, Latin America and the Caribbean Region, World Bank, Washington, DC, 1998.
66. Freeman, R. Why do so many young American men commit crimes and what might we do about it? *J. Econ. Perspect.* 10(1):25–42, 1996.
67. Demeny, P. Population policy dilemmas in Europe at the dawn of the twenty-first century. *Popul. Dev. Rev.* 29(1):1–28, 2003.
68. Wade, R. H. The invisible hand of the American empire. *Ethics Int. Aff.* 17(2):77–88, 2003.
69. Wade, R. H. What strategies are viable for developing countries today? The WTO and the shrinking of development space. *Rev. Int. Polit. Econ.* 10(4):621–644, 2003.
70. Kapur, D. The changing anatomy of governance of the World Bank. In *Reinventing the World Bank,* ed. J. Pincus and J. Winters. Cornell University Press, Ithaca, NY, 2002.
71. U.N. Development Program. *Making Global Trade Work for People.* Earthscan, London, 2003.
72. Wade, R. H. The World Bank and its critics: The dynamics of hypocrisy. *Stud. Comp. Int. Dev.,* 2004.
73. Gopinath, D. Slouching toward a new consensus. *Institutional Investor,* September 1, 1999, pp. 79–87.
74. Wade, R. H. Globalisation, poverty and income distribution: Does the liberal argument hold? In *Globalization, Living Standards and Inequality: Recent Progress and Continuing Challenges,* pp. 37–65. Reserve Bank of Australia, Sydney, 2002.
75. Wade, R. H. World poverty and inequality: Why they are probably rising, and the North-South divide persisting. *New Polit. Econ.,* 2004.

PART IV

Consequences of Neoliberalism and Globalization for Health and Quality of Life

CHAPTER 7

The Scorecard on Development: 25 Years of Diminished Progress

Mark Weisbrot, Dean Baker, and David Rosnick

Over the past 25 years a number of economic reforms have taken place in low- and middle-income countries. These reforms, as a group, have been given various labels: "liberalization," "globalization," or "free market"[1] are among the most common descriptions. Among the reforms widely implemented have been the reduction of restrictions on international trade and capital flows, large-scale privatizations of state-owned enterprises, tighter fiscal and monetary policies (higher interest rates), labor market reforms, and increasing accumulation of foreign reserve holdings. Many of these reforms have been implemented with the active support of multilateral lending institutions such as the International Monetary Fund (IMF) and the World Bank, as well as the G-7 governments, and have often been required in order for countries to have access to credit from these and other sources. But regardless of origin, labels, or political perspectives, there is a general consensus that the majority of developing countries have benefited economically from the reforms, even if they have sometimes been accompanied by increasing inequality or other unintended consequences.[2]

This chapter looks at the available data on economic growth and various social indicators—including health outcomes and education—and finds that, contrary to popular belief, the past 25 years have seen a sharply slower rate of economic growth and reduced progress on social indicators for the vast majority of low- and middle-income countries. Of course it is still possible that some or even all of the policy reforms of the past 25 years have had net positive effects, or that they will have such an impact at some point in the future. But the fact that

---

[1] The latter term, as well as "free trade," is inaccurate as a matter of economics, since the reforms have included very costly forms of protectionism—e.g., increased patent and copyright protection—as well as such policies as fixed exchange rates, which are the opposite of "free market" policies.

[2] "Globalization has brought enormous benefits in growth and efficiency. Yet this same force has brought cross-border financial crises and heightened the imperative to bring into the mainstream those who are being left behind" (1).

these effects have not yet shown up in the data, for developing countries as a group—and that in fact the data show a marked decline in progress over the past quarter-century—is very significant. If the data and trends presented below were well known, it would very likely have an impact on policy discussions and research. Most importantly, there would be a much greater interest in finding out what has gone wrong over the past 25 years.

In order to evaluate the progress of the past 25 years, it is necessary to have a benchmark for comparison. In other words, for the world as a whole, there is almost always economic growth, technological progress, and therefore social progress over time. The relevant question is not whether there has been income growth and social progress, but the rate of such progress as compared with what has been feasible in the past.

For this study, we have chosen to compare the past 25 years (1980–2005)[3] with the previous 20 years: 1960–1980. This is a fair comparison. While the 1960s were a period of exceptional economic performance, the 1970s suffered from two major oil shocks that led to worldwide recessions: in 1974–75, and again at the end of the decade. The 1970s were also a period of high inflation in both developing and developed countries. So this 20-year period is not a particularly high benchmark for comparison with the most recent 25 years. If the 1950s were included, it would have made the benchmark for comparison higher, since the 1950s were generally a period of good growth for the developing world. But there is not much good information for the 1950s; and many of the developing countries did not become independent until the late 1950s or 1960s.

STANDARDS OF COMPARISON

One way to compare the performance of the two periods (1980–2005 and 1960–1980) would be to simply compare how each group of countries did in the first period with the same group of countries' performance for the second period. The problem with such a comparison is that it may be more difficult to make the same amount of progress from a higher level than when starting from a lower level. For example, this is certainly true for some levels of life expectancy: it would be more difficult to raise life expectancy from 70 to 75 years than to raise it from 50 to 55. A comparison of the same countries for the two periods would therefore tend to find a diminished rate of progress simply because of this inherent difficulty that comes from progress during the first period. This is not what we want to measure.

To get around this problem, we divide the countries into five groups, depending on their starting point at the beginning of each of the two periods. For example, if we look at Figure 1, there are groups of countries sorted by per capita income. The middle quintile includes countries with an income per person between

---

[3] For some indicators the most recent data do not extend to 2005—e.g., life expectancy data go only to 2002.

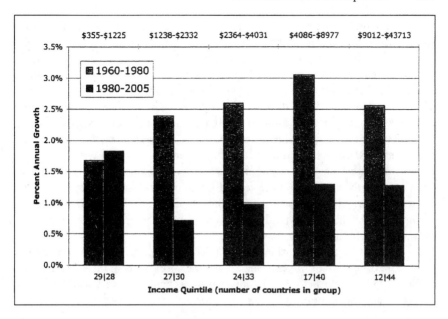

Figure 1. Average annual growth by income quintile and period. *Source:* Penn World Tables 6.1, *IMF World Economic Outlook,* April 2005, author's calculations.

$2,364 and $4,031 (in constant 2000 dollars). These are countries that started out either in 1960 or 1980 with a GDP (gross domestic product) per person in this range. The other quintiles range from the poorest ($355–$1,225) to the richest ($9,012–$43,713).

Looking at the middle quintile, at the bottom of the graph we can see that there were 24 countries that started the 1960s in this range of per capita GDP ($2,364 to $4,031), but 33 countries that started the 1980s in this range. This is to be expected, as some of the countries from the bottom two quintiles moved into the middle quintile as a result of their growth during the first period.[4]

On this basis, we can make a fair comparison, not of the same countries over time, which would suffer from the problems described above, but between all the countries that started the first period at a certain level of income and all the countries that started the second period at that same level. We can do the same for the social indicators as well. In fact, this methodology should bias the data toward finding better results for the second period. There should generally be possibilities for countries to gain by borrowing from the technology and practices

[4] In this data set there are also 65 countries (out of 175) for which there are data only for the 1980–2005 period, and not for 1960–1980. The number of countries in each group also changes as countries move up from one quintile to the next on the basis of progress in the first period.

of other countries that are richer or have achieved higher levels of the various social indicators. As a result of the progress made in the first period, there were far more possibilities for faster improvement in the second period. For example, in the case of life expectancy (see Figure 2 below), there were only 16 countries at the start of the first period (1960) with life expectancy of more than 69 years. This meant that countries in the next lowest grouping, with life expectancies from 63 to 69 years, would have a relatively limited number of countries from which to adopt better public health measures, medicines, or medical practices. However, at the start of the second period (1980), there were 50 countries with life expectancies of more than 69 years. This should have provided a far larger set of practices that the countries in the second grouping (with life expectancies from 63 to 69 years) could adopt to improve health care in their own country in the second period. The same would also be true for all the countries further down the ladder in life expectancy.

In other words, it is reasonable to expect that countries starting at any particular level (e.g., of income or life expectancy) will perform better in the second period (1980–2005), simply because the advance of technology and knowledge over 20 years has created more and better practices that are available to be adopted.

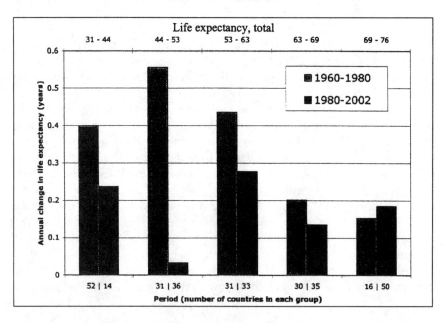

Figure 2. Life expectancy at birth (years), total. *Source:* World Bank, World Development Indicators, 2005.

THE SLOWDOWN IN ECONOMIC GROWTH

The growth of income (or GDP) per person is the most basic measure of economic progress that economists use. Of course this ignores the distribution of income, as well as environmental and health outcomes. And there are things that raise GDP that do not increase human welfare: for example, more people buying cigarettes and alcohol and then having to be treated for resulting health impairment. But as a broad measure of economic progress it is by far the most important. When we look at GDP per person, we are deliberately factoring out population growth, since any growth in the economy that is only due to population growth does not improve living standards. Ignoring for the moment any change in labor force participation, we are really looking at productivity growth. For developing countries especially, it is the increase in productivity over time that enables a country to have higher living standards. As productivity grows, a smaller proportion of the country's resources is allocated to the necessities of life, and more can be dedicated to education, health care, and investment in future growth. In general, and especially over long enough periods of time, productivity growth will improve the lives of the majority of the population, including the poor (e.g., 2).[5] To the extent that any of the reduced progress over the past 25 years measured by social indicators, as noted in subsequent sections of this chapter, is due to economic changes—and much of it is—it is almost certainly due to declining growth rates rather than changes in the distribution of income.[6]

Figure 1 shows the annual rate of growth of GDP (or income) per capita for the two periods (1960–1980 and 1980–2005). The 175 countries are divided into quintiles according to their per capita income at the start of each period, as explained above. There is a pronounced slowdown in growth for each quintile, except for the bottom quintile. Taking the three middle quintiles first, which are all low- and middle-income countries, the difference between the two periods is striking. In the fourth quintile, marked by incomes between $1,238 and $2,332, growth falls from 2.4 percent annually in the first period to 0.7 percent in the second period. To get an idea how much difference this makes over time, at 2.4 percent growth the country's income per person will double in about 29 years; at 0.7 percent growth, it would take 99 years. The declines in the next two quintiles are also severe. The middle quintile, with GDP per capita between $2,364 and $4,031, drops from a 2.6 percent growth rate in the first period to 1 percent in the second. The second quintile ($4,086–$8,977) falls even further:

[5] A remarkable exception to such long-term trends has been the United States over the past 30 years, where the median wage increased only about 9 percent, while productivity increased by more than 80 percent.

[6] This is not to say that redistribution, whether from existing income or wealth, or new income created through growth, is unimportant or undesirable. Indeed, as the UNDP (3) points out, it can potentially make a large difference in poverty reduction.

from 3.1 percent in the first period to 1.3 percent in the second period. Even the top quintile, which at $9,012 to $43,713 contains a mixture of middle-income and high-income countries, shows a sizeable falloff in growth, from 2.6 percent in the first period to only 1.3 percent in the second period. It is worth noting that in the top quintile, the result is mainly driven by the middle-income countries.

As noted above, the comparison in each of these quintiles is not for the same countries over the two periods, but for the countries that start each period at the level of income defined by the per capita income boundaries of the quintile. Some countries will move up to higher levels, as we would expect on the basis of progress between 1960 and 1980. So, for example, Sri Lanka, Indonesia, Lesotho, and the Gambia all started out in the bottom quintile in 1960 but began the second period (1980) in the next quintile up. Morocco, Thailand, and Botswana moved two quintiles, from the bottom to the third (middle) quintile. At the bottom of the table is listed the number of countries in each quintile, for 1960 and 1980 (e.g., 24|33 for the middle quintile).

The only group that does not show a slowdown in growth is the bottom quintile, with per capita income between $355 and $1,225 annually, where growth increases slightly, from 1.7 to 1.8 percent. However, this is still a bad average performance for the poorest developing countries. It is worth noting that this result is reversed without India and China, despite the fact that India and China are counted in the averages here with no more weight than small countries such as Mali or Burundi. That is, the averages are not weighted by either GDP or population. (Since China and India together account for approximately half of the population of the developing world, their experiences are discussed separately in the last section.) So it is only the large jump in their growth rates in the second period that drives the improvement for the bottom quintile. It is also worth noting that the improvement for the bottom quintile is also dependent on the countries that were not in the data set for 1960–1980 but are included for 1980–2005.

In any case, there is no ambiguity about the overall result, which does not depend on how the countries are divided into groups or whether the new countries are included. There is a sharp slowdown in the rate of growth of per capita income for the vast majority of low- and middle-income countries. This is probably the most important economic change that has taken place in the world during the past quarter-century. It is much more difficult to reduce poverty or inequality in the face of such a growth slowdown. When a country's economy is growing, it is at least possible for the poor to share equally or even disproportionately in the gains from productivity growth. When there is very little growth in income per person, such improvements are much harder to achieve, and may be politically impossible to the extent that poverty alleviation depends on actually reducing the current income of the middle and upper classes.

One region that has been particularly affected by this growth slowdown is Latin America. Income for the region grew by 82 percent from 1960 to 1980, but only about 9 percent from 1980 to 2000 and 1 percent from 2000 to 2005. This has been a drastic change. If Brazil, for example, had continued to grow at its pre-1980 rate, the country would have European living standards today. Mexico would not be far behind. Instead, the region has suffered its worst 25-year economic performance in modern Latin American history, even including the years of the Great Depression.

This is a region that adopted many of the policy reforms that have characterized the past quarter-century. The average tariff on imported goods was cut by about half from 1970 to 2000.[7] Controls on the inflow and outflow of investment were either removed or drastically reduced in most countries. Privatization of state-owned enterprises was undertaken on a massive scale: it amounted to $178 billion in the 1990s, more than 20 times the value of privatization in Russia after the collapse of the Soviet Union (4). Latin American countries also adopted more than 80 IMF programs during the past 25 years. These programs generally required higher real interest rates as well as budget cuts, which led to reductions in social spending—as well as other forms of liberalization.

As a result of this long-term economic failure, many Latin Americans have blamed the reforms, which are often labeled "neoliberalism" there. In the past seven years there have been a number of elections—in Venezuela, Argentina, Brazil, Ecuador, and Uruguay—where the winning candidates campaigned against "neoliberalism," and political unrest in other countries based on the same theme. Still, the long-term growth slowdown, whether in Latin America or in the developing world generally, has attracted little attention or debate in policy circles in the United States.

REDUCED PROGRESS IN HEALTH OUTCOMES

As would be expected in a period of sharply reduced economic growth, the past 25-year period also shows slower progress on health outcomes. Figure 2 shows the result for life expectancy, with countries divided into quintiles according to their life expectancy at the beginning of each period. As can be seen in the graph, there is a noticeable slowdown in all groups except the highest quintile, which contains countries where life expectancy is between 69 and 76 years.

The biggest drop was in the fourth quintile, with life expectancy between 44 and 53. These countries saw an average annual increase of 0.56 years for 1960–1980, but almost no progress—0.03 percent—for the second period. Over 20 or 25 years this makes a large difference. For the first period, countries in this quintile increased their life expectancy by about 11 years. If this rate of improvement had continued, the countries in this quintile in the second period would have raised life expectancy by 12 years; instead they saw an increase of

[7] World Bank, World Development Indicators, 2005.

only 0.7 years. The middle and bottom quintiles also show reduced progress. The bottom quintile, with life expectancies between 31 and 44 years, falls from 0.4 to 0.24 years of annual improvement. Over the 22 years of the second period (1980–2002), this means that life expectancy would have increased by 4 years more than it actually did, if not for this falloff in the rate of progress. For the middle quintile, with life expectancies between 53 and 63 years, there is a decline from 0.44 to 0.28 years of annual improvement. The second quintile shows a smaller reduction, from 0.20 to 0.14 years. It is worth noting that even this difference is not insignificant, adding up to a difference of about one year of life expectancy over the 22 years.

A significant part of this story is sub-Saharan Africa, which dominates the bottom two quintiles for the 1980–2002 period and has some impact on the middle quintile. However, even if all the sub-Saharan African countries are removed from the data, there is still a decline in progress for the bottom three quintiles, with no change for the second. So the decline in progress on life expectancy occurs across a broad range of low- and middle-income countries, and is not confined to any particular region. Furthermore, the reduced life expectancies resulting from HIV/AIDS and even the armed conflicts in Africa are not necessarily completely exogenous. Per capita income in sub-Saharan Africa grew by a modest but still significant 36 percent from 1960 to 1980. From 1980 to 2000, income per capita actually declined—a rare event in modern economic history over a 20-year period—by about 15 percent. It is possible that some countries may have been able to deal with the HIV/AIDS and other public health crises at least somewhat more effectively if not for the economic collapse of the second period. Also, the spread of HIV/AIDS is itself partly a result of the increased trade and travel, including migrant and transport labor, associated with international economic integration. For all the benefits that countries can gain as a result of increased commerce, a potential drawback is the more rapid spread of diseases. Finally, it is possible that the continent would have seen less armed conflict over second period if not for the economic collapse that took place.

Figures 3 and 4 show the results for life expectancy for males and females separately. The boundaries for the five quintiles are different from each other and from the overall boundaries in Figure 2, because of the higher overall life expectancy for females. But the quintiles are roughly comparable. The results are similar to the overall result in Figure 2 for the bottom four quintiles, with somewhat more of a decline in the second quintile for females. The top quintile is different, with males actually showing an improvement in the growth of life expectancy in the second period, while females do not. The increase in progress for male life expectancy in the top quintile is driven by high-income countries.[8]

---

[8] This includes Canada, France, Australia, Luxembourg, Belgium, Germany, New Zealand, and Kuwait.

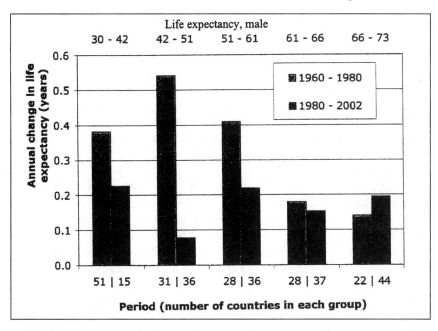

Figure 3. Life expectancy at birth (years), male. *Source:* World Bank, World Development Indicators, 2005.

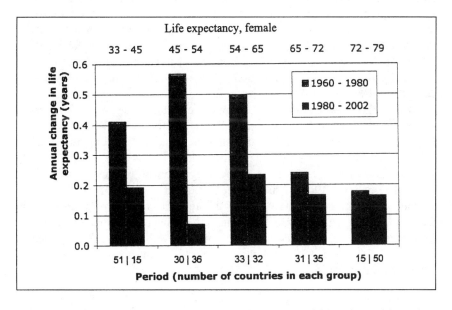

Figure 4. Life expectancy at birth (years), female. *Source:* World Bank, World Development Indicators, 2005.

Figures 5 and 6 show mortality rates for male and female adults, respectively.[9] These are arranged in the opposite direction from the previous charts, with the worst quintiles on the right. For both males and females, the bottom three quintiles show a noticeable reduction in the rate of progress during the second period. For the fourth quintile, with mortality rates between 270 and 415 per thousand for women and 342 and 498 per thousand for men, there is an actual increase in mortality of 3.4 per thousand and 2.6 per thousand annually, respectively, in the second period. The middle quintile for males also has an increase in mortality rates, as compared with an annual average 3.8 per thousand decrease per year during the first period.

For females, the second quintile, with mortality rates of 108 to 165 per thousand, also shows a decline from a 1.7 per thousand annual improvement in the first period to no improvement in the second period. Male mortality for the second quintile (195 to 250 per thousand) shows a slightly better reduction for the second period. In the top quintile, both males and females show improved progress on mortality. As with the data for life expectancy, this improvement is driven by the high-income countries in this quintile.

The trends in mortality are also heavily influenced by sub-Saharan Africa, where the HIV/AIDS crisis and armed conflict have greatly increased mortality. According to the UNDP (United Nations Development Program), the conflict in the eastern part of the Democratic Republic of the Congo has resulted in an estimated 3.8 million "excess deaths" from just 1998 to 2004, as compared with what would have occurred in the absence of war. But the decline in adult mortality for low- and middle-income countries is not determined by sub-Saharan Africa. If the sub-Saharan African countries are eliminated from the data set for Figure 4, the bottom two quintiles still show huge declines in the rate of improvement of mortality, with the middle quintile showing no change. And for the reasons described above, the sub-Saharan region should be included.

Figure 7 shows the data for mortality rates for children under five. This graph shows a declining rate of progress for all five quintiles, although the reduction in progress is relatively small in the top two quintiles. The biggest falloff is for countries in the worst quintile, with child mortality rates of 227 to 390 per thousand. The rate of progress—average annual reduction—falls from 5 per thousand for 1960–1980 to 3 per thousand for 1980–2002.[10] For this second period, the cumulative effect of this reduced progress is an increase in the child mortality rate of 44 per thousand, or more than the entire child mortality rate for the best quintile. The next two quintiles, with child mortality rates of 154 to 227 and 80 to 154 per thousand, also show much reduced progress in reducing child mortality.

---

[9] These mortality rates measure the probability of a 15-year-old dying before age 60 (in deaths per thousand).

[10] For World Development Indicators, February 2005, the last available year for these data is 2002.

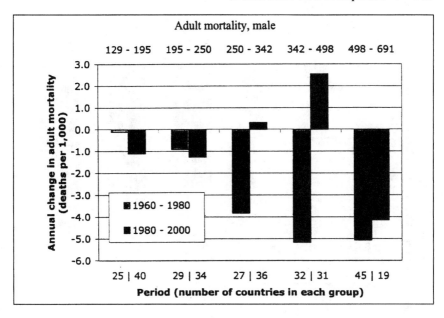

Figure 5. Adult mortality rate (per 1,000), male. *Source:* World Bank, World Development Indicators, 2005.

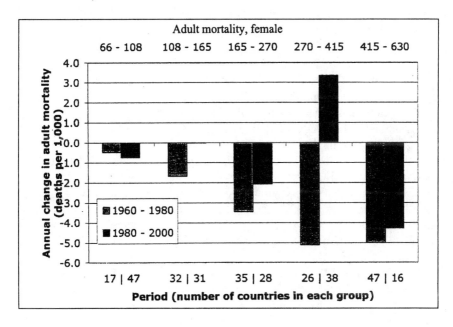

Figure 6. Adult mortality rate (per 1,000), female. *Source:* World Bank, World Development Indicators, 2005.

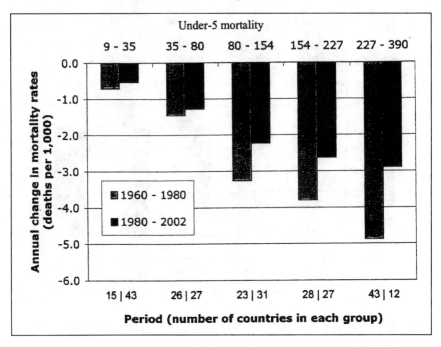

Figure 7. Mortality rate (per 1,000), under 5. *Source:* World Bank, World Development Indicators, 2005.

Figure 8 shows the decline in infant mortality rates for the two periods, arranged by quintiles. Once again, the reduction in progress is across the board. Even the top two quintiles, which are not influenced by sub-Saharan Africa, show declining progress for the 1980–2002 period. The sharpest falloff in the rate of progress is for the fourth quintile, where infant mortality fell by an average of 2.6 per thousand each year from 1960 to 1980, but only 1.3 per thousand from 1980 to 2002. For the period as a whole this means that the average country in this quintile has an infant mortality rate about 29 per thousand more than it would have had if the progress of the first period had continued. For a country at the midpoint of this quintile, say, 122 per thousand, this represents a 31 percent higher infant mortality relative to what could have been achieved just on the basis of past progress.

Summing up the data on health outcomes, there is a significant drop in the rate of progress for the vast majority of low- and middle-income countries. This is true for life expectancy, infant and child mortality, and adult mortality in the second period (since 1980) as compared with the first period (1960–1980). There are a few groups of countries that run counter to this result, but the overall trend is very clear.

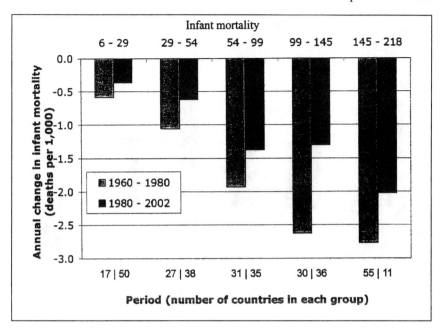

Figure 8. Mortality rate (per 1,000), infant. *Source:* World Bank, World Development Indicators, 2005.

REDUCED PROGRESS IN EDUCATION

Given the sharp slowdown in economic growth, it would not be surprising to find that public spending on education did not increase as much in the second period as in the first, and that is indeed the case. Figure 9 shows the average annual change in public spending on education for the two periods, as a percentage of GDP. There is a reduction in the rate of growth of education spending in all quintiles. For the middle quintile, for example, the rate of growth falls from 0.10 to 0.04 percentage points annually. This would make a difference of about 1.3 percent of GDP over a 20-year period—for illustration, for the United States today this would be $150 billion of education spending per year. The top quintile, with countries spending between 5 and 8 percent of GDP on education, shows an actual reduction of education spending during the second period. Some of this is undoubtedly due to demographics, as the higher-income countries especially experienced a reduction in the number of school-age children. However, this would be less of an explanation in countries that were not already spending a large percentage of their GDP on education. The slower rate of increase in public spending on education for the middle three groups is unlikely to be a result of just demographic changes.

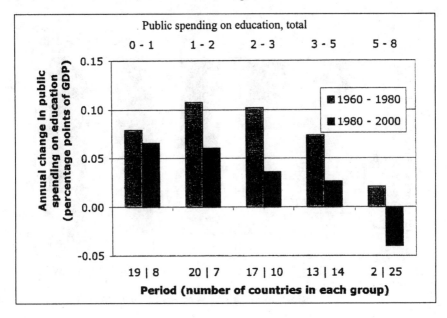

Figure 9. Public spending on education (as % of GDP), total. *Source:* World Bank, World Development Indicators, 2005.

Given the slowing growth in expenditures on public education, we would expect reduced progress in educational outcomes, unless there were large and widespread improvements in the efficiency of education. Figure 10 shows the average annual change in the percentage of students enrolled in primary school. This measures the number of students enrolled as a percentage of their age groups. It is possible for the number to exceed 100 percent, as in the top two quintiles, due to adults taking remedial or literacy classes. The bottom two quintiles show a noticeable decline in the rate of growth of primary school enrollment from the first to the second period. The middle quintile is nearly flat, and the second quintile (with enrollment between 98 and 108 percent) shows some improvement. The top quintile shows a faster rate of decline in the second period as compared with the first, but that is not necessarily harmful; for the higher-income countries, it could represent a reduction in the number of adults that need remedial primary education classes. Figures 11 and 12 look at the same changes in primary school enrollment broken down by gender, for male and female primary school students and school-age children. The overall changes are similar, although the levels of enrollment for females are lower than for males, reflecting a widespread gender bias in education that prevails in many developing countries.

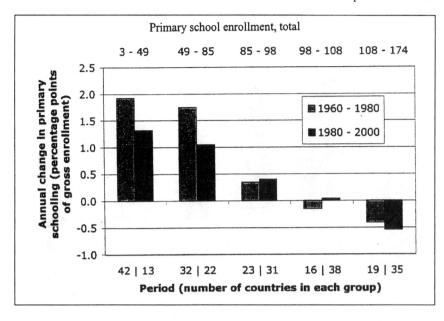

Figure 10. Primary school enrollment (%), total. *Source:* World Bank, World Development Indicators, 2005.

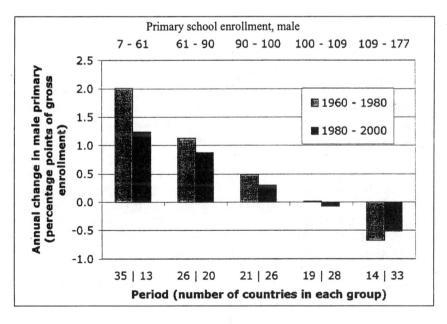

Figure 11. Primary school enrollment (%), male. *Source:* World Bank, World Development Indicators, 2005.

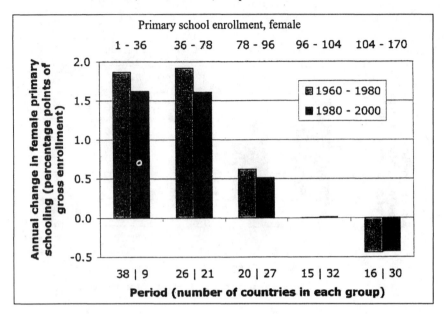

Figure 12. Primary school enrollment (%), female. *Source:* World Bank, World Development Indicators, 2005.

Figures 13, 14, and 15 show changes in secondary school enrollment overall, and for males and females. There is a decline in the rate of growth of secondary school enrollment—again as a percentage of the population in this age group—across all quintiles, from the first period to the second. The only exception is the bottom quintile for females, with an average enrollment of 0 to 4 percent, which is flat. Figure 16 shows the average annual changes in tertiary school enrollment, which is more mixed than the others. Only the fourth quintile, with just 1 to 3 percent of its population in tertiary education, shows reduced progress in the second period. The others are flat or show improvement, with the largest improvement in the second quintile (10–18 percent enrolled), which moves from a 0.7 to a 1.2 percentage point annual increase. Figure 17 shows the average annual percentage point change in literacy. The third and second quintiles, with literacy rates of 56 to 76 percent and 76 to 92 percent, respectively, show a slower rate of progress during the second period. The other quintiles are essentially the same for the two periods.

Summing up the data on education, most low- and middle-income countries made less progress since 1980 in increasing enrollment at the primary and secondary levels of education, as compared with the prior period (1960–1980). This was not true for tertiary education. Public spending on education also increased at a slower rate in the second period, and the rate of progress on literacy

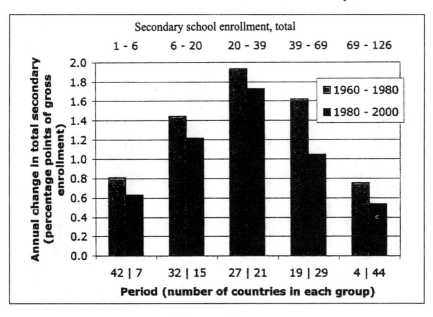

Figure 13. Secondary school enrollment (%), total. *Source:* World Bank, World Development Indicators, 2005.

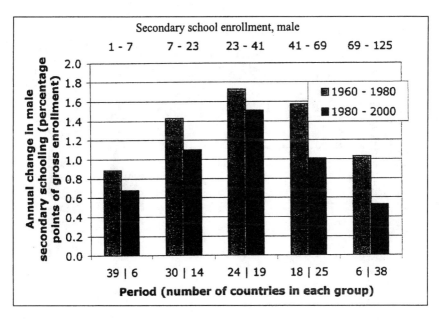

Figure 14. Secondary school enrollment (%), male. *Source:* World Bank, World Development Indicators, 2005.

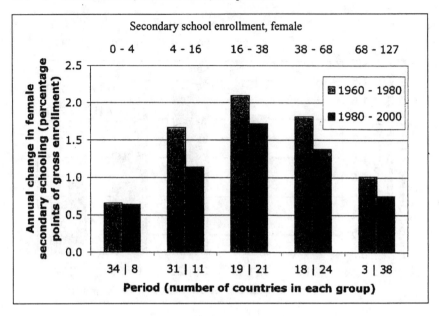

Figure 15. Secondary school enrollment (%), female. *Source:* World Bank, World Development Indicators, 2005.

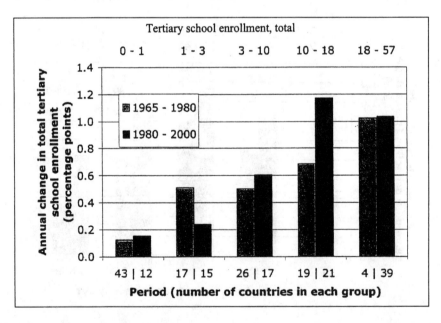

Figure 16. Tertiary school enrollment (%), total. *Source:* World Bank, World Development Indicators, 2005.

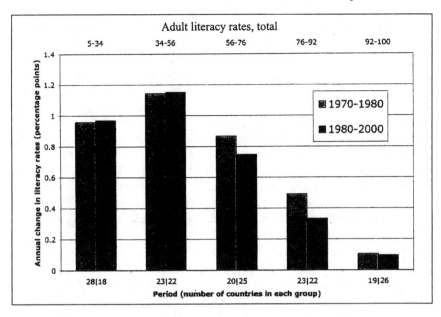

Figure 17. Literacy rates (%), adult total. *Source:* World Bank, World Development Indicators, 2005.

also slowed. This—together with the slowdown in economic growth—could explain the reduced progress for low- and middle-income countries on the educational front. The changes in measures of educational progress are not as pronounced as indicators of health outcomes, or of economic growth, but they are overwhelmingly in the same direction, showing reduced progress since 1980.

EXCEPTIONS: CHINA AND INDIA

A few countries have actually grown much faster since 1980 than in prior decades. Among them are China and India, the world's two most populous countries—China now has 1.3 billion people and India about a billion. Since these countries have adopted some "globalizing" or "liberalizing" reforms over the past 25 years, it is sometimes argued on the basis of these countries' experiences that the overall set of reforms implemented by low- and middle-income countries worldwide has been a success.

There are two arguments here. First, since these two countries contain close to half of the entire population of the developing world, if we look at people rather than countries, the policy changes of the past quarter-century have succeeded. The problem with this argument is that if we are looking at policy changes, we need to look at countries. Individuals do not control the investment, trade, interest rate, budget, and other economic policies that affect their ability to make a living. It is their governments that make these choices. But if a set of policy reforms is implemented over a long period of time in 80 or 90 countries, and only a few show higher growth rates—and the vast majority show slower, and often drastically slower, growth—this provides at least a *prima facie* case that the reforms have failed. This is true even if those few success stories happen to be countries with a lot of people. The other argument is that a few success stories demonstrate that the reforms can work, if only they are correctly implemented. It is possible that all the other countries did not implement them fully enough, or in the right way. One of the World Bank's answers to skeptics has been to group countries into "globalizers" and "non-globalizers" and show that the globalizers have grown faster over the past decade or so. The globalizers were the countries that showed the most rapid increase in trade as a percentage of their economies (5).

But even if it were true that some set of "globalizing" countries—that is, the ones that correctly implemented a set of liberalizing reforms—could be found to do better than the rest during the past 25 years, it would still not explain the long-term drop in the average rate of growth for the period. In Latin America, for example, Chile is the only country that has grown at a faster rate over the past quarter-century than it did previously.[11] Whatever Chile did that was successful, this would not explain why the past 25 years have been such a disaster for Latin America. It is simply not plausible to argue that Chile is the only country in the region that carried through the recommended reforms far enough to achieve benefits. If the nature of the reforms is such that anything less than full implementation leads to sacrifice without gain, and the political obstacles are so great that few countries can attain this level of reform, then most countries would probably be making the right decision by not attempting to follow the reform path. A handful of success stories cannot explain the sharp slowdown in economic growth in the vast majority of low- and middle-income countries.

China has been most often cited as a globalization or liberalization success story, including trade and investment liberalization. And indeed, since 1980 it has had one of the fastest growing economies in world history: GDP per person grew by an incredible average of 7.15 percent, increasing sixfold in 25 years to become the second largest economy in the world. But it did so under a set of economic policies strikingly different from the reforms implemented in the vast majority of low- and middle-income countries.

First, China did not liberalize its trade in most goods until it could compete in those areas in world markets. As late as 1992 its average tariff was still more than 40 percent, about four times the level that Latin America had in 1974, before

---

[11] This is mostly since 1990; the Chilean economy grew by more than 60 percent per capita in the 1990s.

liberalization there. To the extent that trade liberalization contributed to China's growth, it may be because it was done carefully so as not to disrupt existing production—unlike the indiscriminate opening up to imports that was adopted in many other countries. In fact China's transition to a mixed economy—with increasing use of markets—was carried out gradually and carefully. There were pilot projects, Special Economic Zones (in the 1980s) to experiment with foreign capital and technology, and gradual liberalization of prices. All this was deliberately designed so as to be able to correct mistakes and expand upon successes, a logical thing to do when policymakers are entering uncharted territory. As late as 1996, state-owned and collective enterprises accounted for 75 percent of urban employment; even today, 25 years into China's economic transition, they still account for more than one-third of urban jobs (6). This stands in sharp contrast to the "shock therapy," massive and rapid privatization, and rapid decontrol of prices that led to an economic collapse and loss of nearly half of Russia's GDP in five years. That China has been able to manage its transition without any such setbacks—and, by contrast, with record-breaking economic growth over a 25-year period—is a compelling example of how important economic policy decisions can be.

Even today, China's banking system is dominated by four state-owned banks, which have more than 60 percent of the nation's deposits, assets, and credit. Foreign influence in the financial system is minimal. And even after the recent revaluation of the Chinese renminbi, which included some changes to allow more flexibility in its peg to the dollar, foreign currency flows remain strictly controlled.

Foreign direct investment in China has soared from $19 billion in 1990 to more than $53 billion annually today,[12] and it has certainly contributed to China's growth. But even here the government has had a very big role in shaping and directing this investment, and approving investments that would fit in with the country's development goals. These include such priorities as producing for export markets, a high level of technology (with the goal of transferring technology from foreign enterprises to the domestic economy), hiring local residents for managerial and technical jobs, and not competing with certain domestic industries. China's policy toward foreign investment has therefore been directly opposed to the major worldwide reforms of recent decades, including the rules of the World Trade Organization; the same is also true in the important area of intellectual property.

In short, China's economic success over the past quarter-century cannot simply be summed up, as it so often is, as an example of the success of the overall package of reforms that most developing countries have adopted over the past 25 years. The same is true for India, which is a less spectacular but still important exception

---

[12] World Bank, World Development Indicators, 2005 (2003 data for foreign direct investment).

to the general slowdown of growth after 1980. The Indian economy has grown by an average of 3.8 percent annually, per capita, from 1980 to 2005—more than double the 1.6 percent annual rate from 1960 to 1980. But it is difficult to attribute this transformation to "globalizing" reforms. As in China, the big increase in economic growth in India took place more than a decade before liberalization began: India's growth took off in 1980; the liberalizing reforms did not begin until 1991. Tariff revenue, measured as a share of imports or GDP, actually increased significantly during the 1980s, as did other measures of trade protection. Similarly, trade in India increased several times faster in the 1990s than it did in the 1980s. Beginning in 1991, the government embarked upon a rapid reduction of trade barriers, privatization, some deregulation of financial markets, measures to encourage foreign direct investment, and other reforms. But growth did not increase over its 1980s rate. So while there is plenty of room for debate over what caused India to increase its growth rate at a time when most developing countries were moving in the opposite direction, the 1990s reforms do not look like the main answer (7). India's success story also included such non-orthodox policies as strict currency controls. Even after the liberalization of the 1990s, India retained a higher level of protection for its domestic markets than most other developing countries.

CONCLUSION: WHAT WENT WRONG?

The past quarter-century has seen a sharp decline in the rate of growth for the vast majority of low- and middle-income countries. Accompanying this decline has been reduced progress for almost all of the social indicators that are available to measure health and educational outcomes.[13] The methodology of this study precludes the possibility that this reduced economic and social progress was a result of "diminishing returns"—that is, the increased difficulty of progressing at the same rate from a higher level. It is therefore likely that at least some of the policy changes that have been widely implemented over the past 25 years have contributed to this long-term growth and development failure. In some of the financial and economic crises that took place in the late 1990s—for example, in East Asia, Russia, and Argentina—it seems clear that policy mistakes contributed to severe economic losses (8, 9).

But it is generally difficult to show a clear relationship between any particular policy change and economic outcomes, especially across countries. Many changes take place at the same time, and causality is difficult to establish. It is certainly possible that the decline in economic and social progress that has taken place

[13] It is worth noting the limited basis of the comparisons used in this analysis. In particular, it would have been desirable to measure national performances on a variety of environmental measures. Unfortunately, there are no widely available sets of data for most countries on these measures; if such data could be assembled, this would be an important part of a more complete evaluation of the progress of the past quarter-century.

over the past 25 years would have been even worse in the absence of the policy changes that were adopted. But that remains to be demonstrated. In the meantime, a long-term failure of the type documented here should at the very least shift the burden of proof to those who maintain that the major policy changes of the past 25 years have raised living standards in the majority of developing countries, and encourage skepticism with regard to economists or institutions who believe they have found a formula for economic growth and development. Indeed, some economists have recently concluded that more "policy autonomy"—the ability of countries to make their own decisions about economic policy—is needed for developing countries.[14] Most importantly, the outcome of the past quarter-century should have economists and policymakers thinking about what has gone wrong.

Acknowledgments — Egor Kraev, Luis Sandoval, Dan Beeton, Ji Hee Kim, Jamie Strawbridge, and Nihar Bhatt provided research assistance for this chapter.

REFERENCES

1. De Rato, R. (Managing Director of IMF). *Financial Times,* September 14, 2005.
2. Dollar, D., and Kraay, A. *Growth is Good for the Poor.* World Bank, Washington, DC, 2000.
3. United Nations Development Program. *Human Development Report,* pp. 64–71. New York, 2005.
4. World Bank. *Global Development Finance,* tables A4.2 and A4.3, p. 186. World Bank, Washington, DC, 2002.
5. Dollar, D., and Kraay, A. *Trade Growth, and Poverty.* World Bank, Washington, DC, June 2001.
6. Prasad, E. (ed.). *China's Growth and Integration into the World Economy.* International Monetary Fund, Washington, DC, 2004.
7. Rodrik, D., and Subramanian, A. *From Hindu Growth to Productivity Surge: The Mystery of the Indian Growth Transition.* March 2004.
8. Radelet, S., and Sachs, J. *The East Asian Financial Crisis: Diagnosis, Remedies, Prospects.* Harvard Institute for International Development, Cambridge, MA, April 1998.
9. Cibils, A. B., Weisbrot, M., and Kar, D. *Argentina Since Default: The IMF and the Depression.* Center for Economic and Policy Research, Washington, DC, September 2002.
10. Birdsall, N., Rodrik, D., and Subramanian, A. How to help poor countries. *Foreign Affairs* 84(4):136–152, 2005.

[14] This is the conclusion of Birdsall and colleagues (10). With regard to China, the authors ask rhetorically, "Would China have been better off implementing a garden-variety World Bank structural adjustment program in 1978 instead of its own brand of heterodox gradualism?"

CHAPTER 8

The World Health Situation

Vicente Navarro

Analyses of the most important public health issues in today's world show that the greatest problem facing the world population is famine. According to a recent report on children's health, 10 million children die each year, most of them because of starvation and malnutrition (1, 2). This number of deaths is equivalent to 25 Hiroshima bombs exploding every year—and they explode without producing a sound. As a matter of fact, these deaths are so much a part of everyday reality that they do not appear on the front page, or even on the last page, of any prominent newspaper in Europe or the United States. Meanwhile, every two seconds, a child dies of hunger.

The paradox of this reality is that the world has enough food to feed the human population many times over. Let's not forget that the governments of the European Union and the United States are paying farmers not to produce food. Even countries where the majority of people are hungry have enough productive land to feed their populations many times over. According to a recent study, for example, Bangladesh, a country where hunger is endemic, has enough productive land to feed five times its population (3; see also 4). And this is true for most countries where hunger is endemic.

WHY DO WE HAVE THIS SITUATION?

The reason for this state of affairs is the huge concentration of economic, political, social, and cultural power in the world today. The world order—or, better, world disorder—is characterized by a massive concentration of economic, political, and cultural power. As is widely known, a very few countries in the North control or have a major influence over the world's economic, political, and cultural resources. This does not mean, however, that the primary division in today's world is between the North and the South. This idea of a North-South division, constantly reproduced in the documents of U.N. agencies, is wrong, or at least seriously deficient. The Human Development Reports of the U.N. Development Program (UNDP) year after year publish the social status of the world populations, contrasting the amount of money spent by people in the North on taking care of their pets, for example, with the amount spent on food for children in the South. This type of presentation and analysis, besides making people of the North feel guilty, gives the wrong impression that the problem of famine among children in the South could be solved by transferring the funds of those in the North, saved by not feeding their pets, to those in the South, to feed their children. This analysis is naively apolitical and wrong. It is important to stress, again, that the problem of the South is not a lack of resources. The South has enough resources to feed a population many times its size.

The North-South dichotomy ignores the fact that the distribution of economic, political, and social resources is highly concentrated both in the North and in the South. The North has dominant classes and groups and races, as well as a dominant gender, and dominated classes, groups, races, and gender. The same is true in the South: there are dominant and dominated classes, groups, races, and gender in the South as well. Let's not forget that 20 percent of the richest persons in the world live in the South. We can see, for example, that while most populations in the Arab nations are extremely poor, the sheikhs live in opulence.

The world order (or disorder) is based on *an alliance primarily between the dominant classes and groups in the North and the dominant classes and groups in the South against a redistribution of resources that would adversely affect their interests.* The evidence for this is overwhelming (5).

HOW IS THIS SITUATION REPRODUCED?

Within this context, what is the pattern of influences on the world today, including on the health sector? I believe the evidence is very strong: the economic, political, and health establishments of the North, and most especially of the United States (including its federal agencies, foundations, and leading academic institutions), have an enormous influence in shaping the culture, discourse, practices, and policies of the western world, including its international agencies such as the International Monetary Fund (IMF), the World Bank, the World Trade Organization (WTO), the World Health Organization (WHO), and the Pan American Health Organization (PAHO). Dominant ideologies in establishment circles in developed countries (and, again, very much in particular in the United States) appear, for example, in WHO documents shortly after they appear in U.S. "mainstream" medical and economics journals. The latest example of this situation is the document evaluating countries' health systems (*Health Systems: Improving Performance;* 6), prepared by the WHO two years ago (see 7 for a critique of that report). This is a heavily ideological document, reproducing the dominant ideology that has existed in the United States, and to a lesser degree in the United Kingdom, since the 1980s. Since the Reagan administration, managed competition, privatization, and commodification of health services are the name of the game in health policy circles in the United States (and also, since the Thatcher period, in those of the United Kingdom). The administrations of Presidents Reagan, Bush senior, Clinton, and Bush junior in the United States, and of Prime Ministers Thatcher, Major, and Blair in the United Kingdom, have been pushing for the privatization and commodification of medicine. This discourse and practice (such as "clients" rather than patients, health care "markets" rather than planning) has appeared and become dominant in medical and health establishments throughout the world, including the IMF, World Bank, WHO, and PAHO. The introduction of markets and profits in medicine is *in;* national health services are *out.* In the WHO report on health systems, Colombia (which has replaced its national health service with market-determined private health insurance) is rated one of the top countries in Latin America, and Cuba one of the worst. Today, one of the authors of that report—a recent candidate for the post of WHO director-general—is trying to implement an HMO insurance health care system in Mexico, and the other author is promoting the excellence of managed competition in Cambridge, England. We recently saw an article in *The Lancet* in which none other than the editor-in-chief of the WHO report (who resigned in disgust) denounced the manipulation of data to reach the conclusions published in that report (8).

Let me stress that while managed competition, privatization, and for-profit medicine are fashionable doctrine with the U.S. establishment, they are *not* popular at the street level in the United States. The majority of people profoundly dislike insurance companies. Poll after poll confirms this. You may have seen the movie *John Q* (which in the United States means "average citizen"). When the main character in the movie—a blue-collar worker—curses the for-profit health insurance companies, the audiences in many U.S. movie theaters applauded. They clearly hold the private, for-profit health insurance–dominated system responsible for the situation of working people in the United States, where 44 million people lack any form of health insurance and 52 million have insufficient insurance. As I said before, what is pushed forward by the establishments of the North (and their allies in the South) is not the best for the average people of either the North or the South.

ANOTHER EXAMPLE:
NEOLIBERALISM IN THE HEALTH SECTOR

Another consequence of this pattern of influence and control is the reduction of public social expenditures as part of *structural adjustment programs*—sold for many years by the U.S. government and by the international agencies (the IMF and World Bank) over which that government has a huge influence. Structural adjustment programs, with their social austerity policies, have done a lot of damage to the infrastructure of health services in developing countries. Actually, we are also witnessing the application of structural adjustment policies by the

Bush administration in the United States, with great harm to the U.S. population. These policies are also being followed by the German, French, and Italian governments, and they are harming their populations. And in the United States we have an administration that is dramatically cutting federal health expenditures, transferring funds from the health and social sectors to the military sector. Never before have there been so many people in the United States without health insurance. The public sectors are deteriorating rapidly—all done, in theory, to defend the country against terrorism. In practice, however, this is being done to carry out specific class, race, and gender policies aimed at defending class, race, gender, and imperialist purposes.

Also, let me clarify that at a time when even progressive forces have stopped using the word "imperialism," the Bush administration itself, and intellectuals close to it, are proudly using this term. As Michael Ignatieff, Professor of Human Rights at Harvard University and advisor to the Bush administration, said recently, "Imperialism historically has had a bad name. But, although it is politically incorrect to say it, imperialism, as the white burden to expand civilization, continues to be needed" (9). It is most disappointing that, although for a while it looked as if the European Union would oppose such policies, finally it seems to have caved in, allowing the U.S. government to develop an imperial role, parading itself as the defender of human rights, apparently oblivious of the fact that the United States has never signed the U.N. Declaration of Human Rights and does not guarantee its citizens the basic human right of access to health care in time of need. The U.S. government has no credibility in its self-proclaimed role as defender of human rights. And most of the world population, including most of the U.S. population, knows it. Poll after poll in the United States shows that, by an overwhelming majority, U.S. citizens and residents consider the federal government as representative not of their interests, but rather of the interests of specific economic and financial institutions that fund and shape the political process to suit their objectives. The current Bush administration provides confirmation that the U.S. majority's perception of its government is quite accurate—a perception that, according to a recent Pew Foundation International poll, is also widely held among the populations of the western and eastern world (10). Energy, construction, military, insurance, and pharmaceutical interests shape the international and domestic policies of the federal government today. Witness the enormous and successful pressure by the U.S. government to defend the financial interests of the pharmaceutical industry at the cost of letting millions of people in developing countries go without treatment for deadly diseases. It is true that some trade agreements have, finally, been reached on that front, but they are very late and very insufficient.

Yet another example of U.S. influence is policies advocated by the WTO that may force countries with national health services to dismantle these services in order to allow the operation of commercial health insurance companies or medical-business corporations.

In both instances, the WHO, through its collaboration with other international agencies, has been an active participant in the promotion of such policies. The WHO has submerged itself in a type of cultural and ideological environment in which privatization, deregulation, and marketization are common recommendations. Another example is the recent report, from a group chaired by Jeffrey Sachs (the same economist who advised on Russian policies of privatization, and the main economic advisor at Davos), on health development (11)—a report well criticized by Professor Banerji, of India, in the *International Journal of Health Services* (12) and by Professor Waitzkin, of the United States, in the *Lancet* (13). In the WHO report, health investments seem to be evaluated in terms of their contribution to economic development, instead of, as it should be, the other way round.

Actually, the WHO itself has privatized several of its services. One example, among many: WHO-EURO chose to establish its European Primary Health Care Study Center in Catalonia, Spain, because the conservative Catalan regional government offered the most funds, competing successfully with other regional governments that have done a much better job in developing regional public primary health care center networks. Needless to say, the Catalan regional government presented Catalonia as the best site for such a center in recognition of its "excellent" primary health care center network, when actually this network is one of the worst in Spain. This privatization of WHO activities, with the selling of the WHO trademark, is not uncommon.

THE CATEGORICAL VERSUS THE COMPREHENSIVE APPROACH

Another example of influence by the establishments of the North is the emphasis on categorical interventions (a disease-by-disease approach) that weaken the infrastructure of public health services, including national health services. Based on that experience, the eradication of smallpox is a mixed achievement, since its success has inspired many other technical silver-bullet-type solutions that degrade rather than improve countries' public health situations. Professor Banerji has extensively documented the damage caused by such categorical interventions (e.g., 14–16). The pressure from donor agencies to resolve specific disease problems is so overwhelming that most governments cave in and accept programs that have a devastating effect on the health services of their countries. In fact, a similar situation is happening in the United States today, where the smallpox vaccination campaign (part of the highly political anti-bioterrorist campaign, instrumentalized by the Bush administration) is considerably weakening the country's public health services, which are being forced to shift resources to this campaign. As Stephen Cohen put it so clearly in an article in the *Boston Globe,* "we are seeing a seismic shift of priorities that is roiling public health agencies across the nation" (17). School health programs, for example, are being dramatically reduced, while anthrax programs (only five Americans have died in anthrax attacks) have received billions of dollars.

Finally, there is a constant reproduction of the priorities of the developed capitalist countries in the developing ones, ignoring important problems such as famine, which continues to be the primary problem in today's world.

THE ROOTS OF THE PROBLEM

It would be erroneous, however, to put all the blame on the establishments of the countries of the North. The establishments of the developing countries share a large part of the blame. Usually forgotten is that underdevelopment is rooted not only in international power relations but also in the power relations existing within the developing counties—that is, the class and other power relations in those countries. I had the great privilege of being health advisor to the Allende government in Chile. And the fascist coup in Chile, which interrupted major health, social, and economic reforms, was not the imposition by the North (United States) on the South (Chile) of a military dictatorship. Rather, it was the Chilean dominant classes and the Chilean armed forces that stopped the reforms, with the assistance not of the United States but of the U.S. government, whose president, Richard Nixon, was extremely unpopular in the United States. Helping to finance that coup was the pharmaceutical industry, which opposed the health care reforms of the Allende government. The roots of the problem, then, were the dominant classes in Chile that stopped those reforms (with the assistance of the U.S. government and powerful economic groups of the North). This is the point that needs to be stressed: the roots of the problem are to be found in the developing countries themselves—in the patterns of class control over governments, assisted by governments of the North that are heavily influenced by their own dominant classes and dominant economic groups.

The solution, therefore, cannot be the replacement of consultants, academics, or international civil servants of the Northern establishments by their counterparts from the South. We have seen professionals from developing countries directing many international agencies that, while using a more radical discourse, have not behaved very differently in practice. Sometimes they have done even worse.

THE NEED FOR CHANGE

Contrary to what is usually assumed, the solutions to the problems we encounter in the world are not difficult solutions from the scientific point of view. Analyzing the situations in the world, we could easily find the solutions: to empower the dominated populations—the popular classes (in both the North and the South)—to make their governments responsive to their needs. We have enough experience to know how this can be done. And within that new order, the WHO should be a technical agency that supports such empowerment. Part of that support would be the criticism and denunciation of those dominant groups and classes (in both North and South) that, through the governments they so strongly influence, reproduce their interests. We have seen many occasions in which the WHO has failed to stand up to powerful governments and interests whose practices have interfered with the health of populations.

While the solution is easy to see, its application within the pattern of power relations in both the North and the South is very difficult indeed. Difficult, however, doesn't mean impossible. Sometimes, more important than the speed of change is the direction of change. And one direction is to recover many principles and practices that have already proved their worth. On that road we should be guided by the splendid philosophy underlying the WHO Constitution. Let's not forget that the WHO was established after World War II, a victorious war against fascism and Nazism. That war had been fought for a better world, and people all over the world wanted a healthy life for themselves and their children. This is the context in which the WHO Constitution was written—drafted, incidentally, under the influence of public health professionals such as Karl Ewang of Norway, John Brotherston of Scotland, Serg Stampa of Yugoslavia, and others whom I have had the great pleasure of knowing. Karl and John were my teachers in my early years.

The WHO Constitution should guide our work. Some conservatives and liberals have commented that this document is now very old; but something can be antique without being antiquated. The law of gravity is extremely old but not antiquated. And if you doubt it, jump from the fourth floor.

Other documents that continue to be extremely relevant are the Willy Brandt report and the Alma-Ata declaration. They are as urgent, needed, and valuable today as when they first appeared. The Alma-Ata declaration was a positive step (the result of a very different political context) toward responding to the world's needs—though now, of course, it should certainly be updated. But the philosophy behind it is still highly relevant. We have to recover that holistic, comprehensive view of health, in which the merit of an intervention is not evaluated by its contribution to economic growth but rather the reverse: the merit of an economic policy is measured primarily or even exclusively by its impact on the health and welfare of the population.

Some solutions: a health option that enables the empowerment of populations, facilitating their active participation in the shaping of their societies; a health system in which resources are allocated according to need and funds are obtained according to the ability of people to contribute; a health system linked to redistributive policies within each country and between countries—complemented by full-employment policies that ensure adults have the right to satisfactory work in an environment-friendly system of production and distribution, guided by public interventions and regulations. The enormous distance between these solutions (all of them easily doable) and the possibility of achieving them tells us much about the extreme political difficulties we still face.

There are positive signs, however, that the distance between the desired and the feasible can be reduced. We have seen the powerful IMF, World Bank, and WTO being put on the defensive by the anti-globalization movement. I believe that movement will not stop. We also need to put the WHO, and even the UNDP, on the defensive as well, since they are becoming part of the problem rather than the solution. Witness, for example, the UNDP's most recent *Human Development Report* (written by Jeffrey Sachs; 18) in which, once again, there is a clear contradiction between the scandalous situation of the world it documents and the very mild solutions it advocates—moderate to an extreme, so as not to offend the dominant forces that shape the international and national policies responsible for the situation it documents. If you read this report you will not find even a single use of the word "exploitation" or a single recommendation about redistributing resources within and between countries. Quite remarkable!

A FINAL OBSERVATION ON
THE NORTH-SOUTH RELATIONSHIP

While I believe the North-South relationship needs to change profoundly (bilateral "aid" should be discontinued and replaced with multinational transfers, for example), I still feel that the Northern academic institutions could be helpful. They have a wealth of knowledge and practice that can be very useful, if transferable. It is essential to realize, however, that scientific knowledge carries with it the vision and values of the scientific institutions in the countries where it is based, and this vision and these values can be harmful to the populations of the developing countries. Actually, there is a widespread failure to appreciate the extreme dependency of the U.S. academic establishment on the financial and corporate interests that shape and determine the research and tenure policies of the leading universities in the United States, and this dependency preempts any possibility of building a scholarship critical of the U.S. establishment. Europeans are unaware of the enormous limitations on academic freedom in U.S. universities (see Chapter 12 in this volume). Research is aimed at the needs of the U.S. establishment, reproducing its values and discourse.

The consequences of this state of affairs are many. You may have noticed, for example, how under the current Bush administration the term "health inequalities" has been replaced by the supposedly less conflictive term "health disparities," and "hunger" by being "underweight." And as usual, these terms have now become the fashionable ones, along with others such as "social capital" and "human capital," the keywords in current discourse, to an absurd extent. In a recent WHO report (19), for example, the most important problem in the world today is defined as being "underweight"—as if hunger and starvation are simply a weight problem.

I don't want to suggest, of course, that the knowledge derived from leading academic institutions in the United States is all-harmful. Far from it. But that knowledge needs to be channeled through multinational arrangements and institutions that screen the applications of that knowledge.

Also, "North" and "South" must be redefined to encourage relationships between the dominated groups and classes of both North and South. I had the great privilege of being invited by U.S. labor unions of the AFL-CIO to Seattle, where the anti-globalization movement started. The movement was not against globalization, but rather against the neoliberal criteria that the WTO wanted to impose in order to guide the process. In that movement, trade unions, ecological movements, and other social movements from both North and South mobilized together against the WTO's neoliberal rules. The WHO and the foundations should facilitate these international networks, offering resources and/or support. Let's not forget that the WHO is a pulpit that constantly delivers messages. It would be good if the WHO would put forth messages that support these movements, even though that support may be unwelcome in the establishments of the North and South. After all, the discomfort of these establishments might be an indicator that the WHO is on the right track.

Finally, the WHO should require each country, as a condition for membership, to provide health information as well as demonstrate a respect for human and health rights, and should denounce those countries, including the United States, that do not abide by the WHO Constitution. It rarely does that, but it should.

I am aware that this presentation is just a brief sketch of an analysis that should be enriched with the nuances of each case and each situation. Reality is always more complex than it looks, and thus all summaries may appear too simple. But as one of my teachers, Gunnar Myrdal, told me many years ago, "To be simple is not to be simplistic. In the course of your work, you will find out that behind what appears to be very complex and difficult to comprehend, there are fairly simple realities, easy to capture if you just pay attention to them." My 40 years of work on matters of development and underdevelopment have proved my teacher absolutely right. This is what I have tried to do today—to focus on the underlying realities in order to change them.

Note — This chapter is based on the opening speech delivered at the Sixth IUHPE European Conference on Health Promotion and Education, in Perugia, Italy, June 18, 2003.

REFERENCES

1. Black, R. E., Morris, S. S., and Bryce, T. Where and why are 10 million children dying every year? *Lancet* 361:2226–2233, 2003.
2. Drèze, J., Sen, A., and Hussain, A. *The Political Economy of Hunger.* Oxford University Press, Oxford, 1995.
3. *The Malnutrition Problem in Bangladesh.* The Social Policy Program, Paper No. 34. Johns Hopkins University, Baltimore, 2003.
4. Yong Kim, T., et al. *Dying for Growth: Global Inequality and the Health of the Poor.* Common Courage Press, Monroe, ME, 2000.

5. Navarro, V. (ed.). *The Political Economy of Social Inequalities: Consequences for Health and Quality of Life.* Baywood, Amityville, NY, 2002.
6. World Health Organization. *World Health Report 2000: Health System—Improving Performance.* Geneva, 2000.
7. Navarro, V. Assessment of the World Health Report 2000. *Lancet* 356:1598–1601, 2000.
8. Musgrove, P. Judging health systems: Reflections on WHO's methods. *Lancet* 361:1817–1820, 2003.
9. Ignatieff, M. Nation-building lite. *New York Times Magazine,* July 28, 2002.
10. Pew Foundation. *International Attitudes Towards the U.S.* June 2003.
11. World Health Organization. *Report of the Commission on Macroeconomics and Health: Macroeconomics and Health—Investing in Health for Economic Development.* Geneva, 2001.
12. Banerji, D. Report of the WHO Commission on Macroeconomics and Health: A critique. *Int. J. Health Serv.* 32:733–754, 2002.
13. Waitzkin, H. Report of the WHO Commission on Macroeconomics and Health: A summary and critique. *Lancet* 361:523–526, 2003.
14. Banerji, D. Crash of the immunization program: Consequences of a totalitarian approach. *Int. J. Health Serv.* 20:501–510, 1990.
15. Banerji, D. *Serious Implications of the Proposed Revised National Tuberculosis Control Programme for India.* Voluntary Health Association of India and the Nucleus for Health Policies and Programmes, New Delhi, 1996.
16. Banerji, D. A fundamental shift in the approach to international health by WHO, UNICEF, and the World Bank. *Int. J. Health Serv.* 29:227–259, 1999.
17. *Boston Globe,* July 29, 2003.
18. United Nations Development Program. *Human Development Report 2002.* Oxford University Press, New York, 2002.
19. World Health Organization. *Report on World Wide Priorities.* Geneva, 2003.

PART V

European Integration and Its Consequences for Health and Quality of Life

Economic Efficiency versus Social Equality? The U.S. Liberal Model versus The European Social Model

Vicente Navarro and John Schmitt

I. THE ECONOMIC EFFICIENCY OF THE LIBERAL MODEL (U.S.) VERSUS THE SOCIAL MODEL (E.U.)[1]

Is It Valid to Compare the Economic Efficiency of the United States and the European Union?

One of the most influential positions reproduced in economic, financial, and political liberal circles on both sides of the Atlantic is that there is an intrinsic conflict between economic *efficiency* and *reduction of inequality*. As proof of this position, liberal authors hold up the United States as an example of economic *efficiency* (with high economic growth and low unemployment), assumed to have been achieved by tolerating levels of social inequality (the United States has the highest level of income inequality in the Organization for Economic Cooperation and Development) that the European Union would not accept. The low economic growth and high unemployment of the European Union are considered to be a consequence of an excessive concern with equality, a concern that is evident in the European Union's extensive welfare states and its highly regulated labor markets. This idea of a trade-off in *efficiency* and *equality* is almost dogma today in many liberal circles.

As with many dogmas, however, this liberal dogma is reproduced more by faith than by evidence. But before we present the evidence that questions such a trade-off, we should make some observations about a reality that is frequently ignored in comparisons between the United States and the European Union. The first observation is that, when we compare the United States with the

---

[1] This section relies heavily on Navarro and Schmitt (1).

European Union, we are not comparing apples with apples but, rather, apples with oranges. The United States is a federal state with a federal government that has its own economic, social, and fiscal policies. The European Union, however, is primarily an aggregate of 15 nations/states (E.U.-15; recently increased to 25), each with its own economic, social, and fiscal policies. Therefore, to compare the United States with the European Union is not a rigorous project from a scientific point of view. The differences between the United States and the European Union are enormous. To start with, the U.S. federal structure differs substantially from the institutions of government of the European Union. Moreover, the federal government manages 19 percent of the U.S. GNP (gross national product; total U.S. public expenditures represent 30 percent of GNP), enabling the federal government to intervene actively in the management of the economy. (Contrary to what is assumed by many liberal authors, the U.S. federal government is enormously interventionist, shaping large components of research and development in its economy, to mention just one example.) This federal interventionism also allows for active correction of the regional inequalities that exist in the United States.

The European Union, however, does not have a federal government. The "E.U. budget" controlled by the E.U. Commission controls only 1.27 percent of the entire European GNP—a dramatically insufficient amount to have any impact as a stimulant for economic growth or as a corrective for regional inequalities within the European Union, regional inequalities that are, incidentally, much larger in the European Union than in the United States. The unemployment rate differentials between the U.S. regions with highest unemployment and those with lowest unemployment are much lower (7.0 percent in the state with the highest unemployment vs. 3.2 percent in the state with the lowest unemployment) than in the European Union (32 percent vs. 3.8 percent).

Another major institutional difference between the United States and the European Union is the pattern of influences and functions of U.S. institutions versus E.U. institutions. The U.S. Central Bank (the Federal Reserve Board) has a different objective and modus operandi than the European Central Bank, a difference we will expand upon later. These and many other institutional differences greatly limit the comparisons that can be made of the economic efficiency of the U.S. model versus the E.U. model, limitations that become even more apparent when the assumed differences in economic efficiency between the two continents are attributed—as they are by liberal authors—to differences in their labor markets or in the extent of their welfare states, while ignoring the institutional differences that are of paramount importance.

Based on these observations, it would be more reasonable and logical to compare U.S. economic efficiency with the economic efficiency of national states in Europe such as Germany, France, and Italy, among others, or with the Scandinavian countries. If that were done, it could be shown that governments such as those of the Scandinavian countries (which have been governed for long periods of time since World War II by political parties belonging to the social democratic traditions and which have followed policies opposite to liberal ones) have overseen higher levels of well-being and quality of life of their populations and have been more efficient economically (with greater competitiveness) than the United States. Even the liberal World Economic Forum (also known as the Davos Forum) has recognized (in its latest Report on Competitiveness) these Scandinavian countries as among the most competitive in the OECD (Finland ranked number 1; Sweden, 3; Denmark, 5; Norway, 6; Iceland, 10). Based on these data, it would seem that the logical place for the European Union to look for an economic model should not be to the United States but, rather, to the Scandinavian countries.

Which Has Had Higher Economic Growth:
The United States or the E.U.-15?

The slow economic growth of the E.U.-15 versus the high economic growth of the United States is a constant reference point in liberal discourse. As proof of the major economic efficiency of the United States, liberal authors cite the rate of growth of the U.S. and the E.U. economies during the period 1975–2000. And the data they show seem to prove them right. Dividing the period 1975–2000 into four periods (1975–1985, 1985–1990, 1990–1995, and 1995–2000), we can see that the rate of economic growth for each period is superior in the United States (3.4, 3.2, 2.4, and 3.3 percent) than for the same periods in the E.U.-15 (2.3, 3.2, 1.5, and 2.3 percent).

What those liberal authors (and many others) ignore, however, is that, from these data, one cannot derive the conclusion that the United States is more efficient economically than the E.U.-15. The higher rate of economic growth of the United States is due more to its larger demographic growth (in each of the four periods) than to its assumed larger economic efficiency. Actually, when we analyze *the rate of economic growth per capita,* we can see that the rate is similar on both sides of the Atlantic. During the period 1981–1990, for example, the growth rate per capita was 2.1 percent for the E.U.-15 and 2.2 percent for the United States; for the period 1991–1995, the rate for the E.U.-15 was 1.2 percent, slightly higher than the 1.1 percent rate for the United States; and for the period 1996–2000, the rate for the E.U.-15 was 2.4 percent, only slightly inferior to the rate for the United States at 2.8 percent. In reality, the rates of economic growth per capita have been very similar since 1980, and in fact were much larger in the E.U.-15 than in the United States prior to 1980 (during the period 1960–1980).

But if, rather than comparing the United States with the entire E.U.-15, we compare it—as we should—with individual countries in the E.U.-15, we can see that U.S. economic growth per capita during the 1980s was similar to the growth in the majority of countries of the E.U.-15, and inferior to several of them (U.S. 1.9 percent, about equal to or smaller than Austria, 2.1 percent; Belgium,

1.9 percent; Ireland, 6.6 percent; Netherlands, 2.4 percent; Portugal, 3 percent; Spain, 2.4 percent; and Denmark, 1.8 percent). All these countries have more regulated labor markets and larger welfare states than the United States, and therefore it cannot be said that the economic efficiency of the United States is superior to that of the E.U.-15, and, even less, that this nonexistent superiority of the United States was a consequence of a major deregulation of its labor market or of its limited welfare state.

Which Is Richer:
The United States or the E.U.-15?

If we take income per capita (measured at market prices), as an indicator of wealth, then several European countries are, in fact, richer than the United States. For the year 2002, the United States had a median income of $36,102 per capita, a lower figure than Switzerland, $52,624; Japan, $50,611; Norway, $45,177; Denmark, $44,740; Austria, $38,477; Sweden, $37,870; Germany, $37,150; and Finland, $36,659. All these countries but Japan are European, and many of them have been governed by social democratic parties either alone or in alliance with other political traditions (other than the liberal, which in Europe is a minority political tradition). If, however, rather than using currencies at the market value we use purchasing-power-parity exchange rates (where currencies are standardized so as to compare the ability to purchase goods and services in the market within each country), then the United States is the richest country. But this indicator is potentially misleading, because it is constructed based on a set of assumptions that favor the private sector of the economy. Purchasing-power-parity exchange rates do not adequately account, for example, for services such as education, health care, home care services, social services, public housing, and many other public services that are largely excluded from the market in many E.U. countries. If those products and services were included, then the GDP (gross domestic product) per capita would likely be higher in Europe, because those services are much more expensive in the United States than in the European Union.

Which Is More Productive:
The United States or the E.U.-15?

It is usually assumed that the greater richness of the United States (which, as we have just said, is questionable) is due to its greater level of productivity—the value of the goods and services produced in an hour of work—compared with that of the E.U.-15 (which is claimed to be about 30 percent lower). It is also widely argued that the rate of productivity growth in the E.U.-15 is lower than in the United States.

When we compare the levels of productivity of the United States with the productivity of several countries of the E.U.-15, we can see that, as described by Mishel, Bernstein, and Allegretto (2), several E.U. countries have higher productivity levels than the United States. If we assign the level of U.S. productivity in 2002 a value of 100, then Western Germany would have had a value of 101; Ireland, 103; France, 103; Italy, 105; Netherlands, 106; and Belgium, 111—all of them, incidentally, with more regulated labor markets and higher public social expenditures than the United States.

As to the rate of productivity growth, Morley, Ward, and Watt (3) have shown that, for the period 1986–2003, the E.U.-15 (as an aggregate) had a growth rate of 1.7 percent, larger than the U.S. rate of 1.4 percent. These authors also indicated that since 1994, the U.S. rate of productivity growth has been higher (1.8 percent) than the E.U.-15 rate (1.6 percent), but when Italy (which had a very low rate of productivity growth) is excluded from the E.U.-15, then the rate is very similar on both continents.

Where Do People Work More:
The United States or the E.U.-15?

Another variable that is considered important to explain the income level of a country is the number of hours worked each week and the number of weeks worked per worker each year. The working time per worker is much larger in the United States than in the E.U.-15, a situation that should not be evaluated negatively for the E.U.-15, since this factor helps to explain the higher level of health and quality of life in the E.U.-15 than in the United States. The average vacation time per year in the United States is only two weeks, while it is six weeks in the E.U.-15.

Participation of the Adult Population
in the Labor Market

Another factor that helps to explain why the income level per capita is higher in the United States than in the E.U.-15 is the fact that a larger percentage of the adult population works in the United States (71.2 percent) compared with the E.U.-15 (64.8 percent), which is primarily the consequence of a larger percentage of working women in the United States (65.7 percent) than in the E.U.-15 (56.1 percent). If we compare the United States not with the E.U.-15 but with specific countries of the E.U.-15, however, such as the Scandinavian countries (of a social democratic tradition), we find that the percentage of women working is actually higher in these countries (Denmark, 75.1 percent, and Sweden, 73.6 percent, for example) than in the United States.

Other Variables

The *unemployment* rate in 2002 was lower in Ireland (4.3 percent), the Netherlands (2.7 percent), Norway (3.9 percent), Sweden (4.9 percent), Switzerland (3.2 percent), Portugal (5.1 percent), Denmark (4.6 percent), Austria (4.3 percent), and Great Britain (5.1 percent) than in the United States (5.8 percent). For more information on this subject, see the volume edited by David Howell (4), which analyzes the different experiences the OECD countries have had with unemployment and questions the utility of labor market deregulation as a strategy for lowering unemployment. The *annual rate of job production* during the 1995–2002 period was only slightly superior in the United States (1.4 percent) to that in the E.U.-15 (1.2 percent), but inferior, remarkably, to that in France (1.5 percent), among other countries.

Wage differentials, the difference between well-paid workers (the 90th percentile wage earner) and poorly paid workers (the 10th percentile worker), are much larger in the United States—4.8 times for men and 4.6 for women—than in the majority of countries of the E.U.-15. In Sweden the differential is 2.3 and 1.9, respectively. Moreover, wage differentials have been increasing in the United States due to the lowering of wages for the worst-paying jobs, in contrast to many countries in the E.U.-15, where wage differentials have been constant and even declining as a consequence of rising real wages across the full wage distribution. It is also worth noting that all E.U. countries with higher labor productivity levels than the United States have lower wage differentials than the United States.

The *household income* differentials of the United States (using the same difference between the 90th and 10th percentiles of the income distribution) are the highest in the OECD, with a ratio of 5.5. As with wages, all countries in Europe that have higher productivity than the United States still manage to maintain lower household income differentials, calling into question the efficiency–equity trade-off.

The *poverty level* is much higher in the United States than in any European country. Using international definitions, based on relative poverty rates, about 17 percent of the U.S. population (21 percent of children, 24.7 percent of the elderly) lives in poverty, compared with 6.5 percent of the adult Swedish population (only 4.2 percent of children and 7.7 percent of the elderly), 6.4 percent (3.4 percent and 11.9 percent) in Norway, and 5.4 percent (2.8 percent and 8.5 percent) in Finland, and so on, in a large list of other countries.

Given these data, it is surprising that the deregulation of U.S. labor markets and the limited development of its welfare state are presented as a model for the European Union. The economic efficiency of the United States is actually less than that of the E.U.-15. What would the economic efficiency of the United States be if it were subject to the institutional constraints of the E.U.-15 (i.e., the budget deficit limitations, the high interest rates of the European Central Bank, and the minuscule E.U. budget)?

The data presented so far do not demonstrate that the U.S. economy is more efficient than the E.U.-15. Indeed, these data show that, in many respects, the E.U.-15 has been as efficient as the United States, if not more so—a comparison that is even more favorable to the E.U.-15 when the United States is compared with specific members of the E.U.-15, all of them with more regulated labor markets and larger welfare states than the United States. *In the light of this information, it is a profound error for E.U. governments to follow liberal solutions (deregulation of labor markets and reduction of welfare states), because these not only would reduce the quality of life of their populations but also are likely to reduce the efficiency of their economies in important dimensions.*

II. THE LIMITATIONS OF THE EUROPEAN UNION: WHAT ARE THE PROBLEMS IN THE E.U.-15?

The Liberal Dimensions of Some of the Institutional Framework of the E.U.-15

Recently, the rate of economic growth in the aggregate of the E.U.-15 has been below that of the United States—about 1.3 percent in the last nine months of 2003 and the first four months of 2004 in the European Union, for example, compared with 4.8 percent for the same period in the United States. Within the E.U.-15, the rate in Great Britain was 3.7 percent; Germany, 1.5 percent; France, 1.7 percent; and Italy, 0.8 percent. This slower economic growth of the E.U.-15 than the United States is due to several factors. One is that the interest rates defined by the European Central Bank (ECB) have been historically higher and have been declining more slowly than interest rates in the United States, even though inflation has been practically the same on both sides of the Atlantic. Actually, there is no evidence of inflation pressure in Europe, which is a result of the very weak internal demand that characterizes the economic situation in the E.U.-15.

There is almost a consensus that the reason for interest rates being higher in the E.U.-15 (until very recently) and declining much more slowly than in the United States is not a higher risk of future inflation in the European Union. Why, then, this higher interest rate in the European Union? *The answer is a political one:* it is the enormous power of financial capital in Europe, also responsible for the Stability Pact (also referred to, paradoxically, as the Growth Pact), a pact that has created a lot of stability, but very little growth. The Stability Pact limits central governments' budget deficits to 3 percent of GNP, an amount that, under current recession conditions, is insufficient to stimulate internal demand and economic growth. Moreover, this high interest is contributing to a strengthening of the euro versus the dollar. In that respect, it is surprising that liberal authors take the deregulation of U.S. labor markets as the model to follow without taking other characteristics of the "U.S. model" as points of reference. One such characteristic is the behavior of the Federal Reserve Board and of the federal government (they have tolerated deficits of 5.4 percent of GNP). Contrary to what is believed in liberal circles, the Federal Reserve Board is highly centralized and, at least in theory, cannot ignore the political positions of the U.S. Congress. The ECB, however, is insensitive to the opinion of the E.U. Parliament, with a degree of independence that does not exist in the U.S. Federal Reserve Board (or any other central bank in any major country). The ECB has a highly decentralized structure, with the directors of the central banks of the E.U. member states holding great power. The meetings of the ECB Board of Directors are secret, and there are no public minutes of these meetings. There is not even a semblance of public accountability. The Federal Reserve Board, on the contrary, publishes minutes of its meetings, and its director meets regularly with the U.S. Congress. The minutes are publicly available, and the public can learn which decisions are taken and the rationale for taking them. Not so in the European Central Bank, where control by the banking community of the ECB is almost absolute. It is because of this situation that the primary mandate of the ECB is the control of inflation (and only theoretically the stimulation of economic growth).

This responsibility and governance is clearly spelled out in the E.U. Constitution and is one of the major reasons for the slow economic growth in the E.U.-15. What is happening now in Europe is very similar to what happened in Spain in the 1980s. At that time, the high unemployment in that country was attributed to the rigidity of the labor market and to the "excessive generosity of the Spanish welfare state," as the director of the Spanish Central Bank, Mr. Rojo, once complained. (Spain has one of the lowest percentages of GNP in public social expenditures in the E.U.-15.) The actual cause of the high unemployment, however, was the very high interest rates (the highest in Europe) that made it very costly for business to invest and for consumers to consume. We are seeing the same process now in the European Union. As in Spain in the 1980s, banking in Europe is enjoying some of the highest profits of the past 30 years (see 5). Meanwhile, some of the business associations (and very much in particular, mid-sized and small business associations, such as the EUAPME, the representative body of Europe's Small and Middle Size Enterprises) are protesting the ECB policies.

A significant decline of interest rates is indeed a requirement to stimulate economic growth. The reduction of interest rates, per se, is insufficient, however, unless there is an expansion of consumption and investment, stimulated by a considerable growth of public expenditures, allowing for larger public deficits. Part of those public expenditures should be invested in facilitating the integration of women and young people into the labor force. Such integration requires major investments in the development of networks of services, such as childcare centers, home care services, housing, and others that facilitate such integration. In that respect, it is a mistake to try to stimulate internal demand by tax cuts, which tend to be highly regressive and have a very limited effect in stimulating the economy. Public expenditures, particularly public social expenditures, have much more effect in stimulating the economy than do tax cuts. Public expenditures tend to benefit the popular classes, which are the ones with a higher propensity to consume. Another major obstacle for stimulating economic growth in the European Union is the lack of coordinated economic and fiscal policies as well as the very limited resources that exist for redistributional purposes. As we mentioned before, the budget available to the European Commission represents only 1.27 percent of GNP, much smaller than the U.S. federal budget, which is 19 percent of GNP. It is very difficult to correct regional differentials under these conditions. It is worth clarifying here that when the Economic and Monetary Union was first established in the 1970s, some of its original proponents (such as the Chief Advisor to the U.K. Treasury, Sir Donald MacDougall) thought the E.U. budget should be 5 to 7 percent of the combined European GNP, if it was to be used as an instrument in influencing the business cycle. This figure was not accepted. The current figure of 1.27 percent was fixed at the Berlin Summit of 1999 for the period 2000–2006.

Is the Welfare State in Europe Sustainable?

Another position widely promoted by liberal authors (and by the European Central Bank) is that, due to the aging of the E.U. population, the welfare state in Europe is not sustainable without dramatic and substantial cuts in social benefits. An article in the fall 2004 bulletin of the ECB indicated that health services can no longer be sustained as universal (i.e., distributed to all citizens and residents as a matter of right), and rather must become an assistential program (i.e., a means-tested type of program). A less dramatic proposal is the one put forward by some political leaders, even some within the social democratic tradition, of reducing social benefits, with a guarantee, however, of a minimum benefit for everyone. That minimum would be complemented with privately funded provisions of services and benefits. There is active pressure to privatize social transfers and public services, reducing the size of the public's responsibility for maintaining the social well-being of the population.

The theoretical justification for the majority of these positions is the demographic transition that is taking place in the E.U.-15, an outcome of the lowering of fertility rates and the lengthening of life expectancy. It is assumed that demographic transition means a lowering of the number of contributors to the social security trust funds (most concerns about the sustainability of the welfare state focus on pensions and health care) and an extension of the number of years that the elderly enjoy the social benefits.

These arguments are important ones. And they seem to be plausible. Indeed, the growth of the percentage of elderly in the whole population plus the increasing number of years that elderly people live translates to a substantial growth in pension expenditure, as well as health and social expenditures (such as home care services, convalescent homes, homes for the elderly, and others), since the elderly are the people who use health and social services most extensively.

Before reaching these catastrophic conclusions, however, we need to consider several factors. One is that the sustainability of public social programs depends not only on the extension of public social expenditures, but also on the amount of public resources available. This amount depends on, among other factors, the rate of economic growth, the rate of productivity growth, and the percentage of the population that works. If, for example, the percentage of women working in Spain were the same as in Sweden, the sustainability of pensions would be guaranteed in Spain until 2050. Also, a growth in productivity would enable the state to receive higher contributions without reducing the standard of living of the taxpayer. Let's assume, for example, that today we have three workers (the majority of taxpayers are salaried people) earning 1,000 euros per week. Together they earn 3,000 euros. If each worker pays 167 euros to sustain a pensioner (who receives 500 euros), he or she keeps 833 (1,000 − 167) euros. In 2040, if the growth of productivity of each worker in the coming 40 years remained the same as during the last 50 years (a conservative estimate, since it is likely that productivity will grow more rapidly), then each worker should produce double that amount—that is, 2,000 euros. In that case, it would require only two workers to produce 4,000 euros, a larger amount than that produced today by the three workers. If the pensioner were to receive, in 2040, a pension that is double what a pensioner now receives, he or she would be getting 1,000 euros per week; this would derive from 500 euros per contributor, who thus would retain 1,500 (2,000 − 500) euros each, much larger than the amount a contributor retains today. Due to the growth of productivity, both the worker-contributors and the pensioners can have increased incomes (in this estimate, the impact of inflation has been taken into account by using euros with the same purchasing power). Thus, it is important to stress that most catastrophic predictions of the unsustainability of the welfare state are based on exaggerated rates of decline in the growth of the economy and productivity.

Another argument that is usually put forward for the unsustainability of the welfare state is that the growth in numbers of the elderly increases the ratio of dependency (i.e., the number of beneficiaries per contributor). Thus, it has been estimated that this ratio would increase in Europe over the coming 25 years by 40 percent. If, however, we add in children as dependents, then we can see that, due to the reduction in the percentage of children in the population, the ratio of *total* dependency (elderly plus children) will increase only 10 percent during the coming 25 years, since the growth in numbers of elderly will be compensated for by the decline in numbers of children.

On the other hand, Francis Castles (6) has shown that during the past 30 years, there has not been a statistically significant relationship between aging and growth of public social expenditures. The European countries that have seen a larger growth in public social expenditures (Switzerland, Sweden, Norway, and Denmark) have not experienced a specifically higher growth of the elderly in their populations (except Sweden). And, vice versa, Spain,

Greece, and Italy *have* seen a large growth of the elderly in the population (the elderly being a higher proportion of their populations than the OECD average) without a large growth of public social expenditures (lower than the OECD average).

As these data show, there is not a universal tendency toward larger public social expenditures as a result of the growth of the elderly population. Indeed, between aging and public social expenditures, there is a whole set of political, cultural, and institutional variables that preempts the possibility of establishing a direct relationship between aging and public social expenditures. It cannot be said that one will determine the other. It depends on a whole set of variables that dilute the impact of one on the other, bringing into question the idea that the growth of aging means a crisis of pensions or of the welfare state. Actually, the sustainability of the pension system depends much more on the intensity and levels of coverage of these benefits (political variables) than on demographic variables. There is not, therefore, a demographic determinism that leads unavoidably to the crisis of the public pension system or of the welfare state. The large variability in the pattern of public social expenditures is explained much more by political than by demographic considerations, as a consequence of the ability of each state to respond to each specific situation. This variability of public social expenditures also brings into question the theories about the convergence of public social policies in Europe due to demographic transitions.

Finally, one last factor that has been presented as determined by changes in demographics is the need to rely on the immigrant population as a way of resolving the problem created by a diminishing fertility rate. Frequently, immigration is presented as the solution to the problem of the E.U. pension system. Putting aside that there is no pension problem, such an argument ignores the fact that the impact of immigration on the fertility rate will be a rather short one, since immigrants' fertility rates soon adapt to those of their adopted country. But more importantly, this argument ignores the political nature of the problem. The rate of immigration in a country is also a political variable. Southern E.U. countries (such as Spain) with a very low participation of women in the labor force have chosen to resolve·the shortage of labor by relying on immigration rather than by encouraging women to enter the labor market. Spain (where the Chamber of Commerce calls for 100,000 immigrants per year) would have 6 million more workers (and taxpayers) if its rate of women's employment were similar to Sweden's. Spain's choice of immigration rather than women's integration is the result of class power relations (unions are very weak in Spain) and gender power relations (sexism is still very powerful in Spain). The reverse occurs in Northern Europe, where fertility rates, incidentally, are much higher than in Spain.

The social investments, such as the previously cited networks of family supportive services that are aimed at integrating women into the labor force, are very important to guarantee the sustainability of the welfare state. The fertility rate in an E.U. country depends on the availability of these services as well as on a labor market that allows women to gain their autonomy and independence, enabling them to combine their personal professional projects with their family commitments and responsibilities. In that respect, the Northern European countries have been successful in reversing their declining rates of fertility by providing the supportive family conditions that can resolve this situation.

Conclusion

In this section we have shown that the liberal policies now being advocated (which include deregulation of the labor market and reduction of social benefits), even by social democratic governments in Europe, are economically and socially inefficient. Moreover, the liberal elements built into the framework of the E.U. institutions (and reflected in some articles of the E.U. Constitution and in the Nice Treaty) are responsible for the slowing of economic growth and for the high unemployment that have recently characterized the E.U.-15—a situation that explains the growing disenchantment with the European project of large sectors of the population, and especially the popular classes that are most negatively affected by these liberal policies. The alternative is to change some elements of the framework to incorporate elements that have proven successful in other settings, including in the United States (a dimension of the "Anglo-Saxon liberal model" that is ignored by liberal thought)—that is, lower interest rates, more public accountability of the European Central Bank, and the development of a federal structure, with larger resources available to the E.U. government for distributional purposes and with a higher level of democratic participation and economic and fiscal coordination.

III. WHAT CAN BE DONE TO MAINTAIN AND EXPAND THE SOCIAL MODEL IN EUROPE?[2]

A Brief Historical Review: Where We Are Coming From

As the previous sections of this chapter have shown, the establishment of the social model in Europe—one of the most important developments in the 20th century—was both the cause and the consequence of a very efficient economy, which was in many important dimensions more successful (and continues to be so in many economic areas) than the liberal model in existence in the United States.

---

[2] This section is influenced by George Irvin (7) and by a discussion at the CIDEL Workshop "Which Social and Tax Policy for Which European Union?" that took place in Stockholm, June 10–11, 2005, at which a draft of this chapter was presented.

The European social model was based on full-employment policies predicated on a social pact between labor and capital, led by the two major political traditions in existence in Europe: the social democratic and the Christian democratic (or conservative, based on Judeo-Christian values) traditions. Needless to say, that economic growth was greatly assisted at the beginning of the post World War II period by the Marshall Plan, funded by the United States. The primary stimulus for the growth, however, was the enormous increase in the public sector, which increased its share of GNP by 10 percentage points in just ten years between 1950 and 1960 (from 30 to 40 percent) (7).

This economic growth was rooted also in the economic stability provided by the currency exchange program based on the U.S. dollar. The growth of Europe (and Japan) led to a multipolar world capitalist economy in which the strength of the dollar weakened the competitiveness of the U.S. economy. This situation led to the deliberate collapse of the Bretton Woods agreement, allowing first for a realignment of exchange rates with respect to the U.S. dollar in 1971 and later, in 1973, a complete floating of the exchange rate system. This explains why Helmut Schmidt, chancellor of West Germany, and Giscard d'Estaing, French president, established the European Monetary System in 1979, an exchange rate mechanism among the European currencies and the first step toward a single European currency, the euro. A lesser cited cause for the establishment of monetary stability in Europe was the growing labor unrest, a result of seemingly unstoppable inflation. This unrest stimulated the radicalization of labor relations and the strengthening of the conservative response, which led in the United States to the election of President Carter (the most conservative Democratic Party president the United States has had) and later President Reagan, and in the United Kingdom to the defeat of Callaghan (due to the "winter of discontent") and the victory of Thatcher. Let's not forget that, in 1979, Paul Volcker, governor of the Federal Reserve Board, engineered a dramatic increase of interest rates that created a worldwide recession. This policy also had the intention of creating high unemployment rates as a way to discipline labor. It was the beginning of the substitution of Keynesianism with monetarism and supply-side economics, which depend on the elimination of demand management and its replacement by what Susan George has called the 3D's: *deregulation, devaluation,* and *deflation.* The International Monetary Fund (IMF), whose credits were called upon then more than ever (due to the worldwide recession), became a major worldwide promoter of neoliberalism. The bases for the *Washington consensus* were established at that time, the end of the 1970s and beginning of the 1980s.

The Brussels Consensus

The European translation of the Washington consensus was the *Brussels consensus,* which appeared in the 1980s, along with the Maastricht economic rules, when inflation was very high in Europe and public debt was growing very rapidly in many countries. In Belgium, Greece, Italy, and Ireland, public debt exceeded 100 percent of GDP, and public deficits were close to 10 percent of GDP. Germany and the northern European countries were afraid of the recklessness of the southern European countries. These fears explain the attractiveness of monetarism to the architects of the Maastricht Treaty. Moreover, the Mitterrand failure to stimulate the French economy by stimulating Keynesian public policies (with the subsequent decline of the French currency, vulnerable to the financial market's speculative pressures) further strengthened the attraction of monetarism and supply-side economics. And at the time the Maastricht Treaty was signed in 1992, many of the European currencies (Italian lira, French franc, British sterling, and others) were in trouble. The attractiveness of the *Washington consensus* in Europe was thus very powerful. The Maastricht criteria, with their primary objective to reduce inflation (no higher than 2 percent on average) and calling for a balanced budget for the entire economic cycle (no more than 3 percent of public deficit) and a public debt of no more than 60 percent of GDP, were thus established. These policies were highly successful in reducing inflation and in establishing a certain monetary stability in Europe, even though individual currencies would still be subject to speculative attacks by the ubiquitous financial markets.

That limitation of inflation had a cost, however: slower economic growth, higher unemployment, and slower growth of public expenditures, including public social expenditures, in the 1980s and 1990s than in the previous period of the 1950s to 1980s. In 1999, the euro was established. The supposed wisdom of *monetarism* was also apparently demonstrated in the United States when elimination of the federal deficit by Clinton was wrongly presented as the cause for the substantial growth of the U.S. economy in the 1990s. Actually, U.S. economic growth after elimination of the federal deficit was remarkably slow, and only after 1995 did it grow significantly as a result of stock market speculation centered around technology stocks (the famous Wall Street bubble).

The euro has indeed been a success in providing monetary stability. But its greatest success has been to make that currency (like the U.S. dollar) more resistant to financial market speculators. Because of its size (like the dollar and the yen), the euro is difficult for speculators to attack, and the ECB could respond fairly easily to these kinds of activities. This means that, once the euro had taken root, successful *Keynesian policies could indeed be implemented.* As was seen in the United States under Reagan and Bush (and in Japan), large deficits— well beyond the limits set by the SGP (see below)—could be carried without accelerating inflation or speculative attacks.

Moreover, as George Irvin (7) has highlighted, the Maastricht criteria of the Stability and Growth Pact (SGP) have major problems, which include: (*a*) an excessively low inflation rate as an objective, which interferes with economic efficiency; (*b*) the arbitrary nature of its fiscal indicators (why a 3 percent deficit ceiling and not 5 percent, for example?); (*c*) fiscal limits that are no longer necessary now the euro has been established; (*d*) a lack of sensitivity about the different types of deficits (current vs. capital public expenditures); and (*e*) the deflationary impact of the requirement to achieve balanced budgets over the economic cycle, which can require surpluses of up to 3 percent of GNP in good times to compensate for deficits of up to 3 percent in bad times.

Where Was the Social Dimension of the Maastricht Treaty?

It would be unfair, however, to see the *Brussels consensus* as a mere reproduction of the *Washington consensus*. Indeed, parallel to the monetary policies outlined above, there was a series of proposals that were presented as "socially friendly." The Delors White Paper even warned against "wholesale labor market regulations," and the Lisbon European Council in 2000 introduced the concept of social expenditures as investment rather than consumption (8). Moreover, under the leadership of France and Sweden, the E.U. Council documents spoke about the need for full employment. But these social concerns and dimensions were never fully developed and were never allowed to contradict the monetary policies that characterized the *Brussels consensus*. Actually, even in comparative terms, the *Brussels consensus* was much less socially concerned than the earlier Paris consensus, appearing in the Treaty of Paris of 1951, which established the European Coal and Steel Community (ECSC), the precursor of the European Union. In that treaty, the top authority of the ECSC had the power to penalize firms that used low-paid workers to undercut competitors. Later, the Treaty of Rome of 1957 encouraged the establishment of a central coordinating agency responsible for promoting the development of employment law, social security, vocational training, and occupational health, with a mandate to harmonize these conditions.

The process that started with Maastricht, however, evolved to become much less socially concerned, leading to the situation of social insensitivity that appears in the Bolkestein directive, the draft of which (in 2004) was prepared under the auspices of the European Commission presided over by Prodi (paradoxically, the candidate of the social democratic parties). Such directives allowed services provided in other E.U. countries to abide by the laws of the countries "of origin," which basically meant that plumbers from Poland, for example, could work in Germany and get paid according to Polish wages and Polish regulations. This directive was a frontal attack on labor in the E.U.-15 countries. Resistance to the directive led to the modification that workers from new E.U. countries, when foreign workers in other E.U. countries, would be paid at least the minimum wage of the recipient country, thus establishing two levels of salaries for each occupational sector: a minimum wage for immigrant workers and a labor market wage for local workers. This arrogance of capital and clearly aggressive anti-labor intervention was one of the mobilizing forces for the *no* vote against the European

Constitution in France and the Netherlands and the growing unpopularity of the European Union among the European working classes.

Actually, the Bolkestein directive is just the extreme form of a normal situation in which European labor has been weakened considerably. There is, for example, no legislative space in the European Union to allow for a European collective bargaining agreement. Although monetary policy is centralized, economic fiscal, social, and labor policies are decentralized to the national levels, weakening labor significantly. This means that, at the E.U. level, workers can defend themselves individually (against discrimination) but not collectively. As Bercusson (9) has indicated, labor law in the European Union resembles labor law in the United States, whereby the absence of federal legislation on collective bargaining means that the only way that workers can protect themselves is through anti-discriminatory federal legislation—which explains the enormous development of anti-discriminatory legislation in the United States. Needless to say, this situation favors employers and disfavors labor.

The Need for Change

These limitations explain the need for a substantial change in the framework of the European Union, in the directions outlined in Section II of this chapter. There is a need for *more* Europe to save Europe. The state of the current Europe, a result of the excessive power of financial capital and, to a lesser degree, corporate business interests at the cost of labor, explains the growing unpopularity of Europe among the working classes, who saw Europe as the social Europe they had fought for and had hopes for. The limited development of the social dimension of the European Union results from its very restrictive democracy.

The orientation of the needed change should be clear. The centralized nature of monetary policy has to be accompanied by centralized economic, fiscal, social, and labor policies to dilute the excessive power of monetarist interests. Then there is a need to dramatically change the SGP by eliminating it. It should be replaced with a new coordinating committee that goes much further than the current Broad Economic Policy Guidelines. A European Stabilization Fund (ESF) could be administered by the European Investment Fund (EIF), with each member state developing plans for responding to recessions and overheating, and the possibility for the fund to respond to excessive contraction or expansion (more than 2 percent of GNP) (10, 11). The activation of the ESF could be approved by the Council for Economic and Financial Affairs (ECOFIN), and its principles by the European Parliament. The ESF would also promote long-term investments at the E.U. level.

Another possible intervention could be the establishment of a federal E.U. budget of 5 to 7 percent of the European GDP, an amount large enough to be used as an instrument to regulate the European economic cycle. This budget should be funded only partly by a value-added tax (which is regressive) but also by progressive taxation by the states. Also, some form of tax coordination (although not harmonization) should be developed.

These fiscal and economic policies should be complemented by the development of common welfare state policies to guarantee social rights, established in a new constitution and developed operationally under the guidance of criteria developed by the European Parliament, and developed in such a way that no country will see a reduction in its welfare benefits. Only under these conditions can the European project become attractive to European populations—and in particular to the popular classes that have been directly threatened by the monetary and fiscal policies that have been the product of the *Brussels consensus*.

Note — This chapter is adapted from a paper presented at the CIDEL Workshop "Which Social and Tax Policy for Which European Union?" held in Stockholm, Sweden, June 10–11, 2005.

REFERENCES

1. Navarro, V., and Schmitt, J. A donde va el Socioliberalismo? In *Principios: Estudios de Economia Politica*. Fundación Sistema, May 2005.
2. Mishel, J., Bernstein, J., and Allegretto, S. *The State of Working America, 2004–2005*. Economic Policy Institute, Washington, DC, 2005.
3. Morley, J., Ward, T., and Watt, A. *The State of Working Europe*. E.T.U.I., Brussels, 2004.
4. Howell, D. (ed.). *Fighting Unemployment: The Limits of Free Market Orthodoxy*. Oxford University Press, Oxford, 2004.
5. Navarro, V. *La economia politica de la Banca en Espana*. Ariel Economica, 1998.
6. Castles, F. G. *The Future of the Welfare State*. Oxford University Press, Oxford, 2004.
7. Irvin, G. *The Implosion of the Brussels Economic Consensus*. International Centre for Economic Research Working Paper. Turin, Italy, May 2005.
8. Gray, A. *Unsocial Europe: Social Protection or Flexploitation?* Pluto Press, London, 2004.
9. Bercusson, B. Labour Law in the EU. Presented at CIDEL Workshop, Stockholm, June 2005.
10. Sapir, A., et al. *An Agenda for a Growing Europe: The Sapir Report*. Oxford University Press, London, 2004.
11. Economic Policy Co-ordination (EPOC) Report. Economic Policy Coordination for Full-employment and Social Cohesion in Europe 2005. www.epoc.ini-bremen.de.

CHAPTER 10

Is the United States a Good Model for Reducing Social Exclusion in Europe?

John Schmitt and Ben Zipperer

Sustained, high levels of unemployment in the majority of Europe's largest economies have led many Europeans to look to the United States as a possible alternative economic model. The political right and center in Europe have emphasized what they see as the flexibility and dynamism of the U.S. economy. Much of the left, meanwhile, has argued that high unemployment in Europe, which is often concentrated in specific geographic regions or demographic groups, is the driving force behind "social exclusion" in Europe today. This has led many Europeans—even some in the continent's social democratic parties—to the reluctant conclusion that the United States may be a good model for reducing social exclusion there.

This chapter reviews several international indicators of social exclusion to assess how well the United Sates has done in using its apparently greater flexibility and dynamism to reduce social exclusion. On most measures of inequality, poverty, health, education, crime, and punishment, the United States does not fare well compared with the much better-funded welfare states in Europe. The gap between U.S. and European performance in many of these dimensions is striking, and not fully acknowledged in the current debate on promoting U.S.-style reforms in Europe. What is more surprising, however, is that the United States, in fact, performs poorly in two areas where U.S. superiority is usually simply taken for granted: incorporating traditionally disadvantaged groups into the paid labor force and providing opportunities for economic mobility.

INCOME INEQUALITY

We start with what is probably the most basic indicator of social exclusion—household income inequality. Table 1 presents data on income inequality for 28 OECD (Organization for Economic Cooperation and Development) countries in various years during the 1990s and in 2000, from Smeeding (1). The final column of the table—which reports data on the Gini coefficient, the most common

Table 1

Household income inequality, late 1990s to 2000

	10th percentile, % of national median	90th percentile, % of national median	Ratio 90th to 10th	Gini coefficient[a]
Australia	45	195	4.33	0.31
Austria	53	178	3.37	0.27
Belgium	53	170	3.19	0.25
Canada	46	188	4.13	0.31
Czech Republic	60	179	3.01	0.26
Denmark	54	155	2.85	0.24
Finland	57	164	2.90	0.25
France	54	191	3.54	0.29
Germany	54	173	3.18	0.25
Greece	—	—	—	—
Hungary	54	194	3.57	0.30
Iceland	—	—	—	—
Ireland	46	201	4.33	0.33
Italy	44	199	4.48	0.33
Japan	46	192	4.17	0.32
Luxembourg	66	215	3.24	0.26
Mexico	28	328	11.55	0.49
Netherlands	56	167	2.98	0.25
New Zealand	—	—	—	—
Norway	57	159	2.80	0.25
Poland	52	188	3.59	0.29
Portugal	—	—	—	—
Slovak Republic	56	162	2.88	0.24
Spain	50	197	3.96	0.30
Sweden	57	168	2.96	0.25
Switzerland	52	188	3.62	0.31
United Kingdom	47	215	4.58	0.35
United States	**39**	**210**	**5.45**	**0.37**

Source: Smeeding (1, Figure 1).
Note: Data for Japan and Switzerland refer to 1992.
[a]The Gini coefficient ranges from 0 to 1, 0 indicating a perfectly equal distribution of income across all households, 1 indicating that all income is concentrated in one household.

measure of income inequality—shows that the United States (0.37) had the second highest Gini coefficient among the countries with available data; only Mexico (0.49) had higher income inequality by this measure. The United Kingdom (0.35) was the European country with the next highest level of income inequality, followed by Ireland and Italy (both 0.33), with most of the remaining countries in Europe below 0.30. The countries with the lowest Gini coefficients were Denmark (0.24) and Belgium, Finland, Germany, the Netherlands, Norway, and Sweden (all 0.25).[1]

Another basic measure of income inequality is the distance between the 10th, the 50th, and the 90th percentiles of the national income distribution. The greater the distance between points in the distribution, the greater the overall inequality. As Table 1 shows, in the United States, the 10th percentile household earned about 39 percent of what the median household earned, while the 90th percentile household earned about 210 percent of the median. The 10th percentile earner in the United States was further below the median than was the case in every other country in the table except Mexico (28%). In every European country except Italy (44%), Ireland (46%), and the United Kingdom (47%), the 10th percentile household made at least 50 percent of median earnings. Among the major OECD economies, 10th percentile households fared best in Norway (57%), Sweden (57%), and the Netherlands (56%).

Meanwhile, the 90th percentile household in the United States (210%) was further above the median than in almost every other country in the table. Only Mexico (328%), Luxembourg (215%), and the United Kingdom (215%) had larger gaps between the 90th percentile and the median. Incomes at the top were closest to the median in Denmark (155%), the Slovak Republic (162%), Finland (164%), and the Netherlands (167%).

Table 1 also shows the ratio of the 90th and 10th percentile earnings, as an additional measure of income inequality (see also Figure 1). Mexico (11.55) had, by far, the highest inequality, as based on this simple gauge of inequality. The United States (5.45) was next, well ahead of the United Kingdom (4.58), Australia (4.33), and Canada (4.13). The countries with the lowest "90-10" gap were Norway (2.80), Denmark (2.85), the Slovak Republic (2.88), Finland (2.90), and the Netherlands (2.98).

By most measures, then, the United States is the most unequal of the major OECD countries, with a higher Gini coefficient, lower relative incomes at the 10th percentile, and a bigger gap between the incomes of rich and poor households than

---

[1] Gini coefficients in the text are calculated using net disposable income, which subtracts taxes and includes transfer benefits. When measured using pre-tax income, the United States is not such an outlier. Based on pre-tax income, the Gini coefficient for the United States (0.45) lies well within the European range of market income inequality (0.39–0.50). Progressive taxes and especially benefits and transfer payments dramatically reduce inequality in most European nations, with only relatively modest effects in the United States.

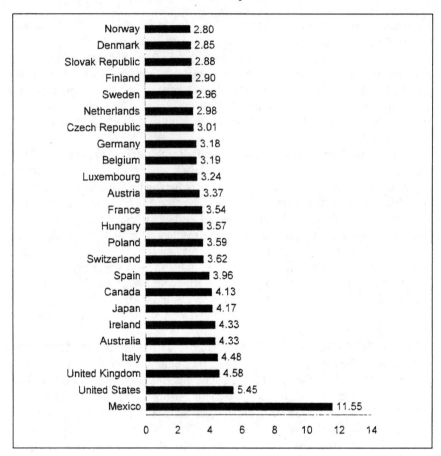

Figure 1. Household income inequality, as ratio of 90th to 10th percentile earnings. *Source:* Smeeding (1, Figure 1).

in any Western European countries. Whatever capacity the United States might have for using its labor market flexibility and dynamism to create jobs and channel potential workers into employment (which we examine below), this capacity has not avoided the emergence of substantial levels of income inequality, with the resulting potential for heightened levels of social exclusion.

POVERTY

Income inequality is, in itself, a cause for social concern (see, e.g., Navarro (2) for a discussion of the health and other effects of inequality), but poverty— extreme relative or absolute deprivation—is generally seen as a more important indicator of potential social exclusion. As Townsend argues, those in poverty have "resources . . . so seriously below those commanded by the average family or individual that they are in effect excluded from ordinary living patterns, customs and activities" (3, p. 31).

Table 2 presents data from Scruggs and Allan (4) on relative and absolute measures of poverty at different points in time over the years 1990 to 2000 for a subset of the countries in the earlier discussion on income inequality. The relative poverty rate is defined as the share of the population in households with incomes below 40 percent of the median (which is obviously closely related to income inequality). Consistent with the earlier results for income inequality, the United States (10.7%) had the highest rate of relative poverty, followed by Ireland (8.0%) and Italy (7.3%). Relative poverty was lowest in Finland (2.1%), Norway (2.8%), Belgium (3.2%), France (3.3%), and Sweden (3.6%).

Absolute poverty is defined here as earning at most 40 percent of the inflation-adjusted 1986 median income in the United States (converted to local currencies with purchasing power parity exchange rates). As shown in Table 2 and Figure 2, the United States, which has a much higher gross domestic product (GDP) per capita than most of the other countries in the sample (see, e.g., 5), does substantially better. About 8.7 percent of the U.S. population was living in absolute poverty by these criteria, well below rates in Italy (18.8%), Australia (16.4%), Ireland (15.4%), and the United Kingdom (11.8%). The United States also does somewhat better than France (10.0%). The rest of the European countries listed in Table 2, however, had lower absolute poverty rates, despite having income levels that are 70 to 80 percent of U.S. levels. Norway (which has a GDP per person close to that of the United States) had an absolute poverty rate of only 2.6 percent; the rate in Switzerland was 3.5 percent.[2]

EDUCATION

Education is arguably the single most important tool available to combat social exclusion. Table 3 shows the educational attainment rates, standardized by the OECD, for our sample of OECD countries for 2003. The first two columns examine the share of the adult population with at least an upper-secondary education (roughly the equivalent of a high school degree in the United States). For all adults age 25 to 64, the United States had the highest share of high school equivalent graduates, with 88 percent. Norway (87%) and the Slovak Republic (87%) trailed close behind. In most of the rest of Western Europe, between 60 and 80 percent of 25- to 64-year-olds had completed the equivalent of high school. The biggest exceptions in Europe were Portugal (23%), Spain (43%), Italy (44%), and Greece (51%).

---

[2] Smeeding (6) defines poverty as half of national median income and finds the pattern of poverty remains largely the same in the analysis by Scruggs and Allan (4).

Table 2

Poverty rates, 1990 to 2000

	Relative rate, % of population	Absolute rate, % of population	Year
Australia	6.6	16.4	1994
Austria	4.0	6.3	1997
Belgium	3.2	7.2	1997
Canada	6.5	6.5	2000
Czech Republic	—	—	—
Denmark	4.9	7.3	1994
Finland	2.1	6.8	2000
France	3.3	10.0	1994
Germany	4.2	7.0	2000
Greece	—	—	—
Hungary	—	—	—
Iceland	—	—	—
Ireland	8.0	15.4	2000
Italy	7.3	18.8	2000
Japan	—	—	—
Luxembourg	—	—	—
Mexico	—	—	—
Netherlands	4.5	7.4	1999
New Zealand	—	—	—
Norway	2.8	2.6	2000
Poland	—	—	—
Portugal	—	—	—
Slovak Republic	—	—	—
Spain	5.2	—	1990
Sweden	3.6	7.9	2000
Switzerland	4.0	3.5	1992
United Kingdom	5.4	11.8	1999
United States	**10.7**	**8.7**	**2000**

Source: Scruggs and Allan (4, Table 1).
Note: Relative poverty is <40 percent of median adjusted disposable income. Absolute poverty is <40 percent of U.S. median income in 1986, adjusted for inflation and converted using purchasing power parity exchange rates.

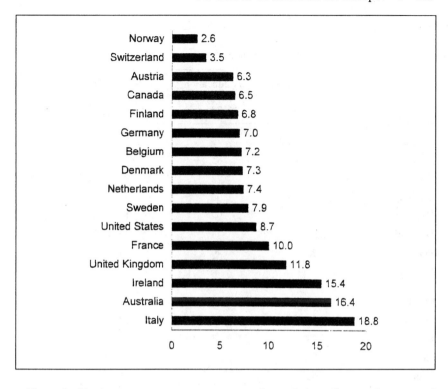

Figure 2. Absolute poverty rate, as percent of population. *Source*: Scruggs and Allan (4, Table 1).

European countries do considerably better, however, when we focus on just 25- to 34-year-olds. High school completion rates for this younger group are generally much higher than for 25- to 64-year-olds, while rates are almost identical across the two age ranges in the United States (87% and 88%). Nevertheless, the United States generally still does better than European countries. The exceptions are Finland (89%), Sweden (91%), the Czech Republic (92%), the Slovak Republic (94%), and Norway (95%); while Austria (85%), Germany (85%), and Denmark (86%) do not lag far behind the United States.

Table 3 also shows the share of the adult population with roughly the equivalent of a four-year college degree or more (tertiary education). Once again, the United States, with 38 percent of 25- to 64-year-olds with college degrees, does well compared with Western Europe. Only Denmark (32%), Norway (31%), and Sweden (33%) had at least 30 percent of their adult populations with college degrees. Most Western European countries fall in the 20 to 30 percent range, with several in the teens.

Table 3

Educational attainment by age, 2003

	At least upper-secondary education, %		At least tertiary education, %	
	25–64 yrs	25–34 yrs	25–64 yrs	25–34 yrs
Australia	62	75	31	36
Austria	79	85	15	15
Belgium	62	78	29	39
Canada	84	90	44	53
Czech Republic	86	92	12	12
Denmark	81	86	32	35
Finland	76	89	33	40
France	65	80	23	37
Germany	83	85	24	22
Greece	51	72	18	24
Hungary	74	83	15	17
Iceland	59	64	26	29
Ireland	62	78	26	37
Italy	44	60	10	12
Japan	84	94	37	52
Luxembourg	59	68	15	19
Mexico	21	25	15	19
Netherlands	66	76	24	28
New Zealand	78	84	31	32
Norway	87	95	31	40
Poland	48	57	14	20
Portugal	23	37	11	16
Slovak Republic	87	94	12	13
Spain	43	60	25	38
Sweden	82	91	33	40
Switzerland	70	76	27	29
United Kingdom	65	71	28	33
United States	**88**	**87**	**38**	**39**

Source: OECD, Education at a Glance, 2005, Web edition, Tables A1.2a and A1.3a.

When we look just at 25- to 34-year-olds, many European countries do almost as well as or better than the United States (39%) with respect to college graduates: Denmark (35%), France (37%), Ireland (37%), Spain (38%), Belgium (39%), and Finland, Norway, and Sweden (all 40%). Several Western European countries, however, still lag far behind the United States: Italy (12%), Austria (15%), Portugal (16%), Germany (22%), and Greece (24%).

Attainment rates are only one way to measure the potential for educational outcomes to contribute to social exclusion. Table 4 presents results tabulated by the OECD from an international standardized test of mathematics administered to 15-years-olds (scores on the Program for International Student Assessment, PISA). In Western Europe, only Greece (445), Italy (466), and Portugal (466) scored, on average, lower than the United States (483). Switzerland (527), Belgium (529), the Netherlands (538), and Finland (544) did the best in Western Europe (see Figure 3).

For purposes of considering social exclusion, however, we may be particularly interested in the scores of the poorest-performing students. Table 4, therefore, also shows the 10th percentile test scores in each country. In Western Europe, only Greece (324), Italy (342), and Portugal (352) scored lower than the United States (356). The best performers in Western Europe for students at the 10th percentile were Ireland (393), Denmark (396), Iceland (396), Switzerland (396), the Netherlands (415), and Finland (438). (For completeness, Table 4 also includes the results at the 90th percentile.)

Table 5 demonstrates that the United States does poorly at both the mean and the 10th percentile,[3] despite spending substantially more on education at the primary level ($8,049 per student) and secondary level ($9,098) than almost every other country in the OECD. Only Luxembourg spends more at both levels ($10,611 for primary and $15,195 for secondary), and Norway more at the secondary level ($10,154). (Table 5 also shows that at the tertiary level, the United States spends substantially more per student per year ($20,545) than all other European countries except Switzerland ($23,714); these expenditures, of course, have no direct impact on the test scores of 15-year-olds.) As Table 6 makes clear, the vast majority of these expenditures at the primary and secondary levels in the United States are in public schools (3.8 percentage points of U.S. GDP in 2002), not in private schools (only 0.3 percentage points of GDP in the same year).[4]

---

[3] The relative performance of the United States is only marginally better at the 90th percentile, as Table 4 also shows.

[4] In the United States, private educational expenditures are more important at the tertiary level: the country spends about 1.2 percentage points of GDP on public higher education and 1.4 percentage points on private higher education.

Table 4

Variation in mathematics performance among 15-year-olds, 2003

	10th percentile	Mean	90th percentile
Australia	399	524	645
Austria	384	506	626
Belgium	381	529	664
Canada	419	532	644
Czech Republic	392	516	641
Denmark	396	514	632
Finland	438	544	652
France	389	511	628
Germany	363	503	632
Greece	324	445	566
Hungary	370	490	611
Iceland	396	515	629
Ireland	393	503	614
Italy	342	466	589
Japan	402	534	660
Luxembourg	373	493	611
Mexico	276	385	497
Netherlands	415	538	657
New Zealand	394	523	650
Norway	376	495	614
Poland	376	490	607
Portugal	352	466	580
Slovak Republic	379	498	619
Spain	369	485	597
Sweden	387	509	630
Switzerland	396	527	652
United Kingdom	—	—	—
United States	**356**	**483**	**607**

Source: OECD, Education at a Glance, 2005, Web edition, Table A4.3.
Note: Data are scores on OECD PISA mathematics scale.

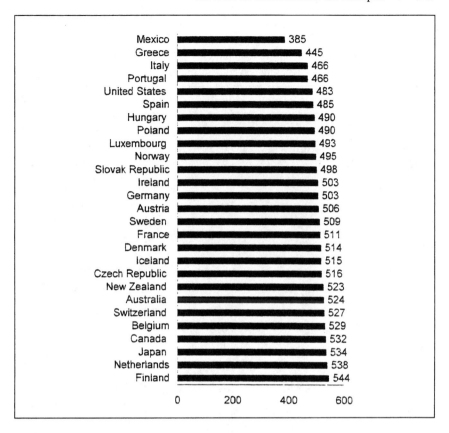

Figure 3. Mathematics performance among 15-year-olds, 2003, PISA mathematics scale scores. *Source:* OECD, Education at a Glance, 2005, Web edition, Table A4.3.

HEALTH

The United States spends much more on health care than any other country in our sample. Table 7 lists total expenditures on health care in 2003, separately for the public and private sectors, based on calculations by the OECD, as a share of national GDP and as expenditures per person per year. The United States spent 15.0 percent of its GDP on health care in 2003 (see Figure 4). The next closest countries were Switzerland (11.5%) and Germany (11.1%); only three other countries spent more than 10 percent (Iceland, 10.5%; Norway, 10.3%; and France, 10.1%) Because U.S. GDP per capita is substantially higher than that of countries in our sample, the gap between U.S. expenditures and those in other countries are even greater when we express health care costs in terms of expenditures per person per year. On average, in 2003 the United States spent

Table 5

Average annual educational expenditures per student, 2002, in U.S. dollars
at purchasing power parity exchange rates

	Pre-primary	Primary	Secondary	Tertiary	Total
Australia	—	5,169	7,375	12,416	7,209
Austria	6,169	7,015	8,887	12,448	8,943
Belgium	4,420	5,665	8,272	12,019	7,933
Canada	—	—	—	—	—
Czech Republic	2,724	2,077	3,628	6,236	3,449
Denmark	4,673	7,727	8,003	15,183	9,261
Finland	3,929	5,087	7,121	11,768	7,304
France	4,512	5,033	8,472	9,276	7,467
Germany	4,999	4,537	7,025	10,999	7,129
Greece	—	3,803	4,058	4,731	4,136
Hungary	3,475	3,016	3,184	8,205	3,872
Iceland	—	7,171	7,229	8,251	7,548
Ireland	—	4,180	5,725	9,809	5,711
Italy	5,445	7,231	7,568	8,636	7,708
Japan	3,691	6,117	6,952	11,716	7,438
Luxembourg	—	10,611	15,195	—	—
Mexico	1,643	1,467	1,768	6,074	1,950
Netherlands	4,923	5,558	6,823	13,101	7,241
New Zealand	4,650	4,536	5,698	—	—
Norway	—	7,508	10,154	13,739	9,560
Poland	2,691	2,585	—	4,834	2,962
Portugal	4,158	4,940	6,921	6,960	6,080
Slovak Republic	2,125	1,471	2,193	4,756	2,300
Spain	3,845	4,592	6,010	8,020	5,914
Sweden	4,107	7,143	7,400	15,715	8,520
Switzerland	3,450	7.776	11,900	23,714	11,334
United Kingdom	8,452	5,150	6,505	11,822	6,691
United States	**7,881**	**8,049**	**9,098**	**20,545**	**11,152**

Source: OECD, Education at a Glance, 2005, Web edition, Table B1.1.
Note: Expenditures for non-tertiary post-secondary education are not shown, but are included in total.

Table 6
Average annual educational expenditures, 2002, as percentage of GDP

	Primary and secondary			Tertiary			Total		
	Public	Private	Total	Public	Private	Total	Public	Private	Total
Australia	3.6	0.7	4.2	0.8	0.8	1.6	4.4	1.5	5.9
Austria	3.7	0.1	3.8	1.1	—	1.1	4.8	0.1	4.9
Belgium	4.1	0.2	4.3	1.2	0.1	1.4	5.3	0.3	5.6
Canada	—	—	—	—	—	—	—	—	—
Czech Republic	2.8	0.1	2.9	0.8	0.1	0.9	3.6	0.2	3.8
Denmark	4.1	0.1	4.2	1.9	—	1.9	6.0	0.1	6.1
Finland	3.8	—	3.9	1.7	—	1.8	5.5	—	5.6
France	4.0	0.2	4.2	1.0	0.1	1.1	5.0	0.4	5.3
Germany	3.0	0.7	3.6	1.0	0.1	1.1	3.9	0.8	4.7
Greece	2.5	0.2	2.7	1.2	—	1.2	3.7	0.2	3.9
Hungary	3.1	0.2	3.3	1.0	0.3	1.2	4.1	0.5	4.5
Iceland	5.4	0.3	5.7	1.0	—	1.1	6.5	0.3	6.8
Ireland	3.0	0.1	3.1	1.1	0.2	1.3	4.0	0.3	4.3
Italy	3.4	0.1	3.5	0.8	0.2	0.9	4.2	0.3	4.5
Japan	2.7	0.2	3.0	0.4	0.6	1.1	3.2	0.9	4.0
Luxembourg	3.9	—	3.9	—	—	—	3.9	—	3.9
Mexico	3.5	0.7	4.1	1.0	0.4	1.4	4.5	1.1	5.5
Netherlands	3.3	0.2	3.4	1.0	0.3	1.3	4.3	0.4	4.7
New Zealand	4.4	0.5	4.9	0.9	0.6	1.5	5.3	1.1	6.3
Norway	4.2	—	4.3	1.4	0.1	1.5	5.6	0.1	5.7
Poland	4.0	0.1	4.1	1.1	0.5	1.5	5.0	0.6	5.6
Portugal	4.2	—	4.2	0.9	0.1	1.0	5.2	0.1	5.2
Slovak Republic	2.7	0.1	2.8	0.7	0.1	0.9	3.5	0.2	3.6
Spain	2.9	0.2	3.2	1.0	0.3	1.2	3.9	0.5	4.4
Sweden	4.6	—	4.6	1.6	0.2	1.8	6.2	0.2	6.3
Switzerland	4.0	0.6	4.6	1.4	—	1.4	5.4	0.6	4.6
United Kingdom	3.7	0.6	4.3	0.8	0.3	1.1	4.5	0.9	5.4
United States	**3.8**	**0.3**	**4.1**	**1.2**	**1.4**	**2.6**	**5.0**	**1.8**	**6.7**

Source: OECD, Education at a Glance, 2005, Web edition, Table B2.1b.

Table 7

Average annual health care expenditures, 2003

	As % GDP			U.S.$ per person per year[a]		
	Public	Private	Total	Public	Private	Total
Australia	6.3	3.0	9.3	1,822	877	2,699
Austria	5.1	2.4	7.5	1,556	746	2,302
Belgium	9.6	0.0	9.6	2,827	0.0	2,827
Canada	6.9	3.0	9.9	2,098	903	3,001
Czech Republic	6.8	0.7	7.5	1,169	129	1,298
Denmark	7.5	1.5	9.0	2,293	470	2,763
Finland	5.7	1.7	7.4	1,620	498	2,118
France	7.7	2.4	10.1	2,215	688	2,903
Germany	8.7	2.4	11.1	2,343	653	2,996
Greece	5.1	4.8	9.9	1,032	979	2,011
Hungary	6.1	2.3	8.4	919	350	1,269
Iceland	8.8	1.7	10.5	2,601	514	3,115
Ireland	5.8	1.6	7.4	1,912	539	2,451
Italy	6.3	2.1	8.4	1,696	562	2,258
Japan	6.4	1.5	7.9	1,743	396	2,139
Luxembourg	6.2	0.7	6.9	3,331	374	3,705
Mexico	2.9	3.3	6.2	271	312	583
Netherlands	6.1	3.7	9.8	1,857	1,119	2,976
New Zealand	6.4	1.7	8.1	1,484	402	1,886
Norway	8.6	1.7	10.3	3,186	621	3,807
Poland	4.5	2.0	6.5	520	224	744
Portugal	6.7	2.9	9.6	1,253	544	1,797
Slovak Republic	5.2	0.7	5.9	686	91	777
Spain	5.5	2.2	7.7	1,307	528	1,835
Sweden	8.0	1.4	9.4	2,303	400	2,703
Switzerland	6.7	4.8	11.5	2,212	1,569	3,781
United Kingdom	6.4	1.3	7.7	1,861	370	2,231
United States	**6.7**	**8.3**	**15.0**	**2,502**	**3,133**	**5,635**

Source: Authors' calculations based on OECD Health Data 2005, Web edition.
[a]U.S. dollars at purchasing power parity exchange rates.

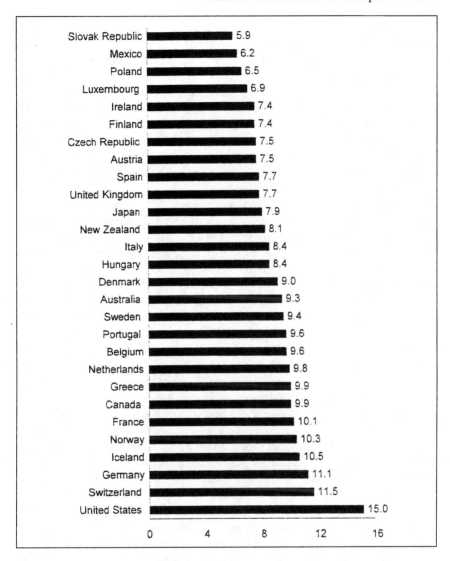

Figure 4. Annual health care expenditures, 2003, as percent of GDP. *Source:* Authors' calculations based on OECD Health Data 2005, Web edition.

about $5,635 on health care per person per year. Of the remaining countries, only four others spent more than $3,000 per person per year: Norway ($3,807), Switzerland ($3,781), Luxembourg ($3,705), and Canada ($3,001).

Table 7 also breaks down health care expenditures by whether they are in the public or private sector. The United States is the only country, except Mexico, in which expenditures in the private sector (8.3% of GDP) exceed those in the public sector (6.7%). Greece and Switzerland are the only other countries where private sector health expenditures exceed 40 percent of the total. Even though private expenditures represent the bulk of health expenditures in the United States, public sector health costs in the United States still fall in about the middle of the range for public expenditures in Western European countries. Denmark (7.5%), France (7.7%), Sweden (8.0%), Norway (8.6%), and Germany (8.7%) spent more in their public sectors in 2003, but Austria (5.1%), Finland (5.7%), Greece (5.1%), Ireland (5.8%), Italy (6.3%), the Netherlands (6.1%), Portugal (6.7%), Spain (5.5%), Switzerland (6.7%), and the United Kingdom (6.4%) spent the same or less than the United States.

The data in Table 7 establish that the United States spends considerably more on health care than do other rich countries, but other data suggest that the United States nevertheless suffers from high levels of social exclusion with respect to health care. The most obvious element of this exclusion is the high share of the U.S. population without health insurance. The United States and Mexico are the only countries listed in Table 7 that do not provide essentially universal health care coverage. In 2003, 15.6 percent of the U.S. population (about 45 million people, or roughly the population of Spain) was without any form of health insurance, public or private, throughout the entire year (7, p. 14). An additional 12 percent of the U.S. population lacked health insurance for some part of the year (8; 2002 data).

Data on many of the most common health indicators also suggest that the U.S. health care system is highly inefficient, yielding poor outcomes despite high levels of expenditures. Table 8 provides details on several broad measures of health outcomes compiled by the OECD: life expectancy, infant and maternal mortality, and rates of obesity and smoking. Only Mexico and the transition economies of Eastern Europe have a lower overall life expectancy than the United States— 77.2 years, identical to Denmark (Figure 5.) On average, residents of Spain (80.5), Switzerland (80.4), and Sweden (80.2)—the three countries with the longest life expectancies in our sample—live three full years longer than residents of the United States. Among the major OECD economies, the United States also has the highest rate of infant mortality (7.0 per 1,000 live births). The next-highest rate in Western Europe is in the United Kingdom (5.3), while Norway (3.4), Finland (3.1), and Sweden (3.1) have rates that are less than half of those in the United States.

The United States also fares poorly with respect to maternal mortality. At the turn of the century, the United States had 9.1 maternal deaths per 100,000 births, the fourth-highest rate in the table behind Mexico (70.7), Denmark (11.1), and Luxembourg (10.9).[5] As with infant mortality, many Western European countries

---

[5] Only a very small percentage of women die in childbirth, so the data for maternal mortality, typically presented per 100,000 births, can vary substantially from year to year. As a result, Table 8 presents maternal mortality data averaged over the five most recent (available) years. For small countries with few births per year, even a small number of relatively bad years can have a relatively long-lasting impact on maternal mortality rates.

Table 8

Various health outcomes, circa 2003

	Life expectancy, yrs			Infant mortality, per 1,000 live births	Maternal mortality, per 100,000 births	Obesity, % adults with BMI > 30	Smoking, % adults smoking daily
	Female	Male	All				
Australia	82.8	77.8	80.3	4.8	4.7	21.7	19.8
Austria	81.6	75.6	78.6	4.5	3.6	9.1	36.3
Belgium	81.1	75.1	78.1	4.3	7.8	11.7	27.0
Canada	82.1	77.2	79.7	5.4	4.4	14.3	17.0
Czech Republic	78.5	72.0	75.3	3.9	7.7	14.8	24.1
Denmark	79.5	74.9	77.2	4.4	11.1	9.5	28.0
Finland	81.8	75.1	78.5	3.1	6.3	12.8	22.2
France	82.9	75.8	79.4	3.9	8.0	9.4	27.0
Germany	81.3	75.5	78.4	4.2	4.3	12.9	24.3
Greece	80.7	75.4	78.1	4.8	3.9	21.9	35.0
Hungary	76.5	68.3	72.4	7.3	7.1	18.8	33.8
Iceland	82.4	79.0	80.7	2.4	9.7	12.4	22.4
Ireland	80.3	75.2	77.8	5.1	3.1	13.0	27.0
Italy	82.9	76.9	79.9	4.3	3.1	8.5	24.2
Japan	85.3	78.4	81.8	3.0	6.5	3.2	30.3
Luxembourg	81.5	74.9	78.2	4.9	10.9	18.4	33.0
Mexico	77.4	72.4	74.9	20.1	70.7	24.2	26.4
Netherlands	80.9	76.2	78.6	4.8	6.9	10.0	32.0
New Zealand	81.1	76.3	78.7	5.6	6.6	20.9	25.0
Norway	81.9	77.0	79.5	3.4	6.6	8.3	26.0
Poland	78.9	70.5	74.7	7.0	5.6	—	27.6
Portugal	80.6	74.0	77.3	4.1	5.4	12.8	20.5
Slovak Republic	77.8	69.9	73.9	7.9	7.0	22.4	24.3
Spain	83.7	77.2	80.5	4.1	4.2	13.1	28.1
Sweden	82.4	77.9	80.2	3.1	4.2	9.7	17.5
Switzerland	83.0	77.8	80.4	4.3	5.0	7.7	26.8
United Kingdom	80.7	76.2	78.5	5.3	6.5	23.0	26.0
United States	**79.9**	**74.5**	**77.2**	**7.0**	**9.1**	**30.6**	**17.5**

Source: OECD Health Data 2005, Web edition.

Note: Maternal mortality rates are averages for the five most recent years. BMI, body mass index.

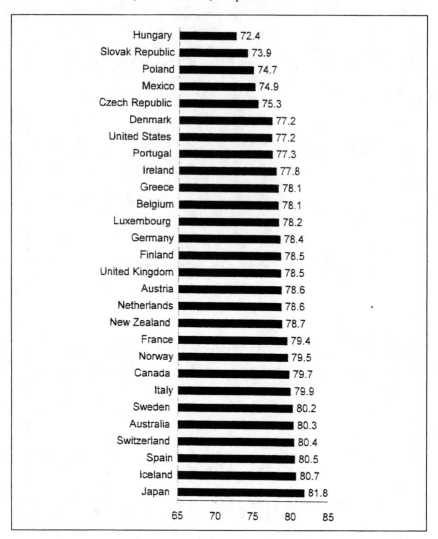

Figure 5. Life expectancy in years. *Source:* OECD Health Data 2005, Web edition.

had maternal mortality rates that were less than half that in the United States: Ireland (3.1), Italy (3.1), Austria (3.6), Greece (3.9), Spain (4.2), Sweden (4.2), and Germany (4.3).

The United States also has a much higher share of its population that exceeds the medical standard of obesity (a body mass index, BMI, of 30 or greater). Just over 30 percent of adults in the United States are obese, compared with 23.0 percent in the United Kingdom, the Western European country with the highest rate of obesity; meanwhile, Switzerland (7.7%), Norway (8.3%), Italy (8.5%), Austria (9.1%), France (9.4%), Denmark (9.5%), and Sweden (9.7%) all have obesity rates below 10 percent.

Public health campaigns against smoking, however, have apparently been much more successful in the United States than in most of Europe. Only 17.5 percent of U.S. adults smoke cigarettes daily. In Western Europe, only Sweden (17.5) has a rate as low. Most of Western Europe has smoking rates around 25 percent, with rates above 30 percent in the Netherlands (32.0%), Greece (35.0%), and Austria (36.3%).

In summary, the United States spends markedly more on health care (as a share of GDP or in dollars per person) than any other country in the world. Yet, more than 15 percent of its population typically finds itself without health coverage—private or public—throughout the entire length of any given year, with more than 27 percent lacking coverage at some point during the year. The additional U.S. expenditures on health care are also associated with substantially worse outcomes for basic health indicators, including life expectancy, infant and maternal mortality, and obesity. The United States, however, has succeeded in lowering rates of adult smoking to the lowest level among the rich, industrialized countries.

CRIME AND PUNISHMENT

Another potential dimension of social exclusion is crime. Table 9 summarizes some basic indicators of both the prevalence of criminal activity and the associated incarceration rates. The most reliable crime data are for murders, because murders are generally reported and accurately recorded. The murder rates listed in Table 9 are based on data compiled by the U.K. Home Office. The United States, at 5.6 murders per 100,000 people, has by far the highest murder rate in the sample of countries in the table. Finland (2.9) is next, followed by the Slovak Republic (2.6), the Czech Republic (2.5), and New Zealand (2.5). The U.S. murder rate is about five times higher than the rate in the safest Western European countries: Austria, Germany, and Portugal (all 1.2); Spain, Sweden, and Switzerland (all 1.1); and Denmark (1.0).

The United States does substantially better with respect to self-reported victimization rates, falling near but not at the top of the countries in Table 9. The table shows criminal victimization rates expressed as reported offenses per 100 people per year, from the 2000 International Crime Victims Survey.[6] In Western Europe, Switzerland (42.6 per 100 per year), Sweden (45.6), the Netherlands (48.1), and the United Kingdom (54.5) had higher victimization rates than the United States (39.5), while Denmark (35.1), France (33.9), Belgium (33.3), Austria (31.4), Finland (28.6), and Portugal (25.8) were all below the U.S. rate.

---

[6] Total of 10 crimes: car theft, theft from car, motor cycle theft, bicycle theft, burglary, attempted burglary, robbery, personal thefts, and assaults or threats.

Table 9

Crime and punishment, 2000s

	Murder rate, per 100,000[a]	Crime victimization, offenses per 100 per year[b]	Prison population rate[c]	
			Rate, per 100,000	World rank
Australia	1.9	54.3	126	60
Austria	1.2	31.4	108	173
Belgium	1.8	33.3	90	138
Canada	1.8	40.4	107	129
Czech Republic	2.5	—	191	156
Denmark	1.0	35.1	77	60
Finland	2.9	28.6	75	122
France	1.7	33.9	88	129
Germany	1.2	—	97	145
Greece	1.4	—	90	80
Hungary	2.3	—	163	107
Iceland	—	—	39	103
Ireland	1.4	—	85	142
Italy	1.5	—	97	198
Japan	1.1	21.0	62	119
Luxembourg	—	—	143	63
Mexico	—	—	191	146
Netherlands	1.5	48.1	127	102
New Zealand	2.5	—	189	93
Norway	1.0	—	68	138
Poland	2.1	39.7	229	92
Portugal	1.2	25.8	123	93
Slovak Republic	2.6	—	169	75
Spain	1.1	—	143	168
Sweden	1.1	45.6	78	157
Switzerland	1.1	42.6	83	160
United Kingdom	1.6	54.5	144	48
United States	**5.6**	**39.5**	**724**	**1**

Sources:
[a]G. Barclay and C. Tavares, "International Comparisons of Criminal Justice Statistics 2001," U.K. Home Office, Research Development and Statistics Directorate, October 24, 2001, Table 1.1. Murders recorded by the police. United Kingdom refers to England and Wales.

[b]J. N. van Kesteren, P. Mayhew, and P. Nieuwbeerta, "Criminal Victimization in Seventeen Industrial Countries: Key Findings from the 2000 International Crime Victims Survey," Appendix 4, Table 2, Ministry of Justice, The Hague. Total of ten crimes: car theft, theft from car, motorcycle theft, bicycle theft, burglary, attempted burglary, robbery, personal thefts, and assaults or threats. United Kingdom refers to England and Wales.

[c]International Centre for Prison Studies (9). United Kingdom refers to England and Wales. Ireland excludes N. Ireland. Ranking out of 213 countries and regions.

Given the United States' high, but not highest overall, victimization rates, all else being constant, we might expect this country to fall somewhere near the top of the list, but not at the top, for the portion of population that is incarcerated. In fact, prison population rates from the International Center for Prison Studies (9) show that the United States has a prison population rate (724 per 100,000) five to ten times those in Western Europe, where incarceration rates range from 68 per 100,000 in Norway to 143 in Spain and Luxembourg and 144 in the United Kingdom. Most of Western Europe, in fact, has incarceration rates below 100 per 100,000, including Finland (75), Denmark (77), Sweden (78), Switzerland (83), Ireland (85), France (88), Belgium (90), Greece (90), Germany (97), and Italy (97) (see Figure 6).

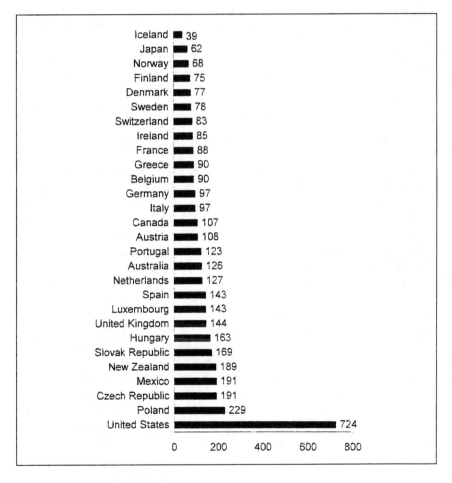

Figure 6. Prison population rate, per 100,000 population. *Source:* International Centre for Prison Studies (9).

The magnitude of the incarcerated population in the United States is sometimes difficult to comprehend. In 2004, U.S. prisons and jails held 2.1 million inmates, about 90 percent of whom were men (10). Given that the adult male workforce aged 16 and older in the same year was about 78.7 million (see 11; data for second quarter 2004, which correspond most closely to mid-2004 prison and jail estimates), this implies that a staggering 2.3 percent of the adult male population of the United States was in prison or jail in 2004.

LABOR MARKET

Based on the evidence reviewed so far, the U.S. economic and social model seems to generate a considerable degree of social exclusion, with high levels of income inequality, high relative and even absolute poverty rates, poor and unequal educational outcomes, poor and unequal health outcomes, and high rates of crime and incarceration. The U.S. model maintains its appeal in the face of poor performance in these areas, however, because supporters believe that the United States offers two compensating advantages: a flexible economy that yields high employment rates, and high income mobility that, in principle, compensates for greater inequality.

As the first column of Table 10 demonstrates, the U.S. experience with overall unemployment (5.6% in 2004) is good, and certainly far better than in Germany (9.9%), France (9.6%), and Spain (11.0%). At the same time, several Western European countries, with decidedly less "flexible" labor markets in the usual sense of that term, had unemployment rates in 2004 that were the same as or lower than in the United States: Ireland (4.4%), Switzerland (4.4%), Norway (4.5%), the Netherlands (4.7%), the United Kingdom (4.7%), Austria (5.3%), and Denmark (5.3%).

Despite the alleged superiority of U.S.-style flexibility, the United States does not do much better on unemployment rates for typically marginalized groups such as young people and those with less education—the kinds of groups most likely to benefit from greater wage flexibility, for example. The third column of Table 10 shows the unemployment rate (in 2004) for 15- to 24-year-olds. The rate in the United States (11.8%) was well below rates in France (21.3%), Italy (23.5%), and Spain (22.0%), but above rates in Switzerland (7.7%), Denmark (7.8%), the Netherlands (8.0%), Ireland (8.1%), the United Kingdom (10.9%), Austria (11.0%), Germany (11.7%), and Norway (11.7%). (The unemployment rate, and even the employment rate, for youth does not necessarily paint an accurate picture of how well the labor market is performing for young people, because many young people are probably best off in school. We examine this issue below.) The fourth column shows a similar pattern for those with the equivalent of less than a high school education. The U.S. unemployment rate for this group (in 2002) was 9.9 percent, higher than the corresponding rates in Norway (3.9%), Portugal (5.7%), Sweden (6.1%), Switzerland (6.1%), Ireland (6.3%), Greece (6.6%), the United Kingdom (6.9%), Denmark (7.2%), and Austria (7.9%).

The unemployment rate, however, is not the only measure of labor market performance. The middle columns of Table 10 give the employment-to-population rates for various demographic groups. Among 15- to 64-year-olds, the United States does manage to incorporate more of the population into jobs (71.2%) than is the case in several major European economies, most notably France (62.8%), Germany (65.5%), Italy (57.4%), and Spain (62.0%) (see Figure 7). Nevertheless, many smaller, "less flexible" Western European economies had higher employment rates than the United States: the United Kingdom (72.7%), the Netherlands (73.1%), Sweden (73.5%), Norway (73.5%), Denmark (76.0%), and Switzerland (77.4%).[7]

The United States has done well in incorporating women into the paid labor force. But, the data in Table 10 show that many Western European countries have also succeeded in this respect. In 2004, 65.4 percent of U.S. women ages 15 to 64 were employed. This was substantially higher than the corresponding rates in Italy (45.2%), Spain (49.0%), France (56.9%), and Germany (59.9%). The U.S. rates, however, were not as high as those in many European economies: Finland (65.5%), the Netherlands (65.7%), the United Kingdom (66.6%), Switzerland (70.3%), Sweden (71.8%), Denmark (72.0%), and Norway (72.7%).

Employment rates for youth (ages 15–24) repeat the now familiar pattern. The United States does better than the large, high-unemployment economies, but not as well as a host of smaller European economies. For youth, employment rates in the United States were 53.9 percent in 2004, well above the rates in Italy (27.2%), France (29.5%), Spain (38.4%), and Germany (41.9%), but not as high as rates in Norway (54.4%), the United Kingdom (60.1%), Denmark (61.3%), Switzerland (62.0%), and the Netherlands (66.2%).

With respect to employment rates for the less-educated, the United States actually underperforms when compared with much of Western Europe. In 2003, 58 percent of the less-educated population in the United States was in work. This rate was near or below rates in Ireland (57%), Spain (57%), Finland (58%), Greece (58%), France (59%), Denmark (61%), Norway (62%), Switzerland (66%), Sweden (68%), and Portugal (72%).

Earlier, we mentioned that using the unemployment rate (and even the employment rate) to measure social exclusion among youth may be misleading. From a societal perspective, we may be just as concerned about whether young people are in school as we are about whether they are in work. The last three columns of Table 10, therefore, report OECD data for 2002 on the share of young people in

---

[7] Schmitt and Baker (12) find that the declining coverage rate of the Current Population Survey (CPS) in recent decades may lead the CPS—the source of the U.S. unemployment and employment rates cited here—to overstate employment by about 1.4 percentage points, with the largest biases for more marginalized groups, especially young black men and young Hispanic women. To the extent that European surveys do not suffer from similar problems, the comparison here would overstate the U.S. performance relative to Europe.

Table 10

Labor-market outcomes, 2004

	Standardized unemployment rate, %				Employment-to-population rate, %				Not in education and not employed, %		
	All 15–64 yrs	Women 15–64 yrs	Youth 15–24 yrs	Less-educated 25–64 yrs	All 15–64 yrs	Women 15–64 yrs	Youth 15–24 yrs	Less-educated 25–64 yrs	15–19 yrs	20–24 yrs	25–29 yrs
Australia	5.5	5.6	11.7	7.0	69.5	62.6	59.4	61	7.0	13.2	17.8
Austria	5.3	5.3	11.0	7.9	66.5	60.1	49.9	55	6.3	11.7	12.4
Belgium	7.4	8.3	17.5	10.7	60.5	53.0	28.1	49	6.8	17.4	17.2
Canada	7.2	6.9	13.4	10.9	72.6	68.4	58.1	57	6.5	14.0	16.7
Czech Republic	8.4	10.0	20.4	19.8	64.2	56.0	28.5	44	6.0	18.1	23.8
Denmark	5.3	5.5	7.8	7.2	76.0	72.0	61.3	61	2.4	7.3	6.7
Finland	8.9	9.0	20.8	11.1	67.2	65.5	38.1	58	14.8	18.8	19.7
France	9.6	10.7	21.3	12.1	62.8	56.9	29.5	59	3.4	14.4	18.2
Germany	9.9	9.4	11.7	18.0	65.5	59.9	41.9	50	4.7	15.9	17.4
Greece	10.4	16.0	26.5	6.6	59.6	45.5	27.4	58	6.2	22.0	25.2
Hungary	6.1	6.1	15.5	10.6	56.8	50.7	23.6	37	8.0	20.3	27.6
Iceland	3.1	3.0	8.1	—	82.8	79.4	66.3	—	—	—	—
Ireland	4.4	3.7	8.1	6.3	65.5	55.8	44.8	57	4.8	10.8	14.7
Italy	8.1	10.6	23.5	—	57.4	45.2	27.2	—	10.5	24.3	24.8

Japan	4.9	9.5	6.7	68.7	57.4	40.0	67	0.0	0.0	0.0
Luxembourg	4.8	18.3	3.3	61.6	50.6	21.4	61	3.0	7.0	11.6
Mexico	3.1	6.4	1.6	60.8	41.3	45.2	63	17.5	26.6	30.6
Netherlands	4.7	8.0	—	73.1	65.7	66.2	—	4.6	7.9	12.9
New Zealand	4.0	9.3	4.9	75.6	66.5	56.8	63	—	—	—
Norway	4.5	11.7	3.9	73.5	72.7	54.4	62	3.2	9.7	10.7
Poland	19.3	40.8	25.9	51.9	46.4	20.0	38	3.1	25.4	31.8
Portugal	7.0	15.3	5.7	67.8	61.7	36.9	72	7.3	12.0	12.2
Slovak Republic	18.2	32.7	44.9	57.0	50.9	26.5	29	15.6	33.9	30.5
Spain	11.0	22.0	11.2	62.0	49.0	38.4	57	7.2	15.1	19.8
Sweden	6.6	17.0	6.1	73.5	71.8	42.8	68	4.6	11.2	8.1
Switzerland	4.4	7.7	6.1	77.4	70.3	62.0	66	4.4	9.7	12.6
United Kingdom	4.7	10.9	6.9	72.7	66.6	60.1	54	8.6	15.3	16.0
United States	**5.6**	**11.8**	**9.9**	**71.2**	**65.4**	**53.9**	**58**	**7.5**	**15.6**	**17.7**

Source: OECD Employment Outlook 2004, 2005, various tables.
Note: Data for less-educated refer to 2003. Data for individuals not in education or employment refer to 2002.

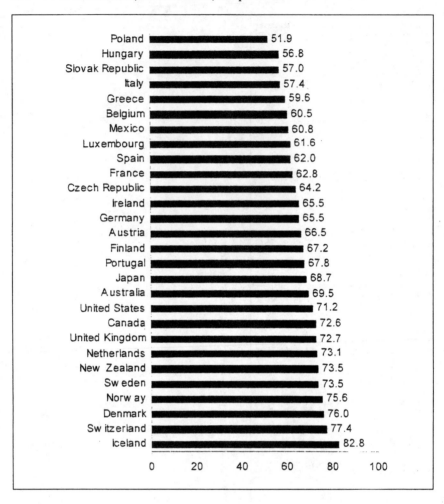

Figure 7. Employment-to-population rate, as percent employed, all individuals ages 15 to 64. *Source:* OECD Employment Outlook 2004, 2005, various tables.

each country that were neither in work nor in education. The United States did not do particularly well among either 15- to 19-year-olds or 20- to 24-year-olds. For the younger group (ages 15–19), only Hungary (8.0%), the United Kingdom (8.6%), Italy (10.5%), and Finland (14.8%) had a higher share of young people out of both work and school (the U.S. rate was 7.5%). For the next-older age group (ages 20–24), the United States (15.6%) did better than some Western European economies—Germany (15.9%), Belgium (17.4%), Finland (18.8%), Greece (22.0%), and Italy (24.3%)—but not as well as Denmark (7.3%), the Netherlands

(7.9%), Norway (9.7%), Switzerland (9.7%), Ireland (10.8%), Sweden (11.2%), Austria (11.7%), Portugal (12.0%), France (14.4%), Spain (15.1%), and the United Kingdom (15.3%).

The review of these data suggests that U.S. labor market performance is generally—though not always—better than that of the four large, high-unemployment European economies (France, Germany, Italy, and Spain). Nevertheless, the United States consistently underperforms relative to many of the smaller Western European economies whose labor markets are conventionally seen as much more rigid than that of the United States.

ECONOMIC MOBILITY

Advocates of the U.S. model also maintain that the country's economic dynamism produces a level of economic mobility that compensates for high levels of inequality and poverty. Economic and social distances may be much greater in the United States than in Europe, but, the argument goes, those at the bottom have a much greater chance to get ahead than they do in Europe. In this final section, we briefly review some international evidence on economic mobility both within and across generations.

Table 11 and Figure 8 present OECD data on short-term income mobility for a subsample of 14 countries. The table gives the share of low-income families

Table 11

Income mobility, 1993 to 1995, as percentage of low-income families exiting low-income status each year

Belgium	48.2
Canada	36.4
Denmark	60.4
France	46.9
Germany	41.1
Greece	38.8
Ireland	54.6
Italy	40.6
Luxembourg	47.4
Netherlands	55.7
Portugal	37.0
Spain	49.6
United Kingdom	58.8
United States	**29.5**

Source: OECD Employment Outlook 2001, Table 2.2.
Note: Low-income defined as earning less than half of the national median income.
U.S. data refer to 1987–1989.

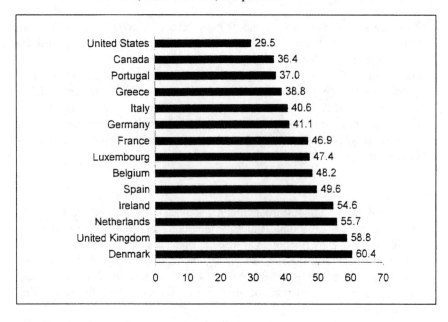

Figure 8. Income mobility, late 1980s to mid-1990s, as percent of low-income families exiting low-income status each year. *Source:* OECD Employment Outlook 2001, Table 2.2.

(with low income defined as earning less than half of the national median income) that managed to escape from low-income status over a three-year period in the mid-1990s.[8] Contrary to the view that the United States offers substantial mobility, this country had the lowest share of low-income workers that exited their low-income status from one year to the next (29.5%). The corresponding rates in several European countries were greater than 50 percent: Ireland (54.6%), the Netherlands (55.7%), the United Kingdom (58.8%), and Denmark (60.4%).

---

[8] The U.S. data refer to 1987–1989. The OECD (13) notes that "the time periods used to study poverty dynamics in the different countries are not fully comparable. The most important instance of non-comparable time periods is that poverty dynamics for the United States are studied for an earlier period . . . than that studied for the other countries, due to data consistency problems in the American data for more recent years. Although the periods chosen are those for which business cycle conditions in the United States approximated those in the other countries studied, this difference means that the results do not reflect the impact on American poverty dynamics of recent reforms in welfare programmes and more generous in-work benefits (i.e., expansion of the Earned Income Tax Credit). On the other hand, the PSID data for income years after 1992 show greater poverty incidence and persistence in the United States, so that the use of these data would reinforce the comparative results for the United States. Exclusion of these data can be regarded as representing a somewhat conservative approach to the assessment of American poverty."

Table 12 summarizes the results from three separate analyses of longer-term intergenerational mobility across countries (14–16). In all three cases, the authors investigated the degree of correlation between fathers' and sons' incomes at different points in time. These intergenerational income coefficients quantify the economic advantage that parents confer on their children: the higher the coefficient, the more likely that children born to poor parents will remain poor later in life.

Table 12

Correlation of income between fathers and sons, as measure
of intergenerational economic mobility

Blanden, 2004 (14, Table 3)	
United States	0.45
United Kingdom	0.27
Germany	0.12
Canada	0.18
Solon, 2002 (15, Table 1 and text)	
United Kingdom	0.57
South Africa	0.44
United Kingdom	0.42
United States	0.40
Germany	0.34
Sweden	0.28
Canada	0.23
Finland	0.22
Sweden	0.14
Finland	0.13
Sweden	0.13
Germany	0.11
Corak, 2004 (16)	
United Kingdom	0.50
United States	0.47
France	0.41
Germany	0.32
Sweden	0.27
Canada	0.19
Finland	0.18
Norway	0.17
Denmark	0.15

Note: The higher the coefficient, the lower the economic mobility.

The top panel of Table 12 summarizes Blanden's findings (14) for Canada, Germany, the United Kingdom, and the United States. Blanden found the lowest level of correlation between fathers' and sons' incomes—therefore, the highest degree of economic mobility—in Germany (0.12), followed by Canada (0.18) and the United Kingdom (0.27). Intergenerational economic mobility was lowest, by a substantial margin, in the United States (0.45). The middle panel presents similar correlation coefficients from a review of international studies by Solon (15; some countries with more than one study). The 0.40 coefficient for the United States is Solon's estimated average based on research in the United States. According to these data, only South Africa (0.44) and, in one of two studies, the United Kingdom (0.57) had lower rates of mobility than the United States (0.40). Canada (0.23), Finland (0.13 and 0.22), Germany (0.11 and 0.34), and Sweden (0.13, 0.14, and 0.28) all seemed to have substantially greater economic mobility across generations than did the United States. Corak (16) reached similar conclusions (Table 12, bottom panel). The United Kingdom (0.50) and the United States (0.47) had the least economic mobility. France (0.41), Germany (0.32), Sweden (0.27), Canada (0.19), Finland (0.18), Norway (0.17), and Denmark (0.15) all offered greater economic mobility than the United States.

What seem to be small differences in intergenerational income coefficients actually imply substantial differences in economic mobility. Take, for example, the case of a family with earnings that are half of the national average. Other factors being constant, if a country has a correlation coefficient for parent–child earnings of 0.20, we would expect that descendants of the poor family would reach the average national earnings in less than two generations, or about 25 to 50 years.[9] In countries with a coefficient of 0.45, a typical level in the estimates for the United States (and, in some cases, for the United Kingdom), descendants of the poor family would not, on average, close the income gap with the average family for more than three generations, or about 75 to 100 years.

CONCLUSION

The U.S. economic and social model is associated with substantial levels of social exclusion, including high levels of income inequality, high relative and absolute poverty rates, poor and unequal educational outcomes, poor health outcomes, and high rates of crime and incarceration.

At the same time, the available evidence provides little support for the view that U.S.-style labor market flexibility dramatically improves labor market outcomes.

---

[9] Intergenerational mobility coefficients are determined by the regression: $\ln Y_{i,t} = \alpha + \beta \ln Y_{i,t-1} + \varepsilon_{i,t}$, where generations are indexed by t. If $G_t = Y_{1,t}/Y_{2,t}$ and nonparental income influences are ignored ($\varepsilon = 0$), the income gaps between two sets of parents, G_0, and their respective children, G_1, satisfy $G_1 = G_0^{\beta}$. Similarly, $G_n = G_0^{\beta^{\wedge}n}$, which implies that $n = \ln (\ln G_n/\ln G_0)/\ln \beta$. The calculations above assume $G_0 = 2$ (the 200% gap between the mean and half the mean), $G_n = 1.05$ (only a 5% gap), and a generation = 25 years.

The U.S. labor market seems to fare consistently better than the four large, high-unemployment economies in Europe—France, Germany, Italy, and Spain— but the United States does no better and often does noticeably worse than many smaller European economies with labor markets that are highly regulated relative to that of the United States and even relative to those of the large, high-unemployment countries.

The data also seem to contradict the belief that greater economic mobility in the United States can somehow compensate for greater levels of inequality and "social exclusion." Despite popular prejudices to the contrary, the U.S. economy consistently affords a lower level of economic mobility, both in the short term (from one year to the next) and in the longer term (across generations), than all the continental European countries for which data are available. Given its high direct levels of social exclusion, and especially its low levels of economic mobility across generations, the United States stands as a poor model for a Europe seeking to combat social exclusion.

Acknowledgments — We thank the Rockefeller Foundation for its financial support of this research at the Center for Economic and Policy Research. We are solely responsible for the views expressed here.

REFERENCES

1. Smeeding, T. M. *Public Policy and Economic Inequality: The United States in Comparative Perspective.* Luxembourg Income Study Working Paper Series no. 367. February 2004.
2. Navarro, V. (ed.). *The Political Economy of Social Inequalities: Consequences for Health and Quality of Life.* Baywood, Amityville, NY, 2002.
3. Townsend, P. *Poverty in the United Kingdom.* Penguin, Harmondsworth, UK, 1979.
4. Scruggs, L., and Allan, J. P. *The Material Consequences of Welfare States: Benefit Generosity and Absolute Poverty in 16 OECD Countries.* Luxembourg Income Study Working Paper Series no. 409. April 2005.
5. Groningen Growth and Development Centre and the Conference Board. Total Economy Database, May 2006. www.ggdc.net/.
6. Smeeding, T. M. Poor people in rich nations: The United States in comparative perspective. *J. Econ. Perspect.* 20:69–90, 2006.
7. DeNavas-Walt. C., Proctor, B. D., and Mills, R. J. *Income, Poverty, and Health Insurance Coverage in the United States: 2003.* U.S. Census Bureau, Washington, DC, 2004.
8. Boushey, H. *Analysis of the Upcoming Release of 2003 Data on Income, Poverty, and Health Insurance.* Briefing paper. Center for Economic and Policy Research, Washington, DC, January 2004.
9. International Centre for Prison Studies, King's College. Entire World—Prison Population Rates per 100,000 of the National Population, London, 2006. www. prisonstudies.org/ (May 2006).

10. U.S. Department of Justice, Office of Justice Programs, Bureau of Justice Statistics. *Prison and Jail Inmates at Midyear 2004.* U.S. Department of Justice, Washington DC, April 2005.
11. Bureau of Labor Statistics, Current Population Survey home page, customized tables, series LNS11000001Q. www.bls.gov/cps/home.htm.
12. Schmitt, J., and Baker, D. *Missing Inaction: Evidence of Undercounting of Non-Workers in the Current Population Survey (CPS).* Briefing paper. Center for Economic and Policy Research, Washington, DC, 2006.
13. Organization for Economic Cooperation and Development. *Employment Outlook 2001: Reconciling Social and Employment Goals.* Paris, June 2001.
14. Blanden, J. International Evidence on Inter-generational Mobility. Unpublished paper. Centre for Economic performance, London, January 2004.
15. Solon, G. Cross-country differences in intergenerational earnings mobility. *J. Econ. Perspect.* 16:59–66, 2002.
16. Corak, M. Do Poor Children Become Poor Adults? Unpublished paper. Statistics Canada, Ottawa, 2004.

PART VI

The Liberal Model in the United States and Its Social Consequences

Labor Markets and Economic Inequality in the United States Since the End of the 1970s

John Schmitt

During the 1990s, international organizations such as the Organization for Economic Cooperation and Development (OECD), the International Monetary Fund (IMF), and the World Bank encouraged both developed and developing economies to restructure their economies in the image of the United States. These proponents of loosely regulated U.S.-style labor, product, and financial markets justified their support for the "U.S. model" by pointing to the country's low unemployment rate, rapid economic and productivity growth, and prodigious capacity for wealth accumulation, especially in national stock markets. These same advocates, however, frequently exaggerated U.S. performance relative to other advanced economies (1) and glossed over the high and rising level of economic and social inequality in the United States.

This chapter seeks to describe the scale and growth of economic inequality in the United States since the end of the 1970s and, then, to analyze some of the economic and political forces that account for these developments. The first section reviews recent trends in three of the most important economic distributions: wages, incomes, and wealth.[1] The second section describes the set of interlocking forces that have, since the end of the 1970s, driven the rise in economic and social inequality. While these forces take many disparate forms—a fall in unionization rates, a decline in the legislated minimum wage, erosion of the generosity of the social safety net, deregulation of product and financial markets, privatization of many state and local government functions, and others—they have a common denominator: each shifts the balance of power away from workers and

---

[1] A complete analysis of economic hardship associated with the "U.S. model" would also require an examination of the rise in hours of work, the high and generally rising levels of job instability and job insecurity, the deterioration of the social safety net, and other developments. Coverage of all these topics is beyond the scope of this chapter. For a comprehensive review of the U.S. labor market in the 1980s and 1990s, including many topics not covered here, see 2; for a detailed analysis of job quality, see 3.

toward their employers. Ultimately, these policy shifts, which reflect the balance of power in society at large, and not technological progress or even the increasing pace of globalization, are the primary culprits behind the widening economic and social disparities documented here.

THREE IMPORTANT ECONOMIC DISTRIBUTIONS

At the end of the 1970s, the United States was probably the most economically unequal of the advanced capitalist economies, and, since the end of the 1970s, economic inequality has almost certainly increased more in the United States than it has in the rest of the world's rich countries. (For an analysis of wage inequality trends in the OECD countries, see 4; for a discussion of income inequality trends, see 5 annex 3; and 6.) This section reviews recent developments in three of the most important economic distributions: hourly wages, annual incomes, and net wealth. While a complete analysis of economic and social inequality would require a thorough discussion of the distribution of access to medical care, adequate housing, quality education, and other fundamental aspects of well-being, the wage, income, and wealth distributions nevertheless provide a compelling, if somewhat incomplete, picture of economic and social inequality in the United States at the turn of the century.

Wages

The first distribution of interest is hourly wages—what workers earn (before paying taxes) for an hour of their work. Table 1 summarizes several important aspects of this distribution for the United States in 2004. The first striking feature of the distribution of wages is that it is highly unequal. As the table shows, the median (50th percentile) worker made $14.00 per hour in 2004—about twice the rate ($6.80) for a low-wage (10th percentile) worker, and about half the rate ($30.46) for a high-wage (90th percentile) worker. A second feature of the wage distribution is that inequality is especially high at the top. Very high-wage workers, such as those in the 95th percentile ($37.34), received about 23 percent more per hour than high-wage workers in the 90th percentile, who were only five percentage points lower in the distribution. A third characteristic of the wage distribution is that men at any given point in the male wage distribution earn substantially more than women do at the corresponding point in their own distribution. In 2004, low-wage (10th percentile) female workers, for example, made about 7 percent less than their male counterparts, while women at the 50th, 90th, and 95th percentiles earned 16 to 20 percent less than men in the same position in the male distribution. A final salient aspect of the wage distribution is that wages differ sharply across racial and ethnic lines. In 2004, the median (50th percentile) white male worker ($17.26) earned 56 percent more than the median Hispanic male worker ($11.09) and 34 percent more than the

Table 1

Hourly wage distribution, by race and gender, United States, 2004

| | Hourly wage, 2003 $, by percentile | | | |
	10th	50th	90th	95th
All	6.80	14.00	30.46	37.34
White	7.28	14.94	32.39	38.74
Black	6.80	12.14	25.28	31.11
Hispanic	6.55	10.62	23.30	28.45
Women	6.80	12.45	27.18	33.61
White	6.80	13.11	28.01	34.31
Black	6.36	11.65	24.27	29.13
Hispanic	6.07	9.71	21.51	26.77
Men	7.28	15.53	33.61	40.05
White	7.77	17.26	35.27	42.01
Black	7.01	12.91	26.89	33.61
Hispanic	6.80	11.09	24.27	29.56

Source: Analysis of CEPR CPS ORG extract, version 0.96.
Note: The white and black categories exclude people of Hispanic origin; Hispanics may be of any race.

median black male worker ($12.91). At the median, white women ($13.11) received about 13 percent more than black women ($11.65) and about 35 percent more than Hispanic women ($9.71).

The inequality visible in the wage data for 2004 is the result of long-standing historical processes including gender and racial discrimination. Since the end of the 1970s, however, these historical forces have been particularly effective in raising wage inequality. Figure 1 graphs changes between 1973 and 2004 in the inflation-adjusted value of wages at the 10th, 50th, and 90th percentiles of the overall wage distribution. In the figure, all wages were set equal to 100.0 in real terms in 1979. Between 1979 and 1985, the real value of the 10th percentile wage fell about 15 percent. Over the same period, real wages at the 50th percentile remained roughly constant, while wages at the 90th percentile rose about 10 percent. As a result, wage inequality, measured as the gap between workers in the 90th percentile and the 10th percentile, grew sharply. Between the mid-1980s and the mid-1990s, wage inequality continued to grow, primarily because wages at the bottom and the middle stagnated at the same time that wages at the top continued to grow at a modest pace. From the mid-1990s through 2001, however, wages rose quickly for workers at all wage levels. Wages grew fastest at the top and bottom, keeping the level of inequality as measured by the differential

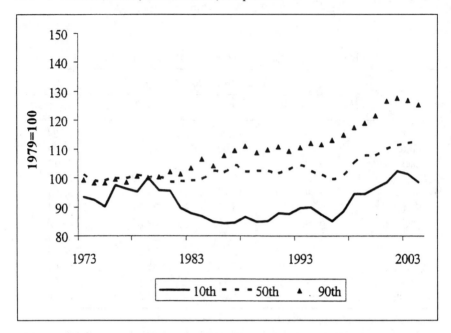

Figure 1. Real hourly wage growth, all U.S. workers, by income percentiles, 1973–2004. *Source:* Analysis of CEPR CPS ORG extract (1979–04) chained to EPI May CPS extract (1973–79), deflated using CPI-U-RS.

between the 90th and 10th percentiles roughly constant. Wages grew slightly slower at the median, contributing to a narrowing of the 50th–10th differential and a slight rise in the 90th–50th differential.

Even after strong wage gains in the late 1990s for low- and middle-wage workers, the wage distribution was still substantially more unequal at the turn of the century than it had been 20 years earlier. Wage growth over the 1980s and 1990s, both in real terms and relative to average productivity, was also well below rates achieved in the earlier postwar period. Real wages for 10th percentile workers, for example, were no higher in 2004 than they had been in 1979, despite a 66 percent increase over the same period in the average output per hour worked (productivity) (1979-2004 growth in average non-farm business output/hour from 7). At the median, real wages rose only 13 percent between 1979 and 2004, an average of less than 0.5 percent per year. Even at the 90th percentile, real wage gains over the same period of 25 percent trailed far behind productivity growth.

The wage data in Figure 1 refer to all workers and mask substantial differences in the underlying developments for men and women, which appear separately in Figure 2. Both the male and female distributions show large increases in inequality, but the graphs reveal two key differences. First, the rise in inequality

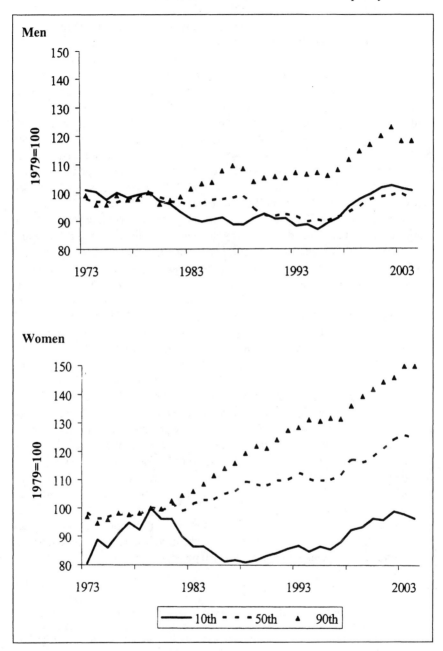

Figure 2. Real hourly wage growth, United States, male workers (top) and female workers (bottom), by income percentiles, 1973–2004. *Source:* Analysis of CEPR CPS ORG extract (1979–04) chained to EPI May CPS extract (1973–79), deflated using CPI-U-RS.

after 1979 (measured by the 90th–10th differential) was larger for women than it was for men. Between 1979 and 2004, the 90th–10th ratio for men grew from 3.9 to 4.6, while the corresponding ratio for women increased from 2.6 to 4.1. Second, across the entire distribution, real wages grew faster (or declined more slowly) for women than they did for men. Between 1979 and 2004, at the 90th percentile, for example, real wages grew about 50 percent for women and only about 18 percent for men; at the 50th percentile, women's real wages increased about 24 percent, compared with about a 3 percent decline for men; and, at the 10th percentile, wages for women were down almost 4 percent compared with no change for men.[2] (As we saw above, even though women's wages grew more rapidly at all points across the distribution, by 2004, women's wages remained below men's wages at comparable points in the two distributions.)

Wages are the most important, but not the only, form of compensation paid to workers. In a country that does not provide low-cost, universal medical care and where the Social Security system, while efficient and effective, is designed only to keep the elderly out of poverty, employer-provided health and pension benefits are two forms of non-wage compensation that are particularly important determinants of workers' well-being.[3] Table 2 presents data on the coverage rates for employer-provided health and pension plans from 1979 through 2002. In 2002, a substantial share of U.S. workers did not have employer-provided health or pension coverage: only 57.3 percent of workers were enrolled in employer-provided health plans and only 45.5 percent were in employer-sponsored pension plans. Moreover, participation in such plans varied substantially across wage level, gender, and race. Among workers in the bottom fifth of the wage distribution, just 26.6 percent had health coverage, compared with 78.5 percent for the top fifth of workers. Men (61.1 percent) were more likely than women (52.8 percent) to have health insurance benefits. Among whites, 57.9 percent had health benefits, compared with 53.8 percent for blacks and just 43.5 percent for Hispanics. Coverage gaps by wage level, gender, and race were also large for pensions. Only 15.0 percent of the bottom fifth of workers had a pension plan at work, compared with 71.2 percent of the top fifth of workers. Again, men (47.2 percent) were more likely than women (43.5 percent) and whites (46.6 percent) were more likely than blacks (39.5 percent) and Hispanics (25.3 percent) to have an employer-provided pension.

---

[2] For a detailed breakdown of real-wage trends for all, male, and female workers, see 2, tables 2.6, 2.7, and 2.8; for a detailed comparison of male and female wage inequality, see 2, table 2.16.

[3] Other important forms of non-wage compensation are paid vacations and holidays, paid family or medical leave, child care, and severance pay. Unlike the European union, which requires employers to provide minimum (and, by U.S. standards, generous) levels of paid leave, the United States does not have statutory requirements for paid leave. U.S. labor law does require employers with more than 50 employees to provide unpaid leave of up to 12 weeks for family and medical reasons. U.S. employers are not required to, and generally do not, provide child care benefits or severance pay.

Table 2

Health and pension benefit coverage rates, United States, 1979–2002

	Coverage rate, %				Percentage point change	
	1979	1989	2000	2002	1979–1989	1989–2002
Health care plans						
All workers	69.0	61.5	63.4	57.3	−7.5	−4.2
Men	75.4	66.8	66.6	61.1	−8.6	−5.7
Women	59.4	54.9	59.3	52.8	−4.5	−2.1
White	70.3	64.0	67.2	57.9	−6.3	−6.1
Black	63.1	56.3	60.2	53.8	−6.8	−2.5
Hispanic	60.4	46.0	44.8	43.5	−14.4	−2.5
By wage quintile						
Lowest	37.9	26.4	33.4	26.6	−11.5	0.2
Second	60.5	51.7	57.7	48.8	−8.8	−2.9
Middle	74.7	67.5	68.3	62.7	−7.2	−4.8
Fourth	83.5	78.0	77.0	72.1	−5.5	−5.9
Top	89.5	84.7	81.2	78.5	−4.8	−6.2
Pension plans						
All workers	50.6	43.7	49.6	45.5	−6.9	1.8
Men	56.9	46.9	51.1	47.2	−10.0	0.3
Women	41.3	39.6	47.6	43.5	−1.7	3.9
White	52.2	46.1	54.6	46.6	−6.1	0.5
Black	45.8	40.7	43.1	39.5	−5.1	−1.2
Hispanic	38.2	26.3	28.5	25.3	−11.9	−1.0
By wage quintile						
Lowest	18.4	12.7	16.0	15.0	−5.7	2.3
Second	36.8	29.0	34.4	33.3	−7.8	4.3
Middle	52.3	44.5	49.9	48.4	−7.8	3.9
Fourth	68.4	60.0	63.6	61.9	−8.4	1.9
Top	78.5	72.8	73.0	71.2	−5.7	−1.6
Defined contrib. plans[a]	16.0	38.0	42.0	42.0	22.0	4.0

Sources: EPI analysis of wage and salary workers, ages 16 to 64, who worked at least 20 hours per week and 26 weeks per year, using March CPS data; adapted from Mishel, Bernstein, and Allegretto (2), tables 2.14 and 2.15. Share of pension participants primarily in defined-contribution plans from Employment Benefit Research Institute, 1998, table 4.

Notes: Coverage defined as being in an employer-provided plan where the employer paid at least part of the coverage.

[a]Data in column one refer to 1980; column two, 1990; columns three and four, 1997; with corresponding changes in last two columns (percentage point changes).

The data in Table 2 also reveal important trends in benefit coverage over time. In the 1980s, both health and pension coverage rates fell across the board. For health insurance, the cutbacks generally hit the most disadvantaged groups (except women) hardest. Between 1979 and 1989, for example, overall health insurance coverage fell 7.5 percentage points, but declined most for low-wage workers (down 11.5 percentage points for the bottom fifth of workers) and least for high-wage workers (down 4.8 percentage points). Declines were also steeper for Hispanics (down 14.4 percentage points) and blacks (down 6.8 percentage points) than they were for whites (down 6.3 percentage points). The fall-off in pension plan participation over the same period, however, was more evenly shared. Between 1979 and 1989, pension coverage fell 6.9 percentage points, with declines about equal at the bottom and top of the wage distribution (both down 5.7 percentage points) and for whites (down 6.1 percentage points) and blacks (down 5.1 percentage points)—though the participation of Hispanics in pension plans fell 11.9 percentage points.

In the 1990s, benefit-coverage rates stabilized in the case of health insurance (up 1.9 percentage points between 1989 and 2000) and, in the case of pension plans, coverage even managed to recoup most of the ground lost in the 1980s (up 5.9 percentage points). With respect to health insurance, disadvantaged groups generally fared best in the 1990s. Coverage rates rose most for low-wage workers—up 7 percentage points by 2000 among the bottom fifth, compared with a 3.5 percentage point decline for the highest fifth. For blacks, rates increased 3.9 percentage points by 2000, slightly faster than the corresponding 3.2 percentage point increase for whites (though Hispanics fell 1.2 percentage points). With respect to pensions, increases between 1989 and 2000 were slightly larger for low- and middle-wage workers than they were for high-wage workers; larger for women (up 8.0 percent points) than they were for men (up 4.2 percentage points); and much larger for whites (up 8.5 percentage points) than they were for blacks (up 2.4 percentage points) or Hispanics (up 2.2 percentage points).

One important reason for the apparent improvements in pension coverage in the 1990s was probably the large shift from "defined-benefit" to "defined-contribution" pension plans. In defined-benefit plans, which were by far the most common form of pension plans in the earlier postwar period, employers guaranteed workers a specific payment in retirement, generally based on the employee's salary history and time with the employer. Employers would set aside and invest a portion of each employee's total compensation and use those invested funds to pay the specified benefit in the employee's retirement. In defined-contribution plans, which have become more widespread since the late 1970s, employers contribute to a pension plan managed individually by each employee. Employees then use the proceeds from their individual accounts to provide for their own retirement. While defined-contribution plans give direct control to employees, these plans also shift all investment risk to employees.[4] The last row of Table 2 shows the share of employees participating in pension plans whose benefits were primarily in the form of defined-contribution program. The share rose from 16 percent in 1980 to 42 percent by the late 1990s, with the fastest shift occurring in the 1980s.

Incomes

The second economic distribution of interest here is annual income—the money families receive in the course of a year from all sources including work, government transfers, profits from investments, and other sources. Table 3 provides a summary of the annual family income distribution in 2001, highlighting several important features. First, the income distribution is even more unequal than the wage distribution. A family in the 80th percentile of the income distribution received almost four times more per year than a family in the 20th percentile of the distribution ($94,150 at the 80th percentile, compared with $24,000 at the 20th percentile). Thus, the gap between the 80th and the 20th percentiles in the income distribution is about the same size as the gap between the 90th and 10th percentiles in the wage distribution. Moreover, as was the case with the wage distribution, income inequality is especially exaggerated at the top. In 2001, a family in the 95th percentile of the income distribution, for example, made 3.2 times more than a family receiving the median income ($164,104, compared with $51,407). For wages in the same year, the 95th percentile was only 2.8 times higher than the median wage.

A second feature of the income distribution is that racial differences are even starker than for wages. In 2001, black and Hispanic families in the middle of their respective annual-income distributions, for example, received less than two-thirds of the income going to a family in the middle of the white distribution (about $42,000 for both blacks and Hispanics, compared with about $65,000 for whites).[5]

Figure 3 shows inflation-adjusted changes in the median family income from the end of World War II through 2004 (with the trend growth for 1947–1973

---

[4] While many employees prefer direct control over their retirement savings, many others don't enjoy the corresponding administrative burden and added financial risk. The poor performance of U.S. stock markets in 2000, 2001, and 2002 has heightened general awareness about the risks inherent in defined-contribution pension plans.

[5] Since most families include males and females, a gender analysis of family income requires more sophisticated analysis than is possible here. A complete gender analysis would involve a review of patterns both across family types (e g., single-parent families, one-earner married-couple families, and two-earner married-couple families) and *within* families, where gender may play an important role in the allocation of family resources.

Table 3

Annual family income distribution, by race, United States, 2001

| | Upper limit of income, 2001 $, by quintile | | | | Lower limit of top 5% |
	Lowest fifth	Second fifth	Middle fifth	Fourth fifth	
All	24,000	41,127	62,500	94,150	164,104
White	26,000	44,000	65,283	97,185	169,501
Black	14,256	26,350	42,400	67,523	110,977
Hispanic	16,000	28,000	41,600	66,040	113,374

Source: Author's analysis of U.S. Census Bureau, Historical Income Tables, Families, tables F-1, F1-A, F1-B, and F1-C.
Note: White families exclude those of Hispanic origin; Hispanic families can be of any race.

projected through 2003). Between 1947 and 1979, the real income of the median U.S. family more than doubled. After 1973, the growth rate decelerated, and family income began to demonstrate a strongly cyclical pattern, falling sharply in downturns (almost unheard of in the earlier postwar period) and rising in booms. Family income growth was particularly rapid in the extended economic expansion of the late 1990s.

The path of median family earnings in Figure 3, however, misses two important characteristics of recent trends in family income. The first is that even as growth in family earnings decelerated after the mid-1970s, the number of hours that families work (particularly married-couple families with children) has expanded greatly. The typical married-couple family with children, for example, as a family, worked almost 15 more weeks per year (about 18 percent longer) in 2000 than it did in 1979 (see 8, table 1.26). Much of the rise in family income that did take place after 1979, therefore, stemmed from family members working more in the course of a year.

The second feature missing from Figure 3 is the distribution of gains across the full distribution. As Figure 4 illustrates, the experience of families at different points of the income distribution varied greatly before and after the mid-1970s. Between 1947 and 1973, the annual growth rate in family income was high and fairly uniform across the income distribution. If anything, families at the bottom and middle saw their incomes rise slightly faster than families at the top. From 1973 through 2003, however, growth rates were much slower across the board and particularly bad at the bottom and middle. In the first part of the postwar period, income growth was rapid and generally equalizing; from the mid-1980s, growth has, on average, been slow and skewed toward the top.

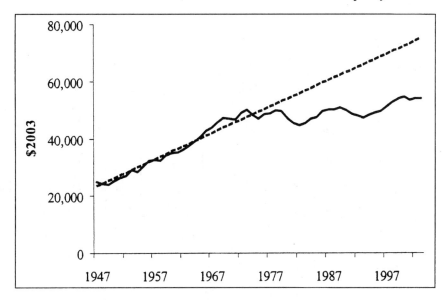

Figure 3. Real median family income, United States, in 2003 dollars, 1947–2003 (dashed line shows 1947–73 trend). *Source:* Analysis of Bureau of the Census, Current Population Survey; deflated using CPI-U-RS.

Wealth

The third economic distribution of interest here is the distribution of wealth—the net value of each household's assets (such as housing, stocks and bonds, savings accounts, etc.) minus its debts (mortgages, credit-card debts, car loans, etc.). Table 4 demonstrates that the distribution of wealth is, by far, the most unequal of the three distributions analyzed here. In 2001, the wealthiest 1 percent of households controlled 33.4 percent of the wealth, an amount equal to about 100 times the 0.3 percent share of all wealth held by the least wealthy 40 percent of households. The differences in net wealth are particularly striking when expressed in dollar terms. The average wealth holdings of the poorest 40 percent of households was just $2,900, compared with $75,000 (primarily housing) for the middle 20 percent of households, and $12.7 million for the top 1 percent.

During the stock-market bubble of the late 1990s, one form of wealth—stock ownership—became the focus of substantial media and political attention. Table 4 shows that, for all but the wealthiest families, stock market wealth actually did not represent a particularly important vehicle for wealth accumulation. The bottom 40 percent of households, for example, held, on average, only about $1,800 in stock in all forms, compared with about $12,000 for households in the middle and $3.6 million for households at the very top.

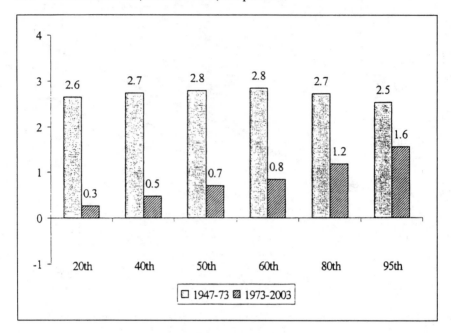

Figure 4. Annual growth rate in real family income, United States, by income per-centile, 1947–2003. *Source:* Analysis of Bureau of the Census, Current Population Survey; deflated using CPI-U-RS.

Consistent with the pattern observed for wages and incomes, wealth holding differs enormously across racial lines. In 1998, for example, the median black household had a net wealth that was equal to just 11 percent of the net wealth for the median white family. Black families were, in particular, far less likely to hold financial assets than white families were (9, table 8; see also 10).

POWER, POLITICS, AND INEQUALITY

The preceding section of this chapter documented the high—and generally rising—levels of inequality in three key economic distributions. To a large extent, changes across these three distributions are linked. Declining wages lowered incomes except where households increased their number of hours of paid work (a fairly widespread phenomenon among married-couple families). Stagnating and declining incomes, in turn, made it more difficult for households to save and, thus, to accumulate wealth, which exacerbated already high levels of wealth inequality. This section attempts to sketch briefly the principal economic and political forces that lie behind these recent, interrelated changes in the distribution of wages, income, and wealth. While the separate forces

Table 4

Distribution of wealth, United States, 1962–2001

	Bottom 40%	Middle 20%	Next 20%	Next 10%	Next 9%	Top 1%
Share of all wealth						
1962	0.3%	5.4%	13.4%	14.0%	33.7%	33.4%
1983	0.9	5.2	12.6	13.1	34.4	33.8
1989	–0.7	4.8	12.3	13.0	33.2	37.4
1998	0.2	4.5	11.9	12.5	32.8	38.1
2001	0.3	3.9	11.3	12.9	38.1	33.4
Average dollar value, 2001, thousands 2001 $						
Stocks	1.8	12.0	41.3	131.9	512.3	3,568.4
+ All other assets	26.6	113.5	234.6	438.4	1,221.1	9,449.5
– Total debt	25.5	50.5	50.5	79.9	122.3	325.8
Net wealth	2.9	75.0	75.0	490.3	1,611.0	12,692.1

Source: Analysis of Survey of Consumer Finance data by Wolff (9), reproduced in Mishel, Bernstein, and Allegretto (2), tables 4.3 and 4.9.

Note: Stocks include all direct and indirect holdings such as mutual funds and 401(k) retirement plans. Net wealth is the sum of stocks and all other assets, minus total debt.

identified take many forms, a common thread runs through all of them: each represents a shift in bargaining power away from workers and toward their employers. In the global North, these policies are associated with the political and economic legacy of Ronald Reagan, Margaret Thatcher, and related "supply-side" and "free-market" politicians and economists. In the global South, a similar constellation of policies has been labeled the "Washington consensus" and is often referred to as "neoliberalism."

Decline of Unions

The most obvious decline in workers' bargaining power over the period was the steep drop in unionization rates. Between 1979 and 2004, the share of workers who were members of unions or who were covered by collective-bargaining agreements fell from just under 25 percent to less than 13 percent of all workers (see Figure 5). The associated reduction in bargaining power made an important contribution to rising wage inequality, especially for men (see, e.g., 11-14).

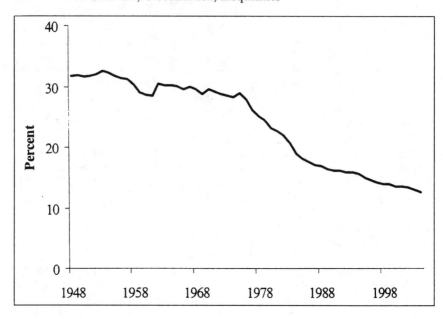

Figure 5. Share of U.S. workers in unions, 1948–2004. *Source:* Analysis of Bureau of Labor Statistics employment data and unionization data from the Labor Research Association.

Falling Minimum Wage

Between 1979 and 1990, the inflation-adjusted value of the minimum wage fell about 30 percent (see Figure 6). After almost a decade without an increase in the nominal value of the minimum wage, Congress set increases in the federal minimum wage four times in the 1990s (1990, 1991, 1996, and 1997). Since 1997, however, the minimum wage has remained at $5.15 per hour, setting off a new round of declining purchasing power. The long-term decline in the bite of the minimum wage effectively has undermined the bargaining power of low-wage workers (especially low-wage women, whose wages closely track the minimum wage) and, thereby, has contributed in an important way to rising wage inequality over the past two decades (see, e.g., 13, 15, 16).

Restrictive Macroeconomic Policy

Many formal models of the labor market emphasize the important role that the unemployment rate plays in determining workers' bargaining power in wage negotiations (see, e.g., 17). When unemployment rates are low, workers can press

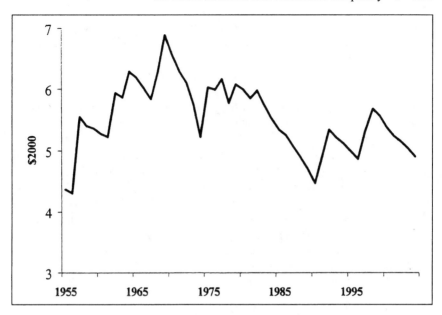

Figure 6. Real value of the minimum wage, as hourly wage in 2000 dollars, 1955–2004. *Source:* Author's analysis of U.S. Department of Labor, Federal Minimum Wage Rates under the FLSA. www.dol.gov/esa/minwage/chart.pdf.

for better wages, benefits, and working conditions because they realize that, even if they lose their jobs in the process, finding new jobs will not be difficult. When unemployment rates are high, however, incumbent workers who demand too much may find themselves out of work in a labor market where their other opportunities are limited. For many of the past 25 years, macroeconomic policy kept the unemployment rate high by historical standards. These high levels of unemployment from the early 1980s through the mid-1990s lowered workers' bargaining power and helped to drive down real wages. (For a discussion of the economic benefits of low unemployment for workers, see 18.) Only after 1995, when the unemployment rate fell below 6 percent, eventually reaching and remaining at a rate of 4 percent, did wages start to rise in real terms for low- and middle-wage workers. Real wages have stagnated again since the downturn of the early 2000s.

Globalization

Over the past two decades, conscious actions to open up U.S. markets to the rest of the world have forced U.S. workers to confront increasing competition from workers in other countries.[6] While trade can, under the right circumstances, improve economic efficiency and increase the domestic standard of living, rising international competition can also reduce employment opportunities and wages for national workers. The net effect of these two opposing forces—rising real incomes stemming from efficiency gains through trade, and declining real income as a result of increased competition for jobs and wages—depends crucially on national economic and social institutions. (For an analysis of trade liberalization and social policy, see 21). In the United States, which starts with high levels of inequality and has only weak redistributive mechanisms, the process of globalization—as implemented so far—has generally acted to lower wages both in manufacturing (through inflows of traded goods, outflows of capital, a rise in "outsourcing," and corporate relocation threats) and in some services (some of which may be traded and many of which can take advantage of largely unprotected immigrant workers).[7] (For a review of the channels through which globalization may affect national wage and employment levels, see 22; for a discussion of the use of relocation threats in the context of NAFTA, see 23.)

CONCLUSION

Wage, income, and wealth inequality in the United States have always been high, but all three forms of economic inequality have grown worse since the end of the 1970s. Wages are not just more unequal. Between 1979 and 2004, wages for workers at the middle and bottom of the wage distribution only just kept pace with inflation—over a period when the output per hour of the average worker grew by over 66 percent in real terms. Over the past 25 years, incomes across most of the distribution have grown more slowly than they did in the earlier postwar period, with rising number of annual hours worked playing an important role in what real gains families did experience. The distribution of wealth has become more skewed toward the very top, with "stock-holder democracy" having little impact on the

---

[6] U.S. markets have opened up considerably since the late 1970s, though some important tariff and non-tariff barriers remain. The United States also continues to subsidize an important portion of its agricultural exports. For a critique of protectionist measures by the United States and other rich countries, see 19 and references therein; for an analysis that suggests the limits of trade liberalization as a path toward economic development in the global South, see 20.

[7] The short discussion here cannot analyze the impact of changes in the current model of globalization on workers in other rich countries or in developing economies. That competition from foreign workers can reduce domestic workers' wages or employment opportunities—in and of itself—has no moral or policy implications. At one level, the same processes discussed here work in the other direction as well, with competition from U.S. workers, all else constant, reducing wages and employment in the manufacturing and agricultural sectors in many developing economies (while any related efficiency gains may act simultaneously to raise living standards in these same receiving countries). At a deeper level, though, the way we carry out economic integration, including decisions about inter- and intra-national mechanisms for redistribution of both current income and any efficiency gains from trade, constitutes the real moral questions posed by globalization.

actual distribution of national wealth. In all cases, these economic divisions are especially sharp across gender and racial lines.

The well-documented decline in union representation, the falling real value of the minimum wage, nearly two decades of restrictive macroeconomic policy, and a forced opening up of much of the U.S. economy to competition from the rest of the world can explain much of the recent rise in economic inequality. These key developments all took place alongside a widespread move toward economic deregulation, the privatization of government services (especially at the state and local levels), and cutbacks in the social safety net (best exemplified in the wholesale restructuring in 1996 of the "welfare" system supporting poor mothers of young children).[8] Separately—but especially in combination—all these forces had, by the turn of the century, greatly reduced workers' bargaining power relative to where conditions stood at the end of the 1970s. While each of these forces bears directly or indirectly on negotiations between workers and employers over wages, benefits, and working conditions, all of these forces had their origin in broader shifts in political power: changes in the legal environment facing unions; legislative decisions about the level of the federal minimum wage; central bank decisions about interest rates; the federal government's attitude toward industry regulation; and public opinion about issues as diverse as the efficiency of markets and the desirability of maintaining a social safety net for those experiencing short- and long-term economic difficulties. Only changes in economic policies will undo the economic inequality generated over the past two decades or so, but only changes in politics ("who gets what") will make these new economic policies possible.[9]

Note — This chapter is adapted from the chapter "Mercados de trabajo y desigualdad en el plano económico en los Estados Unidos desde los finales de la década de los años setenta," in *El trabajo en un mundo globalizado,* edited by Gerardo Fujii and Santos M. Ruesga (Ediciones Pirámide, Madrid, 2004). I thank

[8] In the United States, at least, the impact of deregulation, privatization, and the declining social safety net on wage and income inequality is not as well studied as the links between unionization, the minimum wage, restrictive macroeconomic policy, and globalization. For a discussion of the impact of deregulation on wage inequality, see 24; for a discussion of the impact of deterioration in the safety net, see 8 (the chapter on wages) and earlier editions of *The State of Working America.*

[9] This account gives little attention to the possible role of technological change in explaining rising economic inequality. The conventional story is that the recent rise in economic inequality principally reflects rising economic returns to skills: those with the appropriate skills fare well in the "new economy," which creates an ever-widening gap with respect to those who lack the necessary skills to thrive in the "new economy." But technological change has been a constant in the U.S. economy since at least the industrial revolution, and such change has almost always been, on net, "skill-biased." What is different about the past two decades or so is that the economic institutions that previously ensured equal (and, sometimes, equalizing) growth—even in the face of skill-biased technological growth—no longer seem to have been operating. For a skeptical review of the economic evidence for the skill-biased technological change explanation of rising inequality, see 25, 26.

Theresa Thompson for comments on earlier drafts, and my colleagues Larry Mishel, Jared Bernstein, Heather Boushey, and Dean Baker for their many insights on issues examined in this chapter.

REFERENCES

1. Schmitt, J., and Mishel, L. The United States and Europe: Who's really ahead? In *Unconventional Wisdom: Alternative Perspectives on the New Economy,* ed. J. Madrick. Century Foundation Press, New York, 2000.
2. Mishel, L., Bernstein, J., and Allegretto, S. *The State of Working America 2004–2005.* Cornell University Press, Ithaca, NY, 2005.
3. Schmiu, J. Did job quality deterioraie in the 1980s and 1990s? In *Sourcebook of Labor Markets: Evolving Structures and Processes,* ed. A. L. Kalleberg. Kluwer Academic/Plenum, New York, 2001.
4. Glyn, A. Inequalities of Employment and Wages in OECD Countries. Unpublished paper. University of Oxford, Oxford, 2001.
5. Burniaux, J.-M., et al. *Income Distribution and Poverty in Selected OECD Countries.* Economics Department Working Paper no. 189. Organization for Economic Cooperation and Development, Paris, 1998.
6. Smeeding, T. Globalization, Inequality and the Rich Countries of the G-20: Evidence from the Luxembourg Income Study (LIS). Luxembourg Income Study Working Paper no. 320, 2002. www.lisproject.org/publications/liswps320.pdf.
7. Bureau of Labor Statistics, series PRS85006093, www.bls.gov (April 2005).
8. Mishel, L., Bernstein, J., and Boushey, H. *The State of Working America 2002–2003.* Cornell University Press, Ithaca, NY, 2003.
9. Wolff, E. *Changes in Household Wealth in the 1980s and 1990s in the U.S.* Levy Economics Institute of Bard College Working Paper no. 407. Annandale-on-Hudson, NY, 2004.
10. Wolff, E. Why stocks won't save the middle class. In *Unconventional Wisdom: Alternative Perspectives on the New Economy,* ed. J. Madrick. Century Foundation Press, New York, 2000.
11. Card, D. *The Effect of Unions on the Distribution of Wages: Redistribution or Relabelling?* National Bureau of Economic Research (NBER) Working Paper no. 4195. NBER, Cambridge, MA, 1992.
12. Freeman, R. How much has de-unionization contributed to the rise in male earnings inequality? In *Uneven Tides: Rising Inequality in America,* ed. S. Danziger and P. Gottschalk. Russell Sage Foundation, New York, 1993.
13. DiNardo, J., Fortin, N., and Lemieux, T. Labor market institutions and the distribution of wages, 1973–1992: A semi-parametric approach. *Econometrica* 64(5):1001–1044, 1996.
14. Gosling, A., and Lemieux, T. *Labour Market Reforms and Changes in Wage Inequality in the United Kingdom and the United States.* National Bureau of Economic Research (NBER) Working Paper no. 8413. NBER, Cambridge, MA, 2001.
15. Card, D., and Krueger, A. *Myth and Measurement: The New Economics of the Minimum Wage.* Princeton University Press, Princeton, 1995.
16. Lee, D. S. Wage inequality in the United States during the 1980s: Rising dispersion or falling minimum wage? *Q. J. Econ.* 114(3):977–1023, 1999.

17. Layard, R., Nickell, S., and Jackman, R. *Unemployment: Macroeconomic Performance and the Labour Market.* Oxford University Press, Oxford, 1991.
18. Bernstein, J., and Baker, D. *The Benefits of Full Employment.* Economic Policy Institute, Washington, DC, 2003.
19. Oxfam. Boxing Match in International Trade. Oxfam Briefing Paper no. 32, 2002. www.oxfam.org/eng/pdfs/pp021119_agricultural_trade.pdf.
20. Weisbrot, M., and Baker, D. *The Relative Impact of Trade Liberalization on Developing Countries.* Center for Economic and Policy Research, Washington, DC, 2002.
21. Rodrik, D. *Has Globalization Gone Too Far?* Institute for International Economics, Washington, DC, 1997.
22. Schmitt, J. Globalization and labor markets: A view from the United States. In *Responses to Globalization in Germany and the United States: Seven Sectors Compared,* ed. C. Lankowski. American Institute for Contemporary German Studies (AICGS) Research Report no. 10. AICGS, Washington, DC, 1999.
23. Bronfenbrenner, K. *The Effects of Plant Closing or Threat of Plant Closing on the Right of Workers to Organize.* North American Commission for Labor Cooperation, Dallas, 1997.
24. Peoples, J. Deregulation and the labor market. *J. Econ. Perspect.* 12(3):111–130, 1998.
25. Bernstein, J., and Mishel, L. Seven reasons for skepticism about the technology story of U.S. wage inequality. In *Sourcebook of Labor Markets: Evolving Structures and Processes.* Kluwer Academic/Plenum, New York, 2001.
26. Card, D., and DiNardo, J. *Skill-biased Technological Change and Rising Wage Inequality: Some Problems and Puzzles.* National Bureau of Economic Research (NBER) Working Paper no. 8769. NBER, Cambridge, MA, 2002.

CHAPTER 12

The Politics of Health Inequalities Research in the United States

Vicente Navarro

THE LIMITED DIVERSITY OF U.S. SCHOLARSHIP

Thank you very much for inviting me to share with you my thoughts about scientific practice and discourse, on both sides of the Atlantic, in the areas of social science research in health and medicine, areas in which I have been working for more than 40 years. As you may know, I had to leave Spain for political reasons in 1962, going to Sweden first (where I studied at Uppsala University and at the Karolinska Institute in Stockholm), then to Great Britain (studying at the London School of Economics, Oxford University, and Edinburgh University), and finally to the United States, where I have been on the faculty of the School of Public Health of the Johns Hopkins University since 1965. I have also been a visiting professor at other leading U.S. universities, such as Columbia University, the University of California, Los Angeles, Harvard University, and the University of Michigan. Since the death of the Spanish dictator, General Franco, in 1975, I have also spent considerable time in Spain, where, since 1997, I have directed the Public and Social Policy Program, jointly sponsored by the Johns Hopkins University and the Pompeu Fabra University, in Barcelona. I have therefore been a member of the U.S. academic community for most of my working life, and have been able to compare and contrast it with the European academic institutions where I have also worked. Thus I do believe that I have enough knowledge about academic life on both sides of the Atlantic to be able to comment on it. But before proceeding with my presentation, I want to clarify that I am going to focus on the areas of health and medicine, leaving out other areas of social science research to which my comments may not be applicable. Health and medicine studies are, after all, very conservative sectors of U.S. academia and have their own specificity that distinguishes them from other areas of social science research.

Let me start by saying that one of the very attractive features of U.S. academic life (at least in the universities where I have taught and in the areas in which I have labored) is the richness of the academic infrastructure and the intensity of its intellectual life. Needless to say, a country of this size has universities of all types and all levels of quality, a reality frequently ignored by some European observers who only know or visit the top academic centers. There are many poor-quality universities in the United States, but the leading universities do have the features—a rich and intense intellectual life—that I have just mentioned.

On the other hand, the main weakness of U.S. academic institutions—and a major one—is the very limited diversity in both their faculty and their academic offerings. And by diversity I don't mean number of courses taught, which tends to be very large indeed, but rather a diversity of perspectives, except critical perspectives based on race and gender. Indeed, there are a great many critical analyses of health and medicine (including public health and health policy research) from feminist and black perspectives, for example, but all these are constructed within certain well-defined boundaries. Analyses of U.S. health care from class perspectives, for example, are very rare indeed. If you look at the journals *Health Affairs, Medical Care, Milbank Quarterly,* and *Journal of Health Policy, Politics and Law,* not to speak of *The New England Journal of Medicine* and *JAMA,* you will rarely find articles that use class analysis in their understanding of the realities of U.S. medicine or public health. The only exception is the *International Journal of Health Services,* which frequently presents such analyses in its pages. Otherwise, class analyses are, for the most part, frowned upon in these forums.

Indeed, contrary to what is usually claimed, the academic environment at U.S. universities is profoundly ideological. Simply using the terms "class struggle," "working class," "imperialism," or the like in academic discourse is enough to provoke an emotional response of dismissal. Whoever uses such terms is likely to be dismissed as doctrinaire, and thus marginalized. You may be surprised to know that I have received letters from senior editors on this topic, including one from *The New England Journal of Medicine,* asking me to change some terms I used in my article, such as "working class" and "class struggle"; the editor wanted them changed "for being too doctrinaire"—a direct quotation from his letter of conditional acceptance. My refusal to agree to that condition led to the rejection of the article. Cases like this are many. Other colleagues of mine who use similar types of analysis have reported similar experiences.

To further complicate matters, the degree of knowledge about critical traditions based on class perspective is so limited in the United States that one runs the risk of very easily being labeled a "communist," since, even in scholarly circles, all critical perspectives using class categories are quickly defined as "Marxist," which usually means Marxist-Leninist or "communist." In that respect, it is important to notice that while "mainstream" authors are never labeled with the scholarly traditions to which they belong (such as Weberian or Durkheimian authors), authors who use class perspectives are automatically introduced or referred to as Marxist authors—which, given the very limited diversity and tolerance of academic institutions, may mean academic death for those authors.

Indeed, there is an authentic fear about using certain terms derived from the Marxist or even the Weberian tradition in scientific discourse, a fear, as I mentioned before, of being identified as "red," a coloration that may ruin one's academic life.

You may be surprised to hear this observation, since you may think this happened in the United States in the McCarthy era, but no longer. McCarthyism, however, is alive and well in U.S. academia. Actually, it never was defunct. You know, of course, that the existence of classes and class struggle was indeed accepted by the two prominent sociological traditions in the western world during the 20th century: the Weberian and the Marxist traditions. And you also know, of course, that the difference between Marx and Weber was not in their use of class struggle as a category of analysis, but rather in their definition of the roots of that struggle, based on exploitation in the case of Marx (which he considered intrinsic to capitalist relations) and domination in the case of Weber. But otherwise, they both spoke of class struggle. In the United States, however, someone who speaks about class struggle is liable to being defined as Marxist-Leninist. And that is the end of that scholar. I admit that this discrimination may have been less acute in other areas of social science. In sociology, for example, there was a very rich renaissance of class-based studies in the social sciences in the 1970s and 1980s, which continues today (although in diminished form) in some branches of sociology. But in the areas of health and medicine in which I have worked, this has not been the case. It is an extremely conservative environment in the United States; McCarthyism is still alive and well.

The continuing existence of McCarthyism in the area of health and medicine is explained by the system of funding of most U.S. research and the process for granting academic tenure. Most funding comes from either private foundations, such as the McArthur, Johnson and Johnson, Commonwealth, Rockefeller, and other foundations, or from government agencies, whose peer-review committees tend to be very establishment oriented. Faculty members are under enormous pressure to get significant amounts of funding from these research agencies, since in many centers (such as Hopkins, a top academic health center in the United States), 80 percent of a faculty member's salary (and that of her or his secretary) has to be raised by the faculty member with research funds. Survival in U.S. academia depends not only on the famous dictum "publish or perish" but also on an ability to get research funds, since your salary depends on getting these funds, whether you have tenure or not. So, as you can easily conclude, academic freedom in health and social science research is dramatically reduced (some may even say practically nonexistent) in the United States. Researchers interested in controversial topics (such as the politics of health care) with a class-based outlook, or those who work in disciplines that are not easily funded, such as history or political science, are let go easily. Examples are many: one of the best-known historians of public health in the United States, Professor Elizabeth Fee, was let go from Johns Hopkins School of Public Health (a major U.S. teaching and research public health center) because she could not easily get funds for her research (and thus for her salary). Another example is Professor Jeff Johnson, a leading occupational epidemiologist, who could not get research funds to analyze the negative impact of employers' practices on the health of their workers: he also had to leave. Actually, of the very few critical scholars in health and social science research in the United States, many get their research funding from non-U.S. sources.

Let me clarify that this situation has become much more common since the 1980s than is realized, because of the ending of federal teaching grants that formerly sustained many faculty salaries. President Reagan discontinued these teaching grants and they have never been replaced. This has dramatically reduced the ideological diversity in social science research in health and medicine. As you can see, this system of funding very seriously compromises academic freedom in the United States. The diversity is indeed limited. It resembles the restricted diversity of the American broadcasting industry, where you can find 75 television channels, but not one socialist or even mildly center-left social democrat as a commentator (among 83). In academia, reinforcing this situation is a system of faculty promotion that is clearly skewed against critical perspectives (except race and gender). Exceptions do exist, of course. But they are just that—exceptions.

Academic freedom is indeed dramatically reduced in the United States, to a point that it is practically nonexistent. This is a reality rarely discussed in the United States and rarely presented outside the country. It's as if dirty linen is supposed to be washed at home, but not abroad. But, let me repeat: the main and most obvious characteristic of U.S. academic life is its extremely narrow boundaries and its very limited academic freedom in social science research in health and medicine.

THE RESPONSE OF THE ESTABLISHMENT TO CRITICAL PERSPECTIVES

Of course, critical scholars do exist in the United States, but they operate under huge difficulties. In our field, one of the most creative periods was in the 1960s and early 1970s, when, as a result of the social uprisings taking place in the United States at that time, there was a broad-based questioning of the conventional wisdom. I have written elsewhere about that period and the different critical scholarship traditions it generated (1). One scholarly tradition in the area of health and medicine that became particularly important was what was referred to as "materialist epidemiology," which had the intent of basing social epidemiology in an understanding of the forces that shape society, in which class relations played a critical role. We studied how class relations appear in morbidity and mortality, and how class relations were (and continue to be) reproduced in the institutions, knowledge, and practice of medicine. That way of analyzing our reality—made possible by the intellectually open and questioning atmosphere in the country at that time—also influenced the appearance of radical perspectives in minority- and gender-based studies. That radical thought triggered and stimulated an important process of questioning of our society.

It is interesting to analyze how the U.S. medical and health care establishments, including the foundations and the federal government, as well as their journals and forums, responded to that critical scholarship. They did it in typical and predictable fashion. First, they ignored the radical critiques. Later, as the critiques became too great to ignore, they funded "mainstream" researchers to recycle the critical studies and the issues raised, cleansing them of any political context, changing the terms of the discourse (marginalizing the radical ones), and putting forward analyses and proposals that would be less threatening to the system. This is, indeed, how the medical and health establishments have always functioned in the United States in order to marginalize perspectives they dismiss as "radical." They take over the issues and their radical analysis and recycle them in a form less threatening to the established order. This is the history of the funding of controversial research in the United States. Needless to say, some ex-radicals have assisted in this recycling process for clearly opportunistic reasons, becoming part of the establishment.

Let me say that this situation has also occurred in the U.S. establishment's funding of research on health and medical studies outside the United States, particularly in Latin America and other developing countries. For example, in Latin America during the 1960s and 1970s (with the willing assistance of the Pan American Health Organization, the main transmitter of hegemonic thought from the United States to Latin America), the U.S.-based foundations supported social democratic positions as alternatives to (and in order to put a stop to) communism. Then, when communism collapsed, or was perceived as no longer a threat to international power relations, these same funding agencies began supporting neoliberalism to put a stop to social democracy. You may have seen how the U.S. funding agencies (including the foundations) have recently been promoting managed competition all over the world, using the World Health Organization and PAHO as the instruments of promotion (2). I must admit I am intrigued about what they will support next, although I hope that social democracy in the world will not collapse, as communism did.

AN EXAMPLE: THE EVOLUTION OF STUDIES ON INEQUALITIES AND HEALTH

What I have just said applies to the study of social inequalities and their impact on health, as well. Let me elaborate. In the 1960s, 1970s, and 1980s, considerable work was done on how class relations affect the health of our populations and how class relations are reproduced in the public and private health care institutions of the United States. It was some of the most interesting work in health research. This work was silenced, ignored, or marginalized in establishment forums—which does not mean, however, that it did not have an impact. Indeed, the evidence was pretty overwhelming that the United States (as the *Lancet* once pointed out) is not a classless society. For the most part, these studies did not enjoy government or foundation support. But such studies were part of a larger movement that established the International Association of Health Policy, which soon spread worldwide. And in the United States they triggered the establishment of the Socialist Caucus of the American Public Health Association, where all political traditions of the left—socialists, social democrats, anarchists, communists, and others—cooperated and ran some of the most exciting and well-attended sessions in the annual meetings of the APHA.

How did the U.S. establishment respond to this critical scholarship? The answer is remarkably predictable: by funding studies that presented an alternative to the radical tradition. These studies focused not on class or even on power relations (terms seen as too ideological) but rather on income and status, referring to income and status differentials, rather than class differentials. Thus income and status differentials became the new game in town. The political spectrum in social science research in health and medicine was thus redefined, with the left—the "respectable" left—focusing on the importance of income and status differentials as a determinant of the health of populations, while the right dismissed the idea that income differentials had any relevance for people's health. Soon, and as a result of the huge influence of the United States in the modern world, this focus on income and status differentials rather than class relations (including class, as well as race and gender, exploitation) became the focus of the "respectable" left worldwide. Income and status differentials were *in;* the analysis of how class structure, class exploitation, and class struggle appear, reproduce, and affect the health and quality of life of our populations—all this was *out.* In this theoretical scenario, income is the means by which individuals realize themselves in the world of consumption, the key determinant of status; income and consumption, as well as status, differentials are at the center of analytical debate. And in this new discourse, individuals and how they relate among themselves becomes the main focus of social inequalities research, while concepts such as "social cohesion" and "social capital" become the major trademarks of that discourse. Large income differentials were considered, for example, to be bad for a community because they diluted social cohesion. Large income differentials were also bad because they impoverished the individual's social capital—with social capital defined as an individual's network of contacts and support. Indeed, "social capital" and "social cohesion" became the new terms that must be used to get funding, even from the foundations or the U.S. government. And again, given the enormous power and influence of the United States, these terms and concepts started appearing and becoming widely used worldwide, replacing the concepts of class analysis that, in some European and Latin American countries, had been the most important approach in understanding health and medicine. To get funds even from the European Commission, for example, you must use these code words. Indeed, nowhere in these new studies could you find concepts such as class-consciousness and class solidarity, or class power and its relationship to the state, or collective power resources, such as trade unions or left-wing parties. And those who have continued to work in these areas have been ignored or marginalized by the "respectable" left.

Accompanying these changes was the establishment in the United States of new research networks or research institutions working on inequalities (to replace the socialist associations and networks mentioned above, perceived as "too political"). In these new forums, research and discourse were sanitized to exclude any elements or terms that could be threatening to the establishment or to the funding sources. And all appeared very scholarly, looking at methodological issues, dressed on occasion in extensive statistical apparatuses, and excluding any form of ideological contamination—by which I mean concepts, terms, and proposals perceived as unorthodox and not fundable.

Let me clarify that I am not putting down these income and status studies. On several occasions they have added importantly to the existing knowledge in the area of health inequalities research. What I want to stress, however, is that these studies were presented and put forward as an alternative (less threatening to the sources of class as well as race and gender power) to analyses of realities based on an understanding of class power relations in our societies and their reproduction in the areas of health and medicine. The disregard and marginalization of these class analyses by the income- and status-based researchers carried a major cost, however, revealing the insufficiency of this research in understanding our realities.

A REPRESENTATIVE EXAMPLE OF THE PROBLEM:
THE HEALTH OF NATIONS

Let me focus on one example of this "respectable left": Kawachi and Kennedy's *The Health of Nations: Why Inequality Is Harmful to Your Health* (3). Funded by the McArthur Foundation (the largest funding source for social science research in the United States), this book is authored by two professors from Harvard University. In the advertising brochure, it is presented by Amartya Sen as "the left proposals that the right wing will hate." The first clue about its ideological character (wanting to appear as the respectable left), however, is that none of the researchers who have worked in the areas of health inequalities from a class perspective are mentioned or acknowledged in the book. And the *International Journal of Health Services,* the journal that has published the most work on the issue of social inequalities in health, is cited only once in 235 references. Quite remarkable!

But let me concentrate on the topics covered by *The Health of Nations.* The authors focus on individual income and individual behavior as the point of departure for understanding our societies. At the outset, in the first chapter, they classify countries according to the income and individual consumption of average individuals and average families in each country. Thus they compare the standard of living of countries as diverse as Ethiopia, Mexico, and the United States by comparing the commodities owned by the average family in each country, with photographs of families displaying their possessions—animals, furniture, and other possessions—in front of their houses, following Menzel's well-known photographic work *Material World: A Global Family Portrait.* The countries themselves are ranked by average income per capita, establishing a gradient from the poor to the rich countries. And richness and power are defined by the commodities owned by the average family.

The way the authors of *The Health of Nations* chose to define the countries, however, carries with it a specific understanding of the world, dividing it into high-consuming countries (the rich countries) and low-consuming countries (the poor). The first group of countries, for example, consumes too much food: the people are obese. The second group of countries has the opposite problem: people don't eat enough; they are hungry. Moreover, the problem in the supposedly rich countries is that, besides people consuming too much, they choose a pattern of consumption that is wasteful and even harmful both to themselves and to those in poor countries—they harm the citizens of poor countries because the poor aspire to consume as much as the citizens of rich countries do, using the consumption model of the developed countries as their model and reproducing in the developing countries the patterns of consumption in the developed ones. According to this argument, then, the root of the problem is that the poor in developing countries want to achieve the same pattern of consumption as people in the rich countries. When they cannot achieve that, the poor get frustrated and generate a lot of tension in the world. In a similar fashion, so *The Health of Nations* continues, the major health problem in the United States is that people always want more, to the point that they are working themselves sick, working too many extra hours.

The solution to this situation is for people in the United States and in the developing countries to lower their expectations and change their level and type of consumption by changing their values; they should learn to value friendliness, togetherness, and time spent with friends and family, for example, more than individual competition and consumption. The authors, in their analysis of the predominant health problems in the United States, thus assume that whatever happens in the United States is a result of (*a*) individuals' choice of the type and level of their consumption and (*b*) individuals' political decisions and their effect on the body politic. Indeed, the authors consider that unrestrained individual consumption also leads to the incomplete democracy of the United States, due to the strong influence of money in the country's political system. Although critical of this U.S. political system, still the book concludes that U.S. society is what people have chosen it to be—rather flattering, incidentally, to the U.S. power structures: they are at the top because this is what most people want.

Regarding the developing countries, the authors of *The Health of Nations* conclude that what is imperative is to reduce income disparities in order to prevent envy, frustration, and rancor, and to stimulate better health among their people.

The authors also claim that the solution in the developing countries will be achieved through a change in people's values. How? No more is said. End of book.

THE PROBLEMS WITH THIS ANALYSIS

The problems with the analysis in *The Health of Nations* are many. To start with, individual consumption is a bad place to begin if you wish to understand a society. One society could have lower individual consumption than another yet still have a better standard of living, because it has more collective consumption. To classify countries or families based on the level of individual consumption is to eliminate one of the most important elements that explain a country's quality of life and well-being: its collective consumption, which includes that country's welfare state (public services and social transfers) and infrastructure. So, rather than looking at individual commodities, the book should have included the quality and availability of public schools, public hospitals, public pensions, public childcare and home care services, public transport, and many other aspects of collective consumption (not to mention the nature of work and the public protection of the health and well-being of workers, consumers, and the environment—all of which largely explain a population's health and quality of life (4; see also 5). Measured in this way, the United States would have looked quite poor, much poorer than other countries with much lower individual consumption.

The authors of *The Health of Nations* are aware that defining rich and poor by looking at per capita income is insufficient, since it does not take into account the internal distribution of income within the country. But by the same token, they should have realized that measuring the level of development of a country by individual income and by individual consumption is not only insufficient but wrong, because it does not include collective consumption, which is more important than individual consumption in measuring a population's well-being.

A similar problem appears in grouping countries according to patterns of individual consumption. Actually, when we look at the rich countries, we see that the obese are not found among the wealthiest sectors of the population but among the poorest, contradicting the idea of a gradient from very thin to very fat that parallels the gradient from poor to rich. Countries of both North and South have classes, with different patterns of consumption available to them. Contrary to what the authors seem to assume, the dividing line in the world is not between pet lovers who spend millions of dollars on taking care of their pets in the North and hungry children in the South (an image frequently presented in United Nations Development Program reports, such as the *Human Development Report* 2002 (6), as well as in *The Health of Nations,* constantly appealing to the conscience of readers, making them feel guilty). Rather the division is between the dominant economic groups and social classes of the North that impose specific patterns of production and consumption on the majority of their own populations and, in alliance with the dominant classes in the South, on the majority of the populations and in the developing countries (see Chapter 8 of this volume). Thus the problem is rooted not in the envy of the rich by the poor, but rather in the exploitation (a term never used in the book) of the poor by the rich. And to see the problem as poor people and poor countries making inappropriate choices about what they consume, because they are misled by seeing the consumption by richer people and richer nations, is to ignore the reality that most people have very little choice and very limited decision-making power offered to them by an international and national (dis)order based on enormous exploitation.

The evidence of this reality, ignored by the authors of *The Health of Nations,* is plain overwhelming. Exploitation, not choice, is what moves our world. The extreme weakness of the public transport systems in most U.S. cities, for example, is not the outcome of the average person's preference for a private car. Rather, the influence of the auto and energy industries over the political body is what has destroyed or inhibited the development of public transport. Similarly, the pattern of consumption in poor countries is not a result of people's choices; rather, it is a consequence of an overwhelming poverty based on the exploitation of their labor and resources by economic interests of both North and South. Their frustration is a result not of envy but of an awareness of exploitation. Here again, a failure to see issues such as class (as well as gender and race) power rather than people's choice as the root of the problem puts the blame on the victims themselves—they are making the wrong individual choices. Such a view is also highly uncritical of the U.S. distribution of power, which explains why this view is popular among the social liberals who tend to dominate U.S. funding agencies. But they are wrong.

The authors of *The Health of Nations* cite many polls showing that U.S. citizens do not believe in solidarity and prefer lower taxes and individual consumption to higher taxes and collective consumption. But their presentation of the polling data ignores the fact that responses to the polls are determined by how the questions are posed and by the class, race, gender, and age of the respondent (among other characteristics). Ruy Teixeira and Joel Rogers have polled working-class attitudes and have shown that most working people in the United States would favor an expansion and universalization of the very limited welfare state (including development of a universal health care program that guarantees access to health care in time of need as a human right) (7). If people do not get this, the reason lies in the pattern of economic, corporate, and class influences over the U.S. state and over the country's information- and value-generating systems. As my colleagues and I have shown, wherever the working class is strong and the corporate class is weak, you find very strong and highly developed welfare states. Wherever the corporate class is very strong and the working class very weak, you find very weak welfare states—and this is the situation in the United States. *The Health of Nations* barely touches on this key issue, referring to rather outdated studies and ignoring more recent ones that document a relationship between class power and social inequalities and welfare state development (8).

Class power relations also explain why the United States has one of the least democratic political systems in the western world, a situation rooted in the U.S. Constitution, the rules of the democratic process, and the privatization of the electoral process. Given the continued uncritical promotion of U.S. democratic institutions, let me elaborate on each one. And let me start with the U.S. Constitution. The Constitution established that two senators represent each state in the U.S. Senate. One outcome of this is that half the U.S. population (the half that resides in the most populous and progressive parts of the country) is represented by just 18 senators, while the other half (primarily in the least populous and more conservative states) is represented by 82 senators. This situation "makes the U.S. Senate one of the most underrepresented legislative bodies in the world," in the words of Professor Robert Dahl, former president of the American Political Science Association (9).

Second, on the political rules that guide the electoral process, we find that without a proportional system, and with a "winner takes all" type of political regime, the effect (besides disenfranchising those voters who supported the losing candidates) is to make the establishment of new parties practically impossible (third parties usually hurt the major party closest to them). And third, to make matters worse, the overwhelming influence of corporate and economic interests on the electoral process, with a heavy dependency of the two main parties on these private funds, greatly limits the already structurally deficient democracy in the United States. Indeed, the question one needs to ask is, Is the United States a democracy? The answer is not entirely clear. The answer given by most people in the United States is a strong *no*. Seventy-three percent of U.S. citizens believe the government does not represent them. To present this situation as an outcome of American values and American choice does a serious injustice to the U.S. reality—flattering to those who govern, but profoundly wrong. Here again, we see another victim-blaming situation.

In summary, then, the emphasis of *The Health of Nations* on choice and values rather than on power and exploitation makes its message pretty limited. The message is profoundly apolitical, which leads me back to the point with which I started this presentation.

We need to look for the roots of the problem in the ways that power (class, race, and gender power) is reproduced in the state, in the media, and in the value-generating systems, and to focus on the need to politicize the response by organizing the disorganized, showing them that what they have in common outweighs whatever separates them. In that respect, it is wrong for the authors of *The Health of Nations* to disparage the labor unions. The only time they refer to unions is to note that the head of the city janitors' union of New York draws a salary of $530,000, seventeen times what the average union member makes. While this needs to be denounced, it is profoundly unfair to the U.S. labor movement to present this as representative of the unions. Labor unions have been one of the most consistent forces for change in the United States. A more political analysis would be that public interventions to improve the quality of life of U.S. populations require a set of class mobilizations, with confrontation of rather than adaptation to the U.S. establishment. This is what the authors do not do.

Let me finish these remarks by clarifying, once again, that it is not my intention to castigate research on income inequalities. Income is an important variable, quite handy when other, more important variables are not easy to obtain. But my criticism is directed at those who, ignoring all the work done by critical scholars who for many years have labored in the area of social inequalities from a class perspective, focus instead on income as the dividing line among our citizens, using consumption as the primary area of concern. Consumption is important, but more important are other categories of analysis whose absence, as they are abandoned or discriminated against, weakens and impoverishes the understanding of our realities. In that respect, the whole area of social inequalities research should build upon the very important research work produced from the 1960s through the 1990s that focused on how class power (class, race, and gender power) is reproduced in both political and civil societies and how that reproduction affects the level of health of our populations, in both North and South. Such a focus is not popular in the funding agencies of the North today, but it continues to be the most important.

Note — This chapter is based on a speech given at the Sixth Conference of the International Association of Health Policy, in Barcelona, Spain, March 23, 2003.

REFERENCES

1. Navarro, V. A historical review (1965-1997) of studies on class, health, and quality of life: A personal account. In *The Political Economy of Social Inequalities: Consequences for Health and Quality of Life,* ed. V. Navarro, pp. 13-30 Baywood, Amityville, NY, 2002.
2. Navarro, V. Assessment of the World Health Report 2000. *Lancet* 356:1598–1601, 2000.
3. Kawachi, I., and Kennedy, B. P. *The Health of Nations: Why Inequality Is Harmful to Your Health.* New Press, New York, 2002.
4. Navarro, V. (ed.). *The Political Economy of Social Inequalities: Consequences for Health and Quality of Life.* Baywood, Amityville, NY, 2002.
5. Muntaner, C., and Navarro, V. (eds.). *Political and Economic Determinants of Population Health and Well-Being: Controversies and Developments.* Baywood, Amityville, NY, 2004.
6. United Nations Development Program. *Human Development Report 2002.* Oxford University Press, New York, 2002.
7. Teixeira, R., and Rogers, J. *America's Forgotten Majority: Why the White Working Class Still Matters.* Basic Books, New York, 2001.
8. Navarro, V., and Shi, L. The political context of social inequalities and health. *Int. J. Health Serv.* 31:1–21, 2001.
9. Dahl, R. *How Democratic Is the American Constitution?* Yale University Press, New Haven, 2002.

PART VII

The Situation in Latin America: Alternatives to Neoliberalism

CHAPTER 13

An Alternative to the Neoliberal Model in Health: The Case of Venezuela

Oscar Feo and Carlos Eduardo Siqueira

The objective of this study is to present a synthesis of the proposals put forth by the health sector of Venezuela during the framing of the new Venezuelan Constitution. The goal of these proposals was to create a new constitutional framework for the development of a new health system, confronting the neoliberal platform that has characterized most health sector privatization reforms in Latin America. We summarize the background to the National Constituent Assembly (Asamblea Nacional Constituyente, ANC) and the legal framework that was typical of the health sector during that period, and identify the methodological aspects that substantiated the health themes included in the new Constitution. We analyze the articles that shape the current constitutional health framework in Venezuela, highlighting their most important features and comparing them with points of view common to neoliberal health proposals.

THE RECENT VENEZUELAN POLITICAL CRISIS

Venezuela is a Latin American country with 24 million inhabitants, located in the northern part of South America, just south of the Caribbean Sea. It has been in a deep political crisis over the last year (as of early 2004). In spite of its traditional democratic history, in 2002 Venezuela experienced a failed attempt at a coup d'état and a national strike promoted by an alliance of large corporations, the media, and the largest but poorly representative union confederation, the Central de Trabajadores Venezoelanos. The only objective of both events was to overthrow the democratically elected president, Hugo Chávez. Chávez is a 46-year-old lieutenant colonel who led a national insurrection in 1992 and was elected president in 1998 by 56 percent of the voters, after a hard confrontation with the political elites that had dominated Venezuela for the past 50 years. His main promise in the campaign for the presidency was to call a National Constituent Assembly to write a new Constitution to rebuild the country (1).

The Venezuelan media have severely criticized the Chávez administration, using propaganda tactics to demonize him and to portray his leadership as typical of an authoritarian populist. The Venezuelan government has often opposed the most important aspects of the Bush administration's foreign policy for Latin America. Some of the major U.S. proposals overtly fought by Chávez are the Free Trade Area of the Americas (FTAA), Plan Colombia, the Cuban embargo, privatization of oil companies in Venezuela, and the latest war doctrine euphemistically called the "war against terrorism." For dependent countries such as Venezuela, it is dangerous to disagree with U.S. administration decisions in these times of U.S. hegemony.

For example, during the Summit of the Americas, held in Quebec in 2001, Bush presented the FTAA initiative as a mechanism to integrate markets across the whole continent. Many officials of developing countries in the Americas have significant reservations and fears about the issues discussed, but few dared to express their views publicly at the meeting. Chávez not only refused to sign the final declaration of the summit but also invited Latin American leaders to meet in a smaller Latin American summit to reach a joint agreement before signing the U.S. version of the FTAA agreement.

A similar situation occurred domestically. Many Chávez administration policies have also challenged the usual political and economic rule by business sectors (2). The most important setting for the confrontation between the government and big business has been the Venezuelan oil industry. President Bush, together with powerful sectors of the Venezuelan elite, has supported the privatization of the rich state-owned oil company Petróleos de Venezuela SA. Chávez rapidly blocked their plans, and this led to the national strike at the oil company. Thus it is easy to understand why the corporate-dominated U.S. and Venezuelan media targeted President Chávez as an enemy of freedom and demonized him as an enemy of democracy. In summary, then, the main reason for the social, political, and economic conflicts recently faced by Venezuela is the Chávez administration's clear opposition to neoliberal policies. Within this context, we present the scenario of another area of conflict: the privatization of health services, which was a priority for previous governments but has been blocked by the new Constitution.

BACKGROUND TO THE NEW CONSTITUTION

In 1984 the Presidential Commission for State Reform was created to identify the ways in which the state apparatus should change and respond to the growing loss of legitimacy by the political system. This initiative was designed to promote a constitutional reform, but owing to the lack of capability of the political leadership to renew itself and the country, it never moved forward. For many years, all attempts to change the structures of the state and the Constitution itself did not move beyond Congress. This weak capability for analysis and self-criticism had grave consequences. On February 27, 1989, less than two months after the inauguration of President Carlos Andrés Pérez to his second term as president of the Republic, Venezuela went through a profound political and social upheaval, which started as a spontaneous and uncontrolled popular revolt known as the *Caracazo*. This popular insurrection was a clear demonstration of the high levels of frustration and discontent in the country and was also a spontaneous response by the poor to the impossibility of achieving better living standards. Furthermore, the revolt has been interpreted as a popular response to macroeconomic adjustment policies that had led to the deterioration of material living conditions. Terris (3) witnessed the rebellion in Caracas and reported afterwards on its fundamental characteristics.

This collective frustration brought about, as one of its most important political consequences, the military insurgencies of 1992 led by Lieutenant Col. Hugo Chávez, and opened the possibility for new and deeper social changes. Chávez, once freed from a two-year political sentence, founded the MVR (Fifth Republic Movement) Party with the political goal of framing a new Constitution to reconstruct and reestablish the nation. This political process reached an important climax when President Pérez was overthrown and general elections were announced to elect a new president in 1993. Innovative proposals and strong pro-reform candidates played a fundamental role in the campaign, but progressive candidates did not get enough votes to win. In the end, Rafael Caldera, the senior leader of the Christian Democratic Party, was elected. Then in the following presidential elections in 1998, Hugo Chávez was elected, reflecting the collapse of the old political system and a strong popular rejection of traditional party politics.

The first political act of President Chávez was the announcement of a public referendum so that the people could decide whether or not to call a National Constituent Assembly, mainly to write a new Constitution and lay out the bases for a new regime. On February 2, 1999, the president decreed the date for this referendum. The decree included the following as the justification for his request (4):

> The Venezuelan political system is in crisis and the institutions have undergone a fast process of de-legitimization. Despite this reality, those benefited by the regime, characterized by exclusion of the large majorities, have blocked, permanently, the changes demanded by the people. Because of this behavior the popular forces have been unleashed, and would only have their democratic aspirations met through the call for the Constituent Founding Power. In addition, the consolidation of the "Estado de Derecho" [a state that respects citizen rights and democracy] demands a judicial base that allows for the practice of a Social and Participatory Democracy.

The consultative referendum took place on April 25, 1999, and 81.9 percent approved the call for an ANC aimed at transforming the state and creating a

new judicial order to allow for the effective implementation of social and participatory democracy.

THE CONSTITUTIONAL PROCESS

Four countries in Latin America have implemented constitutional reforms in
recent years: Brazil (1988), Colombia (1989), Ecuador (1994), and Venezuela
(1999). The Constituent Assembly is part of a political project that proposes
the framing of a new Constitution as a mechanism to change the legal and institutional structure of a country, and proceeds to its refoundation by redefining the
bases for the functioning of the nation and the shape of the relationship between
the state, the government, and society. Here our focus is on development of
the health articles in the new Venezuelan Constitution.

Health Background

It is important to note briefly the fundamental characteristics of the current
Venezuelan health system. In the Constitution of 1961, in the chapter dedicated to
social rights, article 76 stated, "All [citizens] have the right to health protection.
The authorities will be responsible for public health preservation and will provide
the means for prevention and health care *to those who lack them*" (5, emphasis
added). This limited view of the role of the state in health matters mandates
the state to be responsible for providing health care only to those sectors of the
population that cannot afford to take care of their own needs. The article focuses
the state's action on the poor and indigent. The bottom line is that, as clearly
expressed today in neoliberal ideas, people must be responsible for satisfying
their own needs in the market. The state should intervene only when individuals
cannot fend for themselves.

The main characteristic of the Venezuelan health system at the time of the ANC
was its fragmentation into three coexisting subsystems: the first, a public system,
free and open to all the population, under the Ministry of Health and Social
Welfare; the second, a subsystem of social security, accessible only to workers
who are part of the formal labor market and contribute to social security; the third,
a private subsystem, which is fed by numerous insurance contracts with the public
sector and generates cross-subsidies between the public and the private sectors.

Methodological Aspects in Writing the Health Articles

On June 16, 1999, rallies were held to elect the 131 Constituent Representatives
who would write the new Constitution as an instrument for transforming the
state and creating a new legal order. The ANC created a Subcommittee for
Health to write the articles that would communicate the view of the majority of
representatives on health issues for Venezuela. As a general framework, the

subcommittee emphasized that the writing of the new Constitution derived from two basic concepts about the role of the state, the citizenry, and society, which support the Constitution:

1. The progressivism and interdependence of human and social rights, reaffirming the role of the state in the construction of collective well-being and fighting the pro-privatization groups that would convert those rights into market commodities.
2. The co-responsibility of the triad state-individuals-society in social participation, which enables citizens and communities to become the main actors in the new society. To achieve this goal, the subcommittee developed the notion of a participatory, federal, and decentralized state, in which decentralization is a basic tool to redistribute power, devolving it to the community.

The Health Articles

Three theoretically informed methodological steps were proposed for writing the language of the Constitution. The first was a situational analysis of the health sector that located its main problems in the functioning of the system and established the need to build alternative proposals. The second step was a literature and document review focused on the health content of the Constitutions of other countries. A synoptic table was developed that included the health subjects of the Constitutions of all the Latin American countries and some countries of Europe and North America that have health systems of well-known quality. This systematic organization of information was an important input for the writing of the Venezuelan Constitution, because it allowed for the collection and synthesis of the experiences of other countries. The third step was a participatory process of public sessions and town meetings to enable key social and political actors to voice their opinions about what themes should be included in the Constitution. Sixteen open and public sessions were held and 80 proposals received and processed, with more than 100 "right to speech" presentations by representatives of several organizations, community representatives, and health experts.

By the end of these three steps, the health aspects with enough relevance to be included in the Constitution were identified: (*a*) the definition of health and the role of the state, (*b*) the type of health system, and (*c*) the financing of the system.

Definition of Health and Role of the State. The ANC entertained a debate of great importance (and of worldwide relevance) on the following issue: is health a social right or a market good? There are two clearly antagonistic positions about this question. Globalization and the dominance of the neoliberal market model have reinforced the trend toward restricting social rights, decreasing the role of the state as guarantor of these rights, converting rights into individual responsibilities, and placing them in the world of the market. A strong public health current has thus been born that posits health as basically an individual good to be acquired within the realm of relationships between the individual, the family, and private health sector providers. In this thinking, the state must intervene only to help those sectors of the population that fail in helping themselves to achieve good health.

This health view has been articulated more clearly in the recent past by the active presence of multilateral financial organizations, such as the World Bank and the Inter-American Development Bank, in the health sector. It promotes health as a market commodity to be bought and sold in the free market, allowing for the free play of supply and demand market forces (6). It is of course understood that countries accepting this neoliberal view end up with privatized health service organizations, with a clear predominance of insurance and financial capital. It is interesting to note that this view is rarely spelled out as visibly as was done in Chile at the beginning of the reforms implemented by the Pinochet regime. More often this model is proposed subtly, without an open recognition of the privatizing consequences of the policies, which are disguised in many different ways.

The Health Subcommittee's view and the ideas that emerged from the popular hearing process of the ANC are radically different. Within the framework of a broad current of progressive thought in Latin America, we think that the living and working conditions of a society determine the people's health (7). Thus improvement of health is closely related to improvements in quality of life. Health cannot be dissociated from the human condition and life; it is consubstantial with human life and therefore a fundamental social and human right, to be guaranteed and protected by the state. Furthermore, health is a vital space for community participation and the construction of social organization and citizenship.

According to this perspective, the first political decision of the subcommittee was that in order to confront this disagreement about health as social right versus market good and to create a process of refoundation and reconstruction of the country, it would be essential to reestablish the value of solidarity and human dignity, and reaffirm the notion that health is a social right to be secured by the state. In addition, all attempts to privatize this right had to be prevented through the build-up of a Public National Health System that ensured the health of all citizens without any kind of discrimination. The first conclusion of the subcommittee, then, was that the first component of the Constitution had to be political, conceptual, addressing the political concept of health as a social right, a duty of all, and a responsibility of the state.

Type of Health System. A second theme in the debate was the mechanisms for executing constitutional mandates. There was a clear understanding that making social rights sacred was not enough. It was also indispensable to lay out the principles and mechanisms that would allow for the implementation of these rights. The subcommittee called them "mechanisms to enforce constitutional mandates." The subcommittee also reached a consensus that the mechanisms to enforce these rights must be included in the Constitution. Within this general perspective, many different ways and possibilities for organizing countrywide health care services and systems were analyzed in detail.

Three significant organizing models, with multiple variations, became evident. The first, typical of countries in Europe, is marked by the concepts of the welfare state that prevailed after World War II. This is typical of old national health or social security systems, such as those in England, Germany, France, Canada, and Spain, where the state is the essential guarantor. The second type is the private system, typical of the United States, which has no national health system and people have to find their own health insurance mechanism (8); this system has a clear dominance of market interests and private insurers. The third type is a fragmented system such as that in Venezuela, that provides health care to people according to their affiliation. This organizing structure has been reframed and "organized" by Frenk and colleagues under the notion of "structured pluralism" (9). The subcommittee considered this the worst organizing structure. Laurell (10) has demonstrated its high cost and inefficiency in several scenarios.

The Constituent Representatives decided that the new Constitution had to ensure a unified health system that was universal, integral, participatory, decentralized, and allowed for increased access to care and quality of care. To achieve these goals the system must (*a*) incorporate the concept of a national public health system as a mechanism to enforce constitutional mandates and (*b*) be directed by the principles of universality, integrality, solidarity, equity, no charge at point of delivery, and participation.

Financing. A detailed analysis focused on three large problems that affect health sector financing: fragmentation, de-financing, and inefficiency. The plan of the previous government followed a financing model partially based on direct payments by users of the services and by contributions. Additionally, it surrendered the administration of the funds to the private sector (privatization plan). The subcommittee proposed to integrate the financing in a single fund, with resources originating basically from the fiscal budget and the possibility of special allocations and contributions, to be progressively integrated into the single fund.

THE HEALTH ARTICLES
OF VENEZUELA'S CONSTITUTION

The health articles of the Constitution were written based on the inputs produced in the three steps mentioned above. The approved constitutional text is as follows (11):

Article 83 Health is a fundamental social right, duty of the state, which will guarantee it as part of the right to life. The State will promote and develop policies oriented towards the increase in life expectancy, the collective well being, and access to services. All individuals have the right to health protection, and the duty to actively participate in its promotion and defense, and to follow the health and sanitation measures that the law establishes, according to the International Treaties and Agreements signed and ratified by the Republic.

Article 84 To guarantee the right to health, the State will create, lead, and manage a public, national health system, intersectoral in nature, decentralized and participatory, integrated with the social security system, directed by the principles of gratuity (free access), universality, integrality, equity, social integration, and solidarity. The public system will give priority to the promotion of health and the prevention of diseases, ensuring prompt care and quality rehabilitation. The public services and goods are propriety of the State and cannot be privatized. The organized community has the right and duty to participate in decision-making about planning, execution, and control of specific policies in the public health institutions.

Article 85 The financing of the public health system is an obligation of the State, which will integrate fiscal resources, mandatory social security contributions, and any other source of financing mandated by law. The State will guarantee a health budget that enables it to implement health policy objectives. In coordination with the universities and research centers, a national human resource development policy to educate professionals and technicians, and a national industry to produce health inputs will be developed. The State will regulate the public and private health institutions.

In these articles health is conceived as a fundamental social right that must be guaranteed by the state, without discrimination of any kind, and as part of the right to life, expressing the link between health, quality of life, and collective well-being. Furthermore, the articles define three mechanisms for enforcing constitutional mandates that will allow translation of this right into reality: first, creation of the Public National Health System; second, fundamental principles that direct this system; third, funding of the system by taxes, which is a responsibility of the state that integrates fiscal resources, mandatory social security contributions, and any other sources established by law. On December 15, 1999, in a referendum for Venezuelans to give their opinion about the new Constitution, 71.37 percent voted in favor of the social right to health, and the mechanisms to ensure it were consecrated in the Constitution of the Bolivarian Republic of Venezuela.

DISCUSSION

After establishing health as a fundamental social right and drawing up the mechanisms of constitutional mandates for its development, there is still work to do on building the legislation and institutional capability for making this legal dream a reality. This requires the design of health policies that:

1. Strengthen the role of the state as manager of the health system and as responsible for the design of intersectoral policies to intervene in the diverse factors that determine the health of the population.
2. Build the Public National Health System, integrating the many existing state agencies, particularly the Ministry of Health and Social Development and the Venezuelan Institute of Social Security, and reinforcing their characteristics of universality, unity, decentralization, and participation.
3. Encourage strong state investments in health to offset the lack of resources, integrate the various sources available today, introduce budgetary mechanisms that include performance measurements, and stimulate the search for higher levels of efficiency in the delivery of services and management of resources.
4. Promote the development of a health care model that reestablishes the integrality of health, emphasizing the need for coherence and harmonization between the biological and the social, the individual and the collective.
5. Allow and promote the real participation of the organized community in the design of health policies and control of services.

CONCLUSION

As Feo (12) notes, a comparative analysis of the Venezuelan Constitutions of 1961 and 1999 shows remarkable progress. First, the 1999 Constitution explicitly endorses the right to health, which was not established in the 1961 Constitution. The most important implications of this are universality and the role of the state as guarantor. Second, the new Constitution establishes individual duties to participate in health promotion. Although the 1961 Constitution established certain individual responsibilities, these were oriented toward compliance with health laws and standards. Third, the new Constitution establishes principles that will govern the health system (as outlined above). Fourth, it establishes mechanisms for the state to enforce the social right to health. Concepts such as decentralization and participation are also incorporated, thus creating a Constitution adapted to the functions that a modern health system must fulfill. The 1961 Constitution did not include those mechanisms or characterize the health system as public, decentralized, participatory, and intersectoral.

Fifth, the new Constitution incorporates the notions of health promotion and disease prevention as priorities of the health system, which were not established in the 1961 Constitution. The new Constitution is less medicalized and less oriented toward curative care, instead focusing on primary care, health promotion, and disease prevention. Sixth, the new Constitution establishes the fiscal nature of financing of the public health system, which has to be administered and governed by the state. Resources originating in the national budget are integrated with social security contributions from workers and businesses. These aspects were not present in the 1961 Constitution. Seventh, inclusion of community and individual participation in health promotion and decision-making on planning, execution, and control of specific institutional health policies represents great progress, in agreement with the organization and functioning of modern health systems. Last, the new Constitution sees health as part of social security. We interpret this to mean that despite being integrated with social security, the health system must be unified and managed by the Ministry of Health and Social Development, the highest authority on health issues.

The new Venezuelan Constitution adopted popular and democratic principles that moved the legal health framework of Venezuela many steps further in the direction of the best health system policies of the 20th century. It is a promising start for the new millennium. Both the procedures by which the new health system has been designed and the principles it embodies belie the slanders about President Chávez.

REFERENCES

1. Beasley-Murray, J. Venezuela: The revolution will not be televised: Pro-Chávez multitudes challenge media blackout. *NACLA Report on the Americas* 36(1):16–23, 2002.
2. Rosen, F., and Youngers, C. Divided society on the brink. *NACLA Report on the Americas* 36(4):8–12, 2002.
3. Terris, M. Witnesses to history: The Caracas explosion and the IMF. *J. Public Health Policy* 10:149, 1989.
4. Presidencia de la República de Venezuela. Decreto No. 3. February 2, 1999.
5. Constitución de la República de Venezuela. Gaceta Oficial No. 662 (extraordinaria). January 23, 1961.
6. Banco Mundial. *Informe sobre el desarrollo mundial 1993: Invertir en salud.* Oxford University Press, Washington, DC, 1993.
7. Waitzkin, H., et al. Social medicine in Latin America: Productivity and dangers facing the major national groups. *Lancet* 358:315–323, 2001.
8. Navarro, V. (ed). *Why the United States Does Not Have a National Health Program.* Baywood, Amityville, NY, 1992.
9. Frenk, J., Londoño, J., and Lozano, R. Pluralismo estructurado, una visión para el futuro de los sistemas de salud en América Latina. In *Salud, Cambio social y política,* ed. M. Bronfman and R. Castro, pp. 253–275. EDAMEX, Mexico, 1999.

10. Laurell, A. C. Avanzar al pasado: la política social del neoliberalismo. In *Estado y políticas sociales en el neoliberalismo,* ed. A. Laurell. Fundación Friedrich Ebert, Mexico, 1992.
11. Constitución de la República Bolivariana de Venezuela. Gaceta Oficial No. 5453 (extraordinaria). March 24, 2000.
12. Feo, O. *La salud en la nueva constitución.* Cendes, Caracas, 2000.

CHAPTER 14

Venezuela's Barrio Adentro:
An Alternative to Neoliberalism in Health Care

Carles Muntaner, René M. Guerra Salazar,
Joan Benach, and Francisco Armada

Health care reforms in most countries since the early 1990s, and particularly in Latin America, have followed a remarkably similar pattern, shifting from a preexisting system of public delivery, financing, and ownership to a greater involvement of the private sector (1–8). In most Latin American countries, including Venezuela, health care became less a human right guaranteed by the state and more a commodity acquired in the marketplace. This shift, often presented as the solution, was mainly fueled by the pressure of the structural adjustment programs (SAPs) adopted by many Latin American countries following the neoliberal paradigm prescribed by international financial institutions (IFIs) concerned with repayment of foreign debt (2).

Nonetheless, there is an exception to this trend: after a decade of adherence to neoliberal reforms, in 1999 Venezuela charted an alternative health care program guaranteed by the state. Driven by local demands through a process of participatory democracy, this new, bold health care reform is playing out in the country's most marginalized and underserved neighborhoods. Moreover, Venezuela's health reform is founded on an international cooperation model that emphasizes "South to South" solidarity, rather than the more typical channels of "North to South" aid. What are the main characteristics of this new, as yet little-known health care model, some of whose beneficiaries say is "the best thing that has happened in Venezuela?"[1]

In this chapter we review the main features of the Venezuelan health care reform, analyzing, within their broader sociopolitical and economic contexts, previous neoliberal health care reforms that mainly benefited transnational capital interests and domestic Latin American elites. We explain the emergence of the

---

[1] Based on interviews conducted by one of the authors in February 2005 in the Caracas *barrio* of Catia, one of the first neighborhoods to implement Misión Barrio Adentro.

new health care program, Misión Barrio Adentro (Inside the Neighborhood), examining its historical, social, and political underpinnings and the central role played by popular resistance to neoliberalism. Finally, we suggest that this program not only provides a compelling health care reform model for other low- to middle-income countries but also offers relevant policy lessons to wealthy countries.

THE SOCIOPOLITICAL AND ECONOMIC CONTEXTS OF HEALTH SECTOR NEOLIBERALIZATION IN VENEZUELA

The deep funding cuts that characterized structural adjustment policies in most Latin American countries after the early 1980s gradually created conditions that fostered neoliberal reforms and the destabilization of the welfare state (2), and erosion of social services such as health care. As a result of SAPs throughout the 1980s, state-administered health care sectors deteriorated in quality, and their inefficiency and inequity increased. The only viable option in the 1990s seemed to be a shift to greater private sector management and delivery of health care services. In 1993, the World Bank's *World Development Report: Investing in Health* marked a second step in health care's neoliberalization (9), advocating for two overarching strategies: limiting state investment in health care to low-cost services that target the poor, and encouraging diversity and competition in the financing and delivery of health services by facilitating greater private sector involvement. These strategies have meant an increase of private, for-profit health insurance plans, coupled with the decentralization of service delivery and administration under ever-shrinking budgets (7, 10). As governments in Latin America privatized health care financing and delivery, several multinational corporations that sell financial, banking, investment, and insurance services entered the new, lucrative markets, often by partnering with Latin American companies owned and operated by wealthy Latin Americans. In Mexico and Brazil, for example, neoliberal health care reforms reduced access to health care services for poor and working-class people, burdened the public health care sector with higher-risk patients, and further compromised the quality of public services, while private insurance companies reported significant profits (3, 7, 11). Although neoliberal health care reforms failed to be fully implemented in most Latin American countries (8), and despite the increasing evidence of the ill effects of these neoliberal reforms on health and well-being (12–15), all countries but Cuba have undergone, to some degree, these health sector changes.

Compared with most of its neighbors, Venezuela jumped on the neoliberal bandwagon relatively late. The slower pace of reform may be attributed in part to Venezuela's large petroleum and natural gas reserves (16), which helped to expand welfare state policies throughout the 1950s and 1960s, even if the benefits were not equitably reaped (17). Nonetheless, fluctuating oil prices and massive spending to pay for imports and national capital projects raised the national debt and decreased oil revenues in the 1980s, contributing to a socioeconomic crisis—in 1989, close to 54 percent of Venezuelans lived in extreme or critical poverty. Seduced by the increasingly dominant neoliberal ideology, the elected president, Carlos Andrés Pérez, sought to address rising poverty in Venezuela by committing to a radical SAP named El paquete, which was supported by the World Bank and International Monetary Fund (18). The Venezuelan government reforms, with deep public spending cuts, privatization, trade liberalization, and restructuring of social programs to target the poor (18, 19), faced widespread public opposition and mobilization that helped spark two failed coup attempts and the impeachment of President Pérez in 1993 (20).

The erosion of welfare institutions throughout the 1990s fueled increasing calls for health care reform, and the new Venezuelan government procured two major health reform loans from the World Bank and the Inter-American Development Bank (21, 22). Both loans contained provisions to facilitate or support the restructuring of health sector financing, with an increased role for private financing and continuing support for the decentralization of social services. Decentralization, coupled with the fiscal austerity measures of the early 1990s, left the newly responsible regional and local levels of government with few options but to carry out an uncoordinated, de facto privatization of many health care services high in demand but short on supply (23). By 1997, 73 percent of health expenditures in Venezuela were private (23). The introduction of user fees in the public system made the deteriorating health services even less accessible.

In the late 1990s, a dramatic drop in oil prices led the Venezuelan government to once again seek loans from the IFIs. By 1999, poor Venezuelans comprised nearly three-quarters of the population, with a very limited access to health care services through a precarious public system. The election in December 1998 of President Hugo Chávez, who campaigned staunchly against further IFI-prescribed neoliberal reforms, set the country in a new direction. Chávez's overwhelming and surprising victory was the political outcome of nearly two decades of popular mobilization against a corrupt Venezuelan regime and its increasingly neoliberal agenda (24). Once elected, and after extensive consultation throughout the country and with all sectors of Venezuelan society, Chávez called in December 1999 for a referendum on a new "Bolivarian" constitution, drafted by a special constituent assembly (25).

THE BEGINNING OF THE BOLIVARIAN
HEALTH ALTERNATIVE

Three main articles in the new constitution had important implications for health care reform (26). First, health is viewed as a fundamental human right that the state is obligated to guarantee (Article 83); second, the state has the duty to create and manage a universal, integrated public health system providing free services and prioritizing disease prevention and health promotion (Article 84); and third, this public health care system must be publicly financed through taxes, social security, and oil revenues, with the state regulating both the public and private elements of the system and developing a human resource policy to train professionals for the new system (Article 85).

Among the alternative redistributive mechanisms to strengthen the Venezuelan welfare state created by the new Bolivarian government are the *misiones*, social programs created as parallel structures either completely outside the scope of government ministries or in collaboration with them, as a means to increase community participation and more efficiently meet the new constitutional imperatives. Misión Barrio Adentro aims to satisfy the constitutional requirements of health as a social right through a public health care system that spans all levels of care. It is a popular program based on the principles of equity, universality, accessibility, solidarity, multisectoral management, cultural sensitivity, participation, and social justice (27).

Barrio Adentro began in December 1999 after Venezuela suffered torrential rains that caused extensive flooding in the state of Vargas, affecting mainly *barrio* dwellers, the marginalized poor living in the hilly periphery of major urban centers. As part of its international solidarity programs, the Cuban government responded to the tragedy by providing a team of 454 Cuban health care workers who offered medical care inside the marginalized *barrios*. Based on this experience, the mayor of the Municipality of Libertador, which has the largest number of poor people in the Metropolitan Area of Caracas, requested the help of Venezuelan physicians in attending to the acute needs of the underserved populace. However, the majority of Venezuelan physicians refused, citing security concerns and a lack of infrastructure as their primary reasons. Behind these explicit objections lay an organized opposition by the Venezuelan medical establishment to the health care reform efforts of the new Bolivarian government (28). In April 2003, after an agreement for a pilot project with the Cuban government, 58 Cuban physicians specializing in integrated family medicine were sent to various *barrios* in Caracas's periphery within the marginalized neighborhoods. A few months later, after witnessing the success of the pilot program, President Chávez officially dubbed the program "Misión Barrio Adentro" and supported its extension to the remaining states and their munici-palities through the coordinated efforts of the Ministry of Health and Social Development and a cooperation agreement with Cuba. In December 2003, a multisectoral Misión Barrio Adentro Presidential Commission was created and charged with the implementation and coordination of a national Primary Health Care Program. Between April and December 2003, more than 10,000 Cuban physicians, dentists, and ophthalmologists began providing primary health care and dispensing free Cuban-supplied medications for poor Venezuelans in hundreds of *barrios*.

ORGANIZATION, ACTIVITIES, AND EARLY ACHIEVEMENTS
OF BARRIO ADENTRO

Today, more than 20,000 Cuban health personnel and a growing number of Venezuelan health professionals make up the human resources in Barrio Adentro (29). Given the continued (though decreasing) reluctance of Venezuela's medical establishment to participate in the program, the government launched a massive training effort to replace, over time, the thousands of Cuban health workers with Venezuelans. According to the Ministry of Health and Social Development Barrio Adentro planning framework, its goal at the primary care level is to provide round-the-clock access through the construction inside historically marginalized communities of one community health center for every 250 families (27). By April 2006, of the more than 8,000 planned community health centers, more than 2,000 had already been built (29). Additionally, many health centers that are part of the preexisting primary health care infrastructure have been incorporated into Barrio Adentro. Each community health center has a multidisciplinary health team consisting of at least one physician specialized in integrated family medicine, a community health worker, and a health promoter. Moreover, each center is stocked with centrally purchased medications to be distributed at no cost to patients, as required. The health team personnel live in the *barrios* themselves. Participating Cuban physicians receive a modest salary of US$250 per month, plus free room and board. In addition to conducting consultations in the health centers, the health teams are responsible for carrying out daily neighborhood rounds to survey residents and making home visits to those too ill to go to the community health centers (27).

This integrated model of care emphasizes a holistic approach to health and illness through the coordination of Barrio Adentro with other *misiones* addressing education, food security, public sanitation, and employment, among other key social determinants of health. For example, people lacking potable water who suffer from recurring intestinal infections are not only prescribed the appropriate antibiotics but also encouraged to organize to demand adequate access to clean water. Health teams and patients are supported by Health Committees comprised of *barrio* residents, which are the organizational mechanisms through which *barrio* residents exercise their participation in primary health care delivery and management. In addition to the 8,000 planned primary health care clinics, Barrio Adentro plans to construct 1,200 diagnostic and rehabilitation centers (secondary care) and to upgrade the existing tertiary care infrastructure of 300 hospitals (29).

In terms of expanding access to health care, the results achieved by Misión Barrio Adentro have been impressive and may well produce a significant improvement in population health status. The next few years will be critical to evaluate the program and to assess its generalizability to other countries.

Despite the overwhelming popularity and success of Barrio Adentro and other *misiones*, these and other proposed reforms have elicited strong opposition from the upper middle class and elite sectors of Venezuelan society. This opposition resulted in a military coup attempt and a debilitating general lockout in 2003 and a presidential recall referendum in 2004, all aiming to remove the democratically elected President Chávez from office (30). However, with a mass mobilization by poor and working-class Venezuelans (who make up the vast majority in the country) in support of their president, all three measures failed (30). At the time of this report, President Chávez has a 75 percent approval rating (31), and the Bolivarian process and its counter-neoliberal health reforms continue to develop.

SOME LESSONS TO BE LEARNED

For the past 25 years, the neoliberal ideology that underpins IFI-sponsored health reform initiatives throughout Latin America has become the new conventional wisdom in policymaking (7). Its influence is surprisingly pervasive, given mounting evidence of its detrimental effects on health and equity throughout the region. Notwithstanding this evidence, numerous countries continue to adhere to neoliberal reform policies. Yet, the Venezuelan experience suggests that the neoliberal way is not inexorable. The Venezuelan example supports the thesis that a country's well-being is determined by policy choices that are more closely related to that country's political and ideological power relations (32)—which themselves are the synthesis of historical popular struggle—than to its income level.

The Venezuelan government, strongly aided by popular participation as explicitly established in its new constitution, has over a short period of time managed to allocate economic and social resources to geographic areas where they can improve the health and well-being of the population. The process is both planned and implemented by government officials and defended and supported by mass organizations such as Health Committees throughout the country. In addition, as the role of Cuba demonstrates, health care reform in Venezuela has been facilitated not by the "policy-based lending" of IFIs but rather by a novel form of international cooperation based on a bottom-up process of democratic local needs assessments and "South to South" mutual aid. Indeed, the unique international cooperation so fundamental to Barrio Adentro suggests a remarkable challenge to the principles of conventional international health "aid." Just as remarkable as the seeming pervasiveness of the neoliberal paradigm for health reform is Venezuela's ability to break with this paradigm that in recent history has dominated the region, though with increasing resistance.

The lessons to be learned from the Venezuelan experience are not exclusive, however, to low- and middle-income countries. The notion, often taken for granted, that international health knowledge and expertise flow only from core to periphery needs to be challenged (33), and the Venezuelan case helps to further debunk this myth. Though many of the elements outlined in the 1984 Ottawa Charter for Health Promotion have failed to gain traction in wealthy countries, they are quite evident in Venezuela's Misión Barrio Adentro. The mechanisms and, more importantly, the social and political contexts that promote and foster community participation in health care management and an emphasis on the social determinants of health in Barrio Adentro may serve as important insights to help increase the access and quality of health care in the marginalized communities of wealthy countries. For the moment, Venezuela has been able to build a compelling alternative to neoliberalism in community health that serves as an as yet little-known international health example for all countries.

Acknowledgment — We thank Professor Anne-Emanuelle Birn for her comments on an earlier draft of this chapter.

Note — Parts of this chapter are adapted from a paper in a special issue of the *Canadian Journal of Public Health*, 2006.

REFERENCES

1. Laurell, A. C. La política de salud en el contexto de las políticas sociales. In *Salud, cambio social y política: perspectivas desde América Latina México*, ed. M. Bronfman and R. Castro. EDAMEX, Mexico City, 1999.
2. Laurell, A. C. Structural adjustment and the globalization of social policy in Latin America. *Int. Sociol.* 15(2):306–325, 2000.
3. Armada, F., Muntaner, C., and Navarro, V. Health and social security reforms in Latin America: The convergence of the World Health Organization, the World Bank, and transnational corporations. *Int. J. Health Serv.* 31(4):729–768, 2001.
4. Birn, A.-E., Zimmerman, S., and Garfield, R. To decentralize or not to decentralize, is that the question? Nicaraguan health policy under structural adjustment in the 1990s. *Int. J. Health Serv.* 30(1):111–128, 2000.
5. Schuyler, G. W. Globalization and health: Venezuela and Cuba. *Can. J. Dev. Stud.* 23(4):687–716, 2002.
6. Abel, C., and Lloyd-Sherlock, P. Health policy in Latin America: Themes, trends and challenges. In *Healthcare Reform and Poverty in Latin America,* ed. P. Lloyd-Sherlock. Institute of Latin American Studies, London, 2000.
7. Iriart, C., Merhy, E. E., and Waitzkin, H. Managed care in Latin America: The new common sense in health policy reform. *Soc. Sci. Med.* 52:1243–1253, 2001.
8. Homedes, N., and Ugalde, A. Why neoliberal health reforms have failed in Latin America. *Health Policy* 71:83–96, 2005.
9. World Bank. *World Development Report: Investing in Health*. Oxford University Press, New York, 1993.
10. Collins, C., and Green, A. Decentralization and primary health care: Some negative implications in developing countries. *Int. J. Health Serv.* 24(3):459–476, 1994.
11. Jasso-Aguilar, R., Waitzkin, H., and Landwehr, A. Multinational corporations and health care in the United States and Latin America: Strategies, actions, and effects. *J. Health Soc. Behav.* 45:136–157, 2004.
12. Kinman, E. Evaluating health service equity at a primary care clinic in Chilimarca, Bolivia. *Soc. Sci. Med.* 49:663–678, 1999.

13. Manfredi, C. Can the resurgence of malaria be partially attributed to structural adjustment programmes? *Parasitologia* 41:389–390, 1999.
14. Garfield, R. Malaria control in Nicaragua: Social and political influences on disease transmission and control activities. *Lancet* 354:414–418, 1999.
15. Jaggar, A. M. Vulnerable women and neoliberal globalization: Debt burdens undermine women's health in the global south. In *Recognition, Responsibility, and Rights: Feminist Ethics and Social Theory,* ed. R. N. Fiore et al. Rowman and Littlefield, Boulder, CO, 2003.
16. Naim, M. *Paper Tigers and Minotaurs: The Politics of Venezuela's Economic Reforms.* Carnegie Endowment for International Peace, Washington, DC, 1993.
17. Hellinger, D. Democracy over a barrel: History through the prism of oil. *NACLA* 27(5):35–41, 1994.
18. Buxton, J. Venezuela. In *Case Studies in Latin American Political Economy,* ed. J. Buxton and N. Phillips. Manchester University Press, New York, 1999.
19. Lander, E. The impact of neoliberal adjustment in Venezuela, 1989–1993. *Latin Am. Perspect.* 23(3):50–73, 1993.
20. Tulchin, J. S., and Bland, G. (eds.). *Venezuela in the Wake of Radical Reform.* Lynne Rienner, Boulder, CO, 1993.
21. World Bank. *Staff Appraisal Report: Venezuela Health Services Reform Project.* Washington, DC, 2005.
22. Inter-American Development Bank. *Program to Strengthen and Modernize the Health Sector.* Washington, DC, 2006.
23. Díaz Polanco, J. El papel del financiamiento en los procesos de reforma del sector salud: el caso de Venezuela. In *La reforma de salud de Venezuela: aspectos políticos e institucionales de la descentralización de la salud en Venezuela Caracas,* ed. J. Díaz Polanco. Fundación Polar, Caracas, 2001.
24. Lander, E. Venezuelan social conflict in a global context. *Latin Am. Perspect.* 32(2):20–38, 2005.
25. Ministerio de la Secretaría de la Presidencia. *Constitución de la República Bolivariana de Venezuela.* Caracas, 2000.
26. Feo, O., and Siqueira, C. E. An alternative to the neoliberal model in health: The case of Venezuela. *Int. J. Health Serv.* 34(2):365–375, 2004.
27. Ministerio de Salud y Desarrollo Social. *Barrio Adentro: expresión de atención primaria de salud: un proceso de construcción permanente.* Caracas, 2005.
28. Jardim, C. Prevention and solidarity: Democratizing health in Venezuela. *Monthly Rev.* 56(8):35–39, 2005.
29. Ministerio de Salud y Desarrollo Social. Barrio Adentro. 2006. www.msds.gov. ve/msds/modules.php?name=Content&pa=showpage&pid=239 (February 15, 2006).
30. Gott, R. *Hugo Chávez and the Bolivarian Revolution.* Verso, New York, 2005.
31. Millard, P. Venezuela Chavez's approval rating at 70.5%. 2005. www.globalexchange. org/countries/americas/venezuela/3036.html (February 15, 2006).
32. Navarro, V. *Globalización Económica, Poder Político, y Estado del Bienestar.* Ariel, Madrid, 2000.
33. Birn, A.-E. Uruguay on the world stage: How child health became an international priority. *Am. J. Public Health* 95(9):1506, 2005.

PART VIII

The Consequences of Neoliberalism in Africa

CHAPTER 15

The Dispossession of African Wealth at the Cost of Africa's Health

Patrick Bond

The South–North drain of African wealth reduces the resources available for development, increases dependency on the global North, and—of considerable importance—can be radically altered by the adoption of bold national policies, notwithstanding an adverse international context (1). Redirecting resources so as to reverse the collapse of African health systems is of perhaps the most critical importance (2; see Chapter 16 of this volume). But this will require a dramatic change in outlook by those in Africa with even a modicum of power to direct resources. Rhetorically, high-profile events during 2005–2006 hinted at prospects for change in the elite circuitry: Britain's governmental Commission for Africa and nongovernmental Make Poverty History campaign, the Live 8 concerts arranged by Bob Geldoff, the Johannesburg-based Global Call to Action Against Poverty, the main creditor countries' debt relief offer, the G8 Gleneagles aid commitments, and increased attention to the United Nations' Millennium Development Goals. In one case, Nigeria, monies looted by Sani Abacha and deposited in Swiss bank accounts were recently returned, and a large debt relief package was granted.

However, what becomes clear from all these events is the establishment's urge to merely revise and restate mainstream conceptions of Africa's plight. Witness Tony Blair's Commission for Africa report, for example (3, p. 13):

> Africa is poor, ultimately, because its economy has not grown. The public and private sectors need to work together to create a climate which unleashes the entrepreneurship of the peoples of Africa, generates employment and encourages individuals and firms, domestic and foreign, to invest. Changes in governance are needed to make the investment climate stronger. The developed world must support the African Union's New Partnership for Africa's Development (Nepad) programme to build public/private partnerships in order to create a stronger climate for growth, investment and jobs.

These sentences distill the mistakes of conventional wisdom regarding the continent's underdevelopment. Blair hosted the G8 and the European Union in 2005, and his chancellor of the exchequer, Gordon Brown, advanced several initiatives on debt, aid, and trade, deploying "Marshall Plan for Africa" rhetoric. Below, I consider the way the Africa Commission co-opted key African elites into a modified "neoliberal"—free market—project.

To set the tone at the outset, it would be more logical to reverse all of the above allegations in the Commission for Africa report and reconstruct the paragraph as follows:

> Africa is poor, ultimately, because its economy and society have been ravaged by international capital as well as by local elites who are often propped up by foreign powers. The public and private sectors have worked together to drain the continent of resources which—if harnessed and shared fairly—should otherwise meet the needs of the peoples of Africa. Changes in "governance"—such as revolutions—are desperately needed for social progress, and these entail not only the empowerment of "civil society" but also the strengthening of those agencies within African states that can deliver welfare and basic infrastructure. The rich world must decide whether to support the African Union's Nepad program, which will worsen the resource drain because of its pro-corporate orientation, or instead to give Africa space for societies to build public–people partnerships in order to satisfy unmet basic needs.

As mainstream economic policy gripped Africa tighter during the 1990s, poverty worsened, leaving three-quarters of the citizenry surviving on less than US$2.15 per day (3). Common—and incorrect—explanations mask both the causes of African poverty and the implications of recent global policy reforms. The International Monetary Fund (IMF), for example, argues unconvincingly that African countries are failing because they have gone "off track" (4, p. 25). Moreover, global reform proposals of 2005 were based on the misperception that Africa is the (often unworthy) beneficiary of significant financial flows. A chart prepared for the Commission for Africa (Figure 1) leaves the impression of a vast inflow of aid, rising foreign investment, sustainable debt payments, and adequate remittances from the African diaspora to fund development (3, p. 106). This analysis ignores the losses due to "phantom aid," the attribution of increased foreign direct investment to just three recipient countries since 1997, a net negative debt service payment since 1990, and the capital flight and brain drain (especially in the health sector) that significantly outweigh remittances.

By contrast, rigorous studies and analyses now confirm the negative consequences of neoliberal policies. A few of these critiques are even emerging from within the Bretton Woods and other institutions responsible for pressuring African countries to adopt structural adjustment and liberalization in the first place. For example, a

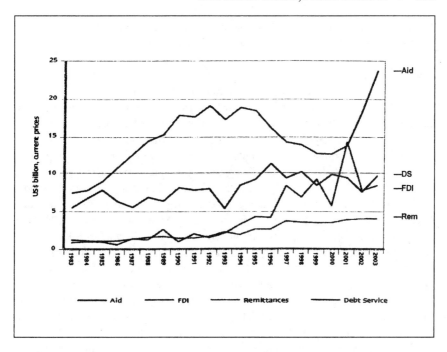

Figure 1. Africa Commission claims of financial/investment flows to sub-Saharan Africa: aid, debt service (DS), foreign direct investment (FDI), and remittances (Rem). *Source:* Commission for Africa (3, p. 106).

mid-2005 study by London research/advocacy charity Christian Aid reaches devastating conclusions (5, p. 1; see also 6):

> Trade liberalisation has cost sub-Saharan Africa $272 billion over the past 20 years. Had they not been forced to liberalise as the price of aid, loans and debt relief, sub-Saharan African countries would have had enough extra income to wipe out their debts and have sufficient left over to pay for every child to be vaccinated and go to school. Two decades of liberalisation has cost sub-Saharan Africa roughly what it has received in aid. Effectively, this aid did no more than compensate African countries for the losses they sustained by meeting the conditions that were attached to the aid they received.

Overall, an analysis of the most recent data contradicts reform proposals to reverse African poverty through "a stronger climate for investment." The first step to effect genuine growth and deliver resources to health services, welfare, and basic infrastructure is, instead, for African societies and policymakers to identify and prevent the vast and ongoing outflows of the continent's existing and potential wealth. Northern governments, multilateral agencies, and international banks and corporations maintain an explicitly financial stranglehold on Africa, with enabling collaboration from some African business interests and some governments.

Africa's political economists have, for many decades, documented the roles of finance, trade, and foreign direct investment in the continent's ongoing under-development, and the following information largely updates rather than supplants the basic thesis of excess Northern power offered by Tajudeen Abdul-Raheem, Charles Abugre, Adebayo Adedeji, Jimi Adesina, Claude Ake, Neville Alexander, Samir Amin, Peter Anyang'Nyong'o, A. M. Babu, Ahmed Ben Bela, Steve Biko, Dennis Brutus, Amilcar Cabral, Fantu Cheru, John Daniel, Jacques Delpechin, Demba Dembele, Ashwin Desai, Yasmine Fall, Frantz Fanon, Ruth First, M. P. Giyose, Yao Graham, Pauline Hountondji, Eboe Hutchful, Khafra Kambon, Dot Keet, Rene Loewenson, Sara Longwe, Patrice Lumumba, Samora Machel, Archie Mafeje, Ben Magubane, Amina Mama, Mahmood Mamdani, Achille Mbembe, Henning Melber, Guy Mhone, Darlene Miller, Thandika Mkandawire, Dani Nabudere, Léonce Ndikumana, Trevor Ngwane, Njoki Njehu, Kwame Nkrumah Julius Nyerere, Georges Nzongola-Ntalaja, Oginga Odinga, Adebayo Olukoshi, Oduor Ongwen, Bade Onimode, Haroub Othman, Mohau Pheko, Kwesi Prah, Brian Raftopoulos, Thomas Sankara, Issa Shivji, Yash Tandon, Riaz Tayob, Aminata Traoré, Dodzi Tsikata, Kwame Ture, Ngugi Wa Thoing'o, Ernest Wamba dia Wamba, Harold Wolpe, Tunde Zack-Williams, and Paul Zeleza. As these and other authors have shown, resources are drained through finance (including debt and aid), through unequal trade, and through foreign direct investment. Consider each in turn.

DEBT, FINANCE, AND AID

North–South inflows in the form of "aid," loans, or investment come with conditions. Pressure through such funding—even on "concessional" (below-market interest rate) terms—intensified Africa's disadvantageous integration into the world economy. The reduction of barriers to financial transactions, and to movements of goods and capital (though not necessarily of labor) in the process, weakened state power that might otherwise have been used constructively. These neoliberal measures intensified a preexisting drain of African wealth.

To illustrate, Africa's debt crisis worsened during the era of globalization. The continent now repays more than it ever received, with outflow in the form of debt repayments equivalent to three times the inflow in loans and, for most African countries, far exceeding export earnings. The debt relief measures announced in mid-2005 by the G7 finance ministers have not disturbed either the draining of Africa's financial accounts or the maintenance of debt-associated control functions. Underlying the Gleneagles proposals was the notion of "sustainable" service repayments (varying by country but typically not exceeding 20 percent of export earnings). Africa has repaid more than it received in new loans since the 1990s. Overall, during the 1980s and 1990s, Africa repaid $255 billion (U.S. dollars), or

4.2 times the original 1980 debt. For some countries (including Cameroon, the Gambia, Mauritania, Senegal, and Zambia), servicing the debt far exceeded government health spending.

In 1980, inflow was comfortably higher than the debt repayment outflow, but soon thereafter Africa suffered from the U.S. Federal Reserve's tripling of U.S. interest rates. Paying abnormally high interest rates to service loans required new loans. By 2000, the net flow deficit reached $6.2 billion, as the new loans no longer paid the interest on old loans. For 21 African countries, the debt reached at least 300 percent of exports by 2002, and for countries such as Sudan, Burundi, Sierra Leone, and Guinea-Bissau, it was 15 times greater than their annual export earnings (7).

Moreover, in at least 16 African countries, according to Eric Toussaint (8), debt inherited from dictators could be defined as legally "odious" and therefore eligible for cancellation, because citizens were victimized both in the debt's original accumulation (and use of monies against the society) and in subsequent demands that it be repaid. These amounts easily exceed 50 percent of Africa's outstanding debt: Nigeria under the Buhari and Abacha regimes, 1984–1998 ($30 billion); South Africa under apartheid, 1948–1993 ($22 billion); the Democratic Republic of the Congo (DRC) under Mobuto, 1965–1997 ($13 billion); Sudan under Numeiri, 1969–1985 ($9 billion); Ethiopia under Mengistu, 1974–1991 ($8 billion); Kenya under Moi, 1978–2002 ($5.8 billion); Congo under Sassou, 1979–2005 ($4.5 billion); Mali under Traore, 1968–1991 ($2.5 billion); Somalia under Siad Barre, 1969–1991 ($2.3 billion); Malawi under Banda, 1966–1994 ($2.2 billion); Togo under Eyadema, 1967–2005 ($1.4 billion); Liberia under Doe, 1980–1990 ($1.2 billion); Rwanda under Habyarimana, 1973–1994 ($1 billion); Uganda under Idi Amin Dada, 1971–1979 ($0.6 billion); and the Central African Republic under Bokassa, 1966–1970 ($0.2 billion). Other nondemocratic countries— including Zimbabwe under Mugabe in recent years ($4.5 billion)—could also be added to this list (8, p. 150).

Aside from credits, other financial "portfolio" investment has mainly taken the form of "hot money"—highly risky speculative investment in stock and currency markets—with erratic and overall negative effects on African currencies and economies. The director of the U.N. Research Institute for Social Development, Thandika Mkandawire, observes: "It is widely recognised that direct investment is preferable to portfolio investment, and foreign investment in 'green field' investments is preferable to acquisitions. The predominance of these [portfolio and acquisition] types of capital inflows should be cause for concern" (9, p. 7). In 1995, for example, foreign purchases and sales were responsible for half the share-trading on the Johannesburg Stock Exchange, once exchange controls were relaxed. Such flows have had devastating effects on South Africa's currency, with more than 30 percent crashes over a period of weeks during runs in early 1996, mid-1998, and late 2001 (10). In Zimbabwe, the November 1997 outflow of hot money crashed the currency by 74 percent in just four hours of trading (11). The result has been extremely erratic performance by the eight major African stock markets (in South Africa and, to a much smaller extent, Nigeria, Kenya, Zambia, Mauritius, Botswana, Ghana, and Zimbabwe), sometimes returning impressive profits to foreign investors and sometimes generating large losses. Few exchange controls prevent foreign repatriation of dividends and profits from South Africa, including excessive outflows to the several huge London-registered corporations— Anglo American, DeBeers, Miller–South African Breweries, Old Mutual, Liberty Life, Didata—that were once South African (10).

Other problems emerge on the aid side of the financial accounts. Africa is commonly and mistakenly represented as the (unworthy) recipient of a vast aid inflow. Aid fell in the wake of the West's Cold War victory—dropping 40 percent during the 1990s—but the general decline had begun in the late 1960s. Moreover, purported aid figures must be corrected for tied aid (money spent in the donor country) and phantom aspects such as debt relief and aid bureaucracy. In any case, aid from most developed countries (except Scandinavia and the Netherlands) falls well below the 0.7 percent of gross domestic product (GDP), the U.N. target set 35 years ago. The U.S. and Japanese figures of 0.12 and 0.23 percent of GDP, respectively, are most egregious. Of total official aid, nongovernmental organizations estimate that just over a third takes the form of "real" aid that reaches poor people, according to Action Aid's 2005 study (12). Only a small proportion of aid is technically "untied." That amount rose from $2.3 billion in 1999 to $4.3 billion in 2003, but declined as a proportion of total "aid."

At the 2002 Conference on Financing for Development, held in Monterrey, Mexico, governments agreed that debt relief should be considered "additional" to existing and rising aid, not used to boost aid figures—a promise broken when exaggerated aid commitments were made at the Gleneagles G8 meeting in 2005. Belatedly recognizing the unsustainability of debt financing, the World Bank and IMF introduced the Highly Indebted Poor Countries (HIPC) initiative in 1996. Nine years later, in June 2005, the plan was augmented by the finance ministers' debt relief concessions for 18 countries that were near or at the HIPC "completion point." Of these, 14 are African: Benin, Burkina Faso, Ethiopia, Ghana, Madagascar, Mali, Mauritania, Mozambique, Niger, Rwanda, Senegal, Tanzania, Uganda, and Zambia (the other 4 are Bolivia, Guyana, Honduras, and Nicaragua). Ten other countries due for relief once they pass the HIPC initiative hurdles are Burundi, Cameroon, Chad, the DRC, the Gambia, Guinea, Guinea-Bissau, Malawi, Sierra Leone, and São Tomé and Principe. At least another 8 African countries are waiting to enter HIPC: the Central African Republic, Comoros, the Republic of the Congo, Côte d'Ivoire, Liberia, Somalia, Sudan, and Togo.

The first point to make in relation to this strategy is that HIPC debt relief has largely applied to loans that *weren't being paid in any case*. Most of the countries listed in Table 1 have vast debts—measured as a proportion of GDP—that can never be repaid; the countries are, in accounting terms, bankrupt. The notional reduction of these debts is effectively meaningless. The average official multilateral

Table 1

Sub-Saharan African debt to official creditors, 2005, as percent
of gross domestic product

Oil-producing countries			
Angola	25.0		
Cameroon	34.0		
Chad	33.9		
Congo, Republic of the	71.4		
Côte d'Ivoire	48.4		
Equatorial Guinea	4.0		
Gabon	40.9		
Nigeria	32.4		
São Tomé and Principe	425.6		
Non-oil-producing countries			
Benin	35.9	Mali	60.5
Botswana	3.1	Mauritius	8.1
Burkina Faso	33.6	Mozambique	66.4
Burundi	191.5	Namibia	5.6
Cape Verde	46.6	Niger	50.6
Central African Republic	88.1	Rwanda	73.7
Comoros	75.9	Senegal	41.8
Congo, Democratic Republic of the	157.0	Seychelles	39.9
Ethiopia	69.6	Sierra Leone	103.5
Gambia, The	122.1	South Africa	2.2
Ghana	73.2	Swaziland	14.0
Guinea	87.7	Tanzania	47.1
Guinea-Bissau	282.3	Togo	93.2
Kenya	27.0	Uganda	49.6
Lesotho	51.6	Zambia	60.8
Madagascar	100.3	Zimbabwe	32.2
Malawi	144.1		
Total for sub-Saharan Africa	**26.4**		

Source: International Monetary Fund, *Regional Economic Outlook: Sub-Saharan Africa*, p. 27.
Washington, DC, September 2005.
Note: The figures do not include commercial debt.

debt of HIPC completion-point countries in 1997–2001 was 80.3 percent of GDP, a figure reduced to 57.3 percent by late 2005. For all of sub-Saharan Africa, the equivalent figures fell from 44.0 to 26.4 percent. Yet only very small increases in available fiscal resources resulted, with even smaller social spending increments. Moreover, for 6 of Africa's 14 HIPC completion-point countries—Ethiopia, Ghana, Madagascar, Niger, Rwanda, and Uganda—there was insubstantial debt relief, leaving debt/GDP levels in 2005 at roughly the same burden as when the program started nine years earlier. In another 5 HIPC cases—Burundi, the Gambia, Guinea–Conakry, Malawi, and Sierra Leone—there has been no progress in paying down the debt (1).

A second point is that aid reductions and debt relief may simply cancel each other out in many cases. According to Alex Wilks, of the European Network on Debt and Development (13):

> The eighteen-to-thirty-eight beneficiary countries will eventually have their debts cancelled, but will also have a corresponding amount cut from the aid flows they were likely to receive. . . . Zambia will stop paying its debts to three creditors, but will not receive the equivalent amount in aid to spend, likely less than 20% of the amount of debt cancelled. In order to get what little extra money they are eligible for, the governments of developing nations will have to accept harsh World Bank and IMF conditions. This typically means privatization and trade liberalization, misconceived policy measures which often harm poorer people and benefit international traders.

Indeed, HIPC country programs and associated Poverty Reduction Strategy Papers still require macroeconomic austerity and services privatization. And in the most important non-HIPC country that received debt relief in 2005, Nigeria, a new Policy Support Instrument was applied with quarterly "on/off signals" for donors that include first and foremost, "macroeconomic performance and policies" but also "structural reforms that are either macro-economically critical, or within the Fund's core areas (e.g., tax system, exchange system, financial sector)" (14, p. 25). While it received a notional $30 billion in debt relief, the immediate cost to Nigeria was a huge debt payment. According to the leader of Nigeria's Jubilee network, Rev. David Ugolor (quoted in 15):

> The Paris Club cannot expect Nigeria, freed from over 30 years of military rule, to muster $12.4 billion to pay off interest and penalties incurred by the military. Since the debt, by President Obasanjo's own admission, is of dubious origin, the issues of the responsibilities of the creditors must be put on the table at the Paris Club. As desirable as an exit from debt peonage is, it is scandalous for a poor debt distressed country, which cannot afford to pay $2 billion in annual debt service payments, to part with $6 billion up front or $12 billion in three months or even one year.

The Global AIDS Alliance made similar remarks (16):

> The creditors should be ashamed of themselves if they simply take this money [$12.4 billion]. These creditors often knew that the money would be siphoned off by dictators and deposited in western banks, and the resulting debt is morally illegitimate. They bear a moral obligation to think more creatively about how to use this money. Nigeria has already paid these creditors $11.6 billion in debt service since 1985.

Finally, on the financial accounts, there is the matter of capital flight. Flows of private African finance shifted from a net inflow during the 1970s, to gradual outflows during the 1980s, to substantial outflows during the 1990s. Using Bank for International Settlements data, Eric Toussaint (with the assistance of Damien Millet) estimates that the total overseas accounts of African citizens in Northern banks and tax havens in 2003 were $80 billion (8, p. 150). At the same time, African countries owed $30 billion to those very banks. The two leading scholars of capital flight, James Boyce and Léonce Ndikumana (17), conclude that "sub-Saharan Africa thus appears to be a net creditor vis-à-vis the rest of the world," since a core group of sub-Saharan African countries whose foreign debt was $178 billion suffered a quarter century of capital flight by elites—from 1970 to 1996—that totaled more than $285 billion (including imputed interest earnings). The sub-Saharan African countries with the worst capital flight problems are Nigeria ($98 billion more than its foreign debt, when interest on capital flight is also added), the Ivory Coast ($15 billion), the DRC ($10.1 billion), Angola ($9.2 billion), and Zambia ($5.5 billion) (17). Capital flight from Africa is a lower figure than that from other regions, but a higher proportion of a continent's GDP than anywhere else. More than $10 billion has left Nigeria, Côte d'Ivoire, the DRC, Angola, and Zambia collectively per year since the early 1970s. In 2004, the IMF found that resident African official outflows from Africa had exceeded $10 billion a year, on average, since 1998 (18, p. 196). A large portion of this amount reflects changes in South African capital controls that permitted residents to offload shares of the largest Johannesburg firms to London purchasers. However, very high outflows continued even after those share deals had their one-off impact.

While this sort of financial liberalization has taken root in Africa, even its proponents admit that it has manifestly failed to achieve growth and stability. Nonetheless, the South African government is committed to providing a hub for global business, in order to amplify liberalization in sub-Saharan Africa. IMF researchers—including the then chief economist, Kenneth Rogoff—finally acknowledged in 2003 that two decades of financial liberalization had wrought severe damage. Rogoff and his colleagues (Eswar Prasad, Shang-Jin Wei, and M. Ayhan Kose) admitted "sobering" conclusions (19, p. 6):

> A systematic examination of the evidence suggests that it is difficult to estab-
> lish a robust causal relationship between the degree of financial integration
> and output growth performance. . . . Recent crises in some more finan-
> cially integrated countries suggest that financial integration may in fact
> have increased volatility.

TRADE TRAPS

In addition to finance, trade has been a source of wealth depletion for Africa, dating back centuries to early versions of plunder, including 12 million slaves. In the past five years, a slight upturn in the terms of trade for African countries has only begun to mitigate the damage done by export-led growth policies foisted on Africa since the 1980s.

Given that many of the continent's elites and allied aid agencies persistently believe that it is possible to achieve growth through exports, a recent report by the World Bank is important to cite at the outset. By considering the natural resources depletion associated with extractive trade, even Bank economists now concede that much of Africa is poorer not wealthier than it would have been had the minerals, petroleum, and indigenous timber stayed put. The Bank report *Where Is the Wealth of Nations?* (20) finds that some countries have lost massive amounts of wealth. For example, Gabon's citizens lost $2,241 each in 2000, followed by citizens of the Republic of the Congo (–$727), Nigeria (–$210), Cameroon (–$152), Mauritania (–$147), and Côte d'Ivoire (–$100) (20, p. 66). This problem is particularly acute in oil-rich countries on the Gulf of Guinea. Most of the dollar value of Africa's exports in recent years is petroleum-related, largely from Nigeria and Angola.

This long-standing problem of dependence on export of primary products was identified by Frantz Fanon, just as the African countries were achieving independence (21):

> The national economy of the period of independence is not set on a new footing. It is still concerned with the ground-nut harvest, with the cocoa crop and the olive yield. In the same way there is no change in the marketing of basic products, and not a single industry is set up in the country. We go on sending out raw materials; we go on being Europe's small farmers who specialize in unfinished products.

Like financial imbalances, distortions in trade (and related currency valuation)—including the rising trade surplus that South Africa runs with the rest of the continent (while its deficit with the West grows)—are another route for the extraction of superprofits. The continent's share of world trade declined over the past quarter century, but the volume of exports increased. "Marginalization" of Africa thus occurred not because of insufficient integration, but because other areas of the world, especially East Asia, moved to the export of manufactured goods, while Africa's industrial potential declined thanks to excessive deregulation associated with structural adjustment.

To be sure, this is a long-standing problem of differential power relations in trade and exchange rate deviations (together termed "unequal exchange"), which according to Samir Amin and Gernot Köhler (as published by Köhler (22)), generated surplus transfers approaching $1.8 trillion per year by the late 1990s (Figure 2). Whereas the average currency value of Second and Third World countries (i.e., non-members of the Organization for Economic Cooperation and Development) in relation to First World currencies was 82 percent in 1960, it had declined to 38 percent by the late 1990s, according to Amin and Köhler.

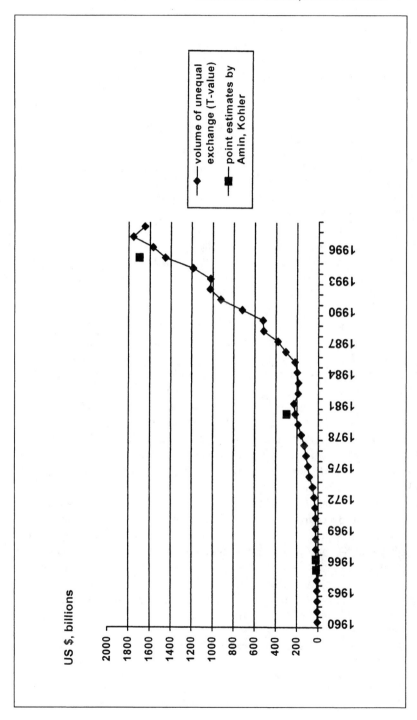

Figure 2. South–North "unequal exchange" transfers, 1960–1998. *Source:* Köhler (22).

Considered in another form, the importance of unequal exchange is witnessed in the difference between export volume and the value-added that goes into the exports. According to Jayati Ghosh, this is a matter not merely of dependence on primary commodity export but also of the nature of manufacturing output in the global division of labor (23):

> While developing countries as a group more than doubled their share of world manufacturing exports from 10.6% in 1980 to 26.5% in 1998, their share of manufacturing value added increased by less than half, from 16.6% to 23.8%. By contrast, developed countries experienced a substantial decline in share of world manufacturing exports, from 82.3% to 70.9%. But at the same time their share of world manufacturing value added actually increased, from 64.5% to 73.3%.

Whether it is a function of real currency changes or of the character of what is being produced (raw materials or low-value manufactured goods), the volatile trade-related underdevelopment captured in these figures is most important during epochs of "globalization" such as the 1910s–1920s and 1980s–1990s. The volatility is, of course, global in scale, as the U.S. current account also suffers from extreme trade/investment instability: from surpluses associated with the weak dollar in 1980, followed by dramatic declines to dangerous levels in the mid-1980s (–3.5 percent of GDP), reversed by surpluses during another weak-dollar period from 1991, but again falling rapidly from the mid-1990s (down to –5 percent of GDP and worse). Once the dot-com boom was finished in 2000, the U.S. share of global foreign direct investment also fell substantially, from $321 billion in 2000 to as low as $40 billion in 2003 (18, Appendix).

Notwithstanding overwhelming evidence of the dangers of export dependency under these circumstances, the policy debate continues. As Nancy Alexander of the Services for All campaign in Washington, D.C., has shown (24), a 2002 World Bank paper promoting export-led growth revealed how two economists, David Dollar and Aart Kraay (25), creatively twisted data to prove their point that only exporting countries could finance internal growth. Dollar and Kraay termed certain countries "globalizers"—including China and India—and others "non–globalizers"—mainly commodity producers whose prices fell dramatically during the 1980s–1990s, even if during that period they were *more* not less dependent on the whims of globalized markets. By adding a commodity dependence dummy variable to the Dollar–Kraay growth equation, Alexander notes, the importance of openness to growth falls by at least half (24):

> These findings are significant because, whereas some development experts assert that low-income countries are caught in a "poverty trap," they are actually caught in a "commodity trap"—signified by a long-term decline of commodity prices, especially relative to the cost of manufactures. . . . In their calculation of the impact of openness on growth, Dollar and Kraay use

changes in the volume of trade as a proxy for changes in trade policy. However, volumes of trade vary due to many influences other than policy changes. . . . Openness is generally the outcome of growth rather than its cause; its "fruit, not its root." The most successful globalisers in the World Bank study, such as China and India, follow heterodox policies, rather than those advocated by donors and creditors.

China and India have substantial tariffs to protect their own agricultural industries, as well as rigorous exchange controls that shielded them from the turmoil that rocked their Asian neighbors in 1997–1998, for example.

At least other Bank economists, Ataman Aksoy and John Beghin, were honest enough to admit that their employer "oversold" the benefits of exporting commodities in a context of diminishing world prices: "A development strategy based on agricultural commodity exports is likely to be impoverishing in the current agricultural policy environment" (26). They also conceded that from 1970 to 1997, the cumulative loss resulting from declining terms of trade for sub-Saharan African non-oil-exporting countries amounted to 119 percent of their total GDP.

None of this is particularly new. Under colonialism, Walter Rodney showed (27):

> The unequal nature of the trade between the metropole and the colonies was emphasised by the concept of the "protected market," which meant even an inefficient metropolitan producer could find a guaranteed market in the colony where his class had political control. Furthermore, as in the preceding era of pre-colonial trade, European manufacturers built up useful sidelines of goods which would have been sub-standard in their own markets, especially in textiles.

In contemporary times, Northern agricultural subsidies have risen to the point, at several hundred billion dollars a year, that campaigners joke how a typical European cow receives a $2 per day subsidy for merely living, while a vast number of Africans are expected to survive on even less. According to Delhi-based agricultural trade researcher Devinder Sharma, Europe especially has taken advantage of Third World powerlessness in the World Trade Organization (28):

> Between 1995 and 2004, Europe alone has been able to increase its agricultural exports by 26%, much of it because of the massive domestic subsidies it provides. Each percentage increase in exports brings in a financial gain of $3 billion. On the other hand, a vast majority of the developing countries, whether in Latin America, Africa or Asia, have in the first 10 years of WTO turned into food importers. Millions of farmers have lost their livelihoods as a result of cheaper imports. If the WTO has its way, and the developing countries fail to understand the prevailing politics that drives the agriculture trade agenda, the world will soon have two kinds of agriculture systems—the rich countries will produce staple foods for the world's

6 billion plus people, and developing countries will grow cash crops like tomato, cut flowers, peas, sunflower, strawberries and vegetables.

FOREIGN DIRECT INVESTMENT AND DISINVESTMENT

Even within the narrow terms of the neoliberal argument, foreign direct investment fails to benefit African economies. Inflated risk factors discourage investment; common perceptions are based on overestimated investment levels; financial sector investment and acquisitions far outweigh investment in new "greenfield" manufacturing; and corrupt elites distort any potential prospects for reinvestment.

In the brief rise of foreign investment into sub-Saharan Africa noted by the Blair Commission (Figure 1), especially from 1997, peaks seem to be associated with special circumstances (Figure 3). The Angolan 1999 oil investment peak was limited to the offshore Cabinda fields at a time of civil war. The 1990s investments in Nigerian oil occurred largely under Sani Abacha's 1990s military rule and were offset by his looting of state resources and transfer to private Swiss and London accounts.

South Africa's investments were mainly accounted for by two processes: the partial privatization of the telecommunications parastatal in 1997 and the relisting of huge domestic corporations offshore from 1998 onward. The implications of the telecommunications investments are now well known, in the wake of the 30 percent share purchase in the state-owned Telkom by a Houston–Kuala Lumpur alliance. Critics such as the Freedom of Expression Institute (www.fxi.org) point to subsequent problems inexorably related to foreign direct investment and privatization, including the skyrocketing cost of local calls as cross-subsidization from long-distance (especially international) calls was phased out; the disconnection of 2.1 million lines (of 2.6 million new lines installed) due to unaffordability; the firing of 20,000 Telkom workers, leading to ongoing labor strife; and an initial public offering on the New York Stock Exchange in 2003 that raised only $500 million, with an estimated $5 billion of Pretoria's own funding of Telkom's late 1990s capital expansion lost in the process. Ironically, the South African state repurchased the shares of Telkom held by the foreign investment consortium in 2004 (although Pretoria did not materially change policies and practices subsequently). There are several similar experiences with failed foreign investment in South Africa's other privatized state assets, including transport (renationalization in the cases of Sun Air and SAA), water (remunicipalization in the case of Suez in Nkonkobe, and likely to occur in Johannesburg), and electricity.

Aside from the expansion of automobile export and component parts manu-facturing capacity in the late 1990s, the only other large foreign direct investment inflow occurred when Barclays purchased the country's largest bank in 2005 (with all that this entailed for shifting funding relationships). South Africa witnessed very few foreign investments in greenfield projects. Behind the overall slowdown in South African fixed investment lie not only global overcapacity combined with

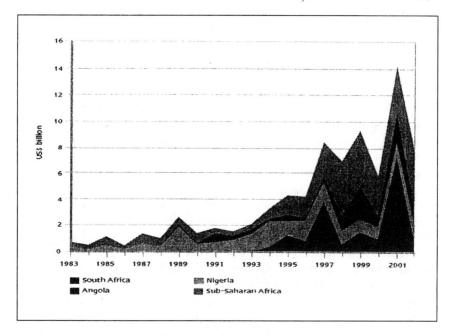

Figure 3. African recipients of foreign direct investment: sub-Saharan Africa (top, gray curve), Angola (second, black), Nigeria (third, gray), and South Africa (bottom, black). *Source:* Commission for Africa (3, p. 295).

national industrial uncompetitiveness, but also South Africa's own overcapacity constraints to new investment, given the long-term decline in manufacturing capacity utilization resulting from overproduction and excessive oligopolistic concentration in the major industrial sectors. South Africa is thus a more complicated and perhaps extreme example of so many other African countries where the private sector was stagnant and in need of privatization opportunities yet, in spite of the fire-sale character of privatization, did not subsequently succeed in turning acquisition fire-sale investments into sustained productive investments (10).

As for the damage done by foreign direct investment in petroleum/mineral sector activity, it is partly economic (as *Where Is the Wealth of Nations?* (20) documents) but also political. With an estimated 3 million dead in Central African wars, thanks largely to the victims' proximity to coltan (a niobium- and tantalum-containing ore) and other mineral riches, conflicts worsened between and within the Uganda/Rwanda bloc, vis-à-vis the late 1990s alliance of the DRC, Zimbabwe, Namibia, and Angola (itself the site of a 30-year civil war fueled by oil and diamonds). Only with DRC leader Laurent Kabila's 2001 assassination and Pretoria's management of elite peace deals in the DRC and Burundi are matters settling, however briefly, into a fragile peace combining neoliberalism and opportunities for minerals extraction. Another particularly difficult site is Sudan, where U.S. Delta Force troops have been sighted in informal operations, perhaps because, although China broached oil exploration during the country's civil war chaos, U.S. firms have subsequently arrived. And bridging sub-Saharan Africa and North Africa—in another subregion of crucial importance to U.S. imperialism—not only is Libya being brought into the fold of weapons certification and control. Already, U.S. troops have been deployed for small-scale interventions in Mali, Chad, and Mauritania. In Chad, World Bank President Paul Wolfowitz has been active in managing (under the guise of funding control) corruption involving U.S. oil firms and Chadian government arms purchases and repression. A site of future extraction lies between northern Nigeria and southern Algeria, where gas pipeline options have been contracted by the U.S. multinationals Halliburton and Bechtel. The major petro prize remains the Gulf of Guinea, given that African routes to Louisiana oil-processing plants are many weeks less time-consuming for tanker transport than the Persian Gulf. West Africa's offshore oil fields have low sulfur output more attractive to U.S. refiners. Moreover, in settings ranging from oil-rich Sudan to Nigeria and Algeria, Africa remains an important site in Washington's campaigns against militant Islamic networks. The "resource course" thus is not just about the tendency of local elites to become rentiers, but is also inextricably tied to petro-military processes that link Texas oil barons, the Pentagon, the World Bank, Wall Street, and their European counterparts, with Pretoria generally serving as subimperial ally (1, 30, 31).

In a related category, the North owes the South, especially Africa, a vast amount in "ecological debt," because developed countries use or destroy a hugely disproportionate measure of the global "commons." A member of the U.N. International Panel on Climate Change calculates that forests in the South that absorb carbon from the atmosphere in effect provide Northern polluters with an annual subsidy of $75 billion (1, 32).

A pedestrian—if nevertheless crucial—query is also worth raising: to what extent do the foreign investors cover their own initial equity stake? The case of the partially privatized Airports Company of South Africa is instructive. Aeroporti Di Roma earned a vast profit—R785 million—on its initial 1998 investment of R890 million for 20 percent of the South African company. In September 2005, the South African state's investment arm bought back the stake for R1.67 billion. Adding the R180 million in dividends paid since 1998, the Italian firm took home more than a 108 percent rate of return over seven years—exceptionally high by any measure (1). At the same time, the repurchase of the company by a state agency showed there was no particular reason to have a foreign investor in the first place. Although "technical expertise" is sometimes considered a valid reason for inviting foreign investment, the South African air transport industry's management and logistics operations were always sufficiently sophisticated to handle the expansion of airports.

These experiences are not uncommon, according to Transparency International's Lawrence Cockcroft (33, p. 2):

> The most common and important form of corruption has been one in which, in spite of a conventional bidding process, an award has been made to a company which has committed itself to specific additional investment often amounting to large sums. The real, but very untransparent arrangement, has been that a key figure in the privatization panel has taken a bribe for the award of the contract and will ensure that no further investment need be made, and even that the initial downpayment should be very modest. This is certain to have disastrous consequences for the long term viability of the operation in question.

Moreover, official statistics have never properly picked up the durable problem of transfer pricing, whereby foreign investors misinvoice inputs drawn from abroad. Companies cheat Third World countries on tax revenues by artificially inflating their imported input prices so as to claim lower net income. One can only guess the vast scale of the problem on the basis of case studies. The Oxford Institute of Energy Studies estimated that in 1994, 14 percent of the total value of exported oil "was not accounted for in national trade figures as a result of various forms of transfer pricing and smuggling" (33; see also 2). According to a 1999 U.N. Conference on Trade and Development survey on income shifting as part of transfer pricing (34, p. 167):

> Of the developing countries with sufficient evidence to make an assessment, 61% estimated that their own national transnational corporations (TNCs) were engaging in income shifting, and 70% deemed it a significant problem. The income-shifting behaviour of foreign-based TNCs was also appraised. 84% of the developing countries felt that the affiliates they hosted shifted income to their parent companies to avoid tax liabilities, and 87% viewed the problem as significant.

In all of this, patriarchy is amplified in the South so as to maintain and increase the profitability of debt/finance, trade, and investment. It is impossible to put a monetary value on the loss of wealth to Africa that is due to persistent patriarchal repression. But it is now well recognized that women are the main victims of neoliberal policies, whether in (increasingly sweatshop-based) production or in the sphere of household and community reproduction. In areas characterized by migrant labor flows, such as southern Africa, the super-exploitation of rural women in childrearing, health care, and elder care is especially evident. More broadly, this is part of what Isabella Bakker and Stephen Gill term "the reprivatisation of social reproduction," entailing these trends (35, p. 136):

- household and caring activities are increasingly provided through the market and are thus exposed to the movement of money;

- societies seem to become redefined as collections of individuals (or at best collections of families), particularly when the state retreats from universal social protection;
- accumulation patterns premised on connected control over wider areas of social life and thus the provisions for social reproduction;
- survival and livelihood. For example, a large proportion of the world's population has no effective health insurance or even basic care.

For Africans, the denial of access to food, medicines, energy, and even water is the most extreme result; people who are surplus to capitalism's labor requirements find they must fend for themselves or die. The scrapping of safety nets in structural adjustment programs exerts greater pressure on the family during economic crises, which makes women more vulnerable to sexual pressures and, therefore, HIV/AIDS. A comprehensive African literature review by Dzodzi Tsikata and Joanna Kerr shows how patriarchal "biases have affected the perception of economic activities and have affected economic policies in ways that perpetuate women's subordination" (36).

POLICY AND POLITICAL OPTIONS

Progressive responses to the outflow of wealth from Africa fall into three main areas:

1. Bottom-up activism, in which policies and strategies draw from civil society campaigns and from grassroots and shop-floor social action movements, both historical and contemporary.
2. Global governance and policy reform, which tend to downplay the structural causes of outflows in the global and African political economy. Regrettably, with the Bush regime in the United States, not even the welcome power shifts in Latin America are likely to change the global balance of forces in the near term so as to initiate and enforce positive global-scale measures (such as proposed ecological reparations, or taxes on currency transactions and arms deals). Much "global governance" reform is therefore a waste of time and energy.
3. National policy opportunities for progressive initiatives to reverse outflows of African wealth and divert resources toward health care and other genuinely needed investments.

But for the national policy space to open, and indeed for new governments to win election in Africa, popular campaigns to reverse resource flows are critical. These are already emerging from African grassroots struggles, such as:

- "Decommodification" movements to establish basic needs as human rights, rather than as privatized commodities that must be paid for

- Campaigns to "de-globalize" capital, such as defunding the World Bank, resisting biopiracy, and securing the right to produce local, generic medicines (especially anti-retrovirals) instead of suffering transnational corporate patent monopolies
- Demands for civil society oversight of national budgets
- Activism to ensure equitable redistribution of resources in ways that benefit low-income households, grassroots communities, and shop-floor workers

Urgently needed national policies to reverse the continent's socioeconomic collapse must draw on bottom-up activism and critiques from Africans themselves. Options that would immediately present themselves to policymakers in states with new, more progressive governments—and that have been successfully tried in recent years—include:

- Nationalization of natural resources
- Systematic default on foreign debt repayments
- Strategies to enforce domestic reinvestment of pensions and other funds
- Reintroduction of currency exchange controls and prohibition of tax-haven transfers
- Refusal of tied and phantom aid, along with naming and shaming fraudulent "aid"
- Inward-oriented import-substitution development strategies
- Refusal of foreign investments that prove unfavorable when realistic projections factor in costs such as natural resource depletion, transfer pricing, and profit/dividend outflows
- Reversal of macroeconomic policies that increase inequality

But intensified bottom-up African activism—as well as further examples from Latin American leaders—are the prerequisites for any such progress. If the top-down campaigns on Africa of 2005 taught the world anything, it is to treat Northern-centric, charity-oriented, and capital-integrating strategies with great skepticism. This is not just because the dispossession of Africa's wealth will worsen if the Global Call to Action Against Poverty continues to divert African activists' attention into fruitless campaigning for Millennium Development Goals, or Live8 concerts and rock stars such as Bono and Geldoff muddy the political terrain, or Oxfam succeeds with its export-oriented trade strategy, or the Make Poverty History coalition again legitimizes 10 Downing Street, other G8 elites, the World Trade Organization, and the Bretton Woods institutions (1). Not only did these efforts represent and reinforce status quo power relations, but it is obvious from the 2005 initiatives that they cannot work even on their own limited terms (1, 30). The G8 granted a very minor amount of debt relief (with intensified neoliberal conditionality); the increases in aid are still largely of a "phantom" nature, not alleviating poverty but instead serving geopolitical, administrative, or corporate-accumulation strategies; trade patterns have remained undisturbed; and investors today have even more capacity to dispossess Africa of its valuable resources through ongoing liberalization pressure.

In contrast, serious grassroots activism against accumulation by dispossession in Africa has recently included the following: Jubilee and reparations campaigners attempting to turn repeated "IMF riots" into longer-term strategies; Treatment Action advocates breaking the hold of pharmaceutical corporations on monopoly anti-retroviral patents; activists fighting Monsanto's genetically modified crops/food drive from the United States to South Africa to several African countries; blood-diamonds victims from Sierra Leone and Angola generating a partially successful global deal at Kimberley; Kalahari Basarwa-San Bushmen raising publicity against forced removals, as the Botswana government clears the way for DeBeers and World Bank investments; Lesotho peasants objecting to displacement during construction of the continent's largest dam system (solely to quench Johannesburg's irrational and hedonistic thirst), along with the actions of Ugandans similarly threatened at the overly expensive, corruption-ridden Bujagali Dam; a growing network questioning Liberia's long exploitation by Firestone Rubber; Chadian and Cameroonian activists pressuring the World Bank not to continue funding repression and environmental degradation; Oil Watch linking of Nigerian Delta and many other Gulf of Guinea communities; and Ghanaian, South African, and Dutch activists opposing water privatization.

How far these activist movements go depends in part on how far valued allies in the advanced capitalist financial and corporate centers recognize the merits of their analysis, strategy, and tactics—and offer the solidarity that African and other Third World activists can repay many times over, once the Northern boot is lifted from their countries' necks and they gain the space to win lasting, emancipatory objectives such as a sufficient flow of resources back into African health care.

Acknowledgment — The research for this chapter was funded through the Harare-based health research network Equinet with support from the Canadian International Development Research Centre and Swedish International Development Aid; these funding sources are not responsible for the content of the arguments found herein.

REFERENCES

1. Bond, P. *Looting Africa: The Economics of Exploitation.* Zed Books, London, 2006.
2. Bond, P., and Dor, G. Uneven health outcomes and political resistance under residual neoliberalism in Africa. *Int. J. Health Serv.* 33:607–630, 2003.
3. Commission for Africa. *Our Common Future.* London, 2005.
4. International Monetary Fund. *Regional Economic Outlook: Sub-Saharan Africa.* Washington, DC, May 2005.

5. Christian Aid. *The Economics of Failure: The Real Cost of "Free" Trade for Poor Countries.* London, 2005.
6. Kraev, E. *Estimating Demand Side Effects of Trade Liberalization on GDP of Developing Countries.* Christian Aid, London, 2005.
7. World Bank. *Global Finance Tables.* Washington, DC, 2002.
8. Toussaint, E. *Your Money or Your Life.* Haymarket Books, Chicago, 2004.
9. Mkandawire, T. Maladjusted African economies and globalization. *Africa Dev.* 30(1–2):2005.
10. Bond, P. *Elite Transition: From Apartheid to Neoliberalism in South Africa.* University of KwaZulu-Natal Press, Pietermaritzburg, 2005.
11. Bond, P., and Manyanya, M. *Zimbabwe's Plunge: Exhausted Nationalism, Neoliberalism and the Search for Social Justice.* Merlin Press, London, 2003.
12. Action Aid. *Real Aid: An Agenda for Making Aid Work.* Johannesburg, 2005.
13. Wilks, A. *Selling Africa Short.* European Network on Debt and Development, Brussels, June 21, 2005.
14. International Monetary Fund. *Policy Support and Signaling in Low-Income Countries.* Policy Development and Review Department, Washington, DC, 2005.
15. Jubilee USA. Nigerian Threat to Repudiate Helps Force Paris Club to Deliver Debt Cancellation. Press release, Washington, DC, October 20, 2005.
16. Global AIDS Alliance. Nigeria's Creditors Should Be Ashamed. Press release. Washington, DC, October 20, 2005.
17. Boyce, J., and Ndikumana, L. Is Africa a Net Creditor? New Estimates of Capital Flight from Severely Indebted Sub-Saharan African Countries, 1970–1996. Occasional paper, University of Massachusetts–Amherst Political Economy Research Institute, 2000.
18. International Monetary Fund. *Global Financial Stability Report.* Washington, DC, 2004.
19. Prasad, E., et al. *Effects of Financial Globalization on Developing Countries: Some Empirical Evidence.* International Monetary Fund, Washington, DC, March 17, 2003.
20. World Bank. *Where Is the Wealth of Nations?* Washington, DC, 2005.
21. Fanon, F. *The Wretched of the Earth.* Grove Press, New York, 1963.
22. Köhler, G. Unequal Exchange 1965–1995: World Trends and World Tables. World-Systems Archive, working papers, 1998. http://csf.colorado.edu/wsystems/ archive/papers/kohlertoc.htm.
23. Ghosh, J. Why More Exports Have Not Made Developing Countries Richer. www.networkideas.org/themes/trade/may2002/print/prnt110502_Exports_Developing _Countries.htm (May 11, 2002).
24. Alexander, N. The Ideological Economics of Commodity Production. Services for All listserve, December 9, 2005.
25. Dollar, D., and Kraay, A. *Trade, Growth and Poverty.* World Bank, Washington, DC, 2002.
26. Aksoy, A., and Beghin, J. *Global Agricultural Trade and Developing Countries.* World Bank, Washington, DC, 2005.
27. Rodney, W. How Europe Underdeveloped Africa. 1972. www.marxists.org/subject/africa/rodney-walter/how-europe/.
28. Sharma, D. Much Ado about Nothing. ZNet Commentary, December 24, 2005.
29. Daniel, J., and Lutchman, J. South Africa in Africa. Paper presented at South African Association of Political Studies Colloquium, Pietermaritzburg, September 22, 2005.

30. Bond, P. *Talk Left, Walk Right: South Africa's Frustrated Global Reforms*. University of KwaZulu-Natal Press, Pietermaritzburg, 2006.
31. Ferguson, J. *Global Shadows*. Duke University Press, Durham, NC, 2006.
32. Martinez-Alier, J. Marxism, Social Metabolism and Ecologically Unequal Exchange. Paper presented at Lund University Conference on World Systems Theory and the Environment, September 19–22, 2003.
33. Cockcroft, L. *Corruption as a Threat to Corporate Behaviour and the Rule of Law*. Transparency International UK, London, 2001.
34. U.N. Conference on Trade and Development. *Transfer Pricing*. Geneva, 1999.
35. Bakker, I., and Gill, S. Ontology, method and hypotheses. In *Power, Production and Social Reproduction,* ed. I. Bakker and S. Gill. Palgrave Macmillan, Basingstoke, England, 2003.
36. Tsikata, D., and Kerr, J. *Demanding Dignity: Women Confronting Economic Reforms in Africa*. North-South Institute, Ottawa, and Third World Network–Africa, Accra, 2002.

CHAPTER 16

Uneven Health Outcomes and Political Resistance Under Residual Neoliberalism in Africa

Patrick Bond and George Dor

In the wake of the devastation wrought in Africa by two decades of "neo-liberalism"—that is, state policies that are market-oriented, export-led, subject to fiscal austerity, and characterized by the commercialization/privatization of public sector functions—this question repeatedly arises: have matters improved now that the Bretton Woods Institutions (the World Bank and International Monetary Fund) and major donor governments are permitting countries to improve their state health systems and increase spending? And what are civil society watchdog groups and debt advocacy movements such as the Jubilee network saying about recent modifications to neoliberalism, especially the Poverty Reduction Strategy Papers and Highly Indebted Poor Countries debt relief initiative?

Several issues have been associated with the direct impact of structural adjustment programs—and neoliberalism more generally—on health and health services in Africa. Effects included disincentives to health-seeking behavior, witnessed by lower utilization rates and declines in the perceived cost and quality of services. Household expenditures on health care and ability to meet major health care expenses dwindled, as did nutritional status. Health services price inflation and additional costs put often unbearable burdens on household disposable incomes and on food consumption. A dramatic decline in employment status had a negative effect on disposable income, time utilization, and food purchasing. Other symptoms of neoliberal policies such as urban drift and migrancy contributed to the HIV/AIDS pandemic.

Effects on health workers were also mainly negative, including cuts in the size of the civil service, wage and salary decay, declining morale, and the brain drain of doctors and researchers. Likewise, the effects on health system integrity included declining fiscal support; difficulties in gaining access to equipment, drugs, and transport (often due to foreign exchange shortages accompanying excessive debt repayment); and the diminished ability of health systems to deal with AIDS-related illnesses. Finally, other aspects of structural adjustment programs and neoliberalism introduced adverse health implications, such as the increasing commodification of basic health-related goods and services (such as food, water, and energy) that made many unaffordable.

The broader context was one of contraction of the economies of sub-Saharan Africa and a decline in the most critical health indicators, alongside growing criticisms of the Bretton Woods Institutions' role. With respect to governance, "IMF riots"—urban uprisings catalyzed by the reduction or elimination of subsidies (on food, transport, or other necessities)—occurred increasingly across Africa during the 1980s, culminating in the sweep from state power of no fewer than 35 ruling parties between 1990 and 1994, mainly through elections.

Meanwhile, the HIV/AIDS pandemic was putting enormous pressure on the continent's health services. According to a World Bank discussion document, HIV/AIDS patients occupy between 30 and 80 percent of hospital beds in countries in the southern African region (1). The beds needed for HIV/AIDS patients will exceed all available beds in 2002 in Botswana, in 2004 in Swaziland, and in 2005 in Namibia. On the assumption that health staff have similar prevalence rates as the population as a whole, there will need to be an increase in training of 25 to 40 percent just to keep staff numbers constant. Assuming a cost of U.S.$1,100 (all dollar amounts in U.S. dollars) per patient per year, providing triple therapy to cover 10 percent of those who need treatment amounts to 0.2 percent of Botswana's gross domestic product and 2.4 percent of that of Malawi; these figures rise to 0.5 and 4.0 percent, respectively, for 2010.

Such statistics call for a massive rethinking of the allocation of resources to the health sector. Yet one World Bank researcher concludes that aside from the "possible exception" of Botswana and South Africa, "none of the countries in the region will be able to offer general access to highly active anti-retroviral therapies through the public health service. . . . Given the serious shortages in personnel and infrastructure the health sector is facing, the scope for alleviating the impact of HIV/AIDS on the health sector through financial aid is limited" (1).

Meanwhile, from 2002 into the foreseeable future, a food crisis has affected an estimated 20 million people across the southern African region, including Malawi, Zimbabwe, Zambia, Mozambique, Angola, Lesotho, and Swaziland. Oxfam (2) has documented the role of neoliberalism in the famine:

> The food crisis has many causes, which vary in magnitude from country to country. Climate, bad governance, HIV/AIDS, unsustainable debt, and collapsing public services have all contributed. However, one major cause of the food crisis is the failure of agricultural policies. This paper asks why, after years of World Bank and IMF designed agricultural sector reforms, do Malawi, Zambia, and Mozambique, face chronic food insecurity. The simple answer is that the international financial institutions designed agricultural reforms for these countries without first carrying out a serious assessment of

their likely impact on poverty and food security. Far from improving food security, World Bank and IMF inspired policies have left poor farmers more vulnerable than ever.

In addition, as we consider in more detail below, the commodification of Africa's water also provides evidence of persistent neoliberalism. In March 2000, the Bank's Orwellian-inspired *Sourcebook on Community Driven Development in the Africa Region* (3) laid out the policy on pricing water: "Work is still needed with political leaders in some national governments to move away from the concept of free water for all. . . . Promote increased capital cost recovery from users. An upfront cash contribution based on their willingness-to-pay is required from users to demonstrate demand and develop community capacity to administer funds and tariffs. Ensure 100 percent recovery of operation and maintenance costs." One implication of the enforcement of this policy in 2000 was a disconnection of water to low-income South Africans that was the most direct cause of the country's worst-ever cholera epidemic (4).

In short, doubts remain about whether the Bretton Woods Institutions were, indeed, ever serious about reforming the core neoliberal philosophy that had been dogmatically pursued over the preceding two decades: user fees based upon full cost-recovery, fiscal cutbacks, and privatization. Nevertheless, several features of modified neoliberalism deserve discussion. The Bretton Woods Institutions' response to the worsening economic and health crises in Africa and many other developing world settings included the late 1990s introduction of limited debt relief and Poverty Reduction Strategy Papers.

As we will see, however, these have been criticized as a whitewashing technique by civil society, and as inadequate by the World Health Organization. Contested claims about implications for health spending reveal the inadequacy of official attempts to modify neoliberalism. At this stage, a broader rejection of the Bretton Woods Institutions' modified neoliberal poverty and debt relief strategy is necessary to roll back conditionalities, free up resources, and assure the associated decommodification of essential health-related services (such as water and energy) that are crucial for improving Africa's health. These topics are discussed in turn.

NEOLIBERAL MODIFICATION THROUGH POVERTY REDUCTION STRATEGY PAPERS

Facing criticisms of neoliberal overreach, the Bank and IMF adopted the Highly Indebted Poor Countries (HIPC) initiative in 1996 and Poverty Reduction Strategy Papers (PRSPs) in 1999. According to the IMF External Relations Department (5):

> The World Bank Group and the IMF approved an approach that recognized that nationally-owned participatory poverty reduction strategies were the most promising means of securing more effective policymaking and better partnerships between countries and donors. To ensure that assistance is well

used for poverty reduction, Poverty Reduction Strategy Papers would henceforth be the basis of all their concessional lending, and for debt relief under the enhanced Heavily Indebted Poor Country Initiative.

There has been widespread acceptance of the PRSP approach. Today, these processes are taking hold in some 60 low-income countries, and are helping promote a more open and inclusive national dialogue on the most effective policies and public actions for poverty reduction. And the approach has increasingly been embraced by countries' external development partners. Because it is based on the two pillars of country self-help and support from the international community, the PRSP approach promises to make development assistance more effective. Nevertheless, the process is continually being refined, including through a 2001/2002 review that identified good practices in the PRSP approach, for countries and their partners alike.

The review showed that there is room for improvement. Further actions are required to make participation processes more open and to develop and promptly implement policies that accelerate economic growth. And donors must better align their assistance with PRSPs, simplify and harmonize their procedures, and work for more predictable aid flows.

There has indeed been a significant response to the World Bank and IMF decision on PRSPs, even if the Bretton Woods Institutions do not acknowledge the intense criticism of most civil society groups. In southern Africa, for example, social movements, nongovernmental organizations, labor, and environmentalists have organized in various ways to become involved in the PRSP process. In Zambia, a network—Civil Society for Poverty Reduction—was established specifically to engage with the process. The Malawi Economic Justice Network arose out of meetings of civil society organizations to develop a common approach to PRSPs. In Tanzania and Mozambique, civil society is also organizing around PRSPs. Jubilee 2000 Angola drew representatives of civil society together from across the war-torn country to participate in a conference on PRSPs.

In most instances, expectations of the PRSP process have been dashed and experiences are at odds with claims made by the IMF and World Bank. Concerns have been raised around the commitment of governments and the international institutions to the participatory process, the issues that have been opened for participation and those that have not, the degree to which the voices of civil society have been incorporated into the poverty reduction strategy papers, and the role of the World Bank and IMF as final authorities on the content of the papers.

Jubilee South organized conferences in Latin America, Asia, and Africa to assess PRSPs in these regions. The African conference took place in Kampala, Uganda, in May 2001 and included national Jubilee campaigns, debt and development organizations, NGOs, women's organizations, and church representation. A mix of organizations had been participating in PRSP processes in their countries, while others had decided not to take part. The conference thus allowed for the full sweep of debate on the implementation of PRSPs on the continent. It concluded with a declaration entitled "Poverty Reduction Strategy Papers: Structural Adjustment Programs in Disguise," which included the following points (6):

> The experiences of the functioning of PRSPs in our countries raise a number of additional concerns with regard to the involvement of organizations of civil society:
> - The PRSPs are not based on real people's participation and ownership, or decision-making. To the contrary, there is no intention of taking civil society perspectives seriously, but to keep participation to mere public relations legitimization.
> - The lack of genuine commitment to participation is further manifested in the failure to provide full and timeout access to all necessary information, limiting the capacity of civil society to make meaningful contributions.
> - The PRSPs have been introduced according to pre-set external schedules which in most countries has resulted in an altogether inadequate time period for an effective participatory process.
> - In addition to all the constraints placed on governments and civil society organizations in formulating PRSPs, the World Bank and IMF retain the right to veto the final programs. This reflects the ultimate mockery of the threadbare claim that the PRSPs are based on "national ownership."
> - An additional serious concern is the way in which PRSPs are being used by the World Bank and IMF, both directly and indirectly, to co-opt NGOs to "monitor" their own governments on behalf of these institutions.

What are the implications of a residual—but modified, "participatory"—neoliberalism for the health sector in Africa?

POVERTY REDUCTION STRATEGY PAPERS
AND HEALTH SPENDING

It is still too early to get a clear sense of the degree to which PRSPs are likely to affect health, but certain trends are already evident. Most important, the disparity between resources being released for health care under the PRSP initiative and the resources required to provide decent health services, together with the seemingly unconcerned approach to the health crises facing the region, suggests that the PRSPs under the direction of the World Bank and IMF do not represent an appropriate solution to the health needs of the region.

As regards health expenditure, the early projections suggest instances in which there may be significant increases in percentage terms, even if overall figures of actual expenditures reveal no or very little change. Indeed, where there are increases, these are above an extremely low base and are not likely to make any significant impact on the health of the poor. Nevertheless, the Bretton Woods Institutions make impressive claims. The IMF and World Bank conducted a study of the 24 HIPC countries that reached their decision points by November 2001. According to their report (7):

- The average debt service due in 2001–3 is roughly 30 percent less than the amount paid before HIPC relief in 1998-99;
- During 2001–3, the World Bank and IMF will reduce debt service payments by 65 and 55 percent, respectively, by providing interim relief;
- Debt service drops sharply in relation to exports or fiscal revenues over this period. On average these ratios fall by one-half;
- In all cases, social expenditures are expected to increase in 2001–2 from the levels in 1999. Average social spending in 2001–2 is expected to be more than 45 percent higher than in 1999, with HIPC savings accounting for a sizable proportion of this increase;
- Average debt service during 2001–2 will be $2 billion;
- Average social expenditure, at about $6.5 billion, will be more than three times higher than average debt service; and
- Average net resource flows (loans + grants – debt service payable) to this group of countries will increase from $3.8 billion (1.2 times debt service) in 1998–99 to $7.2 billion (3.7 times debt service) in 2001–3.

The WHO conducted a study of PRSPs in ten countries, including Mozambique and Tanzania (8). The study revealed variable changes and projected changes in government health budgets and health expenditure per capita. The figures for Mozambique and Tanzania are provided in Table 1. The wild fluctuations in the government budget as a percentage of GDP for Mozambique; the variations in health spending as a percentage of government expenditure, in particular the steep

Table 1

Mozambique and Tanzania health spending, 1999–2003

	1999	2000	2001	2002	2003
Government budget, as percentage of GDP					
Mozambique	22.9	27.7	35..4	29.6	27.1
Tanzania	16.9	16.5	17.3	16.8	N.A.
Health spending, as percentage of government expenditure					
Mozambique	12.5	11.6	9.3	12.7	9.8
Tanzania	2.1	6.0	6.0	6.6	N.A.
Government health expenditure per capita in real terms, 1999 U.S.$ million					
Mozambique	5.05	6.41	7.13	9.31	9.83
Tanzania	0.85	2.41	2.49	2.90	N.A.

jump in the Tanzanian figure from 1999 to 2000; and the poor correlation between health spending as a percentage of government expenditure and health expenditure per capita for Mozambique—all raise questions about the accuracy of the statistical information available from the countries.

~ Nevertheless, the figures for Mozambique suggest an increase in government health expenditure per capita of 53 percent from 1999 to 2003; those for Tanzania, an increase of 242 percent from 1999 to 2002. The increase in the case of Tanzania is largely accounted for by the large step between 1999 and 2000, before implementation of PRSPs. These figures, even taking the likely statistical inaccuracies into account, appear to suggest impressive improvement. However, they need to be put into a broader context. They mask the lack of data on actual spending, due to a combination of the recent introduction of PRSPs and the poor tracking of PRSP program spending.

The WHO takes issue with the quality of PRSPs, because of the lack of information on health sector financing in the papers. It says this is "particularly striking as all ten countries reviewed have health-related financial analyses in Public Expenditure Reviews, and or National Health Accounts." The WHO expresses concern about the lack of clarity around financial resources available for health care, including whether governments are now allocating funds over and above those identified in medium-term plans, whether stated increases reflect existing government spending plans or refer to PRSP-related debt relief, and whether debt relief funds will partly replace or be fully additive to government funds for the health sector. In Burkina Faso, the information available suggests that the HIPC debt relief allocation for health partly replaces government funds that would otherwise have been available to the health sector. The WHO also questions whether the projected increases will be realized, given the seemingly overoptimistic estimates for economic growth in PRSPs. It also notes that PRSPs are largely silent on questions of the distribution of health expenditure, thus making it difficult to assess whether resources will be increasingly allocated to benefit the poor.

Uganda provides an illustration of health expenditure becoming the subject of divergent interpretations. According to the IMF's Timothy Geithner (9), health expenditures in Uganda have increased from 0.7 percent of GDP in 1997–98 to 1.5 percent in 2001–2 and are projected to increase to 1.8 percent of GDP by 2004–5. It is not clear whether these figures include both public and private expenditure and what the changing composition of this expenditure is over the years in question, but Geithner adds that public expenditure on primary health care has shown an even larger increase over this period.

The Uganda National NGO Forum argues that these increases have failed to translate into improved health for the population. According to the forum, price rises in the health sector have exceeded inflation and thus offset the budgetary increases. It suggests numerous other reasons, including the poor standard of service provision in the health sector and shortcomings in other sectors affecting health—for example, the failure of rural policy to reach the majority of the poor and the lack of gender sensitivity in budgetary allocations and programs (10).

Daniel Giusti (11) of the Health Office of the Catholic Bishops Conference in Kampala suggests that the expectation of a growth in the Ugandan health budget has been dashed. Only $9 per capita is available for public sector spending. This figure incorporates all resources assigned to health, including the government budget allocation, donor funding via the budget, donor funding outside the budget, and user fees. Giusti argues that this inadequate amount is due to macroeconomic policy constraint, not resource constraint. Seven levels of budgetary decision-making must be hurdled, including macroeconomic stability targets, resource envelope determinants, a Medium Term Expenditure Framework expenditure ceiling, and sectoral budget ceilings. The Bretton Woods Institutions dictate the fiscal decisions at the higher levels of decision-making, and the social service ministries are involved only at the lower levels. In other words, the Ministry of Health is forced to compete with other social service ministries for resources within a given limit set by the World Bank and IMF, and has to allocate expenditure within a restrictive budget (11).

By March 2002, the Bank and IMF had received data on PRSP-defined poverty reduction spending for 2000 from only four countries, namely Burkina Faso, Honduras, Mozambique, and Uganda. These initial data appear to endorse the perspective that health budgets have remained largely unchanged under PRSPs. According to a paper released by these institutions, spending on education in these four countries increased from the pre-PRSP year to 2000. But the picture for health was different. Spending on health in these four countries amounted to an overall figure of 2.2 percent of GDP in the pre-PRSP year and only 2.1 percent in 2000. Health accounted for 8.5 percent of total government spending in the pre-PRSP year and 8.7 percent in 2000. In other words, health spending as a percentage of GDP declined after the introduction of PRSPs, and health spending as a percentage of total government spending increased only fractionally. A further look at projected spending for health in these four countries and Bolivia, Mauritania, and Tanzania reveals similarly disconcerting figures. Spending on health across these countries amounted to 2.4 percent of GDP and 9.9 percent of total government spending in the pre-PRSP year. The projected figures for 2001–2 are 2.6 percent and 10.0 percent in both instances: the most marginal of increases (12).

There is every chance that the implementation of PRSP programs in those countries outside the four that have collected data will be even poorer. According to the Malawi Economic Justice Network (13),

> Reports from the ministry of Finance and related line ministries indicate that not a single Kwacha has been used from the much-publicized HIPC debt relief. Several explanations are given for this unfortunate behavior realizing how "scarce" resources are to our national programs.

First it's the procedure. It is said that the World Bank/IMF have got very vertical procedures for the government to access the funds, so much so that the time required to move around the special HIPC form is not worthy the amount.

Secondly, the Ministry of Finance itself is said not to have put in writing yet the instructions to line ministries how to access these funds.

Other people feel that the line ministries themselves are not taking initiatives to get the funds. Surely no "unclean hand" would wish to take on these highly watched funds.

The occurrences are of great concern to Malawians. The budget being implemented now contains Priority Poverty Expenditures (PPEs). The question arising now is, how will the PPEs be delivered without this additional funding from HIPC?

The figures represent negligible change from a very low base. According to the WHO, only 11 percent of the global health budget is spent in the low- and middle-income countries, which account for 84 percent of the global population (14). The World Bank concedes that the median per capita health budget for sub-Saharan Africa is $6 and that the mean for the lowest-income African countries is $3 (15). WHO and World Bank data show total health expenditure in southern Africa ranging from a low of $9 per capita in Malawi to a high of $203 in South Africa (1).

According to the WHO, $60 per person per annum is required to deliver a basic level of health care. The WHO director-general, Gro Harlem Brundtland (16), argues, "It is clear that health systems which spend less than $60 or so per capita are not able to even deliver a reasonable minimum of services, even through extensive internal reform. It does not matter how good the structure is—as long as you can't afford to pay your doctor and nurses proper salaries and fill the shelves with essential medicines and vaccines, a health system will not be performing at a reasonable level." Sometimes, the WHO is reported as suggesting lower figures. The WHO Commission on Macroeconomics and Health, chaired by Jeffrey Sachs, calculates a per capita spending of $34 for a minimum package of health services. The WHO Submission to World Bank/IMF Review of PRSPs refers to "the minimum of $30–40 per capita needed to provide decent health care" (8).

For most countries in the southern African region, health expenditure is well below all the WHO estimates of the per capita spending required to provide a minimum level of health care. The figures for Malawi and South Africa translate, respectively, into 0.2 and 4.1 percent of the per capita expenditure in the United States. Even when converted to reflect purchasing power parity, the figures of $45 for Malawi and $552 for South Africa amount to, respectively, 0.9 and 11.1 percent of per capita spending in the United States (1).

This low base is itself a reflection of years of structural adjustment policies that entailed the slashing of government expenditures, notably on health and education. As can be seen in Table 1, the low figures for government budget as a percentage of GDP for Tanzania reflect the end result of such cuts. The budget-to-GDP figures remain constant for the period 1999 to 2002, indicating that the Tanzanian PRSP process is not translating into a redress of this situation. These low levels of expenditure correlate with extremely low levels of service. For example, in Malawi and Mozambique, there are only three physicians per 100,000 people—a mere 1 percent of the number of physicians per 100,000 population in the United States and other northern countries.

In the context of largely unchanged allocations for health expenditure, health ministries are left with just the option of reallocating existing budgets to reflect the health sector priorities raised in PRSPs. The Kenyan PRSP sets itself an objective to "enhance equity, quality, accessibility and affordability of health care." It then identifies the means by which it aims to meet this objective, namely "An application of rational, transparent and poverty focused resource allocation criteria and weights for the Government of Kenya Ministry of Health budget for districts; criteria and weights to be gradually phased in beginning with FY 2001/2002 budget." The first three commitments it makes in this regard are as follows:

- Reduction of the budget allocation for the Kenyatta National Hospital, as a share of the total Ministry of Health recurrent budget, from approximately 15 percent in F.Y. 1999–2000 to 10 percent by F.Y. 2004;
- Establishing an acceptable maximum recurrent budget allocation for provincial hospitals; and
- Establishing maximum recurrent ceilings for district hospitals as a percentage of total district health recurrent budget.

In other words, the first notable impact of the PRSP on the health sector is a financial squeeze on the hospital sector. South Africa underwent a similar experience in the latter half of the 1990s, with devastating consequences. The World Bank was centrally involved in developing Pretoria's macroeconomic policy, the Growth, Employment, and Redistribution Strategy, which included extreme fiscal constraint. In contrast, the Reconstruction and Development Program, developed by anti-apartheid civil society organizations and adopted by the African National Congress government as its mandate to govern, stressed the need to expand primary care so as to make health care accessible to all. Within the constraint of shrinking budgets, the new government slashed hospital budgets so as to release some funds to meet the program objectives. The outcome included a disintegration of the public hospital sector as well as an erosion of the capacity of the health sector to establish, provide training for, and sustain a comprehensive primary health care sector.

A NARROW VERSUS BROAD APPROACH
TO HEALTH

The World Health Organization has identified numerous other concerns in its critique of the impact of Poverty Reduction Strategy Papers on health. The PRSPs in each of the ten countries reviewed were led by a small team in a finance, economic, planning, or related ministry, and excluded the ministries of health and other line ministries. In some countries, inter-ministerial committees were established to get input from health and other ministries. In others, health ministries were approached on a one-to-one basis. In either case, health ministries were limited in the contributions they could make to the PRSPs. In Uganda and Rwanda, there was not enough time for consultation with line ministries, particularly on budgeting and program planning. In Vietnam, the Ministry of Planning and Investment took the lead on the Interim PRSP, despite the Ministry of Labor, Information, and Social Affairs having previously prepared the Hunger Eradication and Poverty Reduction Strategy. The Vietnamese Ministry of Health has not been active in the development of the PRSP.

The WHO review also points to concerns raised that the World Bank and IMF are playing a dominant role, in terms of both their control over the process and their involvement in the development of PRSPs. It cites a health-related example from Cambodia, namely that the Ministry of Health was not consulted on the health component of the PRSP until after a World Bank consultant had prepared an initial draft. The WHO insists that the degree to which ill-health results in poverty and the role that improved health can play in reducing poverty are not adequately reflected in PRSPs and do not find expression in the programs of action (8):

> Ill health is typically described as a consequence of poverty, rather than a cause. Thus many PRSPs provide data on health status by income quintile, showing that the poor are more likely to suffer from ill health, but very few calculate the impoverishing effects of ill health such as out-of-pocket medical costs, lost income, or the consequences of ill-health disability of the bread-winner. The gap in analysis is particularly striking as many PRSPs contain the results of a participatory poverty assessment (PPA) in which poor people themselves identify ill health as a cause of poverty.
>
> As a result of this analysis, PRSPs characterize health as an outcome of development, rather than a means of achieving it. Most PRSPs contain several strands, one or more on increasing the rate of economic growth and/or maintaining macroeconomic stability, and one strand on improving human capabilities. The "growth" strand covers sectors traditionally considered "productive" (business, tourism, manufacturing, etc.) while the "human capa-bilities" strand covers the provision of basic services, including health.
>
> This division creates obstacles to improving health status, and limits the potential of improved health to positively benefit other sectors. For example, improved health is key to worker productivity, to creating and sustaining rural livelihoods, and to educational achievement. Similarly, employment,

agriculture, the environment and other sectors all have an impact on health status. Most PRSPs fail to make these links. . . .

PRSPs reflect traditional definitions of health as a social sector, and health spending as consumption rather than investment. This suggests that within the PRSP framework health will remain under-resourced and marginalized as it has been in the past, and that opportunities to reduce poverty through improving health will be missed.

In preparation for the 2000–2001 World Development Report, the World Bank conducted an extensive study of people's perspectives and experiences of poverty, entitled Voices of the Poor. This included interviews and group discussions with 60,000 people in 60 countries and a review of 81 participatory poverty assessments. Thereafter, the WHO and the World Bank collaborated on a report on the health issues raised in the study, released in 2002 under the title *Dying for Change*. According to the coauthored foreword to the report, "It aims to illuminate . . . how poverty creates ill-health and how ill-health leads to poverty. It also highlights the link between good health and economic survival. Poor people everywhere say how much they value good health. A fit, strong body is an asset that allows poor adults to work and poor children to learn. . . . The poor have long recognized the link between good health and development. But until recently, this link has been neglected in mainstream development thinking" (17). The Bank's track record in the health sector reflects this neglect. In addition to its role in slashing public health services by means of structural adjustment programs, World Bank health projects have also in the main performed poorly. The Bank's Operations Evaluation Department conducted an evaluation of its Health, Nutrition, and Population (HNP) projects between 1970 and 1997 and found that fewer than half the projects were sustainable after completion. Running costs were underestimated and governments' ability to repay the loans was overestimated. Only 21 percent of projects contributed to institutional development and policy change in the health sector.

In a further internal review of the 17 projects started in 1999, 59 percent of projects were found to have failed to address the constraints faced by the poor using HNP services, such as the distance to the projects, lack of drugs, and payment for services. Researchers at the Dutch health NGO Wemos comment, "None of the projects had explicit mechanisms to protect the poor from possible adverse impacts of reforms in the health sector. Not a single project addressed the impact on the poor of shocks or reforms outside the health sector such as structural adjustment, economic shocks, and disasters" (14).

The amounts of money involved in the program are substantial. The HNP portfolio amounts to almost $16 billion across 92 countries. Average annual commitments come to $1.3 billion. This vastly outweighs the WHO's total annual budget of $90 million (18). Shortcomings are admitted in the evaluation and review, but the World Bank fails to take financial responsibility for its mistakes.

The net result in all too many instances is governments being saddled with debts for projects that do not add to the capacity to deliver health care.

The combination of the problems encountered by civil society in participating in PRSPs, the limitations placed on the ministries of health and related line ministries in making their contributions, and the failure to listen to the voices of the poor or heed the participatory poverty assessments has resulted in PRSPs that are unlikely to address the health needs of the poor. Moreover, according to the WHO PRSP review, many PRSPs simply incorporate existing health policy. They focus on improving average indicators and do not include strategies specifically targeted to improve the health status of the poor. The WHO thus questions whether stated interventions will actually reach the poor across the respective countries and highlights the lack of monitoring plans to ascertain the impact of PRSPs on the poor.

Researchers at Wemos characterize the PRSPs reviewed by the organization as being rooted in a narrow approach to health. The papers are selective in that they identify a few communicable diseases, focus on technical solutions to these diseases, and divert attention and resources away from the need to strengthen health systems. They encourage public-private partnerships for limited interventions and continue to downsize government's role in service provision. The World Bank actively promotes the privatization of health care, as evidenced by its 2002 Private Sector Development Strategy and the drive by its private sector development wing, the International Finance Corporation, to increase investments in private health care.

Oscar Lanza (19) of Accion Internacional para la Salud describes the process in Bolivia. The money from the HIPC program for health was earmarked to contract more doctors for work in rural areas and to purchase drugs, thus medicalizing the problem of ill-health. The pressing need for health facilities, clean water, and sanitation remains unaddressed.

USER FEES AND HEALTH CARE COMMODIFICATION

The issue of user charges for health services remains a critical area of concern. The WHO and World Bank publication *Dying for Change* repeatedly refers to the voices of the poor on the financial burden of illness (17):

> Sickness of the family breadwinner is something that poor people particularly fear. It means food and income suddenly stop. Paying for treatment brings more impoverishment—assets may have to be sold and debts incurred. A downward spiral of poverty begins: food becomes scarce, causing malnutrition, and children are withdrawn from school and sent to work. If a working adult dies, then the ratio of dependents to adults increases. If he or she is permanently disabled, then another dependent is created.

>Illness as a cause of destitution was cited often throughout the study. Of the 15 causes of a downward slide into Poverty mentioned by interviewees, this was the most frequently mentioned—ahead of losing a job, which took second place.

In Nicaragua, one civil society response to the PRSP was to conduct a social audit to generate its own information as a basis for informed discussion. The results of the first audit indicate that 45 percent of those audited thought their family was worse off than a year before. As to the reason for this deterioration, 73 percent pointed to the economic situation, of which 39 percent mentioned the negative impact of paying for illness. The audit identified the cost of illness as being a major drain on household budgets, revealing that this accounted for 21 percent of monthly income (20).

Yet PRSPs continue to include user fees for health care. To cite a few examples: Uganda intends to recover 50 percent of the cost of its total health budget with the help of "pro-poor implementation of cost recovery." Kenya is continuing to charge user fees but is amending its "cost-sharing guidelines" to include "waivers and exemptions for vulnerable groups." Ghana is implementing user fees with exemptions and safety nets. Notwithstanding the stated commitment to exemptions, the insistence on continuing to rely on user fees as a key source of finance for the health system can only lead to a further deepening of poverty, given the extent of poverty, marginalization, and vulnerability in the PRSP countries.

In November 2000, the U.S. government enacted legislation that compels the U.S. Executive Directors at the international financial institutions to oppose any loan agreement or debt reduction arrangement that imposes user fees or service charges for primary education and basic health care. But according to leaked minutes of the IMF and World Bank board meeting of December 2000, there was no opposition from the United States on the inclusion of user fees for basic services in the Tanzanian PRSP (21).

It must be remembered that the World Bank and IMF introduced PRSPs with much fanfare about prioritizing education and health care. This can only lead to a further deprioritization of services outside the health care sector that also have a fundamental bearing on people's health, such as water supplies (water-borne diseases kill 2.7 million people each year) (22). Here, at the microdevelopmental level, neoliberalism has become more acceptable, notwithstanding enormous damage. Even the WHO's Sachs Commission background report favorably cited the 1993 World Bank *World Development Report* on health, to the effect that earlier state investments in water systems were wasted: "Not only is improved water and sanitation not particularly cost effective as a health measure, it is also high in total costs. . . . Between 1981 and 1990, more than US$134 billion was invested in efforts to expand water supply and sanitation services, approximately 34 percent of the sum coming from donors. Although some regions were able to make progress in improving access, few attained any of the goals set" (22). But inexplicably, the WHO report failed to recognize that at the same time, the Bretton Woods Institutions were forcing dramatic cuts in operating subsidies on debtor countries, a practice that, as we noted at the outset, continues today (3). When impoverished water consumers could no longer maintain the systems—such as refilling diesel tanks to run boreholes, or replacing broken piping—naturally, the capital investment was lost.

Yet from this experience, which should have encouraged advocacy on behalf of higher state operating subsidies, the Sachs team drew the opposite lesson, namely that "improved water and sanitation [are] not particularly cost effective as a health measure" (22). Moreover, the researchers endorsed regulated water privatization as "an important tool to ensure the delivery of expanded [privatized] services to the poor." One tautological rationale—again, without conceding that Washington financial bureaucrats ordered cuts in social and infrastructural spending—was, "In many places it is the poor themselves, rather than their governments, who are acting to improve their lives by investing in water and sanitation."

The Mozambique PRSP illustrates the problems that lie ahead. In the wake of HIPC conditionality that included a 1998 requirement (described in a letter from World Bank president James Wolfensohn to Mozambican president Joachim Chissano) of a fivefold increase in health clinic cost recovery and the retreat of the state from both urban and rural water systems, the country's health system was devastated, especially in the rural areas (23). Yet while the 2001 PRSP's section on agriculture and land promotes small farmers, public institutions, rural service delivery, and infrastructure, state funding for rural development is projected to decrease (10).

Rachel Marcus and John Wilkinson (24) of the Childhood Poverty Research and Policy Centre assessed 20 PRSPs to evaluate their approach to social protection—that is, policies and practices to protect and promote the livelihoods and welfare of those people most vulnerable to economic and social change, shocks, and disasters. Their analysis backs up the WHO perspective that PRSPs are not explicitly pro-poor and thus are unlikely to address the needs of the poorest. Social protection issues are discussed in about two-thirds of the papers reviewed, but they focus on alleviating the worst effects of poverty and fail to identify strategies to help people out of poverty. Gender analysis is largely missing from the reviewed PRSPs, and childhood poverty is on the whole not prioritized. The social protection measures most commonly discussed include cash-for-work programs, direct cash transfers, and bursaries for poor children to attend school. Food subsidies, nutritional supplementation schemes, and water and energy subsidies are the least common. The measures appear to be at best weakly distributive. The responsibility for social protection is placed with the state and communities, and there are no expectations of the private sector. Marcus and Wilkinson conclude, "In general, we believe this is a missed opportunity for making the most of social protection—ensuring that it can both contain the effects of poverty and help people escape. On the whole, changing international policy discourse in this area seems to have had little impact" (24).

THE NEW PARTNERSHIP FOR AFRICA'S DEVELOPMENT: HOMEGROWN NEOLIBERALISM

As a final confusing element within the modified neoliberal project, several key African rulers, led by South African president Thabo Mbeki, launched the New Partnership for Africa's Development (Nepad) (25; for a set of critiques see 26). In 2002, Nepad was the most discussed initiative in Africa. It won endorsement at a U.N. heads-of-state summit in September 2002, and for a few weeks was one of the main agenda items at the World Summit on Sustainable Development in Johannesburg. Weeks earlier, Nepad won crucial official state and business endorsements at the June summit of the G8 leaders (the Group of Eight main industrial powers) in Alberta, Canada, immediately followed by the southern African gathering of the World Economic Forum in Durban, and the July launch of the African Union (replacement for the Organization of African Unity), also in Durban. Nepad's evolution had occurred under conditions of secrecy, in close contact with the G8 in Okinawa in 2000 and Genoa in 2001, the Bretton Woods Institutions, and international capital through the World Economic Forum at Davos in 2001 and New York in 2002. Nepad has gone by various names, including the African Renaissance (1996–2000), the Millennium Africa Recovery Plan (2000–July 2001), and the New African Initiative (July–October 2001).

The document's core premise is that poverty in Africa can be cured, if only the world elite gives the continent a chance. Nepad suggests, "The continued marginalization of Africa from the globalization process and the social exclusion of the vast majority of its peoples constitute a serious threat to global stability." The argument depends upon a depoliticized view of globalization: "We readily admit that globalization is a product of scientific and technological advances, many of which have been market-driven."

Likewise in areas such as debt and structural adjustment, Nepad offers only the status quo. Instead of promoting debt cancellation, as do virtually all serious reformers, the Nepad strategy is to "support existing poverty reduction initiatives at the multilateral level, such as the Comprehensive Development Framework of the World Bank and the Poverty Reduction Strategy approach linked to the Highly Indebted Poor Country debt relief initiative." Only after trying these discredited strategies, replete with neoliberal conditions such as further privatization, would African leaders "seek recourse" through Nepad. Malawi's 2002 famine, resulting from sale of the country's grain stocks following IMF advice to first repay commercial bankers, is telling.

The same approach is apparent in the health sector, where Nepad offers just six paragraphs' worth of analysis. It is worth considering each in turn.

126. Objectives

- To strengthen programs for containing communicable diseases, so that they do not fall short of the scale required in order to reduce the burden of disease;
- To have a secure health system that meets needs and supports disease control effectively;
- To ensure the necessary support capacity for the sustainable development of an effective health care delivery system;
- To empower the people of Africa to act to improve their own health and to achieve health literacy;
- To successfully reduce the burden of disease on the poorest people in Africa;
- To encourage cooperation between medical doctors and traditional practitioners.

These objectives are laudable. But the last two decades have witnessed the systematic weakening of African health systems due to underfunding and the imposition of cost-recovery provisions. The result has been particularly onerous for women and girls, for whom the decline in health care utilization rates is most damaging in both personal and social terms. Nepad does nothing to suggest these trends will be reversed. Especially worrisome is that the continent's richest and medically most advanced country, South Africa (sponsor of Nepad), has performed very poorly in this regard since 1994, and the difficulty in getting even simple essential medicines at rural clinics is evidence of the state's lack of commitment to its poorest citizens. To target the poorest would require a radical reorientation of the public-private combination of health services, as well as dramatic increases in water, electricity, nutritional, and transport services (among others) to the poorest people. Nepad contains no information to suggest that this is a genuine objective—and indeed, its orientation to public-private partnerships in the provision of infrastructure suggests that the poorest will actually be ignored. The actions proposed are incapable of solving the problems.

127. Actions

- Strengthen Africa's participation in processes aimed at procuring affordable drugs, including those involving the international pharmaceutical companies and the international civil society, and explore the use of alternative delivery systems for essential drugs and supplies;
- Mobilize the resources required to build effective disease interventions and secure health systems;
- Lead the campaign for increased international financial support for the struggle against HIV/AIDS and other communicable diseases;
- Join forces with other international agencies such as the WHO and donors to ensure support for the continent is increased by at least US $10 billion per annum;

- Encourage African countries to give higher priority to health in their own budgets and to phase such increases in expenditure to a level to be mutually determined;
- Jointly mobilize resources for capacity-building in order to enable all African countries to improve their health infrastructures and management.

Judicious use of drugs—"treatment"—is one of the most crucial ways to address disease, and it is important to highlight drugs at the outset, alongside disease prevention. The single greatest advance in acquiring medicines at an affordable cost was the withdrawal (due to international public outrage) in April 2001 of 39 pharmaceutical companies from a lawsuit against the South African government. The lawsuit, had it been successful, would have prevented Pretoria from implementing the 1997 Medicines Act provisions allowing for parallel import, compulsory licensing, and generic production of lifesaving drugs. But in the year following that opportunity, Pretoria failed to take advantage of the withdrawal and made no efforts to activate the Medicines Act clauses. If this is the leadership that Nepad offers Africans in the vital area of medicines access, then progress will be nonexistent. Nepad does not mention the options available through the Medicines Act, or the provisions in the World Trade Organization's Trade in Intellectual Property provisions that allow for patent violation in the event of a medical emergency.

As for "resources required," they are infinite, of course. But Nepad could attempt to specify ways in which the U.N. Global Fund (targeting AIDS, malaria, and TB) would be utilized in Africa. But Nepad does not specifically mention this fund, nor the longstanding debate over the fund's need to prioritize the financing of treatment. Pretoria's leadership on HIV/AIDS will likely be as great a disaster for Africa as it is for South Africa. The "$10 billion" reference apparently refers to the United Nation's attempt to raise money for the Global Fund to address health crisis in *all* parts of the world (not just Africa). The more funding received the better—but Nepad does not engage in the heated debates about where such funds should be prioritized and who should control them. Finally, the "mutual determination" of health budgets harks back to the structural adjustment era (1980s–present) in which budgets are determined in Washington. There is no indication in Nepad as to what sustainable health budgets are and should be, and in view of the systematic destruction of public health system capacity and the rise of private health care options for Africa's ruling classes, the lack of detail and vague references to external funds is worrisome.

Still in the category "Action" Nepad continues,

128. Africa is home to major endemic diseases. Bacteria and parasites carried by insects, the movement of people and other carriers thrive, favored as they are by weak environmental policies and poor living conditions. One of the major impediments facing African development efforts is the widespread incidence of communicable diseases, in particular HIV/AIDS, tuberculosis

and malaria. Unless these epidemics are brought under control, real gains in human development will remain a pipe dream.

The only "action" implied here is bringing the diseases under control. But Pretoria's failure to address HIV/AIDS, in part by promoting dissident analysis in South Africa's Presidential Commission on AIDS, as well as the ongoing cholera and diarrhea epidemics caused mainly by lack of clean water, suggest that Nepad's own authors are not serious about these problems.

> 129. In the health sector, Africa compares very poorly with the rest of the world. In 1997, child and juvenile death rates were 105 and 169 per 1000, as against 6 and 7 per 1000 respectively in developed countries. Life expectancy is 48.9 years, as against 77.7 years in developed countries. Only 16 doctors are available per 100 000 inhabitants against 253 in industrialized countries. Poverty, reflected in very low per capita incomes, is one of the major factors limiting the populations' capacity to address their health problems.

This is an obvious point, but contains no information about "actions" to be taken. Moreover, the phraseology here implies that individuals are responsible for their health status, which takes the burden off the state. Given that individuals' incomes are so low in most of Africa and that health status indicators have fallen so quickly during the era of structural adjustment, the logical conclusion is that market failure requires massive state intervention, but Nepad notably fails to promote this conclusion.

> 130. Nutrition is an important ingredient of good health. The average daily intake of calories varies from 2384 in low-income countries to 2846 in middle-income countries to 3390 in the Organization for Economic Co-operation and Development (OECD) countries.

Again, this point cannot be contested, but Nepad contains no information about actions to be taken. If nutrition were taken seriously as a component in Nepad, some additional state intervention in basic food markets and in food-related subsidization would be on the agenda. But it is not.

> 131. Health, defined by the World Health Organization (WHO) as a state of complete physical and mental well-being, contributes to increase in productivity and consequently to economic growth. The most obvious effects of health improvement on the working population are the reduction in lost working days due to sick leave, the increase in productivity, and the chance to get better paid jobs. Eventually, improvement in health and nutrition directly contributes to improved well-being as the spread of diseases is controlled, infant mortality rates are reduced, and life expectancy is higher. The link with poverty reduction is clearly established.

This information is correct, but again contains no suggestions about actions to be taken. For example, if externalities associated with health care, water, sanitation, and electricity were incorporated into national and local economic strategies, then increased subsidies would be a logical way to translate those externalities into real economic gains. But Nepad is silent about such implications. Likewise, were the system of national accounts in African countries to be recalculated to take into account the health-poverty linkage, and especially to calculate the importance of women's (unpaid) labor in maintaining the health of the society, this might make it easier to better compensate health workers and women and to improve their status. Again, Nepad shies away from any such conclusion, and the document's lip service to gender equity is unveiled as mere rhetoric, when opportunities to improve women's well-being, such as this example, are ignored.

Finally, Nepad is at its most self-contradictory when appealing "to all the peoples of Africa, in all their diversity, to become aware of the seriousness of the situation and the need to mobilize themselves in order to put an end to further marginalization of the continent and ensure its development by bridging the gap with the developed countries." The hypocrisy is breathtaking. Africans, particularly women, falling further into poverty as a result of leadership compradorism and globalization, do not need to "become aware of the seriousness of the situation" as much as do the elite rulers, who generally live in luxury, at great distance from the masses. And when Africans in progressive civil society organizations express "the need to mobilize themselves," they are almost invariably met with repression.

CONCLUSION: BEYOND THE WORLD HEALTH ORGANIZATION—TO AFRICAN SOCIAL MOVEMENTS

The WHO review of Poverty Reduction Strategy Papers (8) recommends the following:

- A conceptual change in the understanding of health's contribution to development: from a "basic service" that helps to mitigate the impact of poverty, to a prerequisite of growth and poverty reduction.
- That health outcomes are distinguished from the provision of health services. The latter are important, but not sufficient to ensure the health of the poor. Explicit health objectives need to be incorporated into sectors which influence—and are influenced by—health.
- That ministries of Health take a more active role in the development of PRSPs and other poverty reduction strategies. This will require improved capacity within health ministries, and greater openness within those leading the PRSP process.
- That health and health-related programs are adequately and equitably financed. This means greater resources for health, and a shift of resources within the health sector to favor the poor.

The contrast between the PRSPs being developed under the dominant hand of the World Bank and IMF and the approach to health embodied in the WHO critique is instructive. The approach of the Bretton Woods Institutions remains fundamentally unchanged from the narrow and selective strategy for health that took increasing hold over countries in the South under the imposition of structural adjustment programs.

The WHO critique, on the other hand, incorporates elements of the somewhat more comprehensive approach to health identified at Alma-Ata in 1978, in terms of its conceptualization of both the interrelationship between health and poverty and the need for a coordinated approach to health across social and economic sectors. At this early stage in the history of PRSPs, the indications are that the approach to health embodied therein and the financial resources being committed to the identified programs fall short of what is required. To be sure, as discussed above, the WHO Commission on Macroeconomics and Health conceded crucial microdevelopmental ground to neoliberalism, especially in relation to water (22).

Most of the civil society advocacy networks now working on these issues are offering critiques (26). The challenge will be to turn what is being termed the "African Social Forum" into a vehicle that can transcend the terribly weak homegrown-neoliberal Nepad strategy and PRSPs, and introduce a more genuine African People's Consensus that will give African activists more confidence for future struggles. In January 2002, dozens of African social movements met in Bamako, Mali, as the African Social Forum, in preparation for the Porto Alegre World Social Forum. It was one of the first substantial conferences since the era of liberation to combine progressive NGOs and social movements from all parts of the continent. This was followed by African Social Forum sessions in Johannesburg (August 2002) and Addis Ababa (January 2003). The Bamako Declaration included the following paragraphs:

> A strong consensus emerged at the Bamako Forum that the values, practices, structures and institutions of the currently dominant neoliberal order are inimical to and incompatible with the realization of Africa's dignity, values and aspirations.
>
> The Forum rejected neoliberal globalization and further integration of Africa into an unjust system as a basis for its growth and development. In this context, there was a strong consensus that initiatives such as Nepad that are inspired by the IMF-WB strategies of Structural Adjustment Programs, trade liberalization that continues to subject Africa to an unequal exchange, and strictures on governance borrowed from the practices of Western countries and not rooted in the culture and history of the peoples of Africa.

It is this spirit—and an emerging African People's Consensus that can act as an alternative pole for advocacy—that provides hope for genuine social and health progress in Africa, not the minor modifications of neoliberalism apparent in PRSPs and Nepad.

Acknowledgments — The research for this report was funded through the Harare-based health research network Equinet and the Canadian International Development Research Centre (which are not responsible for the content of the arguments found herein). The authors are grateful to Rene Loewenson and Christina Zarowsky for helpful comments.

REFERENCES

1. Haacker, M. Providing Health Care to HIV Patients in Southern Africa. World Bank Research Department Policy Discussion Paper. Washington, DC, October 2001.
2. Oxfam. Death on the Doorstep of the Summit. Briefing Paper 29. Oxford, August 2002.
3. World Bank. *Sourcebook on Community Driven Development in the Africa Region: Community Action Programs.* Africa Region, Washington, DC, March 17, 2000.
4. Bond, P. *Unsustainable South Africa: Environment, Development, and Social Protest.* Merlin Press, London, 2002.
5. International Monetary Fund. Press Statement. External Relations Department, April 2002.
6. Jubilee South. *Pan-African Declaration on PRSPs.* Kampala, May 12, 2001.
7. International Monetary Fund and International Development Association. *The Impact of Debt Reduction under the HIPC Initiative on External Debt Service and Social Expenditures.* Washington, DC, November 16, 2001.
8. World Health Organization. *Health in PRSPs: WHO Submission to World Bank/IMF Review of PRSPs.* Department of Health and Development, Geneva, December 2001.
9. Geithner, T. *Reply to Mariska Meurs, Wemos Foundation.* Policy Development and Review Department of the IMF, Washington, DC, August 22, 2002.
10. Gomes, R. P. Lakhani, S., and Woodman, J. *Economic Policy Empowerment Program.* Eurodad, Brussels, 2002.
11. Giusti, D. *Input to Wemos, Consumer Information Network and Cordaid Conference: A Healthy PRSP? Towards a Stronger Voice of Health Organizations in Poverty Reduction Strategy Papers.* Nairobi, September 18–20, 2002.
12. World Bank and International Monetary Fund. *Review of PRSP Approach: Early Experiences with I-PRSPs and Full PRSPs.* Washington, DC, March 26, 2002.
13. Malawi Economic Justice Network. *Civil Society PRSP Briefing,* Issue 8. Lilongwe, December 21, 2001.
14. Verheul, E., and Cooper, G. *Poverty Reduction Strategy Papers: What Is at Stake for Health?* Wemos, Amsterdam, September 2001.
15. World Bank. *Can Africa Claim the 21st Century?* Washington, DC, 2000.
16. Brundtland, G. H. Speech to Winterhur Massive Effort Advocacy Meeting. Winterhur, October 3, 2000.
17. World Bank and World Health Organization. *Dying for Change.* Washington, DC, 2002.
18. Verheul, E., and Rowson, M. Where is health? *Trop. Med. Int. Health* 7(5):391–394, 2002.
19. Lanza, O. *Input to Wemos, Consumer Information Network and Cordaid Conference: A Healthy PRSP? Towards a Stronger Voice of Health Organizations in Poverty Reduction Strategy Papers.* Nairobi, September, 18–20, 2002.

20. Quiros, A. *Input to Wemos, Consumer Information Network and Cordaid Conference: A Healthy PRSP? Towards a Stronger Voice of Health Organizations in Poverty Reduction Strategy Papers.* Nairobi, September 18–20, 2002.
21. Naiman, R. *Is the US Treasury above the Law?* Centre for Economic and Policy Research, Washington, DC, June 2001.
22. World Health Organization. *Improving Health Outcomes of the Poor: The Report of Working Group 5 of the Commission on Macroeconomics and Health.* Geneva, 2001.
23. Bond, P. Mozambican parliament questions debt management. *Sunday Independent* (Pretoria), December 21, 1998.
24. Marcus, R., and Wilkinson, J. *Whose Poverty Matters? Vulnerability, Social Protection, and PRSPs.* Childhood Poverty Research and Policy Centre, London, 2002.
25. New Partnership for Africa's Development. http://www.nepad.org
26. Bond, P. (ed.). *Fanon's Warning: A Civil Society Reader on the New Partnership for Africa's Development.* Africa World Press, Trenton, NJ, 2002.

CHAPTER 17

The International Monetary Fund
and World Bank in Africa:
A "Disastrous" Record

Demba Moussa Dembele

This year [2004] marks the 60th anniversary of the International Monetary Fund (IMF) and the World Bank. Through their propaganda machines, both institutions will attempt to highlight their "assistance" to Africa. But in reality, since the 1970s, these institutions have gradually become the chief architects of policies, known as "the Washington Consensus," which are responsible for the worst inequalities and the explosion of poverty in the world, especially in Africa.

Yet, when they began to intervene on that continent in the late 1970s and early 1980s, their stated goal was to "accelerate development," according to a World Bank document, familiarly known as the "Berg Report," published in 1981. But as the following will show, the actual record is just disastrous.

The main pretext for their intervention was to "help solve" the debt crisis that hit African countries in the late 1970s, following the combination of internal and external shocks, notably sharp fluctuations in commodity prices and skyrocketing interest rates. The remedy they proposed, known as stabilization and structural adjustment programs (SAPs), achieved the opposite, and contributed to worsening the external debt and exacerbating the overall economic and social crisis.

In 1980, at the onset of their intervention, the ratios of debt to gross domestic product (GDP) and exports of goods and services were respectively 23.4 percent and 65.2 percent. Ten years later, in 1990, they had deteriorated to respectively 63.0 percent and 210.0 percent! In 2000, the debt to GDP ratio stood at 71.0 percent while the ratio of debt to exports of goods and services had "improved" somewhat, at 80.2 percent, according to the World Bank's Global Development Finance.

The deterioration in debt ratios is reflected in the inability of many African countries to service their external debt. As a result, accumulated arrears on principal and interests have become a growing share of outstanding debt. In 1999, those arrears accounted for 30 percent of the continent's debt, compared

369

with 15 percent in the 1990s and 5.0 percent for all developing countries. To compound the crisis, African countries are getting very little, in terms of new loans, except to pay back old debts. As a result, since 1988, the part of accumulated arrears in "new" debt is estimated at more than 65 percent.

Between 1980 and 2000, Sub-Saharan African (SSA) countries had paid more than $240 billion as debt service, that is, about four times the amount of their debt in 1980. Yet, despite this financial hemorrhage, SSA still owes almost four times what it owed more than twenty years ago! One of the most striking illustrations of this apparent paradox is the case of the Nigerian debt. In 1978, the country had borrowed $5 billion. By 2000, it had reimbursed $16 billion, but still owed $31 billion, according to President Obasanjo.

The Nigerian case is a good example of the structural nature of Africa's debt crisis and of the power imbalance that characterizes world economic and financial relationships. It is this general context that allowed the IMF and World Bank to increase their influence in African countries. One good illustration of this has been the rapid rise in the share of the World Bank and its affiliate, the International Development Association (IDA), in SSA's debt. The combined share of both, which was barely 5.1 percent of SSA's total debt in 1980, had jumped to 25.0 percent in 1990 and to more than 37 percent in 2000, according to the World Bank. In other words, the World Bank group has become the principal "creditor" of many Sub-Saharan countries, which explains the enormous sway it holds over these countries' policies.

One way they exercise this influence is through the imposition of stiff conditionalities on African countries in exchange for loans and credits. Financial liberalization, aimed at attracting more foreign investments to compensate for shortfalls in export revenues, instead fostered more instability, due to the volatility of exchange rates resulting from speculative short-term capital flows. This, combined with higher interest rates, "crowded" out both public and private investments. For instance, investments as a percentage of gross domestic production fell from an annual average of 23 percent between 1975 and 1979 to an average of 18 percent between 1980 and 1984 and 16 percent between 1985 and 1989. They recovered somewhat in the 1990s, but averaged only 18.2 percent between 1990 and 1997, according to UNCTAD. These statistics are consistent with those given by the World Bank, which show that the annual investment ratio averaged 18.6 percent and 17.2 percent in 1981–1990 and 1991–2000, respectively.

These low investment ratios resulted in a contraction of output. Real GDP growth, which averaged 3.5 percent in the 1970s, fell to 1.7 percent between 1981 and 1990, according to the World Bank. However, this masks the sharp declines recorded in the 1980s, dubbed "the lost decade" for Africa. This is better illustrated by the negative growth rates of both GDP and consumption per capita. They fell respectively by 1.2 percent and 0.9 percent a year between 1981 and 1990. It is estimated that in 1981–1989, the cumulative loss of per capita income for the continent as a whole was equivalent to more than 21 percent of real GDP.

In a report released in September 2001, UNCTAD indicated that the average income per capita in SSA was 10 percent lower in 2000 than its 1980 level. In monetary terms, average income per capita fell from $522 in 1981 to $323 in 1997, a loss of nearly $200. The same report said that rural areas experienced an even greater decline in income. These statistics were confirmed by the World Bank, which says that income per capita in Sub-Saharan Africa contracted by a cumulative 13 percent between 1981 and 2001.

The 2004 edition of the World Development Indicators says that SSA is the only region in the world where poverty has continued to rise since the early 1980s, that is at the onset of IFIs' (International Financial Institutions) intervention. According to that document, in 1981, an estimated 160 million people lived on less than $1 a day. In 2001, the number had risen to 314 million, almost double its 1981 level. This means that approximately 50 percent of Africa's population lives in poverty. When the threshold is $2 a day, the numbers rise from 288 million to 518 million, during the same period.

THE COSTS OF TRADE LIBERALIZATION

According to the IMF and World Bank, one of the sources of Africa's crisis is its inward-looking trade system, characterized by the protection of domestic markets, subsidies, overvalued exchange rates and other "market distortions" that made African exports less "competitive" in world markets. In place of this system, they propose an open and liberal trading system in which tariff and non-tariff barriers are kept to a minimum or even eliminated. Such a system, combined with an export-led growth strategy, would put Africa on a solid path to economic recovery, according to both institutions.

The costs associated with trade liberalization have largely offset any potential "benefits" African countries were supposed to derive from that liberalization. First of all, trade liberalization has translated into substantial fiscal losses, since many countries depend on import taxation as their main source of fiscal revenues. Therefore, the elimination of, or reduction in, import tariffs has led to lower government revenues.

But one of the most negative impacts of trade liberalization has been the collapse of many domestic industries, unable to sustain competition from powerful and subsidized competitors from industrialized countries. In fact, Africa's industrial sector has been among the biggest victims of structural adjustment.

From Senegal to Zambia, from Mali to Tanzania, from Côte d'Ivoire to Uganda, entire sectors of the domestic industry have been wiped out, with devastating consequences. Not only has the industrial sector contribution to domestic product continued to fall, but also the industrial workforce has continued to shrink dramatically. In Senegal, more than one third of industrial workers lost their jobs in the 1980s.

The trend was accentuated in the 1990s, following sweeping trade liberalization policies and privatization imposed by the IMF and the World Bank,
especially after the 50 percent devaluation of the CFA Franc, in 1994. In Ghana,
the industrial workforce declined from 78,700 in 1987 to 28,000 in 1993. In
Zambia, in the textile sector alone, more than 75 percent of workers lost their
jobs in less than a decade, as a result of the complete dismantling of that sector by
the Chiluba presidency. In other countries, such as Côte d'Ivoire, Burkina Faso,
Mali, Togo, Zambia, Tanzania, etc., similar trends can be observed.

In several annual and special reports, the International Labor Organization
(ILO) has documented the devastating impact of SAPs on employment and
wages. The African Union seems to have come to grips with that devastation. It
organized a special Summit on Employment and Poverty, in the capital of Burkina
Faso, September 9 and 10, 2004. It was revealed during that Summit that only
25 percent of the African workforce is employed in the formal sector. The rest,
75 percent, is either in the subsistence agriculture or in the informal sector. In
light of this reality, the Summit issued a Plan of Action aimed at exploring
strategies to foster job creation. But such a Plan will only be credible if African
countries are ready to move away from IMF and World Bank recipes, which were
harshly criticized during the Summit.

UNCTAD has reported that more than 70 percent of Africa's exports are still
composed of primary products, more than 62 percent of which are non-processed
products. This helps justify the need for more liberalization and deregulation to
make African exports more "competitive." The second objective is to help justify
the need for more liberalization and deregulation to make African economies
more "competitive" and "attractive" to foreign direct investments. This also
explains the push for more privatization.

In the name of "comparative advantage," the export-led growth strategy
forces African countries to compete fiercely for market shares, leading them
to flood the same markets with more of their commodities. As a result,
trade liberalization has accentuated the volatility of African commodities,
whose prices experienced twice the volatility of East Asian commodity prices
and nearly four times the volatility that industrial countries experienced in
the 1970s, 1980s, and 1990s. This has contributed to worsening Africa's terms
of trade.

According to UNCTAD, if Africa's terms of trade had remained at their
1980 level:

- Africa's share in world trade would have been twice its current level
- the investment ratio would have been raised by 6.0 percent per annum in
  non-oil-exporting countries
- it would have added to annual growth 1.4 percent per annum
- it would have raised GDP per capita by at least 50 percent to $478 in 1997,
  compared with the actual figure of $323 during that year.

THE COSTS OF FINANCIAL LIBERALIZATION

One of the main objectives of financial liberalization is to make African countries "attractive" to foreign direct investments. But as the experience of development shows, foreign direct investments follow development, not the other way around. In addition, despite all "the right financial policies," foreign investments continue to elude Africa, with less than 2 percent of flows to developing countries, despite having among the highest rates of return on investments in the world. And these flows are concentrated in a few oil-producing and mineral-rich countries, according to UNCTAD and the World Bank.

In reality, financial liberalization has yielded little gains. For most African countries, it has been associated with huge costs. First, it entails higher levels of foreign exchange reserves to protect domestic currencies against attacks resulting from speculative short-term capital outflows. Second, financial liberalization has increased the likelihood of capital flight, in part as a result of a greater volatility of domestic currencies. The high costs of trade and financial liberalization further weakened African economies and opened the way to the privatization of the continent.

THE PRIVATIZATION OF AFRICA

Privatization, like financial liberalization, is seen by the IMF and World Bank as an instrument to promote private sector development, which has been elevated to the status of "engine of growth." The privatization of State-owned enterprises (SOEs), including water and power utilities, has been one of the core conditionalities imposed by the two institutions, even in the context of "poverty reduction."

Most of the foreign direct investments registered by African countries in the 1990s came as a response to privatization of SOEs. No sector was spared, even those considered as "strategic" in the 1980s, such as telecommunications, energy, water, and the extractive industries. In 1994, the World Bank published a report assessing the process of privatization in SSA. After complaining about the slow pace of privatization throughout the region, it issued a warning to African governments to accelerate the dismantling of their public sector, accused of being "at the heart of Africa's economic crisis." The process of privatization peaked in the late 1990s and ever since has leveled off, despite more deregulation, liberalization, and all kinds of incentives offered to would-be investors.

To date (2004), it is estimated that more than 40,000 SOEs have been sold off in Africa. However, the "gains" from privatization, projected by the World Bank and the IMF, have been elusive. In fact, many privatization schemes have failed and contributed to worsening economic and social conditions. Almost everywhere, privatization has been associated with massive job losses and higher prices of goods and services that put them out of reach of most citizens.

BUILDING A NEOLIBERAL STATE

The concept of "good governance" was promoted by the IMF and World Bank to explain the failure of SAPs. It tends to convey the idea that SAPs have failed, in large part, because African States are "corrupt," "wasteful," and "rent-seeking" and because of the "poor implementation" of policies. In other words, SAPs were basically "sound," it is the combination of "rampant corruption" and lack of qualified personnel that led to the failure of these policies. Thus, "good governance" means nothing else than the need to build a neoliberal State, subservient to the IFIs, able to effectively implement "sound policies" and to protect the interests of foreign investors.

Indeed, one of the main goals of the IMF and World Bank has been to discredit State-led development strategies in favor of market-led strategies. This is why one of the main targets of these institutions has been the role of the African State in economic and social development. To discredit that role, a two-track strategy was adopted. The first track was to attack the credibility of the African State as an agent of development. To achieve that goal, an abundant literature has been published by the two institutions, highlighting the "corrupt," "predatory," "wasteful," and "rent-seeking" nature of the African State.

To justify these epithets, the IFIs pointed to the "mismanagement" of the public sector, accused of being an obstacle to economic growth and development. These attacks helped make the case for the sweeping restructure of the public sector, which, in many cases, led to its dismantling in favor of the private sector.

The second track in weakening the role of the State in development was to deprive it of financial resources. Trade and financial liberalization achieved in part that goal. As already indicated, trade liberalization not only led to a greater loss of fiscal revenues, following lower tariff barriers, but it also led to huge trade losses. This was compounded by financial liberalization which entailed further fiscal losses resulting from tax holidays and low income tax rates. To make up for these losses, the African State had to resort to more and more multilateral and bilateral loans and credits, which further alienated its sovereignty.

As a result, many African States have been stripped of all but a handful of their economic and social functions. Cuts in spending mostly fell on social sectors. State retrenchment primarily aimed at eliminating subsidies for the poor, removing social protection, and abandoning its role in fighting for social justice through income redistribution and other social transfers to the most disadvantaged segments of society. This explains, among other things, the degradation of many basic social services and the explosion of poverty in Africa, since 1981, as the World Bank itself has acknowledged.

While dismantling or weakening the economic and social roles of the State, the IMF and World Bank have sought to build or strengthen the functions most useful to the implementation of neoliberal policies and the promotion of private sector development. This explains the insistence on "capacity building" or on "institution building," heard over the last few years. However, the institutions that the IMF and World Bank talk about are not for development, but for markets. In other words, they propose building institutions supportive of neoliberal policies and in the service of the private sector, especially foreign investors.

Thus, the "institution building" agenda promoted by the IMF and the World Bank has nothing to do with promoting democracy and protecting human rights. In fact, the neoliberal conception of governance undermines both since it deprives representative institutions of their role in formulating public policies following open and democratic debates. They are reduced to implementing what the IMF and World Bank and their G8 masters decide for African countries and their people.

FROM STRUCTURAL ADJUSTMENT TO POVERTY "REDUCTION"

After producing poverty and deprivation on a massive scale in Africa and elsewhere, the IFIs' focus on "poverty reduction" since 1999 could not be more suspect. But to make this shift a bit more credible, the IMF's Enhanced Structural Adjustment Facility (ESAF) was renamed "Poverty Reduction and Growth Facility" (PRGF), and the World Bank has set up a "Poverty Reduction Support Credit" (PRSC).

There is no doubt that the shift in the rhetoric of the IFIs amounts to an admission of failure of past policies, which put too much emphasis on correcting macroeconomic imbalances and "market distortions" at the expense of economic growth and social progress. The disastrous record of SAPs and the continued deterioration in the economic and social situation of countries subjected to IMF and World Bank programs put into question the credibility and even the legitimacy of these institutions. Their crisis of legitimacy was exacerbated by stepped up attacks by the Global Justice Movement and growing criticism from mainstream economists, especially from Joseph E. Stiglitz, former World Bank Chief Economist.

THE NATURE OF POVERTY REDUCTION STRATEGY PAPERS (PRSPs)

The PRSPs are supposed to provide more freedom to developing countries in formulating their policies. This is what the Bank and the Fund call "national ownership." Representatives from the government, the private sector, civil society organizations—and even the poor—are supposed to "participate" in drafting the PRSP of each country to decide on how to use the proceeds released by "debt relief" to achieve "poverty reduction."

In reality, the macroeconomic framework that underpins the PRSPs is the same as that which underpinned the now discredited SAPS. That framework is non-negotiable and includes fiscal austerity, trade and financial liberalization, privatization, deregulation and State retrenchment, etc. In essence, despite the disastrous outcome of their past policies, the IMF and the World Bank still believe that those policies are in the "interests of the poor." In particular, they think that trade liberalization and openness are the best—if not the only—road to growth, which they see as a "prerequisite" for poverty reduction. Hence the export-led growth strategy advocated by the two institutions, but which has been a big failure in African and other developing countries.

A survey of 27 African PRSPs by UNCTAD in 2002 has demonstrated that all of them, without exception, contain the policies outlined above. Policies which are at odds with both the wishes and the interests of the poor, observes the document. It is this straight jacket that ties up developing countries' hands and prevents them from achieving any substantial gain in poverty "reduction." Most of the time, countries have failed to implement these conditions, leading to the suspension of their programs.

In fact, the IFIs' conception of poverty views it as an isolated aspect of overall economic and social development that should be dealt with by short-term measures. Hence, the emphasis in the PRSPs on more spending for primary education and health, among others. Thus, PRSPs contain some short-term measures aimed at mitigating the negative impact of macroeconomic policies and structural reforms on the most vulnerable groups, notably the poor. However, the tools the World Bank and the IMF have proposed to achieve this goal are the same as those already tested in the past and that have aggravated poverty and deprivation in much of Africa.

In reality, PRSPs are SAPs with more conditionalities and less resources. As already indicated, a new "generation" of conditionalities have been added to old conditionalities, with the concept of "good governance," analyzed above. UNCTAD (2002) has revealed that between 1999 and 2000, 13 African countries had signed programs containing an average of 114 conditionalities, 75 percent of which are governance-related conditionalities. One can imagine the enormous human and financial resources needed to deal with such a number of conditionalities. For this reason, the degree of compliance with IMF and World Bank–sponsored programs has significantly declined since the mid-1990s. For instance, the rate of compliance was estimated at about 28 percent of the 41 agreements signed between 1993 and 1997, according to UNCTAD.

With the PRSPs, the IMF and the World Bank pursue three objectives. First, mislead world public opinion, especially in Northern countries, in making believe that they are really serious about "reducing poverty." And the World Bank alone counts on a huge and sophisticated propaganda machine to achieve this. With the more than 300 staff of its External Relations Department—Propaganda Department, one should say—the Bank has all the means it needs to "explain" effectively its policies. It has achieved some success, since some big Northern NGOs, once very critical of SAPs, see the PRSPs as a "positive shift" in the IFIs' policies.

The second objective of the PRSPs is to enlist a broad support within each country to help rehabilitate discredited and failed policies. This is what "national ownership" and "participation" of civil society organizations are supposed to achieve. While insisting on the "participation" of civil society organizations, their most vocal critics, the IMF and World Bank tend to sideline representative institutions, like National Assemblies. This is another illustration of these institutions' contempt for the democratic process in Africa. Finally, with PRSPs, the IMF and the World Bank seek to shift the blame to African countries and citizens, for the inevitable failure of these "new" policies.

CONCLUSION

The IMF and World Bank have utterly failed in "reducing poverty" and "promoting development." In fact, they are instruments of domination and control in the hands of powerful states whose long-standing objective is to perpetuate the plunder of the resources of the Global South, especially Africa. In other words, the fundamental role of the Bank and Fund in Africa and in the rest of the developing world is to promote and protect the interests of global capitalism.

This is why they have never been interested in "reducing" poverty, much less in fostering "development." As institutions, their ultimate objective is to make themselves "indispensable" in order to strengthen and expand their power and influence. They will never relinquish easily that power and influence. This explains why they have perfected the art of duplicity, deception, and manipulation. In the face of accumulated failures and erosion of their credibility and legitimacy, they have often changed their rhetoric, but never their fundamental goals and policies.

This is why they cannot be trusted to bring about "development" in Africa. If the experience of the last quarter of a century has taught Africa one fundamental lesson it is that the road to genuine recovery and development begins with a total break with the failed and discredited policies imposed by the IMF and the World Bank.

In fairness to both institutions, we must recognize, however, the complicity of African leaders in the disastrous outcome of neoliberal policies. Many governments and senior civil servants have bought into the agenda promoted by the IMF and World Bank. Therefore, they bear a great responsibility in the current state of the continent. Thus, to put an end to the influence of these institutions, African social movements and progressive forces must explore strategies aimed at promoting a new kind of leadership able and willing to challenge these institutions in favor of genuine alternative development policies.

Note — This chapter was originally published in *Pambazuka News,* 175, a Weekly Electronic Forum for Social Justice in Africa (www.pambazuka.org).

PART IX

Analysis of Proposed Solutions to Current Health and Social Problems

The Sachs Report: *Investing in Health for Economic Development*—Or Increasing the Size of the Crumbs from the Rich Man's Table?

Alison Katz

INTRODUCTION

The report of the Commission on Macroeconomics and Health (CMH) (1), presented in December 2001 to the World Health Organization's director general, Gro Harlem Brundtland, has been heralded as provocative, bold, intelligent, insightful—even "groundbreaking, compassionate and cost effective," in the words of the chairman of the CMH, Jeffrey Sachs, himself (2).

In this chapter, it is argued that the CMH report is deeply conservative and unoriginal. The report encourages medico-technical solutions to public health problems; it ignores macroeconomic determinants and other root causes of both poor health and poverty; it reverses public health logic and history; it is based on a set of flawed assumptions; and it reflects one particular economic perspective to the exclusion of all others. In short, the CMH represents "more of the same." It recommends greater amounts of charity while preserving the status quo. It faithfully reproduces conventional, "free" market, "free" trade prescriptions that have been so resoundingly successful in accelerating poverty and social inequality—and in turn poor health status of populations—over the past 20 years.

At the turn of the century, we confront overwhelming evidence of the failure of such prescriptions. To adopt the report of the WHO's Commission on Macroeconomics and Health as the blueprint for global or national health policy and strategy is nothing short of willful neglect. The lives and well-being of half of humanity are at stake—the half that survives on less than two dollars a day. Alternative perspectives and strategies abound, and evidence to support their value is available. If the international health community persists in ignoring them, it will go down in history as having closed its ears and its eyes to the tremendous movement for social justice occurring at the start of the new millennium. It is our duty to undertake an objective assessment of the impact of neoliberal policy on poverty and health over the past 20 years (or indeed, examine the wealth of evidence already available) and to carefully consider alternative policies and strategies—and the evidence of their success.

A Restricted Mandate and a Reversal of Logic

The CMH was established by the WHO director-general in January 2000 with "a two year mandate to debate, research and reach conclusions about the role of health in economic development" (3). One might assume that a commission on macroeconomics and health would examine the relationship as a whole. The relationship between health and poverty is two way but it is *not symmetric*. Poverty is the single most important determinant of poor health. But poor health is very far from being the single most important determinant of poverty. Poor health exacerbates existing poverty. Both the vicious cycle and the "virtuous" cycle of health and poverty are misleading images, as they imply equal weight of the two poles of health and economic development.

Nonetheless, over the past decade or so, a curious reversal of logic has appeared in the literature on poverty and health, particularly in U.N. documents, in which it is claimed that attention to a few diseases will bring prosperity to individuals, their communities, and even whole nations (4). To justify this, authors, including Sachs, invariably claim that until now, the role of health in economic development has been less appreciated (than the role of economic development in health). This chapter argues that it has been less appreciated for the very good reason that it is significantly less appreciable. By comparison with the substantial and sustainable population health gains that can be achieved through simple measures such as ensuring reliable supplies of food and water (which themselves require relatively modest financial inputs), it plays a very insignificant role indeed.

No amount of excellent medical interventions delivered to Haitians or Tanzanians today are going to make them or their country prosperous tomorrow if the national economy is strangled by debt, unfair terms of trade, and the continued pillage of natural resources and is destabilized by uncontrolled financial out-flows, wildly fluctuating commodity prices, and outside interference in matters of national sovereignty. Haitians and Tanzanians receiving medical treatment today may survive where others die in very precarious conditions, allowing them to contribute for a couple more months to gross national product (GNP), just until the next bout of illness—unless, while the medical technology is being delivered, attention is paid to the underlying causes of the population's poor health status, such as miserable living conditions.

No Basis for Comparison

A report entitled *Investing in Health for Economic Development* has clearly confined its analysis to the less significant part of the two-way relationship between poverty and health, and it would be helpful if the reasons for this were set out. At the very least, such a report should acknowledge that any benefits to economic development accruing from health interventions *must be compared with the benefits that would accrue from attention to the more significant part of the relationship,* in terms of both health and economic improvements and in terms of the expected duration and sustainability of such benefits. In other words, in order to assess the usefulness and cost effectiveness of the strategies proposed by the CMH, policymakers need a comparison of the health and economic benefits to a country of investments in, for example, food and water or public service infrastructure, with investments of the same order in health interventions. Policymakers cannot be expected to endorse, let alone implement, CMH recommendations without such a comparison.

More critically, policymakers in many developing countries need to assess the benefits and losses of their participation in the global "free" market *as it is currently organized and constituted.* In particular, they need to assess the long-term costs and benefits that would accrue from defaulting on odious debt, from protecting national and local production especially in relation to food sovereignty, from providing basic health and education services, from imposing strict controls on financial flows (including to tax havens) and foreign investment, and from securing fair terms of trade. In other words, they need to compare the benefits of larger crumbs from the rich man's table with the benefits of a brand new table—a rational, fair, international economic order— upon which to place whole loaves of bread baked by themselves for their own consumption!

This chapter does not question the accuracy of the CMH estimates of benefits to economic development of the set of interventions proposed—though some researchers have (5, 6). Rather, it points to the fact that these benefits are insignificant, short lived, and unsustainable compared with the benefits—in terms of the economies of poor nations and the health of their peoples—that would result from a set of very simple macroeconomic measures to address root causes of poverty so that basic needs can be met. Such an approach would be based on a very different set of assumptions and would have vastly different implications for strategy and action—and for the future global distribution of power and wealth. It would, however, result in substantial and long-term improvements in population health of poor countries—as those in the rich countries know from their own happy experience between 50 and 100 years ago (7, 8).

Furthermore, if the ultimate goal is for nation states to meet their people's basic needs, including health care, reliably and in the long term, the CMH recommendations are likely to be harmful rather than merely ineffective. This chapter argues that the approach advocated by the CMH is likely to bind poor countries ever more closely into the exploitative North-South relationship that has so devastated their economies (and so enriched the economies of the North) for decades, even centuries.

Central Thesis and Key Recommendation

The central thesis of the Sachs report is that "improvements in health translate into higher incomes, higher economic growth and reduced population growth" (p. 3).[1] The main recommendation is "to scale up access of the world's poor to essential health services, including a focus on specific interventions" (p. 4). The plan is predicated on "donor financing [which] creates the financial reality for a greatly scaled up, more effective health system" (p. 4).

This chapter begins with an examination of the assumptions that underpin the CMH report, in which health is conceived as an input to productivity and economic growth. It proposes an alternative set of assumptions that are critical to a social justice and human rights approach to health and to the goal of *long-term, reliable* improvements in health and material well-being. I then summarize the main findings, recommendations, and "messages" of the report, and identify what is genuinely positive and (some of) what is misleading, biased, or plain wrong. Above all, this discussion points to the disproportion between the benefits that would result from following the CMH recommendations and those that would result from simple, macroeconomic measures directed toward social and economic justice.

Overall, the chapter identifies, as the ultimate source of the poor health status and miserable conditions of popular majorities in poor countries, the extreme concentration of power, worldwide, in the hands of the few. It proposes the establishment of a new macroeconomic commission which, this time, would have a mandate to report on the relationship between poverty and health in its entirety. This commission would thoroughly review and make recommendations on alternative development and economic models designed specifically for sustainable distribution of goods and services according to people's needs within a rational, fair, international economic order.

FATAL FLAWS AND GAPING GAPS

In this section, I argue that the assumptions underlying the Sachs report—referred to as "fatal flaws and gaping gaps"—derive from a neoliberal approach to health. A corresponding set of alternative assumptions is proposed that derives from a human rights and social justice approach to health. Table 1 presents the underlying and alternative assumptions and a comparative summary of the key features of neoliberal and social justice approaches to health.

Each of the underlying assumptions referred to as "fatal flaws and gaping gaps" derives from a very particular world view, sometimes referred to as TINA—There

---

[1] In this chapter, "CMH report" and page numbers refer to *Investing in Health for Economic Development: The Report of the Commission on Macroeconomics and Health*, WHO, 2001, which presents a summary of the reports of the six working groups.

Table 1

Neoliberal versus social justice approaches to health: A summary

Neoliberal approach to health	Social justice/human rights approach to health
Underlying assumptions	*Alternative assumptions*
Economic growth, within a globalized "free" market, is the aim.	Fair distribution and sustainable use of resources is the aim.
Health is what you get from a health service.	Health is what you get from meeting basic needs.
International aid, with conditionalities to enforce certain policies, is the only way to finance health.	Sovereign and solvent states must provide for their people's basic needs without outside interference.
Democracy is alive and well in the developed world and is the model for the developing world.	Democracy is in crisis everywhere; self-determination of nation states and a rules-based system of international governance are required.
Key features	*Key features*
Addresses symptoms, short term	Addresses root causes, long term
Promotes "magic medical bullets"	Promotes the meeting of basic needs
Promotes interventions delivered through health services	Promotes public works to free people from miserable living conditions
Identifies charity and international aid as the only sources of funds for health	Identifies redistribution and economic justice as sources of funds for health
Maintains the status quo of extreme concentrations of wealth and power	Demands a fair and rational international economic order
Focuses on individual behavior and tends to blame victims	Focuses on structural poverty and violence and tends to blame the "system"

Is No Alternative—as famously asserted by Margaret Thatcher. This view has come to dominate the international health community as much as it has come to dominate world politics. It is a shamelessly totalitarian justification of the status quo—unregulated, monopolistic, corporate capitalism—which has successfully stifled dissent for a decade or more (9). However, hope springs eternal and people everywhere are convinced that "another world is possible" (10, 11). Fortunately for the human race, intellectual curiosity and an obstinate refusal to accept that the powerful either know or do what is best for the powerless are forcing TINA into retreat. The implications for poverty, health, and development of the underlying and alternative assumptions corresponding to neoliberal and social justice approaches are explored below.

Economic Growth Is the Aim?

The CMH proposes that the world invest in health for economic development. Economic development is not defined, but the term is used more or less interchangeably with "economic growth" throughout the text (e.g., p. 1 of the Executive summary). Sachs berates the "blithe optimists" for believing that "health goals will take care of themselves as a fairly automatic by-product of economic growth" (p. 3). This is a recent and welcome insight from Sachs— though scarcely original. He is one of several eminent economists[2] now conceding that very little "trickles down" from economic growth without deliberate and specific state intervention (12).

However, Sachs's statement is a misrepresentation of the argument which asserts that economic improvements in terms of meeting basic material needs will indeed result in substantial improvements in population health status. Enthusiasts for "evidence" will concede that no research is required on this particular question. We have 100 years of solid public health experience demonstrating that access to decent food, clean water, adequate sanitation, and shelter are the major determinants of health (13).

If we accept CMH logic for a moment, that investing in health will lead to economic development, then the first and principal recommendation of the report ought to be the meeting of basic needs—which is the fastest, cheapest, and simplest route to good health. Curiously, it is neither the first recommendation, nor even a recommendation at all. In order to understand this, we need to examine the second flawed assumption (see below under "Health Is What You Get from Health Services?").

Economic growth, as Sachs himself points out, has no necessary relationship to improvements in health, or for that matter to improvements in human welfare generally—as this depends largely on how profits or extra resources are distributed or whether increases in GDP (gross domestic product) translate into improvements of any kind in the living conditions of the majority (14). Despite this admission, the CMH report consistently presents growth as the ultimate goal, and the "free" market (albeit a softened and more humane version) as the way to achieve it. Growth as an aim is incompatible with sustainable and equitable use of resources (15), which itself is a prerequisite for peace, social justice, and the Alma-Ata goal of Health for All (16). Furthermore, "free" market policies have failed (17), as many of their keenest proponents such as Stiglitz, Bhagwati, Soros, and Sachs himself are now admitting (18).

The U.N. Development Program's 2003 report (19) finally concedes that neoliberal triumphalism is misplaced and that neither the "invisible hand of the

---

[2] The "prodigal sons" of neoliberalism also include Joseph Stiglitz, who has been given a hero's welcome home for his rather unoriginal critique of the IMF. The most interesting aspect of his well-written book is that he was once chief economist at the World Bank.

market" nor growth, nor technological advances will bring an end to misery on earth. With careful understatement it even admits that "poverty is often a political problem." This UNDP report confirms what many social justice movements and nongovernmental organizations have been saying for 20 years and what its own figures have consistently demonstrated, which is that neoliberal policies hit first and hardest not only the most vulnerable (sub-Saharan African countries) but also, the unkindest cut of all, those who have followed neoliberal recipes most closely—Eastern European and Latin American countries.

Weisbrot and coauthors (20) report that the last 20 years of globalization (1980–2000) have shown clear declines in progress as compared with the previous two decades. This is important because claims about continued increases in growth in the era of globalization have consistently failed to distinguish between the two periods. In the latter period, per capita GDP growth has been considerably worse in all countries than in the two previous decades. The poorest countries experienced *negative* growth in the globalization period. Furthermore, progress in life expectancy, and infant and child mortality, was considerably slower during globalization—and these results cannot be explained by the AIDS pandemic.

Cornia and Court (21, p. 1) have shown that income inequality has risen in most countries since the early to mid 1980s, and in many cases sharply. The widespread surges in inequality are *"due to 'new causes' linked to the excessively liberal economic policy regimes* and the way in which economic reforms have been carried out" (emphasis added). Their analysis also reveals that "the higher the level of inequality, the less impact economic growth has in reducing poverty—for any rate of economic growth."

Less attention has been paid to the *irrationality* of the current order than to its grotesque unfairness. One of the most striking statistics, familiar even to lay people, shows that the world's 225 richest individuals have a combined wealth of more than a trillion dollars—equal to the annual income of the poorest 47 percent of the world's population (22). I will not, therefore, elaborate on the unfairness of the current order. The reader is referred to some key texts (23–25).

The rationality of a capitalist system has always been put forward as its strongest argument. "Free" market advocates of corporate capitalism claim that the system works (or rather will work) for everyone. With exponentially increasing inequalities, through a globalized, monopolistic, corporate-led form of capitalism, this claim is becoming increasingly difficult to support. A few of its most fervent exponents are now asserting that "it will have to get worse before it gets better" and that a little more time is needed for the benefits to be felt.

Some of the most irrational aspects of the current system, often described as "chaotic," "anarchic," or "casino economics," are set out below. They provide an indication of what will be required of alternative economics for people-centered, environment-friendly, and health-enhancing arrangements.

388 / Neoliberalism, Globalization, Inequalities

- Driven by short-term profit for a minority (of shareholders) rather than long-term needs of the majority (of human beings)
- Characterized by boom and bust, inherently unstable
- Results in overproduction of goods, which are increasingly maldistributed
- Creates demand for useless and/or harmful products but fails to supply necessities
- Produces a net transfer of resources from South to North
- Concentrates wealth in line with the sacred principle that "to he who has, more shall be given"
- Favors short-term speculation over long-term productive investment
- Is increasingly virtual, bearing no relation to human activity, productive or otherwise
- Ensures that consumerism triumphs, but the circle of consumers is getting smaller

Perhaps the most striking irrationality in relation to health and sustainable development is that war and militarism are simultaneously public health catastrophes (26), affecting mostly the poor, and motors of the economy, affecting mostly the rich (27, 28). Suffering, death, and devastating environmental damage from war are neither here nor there in assessments of an economy's "health" or efficiency. But billion dollar reconstruction contracts (29) following billion dollar contracts for arms supplies (30), and other contributions of the military-industrial complex to the economy, are critical.

The "health" of the economy takes precedence over the health of people, and the economy drives policy rather than vice versa. At the global level, this is exemplified by the fact that the only international bodies with any meaningful influence on world affairs are the international financial institutions (IFIs): the World Bank, the International Monetary Fund (IMF), and the World Trade Organization (WTO) (31).

The irrationality of the current economic system is compounded by public relations "doublespeak" and outrageous bad faith. "Free" trade is far from free; it is very carefully fixed in the interests of private capital and the rich nations (32). The unemployed are characterized as parasites of the state, even though a rate of at least 10 percent unemployment in theory and often 25 percent or more in practice is viewed and then constructed as a natural and necessary component of an efficient market economy (33).

Chief executive officers of transnational corporations, who are rarely characterized as parasites, vaunt the "independent spirit of enterprise" while their companies are buttressed, made viable, and bailed out through massive state subsidies—even after disastrous mismanagment (34, 35). Profits are privatized and losses and debts are nationalized. The benefits of competition are loudly hailed while mergers and acquisitions between already giant companies create near perfect monopolies (36, 37). Finally, economic liberalization is cynically made synonymous with political democracy (38) while entire populations are reduced to bonded labor through debt and their governments reduced to puppets in the hands of the IFIs.

There is a rich and inspiring literature on alternative economics[3] (often termed "green" or "distribution" economics), which continues to be ignored in mainstream development discourse and has so far had virtually no impact on global health policymaking. If the international health community maintains Health for All as a goal, it cannot continue to ignore the range of options provided by alternative economics. We should not forget that the Alma-Ata Declaration on Primary Health Care in 1978 endorsed in effect "distribution economics" through its support for a new international economic order. The new element today ("new" in the sense of being properly recognized) is green economics to preserve the earth's resources and ensure their equitable and sustainable use.

The link between fair and sustainable use of the earth's resources and countries' capacities to meet people's basic needs for health is difficult to dispute, in ethical and commonsense terms—and as the accumulated evidence shows (16, 39, 40). The argument linking Health for All to both fair distribution and sustainable resource use—economy with ecology—is as follows:

- People are unwell because they are poor.
- People are poor because of structural man-made—not god-given—arrangements.
- The world has plentiful resources, but they are finite and their careless production and consumption damage both the environment and people's health.
- The earth's eventual carrying capacity is probably insufficient for 6 let alone 12 billion people (41).
- One-third of the global health burden is attributable to environmental factors (42).
- Environmental problems disproportionately affect the poor.
- However, overuse and misuse of resources, degradation, and pollution are overwhelmingly the responsibility of the wealthy nations (43).
- Basic needs for health, including a safe environment, can be met for all the world's people and their descendants only if its precious resources are distributed fairly and produced and consumed carefully.

---

[3] Alternative economics draws from and has obvious implications for many other fields, including philosophy, biology, ethics, sociology, psychology, and spirituality, and its scope is enormous. It has stimulated much creative new thinking. Some writers address the environment as a priority, others a fair economic international order. Some explore the potential of regional structures and arrangements or of selective "delinking" from the current corporate-driven globalization process, and of course there is an enormous literature on alternative development paths.

In relation to the earth's carrying capacity, it should be understood that when activists claim that the world produces enough food today for 12 billion people, they are not recommending that figure as a target; they are stating a simple fact, one that supports the ethical imperative of food for all today through fair distribution (44, 45).

The neoliberal approach to health has turned the above reasoning on its head by asserting that people are poor because they are ill, because there are too many of them, because they place a strain on scarce resources, and—to add insult to injury—because they behave irresponsibly.

Some common strands of thought in alternative economics, of relevance to health and sustainable development, are summarized below:

- The current system is inherently unstable and must be regulated, made transparent and accountable, and brought under democratic control.
- The economic system and structures should be informed by ethical values of social justice and human rights.
- It should be designed to provide a good and satisfying life for everyone, in sustainable balance with the earth and all its life forms.
- There is an urgent need to democratize the debate on economics and to encourage public action on global financial issues, especially as the poor suffer first and most from recurrent crises.
- Production of goods and services to meet the basic needs of all should be encouraged, and harmful overconsumption by the already rich should be curbed.
- In the interests of local communities, their environment, the quality of goods (in particular of food), and national sovereignty, economic arrangements should facilitate and encourage local and national production and self reliance.[4]
- Sustainable local communities should produce the essentials of life from the resources of their area and trade only to increase a population's choice (by swapping one commodity for another on equal terms of trade).
- Regional economies and a world economy would support and protect national local economies, reversing the pattern of centuries and halting the continual impoverishment of the periphery through transfer of resources to the center (46).

In conclusion, *economic growth* must be replaced by *fair distribution and sustainable use of resources* as the assumption underlying economic arrangements for health and development. This does not mean that economic growth is never

---

[4] This is a recommendation not for autarchy but for rational and fair internationalism, which, as opposed to globalization, implies cooperation between sovereign nations for mutual benefits as decided by the people.

to be pursued but that when it is pursued, this is because it has been correctly identified as the best means to a particular end, such as improvement in material conditions of life—not achieved at the expense of other people or the environment.

Health Is What You Get from Health Services?

According to the CMH report, health is achieved and health problems are solved through technical interventions delivered through health services. The major recommendation of the report is to "scale up the access of the world's poor to essential health services including a focus on specific interventions" (p. 4). There appears to be no recognition that the major interventions required for improvements in population health status lie outside the health sector; evidence for this has been available for decades (47; see Chapter 20 in this volume). Furthermore, recently published studies (48) confirm that societies' socioeconomic, political, and cultural variables are the most important factors in explaining population levels of health. Data from OECD countries for the period 1950–1998 show that redistributional, universalistic public policy interventions that reduce inequalities in the distribution of economic and social resources are of paramount importance in improving quality of life and level of health of populations.

The findings from the research projects on the political and social contexts of health (summarized in 48) indicate the need for comprehensive policies in which health policy interventions are truly more than health interventions. (The implications of these critical findings for financing interventions for health improvements are discussed below.)

Sachs explains the failure to consider non-health-sector interventions as follows: "Though we advocate a greatly increased investment in the health sector itself, we stress the need for *complementary, additional investments* in areas with an important impact on poverty alleviation (including effects on health). These include education, water and sanitation, and agricultural improvement" (p. 10, emphasis added). In one sentence, Sachs has disposed of the major determinants of health as "complementary and additional" rather than central. In this way, the key question requiring an answer from the CMH has been removed from the discussion.

The question is as follows: What would be the cost of ensuring reliable, long-term supplies of food, water, sanitation, and shelter to all the people of this world? What would be the result of this investment in terms of improvements in health, and in turn, economic development?

The composition of the CMH was heavily weighted toward economists, with comparatively few public health experts.[5] Nevertheless, this does not explain

---

[5] The 18 CMH commissioners formed a homogeneous group; 14 completed university education in the United States; 10 have worked for one of the following: World Bank, IMF, WTO, or OECD; only 4 are women; and only 4 have neither worked for an IFI nor served as director of a private company (see the biographies in the CMH report).

the report's almost total neglect of the classic public health lessons of the late 19th/early 20th century (8). Sachs concedes that improvements in "health infrastructure" contributed to increased life expectancy and reduced morbidity prior to "the most potent health interventions of the 20th century such as immunizations and antibiotics," but he includes within this infrastructure the need for "critical investments in technological advancement not only in biomedical approaches but also in agriculture (e.g., nutritionally fortified crops, or high yielding crops . . .)" (p. 74).

The most potent public health interventions—whatever the century—remain food and water. As for technological advancement, if the aim is to reduce the greatest burden of disease, which everyone agrees is attributable to unclean water and malnutrition, it is neither critical nor urgent. The technology is there and has been for decades. For reasons discussed below, it appears that classic public health lessons are not regarded as applicable to poor countries today. The international health community has been recommending technologies to fight disease in developing countries for at least two decades— drugs, bednets, condoms, and the like—cosmetic, unsustainable, stop-gap measures.

The CMH report fails to acknowledge that poor countries today might wish to rid themselves of the scourge of disease reliably and once for all, just as the rich countries did, rather than for a couple of months while supplies—often acquired expensively from Northern pharmaceutical companies—last.

And yet WHO's own figures, year after year, readily available to the CMH, show that determinants of disease in poor countries today are roughly the same as they were in today's rich countries 100 years ago. (Note that the basic determinants are the same, but many developing countries carry a double burden of traditional risks and "modern" risks—chemical pollution, poor diet, deteriorating environment, etc.) The proportion of disease attributable to factors lying outside the health sector that cannot be addressed through health services is overwhelming. For example, 50 to 70 percent of lower respiratory infections, diarrheal disease, malaria, and measles (the big killers) in childhood are due to undernutrition; 88 percent of diarrheal disease is due to unsafe water, sanitation, and hygiene, and 99.8 percent of deaths due to this risk factor are in developing countries (49). Through malnutrition, poverty seriously impairs immune function, making children more vulnerable to disease of all kinds.

In conclusion, I would argue that the underlying assumption—health is what you get from a health service—should be replaced with the alternative assumption—health is what you get from meeting basic needs. Primary health care is, of course, one of the public services required to provide the conditions for good population health. The costs and benefits of meeting basic needs for health need to be presented to countries as a basis for comparison with the action agenda proposed by the CMH.

International Aid Is the Only Way to Finance Health?

Another striking omission from the Sachs report is the concept of distribution of wealth in the world, fair or otherwise. There is no discussion of how today's distribution came about or of how it is maintained. As Banerji (5) has pointed out, this is an ahistorical and apolitical report (see Chapter 19 of this volume).

The CMH report concedes that *"poverty itself imposes a basic financial constraint"* (emphasis in original) and then asserts that "the gap between financial means and financial need *can only be filled by the donor world"* (emphasis added) (p. 6). Are 19 of the world's most eminent economists seriously suggesting that there are no ways of distributing income and assets between countries other than through international aid? This narrow and static vision of economic arrangements in the world is one in which there are rich, donor countries and poor, recipient countries, and never the twain shall meet. The social justice approach to health rejects poverty as a fact of life and focuses attention on impoverishment as a process inherent to capitalist accumulation and the inevitable concentration of power and wealth.

The findings of the research projects on the political and social contexts of health (summarized in 48), referred to above, underline the importance of political cultures that support social cohesion and solidarity. The studies show that in order to improve the health of a population, it is far more effective to develop universal programs that reduce inequalities than to develop programs specifically targeted at reducing poverty (by focusing on means-tested programs for the poor). Specifically, countries and regions where economic resources (such as income and employment) and social resources (such as health care education and family supportive services) are better distributed have better health indicators. In other words, public policies that improve health and social well-being matter, but the politics determining those public policies also matter.

In the CMH vision of the world, there are no connections between the rich being rich and the poor being poor. And yet those connections are well documented. The factors that allowed today's rich countries to "develop" were cheap raw materials and cheap labor in the colonies; control over trade and technology; a strong state role; particularly in protecting national production and strictly controlling financial flows; and (for European countries) an outlet for excess population through emigration to North America. With the exception of the latter, these are still, today, the factors that allow the North to flourish, the South to wither, and the disparities to widen. And it is almost too obvious to point out that, unfortunately, poor countries will not benefit from any of these factors. If "they" are to escape from poverty, all of "us" will have to find other ways to "develop."

Sachs claims that "donor assistance will be required for a sustained period of time, perhaps 20 years, but will eventually phase out as countries achieve higher per capita incomes" (p. 12). How the time period of 20 years is calculated is not clear. Unless economic arrangements are fundamentally altered, it is difficult to understand how higher per capita incomes for all will be achieved. All nations cannot possibly benefit from unfair terms of trade. Stated simply, we cannot all pay peanuts for bananas, both of which are produced by people on starvation wages in poor countries for consumption by people in rich countries—with vast profits exported out of the producing countries by transnational corporations (50).

International aid is not designed to change the structure and dynamics of relations between North and South. On the contrary, it is fully integrated into the current international financial architecture in terms of its goals and values— and its architects. The pursuit of freedom for capital (rather than people) by leading Western and U.S. elites, bankers, fund managers, media magnates, captains of industry, political leaders, and military chieftains has included the aid system in its sweep. "Aid monies and most of their destinations may be of piffling importance alongside the big stakes in trade wars and military balances, but aid is the home and *raison d'être* for institutions of major significance for those elites" (51, p. 48).

The institutions of major significance to international aid are the World Bank and the IMF, largely controlled by the U.S. Treasury and the U.S. Federal Reserve (52, 53). The policies they promote—retreat of the state, privatization of national assets, deregulation (which in effect removes key areas of the economy from democratic control), and export-oriented production at the expense of national self sufficiency—would all appear to be incompatible with sustainable and emancipatory development.

Aid "is an instrument to project power beyond national borders, a tool of foreign policy" (51). Ideology and the pursuit of commercial advantage are the main determinants of aid (54). Today, aid is seen by many as "a means to hitch low income wagons to turbo-charged global markets." Given these motivations, it is not entirely surprising to learn that aid has some very negative effects on recipient countries, including actually making them poorer. Invitations to poor countries to integrate into the globalized economy today are about as attractive as invitations to integrate into colonialism. It rather depends on whether you are the colonial or the colonized, at the "center" or the "periphery" (55). Furthermore, it can be argued that many poor countries are already thoroughly "globalized," to their cost—as sources of bonded labor and raw materials for the rich countries, as they have been for centuries.

Aid, then, inevitably results in undue influence if not outright interference in public policy. The supposed beneficiaries (the people) are very rarely consulted, but then neither are their elected representatives. It does not appear to have occurred to the CMH that aid, like debt, undermines the democracy it is so keen to promote (as discussed in more depth below).

The question of who are the real donors and the real recipients, taking into account all international transfers of resources, material and financial, is covered later in this chapter. Suffice to say here that even in the case of foreign aid, the transfers are not in the expected or desired direction. About 65 percent of

Dutch aid in 1995 was spent in the Netherlands (or flowed back there); the figure for the United States was around 80 percent (51, p. 70).

The social justice approach to health rejects the assumption that international aid is the only way to finance health and proposes an alternative assumption: A fair and rational international economic order so that sovereign and solvent states may meet the needs of their people sustainably and without external interference. Such an assumption is respectful of human rights, national sovereignty, and democracy and offers a sustainable and equitable approach to health and development.

Models of Democracy and Respect for Human Rights?

The CMH commissioners appear to have absolute faith in democracy and respect for human rights—as practiced today in rich countries and preached to poor countries. Unstated assumptions about these "pillars of Western civilization" underlie most of the report's recommendations. Ironically, the report is prescribing to countries a very particular strategy (which will no doubt shortly be *imposed* on countries) in matters that are properly of national sovereignty—such as budget levels for health, or indeed choice of economic policy. But there is no indication that people will ever be consulted on this strategy, through parliament or any elected representatives. Neither is there any consideration of whether or not this strategy would meet with their approval or whether these policies might violate (or have already violated) their human rights, in particular their economic rights.

In fact, there are strong indications that the same coercion that was applied for implementation of Structural Adjustment Policies will be applied for Poverty Reduction Strategy Papers—through various conditionalities (56, 57). On page 10 of the CMH report, for example, there are ominous references to the need for countries to ensure "consistency with a sound macroeconomic policy framework," and on page 4 to "the chicken and egg problem of deciding whether reform or donor financing must come first." There is no need to specify which macroeconomic policy or which reform, as it is understood that these are "laissez-faire" market policies and reforms accompanied by deregulation, liberalization, and privatization. At least three questions beg to be answered:

- Can national or international democracy be enhanced through imposition of fiscal, monetary, and economic policy by a "donor" country on a "recipient" country?
- Can a "donor" nation consider itself democratic if it consistently undermines democracy in other countries?
- Is a meaningful debate on democracy even possible when wealth and power are so grotesquely concentrated in so few hands?

There is a crisis in democracy today, nationally and internationally, which goes far beyond the minor imperfections that have always been acknowledged and are occasionally addressed. The more imperfect our democracies become, the louder our leaders proclaim their attachment to its principles and the more loosely they use the term (58). Behind the scenes, many of them violate its most fundamental principles with increasing impunity. At the same time, all five of the indivisible human rights (political, civil, social, economic, and cultural) are grossly violated by the same forces that are undermining democracy (59, 60).

At best, the industrialized countries enjoy what has been described as "low intensity democracy" (61), consisting of participation at the ballot box, by a minority of the population—a substantial proportion of whom now vote blank as their last and only means of democratic protest (62). Their legitimate complaint is that no choice is on offer. As Chomsky (63) has said of the United States, and it is increasingly true of all the industrialized "democracies": there is one business party with two factions.

At the international level, gross interference in the democratic processes of developing countries by the powerful nations, in particular the United States, is well documented (59, 64). Suffice to say that almost every legitimate people's movement for democracy in developing countries has been crushed, with violence that ranges from sudden, extreme, and overt to slow, long drawn-out, and covert. It would take the International Criminal Court in the Hague several centuries to investigate crimes against humanity and war crimes perpetrated by the West in dozens of countries since World War II in the name of "democracy" and "freedom" (65). As Arundhati Roy (66) points out, "every kind of outrage is being committed in the name of democracy. . . . Free elections, a free press and an independent judiciary mean little when the free market has reduced them to commodities available on sale to the highest bidder."

The international institutions have played their part in the current crisis— and not just the World Bank, IMF, and WTO. The United Nations, with the power of veto of five permanent members of the Security Council, makes a mockery of its very title (67). Reform of the United Nations, which has wide support, even from its fiercest critics (who are also the fiercest defenders of its original mandate), will have to confront "the very nature of the United Nations . . . as well as the primary raison d'être of its founders, [which] had far more to do with maintaining the power of the World War II victors than with extending democracy, whether political or economic, across the globe" (68).

The Special Rapporteur to the Commission on Human Rights on the Right to Food, Jean Ziegler (44), urges states to confront the profound internal contradictions in the U.N. system: "On the one hand, the U.N. agencies emphasize social justice and human rights. . . . On the other hand, the Bretton Woods institutions along with the government of the United States of America and the WTO oppose in their practice the right to food by means of the Washington Consensus, emphasizing liberalization, deregulation, privatization and the compression of

States' budgets—a model which in many cases produces greater inequalities." The United Nations has only fourth-rate status behind the Bank, IMF, and WTO. However, under its auspices, socially progressive charters, declarations, and conventions and the essentials of international law are developed and formalized, and it therefore remains an important focus for advocacy and action.

For a full appreciation of the dimensions of the crisis in democracy and a consideration of the alternatives, the reader is referred to Aksu and Camilleri (69). In relation to health and sustainable development, four further aspects of the crisis deserve mention: the WTO, the transnational corporations, international aid, and—a key element among the checks and balances of democracy—an independent media.

The *World Trade Organization* regards itself, with a lot of truth but with no sense of irony, as a de facto world government. As one director-general stated, "We are writing the constitution of a single global economy" (70). People are unaware that many (shortly it will be most) aspects of their lives are determined by negotiations at the WTO in trade, agriculture, public services, investment, and intellectual property rights. Levels of secrecy are such that even ministries of health and education are often unaware of what has already been negotiated "for them" (71). The actual operations of this organization are profoundly undemocratic, as an important recent study has shown (72).

The colossal economic power of *transnational corporations* (TNCs) is perhaps the most serious threat to democracy today. The turnover of the 200 largest TNCs is equivalent to the combined incomes of four-fifths of humanity. In the international economy, Ford is roughly equivalent to Norway; Mitsui is worth slightly more than Saudi Arabia (73). TNCs are private, globalized bureaucracies that transcend all democratic control and, at the same time, exercise decision-making power over entire populations (37, 74). TNCs are fully represented in IFIs, government finance ministries, and central banks and exert enormous influence over their policies. There is no international legal or political framework to regulate their supranational activities (75). As resistance to corporate rule increases, TNCs make ever greater efforts to legitimize their activities and their power. Some of these efforts, such as the creation of charitable foundations or public-private partnerships, including notably the Global Compact with the United Nations (76), may represent even greater threats to democracy, as they disguise the true nature of the interaction and allow TNCs even greater illegitimate influence in public policymaking (77).

The proclaimed goals of *international aid* today are the promotion of good governance and democracy within countries themselves. However, for quite obvious reasons (and as discussed above), aid undermines efforts to achieve these goals (78). Leaders of recipient countries become accountable to powerful outsiders, including donors and lenders, rather than to their own people. Worse still, evidence shows that the greater a country's dependence on aid, the worse the quality of its public institutions (79). The fundamentally anti-democratic nature of aid conditionalities has long been recognized (80), but few are aware of the extent of this interference. "The IMF and [World Bank] have occasionally conditioned their loans on parliamentary enactment of specific laws. They might as well use recipients' constitutions to wipe their boots" (51, p. 130). Just as striking in this regard is that major aid recipients have traditionally been those with the worst human rights records (81). Barya states, "Freedom and liberation from autocratic rule, as well as democracy and accountability cannot be decreed. They must have a social basis in which they arise, are nurtured and sustained" (82). There is evidence that donor countries have vigorously discouraged the "social basis" for democracy through interference of various kinds, including aid (83), precisely because people's democracy in poor countries would spell the end of client regimes installed to serve powerful nations' economic interests.

Freedom of information is fundamental to democracy. Yet, a handful of corporations dominates the world's media and communications (84). In 1982, 50 firms dominated the media and communications market; by 2001 there were fewer than 10 (85). Furthermore, the media promote the ideology and propaganda of Western power (86). They also promote consumer capitalism. As Pilger (87) points out, advertising crowds out serious news, and public relations substitutes for real journalism: "One of the most pervasive myths is that we live in an information age. We actually live in a media age in which most of the available information is repetitive, politically safe, and is limited by invisible boundaries." The problem is no longer simply that private corporations exert undue influence on the media. They are the media. Concentration of ownership and cross-alliances in telecommunications, media, computer software and beyond justify use of the term "totalitarian" (88). Vivendi, for example, best known as the colossus of the privatized water industry, merged with media company Seagram in 2000 as Europe's answer to the United States' AOL Time Warner (89). Finally, far from increasing the exchange of information between nations, the globalizing media empire shrinks international coverage and, through enforced privatization followed by takeovers, floods the South with cheap Western products and values. In 1980, when ÚNESCO called for a new world information order and the creation of independent international news agency, the United States and United Kingdom called it an attack on free speech and pulled out (90).

Monopoly over media and communications is just one of several monopolies, the others being those that control the planet's natural resources, technology, worldwide financial markets, and weapons of mass destruction (91). Together, these close the loop and make independent, democratic action by individuals or states near impossible. "Plutocracy" far better describes the system we have created than does "democracy." Money rules in a world in which everything is a commodity, the value of which is measured by cost and consumption.

The assumption that the powerful nations responsible for today's world order are models of democracy and respect for human rights must be recognized for what it is: pure propaganda. The alternative assumption, one that will allow real progress, recognizes that democracy is in crisis everywhere and that self-determination of nation states and a rules-based, international system of governance are urgently required.

CENTRAL THESIS AND KEY RECOMMENDATION

To summarize the chapter thus far, the central thesis of the CMH report is that "improvements in health translate into higher incomes, higher economic growth and reduced population growth." The main recommendation is "to scale up access of the world's poor to essential health services, including a focus on specific interventions." The plan is predicated on "donor financing [which] creates the financial reality for a greatly scaled up, more effective health system" (pp. 3–4). The four underlying assumptions of the CMH report are as follows: economic growth is the aim; health is achieved through interventions delivered through health services; international aid, with conditionalities to enforce certain policies, is the only way to finance health; and democracy is alive and well in the developed world and is the model for the developing world. My proposed alternative assumptions are: fair distribution and sustainable use of resources is the aim; health is what you get from meeting basic needs; sovereign and solvent states must provide for their people's basic needs without outside interference; democracy is in crisis everywhere; and self-determination of nation states and a rules-based system of international governance are urgently required.

WHAT IS POSITIVE AND ORIGINAL IN THE CMH REPORT?

A number of statements and recommendations in the report are welcome and are genuinely positive in the sense that they unambiguously support principles underlying Health for All. These include statements on the following:

- Universal coverage for priority interventions (p. 6)
- Guarantees by the state for financing of services (p. 7)
- Significant scaling up of financing for global research and development (R&D) on the heavy disease burden of the poor (p. 8)
- The fact that "it is no accident that millions of people die unnecessarily each year" (p. 13).
- The fact that "user fees end up excluding the poor from essential health services while at the same time recovering only a tiny fraction of the costs" (p. 61).

Taken alone, these are useful advocacy statements, and indeed, if the key message transmitted by the Sachs report is that medical care is affordable and that funds can be found, that is of value—though not new. Development charities and activists for social justice have made it widely known for decades that only a minute proportion of resources devoted to military spending or speculative activities would be required to meet the basic needs of the world's population for health services and indeed for food, clean water, education, and social services. However, this is a very small part of the key advocacy statements that need to be transmitted in relation to macroeconomics and health. As discussed earlier, health interventions are but one small factor determining population health status, and reliance on donor funds is highly restrictive and of dubious value— if the aim is long-term, significant, and reliable improvements.

Among the ten "findings" resulting from the CMH's two years of work, it is hard to find a single piece of information that could be described as original— let alone as "bold or inspired," in the words of the chairman himself. Readers will judge the originality of the set of ten findings (pp. 16–17) for themselves. Did the international health community not know until the end of 2001 that "a few health conditions are responsible for a high proportion of the health deficits," or that "the HIV/AIDS pandemic is an unparalleled catastrophe," or that "the level of health spending in poor countries is insufficient to address the health challenges they face"?

WISHFUL THINKING, IDEOLOGY, AND UNTRUTHS

The stated aim of the CMH report is to legitimize globalization (p. 29). This has the merit of being transparent. Unfortunately, most explicitly political positions promoted in the report are presented as neutral and established facts. Only a fine line divides wishful thinking from ideology and ideology from untruth, as the following examples show. At the very least, Sachs and his commissioners should have acknowledged that alternative positions exist. In the interests of fairness and objectivity, these positions should have been presented.

There are dozens of examples of ideology disguised as fact in the CMH report, but just three are briefly discussed here: pharmaceutical research and development in relation to access to medicines; trade in services, including health services; and the heavily indebted poor country (HIPC) initiative.

Pharmaceutical R&D and Access to Essential Medicines

Finding number ten states, "Coordinated actions by the pharmaceutical industry, governments of low income countries, donors and international agencies are needed to ensure that the world's low income countries have reliable access to essential medicines" (p. 17). Sachs and others may wish to believe that all these actors are devoted to universal access to medicines, but even a superficial glance at the literature would have revealed quite another perspective—and one that surely deserves mention.

The critical role of nongovernmental organizations (NGOs) and political activists in increasing access to medicines is omitted from Sachs's statement, as is the fact that pharmaceutical industries in particular, some international institutions (the WTO), and some governments (the Quad: United States, Canada, European Union, and Japan) have actively promoted policies and legislation that decrease access (92)—not because they wish poor people to be deprived of medicines but because the pursuit of profit is the raison d'être of the powers directing them, and the pursuit of profit is rarely compatible with the pursuit of universal access or any other manifestation of equity.

Sachs reproduces the pharmaceutical industry's own justification of its outsize profit margins (more than 18 percent, compared with around 7 percent on average in other industries; pharmaceutical executive quoted in 93) in terms of its R&D needs. Yet, this myth was debunked between 15 and 20 years ago (94). The proportion of profits devoted to R&D is far lower than that devoted to marketing of pharmaceutical products—11 percent versus 27 percent (95). Furthermore, the amount devoted to basic research (the R part) is much lower than the amount devoted to development (the D part), which itself has always had far more to do with marketing than with research (96). This is because the majority of "new" products are in fact close copies of competitors' best sellers—just one molecule apart, in order to obtain patent protection.

Rarely mentioned either is the fact that much basic research is publicly funded, with the pharmaceutical industry leaping onto the bandwagon to develop the drug (or rather its market niche) when success looks likely. Most AIDS drugs, for example, were produced through public financing (even through clinical trial stages), and 85 percent of the basic and applied research for the five top-selling drugs on the market was produced through taxpayer funding (97, 98). So much for the corporate contribution to bold, "leap-in-the-dark" scientific endeavor.

Sachs is equally uncritical of current arrangements for pharmaceutical product development. He laments the near total failure to develop drugs for diseases of the poor, but fails to make the connection between this spectacular inefficiency and the fact that the research agenda is largely determined by multinational corporations, which have a legal obligation to make a profit for shareholders. The notion that greater efficiency might be achieved if R&D for essential drugs were to be placed in the public domain, in order to respond to people's needs, is not considered. It should be noted that the Global Health Research Fund, as currently constituted and organized, is *not* what is required for publicly funded and directed research for the diseases of poverty. It is highly likely to encounter the same funding problems as the Global Fund and to be donor driven and or unduly influenced by its "benefactors" and corporate interests.

Trade in Services

Trade in services also receives uncritical mention, as if this were an entirely uncontroversial development arising out of democratic debate. On the contrary, the General Agreement on Trade in Services (GATS) may represent the most serious threat to welfare provision over the past 50 years (99), and like many WTO operations, it is being negotiated mostly behind closed doors (72). Knowledge about, and therefore opposition to, GATS is negligible—even among public sector workers—though its implications are huge (for detailed reviews, see 100, 101)

Trade in services requires first that services be privatized. Conveniently, the ground has been prepared in developing countries through making their deregulation and privatization an SAP (structural adjustment program) conditionality (102). Trade in services will disproportionately benefit the European Union and the United States. As the U.S. Coalition of Service Industries states, "Any increase in consumption of services anywhere in the world effectively means an increase in consumption of U.S. services" (103).

Private provision of services to meet basic needs—whether these be for health, education, water, energy, or transport—invariably results in escalating costs and inequitable access. "Virtually every credible study ever done has shown that private, for profit health care is more expensive, less efficient and of lower quality than public health care" (104). As Sen (105) reports, "In the USA, administrative costs are high, choices are limited and quality is not assured since health need is determined by cost and profit margins for shareholders. In Cuba on the other hand, the per capita costs are much lower and although the choices for the type of care available are limited, the system delivers universal coverage with among the best health indicators in the world." Cuba achieves this with one-sixth the GDP of the United States (19) and with a particularly strict, cruel (and illegal) embargo, but the macroeconomic miracle that this represents receives no mention in the CMH report.

"A market based approach to health not only drives up the costs of health care but it can also lead to disinterest in the factors that make people ill. A consumer society promises—falsely—that medical technology can fix diseased individuals, and that good health can be bought and sold in the marketplace rather than being something to promote or work for" (G. Rayner, quoted in 106). In short, private provision of health services sacrifices the public health goals of prevention of disease and promotion of health.

Heavily Indebted Poor Countries Initiative

There is no indication whatsoever in the CMH report that the HIPC initiative has failed. The myth that developing-country debt is at last being fairly and constructively addressed is reproduced here. This is a serious omission, because debt is the only macroeconomic factor of significance that is mentioned in the report. Between 1996 (when the HIPC initiative started) and 1999, debt service in the HIPC countries increased by 25 percent, according to World Bank figures (107). It should be noted also that the HIPC initiative concerns only 9 percent of third world debt. Twenty of the most heavily indebted countries are excluded from the initiative. The combined debt of the 22 HIPC countries that were accepted by the initiative will be reduced from U.S.$53 billion to $20 billion (108).

The explicit purpose of the initiative is to make, the debt *sustainable.* In the opinion of a member of the Paris Club, it is "to protect the financial integrity of the International Financial Institutions [IFIs]" (107, p. 41). For many analysts, it is clearly an instrument to keep up pressure on countries to adopt neoliberal reforms that are favorable to the interests of their "creditors." People's Tribunals and World Social Forums insist on immediate cancellation followed by reparation, and they bring ample evidence to support this position (109, 110).

JUSTIFYING THE REVERSAL OF LOGIC

As mentioned earlier in the chapter, there is a curious reversal of logic in recent literature on health and economic development, in which it is asserted that attention to a few diseases will create prosperity. As this is the raison d'être and the central thesis of the CMH report, it is important to examine the arguments presented to justify the assertion. Let us start, though, with some commonsense observations:

- Individuals and families in poor communities, even when they are healthy, are not rich and are not going to become rich.
- Their poverty is very likely to make them ill repeatedly. And the chances are quite high that it will kill them prematurely.
- When people are in good health (and under miserable living conditions this is usually a temporary situation), they are able to make the best of their immediate environment—however unfavorable—which has, of course, a real value.

In short, health might *rhyme* with wealth but unfortunately, *it is not wealth.* Once again, this reasoning may sound obvious, but it needs stating because the CMH report, despite its title, ignores all the major macroeconomic factors that determine poverty and "underdevelopment." Quotation marks are used because in the logic of globalized capitalism, the poor countries have been developed precisely as intended, as cheap sources of primary materials and labor for the rich countries. In our environment-conscious age, the materials are now frequently returned for disposal to their original owners in the form of toxic waste products.

With the exception of debt relief—which is dealt with in one sentence as something that should be "deepened"—the report fails to mention a single element of significance to the international economic order (such as those discussed in the next section of this chapter). These are the root causes of miserable living conditions in poor countries, and unless they are tackled, their people will struggle as best they can through bouts of frequent avoidable illness, sometimes ending in premature death.

The CMH report makes a quite unjustified extrapolation from the level of the individual and household to the level of the national economy: "As with the economic well being of individual households, good population health is a critical input into poverty reduction, economic growth and long term economic development at the scale of whole societies" (p. 21).

Individuals and families may be thrown into destitution by illness in many countries, including the United States; this does not happen, of course, in countries where health care is socialized. As already discussed at length, the state of countries' economies is determined by macroeconomic factors of the larger international financial architecture, operating way beyond the arena of people's health. In difficult circumstances, health permits survival and, conversely, an episode of illness may tip already deprived people into destitution, but neither health nor illness make countries rich or poor, respectively.

On closer inspection, the examples cited to back up Sachs's health-to-wealth argument appear to support the opposite thesis. For example, malaria was controlled in southern Europe (p. 39) as it was in the United States—prior to the introduction of DDT—through "environmental cleansing," public health engineering in water management to canalize rivers and remove the breeding grounds for mosquitoes (111). Europeans would not have been satisfied with bednets, drugs, and insecticides at that juncture. By that time, European citizens benefited from sovereign and solvent states and a degree of democracy allowing them to insist on substantial state intervention for the greater good of all. This, of course, is what citizens of the developing countries still lack and continue to be denied, not least by the international economic and political order.

Sachs's explanation of "Africa's chronic poor performance" (p. 24) compared with the high growth countries of East Asia is at odds with that of other experts—Stiglitz (112), for example—who attribute the "miracle" to the fact that these countries stubbornly ignored all IFI prescriptions and instead implemented policies very similar to those used by today's rich countries to establish a productive base to their economy: a strong state role, particularly in provision of public services and protection of national production and control over financial flows. A careful reading of international history and politics reveals Africa's *outstanding performance* in merely surviving the onslaught of centuries of brutal oppression and exploitation.

The CMH report would have us believe that the recommended health interventions will "jump start" the economies of poor countries and that in 20 years time, they will all have achieved development. This is equivalent to refilling a bucket that has holes in it rather than repairing the holes or buying a new bucket. The report offers no sustainable solutions to health problems. It assumes that each time a person falls ill, she or he will get the appropriate drugs. Public works that require infrastructural investment by the state are not mentioned. Yet these are the only public health interventions that reliably and sustainably improve population health status and are designed to eradicate problems once and for all.

These are the investments that must be costed and presented to policymakers. Can poor countries afford to refill buckets for 20 years when they could repair the bucket or buy a new one for a fraction of the cost and for incomparably more significant and long-term benefits?

THE DISPROPORTION: MILLIONS THROUGH CHARITY, OR BILLIONS AND TRILLIONS THROUGH A FAIR INTERNATIONAL ORDER?

Sachs states, "It is important to put the total donor assistance into perspective" (p. 12). This is indeed a critical analytical step. Unfortunately however, Sachs's perspective does not extend beyond donor assistance—it merely compares *current* to *required* levels.

The perspective that is lacking relates to the billions and even trillions that would be released (for health and other projects) through a set of simple macroeconomic measures, or conversely, relates to the amounts that are lost to poor countries daily through a range of international transfers. The latter include debt, unfair terms of trade and Northern protectionism, tax havens and capital flight, free trade zones, SAPs and PRSPs (poverty reduction strategy papers), foreign direct investment, intellectual property and TRIPS, the brain drain, and finally—aid itself. There is a wealth of literature on each of these subjects, and readers are referred to key texts on each: on debt (110); on structural adjustment (113); on tax havens and banking secrecy (114); on foreign direct investment (115); on financial flows (35); and on trade (50).

There is a striking disproportion between the sums that could reasonably be raised through international aid—usually not exceeding millions—and the sums that would be released through simple macroeconomic measures—billions and trillions. The baseline for assessing the disproportion is the CMH's figure of U.S.$27 billion required per year in the form of donor contributions and $38 billion by 2015 to avert 8 million deaths per year by the end of 2010, with economic gains of $360 billion per year during the period 2015 to 2020.

Debt

Among the different mechanisms of South-North transfers of wealth, debt has received by far the most attention. *Illegal, immoral, irresponsible,* and *impossible* are terms that are increasingly understood by the general public in relation to third world debt—thanks to awareness-raising by groups such as Jubilee 2000, CADTM (Comité pour l'Annulation de la Dette du Tiers Monde), and ATTAC (Action pour un Taxe Tobin pour Assister le Citoyen). A few facts are in order before looking at estimates of the losses incurred by developing countries.

First, third world debt—U.S.$2,500 billion in 2001—represents a tiny proportion of total world debt, the largest being that of the United States—$22,000 billion (109). Debt cancellation is not without precedent and is entirely feasible. Interestingly, the major bankruptcies of the capitalist world have been absorbed by the state—in other words paid for by the people. Debt is a key structural arrangement in the international financial architecture and, as made explicit by the HIPC initiative, the aim is to make it *sustainable,* not to cancel it (107). The political and economic leverage that it provides to the North makes it far too valuable for cancellation.

Furthermore, the size of the debt owed by the North to the South over centuries of pillage, often achieved through violent oppression, is calculable but unpayable—at least in its entirety (see the letter from Aztec chief Guaipuro Cuauhtémoc (116) to European governments on the 185 thousand kilos of gold and 16 million kilos of silver "borrowed" by Europeans between 1503 and 1660—a sort of original Marshall Plan for European development—the capital and interest of which has still not been paid back). Imperative, as the first step in reparation, is the removal, at long last, of the obstacles to development that the North continues to impose on the South.

In 2001, development aid stood at U.S.$51 billion (109), but the indebted countries paid out $382 billion in debt repayment. This is $22 billion more than Sachs's estimates of the gains per year by 2015—$360 billion (see above). Between 1980 and 2000, debt has cost these countries $4,500 billion, six times the level of the debt in 1980. The debt/export ratio is extremely high—164 percent (107). In some African countries, debt repayments are four times the amounts spent on health and education together. For every dollar received in aid, three go back to rich countries to service the debt. Debt, which can be seen as bonded labor at the level of nations, is itself a major impediment to development.

Trade

Trade has never been free or fair, but it has served the powerful nations as a weapon of control, oppression, and exploitation for centuries and continues to do so (117). The losses incurred through unfair terms of trade have been devastating, as Davis (118) shows in his account of the famines in India, China, and Africa in the last quarter of the nineteenth century. They have their parallels today as millions of poor farmers are ruined and driven off the land by neoliberal policies (119) and tens of thousands go hungry every day in countries that were self-sufficient in food in the 1960s (45).

The world's poorest economies are forced to export more and more basic primary commodities, resulting predictably in a glutted market, a fall in the cash value of their exports, and decreased incomes for the poor. The rewards of liberalizing world trade are grotesquely skewed toward the rich. The U.N. Secretary General's predictions (120) that the high-income countries stood to gain U.S.$141.8 billion while Africa stood to lose $2.6 billion are being confirmed.

The U.N. Conference on Trade and Development (121) has calculated that barriers to exports from developing countries by the rich countries cost U.S.$700 billion in lost export earnings, and in its 2002 report (122) shows that market distortions and northern protectionism keep one billion people in poverty.

Tax Havens and Capital Flight

Currency speculators gamble U.S.$1.5 trillion daily. ATTAC, which is now an international movement, proposes taxing these activities. At 0.25 percent this would earn $250 billion a year—enough to provide food, basic health care, and education to all the developing world. Experts have said there would be no particular difficulty in introducing this tax (123).

The losses to poor countries—and to poor people in the rich countries—through tax-free offshore accounts (OFCs) are colossal but have received less attention than other international transfers. These "tax havens" play an essential and rapidly growing role in international finance (and international crime). It is estimated that half of all international capital flows pass through or reside in tax havens, including between U.S.$360 and $500 billion in illicit funds per year, compared with $85 billion ten years ago (124). They impose severe constraints on the developing countries by channelling out capital through dubious means. According to conservative estimates, about 30 percent of third world debt has found its way into OFCs (125). Because they significantly undermine the tax base of countries, and therefore states' capacities to provide public services, these losses disproportionately affect the poor. The IMF estimated that if a 40 percent tax were to be paid on earned income (about 5 percent per year) from offshore accounts that contain around U.S.$8 trillion, $160 billion annually would be raised—almost double what it would take for all countries to guarantee basic social services (25).

Free Trade Zones

Free trade zones are an investor's paradise, but their effects on the people in the zones are less than positive and include collapse of small and medium-sized enterprises, progressive elimination of small farmers, loss of food sovereignty, ecological disaster, cultural aggression, and overall increases in poverty (126).

Foreign Direct Investment

Foreign direct investment (FDI) has been heralded as the key benefit that globalization now offers the South and the principal mechanism to jump start economies into rapid growth. FDI and equity investment increased by 440 percent between 1990 and 1996. Woodward (115) points to the ominous similarities of these trends to the buildup of the debt crisis, and argues that they may herald the next crisis. They imply a transfer of ownership of the capital base and productive potential of developing countries to entities outside their borders, with all that this implies for sustainable development and loss of government control over the economy. The rates of return on these investments are astronomically high, particularly for investments in very poor countries. Once again, the winners are the transnational corporations and their shareholders.

Foreign Aid

Finally, as discussed above, foreign aid clearly serves donor interests, both commercial and political, and, with conditionalities, it increases the stranglehold of powerful institutions and interests, all of which, as we have seen, contribute to the net transfer of resources from South to North. The latest players in the aid industry are the charitable foundations of multibillionaires, their spouses, and their companies. The major outcome of their ventures into celebrity philanthropy is illegitimate influence in public policymaking and the furtherance of corporate interests—including their own (127, 128). Furthermore, a long-term and coherent solution to the problems of poverty and inequality will require reasonable remuneration of our "captains of industry" and proper enforcement of progressive taxation, enabling them at last to contribute fairly to society as citizens of the world—albeit through rather conventional channels.

AN INTELLECTUAL AND ETHICAL DARK AGE

The CMH report occasionally diverges from its grim calculations of cost effectiveness and urges the international community to "dream a bit, not beyond the feasible, but to the limits of the feasible" (see frontispiece of the main report). It makes clear that a number of ethical principles that are fundamental to a social justice approach to health—and about which presumably we might dream—need to be made palatable and "user friendly" for the world's decisionmakers. Principles such as equality, justice, or peace—in addition to being a serious threat to the rich and powerful—are inconvenient to the technocrats, because they do not lend themselves to measurement, interpretation, or manipulation.

Ethical principles have the unfortunate characteristic of being absolute. They cannot be diminished, modified, or disproved with formulas, models, or diagrams, so cherished by mainstream economists. Keen (129) has shown that most of these assumptions are flawed. He presents a wealth of evidence showing that economic theory is internally contradictory. As he says, "Economic reality cannot be shoehorned into diagrams."

There is confusion between ends and means, and between values and strategies, throughout the CMH report. Growth, market economies, competition, decentralization, cost containment, foreign investment—even public-private partnerships—are all presented unquestioningly as desirable *ends*. But all of these are *means* to an end—which itself is not made explicit. Likewise, the term *efficiency* is bandied about without any recognition that it can be assessed only when one is clear about the end that is to be achieved.

Sachs's attempts to make principles more attractive to investors are typical of this confusion. The most obvious example is the lame rationalization that investments to improve the health of the poor will have "spillovers to wealthier members of the society" (p. 16). In the latest "trickle" variant, then, wealth goes up toward the rich. When inducements to the rich and powerful are piggybacked onto declarations of principle, much of the moral resonance of these principles is lost.

According to Sachs, "the MDGs [Millennium Development Goals] are partly an expression of humanitarian concern, but they are also an investment in the well being of the rich countries as well as the poor. The evidence is stark: disease breeds instability in poor countries which rebounds on the rich countries as well" (p. 28). This statement raises two ethical problems. First, if the MDGs turn out to be a very poor investment, as is most likely, should they be abandoned? As ethical imperatives, which might even involve redistribution of resources ("sharing," in the vernacular), the MDGs would appear to be unpromising as an investment. Second, is Sachs suggesting that instability in poor countries is due to disease?

This brings us to quite the most outrageous statement in the report. Sachs cites (p. 28) a curious study undertaken by the CIA (130) of "state failure over the period 1960–1994" showing that infant mortality is "a predictor of state collapse (through coups, civil war and other unconstitutional changes in regime). *The United States ended up intervening militarily in many of those crises*" (emphasis added). Not only did the United States *end up* intervening militarily in these crises, but it *started out* intervening militarily (and in other ways). Furthermore, in an astonishing number of countries, it directed, financed, and often participated in the "coups, civil wars and other unconstitutional changes in regime" (64). Neither the welfare of populations nor the promotion of democracy appear to have been the goal of these interventions. Certainly they were not the result. These ill-advised incursions into the field of ethics reveal at best a limited grasp of international affairs, but at worst, inexcusable ignorance and imperial arrogance.

ASKING THE RIGHT QUESTIONS

If evidence is required—and as stated earlier, much already exists—the kinds of questions that need to be asked will provide answers in the form of estimates of the costs and benefits of creating the basic conditions for good population health. They will allow comparison with the CMH recommendations, not just in terms of costs and benefits but in terms of sustainability of the improvements—as "once-and-for-all solutions."

Countries may decide to undertake no further research but rather to be guided by existing knowledge. Estimates of the amounts required to provide basic education and social and health services, including public works to protect and promote public health, are available, for example, through campaigns such as Jubilee 2000, or social justice NGOs such as Oxfam or the World Development Movement. They have been quoted for decades, for example, in the form of proportions of national and international military expenditure, amounts that would be released through fair trade, a Tobin-type tax on speculative activities, or even as a proportion of the amounts spent on pet food or cosmetic surgery in the rich countries. It is unlikely that countries without these basic amenities will obtain funding for public works of this kind from the donor community, unless they involve substantial returns to the donors' transnational corporations. At that point, critical decisions will have to be made about delinking from this infernal cycle of dependence, exploitation, and deepening poverty and inequality.

Regional alliances and the promotion of maximum local and national self-sufficiency offer possible escape routes and the first steps toward building capacity to meet basic needs. Certainly, poor countries will need to act together to stand any chance against monolithic international structures and arrangements, possibly in concert with social justice and environmental movements in the North to work together to revive the New International Economic Order, which was more or less murdered in its infancy (131). In the postwar years, the anticolonial stance of the least developed countries and growing demands for equality in an unequal world came into direct conflict with western interests and perceptions (132).

Another world is possible. Various strategies have been proposed for escaping from this particular axis of evil—if the colossal greed, extreme violence, and tyranny of today's world regime can be described this way. They are reflected in the literature on alternative "development" paths (10, 11, 133–135).

WHY THE CMH REPORT?

So, why this report? The most obvious answer to this question is, "To maintain at all costs the status quo." In a preliminary comment on the CMH report, Legge (136) suggests that it "may prove to be as significant as the 1993 World Bank Report, *Investing in Health,* providing a 'credible' policy narrative proclaiming concern about the health of the poor while reconciling health development objectives with the continuing operation of a brutal and unfair global economic regime."

As the subtitle of this chapter suggests, the CMH action agenda is a simple recommendation to increase the size of the crumbs from the rich man's table. In this way, it performs at least three functions. The first is to avoid any discussion of structural factors that determine poverty and inequality and, in turn, disease and death. Such discussion is deeply threatening to the existing order. The second may be to provide modest relief to the poor (or at least to be *seen* to be doing so), not in any significant way, of course, but to "defuse" the situation. Sachs is correct in identifying misery as destabilizing (he is quite wrong about its origin); the agony of the poor is indeed a tinder box, just waiting for a spark. If the CMH dampens that spark, it will not have served the cause of global social justice, though it may delay its achievement. The third purpose, which is less significant, may be to provide relief to bad consciences. Global health policy experts often have only a vague understanding of the international financial architecture. For example, many disapprove mildly of the seeming brutality of SAPs, without understanding that these follow logically from the fact that the IMF and World Bank are directed by the U.S. Federal Reserve and Treasury (52, 70).

SAPs and PRSPs, for example, are not misguided; on the contrary, they are finely tuned and perfectly targeted to achieve a specific result (70). However, most of those who implement these policies, lower down the rungs in the international health community, imagine that improving the health of the poor is the eventual aim of policies they implement on the orders of the IFIs. It is often *genuinely* their own aim. However, it is arguable that the experts—including Sachs and including international civil servants implementing policy lower down the ranks—have, through their espousal and promotion of a "bad" system, inflicted great suffering on large numbers of their fellow human beings. For some of these, blind faith was the driving force; for others, blind self-interest. Whichever it was, it is the duty of those who claim to have the people's interest at heart to embrace alternative thinking in humble recognition of the imperfections of their terrifying machine.

The world's people deserve a counterweight to the CMH in the form of a Poverty and Health Commission to examine the relationship in its entirety, as recommended by the People's Health Movement (137) in its submission *Realization of the Right to Health* to the Commission on Human Rights.

PLAYING GOD

The most telling statement in the whole CMH report appears in the foreword, signed by Sachs and his 17 commissioners. It reads, "With bold decisions in 2002, the world could initiate a partnership of rich and poor of unrivaled significance, *offering the gift of life itself* to millions of the world's dispossessed and proving to all doubters that globalization can indeed work to the benefit of all humankind" (emphasis added).

Clearly, the era of hidden agendas is over. The purpose of the CMH report is explicitly to promote and legitimize corporate-led globalization of capitalism. Alternative perspectives are not contemplated. Evidence that this globalization works to the benefit of humankind is rare, perhaps nonexistent. Evidence that it deepens poverty and inequality abounds. But neither of these facts is of interest. The apolitical and ahistorical discipline of economics today requires only blind faith.

Furthermore, it is not "the world" that will "initiate" or "offer" anything; it is the rich and powerful, speaking through the voice of Sachs. Only those with an interest in maintaining the status quo could possibly *wish* for a partnership between rich and poor. This is akin to advocating for a partnership between slave owner and slave. As today's abolitionists know, rich and poor are not divinely ordained categories. The struggle for health is a struggle for the abolition of these stark categories—a struggle against the mechanisms and structures of impoverishment and deepening inequality. This must not be dismissed as utopian. The world was firmly on the path to a fairer international economic order during the welfare decades, when the rich and powerful took fright and rapidly backtracked into neoliberal fundamentalism (138).

Lastly, leaving aside the shameless and extraordinary delusions of grandeur, the fact that a group of U.S.-trained, Chicago-school economists feel that they are in a position to offer "the gift of life" to deprived populations on earth is disturbing in itself. That disproportionate and inappropriately allocated power is the very problem to be addressed.

REFERENCES

1. World Health Organization. *Macroeconomics and Health: Investing in Health for Economic Development.* WHO, Geneva, December 2001.
2. Sachs, J. Letter to readers from the Chair of the Commission on Macroeconomics and Health. Geneva, December 20, 2001.
3. Feachem, R. G. A. Commission on Macroeconomics and Health (editorial). *Bull. World Health Organ.* 80(2):87, 2002.
4. World Health Organization. *Health, a Key to Prosperity: Success Stories in Developing Countries.* WHO/CDS/2000.4. Geneva, 2000.
5. Banerji, D. Report of the WHO Commission on Macroeconomics and Health: A critique. *Int. J. Health Serv.* 32(4):733–754, 2002.
6. Morrow, R. H. Macroeconomics and health. *BMJ* 325:53–54, 2002.
7. Rosen, G. *A History of Public Health,* exp. ed. Johns Hopkins University Press, Baltimore, 1993.
8. McKeown, T. *The Role of Medicine.* Blackwell, Oxford, 1979.
9. McChesney, R. Global media, neoliberalism and imperialism. *Int. Socialist Rev.* August/September 2001.
10. Madaley, J. *A People's World: Alternatives to Economic Globalization.* Zed Books, London, 2003.
11. Centre Tricontinentale. *A la Recherche d'Alternatives—un Autre Monde est Possible.* Alternatives Sud, Vol. VIII(2). L'Harmattan, Paris, 2001.
12. Todaro, M. P. *Economic Development.* Addison-Wesley, Reading, MA, 1997.
13. Berkman, L., and Kawachi, I. (eds.). *Social Epidemiology.* Oxford University Press, Oxford, 2000.
14. Pannenborg, O. An economic and financial look at health in low and middle-income countries. In *Health Matters: Public Health in North-South Perspective,* ed. K. Van der Velden et al., pp. 43–62. Health Policy Series, Part 9. Royal Tropical Institute, Amsterdam, 1995.
15. Wackernagel, M., Monfreda, C., and Deumling, D. *Ecological Footprint of Nations: How Much Nature Do They Use? How Much Nature Do They Have?* Sustainability Issue Brief. Redefining Progress, Oakland, CA, November 2002.

16. World Health Organization. *Our Planet, Our Earth: Report of the WHO Commission on Health and Environment.* Geneva, 1992.
17. Eatwell, J. *International Financial Liberation: The Impact on World Development.* United Nations Development Program, New York, 1996.
18. Bello, W. The crisis of the globalist project and the new economics of George Bush. *New Labor Forum,* Fall 2003.
19. United Nations Development Program. *Human Development Report, 2003.* New York, 2003.
20. Weisbrot, M., et al. *The Scorecard on Globalization 1980–2000: Twenty Years of Diminished Progress.* Center for Economic and Policy Research, Washington, DC, 2001.
21. Cornia, G. A., and Courat, J. *Inequality, Growth and Poverty in the Era of Liberalization and Globalization.* United Nations University, World Institute for Development Economic Research, Helsinki, 2001.
22. United Nations Development Program. *Human Development Report 1998.* New York, 1998.
23. Houtart, F., and Polet, F. *L'Autre Davos: Mondialisation des Résistances et des Luttes.* L'Harmattan, Paris, 1999.
24. Weller, C. E., Scott, R. E., and Hersh, A. S. *The Unremarkable Record of Liberalized Trade.* Economic Policy Institute, Washington, DC, 2001.
25. United Nations Research Institute for Social Development. *Visible Hands: Taking Responsibility for Social Development.* Geneva, 2000.
26. Levy, B. S., and Sider, V. W. (eds.). *War and Public Health.* Oxford University Press, New York, 1997.
27. Agee, P. Producing the proper crisis. Speech by former CIA agent. *Z Magazine,* October 1990.
28. Feffer, J. Foreign Policy in Focus: Globalization and Militarization. Global Policy, February 2002. www.globalpolicy.org/soecon/ffd/2002/02military.htm (November 2003).
29. Beelman, M. *U.S. Contractors Reap the Windfalls of Post-War Reconstruction.* Center for Public Integrity, October 30, Washington, DC, 2003.
30. Schulman, J. *Corporate War Profiteering and Tax Avoidance.* Fact Sheet. Institute for Policy Studies, Washington, DC, 2003.
31. Petrella, R., Udry, C. A., and Aguitton, C. Expropriés du monde: construisons ensemble une autre mondialisation—premiere partie: les mécanismes de l'exclusion. In *L'Autre Davos: mondialisation des résistances et des luttes,* ed. F. Houtart and F. Polet. L'Harmattan, Paris, 1999.
32. Hildyard, N. Maastricht: The protectionism of free trade. *The Cornerhouse,* 1993.
33. Phelps, E. S. Phillips curves, expectations of inflation and optimal unemployment over time. *Economica* 34, 1967.
34. Cassen, B. Les bacchanales des patrons voyous. *Le Monde Diplomatique,* August 2003.
35. Singh, K. *Taming Global Financial Flows: A Citizen's Guide.* Zed Books, London, 2000.
36. Renner, M. Corporate mergers skyrocket. In *Vital Signs.* Worldwatch Institute, Washington, DC, 2000.
37. Centre Tricontinental. *Le Pouvoir des Transnationales: Point de Vue du Sud.* Alternatives Sud, Vol. IX(1). L'Harmattan, Paris, 2002.

38. Chan, S. *Liberalism, Democracy and Development.* Cambridge University Press, Cambridge, 2002.
39. Robinson, N. A. *Agenda 21 Earth's Action Plan.* Oceana Publications, New York, 1993.
40. Platt, A. E. *Infecting Ourselves: How Environmental and Social Disruptions Trigger Disease.* Worldwatch Paper 129. Worldwatch Institute, Washington, DC, 1996.
41. Brown, L., and Kane, H. *Full House: Reassessing the Earth's Carrying Capacity.* Worldwatch Books, Williamsport, PA, 1994.
42. World Health Organization. *Healthy Environments for Children: Initiating an Alliance for Action.* WHO/SDE/PHE/02.06. Geneva, 2002.
43. The Ecologist and Friends of the Earth. Keeping score: Which countries are the most sustainable? *The Ecologist,* March 22, 2001.
44. Ziegler, J. *The Right to Food: Report by the Special Rapporteur on the Right to Food.* Economic and Social Council of the United Nations, Geneva, 2001.
45. Madaley, J. *Hungry for Trade: How the Poor Pay for Free Trade.* Global Issues Series. Zed Books, London, 2000.
46. Chase-Dunn, C., and Grimes, P. World systems analysis. *Annu. Rev. Sociol.* 21:387–417, 1995.
47. Navarro, V. Assessment of the World Health Report 2000. *Lancet* 356, November 4, 2000.
48. Navarro, V., et al. Summary and conclusions of the study (Special Project on the Political and Social Contexts of Health). *Int. J. Health Serv.* 33(4):743–749, 2003.
49. World Health Organization. *World Health Report: Reducing Risks, Promoting Healthy Lives.* Geneva, 2002.
50. Oxfam. *Rigged Rules and Double Standards.* Oxford, 2002.
51. Sogge, D. *Give and Take: What's the Matter with Foreign Aid?* Zed Books, London, 2002.
52. Buina, A. (ed.). *Challenges to the World Bank and the IMF: Developing Country Perspectives.* Anthem Press, London, 2003.
53. Monbiot. G. *The Age of Consent: A Manifesto for a New World Order.* Flamingo, London, 2003.
54. Schraeder, P., et al. Clarifying the foreign aid puzzle: A comparison of American, Japanese, French and Swedish aid flows. *World Polit.* 50:294–323, 1998.
55. Wallerstein, I. *The Modern World-System,* Vols 1 and 2. Academic Press, New York, 1974/1980.
56. Stewart, F., and Wang, M. *Do PRSPs Empower Poor Countries and Disempower the World Bank, or Is It the Other Way Round?* QEH Working Papers Series, Working Paper 108. Queen Elizabeth House, University of Oxford, Oxford, 2003.
57. Gould, J., and Ojanen, J. The Politics of Tanzania's Poverty Reduction Strategy. European Network on Debt and Development, July 15, 2003. www.eurodad.org/articles/default.aspx?id=486 (November 2003).
58. Miliband, R. *Divided Societies: Class Struggle in Contemporary Capitalism.* Oxford University Press, Oxford, 1989.
59. Pilger, J. *Hidden Agendas.* Vintage, London, 1999.
60. Chomsky, N. *Rogue States: The Rule of Force in World Affairs.* Pluto Press, London, 2000.

61. Gills, B., et al. *Low Intensity Democracy.* Pluto Press, London, 1999.
62. Garrigou, A. Derrière la façade démocratique: l'abstention gagne les classes moyennes. *Le Monde Diplomatique,* April 2002.
63. Chomsky, N. *Deterring Democracy.* South End Press, Cambridge, MA, 1992.
64. Blum, W. *Killing Hope: US Military and CIA Interventions since World War II.* Zed Books, London, 2003.
65. Jones, A. (ed.). *Genocide, War Crimes and the West.* Zed Books, London, 2003.
66. Roy, A. Instant mix imperial democracy: Buy one and get one free. *Outlook,* May 26, 2003, pp. 46–56.
67. Mekay, E. Rich Nations Continue to Wield Power in Global Bodies. Interpress Service News Agency. www.ipsnews.net/interna.asp?idnews=18012 (November 2003).
68. Bennis, P. *Calling the Shots: How Washington Dominates Today's UN.* Olive Branch Press, Brooklyn, NY, 1996.
69. Aksu, E., and Camilleri, J. A. (eds.). *Democratizing Global Governance.* Palgrave Macmillan, Basingstoke, 2003.
70. George, S. *The Lugano Report.* Pluto Press, London, 1999.
71. Woodward, D. Trading Health for Profit: The Implications of the GATS and Trade in Health Services for Health in Developing Countries. Global Health, March 15, 2003. www.ukglobalhealth.org/content/Text/GATS_Woodward.pdf (November 2003).
72. Jawara, F., and Kwa, A. *Behind the Scenes at the WTO: The Real World of Trade Negotiations.* Zed Books, London, 2003.
73. United Nations Development Program. *Human Development Report 1993.* New York, 1993.
74. Monbiot, G. *Captive State: The Corporate Takeover of Britain.* Macmillan, Basingstoke, 2000.
75. Alliance for Democracy. Call for UN Convention on Corporate Accountability. Paper presented at an NGO conference on corporate accountability and the WSSD, January 26–28, 2002.
76. Richter, J. *Building on Quicksand: The Global Compact, Democratic Governance and Nestlé.* CETIM, IBFAN-GIFA, and Déclaration de Berne, Geneva, 2003.
77. Deacon, B., et al. *Global Social Governance: Themes and Prospects.* Globalism and Social Policy Programme, Ministry for Foreign Affairs, Department for International Cooperation, Helsinki, 2003.
78. Kapur, D., and Webber, R. *Governance Related Conditionalities of the IFIs.* G-24 Discussion Paper Series, No. 6. UNCTAD, Geneva, 2000.
79. Brautigan, D. Aid Dependence and governance, pp. 16–20. Almquist and Wiksell, Stockholm, 2002. www.egdi.gov.se/pdf/2001pdf/2000-1.pdf (November 2003).
80. Chang, H.-J. *Kicking Away the Ladder—Development Strategy in Historical Perspective.* Anthem Press, London, 2002.
81. Herman, E. *Real Terror Networks.* South End Press, Boston, 1982.
82. Barya, J.-J. The new political conditionalities of aid: An independent view from Africa. *IDS Bull.* 24(1):16–23, 1993.
83. Page, J. *The Revolution That Never Was: Northeast Brazil 1955–1964.* Grossman, New York, 1972.
84. Bagdikian, B. *The Media Monopoly.* Beacon Press, Boston, 2000.
85. Klinenberg, E. Dix maîtres pour les médias américains: obsession du rendement, connivances avec les industrials. *Le Monde Diplomatique,* April 2003.

86. Herman, E., and McChesney, R. W. *The Global Media: The New Missionaries of Corporate Capitalism.* Cassell, London, 1997.
87. Pilger, J. The crusaders: The hidden history of Western media propaganda. *New Internationalist,* No. 333, April 2001.
88. Thomas, P. N., and Nain, Z. (eds.). *Who Owns the Media? Global Trends and Local Resistances.* Zed Books, London, 2003.
89. Megalo media: The voice of globalization. *New Internationalist,* No. 333, April 2001.
90. Ainger, K. Empires of the senseless. *New Internationalist,* No. 333, April 2001.
91. Amin, S. *Capitalism in the Age of Globalization: The Management of Contemporary Society.* Zed Books, London, 1997.
92. Health Action International. *Power, Patents and Pills.* HAI-Europe, Amsterdam, 1997.
93. Big Pharma: Making a killing. *New Internationalist* 362, November 2003.
94. Chetley, A. *A Healthy Business: World Health and the Pharmaceutical Industry.* Zed Books, London, 1990.
95. Mahan, D. *Profiting from Pain: Where Prescription Drugs Dollars Go.* Families USA, Washington, DC, 2002.
96. Health Action International. *Promoting Health or Pushing Drugs? A Critical Examination of Marketing of Pharmaceuticals.* HAI-Europe, Amsterdam, 1992.
97. Young, R., and Surrusco, M. *Rx R&D Myths: The Case Against the Drug Industry's R&D "Scare Card."* Public Citizen, Washington, DC, 2001.
98. Basu, S. AIDS, Empire and Public Health Behaviourism. ZNet, August 2, 2003. www.zmag.org/content/showarticle.cfm?SectionID=2&ItemID=3988 (November 2003).
99. Wesselius, E. *Behind GATS 2000: Corporate Power at Work.* WTO Booklet Series No. 4, Transnational Institute, Amsterdam, May 2002.
100. Whitfield, D. *Public Services or Corporate Welfare: Rethinking the Nation State in the Global Economy.* Pluto Press, London, 2001.
101. Sanger, M. *Reckless Abandon: Canada, the GATS and the Future of Health Care.* Canadian Centre for Policy Alternatives, Ottawa, 2001.
102. Sexton, S. Trading healthcare away. In *Restructuring Health Services: Changing Contexts and Comparative Perspectives,* ed. K. Sen. Zed Books, London, 2003.
103. Vastine, R. Statement before the Senate Finance Committee Subcommittee on International Trade, October 21, 1999.
104. Julian, P. Failure to Stop Privatization in New Deal Increases Likelihood of Trade Attacks (press release). The Council of Canadians, Ottawa, September 11, 2000.
105. Sen, K. *Restructuring Health Services: Changing Contexts and Comparative Perspectives.* Zed Books, London, 2003.
106. Sexton, S. Trading health care away: GATS, public services and privatisation. *The Cornerhouse,* July 2001.
107. Pedraza, G. C. H. La dette externe du Tiers Monde: nouvelles initiatives ou vieilles recettes? In *Raisons et Déraisons de la Dette: le Point de Vue du Sud.* Centre Tricontinentale, L'Harmattan, Paris, 2003.
108. Thiery, J. A. P. Stratégies d'acteurs et dynamique de l'endettement du Tiers Monde. In *Raisons et Déraisons de la Dette: le Point de Vue du Sud.* Centre Tricontinental, L'Harmattan, Paris, 2003.
109. Centre Tricontinental. *Raisons et Déraisons de la Dette: le Point de Vue du Sud.* Alternatives Sud, Vol. IX(2–3). L'Harmattan, Paris, 2002.

110. Millet, D., and Toussaint, E. *Who Owes Who?* Zed Books, London, 2003.
111. Turshen, M. *Politics of Public Health.* Zed Books, London, 1989.
112. Stiglitz, J. E. *Globalization and Its Discontents.* Penguin Press, London, 2002.
113. The Structural Adjustment Participatory Review International Network. *Structural Adjustment: The SAPRIN Report: The Policy Roots of Economic Crisis, Poverty and Inequality.* Zed Books, London, 2003.
114. Guex, S. Le secret bancaire a-t-il un avenir? In *La Suisse dans la Constellation des Paradis Fiscaux,* ed. D. Froidevaux, pp. 171–1982. Edition d'En Bas, COTMEC, Lausanne/Genève, 2002.
115. Woodward, D. *The Next Crisis? Direct and Equality Investment in Developing Countries.* Zed Books, London, 2001.
116. Cuauhtémoc, G. Letter from Indian Aztec chief to European governments. Dial 2126, October 1–15, 2000; *Carta a la Iglesias* (El Salvador), May 2000.
117. Dunkeley, G. *Free Trade: Myth, Reality and Alternatives.* Zed Books, London, 2003.
118. Davis, M. *Late Victorian Holocausts: El Nino Famines and the Making of the Third World.* Verso, London, 2001.
119. Centre Europe Tiers Monde. *Via Campesina: Une Alternative Paysanne à la Mondialisation Néolibérale.* Geneva, October 2002.
120. United Nations. *Secretary General's Report to the UN Committee on Financing for Development.* Geneva, January 2001.
121. United Nations Conference on Trade and Development. *Trade and Development Report 1999.* Geneva, 1999.
122. United Nations Conference on Trade and Development. *Trade and Development Report 2002.* Geneva, 2002.
123. Ul Haq, M., Kaul, I., and Grunberg, I. *The Tobin Tax: Coping with Financial Volatility.* Oxford University Press, Oxford, 1996.
124. Des paradis bien gardés. *Alternatives Economiques* 169, April 1999.
125. Palan, R., Abbott, J., and Deans, P. *State Strategies in the Global Political Economy.* Pinter, London, 1996.
126. Centre Tricontinental. *Les Dessous de l'ALCA: Zone de Libre Echange des Amériques: Point du vue du Sud.* Alternatives Sud, Vol. X(1). L'Harmattan, Paris, 2003.
127. Palast, G. Bill Gates: Killing Africans for profit and PR—Mr Bush's bogus AIDS offer. *Observer,* July 14, 2003.
128. Vidal, J. Bill Gates' generosity. L'express, October 17, 2003.
129. Keen, S. *Debunking Economics: The Naked Emperor of the Social Sciences.* Pluto Press, Australia, 2001.
130. Central Intelligence Agency, Woodrow Wilson Center. State Failure Task Force Report: Phase II findings. *Environmental Change and Security Project Report* 5:49–72, Summer 1999.
131. Waelde, T. W. *A Requiem for the "New International Economic Order": The Rise and Fall of Paradigms in International Economic Law.* Festschrift fuer I. Seidl-Hohenveldern, Centre for Energy, Petroleum and Mineral Law and Policy. Kluwer, Amsterdam, 1998.
132. Tehranian, M. Global governance. In *Democratizing Global Governance,* ed. E. Aksu and J. A. Camilleri. Palgrave Macmillan, New York, 2003.

133. International Forum on Globalization. *Alternatives to Economic Globalization: A Better World Is Possible.* Berrett-Koehler, Williston, VT, 2003.
134. Sweetman, C., and Kerr, J. *Women Reinventing Globalization.* Oxfam, Oxford, 2003.
135. Waterman, P., and Chavez, D. (eds.). Two, Three, Many Social Forums . . . ? Transnational Alternatives and Alternatives Transnacionales, 2002. www.tni.org/tat (November 2003).
136. Legge, D. Globalization on Trial: World Health Warning. Preliminary comment. La Trobe University, Victoria, Australia, 2002. http://users.bigpond.net.au/sanguileggi/PrelimAnalCMHReport.html (November 2003).
137. People's Health Movement. *Realization of the Right to Health.* Joint written statement submitted by the Europe–Third World Centrê and the American Association of Jurists to the Commission on Human Rights in its 59th session, 2003.
138. Chang, H.-J. *Globalization, Economic Development and the Role of the State.* Zed Books, London, 2003.

CHAPTER 19

Report of the WHO Commission on Macroeconomics and Health: A Critique

Debabar Banerji

In the early 1990s, apparently at the insistence of the rich countries that contribute to the bulk of its budget, the World Health Organization looked to economists for help in its major policy formulations for work in the fields of health and health services in poor countries. An exponential increase in the power of market forces has propelled the "dismal science" high up in the prestige hierarchy of academic disciplines. Issues such as health economics, health financing, and health sector reform (whatever that means) have come to occupy increasingly important positions in WHO's fields of interest. Activities in these fields have been synchronized with those of other international agencies over which the rich countries have considerable influence, like the World Bank, United Nations Development Program (UNDP), and International Monetary Fund (IMF). The setting up of the Commission on Macroeconomics and Health (CMH), in January 2000 (1), marks a watershed in the involvement of economists in health. The process of formulation of the CHM's report can provide useful insights into the sociology of knowledge of this rapidly expanding field.

WHO succeeded in persuading 18 outstanding economists to form the CMH. The biographical sketch of the chairman, Jeffery Sachs, notes that the *New York Times* described him "as probably the most important economist in the world" (1, p. 147). Most of the CMH economists, including those from the poorer countries, were educated in some of the most prestigious universities, such as Harvard, MIT, Berkeley, Princeton, Oxford, and Cambridge. Many of them served in key positions in international organizations such as the World Bank, UNDP, and IMF.

The CMH formed six working groups, to go into details in specific areas:

WG1: Health, Economic Growth, and Poverty Reduction
WG2: Global Public Goods for Health

WG3: Mobilization of Domestic Resources for Health
WG4: Health and International Economy
WG5: Improving Health Outcomes of the Poor
WG6: Development Assistance and Health.

It also commissioned a number of papers (see 1, pp. 151–156) by scholars from different parts of the world. Governments and foundations of many rich countries offered generous funds for the commission's activities: the Bill and Melinda Gates Foundation, the U.K. Department for International Development, the Grand Duchy of Luxembourg, the government of Ireland, the government of Norway, the Rockefeller Foundation, the government of Sweden, and the United Nations Foundation.

IGNORING SOME MAJOR INTERDISCIPLINARY DIMENSIONS OF MACROECONOMICS

The CMH report rightly begins by stating that "the importance of health on its own can not be overstressed." It quotes Amartya Sen (2) saying that health (like education) is among the basic capabilities that give value to human life. However, like Sen (3), the commission fails to make a deeper analysis of the historical, political, and sociocultural forces, as well as forces generated by international politics, trade, and military pacts, that led to neglect of the "social support systems" in many poor countries. Sen's approving reference to South Korea (3), for instance, does not take into account the impact of the Korean War, the economic benefits of locating a U.S. military base in that country, the propping up of dictators like Syngman Rhee, huge development assistance and foreign direct investment as a reward for the politically and socially correct behavior of Rhee's government, and formation of an export-led economy. Commenting on the worldview of such like-minded economists, Vicente Navarro (4) points out the absence of an analysis of the power relations that arise and reproduce through national and international institutions. As further analysis of the CMH report will show, this study of the macroeconomics of health is deliberately ahistorical, apolitical, and atheoretical (5).

That the "investment" of so much should have yielded so little speaks of the very poor quality of "economics" in the CMH; its report falls far short of expectations. Indeed, it calls into question the capacity of the commission to take a broad, interdisciplinary view of the two major areas of its mandate—health services and health—so that economists could demonstrate how inputs from their discipline could enrich these areas, as, for instance, was done through the induction of the theories, concepts, and methods of disciplines such as biostatistics, human ecology, sociology, and management sciences.

PRECONCEIVED IDEOLOGICAL ORIENTATION

The members of the Commission on Macroeconomics and Health have adopted a selective approach to their study, which conforms to a preconceived ideology. This appears to have trapped the commission in a straitjacket. Thus, instead of enriching the different facets of its enormous area of study, sometimes it has, unwittingly or otherwise, ended up substantially distorting many of these areas in its attempt to fit them within the boundaries it has constructed. Bringing up the utopian concept of "health as a public good," both nationally and internationally; using the obviously faulty concept of "disability adjusted life years (DALYs) saved"; and frequent consideration of the "global burden of disease," without ensuring the validity and reliability of the database—these are some examples of the issues I will take up in scrutinizing the contents of the report. Considering the great stature of the members of the commission and other supporting staff, the report offers documentary evidence of the dismal quality of intellectual life in the present era of market-driven globalization.

A striking aspect of the report is that it has almost systematically "blacked out" alternative viewpoints on health economics. As early as 1967, a plea was made for the use of concepts and methods of economics that ensure more effective use of limited resources in health fields in developing countries (6). Stig Andersen (7) had suggested how such "optimization of health systems" at various levels could be achieved by using the approach of operational research, which has been demonstrated to be useful in program formulation and evaluation in such diverse fields as tuberculosis control (8), family planning (9), and health systems develop-ment (10) in India. Similarly, although a comprehensive critique of the World Bank's use of an analysis of health sector financing (11) as a tool for policy formulation in India was based on ideas generated in India (12), this criticism too was simply blacked out. I will refer to similar instances of such ideology-driven selective blackouts later in this analysis of the CMH report. This is a very disturbing trend. Navarro has recalled his early scholastic days in the United States (13), when a mere reference to "class" in epidemiological analyses of data was frowned upon. Navarro has rightly called this "intellectual fascism." It is significant that the CMH has chosen to overlook some fundamental scientific infirmities in the conceptualization, planning, formulation, and implementation of the "vertical" or categorical global health initiatives and has shown no hesitation in supporting such ventures (1, p. 68).

STUDYING THE MACROECONOMICS OF
HEALTH SERVICES, NOT OF HEALTH

A consequence of the CMH's questionable academic approach to the assigned task has been patent neglect of some of the basic principles that influence a country's health and health services. Obviously, it would be unrealistic to expect the commission to take into account the famous WHO definition of health as "a state of complete physical, social and mental wellbeing, and not merely absence of disease and infirmity" (14, p. 10). And it is understandable that the commission has endorsed the World Bank's Poverty Reduction Strategy Paper (PRSP) framework (1, p. 9), already under implementation for the previous three years (and showing the now familiar shortfalls in achievements), to take care of the intersectoral and developmental dimensions of health and confine its attention to the still formidable issues of health services development in poor countries. However, if that is what was intended, the commission and its report should carry the term "Health Services" instead of "Health."

Although the titles of the 13 chapters of the report and six of the working groups, as well as the list of commissioned papers, give an impression that the CMH has covered a substantial area, closer scrutiny reveals that it has extensively repeated well-worn and often scientifically suspect writings in the publications of WHO and other international organizations. There is also a lack of appreciation of some important developments in the discipline of public health; the commission could have gained considerable insights into the new developments had it studied more carefully just two of the major publications from WHO: *New Public Health and WHO's Ninth General Programme of Work* (14) and *New Challenges for Public Health* (15). Although the commission makes mention of issues such as social development and intersectoral collaboration, it has overlooked issues such as equality, equity, health promotion, and health systems research for health personnel development, which were given central positions in these earlier publications. In addition, the commission has not paid attention to certain well-established basic principles of public health practice (16), such as taking into account the natural history of a disease in a community (tuberculosis, syphilis, and AIDS could have provided classic examples)—references to Robert Fogel's works in the report (1, p. 22) are rare exceptions—or the natural history of a disease in individuals, epidemiological behavior of community health problems (including their social dimensions), choice and social orientation of technology, and organization and management of health services, with their built-in management information and evaluation subsystems. The CMH has been less than successful in blending basic public health principles with the relevant macroeconomic principles when it set out to write the prescription for improving the health of health service systems covering more than two-thirds of the world's population.

POINTED OMISSION OF ANY REFERENCE TO THE ALMA-ATA DECLARATION

By its pointed act of omitting any mention of the Alma-Ata Declaration of 1978 (17), the CMH makes by far the most significant statement of its report, denoting a frontal clash of two opposing ideologies. The Alma-Ata Declaration on Primary Health Care, which was endorsed by all the countries of the world, gave primacy to people and "subordinated" technological considerations (or donor dictates) to the prevailing cultural, social, economic, and epidemiological conditions. It also endorsed the WHO resolution (18) that promised Health for All by the Year 2000, using the approach of primary health care (HFA-2000/PHC).

Some of the outstanding components of the Alma-Ata Declaration are summarized here:

1. Health (in WHO's sense of the term) as a fundamental human right. This was meant to provide a perspective for action.
2. Health action starting "from the people." Before any action is taken against any health problem, it is essential to compare it objectively with the coping capacity that people have developed through the ages. Use of yoga as a health practice is as an example. People should be the prime movers in the shaping of health services that are meant for them; the health services must add to people's existing coping capacity. Thus the declaration has strong democratic overtones.
3. Health services as a component of intersectoral action in wider fields, such as nutrition, adequate access to potable water, sanitation, proper housing, education, and so on. As early as 1848, Rudolf Virchow had defined medicine as nothing more than the practice of politics on a larger scale (19).
4. Social control over the public health services.
5. Use of technology appropriate to the prevailing conditions.
6. Use of traditional systems of medicine, wherever they are found relevant.
7. Use of drugs confined to carefully chosen essential drugs.
8. Health services offered in an integrated form. The declaration thus rules out vertical programs.
9. Coverage of the entire population, including the hitherto unserved and the underserved.

This could justifiably be considered as merely a wish list of the world's poor. Nevertheless, it does provide a roadmap for the deprived to get their dues. Interestingly, it can also be called a manifesto for self-reliance in health by the world's poor.

WHO and its member states were well aware of the enormous funds that would be needed for full implementation of HFA-2000/PHC. However, if the spirit of the declaration is properly understood, a start can be made with minimal resources, without any help from donors. This approach ensured that it could also be a gradual process, subject, of course, to the powers that be allowing the entrusting of "people's health in people's hands."

The contrast between the HFA-2000/PHC approach and the CMH approach is stark. Instead of giving primacy to the people in shaping their health services, the CMH calls for "donor's" imposition on the world's poor of prefabricated, selectively chosen, market- and technology-driven, externally monitored, and dependence-producing programs. This is a component of a new version of colonialism and imperialism. To ensure "compliance" with its virtually "nonnegotiable" plans for action, the commission dangles the carrot of what it promises will be massive "donor" assistance for compliance, along with a big stick to ensure that poor countries mobilize "domestic" resources as their contribution to an "upscaling" of investment for the plan of action laid down by the donors. It comes as a bit of a surprise that the members of the commission— the crème de la crème of the descendants of the European Enlightenment (which included the leader of the opposition of India's Upper House of the Federal Parliament and the initiator of economic liberalization/globalization, as Finance Minister for five years from 1992)—should have kept their eyes so tightly shut to the long chain of failures of past efforts to counter the ideology of primary health care. The commission's enthusiasm for involving pharmaceutical and other commercial interests in what is often called "public-private partnership" (PPP) may provide an explanation for this anomaly.

THE APPROACH TO THE RECOMMENDATIONS

Apart from adding its own share of recommended new initiatives for improving the health of the poor (like National Commissions for Macroeconomics and Health for individual countries and the "close-to-client" strategy), the CMH has unflinchingly carried the ancient baggage of, and indeed warmly endorsed, such obviously discredited funding programs as the Global Fund to Fight AIDS, Tuberculosis, and Malaria (GFATM), the Initiative for Vaccine Research (IVR), the Global Alliance for Vaccine and Immunization (GAVI), and the Global Health Research Fund (GHRF). Following the same trend, the commission has also endorsed a continuation of international programs such as the Tropical Diseases Research and the Special Program for Research Development and Research Training in Human Reproduction (HRP) (1, pp. 77–84). That the commission failed to notice how little these programs have done over long years to strengthen the actions against specific diseases under field conditions is not very flattering to commission members' analytical and evaluative insights.

A CASE STUDY OF THE UNIVERSAL
IMMUNIZATION PROGRAM

I present here a short case study of the design, implementation, and evaluation of the much-publicized Universal Immunization Program (UIP) of 1985–90 (20–22). No reasonably reliable baseline epidemiological data on the six diseases (diphtheria, pertussis, tetanus, tuberculosis, measles, and poliomyelitis) were available. The aim was to achieve worldwide coverage of more than 85 percent of infants to create "herd immunity" (1, p. 29), so that the selected diseases ceased to be public health problems. No data were available on the protective value of the vaccines under different epidemiological conditions. Launching of the UIP on such a scale was obviously an unrealistic task, even with mobilization of the entire health service system (23). It was meant to cover all infants, 0–12 month of age, in entire populations as a routine work. Some of the vaccines had a very short life and had to be stored at 2°C in a specially developed "cold chain"—from the time of manufacture to arrival at distant places in all corners of the world, many of which had no or no assured electricity supply and had an outside temperature rising to 40°C or 50°C at the peak of summer. The cost of running the program during the first five years of its implementation amounted to several hundred million U.S. dollars. No epidemiological evaluation could be made of such an expensive program, for the simple reason that, as noted above, there were no baseline data on the incidence of the diseases. In any case, the program did not have a reliable information and evaluation system. Even in terms of coverage of infants, no country in the world (except perhaps Cuba) could provide verifiable data of attaining the required 85 percent or more of coverage (23).

THE CASE OF MALAWI

The CMH report makes a passing reference to Malawi: "one of the poorest countries of the world where 20 percent population has no access to health services and less than 50 has access to safe water, [Malawi] has recently committed itself to routine measles immunization and to campaigns to catch those missed out by routine efforts. By 1999, there were no reported children's deaths due to measles in Malawi and only two confirmed cases were seen throughout the country" (1, p. 44). The commission gave no source for this instance of "selective" public health practice in Malawi. A public health scholar would have been tempted to ask for some simple details: Was it reproducible? Was it cost effective? Was it a "donor-driven" program? How reliable are the data? What happened to the children who suffer from other types of diseases? Indeed, what happened to the children who were saved from measles by the immunization drive?

The Malawi case shows how deeply flawed is the thinking pursued by the CMH. It has listed the countries that contain almost all the world's abjectly poor who have little or no access to the most elementary health services. The commission calls for three forms of massive commitment from and for these countries. First, it considers what it calls "close-to-client" (CTC) as a major component of its recommendations for action. Second, it strongly advocates fighting crusades against massive diseases like tuberculosis AIDS, and malaria by launching separate, "vertical," technocentric programs costing billions of dollars. And third, it visualizes health as what economists call a "public good," locally, regionally, nationally, and internationally.

Can donor-driven poor countries (like Malawi), which have so little to show for the four or five decades of innumerable initiatives imposed on them by donors, now control the many communicable diseases (e.g., AIDS, tuberculosis, and malaria) and also respond to the urgent health needs of their peoples—even in the unlikely event of their being able to get the proposed billions from the domestic and donor sources? Can Malawi think of health as a public good?

MACROECONOMISTS AND OPERATIONAL RESEARCH

The CMH report's reference to health systems research reveals that even economists have not been able to understand the meaning of the term "operational research" (OR). This research method has been used (since World War II) to determine the most or more effective (optimal) ways of using scarce resources to formulate programs that involve a complex of many interacting variables. As pointed out earlier, this approach has been used in public health planning in India on a number of occasions. In fact, P. C. Mahalonobis (24) used this approach as early as 1951 to compare outcomes from the resources needed to train a full-fledged physician with those from the same amount of resources used to educate a much larger number of medical assistants.

The CMH is somewhat ambivalent in the use of the term "operational research." It comes nearest to the true meaning when it observes, "We recommend that as a normal matter, country specific projects should allocate at least 5 percent of all resources to project related operational research in order to examine the efficacy, the optimisation of treatment protocols, the economics of alternative interventions, and delivery mode and population/patient preferences" (1, p. 8). However, later, instead of advocating the well-established method of clinical trial for deciding on the choice of antiretroviral drugs, it states that "introduction of HAART (Highly Active Anti-Retroviral Therapy) in low income countries should be accompanied by extensive use of operational research to test effectiveness of alternative regimes and approaches" (1, p. 52). The commission continues to confuse OR with clinical trial when it states, "Operational research involves investigation of health intervention in practice, including issues of patient acceptance of treatment regimens and adherence to those regimens, toxicity, dosing, and modes and costs of delivery" (1, p. 83).

The CMH is thus uncertain about what it means by OR. In his classic book on the subject, Churchman (25) clearly defined six distinctive steps for carrying out OR: (*a*) Define the problem in all its interdisciplinary dimensions. (*b*) Collect available data on all the dimensions of the problem. (*c*) Use the data to forecast, with or without mathematical models, outcomes of alternative hypotheses for problem solution. (*d*) Identify the solution(s) that promise to offer "optimal" results. (*e*) Subject the identified solution(s) to "test runs" under real-life conditions, and check the assumptions that were made in choosing them with built-in feedback information systems. (*f*) Put the optimal solution into large-scale implementation, and continue to monitor through feedback data the assumptions on which the choice of the solution was based. A multidisciplinary approach, formulation of a number of choices before deciding on the optimal one, and test runs are the key elements when considering whether a process is indeed OR.

The commission is far from being scientific when it uses the term "operational research" in its report. While it is almost strident in its advocacy of OR, one does not find evidence of the use of OR to optimize systems when the commission sets out to write the prescription for the ailments of the health service systems of the world's poor. Nor did it occur to the commission that the UIP had so few research inputs, operational or otherwise, when so much of the scarce (both domestic and donor) resources were allocated for its implementation; the program was not even given a decent evaluation before it was removed from the radar screen of the international organizations' global initiatives.

The case of the UIP comes dangerously close to an example of public health quackery.

PRINCIPAL COMPONENTS OF THE COMMISSION'S RECOMMENDATIONS

"Close-to-client" is a new term coined by the CMH to underline one of its key recommendations for action. CTC involves "a basic strengthening of the staff at this level, an adequate supply of drugs, and a minimal capacity for transport. It also involves both hardware of the health sector (physical plants, equipment, telephone and e-mail connectivity of the CTC centres) and the software, meaning better systems of management and supervision, and better accountability to the users through local oversight of the CTC units" (1, p. 64). Incidentally, one might wonder how many of the 38 countries listed by the commission as the "least developed countries," or even the 23 "low income countries" or the 19 "lower middle income countries" (1, Table A2.8, p. 173), have the technical and managerial capacity to cover their entire populations with CTC units. The commission also does not give the crucial information on the number of persons or the geographic area to be serviced by a CTC unit.

All this has a familiar ring for those who are conversant with the literature of rural health services development in different parts of the world, starting probably from the ambitious implementation of setting up a nationwide network of primary health centers (26) as integral components of a still more ambitious "Community Development Program" of India in 1952 (27). These were the outcome of the recommendations of the Health Survey and Development Committee of 1946 (28), set up by the then British Indian Government as a counterpart to the more famous Beveridge Committee (whose report provided the blueprint for "health as a public good" in the United Kingdom!).

Like these committees' reports, the CMH report has also recognized that "this enhanced role of the state in the health sector would have to be realised at a time when the capacity of the governments, particularly in the poorest countries, is limited, and subject to administrative and governance constraints. Addressing these constraints will be [a] necessary part of the challenge faced by the countries and donors alike, if the burden of ill health is to be lifted" (1, p. 58).

Proceeding further, the CMH visualizes hospitals (again, the report does not mention the number of people to be served or geographic area to be covered) within the CTC system, "with at least a doctor and paramedical staff," that (1, p. 65)

> may typically be capable of offering patient care to at least 100 in-patients at a time. The purpose of these hospitals will be to deal with acute and particularly dangerous or complicated cases. In the area of maternal health, they will be the referral destinations for eclampsia, postpartum haemor-rhaging, puerperal sepsis and complications associated with poorly performed terminations. They would be appropriate settings for some case management for severe cases of childhood diseases and malaria and treatment associated with complicated tuberculosis cases. Antiretroviral (HAART) treatment for AIDS patients would probably be best introduced at this level. Such hospitals should have some laboratory capacity and at least one operating theatre, anaesthetic and X-ray facilities, and it will have an all-purpose dispensary.

Has the commission done even the barest work study exercises, not to speak of optimization through OR, before planning to entrust so much responsibility to a 100-bed hospital with "at least a doctor and paramedical staff"?

The commission has emphasized certain well-established prerequisites for successful implementation of such a program: political and administrative com-mitment, strengthening of a country's technical and administrative expertise, substantial strengthening of management systems, and creation of systems of community accountability. As is well known, all these are very scarce com-modities and capabilities.

The CMH clearly did not make any effort to optimize the entire system recommended in its report. It could as well claim that considering its enormous task, it could only outline the broad contours of CTC units, hospitals, and the superstructure. Nevertheless, surely the commission is not contending that such structures have never been planned or set up in at least some of the developing countries and that there are no evaluation data to explain why they could not be sustained or further strengthened in the course of time? The commission is obviously aware that it is not reinventing the wheel. The short case study on the UIP provided above would throw a great deal of light on at least some of the major causes of the decline. This points to yet another of the CMH's "blackouts." The commission was certainly well aware of the costs of adopting such tunnel vision. As will be borne out from the example of India later in this chapter, the sheer waste of several hundred million dollars is but a small part of the cost that was paid by countries in adopting the misconceived program, the UIP. It is a pity that such an obvious waste did not strike the economists.

The recommendations of the CMH on CTC units, hospitals, and the superstructure provide little evidence that the commission has even tried to learn from past mistakes committed in the formulation and implementation of the UIP. On the contrary, the commission not only has totally ignored the very serious warnings that emerged from the UIP misadventure, but it has gone on to advocate aggressively a continuation of the UIP. The commission reports that the annual average financial commitment for 1997–99 from all international health agencies for vaccine-preventable diseases amounted to U.S.$251 million, of a total of $1,743 million. It recommends that of the proposed allocation of $27 billion annually in 2007, which is to rise to $38 billion annually by 2015, as much as $2 billion be spent in 2007, and $3 billion annually from 2015, on research and development, which includes the Global Alliance on Vaccines and Immunization and the Initiative for Vaccine Research (1, p. 95).

While forgetting the disastrous history of WHO's own postwar crusades against many scourges by using "silver bullets" such as DDT, BCG vaccine, streptomycin, para-amino salicylic acid (PAS), penicillin, sulphones, and hetrazan, launched in vertical programs on a global scale (30), the 18 wise members of the commission give a startling display of collective amnesia by stating (1, p. 68):

> Historically, one way of avoiding the problems of limited capacity within health systems has been to adopt a 'vertical' or categorical approach to a particular disease—such as malaria—or family intervention—such as childhood vaccination. Such approaches have attracted a great deal of interest from many outside donors, who appreciate centralised technical and financial control that characterises them and their tendency to be more easily assessed. Many such programs have met with great successes both within given countries and in some cases worldwide. We would strongly advocate that categorical approaches not to be dismantled; there is a great value to the concentration of expertise and commitment that drives such approaches, and we would endorse low income countries maintaining and or establishing national programs on HIV/AIDS, malaria, TB, and perhaps other specific conditions, even as they build the CTC system.

The commission wants to have its cake and eat it too! The terms, "limited capacity," "interest from many outside donors," "strongly advocate," "low income countries," and "even as they build the CTC system" are the key to the proposals. Historically, interest from outside donors has ensured that such vertical programs are given priority over other health service activities, including the CTC-hospital complex in this case. The strong recommendation in favor of vertical programs sounds the death knell for the commission's recommendations on the CTC system. Having praised the achievement of Malawi, does the commission really expect that country to implement the package it has put together?

INDIA'S EXPERIENCE WITH VERTICAL
PROGRAMS

Taking the case of India, the second most populous country of the world, which (unlike China) has to keep its health information system (whatever it's worth!) an open book because of its democratic commitments, the government has (in May 2002) come out with the final version of its *National Health Policy 2002* document (31), in which it makes a forthright "confession" of the degree to which its health service system suffered for agreeing to donor-driven vertical programs (including the UIP and tuberculosis and AIDS programs). It now says (31):

> Over the last decade or so, the Government has relied upon a "vertical" implementational structure for the major disease control programmes. Through this, the system has been able to make a substantial dent in reducing the burden of specific diseases. However, such an organisational structure, which requires independent manpower for each disease programme, is extremely expensive and difficult to sustain. Over a long time range, 'vertical' structures may only be affordable for those diseases which offer a reasonable possibility of elimination or eradication in a foreseeable time frame. . . .
>
> It is a widespread perception that over the last decade and a half, the rural health staff has become a vertical structure exclusively for the implementation of the family welfare activities. As a result where there is no separate vertical structure, there is no identifiable service delivery system at all. The [National Health] Policy will address this distortion in the public health system.

Why, then, this obsession of the CMH to defend the indefensible? Is it to create markets for the new products (e.g., vaccines) churned out by the biotechnology industry? Is it to make poor countries "safer" for expansion of the market for rich countries? Is it resurrection of the primordial terror of "bugs" afflicting the properly programmed, well-sanitized, and sterilized new generations in the rich countries, who are being manipulated by market forces to revert to a long-discredited single-etiology theory of diseases? Is it for the more mundane reason of creating jobs for the unemployed in the rich countries, so that they can live like maharajas in poor countries?

Even if, for argument's sake, we assume that the sole purpose of the commission was to serve the commercial and political interests of the "donors," they could have done a much better job of camouflaging their real intentions. The CMH report lacks finesse. It did not seem to occur to the commission that it has given little or no scientific evidence to substantiate its proposals.

Even if the CMH wanted to defend itself by calling its report a mere hypothesis, the experience with implementation of the UIP would have clearly shown that, if anything, the commission has no leg to stand on even for its hypothesis involving CTC units, the 100-bed hospital, and the superstructure, to be superimposed by a battery of top-priority, massive vertical programs. Seeming to add insult to injury, the commission says that what clearly is atrocious overloading will have beneficial effects on the CTC system (1, p. 68):

> Categorical programs can provide technical assistance at the CTC level, standard disease protocols, quality assured drugs, and monitoring and evaluation focused on specific outcomes, and they can help to build broad political support for the particular program. In many cases, the infrastructure established by these categorical approaches are being used to control other high priority diseases. Many of the industry-supported global initiatives mentioned earlier, which depend on distribution of drugs and other commodities to large populations, have strengthened the national infrastructure needed for CTC delivery of intervention.

The commission is blatantly ahistorical and pathetically propagandist in harboring such expectations.

The CMH seems to have reached rock bottom when it made these recommendations, on the basis of such obviously unsubstantiated and irrational considerations. If the commission had looked into the literature (I cited India's new National Health Policy earlier; 31), it would have discovered a mountain of evidence to show the devastation caused to the infrastructure of health services for the poor by some of the most deeply flawed but richly funded donor-driven and donor-dictated vertical programs imposed by the politically powerful rich countries (see, e.g., 17, 32–36). Did Cuba need such inputs to build one of the world's finest public health systems?

The commission seems to see no contradiction between its assertions of glowing successes of many donor-driven programs and what it asserts elsewhere in the report: "In some of the world's poorest countries, the coverage of many basic interventions is falling, not rising. In many countries the percentage of mothers whose births were attended by trained midwives or doctors is falling. Despite importance of vaccination for child survival, levels of childhood vaccination stagnated or dropped in many poor countries in the 1990s, leaving tens of millions of children uncovered by vaccination" (1, p. 47). What prescription does it offer to such countries? More of the discredited same. Indeed, a special fund was created by multilateral and bilateral agencies, international development banks, foundations, pharmaceutical companies, nongovernmental organizations, and government health programs to launch the Global Alliance for Vaccination and Immunization in 1999, "with a mission to address the flagging interest and to increase support to immunization" (1, p. 189).

THE GLOBAL PROGRAM AGAINST TUBERCULOSIS

Despite the CMH's "strong endorsement" of the vertical programs, it is unlikely that the commission has adequate knowledge about the technical background of the factors that led to inclusion of tuberculosis control in the U.N. secretary-general's Global Fight Against AIDS, Tuberculosis and Malaria.

Following the guidelines developed on the basis of extensive operational research in India (37), which was included in the report of WHO's Expert Committee on Tuberculosis in 1964 (38), poorer countries have been acting on the problem as an integral part of their general health services—conceived long before the invention of the CTC principle. However, the program suffered somewhat when overriding priorities were given to implementation of vertical programs, such as family planning, the UIP, and AIDS control. This led to neglect of the already established, integrated tuberculosis-control activities (37).

It is a profound irony that after the donors failed to achieve the objectives of the UIP, the crusaders identified the global fight against tuberculosis, with directly observed treatment with shortcourse chemotherapy (DOTS) as its centerpiece. Reference to just three elements of this response will suffice to prove how poor the initiative was in conceptualization and poorer still in implementation. First, WHO dutifully declared tuberculosis a global emergency in 1995, without a shred of evidence to justify a declaration of such far-reaching significance (39). The hindsight of the past seven years has confirmed that WHO acted most irresponsibly in making such a serious declaration. Second, WHO made the astonishing sociological presumption that even though diagnostic and treatment services were available to patients free of cost, more than half of the patients did not take the treatment as prescribed (by implication, they would rather die) (37, pp. 32–37). So, a global program was unleashed in 1997 to ensure that these patients were administered DOTS at health centers, to "save" them from death and to prevent the spread of TB. Third, as in the case of the UIP, there were no baseline data to monitor and evaluate the program (37, pp. 38–44). On the contrary, reasonably convincing epidemiological evidence showed that in India, which accounts for about half of world's TB cases, there has been no rise in the incidence and prevalence of the disease over the last half century, even though very few of the infectious cases got efficacious treatment during this period (40, 41). In other words, there was no increase in the pool of infection, even after decades of gross neglect in treating infectious persons in the population. Yet, contrary to compelling scientific evidence, the global tuberculosis program was pushed through with the object of reducing the pool of infection.

Not unexpectedly, WHO's process evaluation of the global TB program paints a grim picture; it could not give any data on epidemiological impact, because there was no baseline. This questions the very purpose of the global program. Nor could it give any reliable data on the very dangerous trend of DOTS patients developing multidrug resistance and spreading it to others. The *WHO Report 2002: Global Tuberculosis Control* states, "the 1.02 million smear positive cases reported only a quarter (27 percent) of the estimated total, and the rate of case finding between 1999 and 2000 was no faster than the average since 1994, a mean annual increment of 133,000 smear positive cases. Globally, DOTS programme must recruit an extra 330,000 each year to reach 70 percent case detection by 2005" (42, p. 1). Considering the nature of the second-line combination of drugs, this result was not unexpected. Having committed its unpardonable mistake, the pharmaceutical industry is coming to WHO's "rescue" by condescendingly offering still more powerful medicines at considerably subsidized rates (1, p. 88).

In the case of India, which has an open reporting system, the Statutory Office of Comptroller and Auditor-General says that the reach of the Indian tuberculosis program has been inadequate. The grants released to the District Tuberculosis Control Societies were used to the extent of 13 to 27 percent during 1996–97 to 2000–2001. The grants to the District Tuberculosis Centers by nongovernmental organizations could be used only to the extent of 12 percent (43).

DAMAGING CONSEQUENCES OF PUBLICIZING UNSUBSTANTIATED WHO/UNAIDS ESTIMATES: THE CASE OF THE AIDS PANDEMIC

Justifiably, the Commission on Macroeconomics and Health pays considerable attention to the AIDS pandemic, with special reference to sub-Saharan Africa (1, pp. 47–52). However, instead of giving a fresh perspective on coping with the staggering pandemic that has struck the world, the commission simply reports on the well-worn, convoluted, and not very convincing descriptions and analyses of WHO/UNAIDS. Of late there has been a tendency in WHO/UNAIDS to take liberties with validity, reliability, and comparability in the use of data. They also sometimes seem to be slipping away from their mandatory role of basing their conclusions on the use of well-validated econometric models and other statistical discourses into which they feed reliable and carefully cross-checked data. Despite these very serious lapses in the scientific validity of their conclusions, WHO/UNAIDS often have no pangs of conscience in giving wide publicity to their deeply flawed "estimates." Making "estimates" on the bases of poor and unreliable data and on questionable assumptions raises serious ethical problems. It is certainly a grave breach of trust.

Unfortunately, the names of these once well-respected and reliable organization give an aura of legitimacy to their "estimates" for the many who still trust in their scientific integrity. But the 18 top economists of the world ought to have a better understanding of the situation. The CMH report is full of many instances of fully trusting "WHO estimates" that do not bear scientific scrutiny. In fact, the commission compounded the folly by extensively using these estimates in mathematical models, which themselves were constructed on highly questionable assumptions. Expressing his concern over this type of trend, Navarro (44) has rightly expressed his dissatisfaction with the use of data that "surround themselves with a statistical and mathematical discourse to give an appearance of rigor that they in fact lack." Unwittingly or otherwise, reports based on such obviously faulty discourses are transformed into politically ideological documents. It is intriguing that such flaws escaped the scrutiny of the members of the commission and the many other scholars of repute associated with them. Is it a case of mere oversight or carelessness, or is it something close to what Navarro has termed "intellectual fascism"?

The commission appears to have overlooked the fact that before the outbreak of the AIDS pandemic there was virtually no public health organization in sub-Saharan Africa, and WHO/UNAIDS had to undertake direct responsibility for dealing with the pandemic when it struck the region with awesome ferocity. The commission should also have noted that the WHO/UNAIDS officials were often found unequal to the task assigned to them. What efforts did the officials make to chalk out the sociological, cultural, and economic dimensions of the epidemiology of the AIDS pandemic? How were these data used to set up a strategy to prevent the spread of the disease? Has there been any evaluation and monitoring of the officials' activities, and were they held accountable for their acts of omission and commission on the basis of a public health audit? Such questions and many more remain unanswered.

Furthermore, presumably because of the quality of the data and the flaws in the models used by UNAIDS, there has been a sharp difference of opinion on the extent of the disease in a billion-strong country such as India. The paucity of knowledge of UNAIDS (and of the CMH) can be discerned from their assessment of the problems in the two most populous countries of the world—China and India. Even though the first case of HIV in India was discovered in 1986 and a countrywide program was launched immediately (incidentally, well before a program was launched in the much admired Thailand), the CMH report, without assigning any evidence, says that countries "such as China, and India, are still in the early phase of the pandemic, so that timely control measures can head off an explosive growth of infections" (1, p. 48). In China, the description of the AIDS situation in government handouts is highly ambivalent, making it virtually impossible to arrive at a reasonably reliable assessment. According to the latest official data quoted by a news agency, "The number of the Chinese infected by the deadly AIDS virus has risen sharply and touched 850,000 by the end of 2001. China's ministry of health said by the end of the last year, 30,736 were confirmed AIDS carriers in the country. Of these, 1594 were full blown AIDS patients and 684 have already died" (45).

RESEARCH INPUTS

The CMH rightly emphasizes the importance of a research basis for public health action. However, it makes no mention of such a research basis when it presents its central recommendations on CTC and 100-bed hospitals and a strong endorsement of vertical programs. It makes reference to the idea of "Essential National Health Research" (ENHR), which formed the centerpiece of the recommendations of the much publicized Commission on Research and Development in

1990 (1, p. 79). Its ideas were considered so important that they were the subject for discussion at a Nobel Symposium in Stockholm. A task force and then a Council of Health Research for Development were formed to promote ENHR (46). The requiem for ENHR was read by Lincoln Chen (secretary to the 1990 Commission on Research and Development), who articulated the assessment of many of those gathered, at the International Conference on Health Research for Development held in Bangkok in 2002: "ENHR has not lived up to its expectations" (47). Why did it take ten long years and a considerable investment of resources to come to the obvious conclusion?

Again, while there has rightly been a strong plea for the use of operational research in health service development in poor countries, OR has been applied in different ways in different places. Echoing the (unfulfilled) promises made at the Nobel Symposium, the CMH also recommends setting aside "at least 5 per cent of all resources to operational research in order to examine the efficacy, the optimisation of treatment protocols, the economics of alternative interventions and delivery modes and population/patient preferences" (1, p. 8). It recommends a Global Health Research Fund, with an annual allocation of U.S.$1.5 billion for research on health service development for the poor (1, p. 189).

USE OF QUESTIONABLE MEASUREMENT TOOLS

Perhaps the worst part of the CMH report pertains to the use of DALYs in calculating the cost of illness among poor people due to different clusters of diseases, and calculating the gains that will accrue from as yet undefined "proper sets of interventions" to reduce the incidence and prevalence of these diseases, in what are mysteriously called "WHO Demographically Developing Regions—1998–2020." The commission obtained these data from the widely criticized *World Health Report 2000* (48, Annex Table 4, pp. 170–175), reproduced as Tables 16a, 16b, 17a, and 17b in the CMH report (1, pp. 104–107). The commission deserves even sharper criticism, because it can be accused of intellectual and ethical lapses—not only for failing to see through the widely discussed errors in the WHO data, but also for not paying heed to the valid criticisms of the *World Health Report 2000,* including the comprehensive critique by Navarro (49; see Chapter 20 in this volume) and the academic debate it triggered.

In the CMH report (following the *World Health Report 2002*), the diseases of the poor are classified into three groups: *Group I:* infections and nutritional deficiencies, maternal conditions, respiratory infections, and prenatal conditions; *Group II:* malignant neoplasms, cardiovascular diseases, and others; and *Group III,* as defined in the *World Health Report 2002.* Nobody with even a nodding acquaintance with the health situation in poor countries will give any credence to the data churned out by WHO and so avidly embraced by the CMH. By far the great majority of the world's poor do not even have a reasonably reliable civil registration system of births and deaths, so how can WHO "estimate" morbidity and mortality under such conditions? In an earlier article, Navarro (50) expressed deep concern about the academic quality of the work done at WHO.

The concept of DALYs itself is bristling with gross infirmities, so the entire exercise undertaken by the CMH is an exercise in futility. When the data used are so patently faulty, no purpose is served by examining the validity of what Navarro has called "modeling and statistical and mathematical discourse" in coming to conclusions about the costs of implementing the commission's recommendations: country-level programs: $22 billion annually by 2007 and $37 billion annually in 2015; research and development for diseases of the poor: $3 billion annually by 2007 and $4 billion annually in 2015; provision of other global public goods: $2 billion annually by 2007 and $3 billion annually in 2015 (1, p. 18). The figures are obviously meaningless.

In any event, one can say with reasonable certainty that the manner in which the CMH has designed its centerpiece—the CTC-hospital-superstructure system and the imposition of the many vertical programs—will meet the same fate as the earlier initiatives, such as the UIP and International Commission on Health Research and Development.

PROBABLE LINKAGE BETWEEN FUNDAMENTAL SHIFTS IN WHO POLICIES AND THE WORKINGS OF THE COMMISSION ON MACROECONOMICS AND HEALTH

The proposals of the CMH discussed in this chapter, which are based on many of the ideas developed by WHO over the past two decades, have led to the formulation of a new line of thinking in the practice of international health, particularly in relation to the poor and the deprived of the world, who form the bulk of the world's population (35). I do not contend that there should be no shifts in ideas and policies. It is but natural to expect upheavals (paradigm shifts?) in the knowledge and practice of public health (and medicine) over a period of time. The theory of a single etiology of a disease in a community; changes in the natural history of diseases in a community as a result of changes in the balance within the triad of human host, causative agents, and the environment; and the Alma-Ata Declaration—these are some examples of such upheavals. WHO's 1995 report *New Public Health and WHO's Ninth General Programme of Work* (14) can also be seen as a shift in thinking.

However, the approach adopted by the CMH in developing its plan for spending $27 billion annually from 2007 and $37 billion annually from 2015 to provide health to the world's poor and deprived is of a qualitatively different kind. It disregards convincing scientific evidence that contradicts its suppositions; it is ahistorical, apolitical, and atheoretical; it pointedly omits certain scientifically well-established public health approaches; and it pays scant attention to the reliability, validity, and comparability of critical data and the validity of many of the mathematical models it uses. This somewhat aggressive approach probably led to the commission's drawing unwarranted conclusions from such scientifically questionable tools as DALYs, using highly questionable data on average per capita income in converting DALYs saved into dollar terms and in calculating the cost of intervention in various gross categories of disease in dollar terms, without paying attention to some key elements of interventions in terms of optimizing costs.

Apparently, the situation at WHO had deteriorated to such an extent that the organization sought advice from a group of experts to examine its functioning. The director-general of WHO commissioned a team of consultants led by Leonard Lerer and Richard Matzopoulos, from the reputed French firm of consultants, Healthcare Management Initiative, to review the managerial process through which the organization planned and monitored its performance (51). As expected, the report was not positive. The consultants titled their case study "'The Worst of Both the Worlds': The Management Reform of the World Health Organization," as an allusion to their overwhelming impression that the senior managers and policymakers in global "public sector" institutions seemed to be adopting what they believed to be current business management ideology—namely, that efficiency and productivity are obtained through harsh, rigid control and that short-term results to satisfy external stakeholders are justifiable at any cost. This approach results in a cruelty and inflexibility in the institution, extreme resistance from the staff, and a range of actions and interventions that are clearly not sustainable. This, according to Lerer and Matzopoulos, is certainly not the current managerial approach in most of the private sector: this is the worst of the world of private sector management. At the same time, WHO exhibits the worst of the "public sector" in its archaic forms of governance, political context of decision-making, and lack of transparency and accountability that are often part of the U.N. system and the global "public" service. The consultants conclude: "We are left reflecting on a way forward and perhaps considering two simple questions: what is the core business of WHO, and who has the courage to grapple with the root causes of its problems?" (51).

Lerer and Matzopoulos's report can perhaps explain how some of the most eminent economists of the world could not avoid being influenced by what these authors called the "cruelty and inflexibility" in the working of WHO. Adoption of some of WHO's highly distorted concepts and data by the Commission on Macroeconomics and Health has, in turn, brought about major distortions in the CMH report. Is it a global phenomenon? This should form an important area for medical sociologists' study of the sociology of knowledge.

REFERENCES

1. World Health Organization. *Report of the Commission on Macroeconomics and Health—Macroeconomics and Health: Investing in Health for Economic Development.* Geneva, 2001.
2. Sen, A. *Development as Freedom.* Knopf, New York, 1999.

3. Sen, A. Health in development. *Bull. World Health Organ.* 77:519–623, 1999.
4. Navarro, V. Development and quality of life: A critique of Amartya Sen's Development as Freedom. *Int. J. Health Serv.* 30:661–674, 2000.
5. McKinlay, J. L. *Issues in the Political Economy of Health.* Tavistock, London, 1984.
6. Banerji, D. Health economics in developing countries. *J. Indian Med. Assoc.* 49:417–421, 1967.
7. Andersen, S. Operations research in public health. *Public Health Rep.* 79(4), April 1964.
8. Banerji, D. Scientific bases of the national tuberculosis programme. In *Serious Implications of the Proposed Revised National Tuberculosis Control Programme for India,* pp. 3–11. Voluntary Health Association of India and Nucleus for Health Policies and Programmes, New Delhi, 1996.
9. Banerji, D. Administration of the family planning programme: A plea for an operational research approach. *Manage. Government* 1(2):48, 1969.
10. Banerji, D. Operational research in the field of community health. *Opsearch* 9:135–142, 1972.
11. Banerji, D. A simplistic approach to health policy analysis: The World Bank team on the Indian health sector. *Int. J. Health Serv.* 24:151–159, 1994.
12. World Bank. *India: Health Sector Financing.* Washington, DC, 1992.
13. Navarro, V. A historical review (1965–1967) of studies on class, health, and quality of life: A personal account. *Int. J. Health Serv.* 28:389–406, 1998.
14. World Health Organization. *New Public Health and WHO's Ninth General Programme of Work.* Geneva, 1995.
15. World Health Organization. *New Challenges for Public Health.* Geneva, 1996.
16. Leavell, H. R., and Clark, E. G. (eds.). *Preventive Medicine for the Doctor in His Community: An Epidemiological Approach,* Ed. 3. McGraw-Hill, New York, 1953.
17. World Health Organization. *Primary Health Care: Report on the International Conference on Primary Health Care, Alma-Ata, USSR, September 6–17, 1978.* Geneva, 1978.
18. WHO Resolution WHA.32.33. In *Handbook of Resolutions and Decisions,* Vol. 2 (1973–84). WHO, Geneva, 1985.
19. Rosen, G. *History of Public Health.* M. D. Publications, New York, 1958.
20. Sokhey, J., et al. *Immunization Programme in India: A Handbook for Medical Officers.* Ministry of Health and Family Welfare, New Delhi, 1984.
21. Banerji, D. Western response to the Alma-Ata Declaration. *Econ. Polit. Weekly* 21, July 12, 1986.
22. Banerji, D. Crash of the immunization program: Consequences of a totalitarian approach. *Int. J. Health Serv.* 20:501–510, 1990.
23. Gupta, J. P., and Murali, I. *National Review of the Immunisation Programme in India.* National Institute of Health and Family Welfare, New Delhi, 1989.
24. Mahalonobis, P. C. An approach of operational research to planning in India. *Sankhya* 24:5–90, 1951.
25. Churchman, C. W., et al. *Introduction to Operations Research.* John Wiley, New York, 1957.
26. Dutt, P. R. *Health Services in India: The Primary Health Centres,* Ed. 2. Central Health Education Bureau, New Delhi, 1965.
27. Bhattacharya, S. N. *Community Development: An Analysis of the Programme in India.* Academic Press, Calcutta, 1970.

29. Government of India. *Health Survey and Development Committee: Report,* Vol. 2. Publications Division, Delhi, 1946.
30. Gonzalez, C. L. *Mass Campaign and the General Health Services.* WHO Public Health Papers No. 29. WHO, Geneva, 1965.
31. Government of India. *National Health Policy 2002.* Ministry of Health and Family Welfare, New Delhi, 2002.
32. Voluntary Health Association of India. *Independent Commission on Health in India: Report.* New Delhi, 1997.
33. Banerji, D. *Family Planning in India: A Critique and a Perspective.* People's Publishing House, New Delhi, 1967.
34. Banerji, D. *Health and Family Planning Services in India: An Epidemiological, Socio-cultural, and Political Analysis and a Perspective.* Lok Paksh, New Delhi, 1985.
35. Banerji, D. A fundamental shift in the approach to international health by WHO, UNICEF, and the World Bank: Instances of the practice of "intellectual fascism" and totalitarianism in some Asian countries. *Int. J. Health Serv.* 29:227–259, 1999.
36. Banerji, D. *Landmarks in the Development of Health Services in Countries of South Asia.* Nucleus for Health Policies and Programmes, New Delhi, 1997.
37. Banerji, D. *Serious Implications of the Proposed Revised National Tuberculosis Control Programme for India.* Voluntary Health Association of India and the Nucleus for Health Policies and Programmes, New Delhi, 1996.
38. World Health Organization. *Expert Committee on Tuberculosis: Eighth Report.* Geneva, 1964.
39. World Health Organization. *WHO Report on Tuberculosis Epidemic 1995.* TB/95/183. Geneva, 1995.
40. Chakraborty, A. K. Tuberculosis situation in India: Measuring it through time. *Indian J. Tuberculosis* 40:215–226, 1993.
41. Grzybowski, S. Epidemiology of tuberculosis with particular reference to India. *Indian J. Tuberculosis* 42:195–200, 1995.
42. World Health Organization. *WHO Report 2002: Global Tuberculosis Control.* Geneva, 2002.
43. News item: Drugs "expire" as do patients: WHO plan to curb TB can't reach patients. *Pioneer* (New Delhi), March 24, 2002.
44. Navarro, V. Science or ideology: A response to Murray and Frenk. *Int. J. Health Serv.* 31:875–880, 2001.
45. News item: AIDS alarm in China. *Statesman* (New Delhi), April 12, 2002.
46. *Research into Action: A Newsletter of the Council of Health Research for Development* 26, October-December 2001.
47. World Health Organization. *International Conference on Health Research for Development.* Bangkok, 2002.
48. World Health Organization. *World Health Report 2000: Health Systems: Improving Performance.* Geneva, 2000.
49. Navarro, V. Assessment of the World Health Report 2000. *Lancet* 356:1598–1601, 2000.
50. Navarro, V. Health and equity in the world in the era of "globalization." *Int. J. Health Serv.* 29:215–226, 1999.
51. Lerer, L., and Matzopoulos, R. "The worst of both worlds": The management reform of the World Health Organization. *Int. J. Health Serv.* 31:415–437, 2001.

CHAPTER 20

Assessment of the
World Health Report 2000

Vicente Navarro

On June 24, 2000, the WHO released a report that assessed the world's health-care systems based on an overall index of performance (1). The report had an immediate and enormous impact and was discussed on the front page of almost every major newspaper in the western world and on the broadcast news. The WHO, the health agency of the United Nations (UN), had assessed health-care systems around the world and everyone wanted to know where his or her country was placed in the health-care system league.

In health-policy circles, the report caused some big surprises. At the top of the WHO's health-care league were countries such as Spain and Italy, whose health-care systems were rarely considered models of efficiency or effectiveness before. In Spain, for example, release of the WHO report, which ranked the Spanish system as the third best in Europe, after Italy and France, coincided with unprecedented demonstrations against the Spanish health-care authorities. Demonstrators were protesting against the long waiting lists for critical life-and-death interventions (which had been responsible for a large number of deaths) and the short consultation times in primary-care centres (an average of 3 mins per consultation). This state of affairs in the Spanish system had forced prominent professional associations, including the Spanish Association of Primary Care Physicians, to denounce the current situation as "intolerable" (these events were widely reported in the Spanish press in June and July; see, for example, the series in *El Pais* in June 2000). The growing popular protest had put Spain's Conservative government on the defensive, until the WHO brought out its report listing the Spanish system as the third best in Europe and the seventh best in the world. Spain's Conservative Minister of Health showed the WHO report to the protesters as proof of the unjustified nature of their complaints and demands.

The protesters, however, were not impressed by the WHO's ranking of Spain's health-care system. Something seemed profoundly wrong in the report's claiming that the performance of the Spanish system was the seventh best in the world. The report's conclusions certainly did not coincide with the perceptions of most Spanish people. In one of the most rigorous surveys of views of the Spanish population regarding health care, Spaniards expressed more discontent with their system than did the population of any other major country in the European Union, except Italy, whose health care was also listed among the "best" in the WHO report. An impressive 28 percent of the Spanish population (and an even more impressive 40 percent of the Italian population) indicated "there was so much wrong with their HCS (health-care system) that they needed to completely rebuild it," and an additional 49 percent of the Spanish population (and 46 percent of the Italian population) stated that "there were some good things in their HCS but fundamental changes were needed to make it better" (2). There was indeed a disagreement about the definition of performance by the WHO and by the Spanish and Italian populations. Who is right? In order to answer this question, we must first understand that the WHO is not a scientific but rather a political institution whose positions and reports must be assessed both scientifically and politically.

The Objective of the WHO Ranking

Why do we need to rank countries according to the performance of their health services? Presumably, an important objective is to see what we can learn from "the best," using them as points of reference on the road to better health. A very important element in the WHO ranking, however, is the credibility of the indicators of performance that it uses. It is therefore important to know how the ranking was developed, the assumptions behind the preparation of the indicators used in the ranking, and the consequences for health policy of choosing one indicator versus another.

Let us start with the nature of the indicators. The WHO report develops three types of indicators. The first is related to the effectiveness of the health-care system (mainly medical care plus traditional public-health services) in reducing mortality and morbidity. The second is related to the responsiveness of the system to the user, understanding responsiveness as the ability to protect the user's dignity; to provide confidentiality and autonomy; to provide care promptly with high-quality amenities; to provide access to social support; and to ensure a choice of provider. And the third type of indicator is related to the fairness of the system, measured by the degree of progressiveness in the funding of health care.

All three types of indicators are weighted and added to create a single indicator, the indicator of performance. It is unclear why the WHO felt the need to come up with one synthetic indicator of performance. There is not, after all, a single UN indicator for ranking countries by economic performance. Rather, the annual UN economic reports use specific indicators to measure different components of economic efficiency such as unemployment, economic growth per capita, rate of productivity growth, and so on. But no single indicator summarizes the many dimensions of the equally complex issue of economic performance. So why did the WHO decide to make a single indicator for performance of health-care systems? The WHO report is silent on this point.

Effectiveness of Health-Care Systems

In the WHO's conceptualisation of medical-care effectiveness, the report uncritically reproduces a major assumption in medical-care cultures that medicine is very effective in reducing mortality and morbidity. I find it astonishing that a prominent public-health agency could state:

> The differing degrees of efficiency with which health systems organize and finance themselves, and react to the needs of their populations explain much of the widening gap in death rates between the rich and poor, in countries and between countries, around the world.

No evidence is given for such a statement. Actually, published literature shows that much of the widening gap in mortality rates within and among countries is primarily related to the growing differentials in wealth and income (3).

> Health systems have played a part in the dramatic rise in life expectancy that occurred during the XX century.

Here again, no scientific data are given to support such a statement. Actually, the evidence shows that the most dramatic declines in mortality and increases in life expectancy occurred during the 20th century before medical care proved effective. Indeed, most dramatic changes in mortality during the century were the result of social and economic interventions (4, 5).

> If Sweden enjoys better health than Uganda—life expectancy is almost exactly twice as long—it is in large part because it spends exactly 35 times as much per capita in its health systems.

Again, no evidence is given for this statement. All the scientific data show there is no link between the level of expenditures in health-care systems and level of mortality. There is evidence, however, for a link between political interventions, wealth and income distribution, and mortality indicators (6).

This enormous faith in the effectiveness of medical care reaches extreme proportions when the WHO report indicates that with "an investment in health care of $12 per person one third of the disease burden in the world in 1990 would have been averted." Thus, the report gives the impression that the major problems of mortality and morbidity are a consequence of the limited resources of health-care systems. Give more money to a health system and more lives will be saved. The report even quantifies how many lives could be saved per dollar invested. Very neat, but profoundly wrong. Nowhere does the WHO report present any scientific evidence to support these wild assertions. Again, most available data show that other factors are far more important in explaining a country's level of health and mortality than are its medical services. Any student of public health knows that medicine is not as effective in reducing mortality and morbidity as the medical establishment believes. Indeed, there is extensive literature on the social, cultural, economic, and political causes of health and disease. That medical care is less effective in reducing mortality than the WHO report assumes does not mean, of course, that medicine is not useful in taking care of patients' medical conditions and improving their quality of life. But it is wrong to explain a country's level of mortality by its medical services. Not even public-health interventions (such as immunising against childhood diseases), which have been far more effective in reducing mortality than have medical-care interventions, can be considered the main reasons for the mortality decline in the 20th century. Social, economic, and political interventions are the primary reasons for this decline.

This mistaken assumption—overestimating the effectiveness of medical and health care—explains why some countries, such as the Mediterranean countries, Spain, Italy, Portugal, and Greece, which traditionally have good health indicators with long life expectancies, earn high marks in the WHO's classification of effectiveness. The report erroneously attributes the low mortality in these countries to the effectiveness of their medical care Actually, these various Mediterranean countries have different types of health services, but all share the characteristic that public expenditures in the health-care system as a percentage of gross national product are among the lowest in the EU. Table 2 (basic indicators for all member states) of the WHO report shows these are among the countries with the lowest probability of dying (per 1000) for children under 5 years and for adults between 15 and 59 years, and with the longest life expectancy in the world. None of them have large health-system expenditures. Their types of funding and organisation are extremely varied—with the common denominator, however, of the populations' high level of dissatisfaction with their health systems. Actually, the WHO report lists these health systems as among the least responsive (to users) of all European systems. In the ranking for responsiveness, Spain is listed 34th, Greece 36th, Portugal 38th, and Italy 23rd, all of them among the least responsive in the EU. It would seem then, according to the authors of the WHO report, that the effectiveness of health-care systems in reducing mortality outweighs their limited responsiveness. They are thus considered user-unfriendly but very effective nevertheless. It is highly questionable, however, whether the good mortality indicators of these countries are the results of health-care system interventions.

Who Defines the Indicators of Responsiveness?

The second component of performance is related to what the report called "responsiveness" of the health-care system to users. The report includes here two major groups of considerations. The first deals with what the report calls "respect for persons," which includes the dignity afforded to the patient, the confidentiality of patients' information, and patients' autonomy. The second group is referred to as "client-oriented attributes," such as prompt attention to the patient, the quality of the amenities, access to social support networks, and choice of provider. It would seem that these characteristics should give a fairly good idea of how responsive a health-care system is to its users.

Conceptually, then, indicators of responsiveness seem to be reasonable. The problem arises when we see that the people who defined the values of these indicators and the weights given to each (derived from questionnaires) are what the WHO report calls "key informants," without specifying who those key informants are. These unknown key informants are most likely experts on health care in the various countries. And the survey of these informants is therefore likely to be a survey of the "conventional wisdom" among experts who define the degree of responsiveness of health-care systems to users. The report does not explain who these key informants are, nor does it explain the criteria for their selection. It is likely, however, that the choice of these informants and experts was highly biased towards what are called health-care-establishment figures. Indeed, the selection of references in the report's bibliography is quite biased and prejudiced against critical positions, issues, or authors. One can find consistent references to conservative and neoliberal authors (such as Alain Enthoven of Stanford University, USA) and mainstream medical journals, but never does the report make reference to critical authors or scientific journals that question established wisdom.

Not surprisingly, therefore, the survey of responsiveness reveals that the countries with more responsive health-care systems are those whose health policies better fit what has become the new conventional wisdom. In this thinking, health-care services that combine public funding with public provision of health care (which has characterised national health services) are out. They are constantly referred to as examples of "heavy handed state intervention . . . the type of intervention discredited everywhere," "highly impersonal and inhuman (as in the pre-1990 Soviet Union)," and "monolithic." The abusive nature of the disqualification of these types of health services is all too clear when the collapse of the Soviet Union is used as an example of the deficiencies of national health services. The fashionable thing now, in current conventional thinking, is an insurance system with a public-private mix that allows for competition between managed care plans, giving patients—referred to as clients—increased choice of providers and permitting more flexibility. The WHO report presents the Thatcher reforms in the British national health service as worth extrapolating to other systems. We should not be surprised that these key informants and experts selected the USA as having the system that is most responsive to users, and Colombia, a Latin American country whose national health service has been replaced by an insurance-based managed care competition model, as having the most responsive system in Latin America.

This profoundly ideological position of the WHO report also comes across in its analysis of what the WHO considers the "failure" of the Alma-Ata approach. The Alma-Ata Declaration was a famous WHO report, written in 1978, which emphasised the importance of primary-care services, combining medical with social interventions at the primary level of care. The new WHO report assumes that implementation of the Alma-Ata report failed because, in designing such primary-care models, too much attention was given to the health needs of the population and not enough to the demand for services; the Alma-Ata report was too oblivious to the importance of the private sector and the market. According to the WHO's June, 2000, report, countries should give far more importance to reforms that aim at "making money follow the patient, shifting away from simply giving providers budgets, which in turn are often determined by supposed needs," as many countries are now doing. The report also indicates that there is a link (nowhere documented) between expansion of private delivery of services and responsiveness of the health-care system. This shift from planning according to need toward demand in the market is a radical change in WHO policy, a change I consider antagonistic to the basic principles of public health.

Not surprisingly, besides choosing the USA as the country with the most responsive system, the WHO report considers the greatest challenge facing government-based health systems is to respond to the need for regulating the private sector, a function, say the authors, that most countries are not prepared for. The model they advocate is that put forward by Enthoven (an author cited approvingly in the report), which inspired the Thatcher reforms in the British national health service.

Consequently, given the political and propagandistic character of the report, nowhere do we find quoted, cited, or argued the huge amount of scientific evidence that questions each of the assumptions made in the report and challenges the superiority of insurance-based health-care systems. (There is an extensive literature critical of insurance-based managed care, mostly published in the *International Journal of Health Services* in the 1990s.) To make the USA the top-ranked country in responsiveness to health-care users not only ignores the large body of scientific evidence that shows just how unresponsive the US health service actually is, but also sets aside any observation of the political context of health policy in the USA. The Democratic Party is now trying to identify managed care and managed competition, and their unresponsiveness to users, with the Republican Party as a way of gaining some political advantage in the coming Presidential and Congressional elections, knowing how unpopular managed care and managed competition are with most citizens of the USA.

Unfortunately, however, the WHO is doing what its American branch, the Pan-American Health Organisation (PAHO), has been doing for years— functioning as a transmission bell for Latin America of the conventional wisdom in US financial and political circles. In recent years we have been witnessing how the PAHO and now the WHO, with the assistance of the World Bank and private foundations, are presenting insurance-based managed care as part of the solution to the burgeoning health-care problems in Latin America (7). The privately managed health-insurance schemes are seen as playing a positive role in complementing and competing with the government health-care systems. In a recent speech to corporate and academic leaders in the USA, the Director General of the PAHO referred to the successful experience of several private health insurance schemes in Latin America, taking Instituciones de Salud Previsional (ISAPRES), the major private insurance scheme in Chile, as an example: "The example of ISAPRES in Chile shows the possible success of the privately managed health and social insurance schemes [in Latin America]" (8).

The question that needs to be asked is, for whom is ISAPRES successful? This private insurance scheme, introduced when the dictatorship of General Pinochet dismantled the Chilean national health service, owes its commercial success to the selection of patients, catering to the upper-income sectors of the population while leaving chronically ill and low-income patients to the public sector, reproducing a well-documented social polarisation in the health sector as characterised by the allocation of resources according to the type of insurance coverage and ability to pay rather than according to need (9). This is the unavoidable result of having insurance, competition, and private entrepreneurship (key words in the dominant discourse) in the health sector. The extreme expression of this model is the health-care system of the USA, which the WHO report presents as exemplary for its responsiveness to users. The US population, however, does not concur. According to a report on a nationwide poll by the American Hospital Association: "the majority of the people in the US see [in the health services they received] neither a planned system nor a consumer-oriented organization except one devoted to maximizing profit by blocking access, reducing quality, and limiting spending . . . They blame most of it on the pursuit of profits by health insurance companies . . . Americans believe that their health insurance companies have too much influence and exert too much control over their care" (10).

Because of the enormous influence of the US government on many international agencies, we are seeing their promotion of dominant US values and practices, including managed care and managed competition. Here it is important to note something that has escaped the attention of most observers: the WHO's protective shell against worldwide criticism of its political positions. The WHO has been surrounded by an aura of humanism and social concern that has protected it from close scrutiny. But, just as the World Trade Organization WTO), the World Bank, and the International Monetary Fund (IMF) have come under increasing criticism, so too should the WHO. It is a political institution, heavily involved in propaganda in the guise of apolitical neutrality, ignoring the critical voices that denounced its behaviour. Debabar Banerji has recently criticised the damage that some WHO policies are causing in developing countries (11). We need to be far more critical of the currents in the WHO that are increasingly attuned to the needs of large interest groups, responding to a culture of entrepreneurship, competition, and market values that conflicts with the needs of our populations, as the US experience with its health-care system clearly shows.

How to Define Progressiveness of Funding

Finally, some concerns need to be raised about the third type of indicator used in the WHO Report, related to the degree of "progressiveness" in funding health services. The authors of the report analysed the percentage of household funds spent on health care by several deciles of the population in each country, assuming that the same percentage spent on health care (as percentage of capacity to pay) by different income groups means fair funding arrangements. As the WHO report indicates, "the way that health care is financed is perfectly fair if the ratio of total health contribution to total non-food spending is identical for all households, independently of their income, their health status or their use of the health system." Fairness is a highly subjective concept. But if by fairness in health-care financing we mean that each person should receive health-care services according to his or her needs while contributing according to his or her ability and command of resources, then a criterion of fairness should be the degree to which the financing of health care is redistributive. According to that criterion, to be authentically progressive, the system of funding should be optimally redistributive—that is, the percentage of household contribution to the funding of health services (as percentage of capacity to pay) should be larger (not the same) as household income increases. But this indicator by itself would also be insufficient to tell us much about fairness or progressivity, since fairness depends on the destiny of the household health spending, a topic untouched in the WHO report. A wealthy family may spend much more on health care than a low-income family without having any bearing on progressiveness, if those higher expenses go into higher or more luxurious consumption without having any redistributive effect. In that sense, progressiveness of funding cannot be analysed independently of the channels through which the funding moves. Progressive funding will have a redistributive effect only when the payments are connected to the same system in which funds are transferred from one group to another.

Conclusions

Most experts in health care would agree that the assessment of health-care systems is not an exact science. As in many dimensions of the scientific project, the barrier between science and ideology is not an impermeable one; on the contrary, it is highly porous. The WHO's June, 2000, report is a good example. The issue under discussion, therefore, is what values sustain the ideology reproduced in the WHO report and whether these values are a help or a hindrance on the road to a healthier world.

The principal values reproduced in the WHO report are those that sustain the dominant conventional wisdom in the foremost medical, financial, and political arenas in the USA and other major more-developed countries, based on two main assumptions. The first is the belief that the most prominent health problems our societies now face can be resolved by technological-scientific medical bullets or interventions, without reference to changes in the social, political, and economic environments in which these problems are produced. The second assumption is that the supposed "failures" of health-care systems are due to an excessive reliance on public interventions without allowing for the development of the (assumed) great potential of the private sectors. Thus, there is a growing call for increased partnership between public and private interests in which the latter are increasingly influential in shaping the nature of public decisions. In the new wisdom, client demand replaces patients' needs, risk is valued over security, market shares dominate over government planning, and entrepreneurship dominates over public services. This conventional wisdom has become almost a dogma, which, like all dogmas, is based more on faith than on evidence. It is wrong for the WHO report to uncritically reproduce this thinking.

Note — This chapter was originally published in *Lancet* 356:1598–601, November 4, 2000.

REFERENCES

1. World Health Organization. *Health Systems. Improving Performance.* Geneva, 2000.
2. Blendon, R., et al. Spain's citizens assess their health care system. *Health Aff.* 10:216–228, 1991.
3. Wilkinson, R. *Unhealthy Societies.* Routledge, London, 1996.
4. Berkman, L., and Kawachi, I. (eds.). *Social Epidemiology.* Oxford University Press, Oxford, 2000.
5. Navarro, V. (ed.). *The Political Economy of Social Inequalities.* Baywood, Amityville, NY, 2000.
6. Navarro, V., and Shi, L. The political context of social inequalities and health. *Soc. Sci. Med.* 52:1–11, 2000.
7. Pan American Health Organization. *Health Services Financing and Private Sector Participation: Developing a Model Incorporating American and Caribbean Experiences.* Technical Report Series No. 65. PAHO Public Policy and Health Program, Washington, DC, 1998.
8. Alleyne, A. O. Health Sector Reform, Financing and the Poor. Presentation to the Global Council's 26th Annual Conference "Who Pays? Health Care Reform and Financing in Developing Countries," Arlington, VA, June 20, 1999.

9. Nunez, M. Inequality in the Utilization of Health Services in Chile: Analysis of the Effects of Individual Income and Health Insurance Coverage on Timely Receipt of Health Care Services. Johns Hopkins University, Baltimore, 2000.
10. American Hospital Association. *Reality Check—Public Perceptions of Health and Hospitals.* A Report from Dick Davidson to American Hospital Association Member CEOs. Chicago, 1997.
11. Banerji, D. A fundamental shift in the approach to international health by WHO, UNICEF, and the World Bank. *Int. J. Health Serv.* 29:227–259, 1999.

CHAPTER 21

Serious Crisis in the Practice of International Health by the World Health Organization: The Commission on Social Determinants of Health

Debabar Banerji

Undaunted by the extremely disappointing outcome of the work of some of the world's top economists at the WHO Commission on Macroeconomics and Health (1–4; see Chapters 18 and 19 in this volume), at the World Health Assembly (WHA) in 2004, WHO Director-General Dr. Lee Jong-wook called for the formation of the Commission on Social Determinants of Health. Operating for three years, beginning in March 2005, the Commission (CSDH) is charged with recommending interventions and policies to improve health and narrow health inequalities through action on social determinants (5, 6). The CSDH aims to lever policy change by turning existing public health knowledge into actionable global and national policy agendas. It is expected to achieve the following:

- Compile evidence on successful interventions and formulate policies that address key social determinants of health, particularly for low-income countries.
- Raise societal debate and advocate for implementation by member states, civil society, and global health actors of policies that address social determinants of health.
- Define a medium- and long-term action agenda for incorporating social determinants of health interventions/approaches into planning, policy, and technical work within the WHO.

The main expectations from the CSDH are as follows:

- *Country work* will illustrate ways of addressing the social determinants of health in national health policies and programs related to the Commission's themes. Partner countries will document their findings with respect to the policy process and health effects. Their reports will inform the commissioners' recommendations, for national and global policies and for ways of working at the WHO.

- *Knowledge networks* comprised of leading scientists and practitioners will compile knowledge on interventions to overcome the social barriers to health, with a focus on low-income countries. The knowledge networks will cover themes that include early child development, health systems, employment conditions, globalization, priority public health conditions, urban settings, social exclusion, and measurement of the impact of social determinants approaches on health outcomes.
- *Commission reports* will outline opportunities for action on the social determinants of health for each theme, and recommend specific areas of policy and institutional change to global and member-state stakeholders.
- A *WHO report* will propose concrete mechanisms for incorporating social determinants of health interventions and approaches into WHO programs.

The WHA is asking the Commission to perform what seem to be impossible tasks, in terms of both the geographic extent and the wide range of formulation of policies, plans, and programs required for individual countries. There is a patent lack of organized thinking when it somewhat grandiosely proclaims that the CSDH "aims to lever policy change by turning existing public health knowledge into actionable global and national policy agendas." For instance, the WHA visualizes the Commission undertaking the formidable task of submitting actionable policy agendas for countries such as China and India, on the one side, and Chad and Bolivia, on the other. To further confound the situation, it goes on to give yet another list of 13 bewilderingly diverse areas for action, which "is dedicated to identifying effective approaches and producing policy recommendations for overcoming the social barriers to health."

- Health inequalities impact assessments
- Health needs assessments for disadvantaged groups
- Prevention and health promotion campaigns targeting vulnerable groups
- "Health action zones" declared for areas deprived of services
- Local authority scrutiny of inequalities
- Occupational health services for all employees
- Job rotation for laborers in high-risk jobs
- Employment protection for chronically ill citizens
- School-based health and nutrition services
- Healthy food catering to workplaces
- Healthy community trainings
- Social welfare programs that make benefits conditional on children's school attendance, regular medical check-ups, and other health-promoting actions

• Integrated public budgeting based on health and health equity objectives for the country

In this list, challenging tasks of assessing the effects of health inequality are listed along with such relatively minor tasks as healthy food catering to workplaces and healthy community training. It is difficult to link the given themes with the overcoming of social barriers and drawing up of actionable agendas.

A CRITIQUE OF THE APPROACH

How does the WHO reconcile its oft-repeated focus on low-income countries with its interventions in such areas, in addition to the ones mentioned for actions under "knowledge networks"? Under the heading "country work," in its plans for the CSDH, it claims: "country work will illustrate ways of addressing the social determinants of health in national health policies and programs related to the Commission's themes. Partner countries will document their findings with respect to the policy process and health impacts. Their reports will inform the Commissioners' recommendations, both for national and global policies and ways of working at WHO." Adoption of such an approach is by far the most critical shortcoming in the conceptualization and design of the work of the Commission. It points to a serious lack of scholarship within the WHO Secretariat. If the WHO Secretariat had looked into the considerable body of already existing literature on this subject within the WHO itself, it would soon have realized that the documents to be produced by "partner countries" of the CSDH already exist within the WHO. It is also intriguing that the members of the Commission overlooked the existence of these documents. Reinventing the wheel?

A mere putting together of a few key documents produced before and after the Alma-Ata Declaration on Primary Health Care in 1978 (7) and a close examination of the Declaration would have covered most if not all of the issues sought to be taken up by the CSDH. Two well-researched books—*Health by the People*, edited by K. W. Newell (8), and *Alternative Approaches to Meeting Basic Health Needs in Developing Countries*, edited by V. Djukanovic and E. P. Mach (9)—contain many country case studies that could have provided the inputs needed by the CSDH in areas such as compiling evidence on successful interventions, formulating policies that address key social determinants, and defining a medium- and long-term action agenda for incorporating social determinants of health interventions/approaches into planning, policy, and technical work within the WHO. Documents produced by the WHO for the top-level interaction between the WHO and the World Bank in the mid-1970s, in exploring joint programs of work on combined action in health and poverty issues (10), would be another rich resource for developing the WHA's thinking on the Commission.

Considerable work on "Health by the People" culminated in the formulation of the Alma-Ata Declaration on Primary Health Care (PHC) in 1978 (7). Very briefly stated, it was to be guided by seven principles that stressed (*a*) the need to shape PHC "around the pattern of the population"; (*b*) "involvement of the local population"; (*c*) "maximum reliance on available community resources" while remaining within cost limitations; (*d*) an integrated approach of promotive, preventive, and curative services for both the community and the individual; (*e*) all interventions to be undertaken "at the most peripheral level of health services by the worker most simply trained for this activity"; (*f*) other echelons of services to be designed in support of the needs of the peripheral level; and (*g*) PHC services to be fully integrated with the services of other sectors involved in community development (7, 11, 12). Socrates Litsios (12) has brought together a large amount of documentary evidence from within the WHO (which, incidentally, included the Soviet Union's repeated insistence that the WHO learn from the socialist experience of health service development) to make an insightful analysis of the interplay of (Cold War) political forces that led to the decision to have the International Conference on PHC at Alma-Ata, then in the Soviet Union. Litsios's analysis of the intense public health debates during encounters between the two rival camps provides a disturbing backdrop to the current thinking that dominates the "unipolar" WHO.

The years immediately following the Alma-Ata Declaration saw an even more creative upsurge in the field of international health in the WHO. Reports of two expert committees—one on New Approaches to Health Education in Primary Health Care (13), and the other on Health Manpower Requirements for the Achievement of Health for All by the Year 2000 through Primary Health Care (14)—and publication of monographs in the WHO's "Health for All Series" to articulate specific aspects of implementation, monitoring, and evaluation of Health for All by 2000 through primary health care (HFA-2000/PHC), were some of the outcomes of these efforts. The report of a special WHO group on Inter-sectoral Linkages and Health Development (15) was published in 1984.

THE RETREAT FROM ALMA-ATA

The abrupt end to this trend and its replacement by what came to be known as selective primary health care (SPHC) (16), which received enthusiastic support from both the WHO and UNICEF—the two sponsors of HFA-2000/PHC—was a most significant turn around in the history of public health practice by the WHO. This change inaugurated a long series of what have been called "international initiatives" or "vertical" or "categorical" programs. In sharp contrast to HFA-2000/PHC, with its focus on social determinants of health, these programs were technocentric and limited to specific diseases, were imposed on the people, and turned out to be far from cost-effective, as was claimed at the time of their launching (16).

As if seeming to take yet another turn, the WHO Secretariat came forward with the document *Ninth General Programme of Work Covering the Period 1996–2001* (NGPW-1996–2001) (17), which was submitted to and later approved by the WHA. The Secretariat also produced a consultation document, *Renewing the Health for All Strategy: Elaboration of a Policy for Equity, Solidarity and Health* (18). It also prepared a discussion paper for an interregional meeting in November 1995 that called for adoption of a "New Public Health" (19). While widely approving these ideas, the interregional meeting made some other suggestions, which included changing the title to "New Challenges for Public Health" (20). Conforming to the trend of the past few years, little action followed along the very promising lines suggested by the WHO and the interregional group. The WHO Secretariat, for instance, did not include these ideas when it set out to define the justification and terms of reference for the CSDH or, earlier, for the Commission on Macroeconomics and Health.

An almost total failure to consider the remarkable experiments and successes in nationwide implementation of integrated health services that took full account of the social determinants of health in the now much-maligned socialist countries, such as the former Soviet Union, the Warsaw Pact countries, China, and Cuba, is yet another disappointing feature of the process that led to formation of the CSDH. Despite suffering from sustained and almost intolerable political and economic attacks from outside, the heroic efforts of the people and the government of Cuba to retain one of the best health care systems in the world ought to have served as a shining example to anybody discussing social determinants of health (5, 21).

Somewhat less successful but highly innovative experiments to take into account social determinants of health had also been carried out by many poor countries that could not or did not take the socialist path. I will make brief references to three such instances.

One of the most massive bloodbaths of the liberation struggle preceded the birth of Bangladesh in 1971. Among others problems, the country faced an almost overwhelming challenge of extending health services to its people. Gonoswasthya Kendra (People's Health Center) (22), which had hitherto been catering to the casualties of the liberation struggle, extended its activities by developing low-cost medical practices to provide services to some of the most acutely suffering people and packaging those services with some other similarly devised low-cost measures to address the social determinants of their sickness. Similarly, when, after Independence, India found itself facing massive health, social, and economic problems, as early as 1952 it made the crucial decision to cover the entire rural population by setting up primary health centers (23) to provide promotive, preventive, and curative health services as an integral part of a country-wide network of community development programs (24). This was meant to become a component of the overall social and economic development process. India also started an ambitious Integrated Child Development Services Scheme (25) to cater to the different needs of the country's very needy children. In 1977, it started the

Community Health Workers' Scheme (26) to entrust "people's health in people's hands." Finally, the government of Iran (during the Shah's rule) also launched a community health workers' scheme to extend what could be called "demystified health services" to its underserved rural population (27).

THE APOLITICAL AND AHISTORICAL APPROACH BY THE COMMISSION ON SOCIAL DETERMINANTS OF HEALTH

An obvious question that ought to have received urgent attention from the WHO—and the CSDH—is, What were the factors that stood in the way of implementing such promising initiatives? Ironically, the very fact that the WHO is so powerfully influenced by the dominant international political forces might have persuaded the organization against making deeper political, social, and technical analyses of the repeated failures of many of its own highly ambitious initiatives (e.g., the Universal Immunization Programs of 1985–1990) or initiatives started by individual political groupings or individual countries. As mentioned earlier, the case of Cuba stands alone, its people and government standing firm in maintaining and sustaining its social, economic, and health service system. Present-day China presents a dramatically different picture. Its zeal to embrace a market economy has led to serious deterioration of the earlier well-nurtured health cooperatives that were part of the wider village commune system (8).

In a Roundtable discussion on the CSDH, held in New Delhi in September 2005 (28), the chairman, Michael Marmot, made a significant statement. Responding to a question, he observed that the CSDH is meant to complement the work of the WHO Commission on Macroeconomics and Health (CMH). This raises three sets of problems. The first is the serious lapse on the part of the WHO, the WHA, and the CMH in overlooking the central role of social determinants when considering health aspects of populations. The second is that, from an examination of the conceptualization of the CSDH and its workings up to its half-way stage, it is not difficult to foresee that it will meet the same fate as the CMH. The third (and undoubtedly most important, as pointed out below) is that there are so many infirmities in the "noncomplementary" portions of the CMH report that its "complementing" the report of the CSDH will create a very undesirable product.

As is now clear, the recommendations of the CMH had little impact on health policies and programs at the international and national levels (2–4). This is not surprising, considering the poor quality of scholarship manifested by the members of that commission. Critics from different parts of the world have drawn attention to vital flaws in the arguments presented by the CMH. Apart from the absence of social determinants of health, the CMH report has been shown to suffer from serious flaws in its understanding of political and economic issues (2, 4). Over and above this, the CMH betrayed a profound lack of understanding of some of the basic principles of public health practice (3). Its analyses of vertical programs, such as the measles immunization program in Malawi; its recommendations on perpetuating the long-discredited vertical programs without producing any evidence base, and given the counter-evidence on the performance of programs such as the Universal Immunization Program; its gross misunderstanding of operational research as a research tool, which got in the way of its advocacy for optimizing health service systems; its simplistic arguments (non-evidence-based) that led it to recommend "Close-to-Home Clinics" and the setting-up of single-doctor-run 100-bed hospitals-cum-health centers; and its advocacy of extra-WHO organizations such as the Global Fund for AIDS, Tuberculosis and Malaria, the Global Vaccine Action Initiative, and the Global Health Research Forum—these are just the most disturbing examples of the CMH's deficiencies (3).

SOME FUNDAMENTAL QUESTIONS ABOUT THE WORKINGS OF THE WORLD HEALTH ORGANIZATION

Even the very limited references made to "successful interventions" to form an integrated system to "improve and lower health inequalities" by increasing access to services, particularly for the low-income countries, raise some fundamental questions about the workings of the WHO and the WHA. After about half of its planned duration, the outcomes of the CSDH's work also raise serious questions about its competence to add anything substantially new to the extensive work already done in this area. Consider, for example, the WHO's formulation of the principles for practicing PHC, then its almost immediately "forgetting" it and replacing it with SPHC, then its resurrection of PHC when the organization reverted to advocacy of a New Public Health, soon forgotten and followed by its setting-up of the CMH and now the CSDH—these cannot be dismissed as mere phases of amnesia within the WHO and the WHA. The possible reason for this sequence of events lies deep in the power relations among the countries of the world. The rich countries make the bulk of the contributions to the WHO budget. As pointed out by Vicente Navarro (29), the rich countries get together to form an alliance with the rich sectors of the poor countries, who control the political power there. This enables the rich to gain control over most of the poor member states and thus acquire a dominant position in the WHA—just as in many parliaments in developing countries. Interestingly, the *World Development Report 2006* (30) makes a similar statement: "economic inequalities result from unfair power structures and political influence and an absence of corrective measures of market failures." This probably accounts for the fact that the member states of the WHA and its executive board have almost routinely followed the agenda backed by the rich countries. This also makes it convenient for the alliance to use the WHO as a lever to influence the health policies and programs in the dependent, "poor" countries. As one chilling example: the imposition of the not-so-imaginative Global Polio Eradication Initiative (31) on low-income countries, where the disease accounts for less than 0.001 percent of the disease load, could save the rich countries billions of dollars annually by enabling them to stop routine polio immunization in their own countries (as was the case with smallpox). The alliance of the rich can also use its power to influence appointments to some key positions in the WHO to further its agenda. This has enabled the WHO Secretariat to get the approval of the WHA and its executive board for such obviously ill-conceived and ill-designed "international initiatives" as the Universal Immunization Program, the Global Program against Tuberculosis, and the Global AIDS Control Program (32).

It seems that the WHO is accountable for such programs and their massive failures mostly to its dominant fund providers, not to the masses of poor people of the world. This lack of accountability to the wider population poses a most serious problem concerning the nature of the democratic functioning of the WHO. This needs urgent action. The WHO has to be brought back to performing in accordance with the directives laid down in its constitution and working in consonance with its famous definition of health, which has lately been reiterated by a former director-general, Halfdan Mahler (33). This has to be a political struggle for the neglected peoples of the world to wrest their rights from the hands of those who are using the organization for their narrow class interests.

Apparently, the situation has deteriorated to such an extent that the WHO has had to seek advice from experts to examine its functioning. The director-general commissioned a team of consultants led by Leonard Lerer and Richard Matzopoulos, from the reputed firm Healthcare Management Initiative of France, to review the managerial process through which the organization plans and monitors its performance (34). Expectedly, the report was not positive. The consultants entitled their case study "'The Worst of Both Worlds': The Management Reform of the World Health Organization." This is an allusion to the authors' overwhelming impression that the senior managers and policymakers in global "public sector" institutions seemed to be adopting what they believed to be the current business management ideology—namely, that efficiency and productivity are achieved through harsh, rigid control and that short-term results are justifiable at any cost to satisfy external stakeholders. This approach results in a cruelty and inflexibility in the institution, extreme resistance from the staff, and a range of actions and interventions that are clearly not sustainable. According to Lerer and Matzopoulos, this is certainly not the managerial approach generally followed in the private sector: it is the worst of the world of private sector management. At the same time the WHO demonstrates the worst of the world of the "public sector," in archaic forms of governance, political contexts of decision-making, and lack of transparency and accountability that are often part of the U.N. system and the global "public" service. The consultants concluded: "We are left reflecting on a way forward and perhaps considering two simple questions: what is the core business of WHO, and who has the courage to grapple with the root causes of its problems?" (34).

Lehrer and Matzopoulos's report can perhaps explain how some of the most eminent economists of the world, as members of the CMH, could not avoid being influenced by the "cruelty and inflexibility" in the workings of the WHO. The CMH's adoption of some of the distorted concepts and data from the WHO has, in turn, brought about major distortions in the CMH report. This could also explain why the CSDH is encountering so many difficulties and ambiguities in its work. It should form an important area for study of the sociology of knowledge of medical sociologists.

ALTERNATIVE THINKING ON SOCIAL DETERMINANTS OF HEALTH

As is apparent from the foregoing analysis of some of the literature on social determinants of health, recommendations on this important subject must take into consideration historical and political aspects. They cannot remain ahistorical or apolitical. An attempt is made here to give some examples to underline the importance of these aspects in making recommendations on social determinants of health, particularly in "low-income countries."

1. The ancient science of Ayurveda visualized health as the maintenance of balance and harmony between environment, body, mind, and soul (35). Health is a permanent contest for preserving such a balance and wholeness and, ultimately, is a reflection of this harmony in a high level of consciousness. Later discoveries of viruses and bacteria were incorporated as a small component of "environment." The holistic trend of Ayurveda was followed by the ancient Chinese and Greeks and, later, by socially sensitive scholars of the pre-bacteriological era, such as Rudolf Virchow (36–38) and René Sand (39).

2. The ushering in of the bacteriological era saw the emergence of the concept of the single etiology of disease and enunciation of Koch's postulates, with the birth of the science of immunology and of the vaccine and sera industry. Discovery of germs and the use of vaccines and sera are undoubtedly important landmarks in the history of medical science, but exploitation of these discoveries by market forces has given rise to a distortion of science.

3. Later studies of the history of public health by scholars such as George Rosen (40) and Thomas McKeown (41), and interdisciplinary work in epidemiology and the ecology of health and disease by socially sensitive scholars such as Henry Sigerist (42) and John Ryle (43), resurrected the concept of the multiple etiologies of disease: although one cannot get tuberculosis without the bacillus, the mere presence of the germ does not indicate a case of tuberculosis; similarly, alcohol does not cause alcoholism, cars do not cause accidents, and so on.

4. Availability of the so-called silver bullets in the postwar period once again tempted authorities to launch "mass campaigns" against scourges such as malaria (with DDT), tuberculosis (BCG vaccination), leprosy (dapsone), trachoma (auramycin), and so on. So enthusiastic were the exponents of the mass campaign approach that they forgot about the primordial importance of the social determinants of health. This lapse caused repeated setbacks in the conduct of the much trumpeted campaigns.

5. After a lull of another two decades following the disappointing experience with the mass campaign approach—years that saw the international community advocate "integrated health services," "basic health services," and "poverty and health" approaches, culminating in the Alma-Ata Declaration—in a most blatant disregard for basic scientific norms, the international community swung back to the mass campaign mode, this time involving the use of technocentric approaches against the six immunizable diseases, AIDS, malaria, leprosy, tuberculosis, poliomyelitis (eradication), and acute respiratory diseases. The power of market forces, as in the era of vaccines and sera and the later era of silver bullets, in resurrecting the single-etiology theory is evident. It has now been given yet another boost with the growth of the biotechnology industry—and, quite possibly, with the reluctance of the ruling classes to attend to some very obvious social determinants of health. Also, an entirely new generation of rich people have grown up, their brains properly sanitized and sterilized by powerful market forces to inculcate an almost congenital fear of "bugs" (44). A TV advertisement in India wants the mother living with her toddler son in a new palatial home to buy a brand of rat poison to protect him from getting infected with germs of rat bite fever, typhus, or plague!

6. After a decade and a half of toeing the line of the WHO's "international initiatives," India, with more than a billion population, discovered that these vertical programs were "not cost effective [and were] unsustainable and gravely damaging to the general health services" (45). Yet the WHO's Commission on Macroeconomics and Health not only strongly advocated these vertical, tech-nocentric approaches but asked for massive investments for programs such as the Global Fund for AIDS, Tuberculosis and Malaria and the Global Vaccine Action Initiative. The political economy of this phenomenon ought to be a subject of study for the current WHO Commission on Social Determinants of Health.

7. It is worthwhile taking note of two instances of overlooking the "people's side": (a) imposing the DOTS (directly observed treatment with short-course chemotherapy) program for tuberculosis on a global scale, on the obviously absurd sociological assumption that people with tuberculosis are so stupid that they would rather die of the disease than take the treatment on their own, if offered to them properly; and (b) the repeated failures of pushing polio immunization in certain ethnic or deprived groups, which led to the "discovery" that these groups feared the polio drops were hidden ways for Americans to sterilize their children.

8. Doggedly refusing to learn from past experience, in September 2005 the European Union unveiled an initial US$4 billion immunization program for Africa, making wild claims about saving the lives of millions of children. Will the children thus saved also be immune to death and disease due to hunger and other causes? This should have been in the agenda of study for the CSDH.

9. As early as 1963, sociological studies in India (46) showed that unfavorable "environments"—in the broadest sense of the term—create conditions for illness in a community, and the community culturally responds to the conditions by

developing its own meanings, perceptions, and actions for coping with them. Health problems, the people informed us, are part of the overall problem of suffering caused by socioeconomic conditions. The suffering reflects the felt needs of the people. If one is to intervene, that intervention must be modulated by the prevailing culture and socioeconomic conditions, which generate the felt needs. Neither the CMH nor the European Union nor probably the CSDH has bothered to consider such fundamental issues.

10. Again, it is tempting to think of solving the problems of deprived people by "donors" simply "giving" them the social determinants of health—accessible, free, integrated health services, good food, clean water, sanitation, education, social justice, human rights, and so on. Who are these donors to "give"? These rights have to be wrested by the people. It is well known that in a socially and economically polarized society, the rich rulers tend to find all sorts of subterfuges to deny deprived people their legitimate dues. Hiring social scientists to project deprived people as "uneducated," "superstitious," and "primitive" (47); distorting science to project some people as mentally retarded when they have suffered from malnutrition in infancy (48); projecting vitamin A and vaccines as "pills against poverty" (49)—all are glaring examples of such subterfuges.

11. Deprived people have to "take" the social determinants of health from their rulers. In India, for instance, the people used their limited democratic powers (in 1977) to overthrow a government that used too much coercion to get people sterilized, and they impelled the rulers to act to "entrust people's health in people's hands" (28). More recently, India's rulers have finally enacted the Right to Information Act and the Rural Employment Guarantee Act. A (faulty!) National Rural Health Mission has been set up by the political leadership to once again repeat its vow to improve the health of the country's deprived people (50).

12. The WHO Commission on Social Determinants of Health had an excellent opportunity to act as a counterweight to the technocentric recommendations of the Commission on Macroeconomics and Health. It seems to have already squandered it.

REFERENCES

1. World Health Organization. *Commission on Macroeconomics and Health: Investing in Health for Economic Development*. Report. Geneva, 2001.
2. Waitzkin, H. Report of the WHO Commission on Macroeconomics and Health: A summary and critique. *Lancet* 361:523–526, 2003.
3. Banerji, D. Report of the WHO Commission on Macroeconomics and Health: A critique. *Int. J. Health Serv.* 32:733–754, 2002.
4. Katz, A. The Sachs report: *Investing in Health for Economic Development*—Or, increasing the size of the crumbs from the rich man's table? Parts I and II. *Int. J. Health Serv.* 34:751–773, 2004; 35:171–188, 2005.
5. World Health Organization. *Commission on Social Determinants of Health*. Geneva, 2004.

6. World Health Organization. *Commission on Social Determinants of Health Newsletter*, April 2006.
7. World Health Organization. *Primary Health Care: Report of the International Conference on Primary Health Care, Alma-Ata, USSR, September 6–12, 1978.* Geneva, 1978.
8. Newell, K. W. (ed.). *Health by the People*. World Health Organization, Geneva, 1975.
9. Djukanovic, V., and Mach, E. P. (eds.). *Alternative Approaches to Meeting Basic Health Needs in Developing Countries*. World Health Organization, Geneva, 1975.
10. World Health Organization. *WHO Official Records*, no. 226, annex 11. Geneva, 1975.
11. Banerji, D. Reflections on the twenty-fifth anniversary of the Alma-Ata Declaration. *Int. J. Health Serv.* 33:813–818, 2003.
12. Litsios, S. The long and difficult road to Alma-Ata: A personal reflection. *Int. J. Health Serv.* 32:709–732, 2002.
13. World Health Organization. *Report of the Expert Committee on New Approaches to Health Education in Primary Health Care.* Technical Report Series No. 690. Geneva, 1983.
14. World Health Organization. *Report of the Expert Committee on Health Manpower Requirements for the Achievement of Health for All by the Year 2000 through Primary Health Care.* Technical Report Series No. 717. Geneva, 1985.
15. World Health Organization. *Inter-sectoral Linkages and Health Development*, ed. G. Gunatillake. WHO Offset Publication No. 83. Geneva, 1984.
16. Walsh, J. A., and Warren, K. A. Selective primary health care: An interim strategy for disease control for developing countries. *N. Engl. J. Med.* 301:967–974, 1979.
17. World Health Organization. *Ninth General Programme of Work Covering the Period 1996–2001.* Geneva, 1994.
18. World Health Organization. *Renewing the Health for All Strategy: Elaboration of a Policy for Equity, Solidarity and Health.* Geneva, 1995.
19. Nkariyana, D. J. *New Public Health and WHO's Ninth General Programme of Work* Discussion paper. World Health Organization, Geneva, 1995.
20. World Health Organization. *New Challenges for Public Health: Report of an Inter-regional Meeting.* Geneva, November 27–30, 1995.
21. De Vos, P. "No one left abandoned": Cuba's national health system since the 1959 revolution. *Int. J. Health Serv.* 35:189–208, 2005.
22. Gonoswasthya Kendra. *From Battle Front to Community: Story of Gonoswasthya Kendra.* Dhaka-1344, 2006.
23. Dutt, P. R. *Health Services in India: The Primary Health Centres*, Ed. 2. Central Health Education Bureau, New Delhi, 1965.
24. Bhattacharya, S. N. *Community Development: An Analysis of the Programme in India.* Academic Publishers, Calcutta, 1970.
25. Government of India. *Integrated Child Development Services Scheme.* Ministry of Education and Social Welfare, New Delhi, 1978.
26. Government of India. *Annual Report 1977–78.* Ministry of Health and Family Planning, New Delhi, 1978.
27. King, M. H. *Primary Health Care in Iran.* Oxford University Press, Oxford, 1982.
28. Voluntary Health Association. *Roundtable on Commission on Social Determinants of Health.* New Delhi, September 27, 2005.
29. Navarro, V. The world situation and WHO. *Lancet* 363:1321–1323, 2004.

30. World Bank. *World Development Report 2006: Equity and Development*. Washington, DC, 2006.
31. Sathyamala, C., et al Polio eradication initiative in India: Deconstructing the GPEI. *Int. J. Health Serv.* 35:361–364, 2003.
32. Banerji, D. A fundamental shift in the approach to international health by WHO, UNICEF, and the World Bank: Instances of the practice of "intellectual fascism" and totalitarianism in some Asian countries. *Int. J. Health Serv.* 29:227–259, 1999.
33. Mahler, H. Inaugural Address. Centro de Investigacion y Desarrollo en Salude, San Salvador, February 24, 2003.
34. Lerer, L., and Matzopoulos, R. "The worst of both worlds": The management reform of the World Health Organization. *Int. J. Health Serv.* 31:415–437, 2001.
35. Leguisaman, C. J. M. Dichotomies of Western biomedicine and Ayurveda: Health-illness and body-mind. *Econ. Polit. Wkly.*, July 23, 2005, pp. 3302–3310.
36. Ackerknect, E. *Rudolf Virchow*. University of Wisconsin Press, Madison, 1953.
37. Reese, D. M. Fundamentals—Rudolf Virchow and modern medicine. *West. J. Med.* 169(2):105–108, 1998.
38. Silver, G. A. Virchow, the heroic model in medicine: Health policy by accolade. *Am. J. Public Health* 77(1):82–88, 1987.
39. Sand, R. *The Advance of Social Medicine*. Staples Press, New York, 1952.
40. Rosen, G. *From Medical Police to Social Medicine: Essays on the History of Health Care*. Science History Publications, New York, 1974.
41. McKeown, T. *Role of Medicine: Dream, Mirage or Nemesis?* Nuffield Hospital Trust, London, 1976.
42. Marti-Ibanez, F. (ed.). *Henry Sigerist on History of Medicine*. MD Publications, New York, 1960.
43. Ryle, J. A. Social medicine: Its meaning and scope. *BMJ*, November 23, 1943, pp. 633–636.
44. Banerji, D. Reinventing mass communication: A World Health Organization tool for behavioral change to control disease. *Int. J. Health Serv.* 34:15–24, 2004.
45. Government of India. *National Health Policy 2002*. Ministry of Health and Family Welfare, New Delhi, 2002.
46. Banerji, D., and Andersen, S. A sociological study of awareness of symptoms suggestive of pulmonary tuberculosis. *Bull. WHO* 29:665, 1963.
47. Banerji, D. Critical review of the role and utilization of social scientists in promoting social science in health fields in India. *Indian Med. Assoc.* 60:145–147, 1973.
48. United Nations. *International Action to Avert Impending Protein Crisis*. New York, 1968.
49. Djurfeldt, G., and Lindberg, S. *Pills Against Poverty: A Study of Introduction of Western Medicine in a Tamil Village*. Scandinavian Institute of Asian Studies, Monograph Series No. 23. IBH Publishers, New Delhi, 1975.
50. Banerji, D. Politics of rural health in India. *Econ. Polit. Wkly.*, July 23, 2005, pp. 3253–3258.

B. Critique of Neoliberal Solutions to World Poverty

CHAPTER 22

A Critique of Jeffrey D. Sachs's
The End of Poverty

Doug Henwood

Jeffrey Sachs is a complicated guy. His first claim to fame was as the doctor who administered "shock therapy" in Bolivia, Poland, and Russia. Now he's Bono's traveling companion. Bono wrote the introduction to Sachs's latest book ("My professor. In time, his autograph will be worth a lot more than mine."), and Sachs gushes all over Bono in the text ("Bono brilliantly brought the AIDS tragedy to the attention of several key leaders of the religious right.").

This book, *The End of Poverty* (Penguin Press, 2005), is a manifesto and how-to guide on ending extreme poverty around the world. The subtitle, "Economic Possibilities for Our Time," echoes Keynes's famous 1928 essay, "Economic Possibilities for Our Grandchildren," which forecast, rightly, that we would be able to meet all the basic material needs of humankind two generations later— essentially today. We could, but we don't. Worldwide, about 1 billion people live on the equivalent of less than $1 a day, the official definition of extreme poverty; 2 billion live on less than $2, which officialdom considers normal poverty. These estimates have been criticized for being too low, and the definition of poverty for being too crude, but still, the numbers are criminally large.

Sachs uses this book to promote the United Nations' Millennium Development Goals (on which he is an advisor to Secretary General Kofi Annan), which were agreed to by 147 heads of state gathered in New York in September 2000. These include halving the numbers of the extremely poor and halving the numbers of the hungry by 2015; achieving universal literacy and primary education; promoting gender equality and the empowerment of women; reducing child mortality by two-thirds; improving maternal health; combating HIV/AIDS, malaria, and other horrid diseases; ensuring environmental sustainability; and developing a global partnership for development (which amounts to a nicer neoliberalism).

Achieving these goals, on Sachs's estimates, would require about $80 billion a year over the next ten years—not much next to current world output of $35 trillion a year. It's equal to about 20 hours of global economic activity. It's not much more, as Sachs shows, than the income of the 400 richest U.S. taxpayers—and that's not counting the rest of the world's rich. But even these modest goals are impossible in the current political environment.

A measure of that environment is Washington's current approach to one of Sachs's obsessions, preventing malaria in Africa, where the disease is ubiquitous. It would cost very little to provide Africans with mosquito nets to sleep under, something that's beyond the means of most Africans. But U.S. policy centers instead around something called "social marketing." Instead of giving away the nets, "social marketers buy advertising, conduct public education campaigns and create brands, hoping to promote the goods at low prices in the commercial marketplace" (as Donald McNeil wrote in the *New York Times*). They claim that the poor will value more that which they have to pay for, and the sales will cultivate an entrepreneurial class. There's no money in the budget for epidemiological studies to see if social marketing works. Of course, it probably doesn't. But Washington has big ideas about freedom—so who cares that 10,000 Africans die every day of preventable diseases?

On one level, Sachs's analysis and agenda are unremarkable. Many have written on how much the poor of the world suffer, and how little it would cost to reduce that suffering. But we've almost lost sight of a remarkable fact: this is Dr. Shock, Jeffrey Sachs!

Early Triumphs

Sachs's first moment in the spotlight came in the mid-1980s, with the "stabilization" of Bolivia, a policy package he designed that brought the country's inflation rate from 40,000 percent to near 0 percent. Sadly, though, it did nothing to relieve Bolivia's poverty—and the current round of almost constant protests, which have driven several presidents from office (and some from the country), suggests that twenty years later, Bolivians still aren't happy with their situation. But the superficial success of what came to be called "shock therapy"—and it must be conceded that almost no one likes hyperinflation—left Sachs well-positioned in the global market for economic expertise when socialism started unraveling at the end of the decade.

Sachs was an advisor to the Yeltsin government in Russia from 1991 to 1994, and also advised Poland, Slovenia, and Estonia as they were beginning their transitions to capitalism. The last three are mixed successes—on the surface, Poland looks like a success to some, but with the transition came higher unemployment, falling real wages, and aimless cycles of political discontent. Russia, though, was a thorough disaster, one of the worst collapses in human history. Living standards fell and the population shrank, an almost unprecedented event in a country not at war.

Bono's new best friend refuses to accept any blame for the disaster, offering the defense that the Russians didn't take his advice, and the West didn't come through with the big aid package he insisted was necessary. Apparently this is a well-practiced strategy. A 1992 *Euromoney* profile notes: "Sachs is reluctant to acknowledge mistakes, defining them in terms of regret when governments do not take his advice." In that case, he blamed Poland for not privatizing fast enough. Contrasting with Sachs's regrets over advice not taken, several governments he's consulted with have since characterized the material produced by him and his associates as irrelevant, or, as a Slovenian official put it at the time, "simplistic kindergarten stuff."

Lethal Gall

But the outcome illustrates precisely the danger of having the likes of Sachs parachute in bearing the timeless truths of neoclassical economics. Anyone who knew Russia knew that any rapid privatization would immediately lead to the creation of a new corrupt elite through massive theft of state property. Anyone who knew Washington knew that no big aid package was ever going to come through; adding to usual U.S. cheapness, a lot of hardliners wanted to see Russia ground into the dirt. In the words of former World Bank economist David Ellerman, who frequently collided with Sachs's work in Slovenia and has followed him intently ever since, "Only the mixture of American triumphalism and the academic arrogance of neoclassical economics could produce such a lethal dose of gall."

During what officialdom called the transition, there were divisions between those who wanted to reform the existing socialist system and experiment with hybrid forms of ownership, and what Ellerman calls the "clean postsocialist revolutionaries," many of them with American economics Ph.D.s, who dismissed the reformers as tainted nomenclature and wanted immediate privatization. Adding to the prestige of the revolutionaries were their trusted foreign advisors, like those from the Harvard Institute for International Development, led by Jeffrey Sachs and partly funded by the U.S. government.

In Poland, Sachs was firmly on the side of rapid transition to "normal" capitalism. At first he proposed U.S.-style corporate structures, with professional managers answering to many shareholders and a large economic role for stock markets. That didn't fly with the Polish authorities, so Sachs came back with a Germanic idea—large blocks of the shares of privatized companies would be placed in the hands of big banks. (As Ellerman recounts it, "Wherever the parade was going, [Sachs] had to be in front.") In both versions the point was to end any hints of worker or social control and institute a conventional capitalist class hierarchy.

His style was always abrasive and domineering; he rebuked the Slovenian parliament for passing a bill without his approval, and dismissed his critics as "idiots" and "self-management imbeciles." Waiting to meet with senior Soviet officials in 1991, Sachs put his feet up on a table. An aide asked him not to do that. Sachs took his feet down for a moment, and when the aide turned away, put them back up. From several public events and an hour-long interview, I can say he comes across as a very unpleasant fellow—cocky, vain, and free of doubt.

Russia

The Harvard Institute for International Development eventually collapsed in scandal, when it was revealed that the principals of its Russian project, Andrei Shleifer and Jonathan Hay, along with their wives (who happened to be mutual fund managers), had been buying Russian stocks and dickering for the privilege of getting the country's first mutual fund license, while dispensing advice to the Russian government. (Shleifer was one of the trinity of so-called Harvard Wunderkinder who were to Russia what the Chicago Boys were to Pinochet's Chile; the other two were Lawrence Summers—and Sachs.) The U.S. government sued, and Harvard shuttered the institute. Sachs, who was not involved in the scandal, decamped to Columbia (it's said there was no going-away party from his Harvard colleagues). At Columbia, he was appointed to head its new Earth Institute, an interdisciplinary enterprise that would bring together physical, health, and social scientists to promote sustainable economic development.

Sachs admits to no responsibility for the Russian catastrophe. When I interviewed him in November 2002, I asked him to comment on the (incontrovertible) fact that he's viewed by scores of millions of Russians, as one journalist has put it, as an emissary either of Satan or of the CIA. He answered that he found this question "disgusting," "perverse," and like nothing he's ever been asked before. The global elite leads a very insulated life.

Regrouping, to dissuade him from hanging up, I asked how he justified the tearing apart of the U.S.S.R. and forcing the country headlong into capitalism when there was little popular support for such a strategy. He responded, illogically, by saying he "wanted to support the democratization of the Soviet Union." He sung the praises of "transparency and honesty in government," even though the Yeltsin regime he was advising was opaque and corrupt. Asked to comment on published reports that he supported creating an inflation, so as to wipe out the savings of Russians (part of the shock therapists' attempts to start post–Soviet Russia with a clean slate), he bristled further, denouncing the quote as "phony," the question as "indecent," and the interview itself as not being in "good faith." In his academic work, however, Sachs argued that since China was only very lightly industrialized, it could afford to take its transition slowly. Russia, however, was burdened with the bad inheritance of Soviet industry, which was hopeless and had to go.

Yet . . .

As the 1990s progressed, Sachs became more prominent as a critic of development orthodoxy, arguing against the International Monetary Fund's austere prescriptions after the 1997 Asian crisis, and pressing for debt relief for the poorest countries. He became an economic advisor to the Jubilee 2000 movement (named after the Biblical exhortation to observe a Jubilee year once every fifty years, in which debts would be forgiven). The harder core of the global justice movement has never fully trusted Sachs; he reportedly lobbied to get himself invited to the World Social Forum at Porto Alegre a few years ago, but was rejected. Along with Joseph Stiglitz, he's one of the leading critics of the economic development establishment who's still a member of the club. But there aren't many of them.

For a member of the club, Sachs does use some strong language. *The End of Poverty* is full of sharp critiques of Western imperialism in Africa and elsewhere. He quotes Mike Davis approvingly on British brutality during famines. He blasts U.S. support of Mobutu and the rest of the posse of Cold War thugs. In late 2003, when Bush asked Congress for another $87 billion to fund the Iraq war, Sachs took to the pages of the *Boston Globe* to denounce the administration for pursuing an expensive war for oil while neglecting 500 million impoverished Africans. In the op-ed, he reviewed the disgraceful history of U.S. alliances with Middle Eastern despots "to keep the oil flowing," and noted vast reservoirs of ill-will towards the United States that that policy had created. He declared that "the world will not tolerate unilateral control by a country that accounts for less than 5 percent of humanity and the American people will end up paying a high price for the fantasy of hegemony." That's far stronger than anything Paul Krugman would write.

The New Sachs wasn't entirely unprecedented in the utterances of the Old Sachs. In the early 1990s, as he was busily transforming Eastern Europe, he told *Euromoney*, a banking trade journal, that you shouldn't press debtor countries for repayment if "there is going to be social catastrophe," and that "reform" programs should be "fair," with "burdens and benefits shared in an adequate way." But those high-minded concerns were overwhelmed by the political realities of the moment, and the results were anything but fair, as poverty and inequality increased in most of the formerly socialist countries (a situation that they've only recently begun to recover from).

People who know Sachs say he's always considered himself on the political left. His father, who died in 2001, was a long-time Detroit labor lawyer and general counsel to the Michigan AFL-CIO. That puts his passion to destroy worker power in eastern Europe in an interesting Oedipal light—and might even explain some of the contradictions of Sachs's politics. But that would be speculative psychoanalysis of a suspect sort, so enough of that.

Incomplete Critique

Heavy debts, IMF austerity programs, and fickle financial markets are Sachs's favorite targets. His views on the rest of the development business are more conventional. In *The End of Poverty*, he writes as if all the poorest countries need to do is get a rung or two up the economic ladder; the problem is their distance from the ladder, not the ladder itself. That stands in odd contrast with the strength of his anti-imperialist rhetoric. It's as if he can't see the financial arrangements (with institutions like the IMF at their center—there's usually a state center to a financial system) as crucial enforcement mechanisms for the maintenance of orthodox policies. Finance is an instrument of class power, locally, nationally, and internationally.

In our interview, Sachs told me that to become internationally competitive, Argentina and Brazil need to develop their educational institutions and technological capacity—as if the history of a couple of centuries of structural subordination and the present of debt service demands haven't made that difficult to impossible. (Africa's long-term prospects, he disclosed, lie in tourism, services, and back-office operations.) There's more recognition of deep structural impediments in this book, but then he offers his reform agenda as if the structurally dominant would easily consent to a weakening of their domination, which is how they see any "aid" program. Asked how he would deal with the enormous political obstacles to his agenda, Sachs pointed to his own efforts at promoting debt relief, which date back to 1985.

We're back to Sachs's enormous ego, which exposes almost anything he does to the suspicion that he's in it mostly for the attention. But while his work in Russia, though it drew attention, was mostly destructive—something he still can't admit to—his concerns today are a lot more admirable. His criticisms of American war-mongering and Western indifference to the poverty of a billion or two of our fellow humans are mostly on the side of the angels. Maybe the best summing up of the latest incarnation of Jeffrey Sachs comes from David Ellerman: "I hope he gets what he wants, but that he doesn't get any credit for it."

Note — This chapter is adapted from an article in *Left Business Observer,* no. 111, 2005.

Contributors

FRANCISCO ARMADA, M.D., Ph.D., is Minister of Health of the Bolivarian Republic of Venezuela. He previously held several high-level positions in the Bolivarian Ministry of Health and Social Development of Venezuela and as hospital administrator. His academic scholarship has focused on uncovering the effects of neoliberalism on health care and social security reforms in Latin America. His study was the first of its kind in public health to uncover the links between international financial institutions, international health organizations, corporations, government, and health care reforms in Latin America. As Minister of Health he has played a key role in the consolidation of Barrio Adentro I and in the creation and implementation of Barrio Adentro II and III.

JAVIER ASTUDILLO is an associate lecturer in the Department of Political and Social Sciences of the Pompeu Fabra University in Barcelona and doctor-member of the Juan March Institute of Studies and Research in Madrid. He graduated in geography and history at the Autonomous University of Madrid (1992), then obtained his M.A. in social sciences at the Juan March Institute (1994) and his doctorate in political sciences at the Autonomous University of Madrid (1998). Between 1998 and 2000 he was a Fulbright Scholar in the Center for European Studies of Harvard University, where he undertook postdoctoral research. Dr. Astudillo works in comparative politics with special emphasis on the role of interest groups in the political processes of western Europe and Latin America, as well as the interaction between citizens and voluntary associations.

DEAN BAKER is co-director of the Center for Economic and Policy Research, in Washington, D.C. Formerly he was a senior research fellow at the Preamble Center in Washington and the Century Fund in New York, and before that was a senior economist at the Economic Policy Institute in Washington. He received his Ph.D. in economics from the University of Michigan. Dr. Baker is the author of *Economic Reporting Review,* a weekly examination of the economic reporting in the *New York Times* and *Washington Post,* and periodic analyses of the federal government's economic data on prices, employment, corporate profits, and GDP. Recent publications include "Projections of Income for the 21st Century" (*International Journal of Health Services,* 2001); "What's New In the Nineties: An Assessment of the Nineties Business Cycle" (in *Alternative Perspectives on the Economy,* edited by Jeffrey Madrick, Century Foundation, 2000); *Pensions for the 21st Century* (Century Foundation, 2000); "After the Fall: The Implications of a Stock Market Crash" (*American Prospect,* 2000); and *The Feasibility of a Unilateral Speculation Tax in the United States* (Center for Economic and Policy Research, 2000).

DEBABAR BANERJI is professor emeritus at the Centre of Social Medicine and Community Health, Jawaharlal Nehru University, New Delhi. After he graduated from the Medical College, Calcutta (1953), he worked as a physician in western Tibet and in the interior Himalayan tribal regions, in order to relate the practice of Western medicine to the conditions in these regions. He continued this line of work at the National Tuberculosis Institute, Bangalore (1959–1964), at the National Institute of Health Administration and Education, New Delhi (1964–1971), and in his present position. Banerji's publications cover a number of facets of the relationships between health technology and people, and the formulation of people-oriented health technologies and programs for India.

JOAN BENACH, M.D., Ph.D., is an assistant professor at the University Pompeu Fabra in Barcelona. Since the early 1990s he has been doing research on social inequalities in health, in particular on small area analysis (health geography) and precarious work (occupational health). He has also been involved in public health advocacy in the European Union with unions and environmental organizations. His most recent book is *Learning to Look at Health* (with C. Muntaner; forthcoming).

PATRICK BOND is a political economist and research professor at the University of KwaZulu-Natal (UKZN) School of Development Studies in Durban, South Africa, where he directs the Centre for Civil Society. He formerly taught at York University (Toronto), University of the Witwatersrand (Johannesburg), and Johns Hopkins School of Public Health (Baltimore). Recent publications include *Looting Africa: The Economics of Exploitation* (Zed Books and UKZN Press, 2006); *Talk Left, Walk Right: South Africa's Frustrated Global Reforms* (UKZN Press, 2006); *Trouble in the Air: Global Warming and the Privatised Atmosphere* (edited with Rehana Dada; CCS and Transnational Institute, 2005); *Elite Transition: From Apartheid to Neoliberalism in South Africa* (UKZN Press, 2005); and *Fanon's Warning: A Civil Society Reader on the New Partnership for Africa's Development* (Africa World Press and CCS, 2005).

FRANCIS G. CASTLES is professor of social and public policy at the University of Edinburgh, Scotland. He was previously a research professor in political science at the Australian National University. He has been working the field of comparative welfare state research since the mid-1970s and has convened and edited the findings of a number of international, collaborative research projects in the area.

DEMBA MOUSSA DEMBELE is director of the Forum for African Alternatives in Dakar, Senegal.

GEORGE DOR is a Johannesburg-based research and activist with Jubilee South Africa and the African Social Forum. He has degrees in medicine and social science from the University of the Witwatersrand and the University of London Institute of Commonwealth Studies.

OSCAR FEO, M.D., M.Sc., is a professor at Carabobo University and the Arnaldo Gabaldon Institute of Advanced Studies in Public Health, Ministry of Health in Maracay, Venezuela. He was a member of and coordinated the Health Commission of the Venezuelan Constituent Assembly.

RENÉ M. GUERRA SALAZAR is an OGS Fellow and Ph.D. candidate in the Department of Public Health Sciences at the University of Toronto.

DOUG HENWOOD is editor of the *Left Business Observer,* a newsletter on economics and politics. His most recent book is *After the New Economy* (New Press, 2005).

ALISON KATZ is a social scientist and clinical psychologist. She has worked in the field of health, poverty, and development for more than 15 years for various U.N. agencies and NGOs. She is a member of the People's Health Movement.

CARLES MUNTANER, M.D., Ph.D., is a social epidemiologist, currently research chair and scientist at the Social Equity and Health Section, Center for Addiction and Mental Health, and professor of Nursing, Public Health Sciences, and Psychiatry at the University of Toronto. Since the late 1990s he has been involved with the Bolivarian revolution on public health-related matters. He has written analyses on how mainstream and liberal media have covered the Bolivarian process. Recent publications include "Venezuela: Chomsky's Tropical Nightmare" (with F. Armada; *Counterpunch,* 2001); "Income Inequality and Population Health in Latin America and the Caribbean" (with F. Armada and V. Navarro; *Hispanic Health Care International,* 2002); "Is Chavez's Venezuela Populist or Socialist?" (*Counterpunch,* 2005); "Cuando las Criticas Son Solo Tropicos" (with J. Benach; *El Viejo Topo,* 2005); and "History Is Not Over: La Revolucion Bonita, 21st Century Socialism, and Health Care in Venezuela" (in press).

VICENTE NAVARRO is a professor of health and public policy, sociology, and policy studies at Johns Hopkins University in Baltimore and professor of political and social sciences at the University Pompeu Fabra in Spain. A founder and past president of the International Association of Health Policy and founder and editor-in-chief of the *International Journal of Health Services,* he has written extensively on health and public policy themes. Navarro is the author and editor of many books and articles on these subjects, translated into many different languages. His most recent publications include *The Politics of Health Policy* (Blackwell, 1996); *Neoliberalismo y Estado de Bienestar* (Ariel, 1997); *Neoliberalismo y Estado de Bienestar,* 3rd Ed. Expanded (Ariel Sociedad Economica, 1999); *Globalizacion, Economica Poder Politico y Estado del Bienestar* (Ariel Sociedad Economica, 2000); *The Political Economy of Social Inequalities* (Baywood, 2001); and *The Political and Social Contexts of Health* (Baywood, 2004).

DAVID ROSNICK is a research associate at the Center for Economic and Policy Research in Washington, D.C. He received his Ph.D. in computer science from North Carolina State University at Raleigh. He has written numerous policy papers, including "The Burden of Social Security Taxes and the Burden of Excessive Health Care Costs (with D. Baker; March 2005).

JOHN SCHMITT is a senior economist at the Center for Economic and Policy Research in Washington, D.C.

CARLOS EDUARDO SIQUEIRA, M.D., Sc.D., M.P.H., is a research assistant professor in the Department of Work Environment of the University of Massachusetts Lowell. He graduated from the School of Medicine of the Federal University of Rio de Janeiro, Brazil (1979), and from the Johns Hopkins University School of Hygiene and Public Health (1986).

ROBERT HUNTER WADE is professor of political economy at the London School of Economics. He has taught at Victoria University of Wellington, University of California, San Diego, Sussex University, Princeton University, MIT, and Brown University. He has held fellowships at the Institute for Advanced Study (Princeton), the Russell Sage Foundation (New York), and the Institute for Advanced Study (Berlin), and has worked as staff economist at the World Bank (1984–1988) and at the Office of Technology Assessment, U.S. Congress (1988–1989). Wade's research has focused on economic development understood in terms of variables that are as much institutional and political as narrowly economic. His research sites have included Pitcairn Island, villages in Italy and India, bureaucracies in India and Korea, the state-at-large in Taiwan, the World Bank, and the "world system." Books include *Village Republics: Economic Conditions of Collective Action in South India* (1988, 1994) and *Governing the Market: Economic Theory and the Role of Government in East Asian Industrialization* (1990, 2004). He received the American Political Science Association's Best Book in Political Economy prize 1989–1991. Recent publications have spanned comparative political economy, international relations, and global political economy.

MARK WEISBROT is co-director of the Center for Economic and Policy Research in Washington, D.C. He received his Ph.D. in economics from the University of Michigan. He is co-author of *Social Security: The Phony Crisis* (with D. Baker; University of Chicago Press, 2000) and has written numerous research papers on economic policy.

BEN ZIPPERER is a research assistant at the Center for Economic and Policy Research in Washington, D.C.

Index

475

THE POLITICAL AND SOCIAL CONTEXTS OF HEALTH

Edited by Vicente Navarro

IN PRAISE . . .

"Do political contexts and social policies matter for life expectancy and infant mortality? Here an international team of experts provides fruitful perspectives, informative analyses, and food for thought on this central but often neglected question."

Walter Korpi, Professor of Social Policy, Stockholm University

"Inequality endangers your health. Few social science findings are as important as the conclusion of these investigations, made in several countries."

Göran Therborn, Professor and Director, Swedish Collegium
for Advanced Study in the Social Sciences, Uppsala, Sweden

"Is politics the key to population health? And if so, how? At last we have a book that asks all the right questions. For anyone with a serious interest in health policy, this is where to start."

Richard Wilkinson, Professor, Division of Epidemiology and Public Health
University of Nottingham Medical School, England

"Over the past four decades in public health at the Johns Hopkins University, Vicente Navarro has established himself as a leading authority on the relation of health and health services to societal factors. One may say, more specifically, that with respect to political factors his authority is unchallenged; his work in this area is unique in public health.

"As editor of this volume, Professor Navarro brings together an array of experienced authors. Two or more authors assemble and analyze the relevant and available data for each of five European countries. Navarro himself leads with an analysis of the overall data for the OECD countries as an entity. The work aims to analyze the mortality effects 'of power relations and solidarity and civic behavior on the social inequalities measured by income equalities and determined by labor market and employment policies as welfare state policies.' The assembled material has obvious value for scholars in several related fields."

Mervyn Susser, Sergievsky Professor of Epidemiology
Emeritus, Columbia University, New York

"Our lives are largely determined by health, and our health is largely determined by the social and political contexts in which we live. This book explains and documents how and why, in a cross-cultural perspective. Edited by the world's leading expert in the political economy of public health, this volume is a major contribution both to scholarly research and to policy debates in the field. It should be mandatory reading for students of social policy and planning, as well as for all concerned citizens facing the consequences of the health crisis around the world."

Manuel Castells, Professor Emeritus of Planning and Sociology
University of California, Berkeley

"This is a well written and thought provoking book. It makes the important point that most public health practitioners only focus on individuals and not the broader cultural, economic, and political systems of societies, which are very important in the overall health of individuals."

Ross M. Mullner, PhD, MPH, University of Illinois
at Chicago, *Doody's Book Review Service*

6" × 9", 246 pages
Cloth, ISBN: 0-89503-296-1, $57.00 + $6.50 p/h
Paper, ISBN: 0-89503-299-6, $42.00 + $6.50 p/h

Baywood Publishing Company, Inc.
26 Austin Avenue, PO Box 337, Amityville, New York 11701
phone 631-691-1270 • fax 631-691-1770 • toll-free orderline 800-638-7819
e-mail baywood@baywood.com • website http://baywood.com

POLITICAL AND ECONOMIC DETERMINANTS
OF POPULATION HEALTH AND WELL-BEING
Controversies and Developments

Edited by *Vicente Navarro and Carles Muntaner*

Policy, Politics, Health and Medicine Series
Series Editor, *Vicente Navarro*

IN PRAISE ...

"*Political and Economic Determinants of Population Health and Well-Being* is a superb compendium of research and debate on a question of fundamental importance—the relationship between social inequality and human well-being. It should convince all serious scholars that the study of class, race, gender, and other forms of inequality should be at the center of the agenda of public health research in the 21st century."

Erik Olin Wright, Vilas Distinguished Professor, University of Wisconsin

"This remarkable collection explores, from many perspectives, some of the most crucial problems of social policy of the coming years, not least in the United States. These penetrating essays range from theoretical and analytic dissection of fundamental moral, political, and economic issues to close investigation of a wide variety of critically important cases. For those concerned about what lies ahead—and what we can and should do about it—the collection is not only valuable but indispensable."

Noam Chomsky, Professor Emeritus, MIT

"It was fascinating for me to go through this mine of information, analysis, and interpretation; to find a rigorous academic documentation interlaced with rejections of injustice; to understand how often the health effects of class, gender, race, and social background are concealed; to see the extent to which conservative assumptions are contradicted by strong evidence; to verify the positive health effects of the work of labor unions; to see how many groups defend health as a public good; and to gain so many ideas and insights for research and for action.

"Last year, the International Bioethics Committee of UNESCO declared: 'Health has a double moral value, because it is essential for the quality of life and for life itself, and is instrumental as a condition for freedom. The inequality between rich and poor—at the level of individuals, communities, and nations—is increasingly deeply felt in the area of health and healthcare, thereby contributing to the desperation and injustice that prevail and continue to increase in other health-related fields such as food, income, and education.' This book provides the best analysis of these conditions, the broadest description of the realities in the United States and worldwide, and the stimulus for further research and action."

Giovanni Berlinguer, University of Rome, Italy

"Vicente Navarro and Carles Muntaner offer readers a splendid collection of 30 essays and research articles about a crucial and controversial topic—the determinants of population health and quality of life. These articles were published in recent years in the *International Journal of Health Services*, and have now been complied into a book that will will appeal to readers across many fields."

Roberta Garner, Sociology Department, DePaul University, *Science & Society*

6" × 9", 584 pages
Cloth, ISBN: 0-89503-278-3, $69.00 + $6.50 p/h; Paper, ISBN: 0-89503-279-1, $48.00 + $6.50 p/h

℔ Baywood Publishing Company, Inc.
26 Austin Avenue, PO Box 337, Amityville, New York 11701
phone 631-691-1270 • fax 631-691-1770 • toll-free orderline 800-638-7819
e-mail baywood@baywood.com • website http://baywood.com

SELECT TITLES IN THE
Policy, Politics, Health and Medicine Series
Series Editor, *Vicente Navarro*

HEALTH AND WORK UNDER CAPITALISM
An International Perspective
Editors: Vicente Navarro and Daniel M. Berman

POLITICAL AND ECONOMIC DETERMINANTS OF POPULATION HEALTH AND WELL-BEING
Controversies and Developments
Editors: Vicente Navarro and Carles Muntaner

THE POLITICAL ECONOMY OF SOCIAL INEQUALITIES
Consequences for Health and Quality of Life
Editor: Vicente Navarro

WHY THE UNITED STATES DOES NOT HAVE A NATIONAL HEALTH PROGRAM
Editor: Vicente Navarro

HEALTH AND MEDICAL CARE IN THE U.S.
A Critical Analysis
Editor: Vicente Navarro

IMPERIALISM, HEALTH AND MEDICINE
Editor: Vicente Navarro

Baywood Publishing Company, Inc.
Amityville, New York